An Introduction
to Mathematical Economics

An Introduction to Mathematical Economics: Methods and Applications

G.C. Archibald
The University of British Columbia

Richard G. Lipsey
Queen's University

HARPER & ROW, PUBLISHERS
New York, Hagerstown, San Francisco, London

HB
135
A76

Sponsoring Editor: John Greenman
Project Editor: Eleanor Castellano
Designer: T. R. Funderburk
Production Supervisor: Francis X. Giordano
Compositor: Ruttle, Shaw & Wetherill, Inc.
Printer and binder: Halliday Lithograph Corporation
Art Studio: Vantage Art, Inc.

AN INTRODUCTION TO MATHEMATICAL ECONOMICS: METHODS AND APPLICATIONS

Library of Congress Cataloging in Publication Data

Archibald, George Christopher.
  An introduction to mathematical economics.

  "Portions of this work were first published in the U.K. as An introduction to a mathematical treatment of economics."
  Includes bibliographical references and index.
  1. Economics, Mathematical.   I. Lipsey, Richard G.,
Date-   joint author.   II. Title.
HB135.A76   330'.01'51   75-42082
ISBN 0-06-040324-1

Contents

(Some sections are starred, thus*. This means they are difficult and their comprehension is not assumed in subsequent material.)

3

SIMPLE LINEAR MODELS 60

4

INTRODUCTION TO CALCULUS: DIFFERENTIATION 104

5

APPLICATIONS OF DERIVATIVES 140

The Competitive Model 141

The Model of Income Determination 144

Miscellaneous Applications 152

MAXIMA AND MINIMA 162

ECONOMIC APPLICATIONS OF MAXIMA AND MINIMA 179

The Competitive Market 179

The Model of Income Determination 182

Miscellaneous Applications 184

Comparative Statics 190

8

FUNCTIONS OF MORE THAN ONE VARIABLE 199

9

APPLICATIONS OF FUNCTIONS OF MORE THAN ONE VARIABLE 227

The Competitive Market 227

The Model of Income Determination 230

Miscellaneous Applications 233

10

CONSTRAINED MAXIMA AND MINIMA 247

11

APPLICATIONS OF CONSTRAINED MAXIMA AND MINIMA 269

12

AN INTRODUCTION TO DYNAMICS 300

13

INTEGRATION AND EXPONENTIAL FUNCTIONS 322

14

APPLICATIONS OF DYNAMICS 347

15

INTRODUCTION TO MATRIX ALGEBRA 378

16

APPLICATIONS OF LINEAR ALGEBRA 411

Preface

When we first began to write this book we cast our minds back over our own trainings in mathematics. Each of us found that we had vivid recollections of mathematics instruction in high school that was less than totally satisfactory! One of us clearly recalls that day when one of the brighter and more adventurous of his fellow students interrupted a class in algebra to ask, "Please Sir, what good will all this be to us when we grow up?" The angry teacher retorted, "Probably none at all, but learning it is good for you." The other author painfully recalls countless tedious hours spent working out answers to such idiotic and useless questions as "How much water will there be in the bathtub one hour after the tap has been turned on to produce a rate of inflow of *alpha,* and 50 minutes after some fool has pulled out the plug to produce a rate of outflow of *beta?*"

When we came to study economics in university we each discovered more or less on our own that economic theory was inherently mathematical in structure and that mathematics was, after all, an intensely practical subject. A few years later, when we began to teach economics, we each vowed that we would give our students more help in understanding the relation between mathematics and economics than we ourselves had been given.

The course on which this book is based had its origins in these early experiences and in our dissatisfaction with the situation that we found when, within a year of each other, we joined the staff of the London School of Economics. At that time it was possible to complete a course leading to the specialist honors degree Bachelor of Science (Economics) while remaining totally innocent of anything beyond grade 11 mathematics! As a result, students who were specialists in economics had only the vaguest—and sometimes the wildest—notions about the role of mathematics in the social sciences.

To ameliorate this unsatisfactory state of affairs the authors introduced a voluntary, noncredit course entitled "An Introduction to the Use of Mathematics in Economics." In this course we sought to build on what students already knew about economics and what they were likely to be currently learning. We also assumed that students had actually been using many mathematical concepts, albeit disguised in verbal or graphical terms. *We used what they knew in economics to help them learn what they didn't know in mathematics. Then we applied the mathematics to problems in economics that could not be handled without it.* From a humble beginning of 9 students, 6 of whom lasted the whole course, attendance grew steadily. When we left the LSE our audience, still voluntary, ran to 40 or 50 students.

In the 1960s we both went to help build the new University of Essex in England. There we made the course compulsory for all economics majors and refined it into the form on which this book is based. In the early 1970s we both moved to Canadian universities, and since that time we have used our method of teaching mathematics through economics to teach students in several North American universities.

In all our courses in mathematical economics, and in the present book, we use mathematics to deal with real problems in economics. We try to eliminate the frustrations of our own early experience with idiotic problems that would not arise in practice. ("For goodness sake, why doesn't someone simply replace the plug?"). Also, we only introduce new mathematical techniques when we have run into problems that we want to handle but *cannot* with the tools already introduced—thus answering that question asked long ago in a high school algebra class with a resounding: "Yes, mathematics *is* of great practical use in many subjects, including the one that readers of this book have already studied—economics."

Many people have helped to make this book possible and we wish in particular to thank all of our past students who have endured our course and, by their active participation, have contributed to its development. Richard Harris did most of the work of writing the Appendix to Chapter 18. Many of the end-of-chapter questions came from our class exercises accumulated and proven over the years, but Patricia Hazwell, Duncan Smeaton, and Elmer Wiens have also contributed to the list. Professors John Black and Christopher Bliss and Mr. Patrick Geary, Alan Popoff, and A. A. Vanags gave invaluable advice at early stages.

Weidenfeld and Nicolson have generously given permission for the use of material that was originally published in the United Kingdom under the title *An Introduction to a Mathematical Treatment of Economics,* copyright 1967 by G. C. Archibald and Richard G. Lipsey.

For all of the remaining errors and blemishes the authors may blame each other, but the reader must blame us both.

G. C. Archibald

Richard G. Lipsey

Chapter *1*

Introduction

We hope in this book to show you how to go about doing economics using mathematical tools. Some of you will feel at this point that this objective is quite beyond you. (What, *me* use mathematical tools? I don't really know what an equation is!) Others will feel that it is not even a desirable goal. (Economics is about people, and mathematics is about things.) We hope in the course of the next 504 pages to persuade you that you both can and should aspire to apply mathematical tools to much of your economics.

1.1 MATHEMATICAL ECONOMICS

Economics is so inherently mathematical a subject that any student who has taken a principles course has already done some "mathematical economics," and demonstrated his capacity to do it. That a principles course is "mathematical" may seem a surprising statement. But consider a sample of the ideas in a principles course, and their mathematical expression.

1. "Quantity demanded depends on price" and "consumption depends on the level of income": these are two of the many applications of the fundamental mathematical notion of a functional relationship.

2. "The equilibrium price is that at which quantity demanded equals quantity supplied": this refers to the solution of a system of two simultaneous equations in two unknowns, price and quantity.

3. "General equilibrium" or "everything depends on everything else": this suggests a very large number of relationships that must, somehow, fit together, that is, a set of simultaneous equations.
4. "Profit maximization": this assumption, and all the associated paraphernalia of marginal cost, marginal revenue, etc., is an obvious application of the mathematical notion of maximization, whether we handle it in words, diagrams, or algebra.
5. "Marginal concepts": all marginal concepts such as marginal cost, revenue, utility, product, propensity to consume, save, import, etc., are the mathematical concepts of first derivatives of the relevant functions, going under other names.
6. "The production frontier," or any other frontier, and the search for "optimal points": this involves an application of the mathematical theory of "constrained maxima."

This list could easily be extended, but we hope we have made our point: the familiar, basic ideas of economics usually turn out to be particular cases of problems that are handled in mathematics; and if one is interested in the particular cases it seems natural to inquire into the general mathematics, in the hope of finding illumination and/or useful technical apparatus. Consideration of this list, however, suggests something more fundamental, that *there is no dichotomy between "economics" and "mathematical economics."* Nevertheless, there is clearly some distinction between "economics" and "mathematical economics," and if the distinction does not reflect a real dichotomy of subject matter, we may ask what it does reflect. The answer is that the distinction is mainly a quantitative one: it is a matter simply of how much mathematical technique a particular problem demands. It also reflects a personal choice, because some economists know more mathematics than others and are interested in problems the solutions of which need more mathematics. As one might expect, there is also division of labor between the more and the less mathematically inclined; but division of labor is a matter of costs and convenience; it reflects no fundamental difference in what is divided.

It is common for the "more mathematical" economist to be interested in questions that do not appear to other people to be of much practical significance: he may be interested in the "generality," or "rigor," or "elegance" of proofs of propositions that we take for granted, as well as in solving technical problems that are too complicated for those with less equipment. The concepts of mathematics are intriguing, and the goals of the really "mathematical" economist are worthwhile. We wish to stress at the very outset that this is not a "rigorous" book: our goals are immediate and practical, and we have not hesitated to employ the easiest routes. This book aims accordingly at a much less ambitious level of mathematics than would satisfy the genuine mathematical economist; but it may also be a stage on the way and help the reader to appreciate what else may be done. There is no nonmathematical economics, only more or less; and we are concerned here with that amount which, we believe, any student can learn and put to immediate use.

1.2 SOME COMMON FALLACIES

Readers who have already completed a "principles" course, and who have been at all persuaded by the argument that even a principles course involves mathematical ideas, probably do not need to be convinced of the possibility of "mathematical social science." Nevertheless, there are so many mistaken ideas in common circulation that it may be worth making a few points.

The argument most commonly encountered is that economics is a social science, and that human affairs are too complex to be adequately represented in mathematical models, which are necessarily crude oversimplifications. A little reflection suggests that this is a perverse argument. Suppose that we have to deal, as we do in the social sciences, with a complicated system of interrelationships among many individuals and institutions, pursuing different goals and impinging on each other in different ways. Suppose also that, guided by our knowledge of human beings, and of institutions and of history, we feel that we can formulate some hypotheses about some, at least, of the behavioral relations of the system. If the way in which the system would then work were clear to us, we would not need mathematics. It is precisely because the logical relations between all the "bits" that we can hypothesize are too complex to be perceived by unaided intuition that we require analytical methods to help us elucidate the properties of what was, in the first place, our own creation.

The more complex we believe society to be, the more we need the sort of help that mathematics can give us. It is consistent, although in our view mistaken, to believe that the world is so simple that mathematics can be dispensed with and verbal argument used instead. It is utterly self-contradictory to believe that the real world is so complex that mathematical methods are inappropriate and verbal reasoning more effective. Indeed, just because mathematics is a very powerful tool for making logical deductions from a set of assumptions about behavior, it forces us to make fewer simplifications of reality than we would have to make if we were to rely on verbal reasoning alone. We shall, of course, always simplify because of the amount we do not know and because of our limited ability to handle complex problems. The limitation, however, is not a virtue: it is one thing to simplify because we wish to, in order to omit irrelevant detail and expose the structure of a problem; it is quite another thing to simplify merely because we are technically incompetent.

In fact, of course, any theory is some sort of "simplification" of human affairs, and we shall discuss later the role of theory (*any* sort of theory, whether ostensibly mathematical or not) in social science. Let us now, however, continue with our discussion of ill-founded objections. Probably the next most frequently encountered objection is that mathematics lends a spurious accuracy to economic analysis, spurious because there is always an unknown or unpredictable element in human conduct, accuracy because it is in the nature of mathematics to be "accurate." This is the argument of the man who knows nothing whatever about either mathematics or mathematical economics but believes the former to be glorified arithmetic and the latter to be a sort of super bookkeeping. As for the "accuracy" of mathematics, we shall discover again and again in this book that its great power and beauty lies in its generality: with the help of mathematical analysis, we are able to make deductions of the form "if this works like this, and that like that, the result must be such and such" without knowing—or caring—what an arithmetic example might look like. Consider how frequently one argues like this in a "nonmathematical" principles course: "If the demand curve slopes down, then an increase in supply will lead to a reduction in price" is a simple mathematical deduction, about the excessive "accuracy" of which no one is likely to complain!

Frequently, however, one does want numbers: if, for example, economics is to serve the ends of macro-policy makers, then it is imperative to have numbers. We want answers to such questions as "how much additional unemployment will be caused next winter if firms now reduce the rate of investment spending by $100 million per annum?" It is hard to see how one can get a better answer than "some" by any nonmathematical means whatever. If we want a quantitative answer, the alternative to using an "econometric model" is crystal gazing, or reliance on the intuition of the wise man. This is fine when the wise man is right, but what happens when he is wrong? All we learn is that he is not wise enough, which is not nearly so useful as finding that we have made a remediable error in our analysis of the economy. Indeed, even when he is right, his uses are limited: to listen to him, we must have faith, and there is more than one prophet! It is more satisfactory to judge an answer reached by logical means, which anyone may evaluate for himself—if he is prepared to learn how. As for the criticism that a numerical answer, provided from a "model" of the economy, has a misleading and spurious appearance of accuracy, its accuracy, spurious or otherwise, is a statistical matter. Economic statisticians, or econometricians, as they are called, have at their disposal a substantial tool kit for working out the confidence that should be attached to their numbers. They will produce results qualified by such remarks as "with a 95 percent chance of being within 10 percent either way." The rules of this game are beyond the scope of this book, but it is simply not the case that the modern econometrician gives you a unique right answer and says "take it or leave it": the subject is a good deal more sophisticated than most of its critics. Indeed if we wish to allow for a degree of uncertainty, error, free will, or call-it-what-you-may, we can build it into our theoretical formulations and then use mathematical analysis to determine both our predictions and their probable range of error. The techniques required are complex, and their understanding requires training in statistics. We can see, however, that if we confine ourselves to verbal reasoning we shall have to be satisfied with nonquantitative qualifications, the effect of which we shall be unable to assess in anything but the vaguest fashion.

There is still, of course, the extreme "anti" position of the man who argues that the essential unpredictability of human conduct is such that we delude ourselves when we pretend that even an answer qualified by "with a 95 percent chance of being 10 percent either way" is anything but bogus. This position is basically that *anything* can happen, and it is thus not a criticism of mathematical social science per se; the position is that *any* social science is impossible. The man who argues like this often feels that he is in some way defending human liberty and dignity, that free will is being "got at" or denigrated when the social scientist ventures to predict behavior, and that the defense of liberty depends not on political action but on the obstinate assertion of hopeless disorder and blessed contrariness in human conduct. We may have some sympathy for him, but he is both misguided and wrong. He is misguided because, if human beings frequently behave in a predictable manner, their liberty to do otherwise is not threatened by the discovery of the fact. And he is simply wrong as to fact. Try to imagine a world in which human conduct was genuinely quite unpredictable: existence would be impossible. Neither law, nor justice, nor airline timetables would be more reliable than a roulette wheel; a kind remark could as easily provoke fury as sympathy — as easily as a harsh one; one's landlady might put one out tomorrow or forgive one the rent. There is not, and could not be, anything in science fiction to match it. One cannot really imagine a society of human beings that could possibly work like this. Indeed a major part of "brainwashing" techniques is to mix up rewards and punishments until the victim genuinely does not know "where he is": unpredictable pressures drive human beings mad. The fact is that we live in a world which is some sort of mixture of the predictable, or average, or "most of the people most of the time," and of the haphazard, contrary, and random. When we try to analyze this world, and apply our orderly models, we need help from specialists in probability — statisticians — but we have not yet found we need the advice of the experts in the behavior of systems in states of total chaos.

There is one last popular objection to mathematical economics that has only to be stated to be seen to be absurd, namely that mathematical economics need not be correct. Mistakes can occur in any chain of reasoning, whether ostensibly mathematical or not: human beings are fallible, and mathematical economists are human beings. Perhaps people feel that a mathematical error is more sinful than some other sort of error because it is harder for the nonmathematician to spot! An alternative criticism is that much mathematical economics is "irrelevant." This might be true, but mathematical economics has no monopoly of irrelevance. And it is absurd to blame the tools for being used for the wrong purpose. The solution, if the tools are powerful, is to employ them to better purpose.

1.3 THE ROLE OF THEORY

"Which comes first, theory or observation?" is a perpetual chicken-and-egg question. We need not try to "solve" it. We can say that without some sort of notion of what one is looking for, observation is pretty hopeless: there is an infinite number of facts that one might observe! And we can say that without some observations, theorizing is pretty hopeless: there is an infinite number of theories that one might construct! What is needed is for theory and observation to proceed closely together, but their original precedence or protocol is of no interest. Observation suggests what phenomena need explaining; theory offers explanation; observation is again required to test the theory, and throw up the next round of problems.

When we say "theory" we mean

  i. a set of assumptions or hypotheses about behavior
 ii. a logical analysis
iii. a set of conclusions or predictions.

The role of mathematical analysis is to help with the second step: "If we assume so and so, what follows?" We are accustomed to doing this by ordinary or verbal reasoning, or, in first-year economics, with the help of some Euclidean geometry. But ordinary reasoning is verbal logic, and Euclidean geometry is two-dimensional logic. "Mathematics" is a catchall title for any sort of logical argument conducted with the help of symbols. We can regard ordinary verbal reasoning as a branch of mathematics if we like, or we can regard mathematics as a development of ordinary reasoning for cases in which verbal methods are cumbersome and inefficient. None of this matters very much. What matters is that we have to take the second step, to discover the logical implications of our assumptions, and we want the logical tools for the job. The selection of the tools in each case is a matter of convenience and our own technical skill. The greater is our command of the tools, the more intricate and potentially fruitful are the theories that we can handle.

Suppose, for example, that the observed phenomena we wish to explain are the behavior of prices, wages, and profits in certain specified circumstances. We must start with some behavioral assumptions, such as profit maximization by firms. We also need to know something about the technological limitations on the firm and thus might assume constant returns to scale as well as diminishing returns to each factor separately. We now have to work out all the implications of these assumptions to discover the testable predictions of the theory. If we have done our job efficiently, the theory will explain (i.e., predict) the behavior we set out to explain, but it is almost certain that the theory will also predict other behavior that we have not yet observed. The theory is tested by seeing if these additional predictions conform to the facts, and for this task we need to know some quite difficult statistical theory. Before we do our testing, however, we wish to discover *all* the implications of our basic assumptions. This purely logical process is one of the tasks undertaken by the economic theorist, and to be efficient in making his logical deductions he will need to use tools appropriate to the complexity of the basic assumptions. If the theory is simple, verbal analysis may be sufficient, whereas if the theory is complex, mathematical analysis will almost always be necessary; the attempt to rely on verbal reasoning alone will only leave us in a state of uncertainty as to whether a particular prediction is or is not logically implied by the theory at hand.[1] Only an obscurantist

---

[1] This point was illustrated dramatically to both authors when they were attending a conference some years ago. The first paper was given by a mathematical economist who presented a four-equation model of the behavior of firms, deduced all its testable implications, and showed how he had gone about testing some of them. Because of the mathematical nature of the tools used to make deductions, the paper was regarded by many of the audience as being "impossibly difficult." The second paper was given by a literary economist. Here the discussion centered (in purely verbal terms) on an important applied problem concerning the workings of the monetary system. The model involved had not been formally specified but must, at a guess, have involved about a dozen unknowns, and their relations over time, as governed by a set of unspecified simultaneous differential equations. Proper specification and solution would have been very difficult. As things stood, we did not even know if the model *had* a solution, but, because the argument was all conducted verbally, no one seemed to think that the economics was difficult. When an essentially complex theory is loosely and informally sketched, the intellectual effort subsequently devoted to its verbal analysis can only be a waste of time. No one could possibly have answered any of the questions posed in that discussion about the implications of the model being discussed without a formal specification and the application to it of some quite complex mathematical analysis. To pretend otherwise was self-delusion.

could regard this as a desirable situation. Thus we see that the mathematical and the verbal economists are not separated by their subject matter or their philosophy of social science, but only by the tools used to accomplish a step common to both: the discovery of all the implications of a stated set of hypotheses.

1.4 SOME FEATURES OF THIS BOOK

1. We assume that students have already taken a principles of economics course and are, or shortly will be, taking intermediate macro- or microeconomic theory. Sections that go furthest in intermediate theory appear later in the book. Material usually not included in intermediate theory courses is, as far as possible, self-contained.

2. Throughout most of the book, each chapter of mathematics is immediately followed by a chapter of economic applications.

3. At the beginning, we assume practically no mathematical background. Students may start reading the mathematics chapters at the point appropriate to their previous training, but they should *not* skip any of the applications chapters.

4. The mathematics in this book is definitely nonrigorous. Many people believe that it is wrong to teach mathematics in this way at all. Their perfectly proper respect for the integrity of mathematics leads them to say to the student, in effect, "Go away to the mathematics department for a year or more, and then we will tell you something interesting (in economics)." This is a good approach for some students, but for many reasons we do not believe that it is the only admissible approach: otherwise we should not have written this book. Two of our reasons deserve further comment.

First, we believe that many students of economics have been frightened off mathematics by being exposed to a tedious, mechanical, and totally unmotivated approach. In the interests of the victim of this treatment who wishes to learn economics, we try to compensate by adopting the rule of introducing no technique until it is evidently needed, and then no more of it than is to be immediately employed.

More fundamentally, however, we believe that mathematics is a subject, like economics, in which the correct teaching technique is to cover the same subject several times with increasing rigor. Historically, the fully rigorous development of a subject does not spring from some genius's mind in a single act of spontaneous creation. Rather, problems occur, and techniques—at first rather crude ones— are invented to handle them. Exploration of further problems sooner or later reveals some inadequacy in the techniques, which are then subjected to close scrutiny, and in due course improved. This process[2] may go on for a long time until the "fundamental underpinnings" of the technique are fully developed to the satisfaction of the mathematical theorists. The "finished article," or final state of the theory or theorem, emerges from the process with the property that it is carefully designed to take care of the problems and criticisms that have contributed to its development. In our opinion it is impossible for a student totally unacquainted with the development to understand and appreciate the final product. He needs to relive some of the historical development—which after all was necessary for his elders and betters. He needs to get an approximate idea of what the calculus is all about, to master the technique of differentiation, and to attack his problems in economics with these tools. Soon he will find that his rudimentary understanding is not sufficient. When he has encountered problems for which his existing knowledge is inadequate, he can return for a further investment in theory motivated by his *need* to know more, and his new theoretical knowledge can then be applied to the problem that led him to seek it. *We view this book as one step in a continuing process.* The student who goes on to further work in "mathematical economics" will need to work through the calculus a second, and possibly a third, time, getting a thorough grounding in its basic theory: otherwise he will be a blind rule follower rather than a master of his tools. But the theory will mean more to him when he knows why he needs it and when he meets problems that cannot be solved with the tools learned here.[3]

5. Some sections are starred, thus *. This means both that they are difficult and that their comprehension is not assumed in what follows. They may therefore be skipped entirely without subsequent penalty. Some exercises are starred too. This means simply that they are difficult. We have *not* adopted the policy, common in mathematical texts, of leaving to you to prove *in the exercises* results that will be *required* in the next chapter. If you cannot do a starred exercise, simply go on and do not be discouraged. At some later stage you will probably come back to it and find it quite easy.

---

[2] For a fascinating study of the process of the historical development of mathematics together with an implied criticism of current pedagogical techniques, see Imre Lakatos, "Proofs and Refutations," *British Journal for the Philosophy of Science*, four-part article, 1963–1964, vol. 14, pp. 1–25, 120–139, 221–245, and 296–342.

[3] This is a pedagogical approach adopted, with or without a conscious decision, by most economists. We go over the same subject matter with more and more rigor and depth several times in elementary, intermediate, and advanced courses. We implicitly recognize that the student cannot appreciate why a formal development of some model is needed until he has used a cruder version of the same model and has begun to encounter problems which his cruder model cannot handle.

1.5 THE CONTENTS OF THIS BOOK

One of our rules in preparing this book has been to introduce no mathematics that we do not use in economic applications, and to use none that we have not explained. This means, of course, that we have been very selective in our choice of mathematical topics, and much is omitted.

We can, in fact, concentrate on elementary calculus methods because of their wide applicability and crucial importance in the development of economics. The development of the calculus, and its application to economics, in alternating chapters, takes us from Chapter 2 to Chapter 11. The next three chapters are devoted to economic dynamics. Here we felt that we had to choose between introducing differential equations or difference equations, not wishing to take the space required to discuss both. We have chosen differential equations because they allow us to extend, albeit very briefly, our discussion of the calculus to the integral as well as the differential calculus.[4]

In Chapter 15 we introduce an entirely new topic, linear, or matrix, algebra. This is followed by three chapters of applications.

For economic applications we have concentrated on two central topics that will be familiar from any first-year principles course: the model of the competitive market and the macro-model (or income-determination model). These models are systematically extended in the chapters of applications. Two topics have been allotted self-contained chapters to themselves, input–output analysis (Chapter 17) and linear programming (Chapter 18). We felt that, having introduced the necessary algebra in Chapter 15, it would be a shame to omit such fascinating applications.

Many other topics, such as utility maximization, welfare economics, monopoly behavior, and production functions are taken up as convenient, to illustrate the use of mathematics in deriving interesting results in economic theory. None of these topics will be given the systematic development of the competitive model and the income-determination model. This is deliberate: this book is not intended as a substitute for the usual texts in intermediate economic theory, but as a complement.

---

[4] There already exist at least two superb introductions to difference equations for economists: W. J. Baumol, *Economic Dynamics: An Introduction*, 2nd ed., Macmillan, New York, 1959, and Samuel Goldberg, *Introduction to Difference Equations*, Wiley, New York, Science Editions (paperback), 1961.

Chapter **2**

Some Fundamental Techniques

Functions and Graphs

Economics is concerned with the behavior of measurable quantities such as wages, prices, national income, and employment, and with the relations between two or more of these quantities. In the first part of this chapter we present some of the basic mathematical ideas that are useful in analyzing relations between quantities. Most of the concepts in the first part are used, whether ostensibly or not, in a principles course, so that you will find many ideas that are familiar. The second part of this chapter contains no new ideas, but some useful tricks. Most of it is in any high school algebra book; it is not important to read it in sequence, and you may, if you wish, go straight on, coming back to the second part only when you find some gap in your knowledge that requires it.

2.1 KINDS OF NUMBERS

Economics is concerned with quantities, and we use numbers to express particular quantities. Such an apparently simple concept as number conceals surprisingly subtle complexities. Although at this stage we wish to avoid such complexities as far as possible, a few points need to be made.

We begin with the concept of an integer. Integers are the whole numbers of common experience, 0, 1, 2, 3, 4, 5, etc., together with their extension in a negative direction, $-1, -2, -3, -4, -5$, etc. We take these as understood, although defining them satisfactorily is actually not such an easy task.

We can use the concept of an integer to define rational numbers. Rational numbers are, or can be expressed as, the ratio of two integers. Numbers such as $\frac{1}{2}$, $\frac{2}{3}$, and $\frac{127}{16}$ are rationals. The class of rational numbers includes whole numbers[1] since any integer x can always be expressed as $x/1$. When expressed in decimal notation, a rational number is either a terminating decimal number (e.g., $\frac{5}{4} = 1.25$) or a recurring one (e.g., $\frac{2}{3} = 0.666$ repeating).

Another class of numbers is composed of the irrationals. These numbers cannot be expressed as the ratio of two integers. Examples of irrationals are $\sqrt{2}$ and π, familiar from school geometry. It is quite easy to prove (indeed it was discovered by Pythagoras) that there is no rational number x such that $x^2 = \sqrt{2}$. If we wish to extend the number system to include such numbers as $\sqrt{2}$, we must include irrationals along with rationals.

The real number system is a wider class of numbers that includes both the rational and the irrational numbers. The real number system does not, however, exhaust all the numbers that we can imagine.

In the manipulation of some quite simple mathematical problems we encounter the square roots of negative numbers, e.g., $\sqrt{-144}$ or $\sqrt{-5.0625}$. If these were positive numbers, they would pose no problem: $\sqrt{144}$ is 12 and $\sqrt{5.0625}$ is $\frac{9}{4}$. There is, however, no real number x such that x^2 is a negative number. We deal with square roots of negative numbers by extending our concept of number to include so-called imaginary numbers. If we take $\sqrt{-144}$, we can rewrite this as $\sqrt{(-1)(+144)}$. Taking the square root of the positive term this is $12\sqrt{-1}$. We now introduce the symbol i to indicate $\sqrt{-1}$. Any imaginary number can be expressed as i *times* a real number. Let there be any negative number $-X$. We write the square root of it $\sqrt{-X}$. This can always be rewritten $\sqrt{(-1)(+X)} = \sqrt{X}\sqrt{-1}$. Writing i for $\sqrt{-1}$ and b for $\sqrt{X}$, we have bi, where b is a real number and i is the square root of minus one. The entire number bi is called an imaginary number. Thus in our earlier example $\sqrt{-144} = 12i$.

Imaginary numbers and real numbers are included in the more general class of complex numbers. A complex number can be expressed in the form

$$a + bi \quad ,$$

where a is called the real part and bi is the imaginary part. Thus we

---

[1] For some purposes it is important to distinguish between an integer such as 2 and the rational number $\frac{2}{1} = 2.000$ repeating, but this distinction need not concern us here.

can look upon real numbers as the class of complex numbers in which $b = 0$ and imaginary numbers as the class in which $a = 0$. In this book we shall rarely have to deal with complex numbers. It may be taken for granted that we are referring to the real number system unless we explicitly say otherwise.

An important distinction within the class of real numbers is between numbers that depend on the units of measurement and numbers that do not, the latter being called *pure numbers*. The length of a field depends on the unit of measurement. It might, for example, be stated as 100 yards or 300 feet or 3600 inches. The *ratio* of the length to the width of the field is, however, a pure number. If the ratio is 2, for example, then the result will be found whatever the unit of measurement. Thus 100 yards/50 yards = 300 feet/150 feet = 3600 inches/1800 inches = 2. (Because when the unit of measurement is changed both the top and bottom of the fraction length/width are multiplied by the same number x, the x cancels out, and the ratio is unaffected.)

2.2 QUANTITIES AND DISTANCES

If we observe that during 1975 one household bought 50 pounds of meat whereas another household bought 90 pounds, we have observed two quantities. It is always possible, and very often convenient, to relate these quantities to distances on a one-dimensional scale. In Figure 2.1 we mark a zero as our point of origin, that is, the point from which all measurement begins; we agree to measure positive quantities to the right of the origin and negative quantities to the left. This is an arbitrary convention, and we could just as well have reversed our directions of measurement. We also select arbitrarily a specific distance to correspond to a specific quantity. In the scale in Figure 2.1 we have used the following relation:

$$\text{1 pound of meat purchased corresponds to } \tfrac{1}{55} \text{ of 1 inch} \quad , \quad (1)$$

or, what is the same thing,

$$\text{1 inch corresponds to 55 pounds of meat purchased} \quad . \quad (2)$$

We now show our two households' expenditures on meat by the dots in Figure 2.1.

In the above example we could not have negative quantities because it is impossible for a household to spend less than nothing on

Figure 2.1

meat. Now, however, consider a firm that is both buying and selling meat. This firm holds a stock of meat in deepfreeze. Sometimes it adds to its stock by buying meat, and sometimes it reduces its stock by selling meat. If we let purchases be positive numbers (they add to stocks) and sales be negative numbers (they subtract from stocks), the transactions in which we are interested can range over negative as well as positive quantities. The lower limit is no longer zero but that set by the total stocks of meat held, since the firm cannot sell more than it has. The firm's purchases and sales are illustrated in Figure 2.2, where it is supposed that in four successive months the firm sells 10,000 pounds of meat, buys 75,000 pounds, buys 40,000 pounds and sells 90,000 pounds (and the scale is obviously different from that of Figure 2.1).

We have now taken one of the initial steps in geometrical development: we have related measurable quantities to physical distances. Before proceeding, you should ponder on the power of abstractions that we normally accept without a moment's thought. What could be less obviously related than one dozen eggs and the distance from New York to Panama, and what could be less obviously related than two dozen eggs and the distance from New York to Freetown? And yet by observing that

$$1 \text{ dozen eggs} = \tfrac{1}{2} \text{ of } 2 \text{ dozen eggs}$$

and that

the distance from New York to Panama
$$= \tfrac{1}{2} \text{ of the distance from New York to Freetown}$$

we are on our way to establishing a formal similarity. Rearranging both expressions we have

$$\frac{1 \text{ dozen eggs}}{2 \text{ dozen eggs}} = \frac{1}{2} \tag{3}$$

and

$$\frac{\text{distance New York to Panama}}{\text{distance New York to Freetown}} = \frac{1}{2} . \tag{4}$$

Because the left-hand sides of (3) and (4) are both equal to $\tfrac{1}{2}$, we can equate them to each other, writing

$$\frac{1 \text{ dozen eggs}}{2 \text{ dozen eggs}} = \frac{\text{distance New York to Panama}}{\text{distance New York to Freetown}} , \tag{5}$$

which tells us: *quantitatively one dozen eggs stands in the same relation to two dozen eggs as does the distance from New York to Panama to the distance from New York to Freetown.* It is this relation of pro-

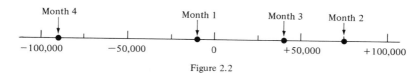

Figure 2.2

portionality that allows us to represent physical quantities such as a number of eggs by distances.

Next we can take two big steps toward abstracting from unnecessary detail. First we use the letter M to indicate meat purchases and sales. In a particular example M will take a numerical value such as 20,000 pounds. In the example of household purchases given above we had $M = 50$ and $M = 90$; and in the second example of the firm's purchases and sales M took the values of $-10,000$, $+75,000$, $+40,000$, and $-90,000$ in four successive months. M is called a *variable*, and it stands for a particular magnitude, meat sales and purchases in this case, but the actual quantity it takes on will, as we have already seen, vary from example to example. As a matter of convention, letters at the end of the alphabet, w, x, y, and z, are commonly used to indicate variable quantities, but we are free to choose other letters, and it is often convenient, as in the above example, to choose a letter as an aid to memory (M reminds us that we are talking about meat).

The second step is to suppress the actual numbers on our scale and deal only in *relative* distances and *relative* quantities. If M takes on two successive values, the second being twice as large as the first, we can show this by points M_1 and M_2 in Figure 2.3. Note that the values of M_1 and M_2 correspond to distances measured from the origin. If we let a stand for the point on the scale at which M_1 is located and b stand for the point at which M_2 is located, then the quantity M_1 corresponds to the distance from 0 to a, which we write $0a$, while the quantity M_2 corresponds to the distance from 0 to b, which we write $0b$. Since we are told that $M_1 = \frac{1}{2}M_2$, we must measure our distances so that $0a = \frac{1}{2}0b$.

The one-dimensional scale we have used in Figures 2.1, 2.2, and 2.3 is often known as the "real line." Each of the real numbers can be regarded as a point on the real line measured with an arbitrary unit of distance from an arbitrary origin. Locating a nonrecurring decimal on the real line poses no problems. The number $\frac{3}{2}$, for example, is located $1\frac{1}{2}$ units to the right of the origin. Recurring decimals, however, do present a problem. Consider, for example, the

Figure 2.3

number $\frac{2}{3}$, or 0.666 repeating. We can locate this only by putting it in an interval "between" two nonrecurring numbers such as 0.6 and 0.7. We can, however, locate it as closely as we like by making the interval as small as we like, e.g., 0.66 and 0.67 or 0.666 and 0.667 and so on. Similarly, the irrationals can always be located in an interval between two nonrecurring decimals. Thus the entire real line may be taken as the geometrical counterpart of the entire system of real numbers.

One of the most important properties of the real number system is that no matter how small an interval we pick there will always be an infinite number of real numbers within that interval. Thus we can never find an interval small enough so that there are no real numbers within it. As an example, suppose that we consider the interval from 0.9 to 1.0. We may subdivide this into ten intervals, and pick one, say 0.99 to 1.0. We subdivide once more, pick one interval, say 0.999 to 1.0. We subdivide and pick one interval again, and so on. We shall not prove, but do assert, that this process may be continued indefinitely without ever producing a "hole," that is, a small interval within which there are no real numbers. This idea is expressed by saying that the real number system is "dense." Both the rationals and irrationals are dense in the sense that between any two rationals, no matter how close together, there is an infinite number of other rationals, and similarly for irrationals.

The geometrical counterpart of the density of the real number system is the "completeness" of the real line. There are no breaks or gaps in the real line: between any two points, no matter how close they are together, there is an infinite number of other points. This completeness is fundamental to mathematical analysis, but discussion of its significance is beyond the scope of this book. We shall simply take for granted the geometrical representation of a real number system with no holes.

2.3 RELATIONS BETWEEN VARIABLES: COORDINATE GEOMETRY

In economics we are not only concerned with variable quantities such as a firm's purchases of meat, but also with the *relation between or among* two or more measurable quantities, such as meat purchases and the price of meat. Suppose that we are told the wholesale prices of meat in the four months for which the firm purchased and sold the quantities of meat recorded in Figure 2.2. We use the symbol p to stand for price. Assume that the values are as follows: month 1, $p = 3.7$, month 2, $p = 2.0$, month 3, $p = 2.7$, month 4, $p = 5.3$. These four prices can be plotted on a price scale as shown in Figure 2.4. You will note that we have allowed for negative as well as for positive prices. These

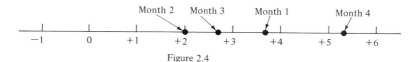

Figure 2.4

will not occur in the present example, but they can be given an economic meaning: a negative price is a subsidy paid to the purchasers of a commodity. Thus if the price of a commodity is $1, the purchaser must give up $1 to obtain a unit; if the price is zero, the commodity is a free good; and if the price is −$1, the purchaser receives a gift or subsidy of $1 on every unit of the commodity that he obtains.

In the present example we are concerned with the *relation* between the two variables, sales and purchases of meat and the price of meat. How can we study this relation? First, we can write the data in a table, such as Table 2.1. But if we wish to *see* the relationship diagrammatically, what shall we do? This problem was solved some 300 years ago by René Descartes. His solution is one of the great landmarks in the history of mathematics: it produced coordinate geometry, and a union between algebra and geometry that we exploit whenever, for example, an economics instructor says "We can express this relation in an algebraic equation or in a graph." The solution, as we all know today, is to set the two scales in Figures 2.2 and 2.4 at right angles to each other with their origins at the same point, thus making it possible for a single point in the diagram to refer to the two separate scales simultaneously. Now we can show the price ruling in a particular month and the amount bought or sold in that month by a single dot. In Figure 2.5 we combine Figures 2.2 and 2.4 in the manner we have just described.

As a matter of convention the horizontal axis is often called the X-axis or the abscissa, while the vertical axis is often called the Y-axis or the ordinate. But this is only terminology, and we shall not again have occasion to use the terms abscissa and ordinate in this book. Some of you may have been frightened by teachers who thought it was more important to memorize names, and to learn by rote how to carry out complex operations, than to understand the essential ideas

Table 2.1

Month	Quantity	Price
1	−10,000	3.7
2	+75,000	2.0
3	+40,000	2.7
4	−90,000	5.3

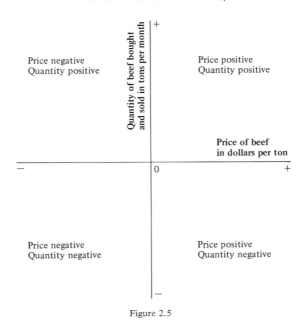

Figure 2.5

behind what you were doing. If so, you may still feel a vague feeling of distaste whenever new terminology is encountered. Of course, naming things is not mathematics, and the purpose of names is only to make discourse easier by providing a commonly understood set of labels.

Setting the two lines perpendicular to each other as in Figure 2.5 divides the total space into four parts, referred to as quadrants or orthants. The upper right-hand quadrant is the one in which both variables are positive (or zero *on* one or other of the axes), and is often referred to as the *positive quadrant*. Except on an axis, everywhere in the lower right-hand quadrant, *y* is negative and *x* positive; everywhere in the upper left-hand quadrant, *y* is positive and *x* negative; everywhere in the lower left-hand quadrant, both variables are negative. In many economic problems we can rule out negative values of all the variables as being impossible, and when we draw graphs to show the relation between such variables we usually give only the positive quadrant (as, say, with the usual textbook demand curve).

We are now ready to take the data from Table 2.1 and plot them on a graph. Each dot in Figure 2.6 shows the quantity of meat bought or sold in a given month *and* the price ruling at the time. Reading upwards, the dots refer to months 4, 1, 3, and 2. Thus, dot 4 is 90,000 pounds below the origin on the quantity scale and 5.3 to the right of the origin on the price scale, indicating that in a month in which the price was 5.3 the firm sold 90,000 pounds of meat.

Thus we see that the relationship between two variables can be shown on a coordinate graph. A single point indicates simultaneously distances along the two scales which have been set at right angles to each other. Let us explore this idea a little further. First, it is general: the method of exhibiting a relationship is not confined to that between the price and quantity of meat sold. We can denote any two quantities in which we are interested by x and y, and use a graph like Figure 2.6 to show the relationship between them. The second point is that, as we have already mentioned, the relationship may be exhibited by this graphical method or by algebra.

In combining Figures 2.2 and 2.4 to produce Figures 2.5 and 2.6, what we have done is set our two real lines at right angles to one another (in such a fashion that the zero points coincide). The resulting *plane* is sometimes known as "Cartesian space." We have already seen that there are no "holes" in the real line. It follows that there are no holes in the plane generated by setting two real lines at right angles. Thus every point in the plane is the geometrical representation of a pair of numbers, one measured on the x-axis and one on the y-axis. Thus the point marked 2, for example, in Figure 2.6, is the geometrical representation of the numbers 2.0, 75,000. This is obviously a different point from that representing 75,000, 2.0. Thus, once we have committed ourselves to labeling our axes, *order* matters: points represent pairs of numbers identified by order. For this reason, the points in

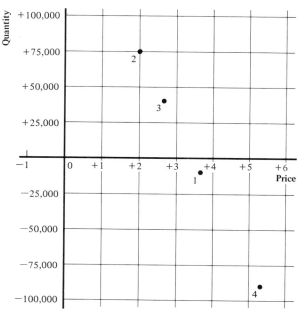

Figure 2.6

our plane are sometimes referred to as "ordered pairs" of numbers.

Application of a ruler to Figure 2.6 will reveal that the four points lie on a straight line. What is called "the equation of a straight line" is

$$y = ax + b \quad .$$

This says that y is equal to some constant amount, a, multiplied by the value of x, plus another constant amount b. Examples of straight lines are

$$y = 2x + 3 \tag{6}$$

and

$$y = 5x - 1 \quad . \tag{7}$$

If you are not familiar with the idea of "the equation" corresponding to "a graph," it would be a good idea to draw your own graph and plot a few points on each of the lines given by (6) and (7). To see that graph and equation convey the same information, consider the following experiment. Suppose that we are told the value of x in example (6) and are asked to find y. If you are told that x is 3, y is found from $y = (2)(3) + 3 = 9$ (where we use parentheses to indicate multiplication). If we had the graph instead of the equation, we could find y by starting at the point corresponding to 3 on the x-axis, moving vertically to the graph of the relationship and then horizontally to the y-axis.

The use of coordinate geometry is not confined to straight lines. In Figure 2.7, we have plotted two curves. Each one of them illus-

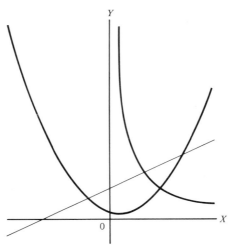

Figure 2.7

trates a possible relationship between x and y, and, in each case, if we were given the x-value, we could read off the corresponding y-value. But if we had the equations for these curves instead of the graphs, we could use them to calculate y for given x. Because we do not have them, and are not bothering with numerical examples, we have suppressed the scale in Figure 2.7. The variables y and x increase in the usual directions along the two axes, but as it is immaterial to our illustration whether 1 inch corresponds to 1 unit of x or to 20, we have omitted the scale entirely. This is a simplification — or suppression of irrelevant detail — which we shall often employ.

2.4 FUNCTIONAL RELATIONS

The idea that there is a relationship between x and y can be expressed quite generally. We may draw illustrative graphs, as in Figures 2.6 and 2.7, but we may also write

$$y = f(x) \quad ,$$

which is read "y is a function of x" or "y equals $f-$of$-x$." This simple way of writing "y is related to x" is an important notational device that requires careful study. We already know that a graph is the geometrical representation of the relationship between two variables, or, as we shall now say, of a function. If we have the graph, we may use it to read off the value of y, given x; and similarly, if we have the function written out algebraically, we can calculate y, given x (in fact, we shall have to do this to draw the graph!). Thus a function provides us with a *rule* for getting the value of one variable given the other. When we say that $y = f(x)$, we assert that a rule exists, although without saying what it is. Our rough intuitive idea of there being "a relationship" between x and y has now become formal: if there is a *rule* which assigns a *single, definite*, y-value to each x-value, then y is a function of x. (Warning: if y is a function of x, it does *not* necessarily follow that x is a function of y. This "inverse" relation is discussed in Section 2.7.)

There are many things to be said about functions and their use and interpretation. Let us start by getting the notation quite clear. In elementary algebra we learn that brackets mean "multiply." Thus

$$a(x + b) = ax + ab \quad .$$

The parentheses in $f(x)$ mean nothing of the sort. $f(x)$ is to be read "function of x," and f is not a quantity with which one may multiply, add, divide, etc.: it stands for the *rule* for getting from x to y, and a rule cannot be operated on as if it were a number.

Since, however, we can multiply or divide or add to or subtract from y in the ordinary way, $ay = af(x)$: multiplying y by a is the same thing as multiplying $f(x)$ by a, since the value of $f(x)$ is y. It is the letter f itself that cannot be treated in this way.

Functions are frequently denoted by Greek letters, such as ϕ and ψ, and other letters from the Roman alphabet such as g. Another notation is to repeat the letter on the left-hand side. Thus $y = y(x)$ means the same thing as $y = f(x)$: there is a functional relationship between x and y. Economists frequently use this notation because it serves to remind us of the variables we are discussing. Thus "investment depends on the rate of interest" can be written $I = I(r)$, and "consumption depends on the level of income" as $C = C(Y)$.

We have said that a function is a rule assigning a single y-value to each x-value. We shall study only what are called "real-valued functions." We know that all points in the Cartesian plane represent pairs of real numbers, which may be denoted by (x, y). A rule for finding y, given x, is therefore a rule to go *from* one real number *to* another. (If we go from x to y, x is called the independent variable or argument of the function.) We may not, however, wish our rule to extend over all possible values of x (or y). Thus if we are dealing with household purchases of meat, we may wish to exclude negative quantities and negative prices. A demand curve expresses a rule for going from market price to household purchases. We exclude negative quantities and prices by saying that the rule is *defined* only for positive values. If in this case we were asked to use our rule to calculate demand for a negative price, we should reply that we had no rule for doing so: the demand curve had been drawn only in the positive orthant.

This suggests that a function needs to be defined over some specified interval of values for x, which is called the *domain* of the function. In economic applications, this is often so obvious that we do not trouble to mention it. For example, we usually exclude negative values of income automatically, and therefore confine ourselves to what is called the "positive half of the real line"; we know that the percentage unemployment rate is defined only over the interval 0 to 100; if we exclude negative quantities as well as prices, then we confine ourselves to rules for going from points on the positive half of the real line to points on the positive half. Thus we restrict the interval within which $f(x)$ may lie as well as the interval over which x may vary. The interval within which $f(x)$ may lie, that is, the values that we may obtain for y under our rule, is called the *range* of the function. In most of our economic applications, we shall not find it necessary even to refer to the domain and range of our functions, but we shall sometimes find that, to avoid mathematical difficulties, it pays to be very careful.

It is probably not at all clear why it helps to have a way of writing down "there is a functional relationship" even if we do not know what it is. The answer is that we may know enough about the functional relationship to advance our discussion even though we are ignorant of the precise form of the function. The converse of this argument is that for some purposes the precise relationship may not matter, but only certain of its characteristics. In this case, we do not want to be encumbered with particular functional forms, and it is a great convenience to have a notation that allows us to dispense with any particular piece of information that is not presently important.

An illustration may clarify some of these ideas. It is widely believed that drinking contributes to road accidents. If we write A for the number of accidents per year, and C for consumption of alcohol per year, we may write $A = f(C)$: there is a functional relationship between drinking and accidents. We do not know the precise form of f, so we do not have the exact rule for going from C to A, but we do know something about it: if drinking increases, we believe that accidents do. This tells us that A is an *increasing function* of C: if C rises, so does A. This is sufficient information to allow us to answer the question "Will a reduction in drinking lead to a reduction in accidents?" This is obvious, but in many cases we do not know if a particular function everywhere increases or decreases, or increases over some values of x and not over others. In such a case it may well be that the mere discovery of this basic property of the function will be sufficient to solve our problem, and the subject of inquiry will therefore be into the direction of change of the function. Again, if this is sufficient to solve the problem, we may not know, and shall not care, what the particular functional form may be, and shall give thanks for a notation that allows us to proceed in general terms.

2.5 SOME SIMPLE FUNCTIONS

We have seen that a function is a precise rule that gets us from x to y. As it is a rule, it tells us what we have to do, when we have the value of x, in order to find the corresponding value of y. Thus the rule might be "add 10," or "divide by 2," or "take the square root" — or do all three of these things in sequence. It is a good deal quicker to write down the rules symbolically. Thus the rule to add 10, divide by 2, and take the square root can be written

$$\sqrt{\frac{x + 10}{2}} \ . \tag{8}$$

Examination of (8) suggests that we have already encountered a case in which we should be careful about the domain of x over which the function is defined. Thus suppose that x is -20. Then our rule leads to $\sqrt{-\frac{10}{2}}$. This is an imaginary number. If, therefore, we wish to confine ourselves to real numbers, we could limit the domain of x in our numerical example by defining the function over positive values of x only. If we wished, we could instead define the function for values of x greater than -10. What we choose to do depends on the application we have in mind.

(8) is an expression that contains only x, without y, as are

$$10 + 2x \qquad\qquad (9)$$

and

$$5 - 2x + x^2 \quad . \qquad\qquad (10)$$

This suggests that, when we are interested in the rule itself, we do not have to write "$y =$" all the time. We can speak of "functions of x," of which expressions (8), (9), and (10) are examples, without having to introduce y. After all, y is only another name for the value of the function, which is the value we obtain when we perform the operations directed by the rule. If our interest is in the rule, and the operations we have to perform, we may talk simply of x and $f(x)$ without y.

Now let us consider the rules in examples (9) and (10). We give x any value we wish, insert that value into the expression in place of x, and calculate the value of the whole expression. Table 2.2 shows the results for selected values of x in (9). We can do the same thing for the other function and obtain Table 2.3.

Table 2.2

x	$f(x) = 10 + 2x$
-100	-190
-1	8
0	10
1	12
10	30
50	110

Table 2.3

x	$f(x) = 5 - 2x + x^2$
-100	10,205
-1	8
0	5
1	4
10	85
50	2,405

You should calculate one or two values for each function to satisfy yourself that you can do it if necessary. This shows that you really do understand what the rules require. Once you are sure that you do know what is going on, further calculation is a purely mechanical exercise. You should never confuse dexterity at extended calculation with mathematical understanding. Unfortunately, they are often confused in school, and all too many students come to believe that they have no taste for mathematics because they are, quite rightly, bored by the repeated performance of routine calculations that could be done faster by machine.

A little experimentation will soon show us that there are families of functions, each family displaying certain common characteristics. The simplest family is that of the linear functions, of which (6), (7), and (9) are members. Here are three other members of the family:

$$-4x + 5$$

$$0.5x$$

$$2x - 10 \quad .$$

We have already encountered the general *linear function*

$$ax + b \quad .$$

In this expression a and b are called coefficients or *parameters*, while x is a variable. Assigning a value to the two parameters singles out a particular member of the family. For any one member of the family, e.g., $2x - 10$, the parameters are constant. Given the values of the parameters, we may read off the values of the function as the value of x is allowed to vary.

Another very common function is the quadratic

$$ax^2 + bx + c \quad . \tag{11}$$

Expression (10) is a member of this family. Any other member is obtained by giving particular numerical values to the parameters a, b, and c, provided that a is not zero.

All members of the quadratic family have certain characteristics in common and are distinctively different from all members of the linear family. These general characteristics are worthy of study since in many practical problems particular linear or quadratic functions will occur.[2] Then our general knowledge of the characteristics of these functions allows us to handle the particular case being studied without having laboriously to rediscover these characteristics in each specific case. We could, of course, always select a large number of

---

[2] For example, we often use linear demand curves which give rise to quadratic total revenue curves (e.g., if $p = 100 - 2q$, $TR = pq = 100q - 2q^2$).

values of x, calculate the corresponding values of $f(x)$, plot these on a graph, and join them up, but if we had to do this each time we encountered a quadratic we would be involved in a lot of tedious calculations. Again, the economy of mathematical abstraction comes to our rescue. It is easy to prove that there is one and only one quadratic that passes through any three points, and thus we need plot only three points from our function to determine its complete shape. It is clearly a great economy to know about the general characteristics of families of functions. Thus a parabola may look something like this: ∪, or this: ∩. In both cases it is symmetrical about a line drawn perpendicularly through its high or low point. A linear function, on the other hand, looks like this: ╱, or this: ╲.

Although there are differences between them, both linear and quadratic functions are members of a wider class of functions called polynominals. Polynominals may be written in the form

$$a_0 + a_1x + a_2x^2 + a_3x^3 + \cdots + a_nx^n$$

(where $a_0, a_1, \ldots, a_n$ are coefficients, and the dots indicate that terms of the same form as those printed have been omitted). The straight line is the special case of a polynominal in which a_1 must be nonzero, a_0 may be zero or nonzero, and all other coefficients must be zero. The quadratic is the special case in which a_2 must be nonzero, a_0 and a_1 may be zero or nonzero, and all other coefficients must be zero. Any combination of zero and nonzero coefficients is, of course, possible, and thus a wide variety of differently behaved functions falls within the general class of polynominals. We could, for example, have $10 + 4x^5 - 2x^{20}$, or $5 - 4x + x^2 + 2x^{64}$, and so on.

It is convenient at this point to go through some taxonomy of functions. You should read this section to become acquainted with the vocabulary, and then refer back to refresh your memory when necessary. An *increasing function* is one the value of which always increases as the value of the independent variable increases. A *decreasing function* is one the value of which decreases whenever the value of the independent variable increases. The classes of increasing and decreasing functions are together called *monotonic functions*, and we may therefore speak of monotonic increasing or monotonic decreasing functions. The straight line $ax + b$ provides an example of a monotonic function. If the coefficient a is positive, we have a monotonic increasing function, as in $2x + 10$. If the coefficient a is negative, we have a monotonic decreasing function, as in $-2x + 10$. If the coefficient a were zero, we would have a horizontal straight line, which is neither increasing nor decreasing. It is sometimes necessary to distinguish between functions, $f(x)$, that *always* increase or decrease as x increases and those that never change direction but stay constant over some values of x, calling the former *strictly monotonic* and the latter simply *monotonic*.

Many functions increase as x increases over some range of values and decrease as x increases over other values. Such functions are not monotonic. A simple example is the quadratic (11). Thus consider $2x^2 - 3x + 10$. You should compare for yourself the effect on the value of the function of increasing x from -4 to -3 and from $+3$ to $+4$.

2.6 CONTINUITY AND SMOOTHNESS

Let us look at a very familiar function, $f(x) = 1/x$. The rule stated by this function is simply to divide x into 1. For positive values of x, the value of the function decreases as x increases. For negative values of x, the domain of the function is the negative half of the real line, and the farther from the origin we take x in the negative direction, the nearer the origin are the (negative) values of $f(x)$. But what happens if $x = 0$? The rule directs us to take $\frac{1}{0}$, but this is impossible: division by zero is not defined.[3] From this we see that, although we may define this function over the positive and negative halves of the real line, we are obliged to exclude the origin. There is a "hole" in the graph of the function at $x = 0$. If we try to trace the graph of $1/x$, we find that we have to "take the pencil off the paper" between the two "arms": we cannot "join up." Wherever this happens, if it happens, we say that there is a *discontinuity* in the function. In this case the discontinuity is forced on us by the fact that division by zero is not defined.

We may illustrate further by considering the simplest formula for a multiplier. If we denote the multiplier by k and the marginal propensity to consume by c, we have $k = 1/(1 - c)$. We see that k is a function of c. Now suppose that we permitted c to take on any value on the real line. If $c = 1$, we have $\frac{1}{0}$, which is not defined. Hence there would be a discontinuity at this value. Economists usually avoid this discontinuity by restricting c to be less than unity but greater than zero, and defining the multiplier only over this domain.

Discontinuities may arise in other ways. Thus suppose that every candidate in an examination who scores more than some preassigned mark, t, receives a prize (perhaps a university place), whereas no one who scores less receives anything. We define a function of x, the percentage mark with range zero to one hundred, to y (prize) as follows:

---

[3] There is no mystery about this. If $a/b = x$, say, then x is the number that, multiplied by b, gives a. In other words, $bx = a$. But suppose that $b = 0$. There *is no number* x such that its product with zero gives a, unless a is also equal to zero. But when we should have $a/b = 0/0$, which is meaningless since we get $0 \cdot x = 0$, which is true for any x.

$$y = 1 \text{ (prize)} \qquad \text{if } x \text{ exceeds } t$$

$$y = 0 \text{ (no prize)} \qquad \text{if } x \text{ is less than } t \quad .$$

(We appear to have omitted the score t itself. We could either rewrite the rule "$y = 1$ if x is t or more," or assume that the examiners will be careful not to award this ambiguous mark.) Representation of "prize–no prize" by 1 and 0 is arbitrary: we could have chosen any other pair of (distinct) numbers. Whatever number we choose, the graph will look like that of Figure 2.8: the function "jumps" at $x = t$, and cannot be drawn without removing the pencil from the paper.

It is clear that we have not yet *defined* continuity: "without taking the pencil from the paper" is a primitive physical analogy, although it captures the idea. We shall not give a formal definition of continuity here, but we may express the idea a little more precisely and without resort to analogy. Suppose that $y = f(x)$ is defined over some domain of x-values. Let us choose a point, say $x = t$, in that interval, and ask if the function is continuous at t. At this point the value of the function is $y = f(t)$, and to deal with the question of continuity we consider a very small change in the value of y, to $y + \epsilon$, say, where ϵ is a number we choose, and are at liberty to make as small as we please. The function $y = f(x)$ is continuous at t if we can find, for any ϵ, an interval around t, which we might denote by $(t - h, t + h)$, so that for any value of x *between* $t - h$ and $t + h$ the difference between $f(x)$ and $f(t)$ is less than ϵ. This definition excludes "jumps" in the value of y. It is illustrated in Figure 2.9. If we can pick the point t anywhere in the interval over which f is defined, then f is continuous over that interval. In this case, there can be no "holes" in y such as occur at $x = 0$ if $y = 1/x$. And if the function is defined over the whole real line,

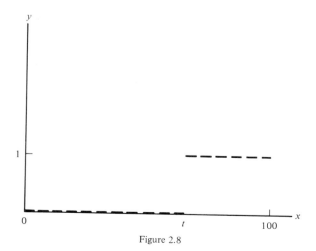

Figure 2.8

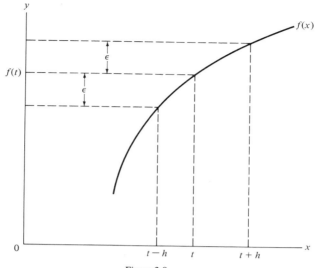

Figure 2.9

and we can choose t anywhere we please, then the function is "everywhere continuous."

The concept of continuity is fundamental to mathematical analysis, but this is as much as we need to know for the purpose of this book. In our economic applications, we shall usually assume, without discussion, that the functions we are dealing with are continuous.

Closely allied to the concept of continuity is the notion of "smoothness," but the concepts are not the same. We shall say more about smoothness below. For the moment, by a smooth curve we mean one that is not only continuous but that has no "corners." A continuous curve may have corners. Thus consider the function illustrated in Figure 2.10, which is

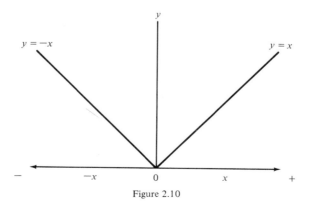

Figure 2.10

$$y = x \qquad \text{if } x \text{ is positive}$$

$$y = -x \qquad \text{if } x \text{ is negative}$$

defined over the whole real line. At $x = 0$, $y = 0$: there are no holes or jumps. Yet there is certainly a "corner" at $x = 0$. Again, in many applications we shall assume without discussion that our functions are smooth as well as continuous. As we shall see below, if we could not make this assumption, our main tools of analysis would not work. This would not be a disaster because there are mathematical tools for handling functional relations that are discontinuous and that contain "kinks." But these tools are not part of the subject matter of this book.

2.7   EXPLICIT AND IMPLICIT FUNCTIONS

We have interpreted a function as a rule assigning a unique y-value to each x-value. It is natural to ask if we can go in the other direction. That is, given the rule f, can we find a rule to go *from y to x?* If we can, we have a new function, which we might write $x = g(y)$. Since this function is derived from f, and reverses the direction in which we go from one variable to the other, it is called the *inverse function,* and is often written f^{-1}. Economic applications are obvious: we sometimes think of price being a function of quantity and sometimes of quantity being a function of price; a consumption function allows us to discover what consumption will be if we know income, but it also allows us to deduce what income must have been if we know consumption; and so on. It turns out, however, that inverse functions do not always exist.

This may sound startling, or suggest some quibble, but it is in fact very simple. Thus consider the function illustrated in Figure 2.10. To every value of x there corresponds a unique value of y, but to every positive y-value there correspond two x-values, one positive and one negative. Now, if we are given y, we do not know which x to choose: we could take a positive or a negative value. Thus we could not formulate a rule. If, of course, we restricted the domain of x to some interval within which the values of x were either all positive or all negative, and defined f over that interval only, the difficulty would disappear: a single value of x would correspond to each y, and the rule f^{-1} would be perfectly clear.

A more extreme example in which there is no inverse is given by the function illustrated in Figure 2.8. This function is not continuous; but suppose that we "join it up" at $x = t$. It is still the case that to each of the two possible values of y there corresponds an infinite number of values of x. No inverse rule can be given.

We may now give the condition for the inverse of a continuous function to exist: $f(x)$ must be *strictly monotonic increasing* or *strictly monotonic decreasing* over the interval. Thus in our first example, the inverse exists over suitably chosen intervals: for $f(x)$, x positive, considered separately, and for $f(x)$, x negative, considered separately. In our second example no patching will yield an inverse. We would have to make the y-value increase or decrease (continuously) over the domain of x to ensure that we could go from *any* y to a *single* value of x. Consider also the horizontal straight line $y = c$ for some domain of x. This is a function because to each x-value we assign a single definite value to y (which is, of course, c). But it has no inverse, because we can assign *any* x-value (within the domain) to the single value of y within the range of the function.

The functions $y = f(x)$ or $x = g(y)$ are written in what is called *explicit form*. We sometimes encounter functions written in the form

$$F(x, y) = 0 \quad .$$

This is known as the *implicit form* and will be of great service later on. It is clear that if we are given $y = f(x)$, we can write the implicit form directly as

$$y - f(x) = F(x, y) = 0 \quad .$$

What is *not* true is that if we are given a function in implicit form, we can always obtain an explicit form. In some cases, it is easy. Thus if $y - 3x^2 + 3x + 10 = 0$, it is simple to write $y = 3x^2 - 3x - 10$.

Consider, however, the pairs of values of x and y which are graphed by the circle illustrated in Figure 2.11. Two possible values

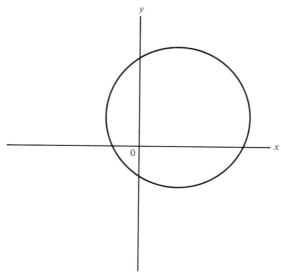

Figure 2.11

of y correspond to each positive value of x, and two to each negative value. Vice versa, two possible values of x correspond to each positive value of y, and two to each negative value. Thus it is clear that we are in trouble: we can express neither y as a function of x nor x as a function of y. Since a circle is, after all, a common object, this might appear scandalous. In implicit form, however, all is well. The equation of a circle with unit radius is

$$x^2 + y^2 - 1 = 0 \quad .$$

(It does not matter if you have forgotten this or never learned it.) This equation cannot be solved for x or y to obtain a function defined on the real line. What the equation does here is give a rule for finding *pairs* of values for x and y that satisfy the condition $F(x, y) = 0$.

The question of the conditions on which we can move from an implicit to an explicit form is much too complicated to settle here. It is, however, useful to know that we can always move in the other direction. Later on, we shall develop methods for dealing with functions in implicit form. These methods are extremely powerful. At the least, they may save us the labor of "unscrambling" an implicit form to obtain an explicit one; and, at the most, they will work even in cases where we can not unscramble.

2.8   FUNCTIONAL RELATIONS AND CAUSAL RELATIONS

When we discussed the relationship between road accidents and drinking, it was very clear that we had a causal relationship in mind. The existence of a rule for going from the value of one variable to the value of another does *not* imply anything about causation. It is important to be clear about this. If we want to deal analytically with a causal relationship, we shall obviously write it in functional form; but the assertion that there exists a definite rule relating two variables says nothing about causes. When we write $y = f(x)$, we are only saying "let y be the value obtained when we operate on x by the rule f." If we also suppose that x stands for some observable quantity and that y stands for another observable quantity, then when we write $y = f(x)$ we only say "the value of y can be found by operating on x in the manner directed." This, of course, means that x and y are systematically associated. This systematic association may be because x influences y, because y influences x, because although x and y are not related they are both influenced by some common causal factor z, or because y and x just happen to have varied with each other by chance.

Let us consider examples of each of these possible interpretations of functional relations. When we write $q = d(p)$, where q is *one* household's quantity of butter demanded and p is the market price of butter, we understand that variations in p cause variations in q but that variations in q do not cause variations in p. When, however, we write $Q = D(p)$, where p is still the market price of butter but Q is now the quantity of butter demanded in the whole market, we understand that changes in Q will now cause changes in p as well as vice versa. Now consider the third possible reason for the existence of a systematic relationship. When we say that over the past three decades there has been a strong positive relation between purchases of motor cars and purchases of phonograph records, which can be written $C = C(P)$, we do not imply that running a car causes people to buy more records, or that having more phonograph records causes people to buy more cars. We do know, however, that purchases of both cars and records are increasing functions of income and that national income has been rising over the past 30 years. Thus the positive relation between C and P follows from no causal relation between these two variables but from a common influencing factor, income. Finally, an example of a relation arising by chance is the famous one between the number of storks nesting in Denmark (S) and the number of births in that country (B). When we write $B = B(S)$, which expresses an empirically observed relation, we are not committing ourselves to the theory that babies are brought by storks, although we *are* saying that storks and births have been observed to vary together in some systematic fashion.

A common case of a functional relation that does not imply any causal relation is a *time series*. Most economic variables vary over time. When we graph any variable on the y-axis with time on the x-axis we obtain a time-series graph. Because, given t, we can then read off the value of the variable x, we can write

$$x = x(t)$$

which is read "x is a function of time." In no sense does this imply that the mere passage of time causes x to vary.

The mathematical language of functions is, appropriately, free of causal implications. Suppose we say that y is always four times as large as x. Two other ways of saying the same thing are to say that x is one quarter as large as y and that y minus $4x$ must be zero. We can write

$$y = 4x \qquad (12)$$

$$x = 0.25y \qquad (13)$$

and

$$y - 4x = 0 \quad . \qquad (14)$$

In other words, we can express this functional relation in the implicit form or in either of its two explicit forms. The term on the left-hand side of each of (12) and (13) is called the dependent variable, and the terms on the right-hand side are called the independent variables. As far as mathematics is concerned, the distinction between dependent and independent variables is arbitrary provided that the inverse function exists: $y = y(x)$ implies that $x = x(y)$. The convention may be used, however, to express information we have about the causal relation between the variables. Assume, for example, that crop yield, C, increases monotonically[4] with the amount of rainfall, R. This allows us to write

$$C = C(R) \quad . \tag{15}$$

In this case we can deduce the amount of crop if we know the rainfall, and we can deduce the amount of rainfall if we know the crop. Thus we also have

$$R = R(C) \quad . \tag{16}$$

As far as mathematics is concerned, it does not matter which of these two forms we choose, (15) or (16). But, of course, the causal relation is clearly defined in this case. The amount of rainfall influences the crop yield; the crop yield does not influence the amount of rainfall.

As a matter of convention, whenever we think we know the direction of the causal link between variables we write the causes as independent variables and the effects as dependent ones. Thus it would be consistent with our ideas about the physical facts to write Eq. (15) instead of Eq. (16). Again, if we wanted to say that crop yield C depended on fertilizer, F, sunshine, S, and rainfall, R, we would write

$$C = C(F, S, R) \quad . \tag{17}$$

In Eq. (17), C is the dependent variable and F, S, and R are the independent variables. This is the first time that we have encountered a function of more than one variable, and we need merely to note here the convention of placing all the variables inside the brackets and separating them by commas. Thus $y = y(x, z)$ says that y is a function of two variables x and z. An example of a function of more than one variable in economics is $P = MV/Y$, where P is the price level, M is the quantity of money, V is the velocity of circulation of money, and Y is national income. If we wished to say merely that the price level was a function of these three variables without committing ourselves to the exact form of the relation in the way that we did above, we would merely write

---

[4] This is a simplification for purposes of illustration, but crop yield certainly depends partly on the amount of rainfall.

$$P = P(M, V, Y) \quad .$$

This is a convenient moment to introduce yet another piece of terminology, knowledge of which will facilitate later discussion. The variables that appear in brackets after the functional symbol are often referred to as the *arguments* of the function. Arguments and independent variables are nearly, but not quite, the same thing, and the distinction can be important. Suppose that we have $y = f(x/z)$, and compare this with $y = g(x, z)$. In both functions, x and z appear as the independent variables. In the first case, however, their ratio appears explicitly, whereas in the second case the variables appear separated by a comma. What this means is that f is an unspecified rule operating on the *ratio* x/z, whereas g is some unspecified function defined on pairs of values of x and z entered separately. In the case of $f(x/z)$ the value of neither variable matters for itself, but only as it affects x/z. Hence in this case we say that x/z is *the* argument of the function, whereas in the case of $g(x, z)$ we say that both x and z are arguments.

Examination of $y = f(x/z)$ suggests another idea. Let us define a new variable, t, by setting $t = x/z$. Thus obviously $y = f(t)$. But t is a function of x and z, which we might write $t = h(x, z)$. Then by substitution $y = f[h(x, z)]$. This is to be read "y is a function of a function of x and z." h gives us the rule for assigning t-values to pairs of x-, z-values, and f in turn gives the rule for assigning y-values to t-values. This idea of a "function of a function" will prove very useful later on.

In drawing graphs of functions, it is the usual convention to plot the independent variable on the x-axis and the dependent variable on the y-axis. The popularizer of graphical analysis in economics, Alfred Marshall, employed a theory that led him to put price on the y-axis and quantity on the x-axis. This practice persists today, although we nearly always take price to be the independent variable and quantity the dependent one. We have decided, in the interest of consistency and convenience, to defy this tradition: all the demand and supply diagrams in this book are drawn with quantity, the dependent variable, on the y-axis. Thus they are the "wrong way up" from the point of view of economics textbooks, but the "right way up" according to general mathematical practice. You must realize that it is only a matter of convenience, and you should be prepared to redraw any familiar economic diagram with the axes reversed.

We have seen that the existence of a functional relationship does not imply dependence in a physical or causal sense. If y and x are variables not related in any way, we shall not, of course, be able to formulate a rule to go from x to y. In the case in which y is a constant for any x it might be felt that to call y a function of x is to stretch the notion of a functional "relation" too far; but, if we wish to be consistent, we must include it. In this case $y = f(x) = c$ is a perfectly well-defined, consistent (and continuous) function. (It is, of course, not single-valued: f^{-1} does not exist.) Thus our definition of function leads us to include the so-called "constant function" and serves to confirm that there is not a two-way relation between the concept of "causality" and the concept of function.

2.9   FUNCTIONS AND EQUATIONS: ROOTS

Suppose that we write

$$f(x) = x^2 - 3x - 10 \quad . \tag{18}$$

This merely spells out the precise function of x. Since it tells us that $f(x)$ *is the same thing as* $x^2 - 3x - 10$, it is true for all values of x. To take another example, $(a + x)^2 = a^2 + 2ax + x^2$ is also true for all values of x. The "equal" sign should in this case be read "is the same thing as" or "is identical with." Relations that are true for all values of x are called identities. When it is important to distinguish an identity from an equality, we write $\equiv$ for the former instead of the ordinary equality sign $=$.

Now suppose that we write the quadratic equation

$$x^2 - 3x - 10 = 0 \quad . \tag{19}$$

Unlike (18) this equation is not true for all values of x; indeed it is true only for $x = 5$ and $x = -2$. Equation (19) does not say that $x^2 - 3x - 10$ is the same thing as, or is identical with, zero; instead it sets $x^2 - 3x - 10$ equal to zero, and thus invites us to find the values of x for which this is true. To do this we shall review the methods of solving quadratic equations.

The function $x^2 - 3x - 10$ is graphed in Figure 2.12. It is apparent from inspection of the figure that there are two values of x for which

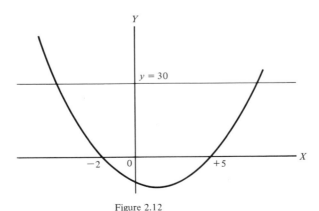

Figure 2.12

the value of the function is zero, -2 and $+5$. They are called the *roots of the function*. There are two standard methods for finding the roots of a quadratic equation (both are taught in high school algebra, so we shall not justify them here). The first method is that of factoring the quadratic

$$ax^2 + bx + c \qquad (20)$$

into an expression of the form

$$(lx + d)(mx + e) \qquad (21)$$

such that[5]

$$ax^2 + bx + c = (lx + d)(mx + e) \quad . \qquad (22)$$

Since we wish to find values of x for which the function has a value of zero, we merely set (21) equal to zero. Now if we have the product of two terms, say PQ, equal to zero, either P must be zero or Q must be zero. Hence to "satisfy" our equation, we must have either

$$lx + d = 0$$

or

$$mx + e = 0 \quad .$$

The first is true if $x = -d/l$, and the second if $x = -e/m$. The result is that $f(x) = 0$ if x has either of these values. In the case of the example in (18) the factoring is easy:

$$x^2 - 3x - 10 = (x - 5)(x + 2) \quad .$$

You can satisfy yourself that this is correct by multiplying out $(x - 5)(x + 2)$. We now know that the roots of the function are $+5$ and -2: the value of $f(x)$ will be zero when x takes on either of these values.

---

[5] In case you have forgotten how to multiply $(lx + d)(mx + e)$, we offer a reminder. Write

$$lx + d$$
$$mx + e$$

multiplying the top line by mx gives $\dfrac{lmx^2 + mdx}{}$;

multiplying by e gives

and adding gives $\dfrac{elx + de}{lmx^2 + (md + el)x + de}$.

Comparison of this with $ax^2 + bx + c$ shows that factoring consists of finding, if we can, values for l, m, d, and e such that

$$lm = a$$
$$md + el = b$$

and

$$de = c \quad .$$

The second method of finding the roots of the equation is to substitute into the formula

$$x = \frac{-b \pm \sqrt{b^2 - 4ac}}{2a} \quad . \tag{23}$$

This expression is derived[6] by straightforward manipulation of the expression $ax^2 + bx + c = 0$.

We might want to know the values of x that cause the whole function to be some value other than zero, say 30. The graphical solution to this problem is shown in Figure 2.12. As long as we have the graph of the function accurately plotted we can read off the answer for any

[6] A derivation of this rule is given below for any reader who wishes to review it.

We want to solve

$$ax^2 + bx + c = 0 \quad .$$

Dividing through by a gives

$$x^2 + \frac{b}{a}x + \frac{c}{a} = 0 \quad .$$

We want an expression that can be arranged to put x^2 on one side and that has no x-terms on the other side, whence x can be found by taking the square root. The trick is called "completing the square." If we *add* and *subtract* the same term, we clearly do not upset the equation. The trick is to add and subtract the square of one half of the coefficient of x, which is $b^2/4a^2$. This gives

$$x^2 + \frac{b^2}{4a^2} + \frac{b}{a}x + \frac{c}{a} - \frac{b^2}{4a^2} = 0 \quad .$$

The first three terms are, however, the square of $(x + b/2a)$. We therefore have

$$\left(x + \frac{b}{2a}\right)^2 + \left(\frac{c}{a} - \frac{b^2}{4a^2}\right) = 0 \quad ,$$

or

$$\left(x + \frac{b}{2a}\right)^2 = \left(\frac{b^2}{4a^2} - \frac{c}{a}\right) \quad .$$

Taking square roots, we have

$$x + \frac{b}{2a} = \pm\sqrt{\frac{b^2}{4a^2} - \frac{c}{a}}$$

$$x + \frac{b}{2a} = \pm\sqrt{\frac{b^2 - 4ac}{4a^2}}$$

$$x + \frac{b}{2a} = \pm\frac{1}{2a}\sqrt{b^2 - 4ac} \quad ,$$

whence

$$x = \frac{-b \pm \sqrt{b - 4ac}}{2a} \quad .$$

value of the function. In this case it is −5 and +8, which are the values of x that give the function a value of 30. Algebraically, however, the solution proceeds as follows. We wish to find x such that

$$x^2 - 3x - 10 = 30 \quad,$$

and by subtracting 30 from both sides of the equality sign we have

$$x^2 - 3x - 40 = 0 \quad,$$

which factors as follows:

$$x^2 - 3x - 40 = (x - 8)(x + 5) \quad.$$

We now set this function equal to zero and discover the roots to be +8 and −5.

Thus any problem of finding the value of x such that the function takes on a stated value, V, can be turned into a problem of finding the roots of a new function that is found by subtracting V from the original function. Thus the problem "find x such that $ax^2 + bx = V$" is the same as the problem "find x such that $ax^2 + bx - V = 0$." For example, the problem "find the number which when multiplied by 3 and added to its square equals 10" can be written $x^2 + 3x = 10$ and solved by finding the roots of $x^2 + 3x - 10 = 0$.

So far we have considered quadratics that have real roots in the sense that there are two real values of x for which the function has a value of zero. Now consider taking a quadratic, such as the one labeled 1 in Figure 2.13, and slowly increasing the value of the parameter c. This shifts the curve upwards, and it is visually obvious from the figure that the roots move closer and closer together. Finally, when we have shifted the curve up so that the curve is just tangent to the x-axis (curve 4), the two roots coincide in a single point. This

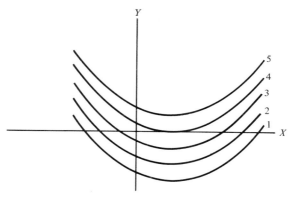

Figure 2.13

means that there is only one value of x for which the whole expression is zero. An example of such a quadratic is

$$f(x) = x^2 - 6x + 9$$

which factors into

$$f(x) = (x - 3)(x - 3)$$

which is zero if, and only if, $x = +3$.

If we increase the value of the constant yet further, the curve rises above the x-axis throughout its whole range. *There is no real value of x for which the value of the function is zero.* In this case we say that the function has no "real roots." If we substitute the values of the parameters into (23), we shall find in these cases that b^2 is less than $4ac$, so that the expression inside the square root sign is negative. Thus we have encountered an imaginary number (see Section 2.1) arising from a quite commonplace operation on a quadratic expression. We do not need, however, to pursue the interpretation of this result further at present: the graphical illustration makes it clear enough that, in these cases, there is no solution in the real number system.

To illustrate the solution of a quadratic, let us consider a demand function. If the quantity of a good demanded depends on its price, we write $q = f(p)$. Consider a linear demand function

$$q = 1{,}000{,}000 - 50{,}000p \quad . \tag{24}$$

Now let us derive the total revenue function. Total expenditure by consumers, which is the same thing as suppliers' total revenue, equals price per unit times number of units bought, so we may write

$$TR = pq \quad . \tag{25}$$

From (24) we already have an expression for q, and substituting that into (25) we get a quadratic in p:

$$TR = p(1{,}000{,}000 - 50{,}000p)$$

$$= 1{,}000{,}000p - 50{,}000p^2 \tag{26}$$

which is plotted in Figure 2.14.

Since (26) is a quadratic, we expect it to have two roots, and inspection of Figure 2.14 suggests that this particular function will have real roots. To find these roots we set the function equal to zero,

$$1{,}000{,}000p - 50{,}000p^2 = 0 \quad ,$$

and, dividing through by 50,000, we get

$$20p - p^2 = 0 \quad .$$

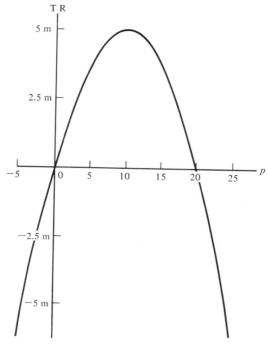

Figure 2.14

Factoring,

$$p(p - 20) = 0 \quad ,$$

so that the roots are seen to be zero and $+20$. This indicates that total revenue is zero both at price zero and at price 20. The first case is obvious: if the product is given away, no revenue is earned. The second point of zero revenue is the price at which quantity demanded falls to zero. [This can be seen by substituting $p = 20$ into Eq. (24)].

2.10 MAXIMUM AND MINIMUM VALUES

We have seen how to discover the values of x for which the value of the function is zero. Very often in economics we are interested in finding the value of x for which the value of the function is a maximum or a minimum. For example, looking for the price at which total revenue is at a maximum is a familiar problem. In the case of a quadratic such as the one we have just studied, the problem is simple since we can make use of the symmetry properties of a quadratic for finding the maximum. If a quadratic cuts the x-axis at zero and 20, it must reach a maximum halfway between these two points. Indeed, we need merely find the two x-values for which the function has some stated value, zero or anything else, and the maximum or minimum point must be halfway between these values.

This simple method will not work in general, and the approach that we must adopt is somewhat different. If we have a function $y = y(x)$, we find a new function $y'(x)$ (which is read "y-dashed of x" or "y-primed of x"), which is derived from $y(x)$, and which has the property that $y'(x) = 0$ if $y(x)$ is at a maximum or a minimum value. Thus the problem of finding maximum and minimum values divides into two parts.

1. First, we must derive from the function $y(x)$ a new function $y'(x)$ such that $y'(x) = 0$ if the original function $y(x)$ is at a maximum or a minimum value.
2. Second, we must solve the equation $y'(x) = 0$, which means finding the value(s) of x for which the function $y'(x)$ is zero.

We already know how to do step 2 in simple cases, and later in this book we shall study the technique of differentiation, which is the method of deriving the desired function $y'(x)$ from the function $y(x)$.

2.11 SLOPES, CHORDS, AND TANGENTS

Consider the linear function $y = ax + b$. Both the parameters a and b can be given specific graphic interpretations. Let us see if we can discover what these interpretations are. To discover the significance of the parameter b we let x take on the value of zero. The equation then reduces to $y = b$. Thus b tells us the value that y takes on when x is zero. Graphically, b determines the point at which the line graphing the function cuts the y-axis ($x = 0$), as is shown in Figure 2.15.

The significance of a is a little less obvious, but basically what a does is to determine the direction and the magnitude of changes in y associated with changes in x. Clearly if a is positive, then the larger is x, the larger is y, so that x and y vary directly with each other; whereas if a is negative, y varies inversely with x. Inspection also shows that the larger is the magnitude of a, the bigger are the changes in y for given changes in x. Geometrically, a corresponds to the slope of the line plotted from the function in question. Let us make certain that this is so.

Give x any particular value designated by x_1 and calculate the corresponding value of y, which we designate by y_1. Then let x take on another value x_2, and calculate y_2, the corresponding value of y. This gives us

$$y_1 = ax_1 + b$$

and

$$y_2 = ax_2 + b \quad.$$

Subtracting one equation from the other gives us

$$y_2 - y_1 = ax_2 - ax_1$$

or

$$y_2 - y_1 = a(x_2 - x_1) \quad. \tag{27}$$

We may now introduce the symbol Δ (read "capital delta," or "cap delta" for short) to indicate the change in the variable before which it is written. In this notation, $\Delta y = y_2 - y_1$, and $\Delta x = x_2 - x_1$. Thus we can rewrite (27) as

$$\Delta y = a\,\Delta x \quad,$$

and dividing through by Δx gives

$$\frac{\Delta y}{\Delta x} = a \quad.$$

Thus the ratio of Δy to Δx is a constant, irrespective of where on the function the change is measured. The ratio $\Delta y/\Delta x$ tells us how one variable changes as the other changes, and it is of particular interest in mathematics and economics. In economics we are constantly asking by how much one variable changes when another variable changes.

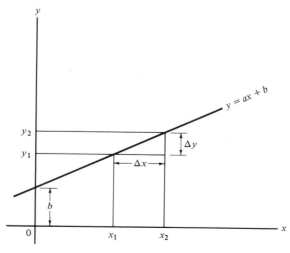

Figure 2.15

We have now shown that it is a property of linear functions that the ratio $\Delta y/\Delta x$ is the same everywhere on the function. That this is not true of nonlinear functions can easily be seen graphically. If in Figure 2.16 we start at point α, where x is $0a$ and y is $0b$, and make a change to the point β, the value of x increases by ac and of y by bd. The ratio $\Delta y/\Delta x$ is bd/ac, which is the slope of the line joining the two points α and β. Now move β to another point β' on the curve, and the slope of the line joining α and β will change. Thus the ratio $\Delta y/\Delta x$ depends on the size of the change in x. What is not shown in the figure (but you can easily check it for yourself) is that the value of $\Delta y/\Delta x$ also depends on the point at which we start and the direction of the change in x.

The line joining α and β is called a *chord*. In general, a chord is a straight line joining any two points on a curve. The slope of a chord between two points always indicates the ratio $\Delta y/\Delta x$, where Δy and Δx are the changes in y and x between the two points in question. This is illustrated in Figure 2.16. The ratio $\Delta y/\Delta x$ is often called the *incremental ratio*.

In Figure 2.16 the line TT is drawn tangential to the curve at α. The slope of the tangent is denoted by dy/dx. Now consider the relation between the slope of the tangent TT and the slope of the chord between α and β as β is brought closer and closer to α. It is visually clear from an inspection of Figure 2.16 that in this case the slope of the chord gets closer and closer to the slope of the tangent as the chord is made smaller and smaller. We write this $\Delta y/\Delta x \to dy/dx$ as $\Delta x \to 0$, where the $\to$ sign is read "approaches." Thus we are saying that in the case shown in the figure the slope of the incremental ratio, which geometrically is the slope of the chord, approaches the slope of the tangent as the increment Δx in x approaches zero (geometrically, as the chord through α gets smaller and smaller).

We can now explain a little more clearly our intuitive notion of a "smooth" function, or one without corners. By a smooth function, we mean one to which there is everywhere a unique tangent. Reference back to Figure 2.10 will illustrate: At $x = 0$ any line with a slope between -1 and $+1$ can be made tangent to the function. Thus at that point there is no unique value of the tangent slope dy/dx that $\Delta y/\Delta x$ can approach as we make Δx approach zero.

Yet another way of expressing the idea of smoothness is to say that the tangent slope, if it changes, must change continuously. There must be no jumps or holes in the range of values taken on by dy/dx. (It goes without saying that a smooth function must itself be continuous.) This is all we shall say about smoothness for now, and we shall take it for granted in the next chapter that our functions are smooth, but in Chapter 4, in which we learn to differentiate, we shall

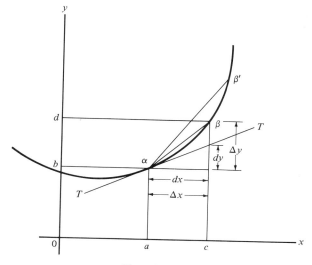

Figure 2.16

find it a very important concept, and shall be able to express it more clearly.

This completes our introduction to those basic ideas of analysis that we require to take the next step in our mathematical treatment of economics. Some of the ideas will have been more familiar than others; but we are prepared to bet that there is not one in this chapter that was not encountered, however disguised, in your economic principles course.

In the remaining part of this chapter, we shall review some useful algebra. Then we shall get on with some economics, and come back to the mathematical technique (in Chapter 4) only when we find that the possession of more equipment is imperative.

Inequalities, Indices, Logarithms

2.12 INEQUALITIES

The symbols used for the relationships "greater than" and "less than" are

$y > c$ meaning "y is greater than c" or "y exceeds c"

$y < c$ meaning "y is less than c."

If we wish to say that some variable is positive, we merely replace c

by zero and write $y > 0$. Similarly, if the variable is negative, we write $y < 0$.

There are rules for manipulating inequalities, just as there are for equalities. These are derived in school algebra, and we shall merely assert and illustrate here the ones that we need.

1. We can add the same number to or subtract it from both sides of an inequality without changing the relation. Thus if $y > x$, then $y + a > x + a$. This allows us to transfer terms from one side of the inequality to the other. If, for example, we are told that $2x > 4$, we can subtract 4 from both sides to obtain $2x - 4 > 0$.

2. We can multiply or divide both sides of an inequality by the same positive number without disturbing the relation. Thus if

$$y > x \quad ,$$

then

$$ay > ax$$

and

$$\frac{y}{a} > \frac{x}{a}$$

for all $a > 0$. Since, for example, $4 > 2$, it follows that $4a > 2a$ for any $a > 0$.

3. If we multiply or divide both sides of an inequality by a negative number, we reverse the relation. Thus if

$$y > x \quad ,$$

then

$$(-1)y < (-1)x \quad .$$

Since, for example, $4 > 2$, it follows that $-4 < -2$.

Suppose now that we do not know that x exceeds some value c but only that it is not less. "Not less" equals "greater than or equal to"; "not more" equals "less than or equal to"; and the symbols are

$$x \geqq c \quad \text{or} \quad x \geq c \qquad \text{meaning "x is greater than or equal to c"}$$

and $\quad x \leqq c \quad \text{or} \quad x \leq c \qquad \text{meaning "x is less than or equal to c."}$

We can use these symbols to say in a compact way that a variable cannot be negative or that it cannot be positive. Thus $x \geqq 0$ reads "x is greater than or equal to zero," or "x is nonnegative," and $x \leqq 0$ reads "x is nonpositive."

The symbols $>$ and $<$ are known as "strong inequalities," whereas $\geqq$ and $\leqq$ are known as "weak inequalities."

2.13 INDICES

There are two simple forms of specific functions that turn up very frequently. One is the "polynomial," which, as we have seen, takes the form

$$a_0 + a_1x + a_2x^2 + a_3x^3 + \cdots + a_nx^n \quad . \tag{28}$$

Here x appears in a series of additive terms in each of which it is raised to a different power. For convenience the powers are usually arranged in ascending or descending order. The general polynomial reduces to a linear relation if $a_2, a_3, \ldots, a_n = 0$ and to a quadratic if $a_3, \ldots, a_n = 0$ and so on. The other function very commonly encountered is the exponential function

$$a^x \quad . \tag{29}$$

In this function the variable x appears as the exponent of the parameter a, hence the name exponential function. An example is $y = 2^x$, which gives $y = 2$ for $x = 1$, $y = 4$ for $x = 2$, $y = 8$ for $x = 3$, and so on. We can postpone a serious consideration of exponential functions for another 11 chapters, but we shall encounter simple examples of polynomials very soon, and it is necessary to recall some elementary results on indices so that we can handle these functions when they occur.

We know that x^2 is merely a shorthand way of writing $(x)(x)$, while x^3 stands for $(x)(x)(x)$, and so on. Thus where n is a positive integer (whole number), x^n is merely a direction that tells us to multiply n x's together. This is very simple for positive integers, but we must wonder if we can give any meaning to x^n either when n is a fraction or when it is negative.

Before we consider this question let us recall the rule for multiplying indices. $(x^2)(x^3)$ is shorthand for $(xx)(xxx)$, which is five x's multiplied together and written x^5 in our notation. Thus $(x^2)(x^3) = x^5$. In general we can simplify $(x^n)(x^m)$ for any n and m without writing all the x's out as we did above by using the rule

$$(x^n)(x^m) = x^{n+m} \quad ,$$

or, *when multiplying merely add indices.* The common sense of this is that if you first take n x's and multiply them together, and then do the same with m x's, and then multiply the two results, you will have multiplied $(n + m)$ x's together. If you are not convinced, try it for a few specific values, for example, $(x^3)(x^4) = (xxx)(xxxx) = (xxxxxxx) = x^7$.

Now let us return to our question about negative and fractional indices. Take negative ones first. Without yet knowing how to interpret x^{-2} let us apply our multiplication rule to $(x^5)(x^{-2})$. According to the rule of adding indices this gives us $x^{5-2} = x^3$. We also know that, if we start with x^5 and wish to obtain x^3, we must divide by x^2. Writing it out in full,

$$\frac{xxxxx}{xx} = xxx = x^3 \quad .$$

Thus if we interpret x^{-2} as $1/x^2$, the application of our original multiplication rule gives us the correct answer. Hence we interpret negative integer indices by

$$x^{-n} = \frac{1}{x^n} \quad ,$$

and this gives us

$$(x^m)(x^{-n}) = \frac{x^m}{x^n} = x^{m-n} \quad .$$

Now let us consider fractional indices. We again start by blindly applying our multiplication rule to a particular example. Take $(x^{1/2})(x^{1/2})$: according to our rule we have

$$(x^{1/2})(x^{1/2}) = x^{1/2+1/2} = x^1 = x \quad .$$

Now we know that the number whose square is x is $\sqrt{x}$. Thus if we interpret $x^{1/2}$ as $\sqrt{x}$, the application of the multiplication rule above produces the correct answer. We also know that $(\sqrt[3]{x})^3 = x$, so if we interpret $x^{1/3}$ as $\sqrt[3]{x}$, we shall again get correct answers when we apply our multiplication rule to $x^{1/3}$. In general then, we have $x^{1/n} = \sqrt[n]{x}$.

An extension of the same line of argument will suggest that $x^{2/3} = \sqrt[3]{x^2}$, and in general $x^{n/m} = \sqrt[m]{x^n}$. If you are not sure of this one, try $(x^{3/2})(x^{-1/2})$ and $(x^{3/4})(x^{1/4})$.

We now know how to interpret indices that are fractions as well as those that are positive and negative integers. We must just check briefly on two particular integers, zero and unity. Consider first x^1. According to the basic rule of the meaning of positive-integer indices, this says "take x once," and the answer to this is clearly x. Let us try applying our rule to $(x^3)(x^{-2})$, which gives

$$(x^3)(x^{-2}) = x^{3-2} = x^1 = x \quad .$$

Proceeding according to first principles we have

$$\frac{xxx}{xx} = x$$

which checks. Thus we have $x^1 = x$.

Finally, to see what meaning we can give to x^0, let us consider a problem that gives x^0 as an answer. For example,

$$(x^2)(x^{-2}) = x^0$$

according to our rule. Now, writing it all out, we have

$$\frac{xx}{xx} = 1 \quad .$$

It is clear that this result holds generally so that

$$(x^n)(x^{-n}) = x^{n-n} = x^0$$

and

$$\frac{nx's}{nx's} = 1 \quad .$$

Thus if our rules are to give us correct answers for multiplying together x's raised to various powers, we must understand x^0 to be unity.

So far we have seen that we multiply two terms with x raised to powers by adding the powers together. Now let us quickly investigate subtraction, multiplication, and division of indices. Consider x^3 and x^2. If we subtract indices, we get x^1, which is the result we would get from x^3/x^2. This result generalizes, and we see that

$$\frac{x^m}{x^n} = x^{m-n} \quad ,$$

which says that to divide x^m by x^n merely subtract the indices.

Now what would happen if we took x^3 and multiplied the index by 2 to get x^6? Since $x^3 = (xxx)$ and $x^6 = (xxxxxx)$, this suggests that we have squared the original number by multiplying its index by 2. Indeed

$$(x^n)^m = x^{nm}$$

means that x^n has been raised to the mth power. Finally, this gives, by analogy, a result we have already obtained: that if we divide the index by some number m, we are taking the mth root of the original number. Thus

$$(x^n)^{1/m} = x^{n/m} = \sqrt[m]{x^n} \quad ,$$

which is a result we have seen before.

All of this may be summarized in the following rules (which should make sense by now and not just be rules blindly committed to memory).

    i. $x^n = n$ x's multiplied together.

ii. $x^1 = x$ [which is obvious from (i)].
iii. $x^0 = 1$ [which is not obvious from (i)].
iv. $x^{-n} = 1/x^n$.
v. $x^{n/m} = \sqrt[m]{x^n}$.
vi. $x^{-n/m} = 1/\sqrt[m]{x^n}$.
vii. $(x^n)(x^m) = x^{m+n}$.
viii. $(x^n)(x^{-m}) = x^n/x^m$.
ix. $x^{nm} = (x^n)^m$.

2.14 LOGARITHMS

Indices are the basis of logarithms, and this is therefore a convenient moment to review logarithms.

Consider the exponential function

$$y = a^x \quad . \tag{30}$$

We may also write

$$x = \log_a y \quad . \tag{31}$$

This says that, if y is equal to a constant a raised to a power x, then we *define* the variable x to be *the logarithm to base a of y*. In less cumbersome language the phrase "the logarithm to the base a of y" means the power to which a must be raised to give it a value equal to y.

The great value of logarithms is that they reduce the processes of multiplication and division to those of addition and subtraction and the processes of finding powers and roots to those of multiplication and division. A major limitation of logarithms, however, is that they work only for positive numbers. Shortly we shall note the reason for this. Let us recall how logarithms can be used. Assume that we have

$$y = (a^{x_1})(a^{x_2}) \quad ,$$

which, simplified by adding exponents, gives

$$y = a^{x_1+x_2} \quad .$$

We can exploit this in multiplying any two numbers, which we denote by y_1 and y_2. If we already know the values of x_1 and x_2 that solve the equations

$$y_1 = a^{x_1}$$

$$y_2 = a^{x_2} \quad ,$$

we merely add these exponents to obtain

$$y_3 = (y_1)(y_2) = a^{x_1+x_2} \quad .$$

If we know the value of $a^{x_1+x_2}$, we have the solution to our problem.

Let us try an example of this technique by performing the multiplications

$$y = 301 \times 562 \times 46 \quad.$$

Now, if some benevolent person has solved for x the equation

$$y = 10^x$$

for all possible values of y and entered the results in a table of logarithms, we only have to look up the values of x that solve the three equations

$$301 = 10^{x_1}$$
$$562 = 10^{x_2}$$
$$46 = 10^{x_3} \quad.$$

The table, in fact, gives us the following results (correct to four decimal places):

$$x_1 = 2.4786$$
$$x_2 = 2.7497$$
$$x_3 = 1.6628 \quad,$$

which says that 10 raised to the power 2.4786 is equal to 301 and so on. We calculate the product as follows:

$$y = 301 \times 562 \times 46$$
$$= 10^{2.4786} \times 10^{2.7497} \times 10^{1.6628}$$
$$= 10^{6.8911} \quad.$$

Now we know that the number we require is 10 raised to the power 6.8911, and we merely consult our table once again to find the "antilogarithm" of 6.8911, which is 7,781,500, and we have our answer. (An antilogarithm merely means the value of y which has that specific number, 6.8911 in this case, as its logarithm.)

Just above, we suggested that some benevolent person had solved the equation $y = 10^x$ for all possible values of y and entered them in a table of logarithms. No matter how benevolent the individual, he could only do the job for $y \geqq 0$ since there is no power x to which 10, or any other positive number, can be raised that will produce a negative result. Thus if y is a negative number, it cannot have a logarithm, whence we cannot use logs to perform calculations involving that number. The use of logs is confined to nonnegative numbers.

If we wish to divide two positive numbers, we merely subtract their logarithms. Say we have

$$y_3 = \frac{y_1}{y_2} = \frac{10^{x_1}}{10^{x_2}} = 10^{x_1 - x_2} \quad.$$

Thus we merely find the logarithms of y_1 and y_2, subtract, and look up an antilogarithm. We present an example:

$$y_3 = \frac{187}{17} = \frac{10^{2.2718}}{10^{1.2304}}$$

$$= 10^{2.2718 - 1.2304}$$

$$= 10^{1.0414} \quad.$$

Now we consult our table of antilogarithms to find that 10 raised to the power 1.0414 is 11 (i.e., 11 is *the* number whose logarithm is 1.0414).

We raise a number to a power by using the relation

$$(y^x)^n = y^{xn} \quad.$$

Assume that we wish to raise 8.6 to the sixth power. We first look up the logarithm of 8.6, which is 0.9345, so that $8.6 = 10^{0.9345}$. Now we can solve our problem as follows:

$$8.6^6 = (10^{0.9345})^6 = 10^{0.9345 \times 6}$$

$$= 10^{5.6070} \quad,$$

and the table shows that the antilogarithm of 5.6070 is 404,550, which is our answer.

Finally, if we wish to take the nth root of a number, we use the relation

$$(y^x)^{1/n} = (y)^{x/n} \quad.$$

Thus we merely divide the logarithm of a number by n in order to take the nth root of the number — a most convenient result! As an example, assume that we wish to find the fifth root of 261. We look up a table of logarithms to discover that

$$261 = 10^{2.4166} \quad,$$

so that

$$(261)^{1/5} = (10^{2.4166})^{1/5} = 10^{2.4166/5} = 10^{0.4833} \quad.$$

The table now shows us that $10^{0.4833}$ is 3.043, and we have found the fifth root of 261, which would have been a laborious task without logarithms. If, instead of the fifth root, we had wanted the 4.72nd root, this would have been really very difficult without logarithms, but, using logarithms, it requires only that we can divide 2.4166 by 4.72 and have the necessary tables.

One limitation of logarithms must now be mentioned. To multiply natural numbers together we add their logs. There is no equivalent in logarithms of the addition of natural numbers. Thus, although the expression ab^x is easily transformed into logs as $\log a + x \log b$, the expression $a + b^x$ cannot be transformed into an equivalent log form.

Up to this point we have been dealing with logarithms to the base 10. These are called common logarithms. Clearly, however, the logarithm "trick" can be worked for *any* base a. Instead of solving the equation $y = 10^x$ for all y's we could just as well have solved the equation $y = 5^x$ for all y's. If we gathered these results in a table, we would have a set of logarithms to the base 5. For practical purposes we use bases for which the values have been worked out in advance. The equation $y = a^x$ has been solved for $a = 10$ for all eight-digit values of x and the values recorded in tables of logarithms.

Later on we shall introduce an entirely new base. There exists a simple method of changing from one base to another, but we shall not need it.

2.15 THE LOG–LINEAR FUNCTION

Arithmetic examples of logarithmic manipulations are undeniably tedious. Let us now show that the principle of logarithms is useful for more than doing sums by looking at a particularly interesting and important function.

Experience in the first part of this chapter, and a little reflection, will suggest that linear relationships are much easier to handle than nonlinear ones. On the other hand, if we refused to work with any nonlinear functions, the models of the world that we might build would be rather restricted. Now consider the function

$$y = ax^b \quad , \tag{32}$$

which says that y is equal to x raised to some given power b, all multiplied by a constant a. This does not look very tractable as it stands, but a very simple trick will do wonders. We simply take logarithms of both sides to get

$$\log y = \log a + b \log x \quad . \tag{33}$$

(33) is *linear in the logarithms of the variables x and y.* If we draw our usual coordinate diagram and put $\log y$ on the vertical axis and $\log x$ on the horizontal, the graph of (33) will be a straight line with intercept equal to $\log a$ and slope equal to b. Thus the incremental ratio is simply given by

$$\frac{\Delta \log y}{\Delta \log x} = b \quad .$$

(You should refer back, if necessary, to Section 2.11.) (32) is, of course, nonlinear in the "natural numbers." (33) is called the *logarithmic transformation* of (32) and is linear in the logs. Comparison of (32) and (33) suggests that we may start with an awkward nonlinear relation and, by making the transformation, get a function that is very easily handled indeed. This circumstance is very widely exploited: functions of the form of (33) are used regularly in economics, and we shall meet frequent examples in this book. When we have learned, in Chapter 4, to take derivatives, we shall discover even more convenient properties.

2.16 NECESSARY AND SUFFICIENT CONDITIONS

In any logical discourse, it is extremely important to distinguish between conditions that are necessary and those that are sufficient for some result to hold. We might wish to prove, for example, that if a is true then b must also be true, and we might conjecture that it would be convenient to reverse the argument and prove this by showing that if b is true then a must also be true. This alone is not valid. The following example shows why the suggested procedure is not valid. The fact that if someone is a man he is necessarily a member of the human race does not prove that if someone is a member of the human race he must be a man (for a woman is also a member of the human race). Clearly, being a member of the human race is necessary if one is to be a man, but it is not sufficient. Also, being a man is sufficient to ensure that one is a human, but it is not necessary — since being a woman will do at least as well!

In general we can state these relations as follows. A necessary condition for a result a is one that must be present if a is to occur, but by itself is not enough to guarantee that a will occur. A sufficient condition for a is one whose presence is enough to guarantee that a will occur; but from the fact that it is sufficient we cannot tell if it is required for a to occur. A condition (or set of conditions) is necessary *and* sufficient for a to occur if it *must* be present for a to occur, and if its presence alone is enough to guarantee that a will occur.

The relations work in both directions, but not symmetrically. If z is a necessary condition for a, then a is a sufficient condition for z. In words: "if z must occur if a is to occur, then the occurrence of a is sufficient to tell us that z must have occurred." If z is a sufficient contion for a, then a is a necessary condition for z. In words, "if the occurrence of z is sufficient for a to occur, then a must necessarily have occurred if z is to have occurred." From these two results it follows immediately that if z is *both* necessary and sufficient for a, then a is also necessary and sufficient for z.

We often distinguish these relations by use of "if" and "only if."

Thus the statement "*a* occurs *if z* occurs" means that *z* is a sufficient condition for *a* and that *a* is a necessary condition for *z*. The statement "*a* occurs *if and only if z* occurs" means that *z* is a necessary and sufficient condition for *a*.

These distinctions are extremely important, and they are probably best clarified by considering examples. A number of examples are included in the questions at the end of this chapter, and you should try them all before reading on to the next chapter.

QUESTIONS

1. Classify each of the following numbers as rational, irrational, imaginary, or complex.
   a. 1.0
   b. $\sqrt{2}$
   c. 1.33
   d. 2.7184/9.812
   e. $12 + 10i$
   f. $\sqrt[3]{-27}$
   g. π

2. Which of the following are pure numbers?
   a. The slope of a demand curve
   b. The elasticity of demand
   c. A firm's total profits
   d. The proportion of a firm's revenue that is profit

3. We know that the real number system is "dense." (a) Is the subset of real numbers called rational numbers dense, that is, can we find a rational number fitting between any two different rational numbers? (b) Is the subset of real numbers known as integers similarly dense?

4. A scale is drawn on a page and points on this scale are numbered 0, 1, 2, 3, 4, ... If the distance between the point numbered 1 and the point numbered 2 is $\frac{1}{2}$ inch, then what would you expect the distance between the point numbered 3 and the point numbered 5 to be?

5. Which of the following notations, if any, would you consider appropriate to indicate a functional relationship between a worker's yearly income and his wages?
   a. $Y = Y(w)$
   b. $Y = f(w)$
   c. $Y = \phi(w)$
   (*Y* stands for yearly income and *w* stands for the wage rate.)

6. Given that $Y = Y(w)$, assume that the possible values of *Y* lie between 0 and 100,000, while the corresponding values of *w* lie between 0 and 20.
   a. Does 15 fall within the range? Within the domain?
   b. Does 1000 fall within the range? Within the domain?
   c. Is the function defined for a wage of 50?

7. Plot enough points on each of the following functions to allow you to sketch the curve.
   a. $x^2 + 3x$
   b. $x^2 + x - 2$
   (*Hint:* What is the value of the function when $x = 0$? Where does it cross the x-axis?)

8. From a demand curve which is known to be linear, you are given the following observations:

$$\text{at } p = 15, \quad q = 35$$
$$\text{at } p = 12, \quad q = 50 \quad .$$

Write down the functional relationship between q and p. In which of the quadrants of the Cartesian plane does this function lie?

9. a. Suppose that y has some constant value, c (say, 100 or 15). Can we say that y is a function of x?
   b. Suppose that we have the following information about pairs of values of x and y:

$$y = 0 \qquad \text{if } x \text{ is less than 3}$$
$$y = 2 \qquad \text{if } x \text{ is 3}$$
$$y = 5 \qquad \text{if } x \text{ is between 3 and 11}$$
$$y = 7 \qquad \text{when } x \text{ is 11}$$
$$y = 50 \qquad \text{if } x \text{ is greater than 11} \quad .$$

Can we say that y is a function of x?

10. In which of the following does the letter f symbolize a function? Identify the argument(s) of the function in each case.
    a. $y = f(x, z)$
    b. $y = f(w/v)$
    c. $y = ax^6 + bx^5 + cx^4 + dx^3 + ex^2 + fx + g$
    d. $y = f(x + z)$

11. Consider $ax^2 + bx + c$.
    a. If $a = 0$, is the function a quadratic? Is it linear?
    b. If $a = 0$ and $c = 0$, is the function linear?
    c. If $b = c = 0$, is the function a quadratic?

12. Consider $f(x) = (x - 3)^2$.
    a. If this function has a kink or discontinuity, does it occur at $x = 0$ or at $x = 3$?
    b. This function could also be written as $f(x) = x^2 - 6x + 9$. Is it a quadratic?
    c. Consider $f(x) = x^2 - 6x + 9$ and the general quadratic $ax^2 + bx + c$. What are the values of a, b, and c in the example?
    d. Now consider another quadratic, $f(x) = x^2 - 3$. What are the a-, b-, and c-values here?

13. a. Can all explicit functions be expressed as implicit functions?

b. Suppose that $y = f(x) = 2x^2 - 10$, an explicit function of x. Is $y - 2x^2 - 10 = 0$ an implicit function of x and y?

14. Suppose that $y = 5x$ has a domain of 0 to 1000 inclusive.
a. What is the range of this function?
b. Inverting the function, we obtain $x = \frac{1}{5}y$. What is the domain now?

15. The scoreboard adds 7 to its display every time our team scores a touchdown (we always convert). Let S be the value on the scoreboard and T be the number of touchdowns.
a. Can we write $T = \frac{1}{7}S$?
b. Is T a function of S?
c. Is S a cause of T?
d. What is the implicit form?
e. Is this a monotonic function, and is it a "strictly" increasing function?

16. Consider $M = f(S, C)$, where M is gas mileage on the highway, S is the average speed, and C is the number of cylinders in the car engine.
a. What are the arguments of the function f?
b. Could this function be equivalently written $M = f(S/C)$?
c. How many arguments would the function $g(S/C)$ have?

17. a. Calculate the roots of
(i) $f(x) = 5x^2 - 6x + 1 = 0$
(ii) $f(x) = x^2 - 2x + 1 = 0$
b. Which of the following statements is true?
(i) The roots calculated indicate the point at which the graph crosses or touches the X-axis.
(ii) The roots calculated indicate the point at which the graph crosses or touches the Y-axis.

18. Calculate the roots of $f(x) = 4x + 5 = 0$. (Remember that what you are trying to determine is the values of x which satisfy the equation.)

19. a. Is it true that $15x^2 + 150x - 60 = 0$ will have the same roots as $3x^2 + 30x - 12 = 0$?
b. Remembering that, for a quadratic to have real roots, $b^2 - 4ac$ must be positive, does this function have real roots?

20. What is the slope of the following?
a. $y = 15x + 856$
b. $y = -x - 10$

21. Consider the following argument. "It is lack of religious belief that undermines marriage and leads to divorce. We have seen in this century declining attendance at church and a shocking increase in divorce, which establishes the point beyond doubt."
a. Using functional notation, write out what is supposed to be a function of what, and say which are supposed to be increasing and which decreasing functions.
b. Which of the functions corresponds to a statement about observed facts, and which to a hypothesis or belief?

c. Given the same observations, can you find another explanation?

d. Do you think the argument is well supported? How might it be further tested?

22. Consider the function

$$y = 1 + x \qquad \text{if } x \text{ is less than } 0$$
$$y = x^2 + x + 1 \qquad \text{if } x \text{ is greater than } 0$$
$$y = 1 \qquad \text{if } x = 0 \quad .$$

(*Hint:* Sketch the graph of the function.)

a. Is y continuous? Is it smooth?

b. Over what interval(s) is y monotonically increasing? Monotonically decreasing?

c. Over what interval(s) is y a linear function? A quadratic function?

d. Express the function implicitly.

23. Starting with

$$3x + 16 \le 18y - 20$$

we get

$$3x \le 18y - 36$$

and then

$$x \le 6y - 12 \quad .$$

a. Were the operations performed on the original inequality valid?

b. If y is 3 and x is 5, is the inequality satisfied?

c. If y is 3 and x is 6, is the inequality satisfied?

24. Given that $-25x < -10y$, is it true that $y < 2.5x$?

25. If $y = a^x$, which symbol is the index?

26. Answer true or false to each of the following statements.

a. $x^2 x^{-2} = x^0 = 1$

b. $9^{2/3} = 3^2 = 81^{1/2} = \sqrt[2]{81} = 6$

c. $x^{3-2} = x$

d. $2^{1/2} = 1/2^2$

e. $2^{-2} = 1/2^2$

27. If $y = a^x$, which symbol is the base?

28. If $y = a^x$, then does $\log y = x \log a$?

29. a. If $\log_{10} 3 = 0.4771$, find, *without using log tables,* $\log_{10} 9$ and $\log_{10} 27$.

b. If $\log_{10} 16 = 1.2041$, find, *without using tables,* $\log_{10} 4$ and $\log_{10} 2$.

c. Find $\log_{10} 6$.

30. If $2x + 3 > 4$, show that x is positive.

31. Can you find a "logarithmic transformation" of the following?

a. $y = 7x^{1/3}$
b. $y = 10 + 3x^b$
c. $y = 2(-x)^3$

32. Given that $\Delta \log y / \Delta \log x = 3$ and $\log y = 1$ when $\log x = 0$, find the function relating x to y in natural numbers.

33. What is $\log_{10} 1$? $\log_{10} 10$? $\log_{10} 100$? $\log_{10} 1000$? Can you generalize these results to get a formula for $\log_{10} 10^n$?

34. $y > 3$ is necessary for $y = 5$; is it sufficient? Is the double condition $y > 3$ and $y < 5$ necessary and sufficient for $y = 4$?

35. If a is necessary and sufficient for z and at the same time b is necessary and sufficient for z, what can you say about the relation between a and b?

36. You are told that (1) *provided the government is not currently running a budget deficit* it will raise its expenditures either (2) *if unemployment rises above 5 percent* or (3) *if there is a balance of payments surplus.* Under no other circumstances would expenditure be raised. Consider the three conditions singly and state whether each is necessary, sufficient, neither, or both to produce the result of a rise in government expenditure. Next take the conditions in pairs and ask if each pair holding simultaneously is necessary, sufficient, neither, or both. Finally, take all three conditions as a single set and ask the same question of this set.

37. You are told that in order to get into an exclusive club you must (1) be a male, or (2) you must be a civil servant, and (3) you must have a reference from an existing member. Take these conditions one at a time, then in pairs, and then all together, and ask if each single or composite condition is necessary, sufficient, neither, or both to gain entrance to the club.

38. For what values of C will the quadratic $x^2 + 2x + C = 0$ have real roots? (*Hint:* Use the formula $x = (-b \pm \sqrt{b^2 - 4ac})/2a$. If $b^2 - 4ac \geq 0$, will the quadratic have real roots?)

39. a. Rewrite the example from page 27 in terms of strong inequalities. Suppose that every candidate in an examination who scores more than some preassigned percentage, t, receives a prize, whereas no one who scores less receives anything. Define a function relating x, the percentage mark with domain 0 to 100, to $y = 1$ (prize) and $y = 0$ (no prize).
b. The marker decides that a score of t should be awarded the prize. Rewrite the above inequalities to reflect this new information.

40. Solve for x:

$$x = \frac{(\sqrt{2^3})(3^4)}{6} \quad .$$

Chapter **3**

Simple Linear Models

A Competitive Market

In this chapter we are going to begin to do mathematical economics. In spite of the very limited set of tools so far at our command, we can go quite a long way providing we are prepared to consider such special cases as demand and supply curves that are linear. We begin with the model of a competitive market and then go on to the standard macro model.

3.1 THE SOLUTION OF A NUMERICAL EXAMPLE

We shall now develop the simple theory of a competitive market. The only additional technique required is the method of solving simultaneous linear equations. If you have forgotten how to do this, there is no need to look it up in a mathematics text, because we shall develop the method we require quite easily as we proceed. The analysis of a simple competitive market is useful not only as an exercise in technique but also because it will serve to illustrate some fundamental ideas that will recur frequently throughout this book. We shall exploit the model itself extensively, handling more and more ambitious questions as our technique increases, until we finally have a very thorough and general treatment of it.

Our simplest case is that in which both demand and supply curves are straight lines, described by the linear functions

$$q^d = a + bp \qquad\qquad (1)$$

$$q^s = c + dp \quad , \qquad\qquad (2)$$

where q^d denotes the quantity demanded and q^s the quantity supplied. (q^d is read "q-superscript d," or "q-super-d" for short.) These are behavioral equations: they state assumptions about market behavior. Since there is no economic meaning in this model for a negative q, and since there are no subsidies that could create a negative price, we define these functions only over nonnegative values of p and q.

The assumption that the functions are linear may look rather restrictive and unlikely to be satisfied in the real world. We shall find, however, that we can learn a good deal, of a general nature, even on this simple assumption; and, besides, a straight line may lie sufficiently close to a curved one over some range that, for small changes at least, the treatment of the curve as though it were a straight line leads to acceptable approximations to the correct answer. (The technique of "linear approximations" to nonlinear relationships is widely used in the physical sciences.) Anyhow, we need more technique before we can drop this assumption, which we shall do in Chapter 9. To complete the theory of competitive price determination set out in (1) and (2), we add the equilibrium condition

$$q^d = q^s \quad . \tag{3}$$

In a specific case, we might know the actual numerical values of the parameters a, b, c, and d. We should then insert them, and solve for equilibrium price and quantity. Thus let us start by solving the numerical example given in Eqs. (4), (5), and (6):

$$q^d = 1200 - 2p \tag{4}$$

$$q^s = 4p \tag{5}$$

$$q^d = q^s \quad . \tag{6}$$

(What value has been given to the parameter c in this example? What must the supply curve look like?) From (6), we know that the price must be at the level that equates supply and demand. Hence we substitute (4) and (5) into (6), which eliminates both q^d and q^s, and we obtain

$$1200 - 2p = 4p \quad . \tag{7}$$

Collecting terms we have

$$6p = 1200 \tag{8}$$

whence

$$p = 200$$

and

$$q^d = q^s = 800 \quad . \tag{9}$$

There are two points to notice about the method of solution, which we shall use again and again.

1. We started with three equations in three unknowns (q^d, q^s, p). By substitution, we obtained a single equation (7) in one unknown, p.

2. Having solved for p, we obtain equilibrium q by substituting the equilibrium value of p into *either one* of the behavioral equations. [You may check arithmetically that, with $p = 200$, $q = 800$ is obtained from (4) *or* (5), but this is no accident. Why not?]

3.2 THE GENERAL SOLUTION OF THE LINEAR MODEL

We are now equipped to start the study of an important and fascinating topic frequently referred to as "qualitative economics." In practice, we frequently do not know parameter values, but only restrictions such as "the demand curve slopes down." Hence we are interested in the question of what, if anything, we can discover about the solution of the model, and its properties, on the basis of qualitative restrictions on the parameters. By "qualitative restrictions" we mean (for the moment) such simple and general notions as "the demand curve slopes down and the supply curve up." Evidently if restrictions like this prove to be *sufficient* to establish some property or result, without need for numbers, we have *general* results. The search for general qualitative results is ambitious and exciting. It unfortunately turns out that in more complicated models qualitative results are rather rare, and it is imperative to have numerical estimates of parameters before definite results can be obtained, but even then it is essential to our own understanding of the model that we know if it yields qualitative results, and if not, why not.

In the present case, we can do quite a lot qualitatively. We must start by specifying the model more carefully, and we now list our qualitative assumptions.

    i. $b < 0$; i.e., the demand curve slopes down.

    ii. $d > 0$; i.e., the supply curve slopes up.

    iii. $a > 0$; the demand curve must have a positive intercept.

    iv. $c < a$, because if this were not true, supply would exceed demand at zero price, and the good in question would not be an economic good; its price would be zero (you should draw a diagram to illustrate this).[1]

---

[1] Usually it is assumed that $c < 0$ so that the supply curve has a positive intercept on the price axis indicating that nothing is supplied below some minimum positive price. But all that is required for present purposes is $c < a$, as explained in the text.

We may now solve the general model of Eqs. (1), (2), and (3), where we only have the parameters in the form a, b, c, d, without numbers. We use exactly the method of our numerical example, and start by substituting (1) and (2) into (3) to obtain

$$a + bp = c + dp \quad . \tag{10}$$

Collecting terms,

$$a - c = dp - bp \quad .$$

Factoring the right-hand side,

$$a - c = p(d - b) \quad .$$

Dividing both sides by $d - b$,

$$p = \frac{a - c}{d - b} \quad . \tag{11}$$

Substituting (11) into (1) we obtain

$$q = a + b\left(\frac{a - c}{d - b}\right) \quad .$$

To simplify the right-hand side, we multiply a by $(d - b)/(d - b)$, which gives $d - b$ as a common denominator, whence

$$q = \frac{a(d - b) + b(a - c)}{d - b}$$

$$= \frac{ad - bc}{d - b} \quad . \tag{12}$$

Equations (11) and (12) are said to "constitute the solution to the system of Eqs. (1), (2), and (3)." This sounds very imposing, but are we any better off contemplating (11) and (12) than we were when we had merely (1), (2), and (3)? To answer this, we must consider what we mean by a "solution," and what use it is. First, we need a little terminology, for convenience of discussion. By an *endogenous variable* we mean one that is determined within the system we are analyzing: it is *dependent*, and, when we start, it is an unknown. Thus our dependent variables in this case are price and quantity. By an *exogenous variable* we mean one not determined within the particular system we are analyzing: from the point of view of the analysis of a single micro-market, Gross National Product (GNP), for example, may be taken as exogenous. (The terms "autonomous" and "prede-termined" are also used. They are nearly, but not quite, interchangeable with "exogenous." The distinctions need not concern us here.) A *parameter* means, as we saw in Chapter 2, a fixed coefficient, such as a, b, c, or d in this model.

In Eqs. (1) and (2), one dependent variable depends on another:

to know one of the unknowns, you must already know the other. This is why we are not content to leave matters here. By a *solution* we mean an equation (or set of equations if there is more than one dependent variable) that expresses an endogenous variable as a function of the parameters and exogenous variables *only*. Hence Eqs. (11) and (12) are solutions in the sense that neither p nor q appears on the right-hand side of either of them. Thus to know q, say, from Eq. (12) it is not necessary to know p: it is only necessary to know the parameter values, and to know that the market is in equilibrium. In this particular example, of course, we have not explicitly introduced any exogenous variables. We may imagine, however, that GNP, prices of substitutes, etc., will have their effects through the values of the parameters. If the commodity in question is not an inferior good, the demand for it increases when income increases. Thus an increase in GNP might be reflected in this model by an increase in the parameter a, the intercept of the demand equation, and perhaps a change in b as well. Similarly, a change in external circumstances that altered the conditions of supply would be reflected by changes in the parameters c and d. Thus for the moment we do not have to introduce exogenous variables explicitly: it is enough to express the endogenous variables as functions of parameters that themselves depend on exogenous variables.

What use, then, is a solution such as that provided by (11) and (12)? First, it is the "general solution" to this linear system. This means, simply, that once it has been done, it need never be done again for any pair of linear supply and demand curves for any market whatsoever. Given numerical values for the parameters, we need never again solve numerically as we did in Eqs. (7), (8), and (9): we substitute any set of parameter values directly into (11) and (12). (You should satisfy yourself that this works.) It is evident that general solutions are potentially labor-saving devices on a grand scale. Second, however, they may be used directly to investigate the qualitative properties of the model. Equations (1), (2), and (3) cannot be used for this, because we have not yet disentangled the endogenous variables from each other and related them directly to the parameters. A numerical example will not do either because we cannot tell if some property that obtains if, say, $q^s = 4p$, will also hold if $q^s = 4.5p$, and we shall get bored long before we have exhausted the (infinite!) number of possible arithmetic examples: this is precisely why we seek "general" methods, and why mathematical analysis is so labor-saving and powerful when it provides them.

We often take it for granted in economic theory that prices and quantities are positive (the interpretation of zero and negative prices was discussed in Chapter 2). It is prudent, however, to check that our model does give a positive price, and this check will also serve as our first example of qualitative analysis. The solution for p was given in Eq. (11), so what we have to do is investigate the sign of the right-hand side of (11). It is now convenient to introduce some new terminology. In dealing with a fractional expression such as a/b, we call a, the part "above the line," the *numerator,* and b, the part "below the line," the *denominator.* It follows from assumption (iv) above, $c < a$, that the numerator of (11) is positive. Furthermore, $d > 0$ and $b < 0$ are sufficient (but not necessary: see Section 3.4) for the denominator to be positive. Hence our qualitative assumptions are sufficient (but, again, not necessary) to ensure that this model always gives a positive price (i.e., the good cannot be a free good).

3.3 SHIFTS IN DEMAND AND SUPPLY

We may now use our model to illustrate the so-called "laws of supply and demand": the effects on equilibrium price and quantity of shifts in the demand and supply curve. Eventually we shall have tools powerful enough to demonstrate these propositions quite generally. At the moment we shall confine ourselves to illustrating them for parallel shifts in our linear demand and supply curves.

To begin, we return to Eqs. (1) and (2) and introduce what are called *shift parameters.* A shift parameter allows a relation to be left in its original form or shifted as desired. The equations are now rewritten as

$$q^d = a + \Delta a + bp \qquad (13)$$

and

$$q^s = c + \Delta c + dp \quad . \qquad (14)$$

Recall that in Section 2.11 we introduced the symbol Δ to stand for a change in some magnitude. Both a and c are now shift parameters, and Δa and Δc are the magnitudes of the shifts. By giving Δa and Δc positive or negative values we can shift the two curves outwards or inwards while leaving their slopes unchanged (i.e., we are confined to parallel shifts of the curves). If these two equations are substituted into the equilibrium condition (3), price can be solved for in exactly the same way as in Section 3.2 to give

$$p = \frac{(a + \Delta a) - (c + \Delta c)}{d - b} \quad . \qquad (15)$$

Anyone not perfectly at home with simple simultaneous equations should make the substitutions to check the result.

As a double check we can notice that when $\Delta a = \Delta c = 0$ Eq. (15)

reduces to (11), which shows that if neither curve shifts we get our original result.

It is simpler now to rewrite (15) to separate out the effects of the shifts:

$$p = \frac{a-c}{d-b} + \frac{\Delta a}{d-b} - \frac{\Delta c}{d-b} \quad . \tag{16}$$

If we let p_0 stand for the original price when $\Delta a = \Delta c = 0$ and p_1 stand for the new price after one or both of the curves shift, we can rewrite (16) as

$$p_1 = p_0 + \frac{\Delta a}{d-b} - \frac{\Delta c}{d-b} \quad . \tag{17}$$

Inspection of (17) produces the results listed below.

  1. If $\Delta a > 0$, $\Delta c = 0$, then $p_1 > p_0$.
  2. If $\Delta a < 0$, $\Delta c = 0$, then $p_1 < p_0$.
  3. If $\Delta c > 0$, $\Delta a = 0$, then $p_1 < p_0$.
  4. If $\Delta c < 0$, $\Delta a = 0$, then $p_1 > p_0$.

These four results illustrate the propositions about the effect on price of shifts in demand and supply curves for the case of parallel shifts of linear demand and supply curves. The effects on quantity are dealt with in Question 2 at the end of this chapter.

3.4   AN EXCISE TAX IN A COMPETITIVE MARKET

We can now use our competitive model to make a qualitative investigation of a problem in public finance: what are the effects on price and quantity sold of the imposition of a specific excise tax? A specific excise tax is a tax of a given amount per unit sold (so much per bottle on 70-proof Scotch whisky), as opposed to an *ad valorem* tax, which is a given percentage of the price. One famous result is that a specific excise tax will raise price, but by less than the amount of the tax per unit—at least, on certain assumptions. We can now use our technique to derive this prediction for the linear case, and to try to find out on what assumptions it depends. This is an example of qualitative analysis, and we shall see how far we can get.

For demand, we shall still assume that

$$q^d = a + bp \quad , \tag{1}$$

but, in place of (2), we now have

$$q^s = c + dp^* \quad , \tag{18}$$

where p^* is the price received by suppliers after paying tax, which is less than market price p by the amount of the tax. p^* and p are therefore related by

$$p^* = p - t \quad , \tag{19}$$

where t is tax per unit. We also have, of course,

$$q^d = q^s \quad . \tag{3}$$

Thus we have a system of four equations, (1), (18), (19), and (3), in the unknowns q^d, q^s, p^*, and p, with parameters a, b, c, d, and t (we may, if we wish, call t an exogenous variable instead of a parameter: it makes no difference). As before, we proceed by substitution to obtain a single equation in one unknown. Substituting (19) into (18) we have

$$q^s = c + dp - dt \quad , \tag{20}$$

which eliminates p^*. Now substitute (1) and (20) into (3) to eliminate q^d and q^s:

$$a + bp = c + dp - dt \quad .$$

Rearranging as before,

$$a - c = p(d - b) - dt \quad , \tag{21}$$

whence

$$p = \frac{a - c}{d - b} + \frac{d}{d - b} t \quad . \tag{22}$$

(22) is another general solution, and we want to discover what properties of the solution, if any, can be established. We want to know, that is, if our qualitative restrictions, assumptions (i), (ii), (iii), and (iv) of Section 3.2, are enough to tell us anything about (22), and, if they are, what happens if we change any of these assumptions. There are four points we may make at once.

1. We had better start by checking that this solution is consistent with that of Section 3.2 (11). The only difference between the two cases is that in one we have a tax and in the other we do not. This suggests that we should ask what happens in the "with-tax" case if the tax rate is zero: we obviously should get the same solution as in the "no-tax" case. Thus we satisfy ourselves that we have not made some frightful blunder by trying $t = 0$ in (22). If we do this, we get $p = (a - c)/(d - b)$, which is what we found in (11).

2. This suggests that we look at the term in (22) that does contain t, and consider the way in which p depends on t. This term is

$$\frac{d}{d-b}t$$

which contains only the slope coefficients b and d: it does not contain the intercept coefficients a and c. Thus we may say that the effect of the tax on price is independent of the intercepts. This rather striking result can be quite easily illustrated geometrically. Draw linear supply and demand curves, add a tax, and find the new price. The easiest way of shifting the intercepts but not the slopes is just to move the axes. Draw the quantity axis an inch to the left and the price axis an inch lower down, and it is obvious that the price effect of the tax is unaltered. You will be asked to investigate in Question 4 the effect of the tax on quantity.

3. Since both d and $d - b$ are positive by assumption, the effect of the tax on price is always positive.
4. We know that $d/(d - b)$ is positive. If we can also show that it is less than unity, we shall have shown that the tax increases price, but by less than the amount of the tax. Since b, the slope coefficient of the demand curve, is negative, subtracting it from d has the effect of *adding* a positive number (this is an application of the rule "minus a minus makes a plus"). Hence $d - b > d$, whence $d/(d - b) < 1$, which is what we wanted to show.

Thus by point 4 we have proved the "tax theorem" for a competitive market with linear demand and supply curves, and have done so quite generally in the sense that we have not had to depend on numerical examples. We have, however, considered only the straightforward case of a downward-sloping demand curve and upward-sloping supply curve. We are still left with some problems:

i. What happens if the demand curve is upward-sloping as well as the supply curve?
ii. What happens if the supply curve is downward-sloping as well as the demand curve?
iii. For what values of the parameters does the solution break down?

We will deal with these problems in Section 3.5, but it would pay to try them for yourself before reading on, and to consider both their graphical illustrations and economic interpretations.

3.5 QUALITATIVE RESULTS WITH AN EXCISE TAX

Discovering the answers to these problems turns out to be fairly laborious: we shall find several possible answers to each, depending on the assumptions we make about the relative magnitudes of the parameters in each case. Our discussion is exhaustive, and has to be. If we did not examine every possibility, we might well overlook such circumstances as, for example, the following: if the demand curve slopes up, but more steeply than the supply curve, and we retain our assumption that $c < a$, which we made originally to be sure of having a positive price, we shall get a negative one! A systematic treatment can clarify many points that may not be immediately obvious to the intuition.

It is helpful to remember that our solution in the tax case is

$$p = \frac{a - c}{d - b} + \frac{d}{d - b} t \quad . \tag{22}$$

Problem (i). If the demand curve is upward-sloping, $b > 0$. This gives rise to three possible cases.

In the first case, the positive slope of the demand curve may be less than that of the supply curve (with q on the vertical axis of the graph, the slope of the demand curve is less steep than that of the supply curve). This means that $b < d$, in which case $d - b$ and $d/(d - b)$ are both positive, p is positive, and the effect of the tax on price is still positive. Since, however, b is positive, we now have $d > d - b$, so that the tax raises price by more than the amount of the tax.

In the second case the demand curve is steeper than the supply curve, so we have $b > d$, which, at first glance, gives the result $d/(d - b) < 0$: the tax lowers the price. If $d - b < 0$, however, we also have

$$\frac{a - c}{d - b} < 0$$

if $a > c$ as we assumed, which means that the curves intersect at a negative price. Thus we do not get a positive price—intersection in the positive quadrant—in this case unless we alter our assumption about the intercepts and put $c > a$, whereupon the tax does lower the price.

Between these two cases (supply curve steeper than demand curve, demand curve steeper than supply curve) there must lie a third, that in which the two slopes are the same. This means that $b = d$ in which case we have $d - b = 0$.

If we try to substitute this into (17), we get nonsense results with denominator terms of zero. Whenever we find that we wish to set some parameter (or combination of parameters) in our solution equation to zero we must check back over all previous algebraic manipulations to make sure that we have not done something with any parameter that is inadmissible when its value is zero. In the present case we note that we divided through by $d - b$ to get the solution equation. Since division by zero is undefined in the real number system, this is an inadmissible operation if $d - b = 0$. (Note that if we wished to set a or c or $a - c$ at zero the operation would be legitimate because we should do nothing but add and subtract these parameters from both sides of the equations, and addition and subtraction by zero *is* defined in the real number system.)

To investigate further the case in which $d - b = 0$ we must go back to our original equations. Take Eqs. (1), (2), and (3) and add the new assumed relation $d = b$ to give

$$a + bp = c + bp \quad ,$$

whence

$$a = c \quad .$$

These equations can thus be simultaneously satisfied only if $a = c$, in which case they hold for *any* p. The geometric interpretation is that not only do the curves have the same slope, but they also have the same intercept: *they are coincident*. In this case $q^d = q^s$ at any p. If, however, we insist on having $a \neq c$, then the equations cannot be simultaneously satisfied. The geometric interpretation is that if two parallel curves are not coincident they can never intersect: there is no equilibrium price.

We now wish to fit taxes into this special case of parallel demand and supply curves. To do this we go back to the tax model of Eq. (21) and substitute $b = d$. To see what this additional restriction implies, we rearrange (21) to get t expressed in terms of the remaining parameters:

$$t = \frac{a - c}{d} \quad .$$

This tells us that if we wish the model to have an equilibrium we are not free to let t take on any value we wish. Specifically, the above equation tells us that if $a \neq c$, so that the demand and supply curves are not initially coincident, a tax of exactly $(a - c)/d$ will cause the two curves to coincide, in which case any price is an equilibrium price. (Note that if the two curves coincide already, then $a = c$, and the tax must be zero.) Any other tax will bring about a situation in which the two curves do not coincide and there is no equilibrium price. (This is shown by the fact that no other t will satisfy the equation.)

These three cases are illustrated in Figures 3.1, 3.2, and 3.3. In Figure 3.1 the result of a tax of AB is to raise price by AC — and to raise quantity, too.[2] In Figure 3.2 it has been assumed that $c > a$, and a tax of EF can be seen to lower the price by DE. In Figure 3.3 the curves are parallel. There is no solution for price in Figure 3.3(a), and there is an infinite number of solutions in Figure 3.3(b).

The example of Figure 3.3 provides an important general warning. If we make an algebraic manipulation, we are implicitly assuming that it is a legitimate one. If we subsequently assume that one of the symbols in our equation take on a value for which the manipulation is inadmissible, the results cannot be used. Examples are dividing through by a symbol subsequently assumed to be zero and transferring into logarithms and later back into natural number symbols subsequently assumed to have negative values.

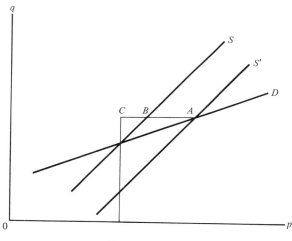

Figure 3.1

[2] In line with the rule laid down in Section 2.8, we have put quantity on the vertical axis in this figure. Thus the case $0 < b < d$, for example, means that the demand and supply curves both slope up, but the demand curve slopes up less steeply than the supply curve. To convert to the Marshallian diagram usually drawn by economists, with p on the vertical axis, it is only necessary to remember that if $q = a + bp$, then

$$p = \frac{-a}{b} + \frac{1}{b}q \quad,$$

so that the slope of the demand curve as conventionally drawn is $1/b$.

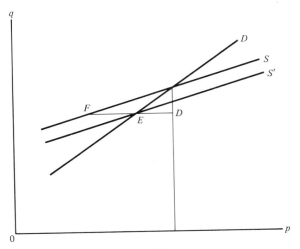

Figure 3.2

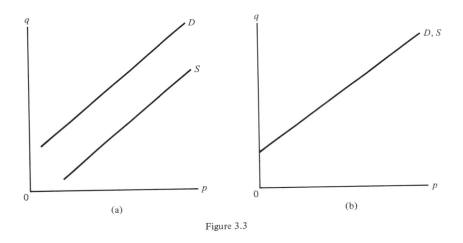

(a)   (b)

Figure 3.3

Problem (ii). What happens if the supply curve is downward-sloping as well as the demand curve? This means that $d < 0$, and again there are three possible cases.[3]

---

[3] $|X|$ is read "the absolute value of X," or "the modulus of X." It is defined as

$$|X| = X \qquad \text{if } X > 0$$
$$|X| = -X \qquad \text{if } X < 0 \ .$$

If b and d are negative, but $|b| > |d|$, then $d - b > 0$ because $-b$ is positive and absolutely larger than the negative d.

i. $|b| > |d|$ in which case $d - b > 0$ and $d/(d - b) < 0$: the tax lowers the price. Notice that since $d - b > 0$, the assumption $a > c$ is in this case required for a positive solution.

ii. $|b| < |d|$ gives $d/(d - b) > 0$: the tax increases price, but we need $c < a$ to get a solution at all.

iii. $b = d$: parallelism again.

This is a good moment to do Question 6.

Problem (iii). For what values of the parameters does the solution break down? To answer this we have only to collect up results from (*i*) and (*ii*). Part of the answer is obviously "if $b = d$." Another part is "if

$$b > d > 0 \quad \text{or} \quad b < d < 0$$

unless we change our assumption about the intercepts."

Looking over these results, we also see that we obtain a positive price with an upward-sloping demand curve and a downward-sloping supply curve, provided we assume that $c > a$. This is why we noted, in our discussion of the "no-tax" case in Section 3.2, that the straightforward assumptions of a downward-sloping demand curve, an upward-sloping supply curve, and a smaller supply intercept than demand intercept, were sufficient *but not necessary* to ensure that the solution gave a positive price.

3.6 LIMITING CASES

Infinite elasticity and zero elasticity, of either demand or supply, are familiar limiting cases, and we may now employ our techniques of qualitative analysis to discover what happens in these cases. Let us start with the case of a perfectly inelastic supply curve. In this case the supply curve is horizontal, and we say that the receipts of suppliers are entirely rents: a change in price leads to no alteration in supply. It is a well-known prediction of economic theory that in this case an excise tax falls entirely on the rent, leaving the market price unaffected. We can easily confirm this. If the supply curve is perfectly inelastic, we simply have the fixed supply

$$q^s = c \quad ,$$

that is, d is zero. If we replace d with zero in Eq. (22), we get

$$p = \frac{a - c}{-b} + \frac{0}{-b} t \quad ,$$

where the effect of the tax on price is zero, as we expected. Notice, incidentally, that we have here a good example of the utility of the general solution. We might have gone right back to Eqs. (1), (18), (19), and (3) of Sections 3.1, 3.2, and 3.4, replaced (18) with $q^s = c$, and solved the system again, but it would have been unnecessary labor: we have found the solution (22), and may substitute directly into it, merely replacing d with a zero whenever it occurs.[4]

The case of perfectly elastic supply produces some interesting problems. The supply curve here is vertical (since price is measured on the horizontal axis), and it is often said that its slope is infinite. If, however, we put $d = \infty$ and substitute into (22), we get

$$p = \frac{a - c}{\infty - b} + \frac{\infty}{\infty - b} t \quad ,$$

which is obviously nonsense. Something has gone wrong! It is important to consider very carefully what the cause of the trouble may be: if it is a comprehensible blunder, it can be understood and corrected and need not recur.

In fact, direct substitution of $d = \infty$ into (22) is a perfectly straightforward blunder in mathematics, and in economics as well. The mathematical blunder is easily understood. A vertical line has no slope — its slope is simply undefined — and if we insist on writing the symbol ∞ whenever we meet something undefined, we may expect to obtain a silly answer: the situation would not be different if we wrote "dog" or "dummy" for the nonexistent slope coefficient. To understand what has happened in economics, we must think out how the model works. If supply is perfectly elastic, there is one and only one price at which any output is produced at all, so equations such as (11) in the no-tax case or (22) in the tax case cannot be solutions *at all:* they provide solutions *when price is an endogenous variable, but here it is fixed.* We must therefore go back to the beginning and get the supply equation right. We still have Eq. (1),

$$q^d = a + bp \quad , \tag{1}$$

but instead of $q^s = c + dp$, we have $p = \bar{p}$ and no equation for the quantity supplied at all. This is intuitively reasonable, since perfectly elastic supply means that suppliers will provide *any* quantity they are asked for *at the given price* $\bar{p}$, so that they determine price, and consumers alone determine quantity. We now have the three-equation model

---

[4] This procedure is valid provided that $b \neq 0$ because we divided through earlier by $d - b$ but not by d on its own.

$$q^d = a + bp \tag{1}$$

$$p = \bar{p} \tag{23}$$

and

$$q^d = q^s \quad . \tag{3}$$

To solve, we merely substitute $p = \bar{p}$ into the demand equation, obtaining

$$q^d = a + b\bar{p} \quad , \tag{24}$$

and note that $q^s = q^d$.

Before we add a tax to the model of (1), (23), and (3), it will be wise to discover the conditions for anything to be sold at all at a positive price. We can no longer use $a < c$, since c has disappeared. What we require is that the intercept of the demand curve on the price axis be larger than the intercept of the supply curve. The latter is, of course, $\bar{p}$. The former we find by rearranging the demand equation:

$$bp = q^d - a$$

or

$$p = \frac{q}{b} - \frac{a}{b} \quad ,$$

whence the intercept is $-a/b$ (remember that $b < 0$), and the condition is $-a/b > \bar{p}$.

We may now analyze the effects of a tax. Recall that, whatever may happen, market price must be equal to suppliers' price plus tax, that is,

$$p = p^* + t \quad , \tag{19}$$

where p is market price and p^* suppliers' net price, as before. But there is a unique supply price, $\bar{p}$, so substitution at once gives

$$p = \bar{p} + t \quad , \tag{25}$$

and it immediately follows that price must rise by the full amount of the tax, the standard result we were trying to get. We also have

$$q = a + b(\bar{p} + t) \quad ,$$

that is, quantity falls by bt.

The analysis of this case suggests two morals that are worth some attention.

1. A great nineteenth-century problem was "Which determines prices, cost of production or value (marginal utility)?" Marshall answered this with the analogy of the scissors: "Which blade cuts the string?" We are so accustomed to the simultaneous determination of price *and* quantity by demand and supply that it is easy to forget that, if one is already fixed, there is only one scissor blade to move.

2. Suppose that we start with a model containing a given set of endogenous variables, and the equations relating them, and work out the solution and its properties. Now someone says "What if one of the variables is actually fixed?" (Many illustrations come to mind: "What if the price is controlled? Wages are sticky? Interest rates are fixed?") It may not be correct to substitute a fixed value into the solution since one or more of the behavioral equations may have been changed, and a new solution needs to be derived. Thus it may be necessary to go back to the original formulation of the model, and see how it is to work.

3.7 QUALITATIVE COMPARATIVE STATICS

In Section 3.2, we introduced the notion of "qualitative restrictions," and suggested that they might be sufficient to establish some properties of the solution of the model. In the last few sections, we have been working out the properties and the relevant restrictions, and have discovered, among other things, that the conditions $b < 0, d > 0$, and $c < a$ are sufficient, though not necessary, to establish the proposition that the tax will increase price but by less than itself. Consider again Eq. (22),

$$p = \frac{a - c}{d - b} + \frac{d}{d - b} t \quad ,$$

the graph of which is presented in Figure 3.4. Equation (22) gives price as a linear function of tax: the intercept is $(a - c)/(d - b)$, which is equilibrium price in the absence of a tax, and the slope is $d/(d - b)$, which measures the increase in price per unit increase in tax.

We may describe our result formally by saying that the slope in (22) is the rate of change of the endogenous variable, p, with respect to the exogenous variable (or "shift parameter"), t. What we have done is to differentiate the equilibrium value of the variable p with respect to the parameter t, and establish the qualitative result that the price rises but by less than the amount of the tax in the case in which $0 < d/(d - b) < 1$. "Differentiating the equilibrium value . . ." sounds formidable, but we have really done it. [In a linear model it happens to be peculiarly easy: it can be done by inspection, almost uncon-

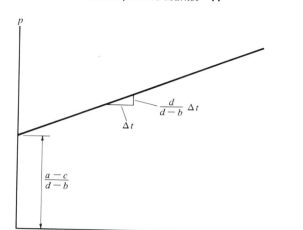

Figure 3.4

sciously. If p were a nonlinear function of t, then the slope (rate of change) would not, of course, be a constant. Later on we shall devote a good deal of attention to techniques that will allow us to find the relevant slope in more difficult cases.] What we are doing is often called "qualitative comparative statics," or even "the qualitative calculus." It is *comparative statics* because we are comparing one equilibrium situation with another, asking what changes in the variables are required when exogenous changes take place, and *qualitative* because we are trying to determine the directions of change without knowing numbers but only the signs of our parameters. In this case, of course, we have succeeded pretty well.

Imagine the situation had we failed. Suppose that the structure of the model were such that, with information such as $b < 0$, $c > 0$, etc., we could not predict the direction of change in price when a tax was imposed or altered. Without numerical estimates of the parameters, we could not compare the model with the real world. Our conclusion would be "price might go up, or it might go down, or it might stay the same." Whatever happened in the world would be consistent with this, and the comparison of events with our model would leave us no wiser. The model predicts that anything can happen, which is to say that it predicts nothing. Such a model is said to be qualitatively empty. It does *not* follow that a qualitatively empty model is irretrievably empty, but only that numerical estimates of parameters are required in order that directions of change may be predicted. A model with qualitative content may be more simply handled and more readily testable than one without, and we may hope that our simpler models, at least, have qualitative content. We shall certainly be concerned to investigate the matter, and to develop more powerful techniques for the purpose.

3.8 ON THE NUMBER OF EQUATIONS AND UNKNOWNS

The method of solution used in this chapter has been to eliminate variables by substitution, find the equilibrium value of the remaining variable, and then find the eliminated variables by substituting this value into the original equations. The model, or system, we started with has in each case been simultaneous in the sense that more than one relation had to hold simultaneously. The question arises: how many equations do we need to determine some given number of variables? So far, we have taken it for granted that we need the same number. (Thus if we wish to determine quantity demanded, quantity supplied, and price, we need a demand equation, a supply equation, and the equilibrium condition $q^d = q^s$.)

Unfortunately, however, equality between the number of unknowns and the number of equations in a system is neither necessary *nor* sufficient for a solution to exist. A complete discussion of the problem would be a large-scale undertaking, but there is no reason why it should be left an utter mystery, and we can quickly get some idea of what is involved.

Suppose, first, that we retain the assumption that all relations are linear. Now suppose that we are given two unknowns, y and x, and the single equation, say,

$$y = 10 + 5x \quad .$$

We obviously cannot "solve" for y, but only say "the equation establishes pairs of values: given x, we can read off y." If we were given another equation, say

$$x = 2 \quad ,$$

we could produce the solution, $y = 20$. We could also find the solution if we were given a second equation such as

$$y = x$$

or

$$y = 20 - x \quad .$$

You should draw a rough graph in each case (and you will have to use the negative quadrants). You will find that each equation gives a straight line and that the solution corresponds to the point where the two lines intersect. $y = x$ defines, of course, the 45° line, and $x = 2$ can be represented by a vertical line through the point $x = 2$: the solution is the value of y at the point where that line cuts the line $y = 10 + 5x$.

This is straightforward. Suppose, now, that we have $y = 10 + 5x$, and $y = x$, and are told that a third relation also holds, say, $y = 2 + 2x$. If you graph these three equations, you will find that they do not all intersect in the same place: it is impossible to satisfy all three relations simultaneously, and the system has no solution, but is said to be "over-determined." If this should occur, it is evidence that there is something wrong with the model in the first place. It might appear now that the rule we need is simply "do not have more equations than unknowns," but unfortunately matters are not quite so simple. There is, first, the possibility of accident: given three straight lines, they *may* all intersect in the same place. This case, however, is not very interesting since, even if one starts with an accidental solution, if one of the lines is moved by some change in data, there will then be no solution. There is, second, a possibility that we may illustrate. Suppose that we still have

$$y = 10 + 5x$$

and are given as a second equation

$$10y = 100 + 50x \quad .$$

Consider what happens if we divide through by 10: we simply get $y = 10 + 5x$. Thus the second equation tells us nothing that the first did not tell us: it gives the same line on the graph, and gets us no nearer to a solution. It is not "independent" of the first equation, whereas $y = x$ is independent of $y = 10 + 5x$ (there is no factor such that multiplication or division of one equation by that factor will produce the other). This suggests that we modify our rule to read "have exactly the number of independent equations as there are unknowns," and this is nearly correct. There remains, however, the sort of case we encountered in Section 3.5. What if we have

$$y = 10 + 5x$$

and

$$y = 20 + 5x \quad ?$$

These two lines are parallel, and we get no solution. With the techniques now at our command we cannot easily produce a general rule to deal with this case, so we shall leave the question for the moment.

If we allow nonlinear functions, matters get a good deal more complicated, as may easily be seen from a little geometrical experiment. A straight line, for example, may intersect a U-shaped curve (say, a quadratic) twice, or nowhere if it passes underneath it, or once if it is tangent to it or vertical. The case of "passing underneath" is the one that gives "imaginary roots" when we try to solve a quadratic that lies everywhere above the x-axis. It is not easy to lay down general rules, and all we can say is "if there appear to be more or less independent equations than unknowns, there is likely to be trouble; and if there are nonlinear functions, there may be no solution or multiple solutions, all depending on the particular case."

Income Determination

3.9 THE MULTIPLIER

We shall now subject a simple Keynesian model to the same sort of analysis that we have just applied to a competitive market. Once again, this is not only a technical exercise: we can illustrate some important ideas, and obtain some very interesting results that illuminate the relationship between economic analysis and economic policy. We shall also return to the model repeatedly in future chapters, tackling more and more ambitious questions as the technique at our command increases. We shall begin with a simple Keynesian model, of the sort that will be familiar from any standard "principles" text in which it is assumed that consumption depends only on current income and that all investment is autonomous. This effectively allows us to ignore the monetary sector, because if we assume that investment is autonomous, we do not have to concern ourselves with the determination of the interest rate and its effect on investment. We also assume, among other things, that prices are constant in spite of income changes, which means that we must assume unemployed resources, and confine ourselves to income changes that do not come too close to the full-employment "ceiling" on real national income.

The simplest case to start with is that of a closed economy with no government, and the first behavior equation we want is a consumption function. In the interests of analytical convenience we shall restrict ourselves to linear functions. Hence we assume that

$$C = a + cY \quad . \tag{26}$$

in which C and Y are consumption and national income and a and c are parameters.

In this case the average and marginal propensities to consume are unequal provided that a is not zero. The marginal propensity is given by

$$\frac{\Delta C}{\Delta Y} = c$$

and the average propensity by

$$\frac{C}{Y} = \frac{a + cY}{Y} = \frac{a}{Y} + c \quad .$$

If we assume that the intercept on the consumption function is positive, that is, $a > 0$, then the average propensity to consume exceeds the marginal propensity. (You should satisfy yourself that, the larger is Y, the more nearly equal are the average and marginal propensities. Illustrate geometrically.) The empirical evidence is not easy to interpret, but there is a good case for thinking that the average and marginal propensities *are* equal. We shall assume that they are equal, which means setting $a = 0$. The consumption function then goes through the origin when C is plotted against Y.

On these assumptions our behavior equation for consumption is

$$C = cY \quad . \tag{26a}$$

Following the usual Keynesian assumption that households consume a part of their income and save the rest, we have the qualitative restriction $0 < c < 1$.

The second behavioral assumption is that investment is an exogenous constant, which we may write as

$$I = \bar{I} \quad . \tag{27}$$

Strictly speaking, we should write $\bar{I}$ every time we refer to investment, but bars over variables to indicate that they are being held constant are costly to print and as long as we remember that investment is held constant we may use I rather than $\bar{I}$ to refer to it.

The model is completed by specifying the equilibrium condition[5] that total expenditure, $C + I$, should equal total income, Y:

$$Y = C + I \quad . \tag{28}$$

The model may now be summarized in terms of its two behavior

---

[5] Because we wish to have a genuine model, this must be an equilibrium condition rather than a definitional identity. The most common way of allowing for this is to say that C and I refer to desired consumption and investment expenditure rather than to the "actual values" as measured by national income statisticians, whereas Y refers to actual output. Thus (28) states the equilibrium condition that desired expenditure $(C + I)$ equals actual output (Y). This orthodox interpretation will suffice for our purposes, but its correct interpretation entails some tricky conceptual problems. (On this subject more advanced readers might wish to consult K. Klappholz and J. Agassi, "Identities in Economic Models," *Economica*, May 1962, and R. G. Lipsey, "The Foundations of National Income Theory: An Analysis of Five Fundamental Errors," in *Essays in Honor of Lord Robbins*, B. Corry and M. Peston, eds., Weidenfeld & Nicolson, London, 1971, Ch. 1.

equations, its one equilibrium condition, and the qualitative restrictions on the parameters:

$$C = a + cY, \qquad a = 0, \ 0 < c < 1 \qquad (26a)$$

$$I = \bar{I} \qquad (27)$$

$$Y = C + \bar{I} \ . \qquad (28)$$

We may now solve the model by substituting (26a) and (27) into (28) (remembering that we have agreed to simplify the terminology by writing I rather than $\bar{I}$ for the constant amount of investment expenditure). This gives us

$$Y = cY + I \ .$$

Collecting terms,

$$Y - cY = I \ .$$

Factoring out the left-hand side,

$$Y(1 - c) = I \ ,$$

and, dividing through by $1 - c$, we obtain[6]

$$Y = \frac{1}{1 - c} I \ . \qquad (29)$$

From (29) we see at once that

$$\Delta Y = \frac{1}{1 - c} \Delta I$$

or

$$\frac{\Delta Y}{\Delta I} = \frac{1}{1 - c} \ . \qquad (29a)$$

$1/(1 - c)$ is, of course, the multiplier, which it will be convenient to denote by k. It is worth noting that we obtain exactly the same multiplier if we assume that there is an intercept in the consumption function. Thus if we substitute (26) instead of (26a) into (28) and solve for Y by the method just adopted, we shall find

$$Y = \frac{1}{1 - c}(I + a) \ .$$

This shows that we may lump all autonomous expenditure together, irrespective of whether it is for consumption or investment, into a

---

[6] Notice that anything that follows will not be valid for the case in which $c = 1$ so that $1 - c = 0$.

single *multiplicand* ("multiplicand" is a useful word, meaning "that which is to be multiplied"), and that the multiplier depends only on those expenditure flows that vary with current income.

It is a familiar qualitative prediction from the Keynesian model that the multiplier is not only positive but greater than unity. If we want a qualitative prediction, however, we should expect to have to impose at least some qualitative restrictions. You should be able to show for yourself that the restriction we have placed on c ($0 < c < 1$) is necessary and sufficient for the result that $1 < k$ in the present simple model. Given the necessary restrictions, the result that $\Delta Y / \Delta I > 1$ is a qualitative comparative static prediction. Just as, in the tax case, we found that price was a linear function of the shift parameter, t, here we have found that income is a linear function of the autonomous variable I. When we try to discover the value of a multiplier, we are doing comparative statics in just the same way that we do when we impose taxes, shift demand curves, etc., in microanalysis. In our analysis of the competitive market, we obtained the result that, given certain qualitative restrictions on demand and supply, a tax would raise price, but by less than itself, which we could express as $0 < \Delta p / \Delta t < 1$. The result that the multiplier is greater than unity, given the restriction $0 < c < 1$, is a qualitative comparative static prediction of just the same sort.

3.10 THE EFFECTS OF TAXING AND SPENDING BY THE GOVERNMENT

A simple extension of this model, to include a government, will allow us to investigate a number of interesting problems in fiscal policy. We shall find our simple algebraic tools sufficiently powerful for an analysis of a number of questions over which there has been serious political controversy, and in the process we shall learn a good deal about the relationship between positive economics and economic policy. Let us assume that the government spends (autonomously) at the rate G on current goods and services, and that it imposes a flat-rate proportional income tax at rate[7] t. In this analysis, t is autonomous; but as it is a coefficient rather than an expenditure flow, it is a *shift parameter*. (A shift parameter is anything that appears in the equations of a model as a parameter, but as one that may be exogenously changed.)

If we assume that households' spending decisions depend on disposable income, we have

---

[7] We might also say "at $100t$ percent." Thus a 20 percent tax rate requires $t = 0.2$, and $100t$ percent $= 20$ percent.

$$C = cY^d \quad , \tag{26b}$$

where Y^d is disposable income. Our equilibrium condition is now

$$Y = C + I + G \quad . \tag{30}$$

Before substituting, however, we must express C as a function of Y instead of Y^d. Since disposable income is income after tax, we have the relation

$$Y^d = Y - T \quad , \tag{31}$$

where T is total tax paid, or "tax yield." Since taxation is proportional, we also have

$$T = tY \quad . \tag{32}$$

Substituting (32) into (31),

$$Y^d = Y - tY \quad , \tag{33}$$

and, factoring the right-hand side,

$$Y^d = Y(1 - t) \quad . \tag{34}$$

We now substitute (34) into (26b), which gives us

$$C = cY(1 - t) \quad , \tag{35}$$

and we have eliminated Y^d, disposable income: in (35) we have managed to express C simply as a function of income, Y, and the parameters c and t. [Recall how, in Section 3.4, when we had p^* and p, we eliminated one by using the relation expressed in Eq. (19): $p^* = p - t$.] If we now substitute (35) into (30), we have

$$Y = cY(1 - t) + I + G \quad . \tag{36}$$

Collecting Y terms we have $Y - cY(1 - t) = I + G$. Factoring as before, we have $Y[1 - c(1 - t)] = I + G$, and, dividing through by $[1 - c(1 - t)]$, this yields

$$Y = \frac{1}{1 - c(1 - t)}(I + G) \quad . \tag{37}$$

In (37) we have a new multiplier, $1/[1 - c(1 - t)]$, of greater generality than the one we found in (29). First, we must check that the two are consistent. If we assume that the rate of taxation is reduced to zero in (37), we have

$$\frac{1}{1 - c(1 - 0)} = \frac{1}{1 - c} \quad ,$$

which is the multiplier of (29), as we should expect. We also expect, for a given value of c, that the multiplier will be smaller for $t > 0$ than for $t = 0$. Thus we wish to confirm the inequality

$$\frac{1}{1 - c(1 - t)} < \frac{1}{1 - c} \quad .$$

Here we have an inequality between two fractions, a relationship that we have not encountered before. We can, however, handle it quite simply. Since the numerators on both sides are the same (both equal to 1), the left-hand side will be smaller than the right-hand side if the denominator of the left-hand side is *larger* than that of the right-hand side. Thus multiplying out the denominator of the left-hand side, the condition for the inequality to hold is that

$$1 - c + ct > 1 - c \quad .$$

We know that we do not disturb an equality if we subtract the same term from both sides, so if we subtract $1 - c$, our condition becomes simply

$$ct > 0 \quad .$$

But this must be true if the marginal propensity to consume and the tax rate are both positive. Hence we have confirmed our inequality: taxation does reduce the value of the multiplier.

The remaining question is, on what qualitative restrictions will the multiplier still exceed unity? For the multiplier to exceed unity, we want

$$1 - c + ct < 1 \quad .$$

Subtracting 1 from both sides and adding c to both sides, the condition is

$$ct < c \quad ,$$

which is true if t is a positive fraction. Thus we have obtained formally the not surprising result that, to obtain a multiplier greater than unity, we require that taxation of income be at less than 100 percent. This confirms something of considerable importance and generality: at no tax rate less than 100 percent do we lose the qualitative prediction of the no-tax case, that the multiplier is greater than unity.

We can explore a number of problems with this model, and a numerical example appears in Question 9. Let us investigate here the following question: what is the effect on the budget deficit (or surplus) of an extra unit of G? We need to be careful here about the meaning of "an extra unit of G," which we will write ΔG. We are doing static equilibrium analysis, and G is therefore the rate of expenditure on current goods and services by the government per unit of time (just as, in static price theory, "demand" is quantity demanded per unit of time). Hence ΔG is the *increment to the rate of expenditure,* for example, \$1 per year. We do not know, in general, whether we start from a deficit or surplus, but it makes no difference to the incremental changes, so we may proceed without bothering about the "starting point." We define

$$\Delta D = \Delta G - \Delta T \quad , \tag{38}$$

where ΔD is the change in the deficit (*note:* the change in the rate of deficit per unit of time, e.g., \$100 per year). Evidently, to find ΔD given ΔG, all we have to do is find ΔT. But $\Delta T = t\,\Delta Y$ and $\Delta Y = k\,\Delta G$, where k is the multiplier, equal here to $1/[1 - c(1 - t)]$; hence

$$\Delta D = \Delta G - tk\,\Delta G$$

$$= (1 - tk)\,\Delta G \quad . \tag{39}$$

Once again, we have expressed an endogenous variable as a function of an exogenous one, but is the expression in brackets in (39) positive, negative, greater than 1, or unknown? First of all, tk is positive, so $1 - tk$ must be less than 1, and the deficit cannot increase as much as G does; here is one qualitative prediction. But could the deficit actually fall? We have to explore the possibility that the increased income consequent upon additional expenditure ΔG is so large that the tax yield from it, at constant tax rates, actually exceeds ΔG. This seems intuitively a little steep, but to rule it out, we must show that $\Delta D > 0$, which it is if the bracketed term in (39) is positive, that is, if

$$1 - tk > 0 \quad .$$

Demonstrating that this inequality holds is rather laborious, but each step is quite straightforward. It is clearly true if $tk < 1$, that is, if

$$\frac{t}{1 - c(1 - t)} < 1 \quad .$$

This is the case if

$$t < 1 - c(1 - t) \quad .$$

Multiplying out the right-hand side, the condition is

$$t < 1 - c + ct \quad ,$$

or, subtracting ct from both sides,

$$t - ct < 1 - c$$

or

$$t(1 - c) < 1 - c \quad .$$

Dividing both sides by $1 - c$, our condition is

$$t < \frac{1-c}{1-c} = 1 \quad . \tag{40}$$

This is true if $t < 1$, as we have assumed, so that (39) must be positive: the deficit cannot fall.

These results are quite important and may be summarized. We have assumed a closed economy with unemployed resources and constant prices. We have also assumed that all investment and government expenditure are autonomous and that consumption is a constant fraction of disposable income. On these assumptions, we have shown that, for an increase ΔG in government expenditure,

$$\Delta Y = k \, \Delta G, \quad k > 1$$

and

$$0 < \Delta D = \Delta G (1 - tk) < \Delta G$$

assuming that $0 < c < 1$ and $0 < t < 1$. In words, an increase in government expenditure leads to an increase in income *greater* than itself, but to an increase in the budget deficit (or reduction in the surplus, as the case may be) *smaller* than itself.[8]

3.11 THE INCOME-DEFICIT TRADE-OFF

Each additional unit of government expenditure leads to an increased deficit as well as to increased income. Thus in this model, society can obtain increased income at the "cost" of increased deficit at some definite rate. We may illustrate this diagrammatically. In Figure 3.5, changes in income are measured on the vertical axis and changes in deficit on the horizontal axis. It is convenient to allow the origin to represent the *status quo ante*, that is, the starting point or initial equilibrium, and to continue to work in increments. Since, if nothing happens, equilibrium is undisturbed, the line relating ΔY to ΔD clearly passes through the origin. Since both the tax rate and the multiplier are constant, we may expect a straight line. It only remains to determine its slope. We know from Eq. (39) that

$$\Delta D = (1 - tk) \, \Delta G$$

and also that

$$\Delta Y = k \, \Delta G \quad .$$

---

[8] Remember that we have not only assumed all investment to be autonomous but have also suppressed the monetary sector.

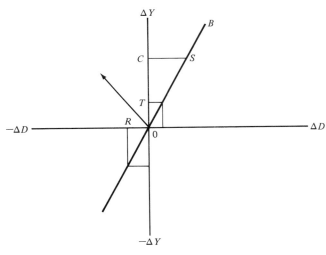

Figure 3.5

The slope is the ratio of ΔY to ΔD; hence we simply divide ΔY by ΔD to obtain

$$\frac{\Delta Y}{\Delta D} = \frac{k \, \Delta G}{(1 - tk) \, \Delta G} = \frac{k}{1 - tk} \qquad (41)$$

as the "trade-off rate" between ΔY and ΔD. We may evaluate this expression in terms of c and t or leave it as it stands: this is purely a matter of convenience (but it is good practice to evaluate it). What we want to do it to find out what we can about its value. We, in fact, already have enough information to determine its sign. We know that $0 < 1 - tk < 1$ from inequality (40) and that $k > 1$. Hence (41) is not only positive, not only greater than unity, but greater than the multiplier, k. This makes economic sense: a unit of ΔG leads to a larger increase in income and a smaller increase in the deficit.

Now, with the apparatus of Figure 3.5, we may illuminate some problems in economic policy. Suppose that the initial equilibrium is a position of unemployment and low income. Suppose further that you have no political objection to increased government spending or deficit. Then you obviously wish to move from the initial equilibrium out along the line $0B$, and you face no policy conflict. (We may also suppose that there is some increment in income $0C$ that would take the economy to full employment; then your policy would be to go to S and live happily ever after.) Consider now a man who wants increased income, is indifferent to deficits, and believes that the government should spend more. He might be of the Galbraith[9] school, believing that insufficient resources are being allocated to collective goods compared with private ones. For this person, too, there is no problem because the two things he wants, Y and G, are *positively associated in the real world:* he too goes to S, sacrificing nothing, and lives happily ever after. The moral is, of course, that if one "good" is independent of everything else that you value, you have no choice problem because there is no opportunity cost: you take as much as is available or as leads to satiety, whichever is the less. Similarly, if two "goods" are positively associated, increasing the amount of one involves no sacrifice of the other, and there is no choice problem.

Now consider a person who dislikes unemployment but also objects to increased government spending and/or deficits. Such a man might hold that citizens can spend their incomes to better advantage than the government, which should therefore refrain as far as possible from using its compulsory powers to do it for them. For simplicity, let us call such a man a fiscal conservative. We have no occasion to argue with his judgments: it is of interest merely to set out his problem. A man who wishes to increase income wishes to move north in Figure 3.5. If he wishes to reduce deficits, he also wishes to move west. Combining the two, he wishes to move in some northwesterly direction suggested by the arrow. But the line through $0B$ stops him: an increment of income of $0T$, say, simply cannot be had without an increased deficit; a reduction of $0R$ in the deficit will cause decreased income. From his point of view, therefore, $0B$ has become a *constraint:* he may choose a point on it but cannot get beyond it. Because he attaches a *negative* valuation to G (or D) and a positive one to Y, while they are positively associated in the world, the fiscal conservative is in a genuine choice situation: to increase the amount of one good, he must give up some of the other (increase a dis-good). And for him, the trade-off rate, $k/(1 - tk)$, represents a genuine opportunity cost ratio.

There are several points to notice here.

1. First-year students of economics are familiar with the production possibility curve or production frontier, which defines the alternative bundles of outputs possible in the economy. It turns out that we may find other constraints that force us to make choices.

[9] See J. K. Galbraith, *The Affluent Society*, River Press, Cambridge, Mass., 1958, particularly pp. 251–253.

2. The shape of the constraint, given by Eq. (41), depends on how society behaves. Our two basic behavioral assumptions here were proportionality in consumption and taxation. We could give the precise location of the constraint only if we knew the numerical values of c and t, but for *any* values of c and t between zero and 1, which is the range of relevant values, the constraint exists and has a positive slope.

3. The relationship between Y and D, being determined by the behavior of society, exists quite independently of whether we find it convenient or inconvenient. This seems to dispose of one major argument in support of the view that positive and normative questions can never be distinguished in social science. Where to go on the constraint depends on value judgments: knowledge of where the constraint is depends on scientific inquiry into the behavior of society. Thus we have a clear distinction between the normative question "where do you want to go?," and the positive one "where is it possible to go?" We shall see the distinction even more clearly in Chapters 10 and 11.

4. Individuals and societies can obviously make better choices (i.e., adopt policies to take them closer to where they want to be, consistent with where it is possible to be) if they know where the constraints are. Economists and econometricians try to find out for them. This conflicts with the view that an economist can give no useful advice, and make no contribution to the welfare of society, unless he actively recommends in the normative sense, and proposes solutions evolved from consideration of value as well as fact. (Some writers say that, as anything the economist can say has value implications, all we can ask is honesty!) The discovery of where constraints are — how society behaves — is no small contribution, and no one need be ashamed of devoting himself to this challenging and useful task.

5. We may wish to move constraints. If we are to do this successfully, we must understand the behavior and structure of the system that determines the location of the constraints. In the case of our illustration, it is obvious that the slope of the frontier depends on the value of t, which is directly under the control of the government, as well as on c, which is not so easily controlled. We now see why a government that wishes to move a constraint but does not wish to change tax rates may be tempted to persuade and exhort, or even to bully and threaten, to induce people to alter their behavior.

6. Since the government controls t, it is natural to ask "how is the slope of the frontier altered by a change in t?" Since, however, the trade-off rate, $k/(1 - tk)$, is not a simple linear function of t (remember that k is a function of t, too), we cannot answer this by simple inspection, as we have in other cases so far. This is a difficult question, as well as an important one, and to answer it we need a more powerful mathematical technique, which will be introduced in Chapter 4.

3.12 TRADE-OFF RATES IN AN OPEN ECONOMY

Many interesting and important policy problems arise from international trade. Governments are frequently much concerned, in particular, with the relationship between national income (and employment) and the balance of payments. A further simple extension of our linear model will allow us to examine this relationship. We consider an open economy with a government. We make the strong simplifying assumptions that exports, X, are autonomous and that imports, M, consisting only of final consumer goods, are proportional to disposable income:

$$M = mY^d \tag{42}$$

(where m is the constant propensity to import).

The difference between exports and imports is the balance of trade. For simplicity, we assume that there is no trade in invisibles and that there are no capital movements other than those necessary to adjust for a discrepancy between exports and imports. There is also a fixed exchange rate so that any discrepancy between M and X is reflected in a change in government-held foreign exchange reserves. Thus, in this simple model, which is sufficiently complex for our purposes, the balance of trade and the balance of payments are the same, and we shall use these two terms interchangeably to refer to $X - M$.

Our equilibrium condition is now[10]

$$Y = C + I + G + (X - M) \quad . \tag{43}$$

It is important to note that (42) and (43) together mean that C stands for *total* consumption, of both domestic and imported goods together.

---

[10] The right-hand side of (43) is aggregate expenditure on domestically produced output. It is necessary to deduct expenditure on imported goods, M, and to add expenditure of foreign spending units on our exports in order to arrive at this total. Hence the last term is *plus* X and *minus* M, which is often referred to as *net exports*.

Thus consumption of home-produced goods is $C - M$, and personal saving is $Y - T - C$, *not* $Y - T - C - M$. (Obviously we could have defined another variable C' as consumption of home goods only, and altered coefficient values accordingly: it is purely a matter of convenience and makes no difference to the results.)

Now $Y^d = Y(1 - t)$ from (34), and we combine this with (42) to obtain

$$M = mY(1 - t) \quad . \tag{44}$$

We retain the other behavioral assumptions of Section 3.11 and thus still have (35),

$$C = cY(1 - t) \quad .$$

Notice now that personal saving is

$$Y - T - C = Y - tY - cY(1 - t)$$
$$= Y[1 - t - c(1 - t)]$$

and that expenditure on domestically produced goods can be written

$$C - M = cY(1 - t) - mY(1 - t)$$
$$= Y(1 - t)(c - m) \quad .$$

As usual, we obviously assume that $0 < c < 1$. We also need $0 < m < 1$ *and* $m < c$.

Substituting these behavior relations for C and M into (43), we have

$$Y = cY(1 - t) + I + G + X - mY(1 - t) \quad .$$

We can use the same method that we used to obtain (29) and (37) to derive

$$Y = \frac{1}{1 - (1 - t)(c - m)}(I + G + X) \quad , \tag{45}$$

which you may check for yourself. This looks a bit cumbersome, but, once again, we can use some constant, k, to denote the multiplier and evaluate subsequent expressions in terms of c, m, and t only if we have to. [It is a good exercise to check that, if m and X are zero, (45) does reduce to (37).]

We now have a more complex model and might investigate a number of problems. Once again, we will look at one of society's choice constraints and find a trade-off rate. There are, in fact, several that we might look at: we could look at the pairs (Y, G), or (Y, M), or (G, M). Indeed, it is clear that "the" constraint requires more than two dimensions: in three, with Y, G, and M, we could see the situation clearly. The trade-off between Y and M, however, is particularly interesting, since with X autonomous, a change in M is exactly matched by a change in the balance of payments surplus or deficit. The government's *policy instruments* are G and t. The analysis of changes in t presents, as we have already seen, some difficulties. We will therefore concentrate on the Y/M frontier faced by a government that can alter G at will. We already know that $\Delta Y = k\ \Delta G$. Working in increments, as before, we define

$$\Delta B = \Delta M - \Delta X$$

as the net change in the balance of payments deficit (*note again:* change in the rate at which the deficit is running per unit of time). Now,

$$\Delta M = m\ \Delta Y^d \qquad [\text{see } (42)]$$
$$= m\ \Delta Y(1 - t) \qquad [\text{see } (44)]$$
$$= m(1 - t)k\ \Delta G \qquad [\text{see } (45)] \qquad (46)$$

and $\Delta B = \Delta M$ on the assumption that X is autonomous ($\Delta X = 0$ in response to any change in G, Y, or M). We now simply take the ratio of the values of ΔY and ΔB in response to ΔG from (45) and (46):

$$\frac{\Delta Y}{\Delta B} = \frac{k\ \Delta G}{m(1 - t)k\ \Delta G} = \frac{1}{m(1 - t)} \qquad . \qquad (47)$$

Equation (47) gives the slope of the frontier facing the government. Suppose, as we may, that the government regards Y as "good" and B as "bad." It is important to know if the frontier has a positive or negative slope. It is obviously positive, since m and $1 - t$ are positive by assumption: increased income, in response to increased G, leads to an increased balance of payments deficit — which is clear enough from our basic behavior assumption in (42) or from (46).

We have now discovered the slope of a constraint which causes governments much concern, and it is worth exploring a little further. The situation is illustrated in Figure 3.6, where ΔY appears on the vertical axis and ΔB on the horizontal axis. Once again, since we are working in increments, the constraint goes through the origin (if nothing happens, nothing happens), and its (positive) slope is given by (47). $-\Delta B$ of course means either a reduction in the deficit or an increase in surplus, depending on the starting point. The arrow indicates the desired direction of movement for a government, or anyone else, who wants higher income but wishes to avoid balance of payments difficulties. A desired improvement in the balance of payments,

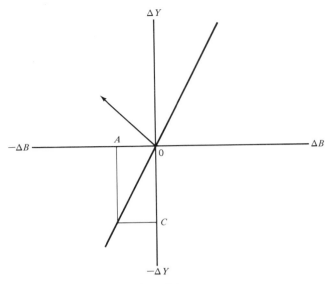

Figure 3.6

such as 0A, can of course be made, but only at the price of reducing G enough to reduce income by 0C. The behavior of the economy, which is summed up by the values of c, m, and t, and their interrelations, has effectively produced a choice constraint. Let us consider a little further, however, the direction in which governments might wish to move. Thus suppose that the origin in Figure 3.6 corresponded to an initial position or "starting point" of considerable unemployment and a substantial balance of payments surplus. A man who wished to avoid deficits might be quite indifferent to a reduction in the surplus, and thus feel that there was no choice problem so long as there was both unemployment and surplus: only when a further increase in employment threatened to run the economy into balance of payments deficit would he start to feel constrained. This suggests that the desired direction of movement, or, what comes to the same thing, whether a given constraint imposes the necessity for choice, may depend on the initial equilibrium values of variables such as Y and B. We return in Chapters 10 and 11 to the subject of optimal choice given a constraint or, as it is technically called, "maximization subject to constraint": it is a central topic of economics, but we shall require a good deal more technique before we can do more than outline the nature of the problem as we have done in this chapter.

There is no need to rehearse the discussion at the end of Section 3.11. What we may notice here is, first, that the effects of changing t

will again be troublesome to analyze, and, second, that an alternative method of changing the structure now appears: operating on m, and perhaps X, by "expenditure-switching" policies that we cannot handle at all in this simple model.[11]

3.13 THE CLOSED ECONOMY WITH MONEY

Let us now see what happens if we relax the assumption that all investment is autonomous and assume instead that it is a function of the interest rate. To study this problem in the simplest possible model we shall revert to the model of Section 3.9 in which there is neither a governmental nor a foreign trade sector.

In standard Keynesian theory the interest rate is determined by the demand for and the supply of money. This is the first time we have introduced money, and we need to be rather careful. The quantity of money is usually defined to include all notes and coins (legal tender) in circulation plus demand deposits at banks. The quantity of money is thus a stock—so many dollars—in contrast to variables such as Y and C, which are flows—so many dollars per unit of time. The demand for money is accordingly a "stock" demand—a demand to hold, on the average, a certain volume of currency and deposits—and it is convenient to speak of the demand for money balances.

An individual's money balances are part of his wealth, *not* part of his income flow. Money is one form in which wealth may be held and individual decision units (households and firms) are thought of as deciding how much of their wealth to hold in liquid form (money) and how much to invest in less liquid assets that yield an interest payment. In a simple model, all these interest-earning assets are lumped together and called bonds (in more complex models, many kinds of interest-earning assets are introduced).

The demand for money is assumed to be an increasing function of income and a decreasing function of the rate of interest. The higher is income, the larger is the stock of money needed for transactions purposes (the transactions motive), and the larger the stock needed to provide a given amount of security against unexpected fluctuations in receipts and payments (the precautionary motive). The higher the interest rate, the greater the opportunity cost of holding cash rather than investing in bonds, and *if investors have some idea of a normal rate around which the actual rate fluctuates*, the larger the possibility of capital gains (the speculative motive) from holding bonds

---

[11] A change in the exchange rate will change the level of exports and also the amount of imports associated with any given level of national income, thus changing m.

when the rate of interest falls back to normal in the future (when the rate of interest falls the price of bonds rises).[12]

If we continue to assume that all demand functions are linear, we may write

$$M^d = d + eY + fr \quad , \tag{48}$$

where M^d is the demand for money, r is the rate of interest, and the parameters are $d > 0$, $e > 0$, and $f < 0$.

In the simplest theory the supply of money is assumed to be determined by the policy of the *central bank*. Although this assumption is now thought to attribute to central banks more power over the money supply than they actually exert, we can go a long way by using it as a convenient simplification. Thus we write

$$M^s = M_0 \quad , \tag{49}$$

where M^s is the money supply and M_0 is a constant amount determined by the central bank.

Equilibrium requires that

$$M^d = M^s \quad ,$$

and, substituting in our behavior Eqs. (48) and (49), we obtain

$$d + eY + fr = M_0 \quad . \tag{50}$$

Equation (50) contains *two* endogenous variables, Y and r. This means that, if we know Y, we can determine the interest rate that will equate the demand for and supply of money, and vice versa, but we cannot simultaneously determine both variables from this one equation. We need help, so let us complete the model.

The model is completed by adding in the expenditures on goods, considered in Section 3.9. We now have investment depending on the rate of interest, which, assuming a linear relation, gives

$$I = b + gr$$

with the parameters $b > 0$ and $g < 0$. We also need a consumption function, which from (26a) is

$$C = cY \quad .$$

Finally, we have for equilibrium in the goods market the condition that income should equal expenditure, which in this simple model has only two components, consumption and investment:

---

[12] This paragraph gives a very compressed summary of the elementary Keynesian theory of the demand for money. It will not be sufficient for those not already familiar with it, and such readers should consult the treatment in any standard text.

$$Y = C + I \quad .$$

We may now gather all the equations together and give them new numbers for ease of subsequent cross-referencing.

GOODS MARKET

$C = cY$	(consumption function)	(51)
$I = b + gr$	(investment function)	(52)
$Y = C + I$	(equilibrium condition)	(53)

$$0 < c < 1, g < 0, 0 < b \quad .$$

MONEY MARKET

$M^d = d + eY + fr$	(demand function)	(54)
$M^s = M_0$	(supply function)	(55)
$M^d = M^s$	(equilibrium condition)	(56)

$$0 < d, 0 < e, f < 0 \quad .$$

Substitution into the two equilibrium conditions gives the following equations:

GOODS MARKET

$$r = -\frac{b}{g} + \frac{(1-c)}{g} Y \quad , \tag{57}$$

and

MONEY MARKET

$$r = \frac{M_0 - d}{f} - \frac{e}{f} Y \quad . \tag{58}$$

Equations (57) and (58) are linear versions of equations that are very frequently used in macro theory, and you should make for yourself the substitutions of (51) and (52) into (53), and of (54) and (55) into (56) to be quite certain you understand their derivation.

Now consider what we have done. We have set up a model consisting of *two pairs* of behavioral equations, (51)–(52) and (54)–(55). We have substituted each pair into the appropriate equilibrium condition and thus obtained a pair of simultaneous equations, (57) and (58), in two unknowns, Y and r.

These are the equations in linear form of the famous *I-S* curve (57) and the *L-M* curve (58). Equation (57) expresses the relation between Y and r that must obtain if the goods market is to be in equilibrium (income equals expenditure), and Eq. (58) expresses the relation between Y and r that must obtain if the money market is to be in equilibrium (demand for money equals supply of money). When plotted on a diagram with r on the vertical axis and Y on the horizontal axis, the well-known *I-S, L-M* diagram results. This is illustrated in Figure 3.7.

Let us first determine the slopes of these relations. Inspection of (57) tells us that $\Delta r/\Delta Y = (1 - c)/g < 0$. Thus the *I-S* curve slopes downward, because an increase in income induces a smaller increase in consumption expenditure, and if total expenditure is to increase as much as income, the rate of interest must fall to induce enough additional investment so that the change in aggregate expenditure matches the change in income; that is, $\Delta Y = \Delta C + \Delta I$.

Inspection of (58) shows that $\Delta r/\Delta Y = -(e/f) > 0$. Thus the *L-M* curve slopes upward, because an increase in income increases the demand for money $(0 < e)$, and, to keep the overall demand equal to the unchanged supply (M_0), it is necessary for the rate of interest to rise sufficiently to leave the overall demand for money unchanged. This may sound rather complicated (which it really isn't), and it may be worth looking at it in another way. If we substitute (54) and (55) into (56) but do not do the manipulation necessary to put them into the form of (58), we have

$$d + eY + fr = M_0 \quad .$$

This is merely the demand for money on the left-hand side (LHS) equated to the supply on the right-hand side (RHS). If we take changes in the variables, we get

$$e\,\Delta Y + f\,\Delta r = \Delta M_0 \quad ,$$

and if we recall our assumption that the money supply is a constant, this reduces to

$$e\,\Delta Y + f\,\Delta r = 0 \quad .$$

Now, since $e > 0$ (i.e., an increase in Y increases M^d) and $f < 0$ (i.e., a fall in r increases M^d), the overall demand for money can be held equal to the unchanged supply if changes in Y are accompanied by appropriate changes in r of the opposite sign to the changes in Y.

Next we ask, how do we discover the equilibrium values of Y and r? Algebraically, we solve (57) and (58) simultaneously to find the values of Y and r consistent with equilibrium in *both* the goods and the money markets. The graphical equivalent is to find the intersection of the *I-S* and the *L-M* curves.

We may now solve the model algebraically by the standard, if

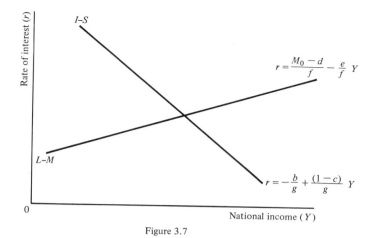

Figure 3.7

tedious, method of substitution. Substituting for r from (57) into (58) we have

$$Y\frac{(1-c)}{g} - \frac{b}{g} = -\frac{e}{f}Y + \frac{M_0 - d}{f} \quad .$$

Collecting terms,

$$Y\left[\frac{(1-c)}{g} + \frac{e}{f}\right] = \frac{M_0 - d}{f} + \frac{b}{g}$$

and

$$Y\left[\frac{f(1-c) + eg}{fg}\right] = \frac{g(M_0 - d) + bf}{fg} \quad ,$$

whence, finally,

$$Y = \frac{1}{(1-c)f/g + e}(M_0 - d) + \frac{b}{(1-c) + eg/f} \quad . \tag{59}$$

To find r, we substitute (59) back into (57) [or (58): you should be familiar with the reason we may use either] to obtain

$$r = \frac{(1-c)}{f(1-c) + eg}(M_0 - d) - \frac{eb}{f(1-c) + eg} \tag{60}$$

(by the application of brute force).

Equations (59) and (60) look unpromising, but they are both linear in M_0, the money supply, and in b, the constant in the investment function.

To study this equation further let us hold the money supply and the parameters in all our behavior equations except the investment function constant. We will shift the investment function parallel to itself by changing the constant, b, in Eq. (52). Now if we express ΔY as a function of Δb from (59) we obtain

$$\Delta Y = \frac{\Delta b}{(1-c)+eg/f}$$

or

$$\frac{\Delta Y}{\Delta b} = \frac{1}{(1-c)+eg/f} \ . \tag{61}$$

This is a multiplier expression for a shift in the autonomous component in investment which we must compare with the multiplier derived from the simpler model in Section 3.9:

$$\frac{\Delta Y}{\Delta I} = \frac{1}{1-c} \ . \tag{29a}$$

The difference between (29a) and (61) is in the additive term eg/f in the denominator of (61). The sign restrictions on the parameters $(f, g < 0 < e)$ are sufficient to establish that the term eg/f is positive. Thus the term increases the value of the denominator and reduces the value of the investment multiplier:

$$\frac{1}{1-c} > \frac{1}{(1-c)+eg/f} \ .$$

The amount by which the new multiplier of (61) is reduced below the simpler multiplier of (29a) depends on the parameters that determine the demand for money (e and f) and the response of investment to a change in the rate of interest (g). The common sense of this result is that a rise in investment increases income; this increases the demand for money, and the interest rate rises to equate M^d with an unchanged M^s; the rise in r chokes off some interest-sensitive investment and so reduces the value of the multiplier below what it is when there is no relation between interest rates and investment.

Now consider what happens in (59) if we hold b constant and change M_0. By inspection we obtain directly

$$\frac{\Delta Y}{\Delta M_0} = \frac{1}{(1-c)f/g+e} \ . \tag{62}$$

We see that this is positive, since $f < 0$, $g < 0$, and $e > 0$.

Equation (62) is usually called a "money multiplier," and we should compare it with the more familiar expressions in (61). In (61), both numerator and denominator are *flows per unit time*. In (62), ΔY is again a flow per unit time, whereas ΔM_0 is a once-and-for-all change in the money *stock*. It follows that the two kinds of multiplier are not directly comparable. In one case we have the response of a permanent flow to a stock change and in the others the response of a flow to changes in flows. We shall return to these models in Chapter 16 when we have more powerful techniques at our command.

QUESTIONS

1. Show that the solution obtained for q in (12) would also have been obtained by substituting (11) into (2) instead of (1). Consider carefully why this will always work.

2. What are the effects of a tax of 75 per unit in the numerical example of Eqs. (4), (5), (6) in Section 3.1?

3. Use shift parameters Δa and Δc to illustrate the effects on quantity of parallel shifts in linear demand and supply curves. What simultaneous shifts in both curves would leave price unaffected? What effect would such shifts have on quantity? Now make simultaneous shifts that leave quantity unaffected and consider their effect on price.

4. It is shown in Section 3.4 that the effect of a specific excise tax on price is independent of the intercept coefficients. What does the geometrical illustration suggest about the effect of the tax on equilibrium quantity? Investigate algebraically. (*Hint:* Substitute (22) into (1) and examine the term that contains t.)

5. In Figure 3.3 the supply curve has been drawn below the demand curve.
   (a) Is this consistent with our assumption about c and a?
   (b) Does it make any difference to the conclusion whether the supply curve is above the demand curve or vice versa for the case $d = b$?
   (c) What happens if $d = b$ and $c = a$?

6. Provide geometrical illustrations of the answers to Problem 2 of Section 3.5.

7. Apply the techniques of Section 3.6 to the cases of perfectly inelastic and perfectly elastic demand.

8. In the model set out below, the equations on the right-hand side give a numerical version of the equations on the left:

$$
\begin{array}{ll}
Y = C + I & Y = C + I \\
C = a + bY & C = 5 + 0.7Y \\
I = e + fY & I = 100 + 0.2Y
\end{array} \quad .
$$

   a. Compute the multiplier for both.
   b. Would a and e represent autonomous expenditure in this model?
   c. Could I be regarded as autonomous expenditure in this model?

9. Assume that, in the model of Section 3.10, the government taxes all income at 20 percent, that the marginal propensity to consume is 0.7, and that the government begins annual expenditures of $5 billion for highway repairs. What would be the impact on the budget deficit?

10. Consider the consumption function

$$C = 5 + 0.9Y \quad .$$

   a. What are the marginal and average propensities to consume?
   b. Are these propensities ever in equality for positive values of Y?
   c. Now consider $C = 0.9Y$, and answer the same questions.
   d. Is the consumption function a behavioral equation?
   e. Take both of these consumption functions, and in conjunction with the following equilibrium equation, $Y = C + I$, compute the values of the multipliers.
   f. Would you characterize this as a comparative static result?

11. a. If $t > 0$, then is $1/[1 - c(1 - t)]$ known as the multiplier, or does the term apply only to the part $1/(1 - c)$?
   b. The value of t is restricted to lie in the range 0 to 1. Calculate the multipliers corresponding to these two extreme values of t. (Assume that $c = 0.95$.)
   c. Now suppose new highway expenditures of $5 billion yearly are approved. What would be the two corresponding values of ΔY for the two values of the multiplier calculated in part b?
   d. Explain the result.

12. Once again assume new highway expenditures of $5 billion annually, and use $c = 0.95$ and $t = 0.25$.
   a. What would be the change in the budget balance as a result of the new expenditure?
   b. If the total government expenditure had been $200 billion per year, would the deficit have changed more or less compared with a situation in which previous government expenditures had been $300 billion per year? Had the question been "Will the change in the deficit be greater than the $5 billion in increased expenditure?," would it have been necessary to perform numerical calculations? (Refer to Section 3.10.)

13. a. What is the economic explanation of the result of Section 3.10, Eq. (39), that $\Delta D < \Delta G$?
   b. It is also shown that $\Delta D > 0$ if $0 < t < 1$. What happens if $t = 1$? (*Hint:* What is the value of the multiplier in this case?)
   c. The Secretary of the Treasury proposing an increase in income tax argues as follows: "National income is 140 million per annum, of which 100 million is personal income subject to income tax at the standard rate, now 15 percent. The increase in the rate from 15 to 20 percent will increase revenue by 5 million." Comment critically on this argument.

14. Show algebraically that $\Delta Y/\Delta D$ [Eq. (41)] exceeds $\Delta Y/\Delta G$ [from Eq. (37)]. Why do you expect this result?

15. Construct a diagram, similar to Figure 3.5, but with ΔY and ΔG on the axes, and determine the slope of the constraint.

16. How is the situation of the Galbraithian changed if society starts at S in

Figure 3.5 instead of 0? Why are the problems of a party that supports the Galbraithian position easier if it is elected at a time of unemployment (besides, that is, getting credit for curing the unemployment)?

17. Assume an economy in which

$$C = 0.8Y^d$$
$$M = 0.2Y^d$$
$$\left.\begin{array}{l} X = 80 \\ I = 120 \end{array}\right\} \text{ both autonomous}$$
$$t = 0.2 \quad .$$

(*Hint:* It will be found more convenient to work in fractions than in decimals.)
a. What will be the equilibrium level of Y if $G = 99$?
b. What level of G will balance the budget?
c. What level of G will lead to balance of payments equilibrium?
d. If full employment income is 700, what level of G will be needed to reach full employment?
e. What will the surplus or deficit in the balance of trade be at full employment?
f. What are the trade-off rates to the government between

i. budget deficit and income?
ii. budget deficit and balance of payments deficit?
iii. income and balance of payments deficit?

Illustrate diagrammatically.
g. Check, at least in part a, that $I + G + X = S + T + M$. How is home investment being financed?
h. Describe the policy problem facing this economy. What would you do?

18. a. Calculate the equilibrium values of r and Y for the following model:

$$C = 0.95Y$$
$$I = 12.0126 - 0.2r$$
$$M^D = 0.25Y - 0.05r$$
$$M^S = 100$$
$$Y = C + I$$
$$M^S = M^D \quad .$$

b. What would be the effect on the equilibrium values of Y and r if the constant term in the investment equation was increased from 12.0126 to 12.0147? Using the solution equations of the full model, which are found in Section 3.13, Eqs. (59) and (60), calculate $\Delta r / \Delta b$ and $\Delta Y / \Delta b$ in terms of the other parameters. Note the relationship of these calculations with those of the first half of the question.

19. List four economic flow variables and four economic stock variables ("economic" can be taken to mean anything that might be found in the literature of economics).

Chapter 4

Introduction to Calculus: Differentiation

If we are to progress further than we did in Chapter 3, we must not confine ourselves to linear relations or to what we can deduce about our relations using only those algebraic tools presently at our command. To go further we need more technique, and in this chapter we shall present enough to enable us to take our study of economics one step further. For those readers who have not yet studied the calculus this chapter is the decisive hurdle.

4.1 ELASTICITY OF DEMAND

Consider what might be known about some of the functional relations in economics. At one extreme we can make only very general qualitative statements about the way in which our variables are associated. In demand theory, for example, we often do not assume more than that in the function

$$q = q(p) \tag{1}$$

quantity is a decreasing function of price. At the other extreme we sometimes know enough to specify a very precise quantitative relationship between the variables. For example, Stone has estimated that the demand for home-produced mutton in Britain during the period between World Wars I and II was given approximately by the nonlinear expression[1]

---

[1] Richard Stone, *The Measurement of Consumers' Expenditure and Behaviour in the United Kingdom*, 1920–1938, vol. 1, Cambridge University Press, London, 1954. The general expression is of the form $q° = ap^a$ but we can remove the constant by dividing through by a and defining our new unit of measurement of demand to be $q = q°/a$, where $q°$ is demand measured in the original units of measurement.

$$q = \frac{1}{\sqrt{p^3}} \quad . \tag{2}$$

In other cases we are able to specify more than just the signs of our parameters, but we are unable to specify their specific values. For example, we may wish to say that the demand for some commodity is given by

$$q = p^\alpha \quad , \tag{3}$$

where $0 > \alpha > -1$. In all these cases we are putting some restriction on the way in which demand varies as price varies, and very often our problem is to discover, with only qualitative restrictions, the direction of change in the dependent variable as an exogenous variable changes. In Chapter 3 we were able to handle such problems successfully when the variables were related by linear functions. We now seek a more general method of handling them when the variables are linked by a nonlinear function as they are in (2) and (3).

We shall begin by considering the elasticity of demand as an example. In elementary treatments the elasticity of demand is often defined as

$$\eta = \frac{\% \text{ change in quantity demanded}}{\% \text{ change in price}}$$

$$= \frac{(\Delta q/q) \cdot 100}{(\Delta p/p) \cdot 100}$$

$$= \frac{\Delta q}{q} \cdot \frac{p}{\Delta p}$$

$$= \frac{\Delta q}{\Delta p} \cdot \frac{p}{q} \tag{4}$$

(η is the Greek letter "eta"). The elasticity measured by (4) is taken to refer to the point (p, q) on the demand curve. The first term in (4) is the incremental ratio measured from the demand function. We have seen in Chapter 2 that when the demand curve is plotted on a graph this ratio shows the slope of the chord joining the two price–quantity points between which the changes are being measured. The second term, p/q, depends solely on the point on the curve representing the original price and quantity.

Consider first the elasticity of the linear demand function $q = ap + b$. In this case we know that the incremental ratio is the same no matter where on the function we measure it. Thus $\Delta q/\Delta p = a$, and we can rewrite (4) as

$$\eta = a\frac{p}{q} \quad . \tag{5}$$

This shows that the elasticity measured at any point (p, q) on the linear demand function will be independent of the size and direction of the change in price that occurs. We say that there is a *unique* elasticity associated with each point on the linear demand function, although, of course, the elasticity is different at each point.

Now consider a nonlinear demand function. Take, for example, the case in which a constant sum, \$1200, is spent on the commodity whatever its price. Since expenditure is constant at \$1200, the equation for the demand function must be

$$pq = 1200 \quad . \tag{6}$$

This is the implicit form, but obviously yields

$$q = 1200p^{-1} \quad . \tag{7}$$

Our elementary economics tells us that this curve should have an elasticity of minus unity, since total expenditure remains constant as price changes. Let us, however, try to measure elasticity by the formula given in (4). Consider the prices and quantities given in Table 4.1, all of which satisfy Eq. (6). Let us take the point $p = 30$, $q = 40$ and calculate elasticity for a change in price to each of the other price–quantity combinations shown in Table 4.1. The results are displayed in Table 4.2. In no case does our calculated elasticity come out to be unity. Furthermore, the answer varies according to the direction and the magnitude of the changes in price that we consider. According to standard theory, elasticity should be minus unity everywhere on this curve. The measure defined in (4), however, provides no unique number for elasticity at the point (30, 40) — and won't elsewhere.

We now have a most unsatisfactory discrepancy between the results of standard theory and those given by Eq. (4). It is a consequence of using incremental ratios on nonlinear functions. In the present case, we are dealing with a curve and not a straight line, and the incremental ratio $\Delta q / \Delta p$ varies with the size and direction of the change in p that we consider and with the value of p, q, at which we seek to measure the elasticity. The geometrical illustration of this is

Table 4.1
Values computed from the demand
function $pq = 1200$

p	q	pq
20	60	1200
25	48	1200
30	40	1200
32	37.5	1200
50	24	1200

Table 4.2
Elasticities of demand measured from the point
$p = 30$, $q = 40$, on the demand function $pq = 1200$

Δp	Δq	$\dfrac{\Delta q}{\Delta p}$	$\dfrac{p}{q}$	η
-10	$+20$	-2.00	0.75	-1.5000
-5	$+8$	-1.60	0.75	-1.2000
$+2$	-2.5	-1.25	0.75	-0.9375
$+20$	-16	-0.80	0.75	-0.6000

given in Figure 4.1 where we illustrate what we first established in Chapter 2, that the incremental ratios in Table 4.1 are the slopes of the chords joining the pairs of points in question. Clearly with any nonlinear demand function the slope of the chord joining one point m to various other points on the curve will vary as the second point chosen varies. What we need is a unique measure of the rate at which quantity demanded is tending to change as price changes at a particular point on the curve. It is now evident that the measure involving the incremental ratio will not serve this purpose. To provide this measure we take the slope of the straight line that is tangent to the curve at the point in question. This is illustrated in Figure 4.1. The line TT is tangent to the demand curve at the point m, and we say that its slope measures the rate at which q is tending to change as price changes at point m. We call the slope of this tangent the *derivative of quantity with respect to price*, and we give it the symbol dq/dp.

Now consider the relation between the slope of the tangent to a curve at any point and the slopes of the incremental ratios measured

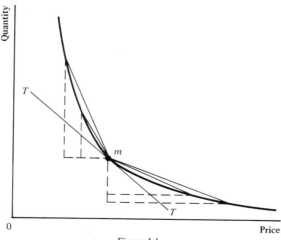

Figure 4.1

from that point. Inspection of Figure 4.1 suggests that, as Δp is made smaller and smaller, the slope of the chord joining the two points on the curve comes closer and closer to the slope of the tangent. Indeed, it looks as though we could make the incremental ratio get as close as we wanted to the slope of the tangent as long as we made Δp small enough. We shall investigate this more fully in Section 4.2, but at present we merely assert, what seems visually clear from the figure, that the ratio $\Delta q/\Delta p$ gets very close indeed to the slope of the tangent as Δp is made very small.

We may now consider what will happen to our measure of elasticity if we substitute the slope of the tangent dq/dp, at the point (p, q), for the incremental ratio $\Delta q/\Delta p$. The tangent to a smooth continuous curve at a point will be unique: there is only *one* dq/dp at any point. We may now redefine elasticity as

$$\eta = \frac{dq}{dp} \cdot \frac{p}{q} \quad , \tag{8}$$

and this will give us a unique elasticity at each point on the curve.

For obvious reasons elasticity defined by (8) is usually called *point elasticity*, whereas elasticity defined by (4) is called *arc elasticity*.

4.2 THE CONCEPT OF A LIMIT

In Section 4.1 we relied on inspection of Figure 4.1 to suggest that the slope of the incremental ratio gets closer and closer to the slope of the tangent as Δp is made smaller and smaller. Indeed we conjectured that we could make $\Delta q/\Delta p$ come as close as we wanted to dq/dp if we made Δp small enough. It is this latter conjecture that we need to clarify and elaborate upon. To do this we introduce the idea of a limit.

In Section 2.6 we considered the function $1/x$. As x takes on larger and larger values, the value of the function becomes smaller and smaller. We can never make it actually become zero by letting x get bigger and bigger, but we can make it get very close indeed to zero. If, for example, $x = 1,000,000$, then $1/x = 0.000001$. Indeed, whatever small number you care to mention, we can make $1/x$ smaller than that by taking a large enough x. In this case we say that the value of the function $1/x$ approaches the limit of zero as x increases without limit. If x increases without limit, we write $x \to \infty$, which may be read "x goes to infinity," or "x increases without limit." We may write

$$\lim_{x \to \infty} \left(\frac{1}{x}\right) = 0 \quad , \tag{9}$$

which is read "the limit of the value of $1/x$ as x increases without limit is zero."

Before giving a formal definition of a limit, let us consider some more examples. The multiplier, $k = 1/(1 - c)$, is a function of c. Suppose that we let the domain of the function be $0 \le c \le 1$. First, what happens if $c = 0$, that is, if the marginal propensity to save is unity? This presents no problem: $k = 1$, and a change in autonomous expenditure changes income by the same amount. If, however, we let $c = 1$, then $k = \frac{1}{0}$, which is undefined. That is why we usually restrict the domain of the function to $0 < c < 1$ (or $0 \le c < 1$). Although we get a nonsense result when we let $c = 1$, we can easily discover what happens to k as we let c *approach* unity. Indeed it is easy to see that k *increases without limit* as c approaches unity. To see this, note that we can make k exceed any finite value we wish to state by picking a c sufficiently close to unity. Suppose, for example, that we choose $k = 1,000,000$. The corresponding value of c is 0.999,999, and for any c for which it is true that $0.999,999 < c < 1.0$ we have $k > 1,000,000$.

As another example, let us take the rectangular hyperbola $xy = c$. Taking y as a function of x, we have $y = c/x$. This is just a variation of the case $1/x$ we have already considered, replacing 1 by the constant c. It is obvious that

$$\lim_{x \to \infty} \left(\frac{c}{x} \right) = 0 \quad .$$

We can also consider $x = c/y$, and in the same way write

$$\lim_{y \to \infty} \left(\frac{c}{y} \right) = 0 \quad .$$

The geometry of this is familiar. The curve $xy = c$ gets closer and closer to each axis the farther out we go but never touches either axis: it cannot, since if either x or y were actually zero, xy would equal zero, not c. Thus as x increases without limit, y approaches zero but never reaches it, and vice versa.

As a last example, we take the function $a + bx^{-1}$. Comparing it with the results we had for $1/x$, it is easy to see that

$$\lim_{x \to \infty} (a + bx^{-1}) = a$$

and that the function increases without limit as x approaches zero (but is undefined at $x = 0$).

We now need to define a limit precisely. To begin with we let ϵ stand for any small number. In general we say that the value of the function $f(x)$ approaches a finite limit L as x goes to infinity if for *any* ϵ as small as is desired there is some X large enough that for *all* $x \ge X$

the difference between the value of the function and L is less than ϵ; that is, $|L - f(x)| < \epsilon$. We use the absolute value of $L - f(x)$ since the notion of a function approaching a limit is independent of the direction from which it approaches that limit. In other words, we are saying that we can make the value of $f(x)$ come as close to the limit as we wish even though we never make it actually reach the limit.

Consider again the value of the function $1/x$ as x approaches *zero*. We cannot just let $x = 0$ because $\frac{1}{0}$ is not defined. But we can let x get as *close* to zero as we like. It is apparent that, as x gets very small, the value of $1/x$ gets very large. Indeed, for any finite number N you care to mention, no matter how small, $1/x > N$ for all $x < 1/N$. In this case we say that the value of the function $1/x$ increases *without limit* as x approaches zero. At $x = 0$, the function $1/x$ is undefined.

Some function $f(x)$ may, of course, have a limit at a value of x, $\bar{x}$ say, other than zero or infinity. It is easy to generalize the above definition by substituting $x \to \bar{x}$ for $x \to \infty$ or $x \to 0$. In what follows we shall be concerned only with functions that have finite limits as the value of the variable goes to zero, so that we need not pursue this generalization.

In Section 4.1 we were concerned with the limiting value of the incremental ratio $\Delta q / \Delta p$ as Δp approached zero. We cannot just insert $\Delta p = 0$ into the ratio because if price does not change, neither does quantity change, and the incremental ratio is $\frac{0}{0}$, which is undefined. Notice that as Δp gets smaller Δq also gets smaller. Further inspection of Figure 4.1 suggests that the slope of the chord approaches the slope of the tangent. The idea of a ratio of two increments not approaching zero as the size of the separate increments approaches zero is not an easy one to grasp. We have illustrated this geometrically in Figure 4.1, and subsequently we shall consider a numerical example.

4.3 DERIVATIVES AND LIMITS

We now assert what we shall be able to prove subsequently, that the slope of the tangent to the demand curve used in Section 4.1 at the point (30, 40) is $-\frac{4}{3}$. When we say that the limit of the value of the incremented ratio measured at the point (30, 40) is $-\frac{4}{3}$, we mean the following: choose any number ϵ, as small as you like; then there will be a corresponding value of Δp, which we will call $\Delta p(\epsilon)$, such that, for all $\Delta p < \Delta p(\epsilon)$, the difference between $-\frac{4}{3}$ and $\Delta q / \Delta p$ is less than $|\epsilon|$. We shall see numerical examples of this later in this chapter when we consider how actually to find the limiting values of incremental ratios. In the meantime note that we can write the assertion that the value of the incremental ratio approaches the slope of the tangent to the curve as Δp gets smaller and smaller as follows:

$$\lim_{\Delta p \to 0} \left(\frac{\Delta q}{\Delta p} \right) = \frac{dq}{dp} \quad . \tag{10}$$

This is read "the limit of $\Delta q/\Delta p$ as Δp approaches zero is *DQ* by *DP*."

Now consider a continuous function $y = f(x)$. The derivative of y with respect to x is denoted by dy/dx, and it is defined as

$$\frac{dy}{dx} = \lim_{\Delta x \to 0} \frac{\Delta y}{\Delta x} \quad . \tag{11}$$

The variables y and x are linked together by the function $f(x)$, and it will be convenient for some work that follows to write the definition of the derivative in a slightly expanded form. First, as a matter purely of notation, we denote the small change in x as h instead of Δx. Next we notice that the change in y (i.e., Δy) is equal to the new value of the function after x has increased by h *minus* the original value. Thus $\Delta y = f(x + h) - f(x)$. We can now rewrite the definition of a derivative as

$$\frac{dy}{dx} = \lim_{h \to 0} \frac{f(x + h) - f(x)}{h} \quad . \tag{12}$$

This is nothing more than a rewrite of (11) since the numerator in (12) merely defines Δy and h is merely another symbol for Δx. The definition of a derivative given in (12) is extremely important and will provide the starting point for further proofs as we need them. You should not read on until you are satisfied that (12) says the same thing as (11).

It is important to note that what we have done is to *define* the derivative of a function $f(x)$: it is the limit of the derived function of h, $[f(x + h) - f(x)]/h$ as h goes to zero, *if that limit exists*. Defining the derivative as a limit does not imply that the limit must always exist: many functions have no limits. Our next task is to learn to find limits as we learn some of the techniques of differentiation. In Section 4.11 we shall consider some examples of functions that do not possess derivatives.

It remains now to discover how to determine the value of dy/dx. It would be possible to plot a graph of the function $y = f(x)$ and then to measure the slope of the tangent at the point in question. This would be a very cumbersome procedure, and it would also have the disadvantage that we would not be able to deal with derivatives in terms more general than their precise numerical values at particular points on the function. Fortunately there are more general and more reliable methods of finding derivatives than drawing curves and measuring the slopes of tangents. It is to the study of these methods that we must now turn.

What you already know about derivatives can first be summarized.

1. The derivative of a continuous function $y = f(x)$ at the point x_1, y_1 is the slope of the tangent to the curve at that point. All we are going to do now is to discover an analytical method of determining this slope.
2. The derivative shows how y changes with x at the point at which it is evaluated. This rate of change is called an instantaneous rate of change to distinguish it from an average rate of change, which is given by the slope of the chord joining two distinct points on the curve.
3. We can discover the derivative by finding the value approached by the slope of the chord as Δx approaches zero. We have seen this already in an intuitive way.

The next step is to consider the power function

$$y = ax^n \quad ,$$

where a and n are parameters and x and y are variables.

4.4 EXAMPLES OF THE EVALUATION OF DERIVATIVES OF POWER FUNCTIONS

Let us take the familiar example

$$y = x^2 \tag{13}$$

and start with some arithmetical experimentation.

How y changes as x changes. First let us consider how y changes as x changes when we start from a particular value of x. If, for example, $x = 6$, $y = 6^2 = 36$. If x now increases to 8, then y rises to $8^2 = 64$. It helps to tabulate this:

$$\text{first value:} \qquad 36 = (6)^2 \tag{14}$$

$$\text{second value:} \qquad 64 = (8)^2 \tag{15}$$

$$\text{or} \qquad 36 + 28 = (6 + 2)^2 \quad . \tag{16}$$

In (16) we show exactly the same calculation as in (15), but instead of just inserting the new value of x we insert the original value of 6 and the increment of 2 in x. The approach used in (16) proves to be helpful when we come to calculate derivatives in general.

Now let us consider how y changes as x changes at *any* point on the function. We begin with any value of x and a corresponding value of y; we let x increase by an amount Δx, and y increases by Δy. Thus we can write

$$y + \Delta y = (x + \Delta x)^2 \quad,$$

which is exactly the same as (16) except that we have letters instead of the numbers of the specific example. Expanding the right-hand side gives

$$y + \Delta y = x^2 + 2x\,\Delta x + (\Delta x)^2 \quad. \tag{17}$$

Next we subtract (13) from (17), thus removing the y from the left-hand side and the x^2 from the right. This gives

$$\Delta y = 2x\,\Delta x + (\Delta x)^2 \quad, \tag{18}$$

which tells us the change in y for any change in x starting from any value of x.

The value of the incremental ratio. To get an expression for this ratio we merely divide (18) by Δx to obtain

$$\frac{\Delta y}{\Delta x} = 2x + \Delta x \quad. \tag{19}$$

This gives us a very neat way of calculating the incremental ratio anywhere on the function $y = x^2$. Let us try an example to check it. What is the incremental ratio when we start from the point $x = 3$, $y = 9$ and let x rise by 2? Using (19) we have

$$\frac{\Delta y}{\Delta x} = 6 + 2 = 8 \quad.$$

[As a check on this formula you should calculate the same ratio by direct substitution into $y = x^2$. You should try a few more examples to be sure you are satisfied that (19) gives you the correct ratios.]

The limit of the incremental ratio as Δx approaches zero. We have already defined dy/dx as the limit approached by $\Delta y/\Delta x$ as Δx approaches zero. Letting Δx *approach* zero does not mean we make $\Delta x = 0$ since $\Delta y/0$ is undefined; it means rather that we let Δx get smaller and smaller and see if $\Delta y/\Delta x$ approaches some limiting value. One might think at first glance that this limiting value would also be zero, but that is not the case. Indeed what happens as Δx is made smaller and smaller is that $\Delta y/\Delta x$ approaches the value of the slope of the tangent to the curve at the point in question. This is, of course, what we wish to determine.

Let us try some examples beginning from the point $(3, 9)$ on expression (13) and letting Δx get smaller and smaller. The calculations are shown in Table 4.3.

Table 4.3

Calculation of some incremental ratios from the point (3, 9) *on the function* $y = x^2$

x	y	Δx	Δy	$\dfrac{\Delta y}{\Delta x}$
3	9	—	—	—
5	25	2	16	8
4	16	1	7	7
3.1	9.61	0.1	0.61	6.1
3.01	9.0601	0.01	0.0601	6.01
3.0001	9.00060001	0.0001	0.00060001	6.0001

If we use expression (19) to calculate these incremental ratios, we shall get the same results, but what is happening will become more obvious. These calculations are shown in Table 4.4.

Evidently as we take smaller and smaller changes in x the ratio $\Delta y/\Delta x$ approaches 6. Looking at expression (19) we see that as Δx gets smaller and smaller the value of $\Delta y/\Delta x$ gets closer and closer to $2x$ because the Δx term becomes more and more insignificant.

This suggests a generalization of great importance, and it gives the clue to our method. For any function f, we want a method of *evaluating* dy/dx. We know that dy/dx is the limit of the incremental ratio $\Delta y/\Delta x$ as Δx approaches zero, but we obviously cannot discover its value by looking directly at $\Delta y/\Delta x$. What we have to do is find, for each function we consider, an expression for $\Delta y/\Delta x$ that allows us to find its limit as Δx goes to zero. This is just what we have in (19) for the function $y = x^2$. We can find a value for the limit of the left-hand side by letting Δx go to zero on the right-hand side.

We shall now repeat our experiments with the function $y = x^3$. Before reading on, however, you should try to do this for yourself. You can expand $(x + \Delta x)^3$ to get an expression analogous to (19) and

Table 4.4

Calculation of some incremental ratios from the point (3, 9) *on the function* $y = x^2$ *from* (19)

When x goes from 3 to	$2x$	Δx	$2x + \Delta x$
5	6	2	8
4	6	1	7
3.1	6	0.1	6.1
3.01	6	0.01	6.01
3.0001	6	0.0001	6.0001

can then substitute into it to see what happens to the ratio $\Delta y/\Delta x$ as Δx gets very small. If you do this you will have gone a long way toward discovering how to differentiate for yourself. We now proceed: if

$$y = x^3 \tag{20}$$

then we can write

$$y + \Delta y = (x + \Delta x)^3 \quad .$$

Expanding the right-hand side gives

$$y + \Delta y = x^3 + 3x^2 \, \Delta x + 3x(\Delta x)^2 + (\Delta x)^3 \quad .$$

Subtracting (20) and dividing through by Δx gives

$$\frac{\Delta y}{\Delta x} = 3x^2 + 3x \, \Delta x + (\Delta x)^2 \quad . \tag{21}$$

Again we see that if we let Δx get smaller and smaller this expression will get closer and closer to $3x^2$ because *all* terms on the right-hand side except $3x^2$ must go to zero as Δx goes to zero. Indeed, by letting Δx be some particular small value the value of (21) can be made to come as close to $3x^2$ as is desired. We say that the limit of $\Delta y/\Delta x$ for the function $y = x^3$ as Δx approaches zero is $3x^2$, and we write this as

$$\lim_{\Delta x \to 0} \frac{\Delta y}{\Delta x} (y = x^3) = 3x^2 \quad . \tag{22}$$

Thus the slope of the tangent to the curve $y = x^3$ is 3 when x is 1, 12 when x is 2, 27 when x is 3, and so on. This tells us what we should see if we actually drew the curve: that the curve gets steeper as x increases. Thus y is more responsive to changes in x the larger is x.

Having found dy/dx for $y = x^2$ and $y = x^3$ the obvious step is to try to find a general rule to cover all power functions $y = ax^n$.

We shall have to consider the case in which n is negative and the case in which it is a fraction, as well as find a general rule for the case in which n is a positive integer, of which we have already handled two examples. We could handle more examples by brute force, but it is much easier to establish some general rules for differentiation and then return to this problem. In Section 4.5 we introduce some useful notation. In Section 4.6 we consider how to differentiate expressions that are formed by combining simpler ones. Then we return to the power function $y = ax^n$ and derive general rules for differentiating it.

4.5 FUNCTIONS OF x

So far in this chapter we have dealt with functional relations between two variables. We can, of course, just look at a function involving x

without necessarily equating it to another variable. For example, we might consider the relation $y = x^3$ and ask what is the instantaneous rate of change of y with respect to x? The answer to this question is provided by taking the derivative of y with respect to x to give $dy/dx = 3x^2$. It might, however, be the case in another example that $z = x^3$ in which case $dz/dx = 3x^2$. Indeed we can just look at the function of x without setting it equal to y, z, or any other variable and write

$$f(x) = x^3 \tag{23}$$

in the manner considered in Section 2.5. In this case we can ask how the value of the function changes as x changes, and we can write

$$\frac{d}{dx}(x^3) = 3x^2 \quad , \tag{24}$$

which tells us how the value of the function is changing as x changes. Equation (24) is read "D by D-X of X cubed is three X squared," and it tells us the rate of change of the value of the function of x for any value of x.

A very convenient notation is a prime mark to indicate the operation of differentiation has been performed on the function. Thus if

$$f(x) = x^3 \quad ,$$

then

$$\frac{d}{dx}(f(x)) = 3x^2 = f'(x) \quad . \tag{25}$$

The last term in (25) is read "F primed of X." One of the characteristics of mathematics is its ability to suppress unwanted detail. In some cases it is actually necessary to differentiate a function such as (23), and, in the case of complicated functions, this can become a very tedious business. In other cases we can often just put the prime mark on $f(x)$ to show that, whatever the function is, we consider it to be differentiated, and this is all we require to prove what we wish. This is a great labor-saving device, and we shall use it many times throughout this book. Some examples of its use are given in the questions at the end of this chapter.

Before going on to what are called "compound expressions," we may check two simple limiting cases. First, what is the derivative of the simplest power function, $f(x) = x$? This is, of course, the equation of the 45° line $y = x$, with constant slope, whence it is easy to see that the derivative must be 1. Nevertheless, let us check it out by the method we have been using. We have

$$y + \Delta y = x + \Delta x \quad .$$

Subtracting $y = x$ and rearranging, we have

$$\frac{\Delta y}{\Delta x} = 1$$

as we expected, and, since the slope is everywhere constant, the ratio $\Delta y/\Delta x$ is the same whether Δx is large or small. Second, what is the derivative of the constant function $f(x) = c$? It is not hard to guess that the answer is *zero*, but we may check again. We have $f(x) = c = f(x + \Delta x)$, or $\Delta y = 0$, whence the answer is indeed zero: a constant has no rate of change.

Earlier we discovered the derivatives of x^2 and x^3. We have now found the derivatives of x^1 and x^0 since $f(x) = x$ is the same thing as $f(x) = x^1$ and $f(x) = c$ is the same thing as $f(x) = x^0$, where $c = 1$.

4.6 RULES FOR COMPOUND EXPRESSIONS

We shall now consider how to extend the concept of a derivative to apply to expressions that are compounded from the simple functional relation $y = f(x)$.

We shall assume that $f(x)$ is *differentiable,* by which we mean that we shall deal only with functions for which it is true that the incremental ratio has a limiting value, $f'(x)$, as the increment approaches zero. We shall then seek ways of finding the limits of functions of differentiable functions. We begin with the simplest case.

A constant multiple. Assume that the whole function, $f(x)$, is multiplied by some constant amount a. This gives

$$af(x) \tag{26}$$

and we want dy/dx for this case.

From the definition of a derivative in (12) we can write

$$\frac{d}{dx}(f(x)) = f'(x) = \lim_{h \to 0} \frac{f(x+h) - f(x)}{h} \tag{27}$$

and

$$\frac{d}{dx}(af(x)) = \lim_{h \to 0} \frac{af(x+h) - af(x)}{h}$$

$$= a \lim_{h \to 0} \left[\frac{f(x+h) - f(x)}{h} \right] . \tag{28}$$

The second expression is obtained from the first merely by factoring out the constant a. But (27) tells us that the expression in the square brackets of (28) is $df(x)/dx$, and substituting this into (28) gives

$$\frac{d}{dx}(af(x)) = a\frac{d}{dx}(f(x)) = af'(x) \quad . \tag{29}$$

Thus the derivative of $af(x)$ is merely a times the derivative of $f(x)$.

The sum of two functions. Suppose that y is given as the sum of two differentiable functions,

$$y = f(x) + g(x) \quad . \tag{30}$$

y might, for example, be equal to $2x^2 + x^3$, or something more complicated. To find dy/dx we need only use the definition in (12). Thus

$$\frac{dy}{dx} = \lim_{h \to 0} \left[\frac{f(x+h) + g(x+h) - f(x) - g(x)}{h}\right]$$

$$= \lim_{h \to 0} \left[\frac{f(x+h) - f(x)}{h} + \frac{g(x+h) - g(x)}{h}\right]$$

$$= f'(x) + g'(x) \quad .$$

Thus the derivative of the sum of two functions is the sum of their derivatives. It is obvious that we can extend this rule to the sum of any number of functions.

There is a point worth noting here. Suppose that we write (30) as $F(x) = f(x) + g(x)$. We do not have to assume in advance that F is differentiable, that is, that the limit $F'(x)$ exists: we have proved that if $f(x)$ and $g(x)$ are differentiable, then F is. This point will come up again.

The difference between two functions. This can be proved in the same way as the addition rule, and we shall not work through it. It is, however, an excellent exercise to demonstrate for yourself that if

$$y = f(x) - g(x) \quad ,$$

then

$$\frac{dy}{dx} = f'(x) - g'(x) \quad . \tag{31}$$

The product of two functions. We now wish to find the derivative, dy/dx, of the product of two differentiable functions: $F(x) = f(x) \cdot g(x)$. By definition

$$\frac{dy}{dx} = \lim_{h \to 0} \left[\frac{F(x+h) - F(x)}{h}\right] \quad .$$

But the expression in brackets is equal to

$$\frac{f(x+h)g(x+h) - f(x)g(x)}{h} \quad .$$

A little manipulation is called for. We add to and subtract from the numerator the term

$$f(x+h)g(x) \quad ,$$

obtaining

$$\frac{f(x+h)g(x+h) - f(x+h)g(x) + f(x+h)g(x) - f(x)g(x)}{h} \quad .$$

We rearrange this to

$$f(x+h)\left[\frac{g(x+h) - g(x)}{h}\right] + g(x)\left[\frac{f(x+h) - f(x)}{h}\right] \quad .$$

Taking the limits as $h \to 0$, the two terms in brackets are $g'(x)$ and $f'(x)$, respectively, and $f(x+h)$ approaches $f(x)$. Thus

$$\frac{dy}{dx} = f(x)g'(x) + g(x)f'(x) \quad . \tag{32}$$

Note that once again we have not needed to assume in advance that the derivative exists: we have proved that if $f'(x)$ and $g'(x)$ exist, so must $F'(x)$.

It is convenient to know another and popular notation for writing the product rule. Set $u = f(x)$ and $v = g(x)$. Then $y = uv$, where both u and v are functions of x. The rule can now be written

$$\frac{dy}{dx} = u\frac{dv}{dx} + v\frac{du}{dx} \quad , \tag{33}$$

which is the exact equivalent of (32) and more easily memorized.

We may extend (33) to the case in which y is a product of more than two functions of x. Thus suppose that we have

$$y = uvw \quad .$$

Application of the procedure we have just applied to the case $y = uv$ now gives

$$\frac{dy}{dx} = vw\frac{du}{dx} + uw\frac{dv}{dx} + uv\frac{dw}{dx} \quad . \tag{34}$$

We shall not work through the proof, which is a simple but rather laborious extension of the one just given. (It might be a good exercise to work it out for yourself.) Instead, we shall state, without proof, the *general product rule*: if y is the product of any number of functions of x (let the number be n), then dy/dx is obtained as the sum of n terms each of which consists of the derivative of one of the functions multiplied by the values of the remaining $n-1$ functions. It is easy to see that this is a straightforward extension of (34).

The quotient of two functions. Finally consider the function $y = 6x^6/2x^2$. We could rewrite this as $y = 3x^4$ and then differentiate it. If we have two unspecified functions of x, we cannot (and in any case we may not find it convenient to) complete the division before differentiating.

To handle such cases we consider the general case of a function $F(x)$ which can be expressed as the quotient of two functions of x, so that

$$F(x) = \frac{f(x)}{g(x)} \quad . \tag{35}$$

We assume, as before, that $f(x)$ and $g(x)$ are differentiable, but this time we will assume in advance that the limit $F'(x)$ exists wherever $g(x)$ is not zero (we shall be able to do better than this below). We simply rearrange (35) as

$$f(x) = F(x)g(x)$$

and apply the product rule to obtain

$$f'(x) = F(x)g'(x) + g(x)F'(x) \quad .$$

Rearranging this, we have

$$F'(x) = \frac{1}{g(x)}[f'(x) - F(x)g'(x)] \quad .$$

Replacing $F(x)$ with $f(x)/g(x)$,

$$F'(x) = \frac{f'(x)}{g(x)} - \frac{1}{g(x)} \cdot \frac{f(x)}{g(x)} \cdot g'(x)$$

$$= \frac{g(x)f'(x) - f(x)g'(x)}{\{g(x)\}^2} \quad , \tag{36}$$

which is the result we require.

Once again, the quotient rule can be expressed conveniently in an alternative notation. If we put $u = f(x)$ and $v = g(x)$, then

$$\frac{d(u/v)}{dx} = \frac{v(du/dx) - u(dv/dx)}{v^2} \quad . \tag{37}$$

As a particular application of the quotient rule, consider the function $1/f(x)$. In the notation u/v we have $u = 1$, $du/dx = 0$, $v = f(x)$, and

$dv/dx = f'(x)$, whence, using (37),

$$\frac{d}{dx}\left(\frac{1}{f(x)}\right) = -\frac{f'(x)}{[f(x)]^2} \quad .$$

[It is, of course, necessary to assume that $f(x)$ is differentiable and not equal to zero.]

We can also derive the quotient rule by another route. We take this in two steps. Let us first try to find the derivative of $F(x) = 1/f(x)$ from first principles, instead of by the quotient rule, as we did above. We assume, of course, that $f'(x)$ exists and that $f(x) \neq 0$. From the definition of a derivative,

$$\lim_{h\to 0}\frac{F(x+h)-F(x)}{h} = \lim_{h\to 0}\frac{1/f(x+h)-1/f(x)}{h} \quad .$$

Rearranging the right-hand side, we have

$$\left[\frac{f(x)-f(x+h)}{f(x)f(x+h)}\right]\bigg/ h \quad .$$

But the limit of $[f(x)-f(x+h)]/h$ as $h \to 0$ is, of course, $-f'(x)$, while the limit of $f(x)f(x+h)$ is $[f(x)]^2$. It follows that

$$F'(x) = \frac{d}{dx}\left(\frac{1}{f(x)}\right) = -\frac{f'(x)}{[f(x)]^2} \quad .$$

Now we appeal to the product rule, which we have already derived from first principles. For two differentiable functions $f(x)$ and $h(x)$, say, we have $(d/dx)[f(x)h(x)] = f(x)h'(x) + h(x)f'(x)$. All we have to do now is to replace $h(x)$ with $1/g(x)[g(x) \neq 0]$ and use the result we have just proved. Thus

$$\frac{d}{dx}\left[\frac{f(x)}{g(x)}\right] = f(x)\frac{d}{dx}\left(\frac{1}{g(x)}\right) + \frac{1}{g(x)}f'(x)$$

$$= -f(x)\frac{g'(x)}{[g(x)]^2} + \frac{f'(x)}{g(x)}$$

$$= \frac{g(x)f'(x) - f(x)g'(x)}{[g(x)]^2}$$

(or $[v(du/dx) - u(dv/dx)]/v^2$), the result we obtained earlier.

Note that, proceeding in this fashion, we now do not need to assume in advance that the derivative of the quotient exists: if $f'(x)$ and $g'(x)$ exist, so does the derivative of the quotient $f(x)/g(x)$.

Functions of functions. We now introduce an extremely useful device called the function-of-a-function rule or chain rule. Suppose that we have the two functions

$$y = 2z^2$$

and

$$z = 3x + 2 \quad .$$

We could substitute one into the other to obtain

$$y = 2(3x + 2)^2$$
$$= 18x^2 + 24x + 8$$

and then differentiate to obtain

$$\frac{dy}{dx} = 36x + 24$$

(using the results of differentiating x and x^2 from Section 4.4 and the rule for the sum of two functions developed earlier in this section). In many cases it may be either convenient or necessary to keep the two functions separate. Thus we have two differentiable functions

$$y = y(z) \tag{38}$$

$$z = z(x) \quad , \tag{39}$$

and we wish to find dy/dx.

We can do this by the following very simple rule. Given (38) and (39) it is true that

$$\frac{dy}{dx} = \frac{dy}{dz} \cdot \frac{dz}{dx} \quad . \tag{40}$$

Equation (40) says that if y depends on z and z depends on x, and if you want to know by how much a change in x influences y, you find out by calculating how much a change in x influences z and how much a change in z influences y, and the product of the two changes gives the answer.

An explanation of this result is given below (a fully satisfactory proof requires a little more technique than can now be assumed).

Equations (38) and (39) tell us that y is a function of z and z is a function of x. Substituting (39) into (38) gives

$$y = y(z(x)) \quad .$$

This operation is not to be confused with simple multiplication. The term $z(x)$ says "operate on x according to the rule z." The expression $y(z(x))$ then says "operate on the result according to the rule y." If we denote the combined effects of these two operations by the single symbol F, we can write

$$y = F(x) = y(z(x)) \quad .$$

By the definition of a derivative we have

$$\frac{dy}{dx} = F'(x) = \lim_{\Delta x \to 0} \frac{\Delta y}{\Delta x} \quad . \tag{41}$$

Now by simple algebra we can multiply the incremental ratio $\Delta y/\Delta x$ by $\Delta z/\Delta z$ to get $(\Delta y/\Delta z)(\Delta z/\Delta x)$ and hence write

$$\frac{\Delta y}{\Delta x} = \frac{\Delta y}{\Delta z} \cdot \frac{\Delta z}{\Delta x} \tag{42}$$

and then rewrite (41) as

$$\frac{dy}{dx} = F'(x) = \lim_{\Delta x \to 0} \frac{\Delta y}{\Delta z} \cdot \frac{\Delta z}{\Delta x} \quad . \tag{43}$$

Again by the definition of a derivative we can write

$$\lim_{\Delta z \to 0} \frac{\Delta y}{\Delta z} = \frac{dy}{dz}$$

and

$$\lim_{\Delta x \to 0} \frac{\Delta z}{\Delta x} = \frac{dz}{dx} \quad .$$

Since by (39) $z = z(x)$, it follows that $\Delta z \to 0$ as $\Delta x \to 0$. Thus we can rewrite (43) as

$$\frac{dy}{dx} = F'(x) = \frac{dy}{dz} \cdot \frac{dz}{dx} \quad . \tag{44}$$

This rule applies only if f and g are indeed differentiable and z does vary with x so that $dz/dx \neq 0$.

The chain rule can be extended as far as we wish: if, for example, $y = y(u)$, $u = u(v)$, $v = v(w)$, $w = w(x)$, $x = x(z)$, then

$$\frac{dy}{dz} = \frac{dy}{du} \cdot \frac{du}{dv} \cdot \frac{dv}{dw} \cdot \frac{dw}{dx} \cdot \frac{dx}{dz} \quad , \tag{45}$$

which is a very convenient result (that we do not prove).

At the beginning of this section we substituted $z = 3x + 2$ into $y = 2z^2$ and differentiated the result to obtain $dy/dx = 36x + 24$. As a check we can now apply the function-of-a-function rule to the two original functions as follows:

$$\frac{dy}{dx} = \frac{dy}{dz} \cdot \frac{dz}{dx}$$

$$= (4z)(3)$$

$$= 12z \quad ,$$

and since $z = 3x + 2$, this gives

$$\frac{dy}{dx} = 36x + 24$$

which agrees with the result obtained earlier.

We shall have occasion to use the function-of-a-function rule many times throughout this book. It is a very powerful tool, and it usually provides us with more than one way of obtaining a result that we want.

4.7 TO DIFFERENTIATE ax^n

We learned in Section 4.4 to differentiate x^0, x^1, x^2, and x^3. Since then, we have taken a long detour through the rules for differentiating compound expressions without learning any more about how to differentiate the individual terms. That is, in fact, a good example of roundabout methods of production paying off. It is now quite easy to extend our discussion of the function ax^n.

First, let us consider the case in which n is a positive integer, such as 2 or 97. We know that the derivative of x^3 is $3x^2$ and of x^2 is $2x$. Suppose that we write

$$y = x^2 = x \cdot x \quad .$$

Now we apply the product rule: If $y = uv$, $dy/dx = u\, dv/dx + v\, du/dx$. Here, we have $u = v = x$, and $dv/dx = du/dx = 1$, whence

$$\frac{dy}{dx} = x + x = 2x \quad .$$

Again, if

$$y = x^3 = x \cdot x \cdot x$$

and we put $u = v = w = x$, the product rule gives

$$\frac{dy}{dx} = xx + xx + xx = 3x^2 \quad .$$

Generally, if

$$y = x^n = x \cdot x \cdot x \cdot \cdots \cdot n \text{ times,}$$

the product rule gives dy/dx as the sum of n terms, each of which is the derivative of x, multiplied by $n - 1$ x's. Thus, since the derivative of x with respect to x is 1,

$$\frac{dy}{dx} = (x \cdot x \cdot x \cdot \cdots \cdot (n-1) \text{ times})$$
$$+ (x \cdot x \cdot x \cdot \cdots \cdot (n-1) \text{ times})$$
$$+ \cdots + n \text{ times,}$$

which is simply

$$\frac{dy}{dx} = nx^{n-1} \quad . \tag{46}$$

The general form in which we are interested is $y = ax^n$. So far in this section, we have assumed that $a = 1$. But it is easy to see that, if

$$y = ax^n \quad ,$$

then

$$\frac{dy}{dx} = anx^{n-1} \quad .$$

This illustrates the rule derived in Section 4.6 that if $y = af(x)$, where a is a constant, then, whatever the derivative of $f(x)$, dy/dx is a times it.

Now let us consider the case in which n is a negative integer, such as -1 or -10. We know that

$$x^{-1} = \frac{1}{x} \quad \text{and} \quad x^{-10} = \frac{1}{x^{10}} \quad ,$$

so if $y = x^n$ and n is a negative integer, we can write

$$y = \frac{1}{x^m} \quad ,$$

where $-m = n$. To differentiate this, we have only to apply the quotient rule as we did above in the case of $1/f(x)$,

$$\frac{d}{dx}\left(\frac{u}{v}\right) = \frac{v\,du - u\,dv}{v^2} \quad .$$

Here $u = 1$, whence $du = 0$, so that

$$\frac{d}{dx}\left(\frac{1}{x^m}\right) = -\frac{(d/dx)\,(x^m)}{x^{2m}} \quad .$$

We know that the numerator is mx^{m-1}, whence

$$\frac{d}{dx}\left(\frac{1}{x^m}\right) = -\frac{mx^{m-1}}{x^{2m}} \quad .$$

To divide x^{m-1} by x^{2m}, we subtract the second exponent from the first, getting x^{-m-1}. Remembering that $n = -m$, we have once again

$$\frac{dy}{dx} = nx^{n-1} \quad .$$

This is, of course, the same expression that we had in (46) but necessarily negative since n is negative.

Let us consider an example of our rule for n a positive integer and n a negative integer. If

$$y = x^{10} \quad,$$

then

$$\frac{dy}{dx} = 10x^9 \quad.$$

If

$$y = x^{-10} = \frac{1}{x^{10}} \quad,$$

then

$$\frac{dy}{dx} = -10x^{-11} \quad.$$

We have not yet found the rule in the case in which n is a fraction, but it is easier to postpone this until we have learned to differentiate inverse functions.

4.8   RECAPITULATION

The material so far introduced in this chapter may seem like a big dose at first sight, but for differentiable compound functions it all boils down to six rules.

1. If

$$y = af(x) \quad,$$

then

$$\frac{dy}{dx} = af'(x) \quad.$$

2. If u and v are two functions of x such that

$$f(x) = u + v \quad,$$

then

$$\frac{df(x)}{dx} = \frac{du}{dx} + \frac{dv}{dx} \quad.$$

3. If

$$f(x) = u - v \quad,$$

then

$$\frac{df(x)}{dx} = \frac{du}{dx} - \frac{dv}{dx} \quad.$$

4. If

$$f(x) = uv \quad,$$

then

$$\frac{df(x)}{dx} = u\frac{dv}{dx} + v\frac{du}{dx} \quad.$$

5. If

$$f(x) = \frac{u}{v} \quad,$$

then

$$\frac{df(x)}{dx} = \frac{v(du/dx) - u(dv/dx)}{v^2} \quad.$$

6. If

$$y = y(z)$$

and

$$z = z(x) \quad,$$

then

$$\frac{dy}{dx} = \frac{dy}{dz} \cdot \frac{dz}{dx} \quad.$$

4.9 SECOND- AND HIGHER-ORDER DERIVATIVES

Consider the linear demand relation, which it is now convenient to write with price as the dependent variable:

$$p = 10{,}000 - 15q \quad. \tag{47}$$

To obtain the total revenue function we multiply through by q:

$$R = pq = 10{,}000q - 15q^2 \quad. \tag{48}$$

We now want to know how total revenue responds to changes in quantity. To do this we calculate marginal revenue:

$$MR = \frac{dR}{dq} = 10{,}000 - 30q \quad. \tag{49}$$

Equations (47) and (49) are both illustrated in Figure 4.2(a). Equation (49), of course, gives us the rate of change of total revenue as the quantity sold changes. Equation (48) is illustrated by the curve in Figure 4.2(b), and two values of (49), for $q = 200$ and $q = 425$, are shown as tangents to the curve.

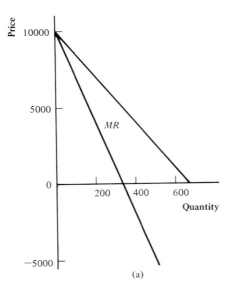

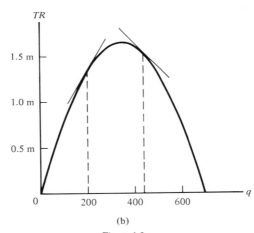

(b)

Figure 4.2

We now ask how marginal revenue is itself varying as quantity sold varies. We wish to know if, for example, marginal revenue is increasing or decreasing as the volume of sales rises and by how much it is rising or falling.[2] In other words we want to find dMR/dq. Evi-

---

[2] It is often thought that as long as the demand curve is downward-sloping the MR curve is also downward-sloping — textbooks always draw both curves in this way. You will find, however, that this is not the case: a downward-sloping demand curve is *not* a sufficient condition for a downward-sloping MR curve.

dently, in the example used above, this can be established by differentiating (49), whence

$$\frac{dMR}{dq} = -30 \quad .$$

In this case marginal revenue is declining at a constant rate of -30 per unit increase in the quantity sold.

A moment's thought will show that what we have done is to differentiate the total revenue function given in Eq. (48) twice with respect to quantity. The first derivative tells us how the function R is behaving as we vary quantity, and the second derivative tells us how its rate of change (i.e., MR) is behaving as we vary quantity.

Consider a general functional relation between x and y, $y = f(x)$ and its derivative $dy/dx = f'(x)$. We can now differentiate this function a second time as we did above and indicate this by the following notation:

$$\frac{d^2y}{dx^2} = f''(x) \quad .$$

This is read "D-two Y by D-X squared." The 2's on the left-hand side and the "double prime sign" on the right-hand side both indicate that we have differentiated the function twice. If dy/dx tells us how y is tending to change as x changes, then d^2y/dx^2 tells us how the rate of change of y with respect to x is itself changing as we change x. Evidently we can continue to ask how a function obtained by differentiation itself changes as x changes as many times as we like. Consider, for example, the following function:

$$y = 10 + 2x - 3x^2 - 5x^3 + 0.1x^4 \quad . \tag{50}$$

Successive derivatives are

$$\frac{dy}{dx} = +2 - 6x - 15x^2 + 0.4x^3 \quad ,$$

$$\frac{d^2y}{dx^2} = -6 - 30x + 1.2x^2 \quad ,$$

$$\frac{d^3y}{dx^3} = -30 + 2.4x \quad ,$$

$$\frac{d^4y}{dx^4} = +2.4 \quad ,$$

and

$$\frac{d^5y}{dx^5} = 0 \quad .$$

We call these functions first, second, third, fourth, and fifth derivatives of (50), respectively. Each of these higher-order derivatives tells us the direction and speed of change of the derivative of the next lower order. Thus, for example, the fourth derivative (d^4y/dx^4) tells us that the value of the third derivative is increasing at a constant rate of 2.4 per unit increase in x.

Now let us look at some general types of functions and consider how the slope of the tangent gradient dy/dx changes as we move about the curve given by $y = f(x)$. Consider first a linear function. It is visually clear that with such a function the tangent gradient coincides with the function and is constant over the entire range of the function. This is easily checked formally: the equation of a straight line is $y = a + bx$, whence $dy/dx = b$ and $d^2y/dx^2 = 0$. The second derivative is zero, which tells us that the first derivative does not vary with x.

Now consider some examples of nonlinear functions. Visual inspection of Figure 4.3(a) makes it obvious that dy/dx is not constant but increases as x increases. An example of a function that, when graphed, looks like Figure 4.3(a) is $y = ax^2$. The first derivative of the function is

$$\frac{dy}{dx} = 2ax > 0 \quad,$$

which tells us that y is an increasing function of x if a is positive. The second derivative is

$$\frac{d^2y}{dx^2} = 2a > 0 \quad,$$

which tells us that the tangent gradient is itself increasing at a constant rate, $2a$, as x increases. It is an instructive exercise to show for yourself that the remarks in this paragraph apply to any function $y = ax^\alpha$ for which $\alpha > 1$. (This does not, of course, exhaust the class of functions to which these remarks apply.)

Now consider the curve in Figure 4.3(b). It is visually obvious that the slope of the tangent gradient dy/dx is getting smaller as x increases: the reaction of y to a change in x is less the larger is x. An example of a function that looks like Figure 4.3(b) is $y = bx^{1/2}$ (with $b > 0$). The first derivative of this function is

$$\frac{dy}{dx} = \frac{1}{2}bx^{-1/2} > 0 \quad,$$

which tells us that y increases as x increases. The second derivative is

$$\frac{dy}{dx} = -\frac{1}{4}bx^{-3/2} < 0 \quad,$$

which tells us that the tangent gradient is decreasing as x increases.

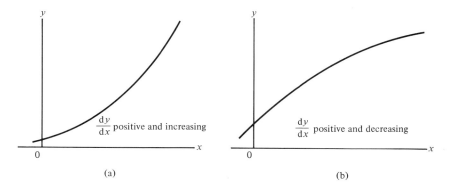

(a)

(b)

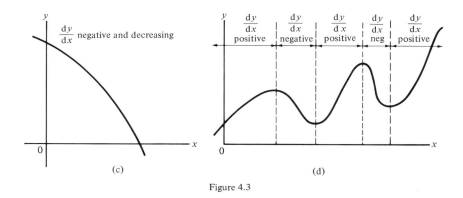

(c)

(d)

Figure 4.3

It is an instructive exercise to show for yourself that the remarks in this paragraph apply to any function $y = bx^\beta$ for which $0 < \beta < 1$ (and $b > 0$).

In Figure 4.3(c), dy/dx is negative throughout and takes on larger and larger negative values as x increases. Can you restrict the values of γ in the equation $y = cx^\gamma$ to give curves such as Figure 4.2(c) and then check the second derivative to see that it is negative?

In Figure 4.3(d) the tangent gradient dy/dx alternates in sign several times as x increases. These alternations are indicated in the figure. Can you indicate similar ranges of positive and negative values for the second derivative d^2y/dx^2?

We shall make use of second derivatives in a later chapter, but we shall seldom have to use derivatives higher than those of the second order. At this stage we need merely note that the operation of taking successive derivatives poses no new problems. If we wish to find a higher-order derivative, we merely apply the rules of differentiation that we have developed to the derivative of the lower order. Full use of second derivatives in an economic application together with a chance to gain some further intuitive feel for their meaning and use must be postponed until we discuss the problems of maxima and minima in Chapters 6 and 7.

4.10 INVERSE FUNCTIONS

We considered inverse functions in Chapter 2. Suppose now that $y = f(x)$ is a continuous strictly monotonic increasing (or decreasing) function of x over some domain. Then we know that the inverse, $x = g(y)$, say, also exists and is continuous and monotonic increasing (or decreasing). The question now is "if we know dy/dx, can we find dx/dy directly, or do we have to find the function $g(y)$ first?"

Intuition, and a little geometry, suggest that we expect to find

$$\frac{dx}{dy} = \frac{1}{dy/dx} \quad .$$

Thus consider Figure 4.4. The derivative evaluated at Q is the tangent slope at Q, the limit of $\Delta y/\Delta x$ as Δx goes to zero. dx/dy is merely the limit of $\Delta x/\Delta y$ as Δy goes to zero. Clearly, it does not matter whether we let Δx or Δy go to zero—the operations are equivalent.

Let us put this a little more formally and then apply it. Instead of writing x and Δx (or x and $x + h$) and y and Δy, let us write x_1 and x_2, y_1 and y_2, where, of course, $y_1 = f(x_1)$ and $y_2 = f(x_2)$. Then we can

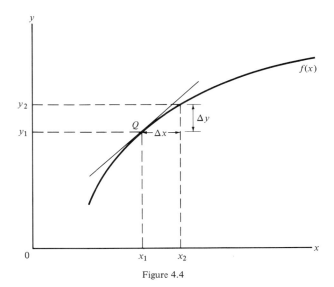

Figure 4.4

write our definition

$$\frac{dy}{dx} = \lim_{x_2 \to x_1} \frac{y_2 - y_1}{x_2 - x_1} \quad . \tag{51}$$

Since, however, the function is continuous, y_2 $[=f(x_2)]$ must go to y_1 as x_2 goes to x_1. It follows that we can replace (51) by

$$\frac{dy}{dx} = \lim_{y_2 \to y_1} \frac{y_2 - y_1}{x_2 - x_1} \quad . \tag{52}$$

Now, by definition,

$$\frac{dx}{dy} = \lim_{y_2 \to y_1} \frac{x_2 - x_1}{y_2 - y_1} \quad . \tag{53}$$

But (53) must be the reciprocal of (52), which is the same as (51), whence

$$\frac{dx}{dy} = \frac{1}{dy/dx} \quad .$$

Let us consider the straight line

$$y = a + bx \quad ,$$

with derivative $dy/dx = b$. If now we solve for x in terms of y, we have

$$x = \frac{y}{b} - \frac{a}{b}$$

and

$$\frac{dx}{dy} = \frac{1}{b} \quad ,$$

which we might have obtained directly from the inverse function rule.

We can now obtain a very useful result. Suppose that $y = x^2$ with $dy/dx = 2x$. The inverse function is

$$x = \sqrt{y} \quad \text{or} \quad y^{1/2} \quad . \tag{54}$$

If we look back, we shall find that we have not yet completed our discussion of how to obtain the derivative of $y = x^n$ for fractional n. We are now in a position to do so, but we see that we must be careful. In (54), we have a square root, so, if we want to avoid imaginary numbers (those involving the square root of minus one), we must be careful to define (54) over the nonnegative half of the real line only: this ensures that it is a monotonic increasing function. We now have immediately $dx/dy = 1/2x$ (since both the range and domain of the function are limited to the positive half of the real line).

Let us generalize this. Suppose that

$$x = y^n \qquad (55)$$

where n is a positive integer. We already know that

$$\frac{dx}{dy} = ny^{n-1} \quad .$$

Now the inverse function is

$$y = x^{1/n} \quad , \qquad (56)$$

and

$$\frac{dy}{dx} = \frac{1}{ny^{n-1}} \quad . \qquad (57)$$

A little substitution will tidy this up. Dividing through (55) by y gives

$$y^{n-1} = \frac{x}{y} \quad .$$

Taking the reciprocals of both sides of (56) and multiplying through by x gives

$$\frac{x}{y} = \frac{x}{x^{1/n}} = x^{1-1/n}$$

whence $y^{n-1} = x^{1-1/n}$. Substituting into (57),

$$\frac{dy}{dx} = \frac{1}{nx^{1-1/n}} = \frac{1}{n} x^{1/n-1} \quad . \qquad (58)$$

Equation (58) is the result we have been looking for. We can now state the general rule for differentiating power functions to deal with fractions of the type $1/n$: bring down the exponent as a coefficient; subtract 1 from the exponent.

We still have not quite finished. What about fractions such as $\frac{3}{4}$ or $\frac{2}{5}$? These are called *rational numbers* (see Section 2.1): they can be written in the form p/m, where p and m are integers. (Warning: we shall not prove the rule for irrational numbers such as $\sqrt{2}$ or π that cannot be written in the form p/m.) It is now very easy to prove the rule for

$$y = x^{p/m} \quad .$$

We look on this as

$$y = x^{1/m} \cdot x^{1/m} \cdots$$

with the term $x^{1/m}$ repeated p times, which we indicate hereafter as $\cdots$ p times.

Using the rule just proved, and the product rule, we have

$$\frac{dy}{dx} = \frac{1}{m} x^{1/m-1} \{\cdot \ x^{1/m} \cdot x^{1/m} \cdot \ \cdots \ \cdot (p-1) \text{ times}\}$$

$$+ \frac{1}{m} x^{1/m-1} \{ x^{1/m} \cdot x^{1/m} \cdot \ \cdots \ \cdot (p-1) \text{ times}\}$$

$$+ \ \cdots \ p \text{ times}.$$

If we collect the exponents of x in each of these p terms, we have

$$\left(\frac{1}{m} - 1\right) + \left(\frac{p-1}{m}\right) = \frac{p-m}{m} = \frac{p}{m} - 1 \quad .$$

Adding up the p terms,

$$\frac{dy}{dx} = \frac{p}{m} x^{p/m-1} \quad , \tag{59}$$

following our general rule.

We are left only with the case of negative rational fractions, such as $-\frac{3}{4}$. We have only to combine the rules used above to prove that if

$$y = x^{-p/m}$$

then

$$\frac{dy}{dx} = -\frac{p}{m} x^{-(p/m+1)} \quad .$$

4.11 SOME DIFFICULTIES

The functions that we encounter in elementary economic theory are usually all *differentiable*, which means that at every point on the function a unique derivative exists. When this is the case we are able to say quite unambiguously how fast y is changing as x changes everywhere on the function. Graphically this means that there is a unique tangent gradient at every point on the function.

As we know, a function is *differentiable* if the limit dy/dx of the incremental ratio $\Delta y/\Delta x$ exists. A function may be differentiable everywhere, somewhere, or nowhere. To be everywhere differentiable, it is necessary but not sufficient that the function be continuous. Consider some examples. The polynomials we studied in this chapter are everywhere differentiable, but in Section 2.6 we studied the continuous function $y = |x|$, illustrated in Figure 2.10. This function has a corner at $x = 0$, where it is not differentiable: we could draw an infinite number of "tangents" to it at this point. Thus $\Delta y/\Delta x$ does not have a unique limit at this point. Another function with a corner at $x = 0$ is illustrated in Figure 12.6. The function illustrated in Figure 2.8 has a derivative where $0 < x < t$ and where $x > t$ (it happens to be zero), but no derivative at the value $x = t$. We can now attach a more precise meaning to the notion of "smoothness": if a function is differentiable over some interval, we may call it smooth. It may have one or more discontinuities, where the derivative does not exist, and it may be continuous without being everywhere differentiable (if it has corners).

In most of the work that follows we shall assume that we are dealing with smooth continuous functions that can be differentiated. There are, however, techniques for dealing with functions that are not everywhere differentiable. In Chapter 18 we shall introduce the method of linear programming, which is not derived from calculus.

We have now done quite a bit of mathematics, but the student who has persevered this far has gone a long way toward mastering the techniques he needs, and we must see without further delay to what use we can put the techniques we have learned in this chapter.

QUESTIONS

1. In Section 4.1 we consider the elasticity of the demand curve $pq = 1200$.
   a. Calculate the elasticity of this curve using the definition

   $$\eta = \frac{dq}{dp}\frac{p}{q} \quad .$$

   b. Show that any demand curve of the form $pq = C$ has an elasticity of unity.

2. Show that the elasticity of demand is the same at all points on the demand curve $q = Cp^{-\alpha}$.

3. a. A colleague suggests the following demand curve: $q^d = -55p$.
   i. Calculate the elasticity of demand.
   ii. Considering that p is restricted to nonnegative values, does this demand function seem reasonable?
   b. i. Now calculate the elasticity of $q^d = 100 - 55p$.
   ii. Over what values of p does this seem reasonable?
   iii. Calculate the specific elasticity when $p = 1$.
   c. Now calculate the elasticities for the following supply curves:
   i. $q^s = 50 + 50p$
   ii. $q^s = 20p$
   and for the following demand curve:
   iii. $q^d = 500p^{-2}$

4. Use the method of Section 4.4 and the rules for compound expressions to find the first derivatives of the following.
   a. $y = \frac{1}{3}x^3$
   b. $y = x + x^2$
   c. $y = (x - 1)(x - 2)$

5. a. Find the first derivative of $y = (x - 1)^2$.
  b. How many of the techniques given in this chapter could have been used in solving the problem?

6. Use the method of Section 4.6 to find the first derivative with respect to x of y where $y = x(1 + x)$ without multiplying out *or* appealing to the product rule, that is, use the definition of a derivative.

7. a. Is $1/x$ everywhere differentiable?
  b. Find the derivative, where it exists, of $y = |x|$.
  c. Consider the function $y = ax$ defined for x a positive integer only. Is it differentiable?

8. a. Calculate the first derivative with respect to x of the following:
  i. $y = 3x$
  ii. $y = 3 + x$
  iii. $y = 50x^{50}$
  iv. $y = 50 + 2500x$
  v. $y = 50(x^{20}x^{30})$ (use the multiplication rule)
  vi. $z = (y + 3)^2$, where $y = (x + 3)^2$
  vii. $y = 1/x^{1/3}$
  viii. $y = x^{-1/3}$
  ix. $y = (x^2 + 1)/(2^2 + x)$
  x. $y = 15x - 10x$
  b. Calculate the second derivative of y with respect to x of i, iii, iv, and vi in part a.

9. Evaluate the first and second derivatives of y with respect to x in each of the following:
  a. $y = 8x^2$
  b. $y = 8x^{1/2}$
  c. $y = 4z^2 + 2z + 5$, where $z = 3x^2 + x$
  d. $y = (3 + 2x^2)^2$ (*Hint:* Let $u = (3 + 2x^2)$ and use the function-of-a-function rule.)
  e. $y = (x^2 + 10)(x - 4)$ (*Hint:* Often it is easier to multiply terms after differentiation than before.)

10. Calculate all the nonzero derivatives of

$$y = 10 + 3x + 5x^3 + 7x^5 \quad.$$

11. Consider the derivation of a marginal revenue curve from a demand curve, first in a numerical example and then in general terms.
  a. The demand for a commodity is given by $q^d = 1000 - 3p$. Derive the total revenue and the marginal revenue functions.
  b. The demand for a commodity is given by $p = a + bq$. Prove that the slope of the marginal revenue curve associated with a linear Marshallian demand curve is always twice that of the demand curve. (This is a most convenient result to know when constructing graphs.)
  c. The demand curve for a commodity is given by $p = f(q)$. Show that marginal revenue is given by $MR = f(q) + qf'(q)$ [don't forget that

$f'(q) = dq/dp$]. (*Hint*: First get an expression for total revenue and then differentiate it, using the product rule, to get marginal revenue.)

12. If the area of a circle is $A = \pi r^2$, how fast does the area increase as the radius (r) is increased?

13. Using $C = a + bY$,
    a. Determine the marginal propensity to consume and the average propensity to consume.
    b. Can you calculate dY/dC for this function, and if so, what is it?
    c. Is the following valid: $APC - MPC = a/Y$?

14. a. Calculate dx/dy for the following:
       i. $y = 5 + 7x$
       ii. $x = 5 + 7y$
       iii. $yx = 5$
    b. Calculate dy/dx and dx/dy for $y = 5 - x^2$ if it is possible; if it is not possible, why not?

15. Consider the following functions defined over nonnegative x only:
       i. $y = 10 + 2x$
       ii. $y = x^2$
       iii. $y = x^3$
    a. Calculate dy/dx for each function.
    b. Calculate dx/dy using the inverse function rule.
    c. Express x as an explicit function of y for each function.
    d. Calculate dx/dy from each of the functions in part c and check that you obtain the same answers as in part b.

16. Assume that $q^d = 1000 - 5p - 0.1p^3$ and $p = 2t^{3/2}$. This says that demand is a function of price and that price is increasing over time. Use the function-of-a-function rule to calculate the rate of change of q^d over time. Check your results by substituting $p = p(t)$ into $q^d = q(p)$ to obtain a single function $p = p(t)$ and then calculate dp/dt directly from this function.

17. A golfer putts the ball so that it rolls x feet in t seconds, where $x = 3t^2 - t^3$.
    a. How fast is the ball rolling at any given time? After how many seconds will the ball stop rolling?
    b. As the ball stops rolling, it falls into the hole. What was the initial distance between the ball and the hole?
    c. Find the acceleration of the ball, $d(\text{speed})/dt$. At what time does the ball stop accelerating and start decelerating?

18. A secretary working in a busy office finds that the more telephone calls she gets, the less typing she gets done. If she spends 8 hours a day at her job, an equation for the actual amount of time, t, spent typing is

$$t = 8 - f(p) \quad ,$$

where p is the percentage of time spent on the phone in 1 day.
    a. What are the upper and lower limits of p? Of $f(p)$?
    b. Find a function $f(p)$ satisfying the given conditions.

19. The functions and their derivatives considered so far have involved simple *operators* (an operator is an instruction to perform an operation) such as $+$, $-$, $\div$, $\times$, and "power." Consider the following functions:

 i. $y = a + |x|$

 ii. $y = (x - 5)^2 + 5$

 iii. $y = 1$ if $x > 10$

   0 if $x \leq 10$

 iv. $y = x/3$ rounded to next highest integer

 v. $y = 1$ if $x > 10$

   0 if $x < 4$

Note that function v is not defined for $4 \leq x \leq 10$.

a. Sketch a graph of each of these functions, and indicate points of discontinuity and points where the graph has a kink.

b. Calculate the first and second derivative for function ii.

Chapter 5

Applications of Derivatives

In Chapter 3 we applied the simple techniques of simultaneous linear equations to the two models of the determination of price in a competitive market and of the determination of national income. The present chapter and all subsequent "applications" chapters are potentially divided into three parts: first, applications of new techniques to the model of the competitive market; second, application to the model of income determination; and third, miscellaneous applications to other parts of economic theory. It is our objective to make a thorough study of the two basic models of a competitive market and income determination. In some cases, however, there are not enough applications to provide a thorough drilling in some new technique, and, in others, obvious applications to other areas of economics suggest themselves. These applications are gathered into the final "miscellaneous" section of each applied chapter. We hope that these applications are useful and enlightening, but we make no pretense of a comprehensive coverage of any area of theory other than the competitive market and income determination. In some chapters, one, or more, of the three possible sections is omitted, either because there are no obvious or very useful applications of a new technique to one of the two basic models, or because there are so many that further miscellaneous applications are not needed.

Most of the applications of calculus to the competitive model require us to find the maximum or minimum values of functions, and so must wait until we have another chapter of mathematical techniques at our disposal. There are, however, two problems that we can begin to study now, although their full solution must wait until later.

The Competitive Model

5.1 CONSTANT ELASTICITY DEMAND CURVES

In our competitive model so far, we have used demand curves that are linear in natural numbers:

$$q^d = a + bp \ .$$

(1)

In much theoretical and empirical work it is convenient to use demand curves that are linear in logarithms:

$$\log q^d = \log A + \alpha \log p \ .$$

(2)

In natural numbers this curve takes the form

$$q^d = Ap^\alpha \ .$$

(3)

We may now establish the important result that this demand curve has a constant elasticity throughout its entire range:

$$\eta = \frac{dq}{dp} \cdot \frac{p}{q}$$

$$= \alpha A p^{\alpha-1} \cdot \frac{p}{q}$$

$$= \alpha A p^{\alpha-1} \cdot \frac{p}{Ap^\alpha} \qquad [\text{from (3)}]$$

$$= \alpha \frac{Ap^\alpha}{Ap^\alpha}$$

$$= \alpha \ .$$

(4)

The elasticity of the log–linear demand function in (3) is a constant equal to α.

Now let us take dlog q/dlog p from (2). Since (2) is linear in the logarithms, we get

$$\frac{d \log q}{d \log p} = \alpha \ .$$

(5)

Equations (4) and (5) show that, with the log–linear function, elasticity is equal to dlog q/dlog p. Thus for this function we have

$$\frac{dq}{dp} \cdot \frac{p}{q} = \frac{d \log q}{d \log p} \ .$$

(6)

We shall see in Section 13.7 that this is a general result. In the meantime, we note that we have discovered the form of the demand functions that have constant elasticities, and have discovered that, with these functions, elasticity is the derivative of the log of quantity with respect to the log of price.

5.2   TAX RATES AND TAX YIELDS IN COMPETITIVE MARKETS

In Section 3.4 we derived the equilibrium price in a competitive market with linear demand and supply curves. The solution for price was originally stated in Eq. (22) and is restated below:

$$p = \frac{a - c}{d - b} + \frac{d}{d - b} t \quad, \tag{7}$$

where t is a specific tax, a and b are the intercept and slope parameters on the demand curve, and c and d are the intercept and slope parameters on the supply curve. Notice the possible confusion arising from our use of d as a parameter in this model. The "d" in differentiation is always written as a Roman character, whereas the "d" used a a parameter is always written in italic. Thus there is no ambiguity for the careful reader.

In Chapter 3 we saw by inspection that $\Delta p / \Delta t = d / (d - b)$. Equation (7) gives p as a linear function of t, and we can easily find the derivative of p with respect to t:

$$\frac{dp}{dt} = \frac{d}{d - b} \quad. \tag{8}$$

In Chapter 3 we studied the conditions for this expression to be positive but less than unity.

Suppose now that we consider the relation between the rate of tax t and the tax yield, which is given by tq. Intuition suggests that, over some range, increases in t will lead to increased tax yields, whereas, over others, tax increases may so reduce the quantity demanded as to reduce yield. The question is obviously of some interest to policy makers. The general answer from standard supply and demand analysis is the familiar "it depends on elasticities," but let us obtain a more specific answer for our linear case. We assume that the demand curve slopes down and the supply curve up. We define tax yield as

$$T = tq \tag{9}$$

and from the demand equation have

$$q = a + b\bar{p} \quad, \tag{10}$$

where $\bar{p}$ is the equilibrium price under taxation,[1] given by (7). Substituting (7) into (10) and (10) into (9),

$$T = t\left[a + b\left(\frac{a-c}{d-b} + \frac{d}{d-b}t\right)\right]$$

$$= at + \frac{b(a-c)t}{d-b} + \frac{bdt^2}{d-b}$$

$$= \frac{ad-bc}{d-b}t + \frac{bd}{d-b}t^2 \quad . \tag{11}$$

What we have done here is to express tax yield, T, as a function of tax rate, t, and (11) shows that it is a quadratic. This is not surprising, since $T = tq$, and we have already found that q is a linear function of t. We now differentiate (11) to obtain

$$\frac{dT}{dt} = \frac{ad-bc}{d-b} + \frac{2bdt}{d-b} \quad . \tag{12}$$

It is not immediately obvious if this is positive or negative, or at what values. The expression $(ad-bc)/(d-b)$ is the solution for q in the absence of tax as may be seen from (7) and (10). With $d > 0$ and $b < 0$, the second term in (12) is obviously negative. Thus (12) is positive if

$$|ad-bc| > |2bdt| \quad ,$$

that is, if

$$ad-bc > 2bdt \quad . \tag{13}$$

We can see that this inequality is satisfied, and dT/dt consequently positive, for at least some values of t. Given the parameters, the left-hand side is constant, whereas the right-hand side varies with t. As t approaches zero, the right-hand side approaches zero, and we know that $ad-bc > 0$ (see Section 3.2). Thus we know that there must exist at least some values of t at which the inequality is satisfied, al-

---

[1] You may have noticed that we have sometimes used $\bar{p}$ to denote the equilibrium price just discovered and sometimes to denote some given constant price. This seems like sloppiness in notation, and we have remarked on the utility of good notation! Both uses of the bar over a variable are common in the literature, and the reason is that mathematics is a subject with a history: notation is invented as circumstance requires — or genius suggests — and there is often neither time nor occasion to standardize. Evidently every writer, in this situation, must accept the responsibility for making himself plain whe he uses any symbol whose meaning is not absolutely prescribed by common usage. Equally evidently, mathematics encounters the common problems of language.

though we cannot discover by this means how close to zero they must be. Now suppose that t is large. For constant $ad - bc$, we can obviously always find a t-value so large that the inequality is not satisfied. Thus we know that there is some value of t at which dT/dt becomes negative, although we do not know how large it must be. If dT/dt is positive for small t and negative for large t, there is evidently some value of t that gives a maximum value of T. Finding this value must again wait until we have a little more technique, but we can at least confirm what common sense requires, that it is a maximum, not a minimum. Let us try putting $t = 0$ in (11): we see that $T = 0$. This shows that the quadratic function $T = f(t)$ goes through the origin. But we have already seen that T has positive values for at least some values of t close to zero, so it must rise to the right of $t = 0$. As it declines at some large values of t, it must have a maximum somewhere in the positive quadrant.

The Model of Income Determination

5.3 THE MULTIPLIER AND THE RATE OF INCOME TAX

In Chapter 3, in the sections on the theory of income determination, we encountered some interesting problems that we could not then solve. One, which is obviously important to government policy, is to find the effect on the value of the multiplier of a change in the tax rate. Presumably every Treasury official would like to know the solution to this problem, as well as to know how a change in the tax rate affects the trade-off rate between government expenditure and the budget deficit. We can handle these problems with the technique we now have, and it is not easy to see how else they could be handled. Let us start with the effect on the value of the multiplier of a change in the rate of income tax. From Eq. (37) of Section 3.10, the multiplier in a closed economy with proportional income tax is

$$k = \frac{1}{1 - c(1 - t)} \quad . \tag{14}$$

Our problem is solved by differentiating k with respect to t, but here the multiplier is a nonlinear function of the tax rate, so simple inspection is not sufficient to discover the derivative. We require

$$\frac{dk}{dt} = \frac{d}{dt}\left(\frac{1}{1 - c + ct}\right) \quad .$$

This may be evaluated by an extremely useful substitution trick (which was suggested in Question 5 in Chapter 4). We introduce a new variable, z, and put

$$z = 1 - c + ct$$

so that

$$k = z^{-1} \quad .$$

Now

$$\frac{dk}{dz} = -z^{-2} = \frac{-1}{(1 - c + ct)^2}$$

and

$$\frac{dz}{dt} = c \quad .$$

By the chain rule

$$\frac{dk}{dt} = \frac{dk}{dz} \cdot \frac{dz}{dt}$$

$$= \frac{-c}{(1 - c + ct)^2} \quad ,$$

which is what we want. It is perhaps more conveniently rewritten as

$$\frac{dk}{dt} = -ck^2 \tag{15}$$

[since from (14) $k = 1/(1 - c + ct)$]. The rate of change of the multiplier with respect to tax rate is negative and is equal to the square of the multiplier itself times the marginal propensity to consume — a result we are hardly likely to have discovered by verbal or intuitive methods!

Notice, incidentally, that in (15) we actually have a second derivative, since k itself is the first derivative of income with respect to autonomous expenditure. If we let A stand for all autonomous expenditure, then

$$k = \frac{dY}{dA} \quad \text{and} \quad \frac{dk}{dt} = \frac{d}{dt}\left(\frac{dY}{dA}\right) \quad .$$

This illustrates the fact, to which we shall return in Chapter 8, that if there is more than one variable in a function, we may evaluate its derivative first with respect to one variable, holding the other constant, and then with respect to a second variable, holding the first constant. Evidently this presents no difficulty: we have just done it, and we shall do it again. (This is a good moment to do Question 3.)

5.4   DEFICITS AND THE LEVEL OF INCOME TAX

Armed with the result in (15), we can tackle the next question arising from Section 3.10. We saw there that an increase in government
spending led to a less-than-equal increase in the deficit because of
the tax yield on the increased income. The question is, would the ratio
$\Delta D/\Delta G$ be larger or smaller if the tax rate were higher? The higher
the tax rate, the smaller the multiplier, as we have just seen, and the
smaller the multiplier, the less the increase in taxable income following upon the extra government expenditure, ΔG. On the other hand,
the higher the tax rate, the greater the yield from whatever increase
in income does take place. So the question is, can we determine, with
qualitative information only, which of these two forces is the stronger?

The relevant equation is (39) from Section 3.10:

$$\Delta D = \Delta G(1 - tk) \quad . \tag{16}$$

We want to discover, if we can, the sign of

$$\frac{\mathrm{d}}{\mathrm{d}t}\,\Delta D = \frac{\mathrm{d}}{\mathrm{d}t}\,[\Delta G(1 - tk)] \quad .$$

For this exercise, ΔG is to be regarded as a constant that by a suitable
choice of units may be made unity: we are interested in the effect
on ΔD, per unit ΔG, of changing t. Thus all we really need is

$$\frac{\mathrm{d}}{\mathrm{d}t}\,(1 - tk) \quad .$$

But k is itself a function of t, so to evaluate this, we require the product rule:

$$\frac{\mathrm{d}}{\mathrm{d}t}\,(1 - tk) = -\left(t\,\frac{\mathrm{d}k}{\mathrm{d}t} + k\,\frac{\mathrm{d}t}{\mathrm{d}t}\right) \quad .$$

But $\mathrm{d}t/\mathrm{d}t$ is obviously unity, and we have just found $\mathrm{d}k/\mathrm{d}t$ in (15),
whence

$$\frac{\mathrm{d}}{\mathrm{d}t}\,\Delta D = -(-ctk^2 + k)$$

$$= k(ctk - 1) \quad . \tag{17}$$

ctk is obviously positive, but is it greater than unity? In Section 3.10,
Eq. (40), we showed that $1 - tk > 0$, that is, that $tk < 1$. Since $0 < c < 1$
by assumption, it follows that $ctk < 1$, so (17) is negative: increasing
the tax rate reduces the increase in deficit per unit ΔG; that is, the
greater tax yield per unit increase in income offsets the effect of a
smaller multiplier. This is another qualitative prediction that we
could hardly have discovered by simpler means.

5.5 INCOME TAX AND THE INCOME-DEFICIT TRADE-OFF

It is now easy to answer a question we raised in Section 3.11 and could not answer there: how is the constraint relating changes in the deficit to changes in income shifted by a change in the tax rate? Since we are working in increments, the constraint must still go through the origin (see Section 3.11): only its slope can be affected. The origin itself, however, now corresponds to different values of Y and D as we shift t. This sounds like a formidable complication, but actually will cause us little trouble. The reason for the shift is that a changed tax rate alters the value of the multiplier, and therefore alters the equilibrium level of income for any given autonomous expenditure. Hence if we assume constant autonomous expenditure, the origin in our incremental diagram, which corresponds to the initial equilibrium or *status quo ante*, is shifted. The $\Delta Y : \Delta D$ constraint, however, goes through the origin by definition, whatever initial equilibrium values may be, and its slope is a function of c and t only, so the effect on its slope of changing t can be considered independently of the effect on the initial equilibrium of changing t. We recall that its slope was given by Eq. (41) in Section 3.11:

$$\frac{\Delta Y}{\Delta D} = \frac{k}{1 - tk} \qquad . \qquad (18)$$

Its rate of change with respect to the tax rate must be

$$\frac{\mathrm{d}(\Delta Y / \Delta D)}{\mathrm{d}t} = \frac{\mathrm{d}}{\mathrm{d}t}\left(\frac{k}{1 - tk}\right) \qquad . \qquad (19)$$

Notice here that we are asking for the derivative of an incremental ratio. This need not trouble us, since we have learned that we may always look for the derivative of a function, $\mathrm{d}f(x)/\mathrm{d}x$, without having to write "$y =$" first. In (18), we see a function that happens to measure a particular slope, and if we take the derivative of that function with respect to t, then we know how that slope is altered by changing t.

Evidently what we want is the sign of (19), and it is not clear what this is going to be. We already know from (17) that increasing the tax rate reduces the deficit-generating effect of increased government expenditure; but we also know from (15) that increasing the tax rate also reduces the income-generating effect of increased government expenditure. What it does to $\Delta Y / \Delta D$ therefore depends on which effect is stronger, and there appears to be nothing for it but to evaluate (19) and look for its sign. Applying the quotient rule to (19), we get

$$\frac{\mathrm{d}}{\mathrm{d}t}\left(\frac{k}{1 - tk}\right) = \frac{(1 - tk)\dfrac{\mathrm{d}k}{\mathrm{d}t} - k\dfrac{\mathrm{d}}{\mathrm{d}t}(1 - tk)}{(1 - tk)^2} \qquad .$$

From Eqs. (15) and (17), we have dk/dt and $d(1 - tk)/dt$, and can substitute in, whence

$$\frac{d}{dt}\left(\frac{k}{1 - tk}\right) = \frac{-(1 - tk)ck^2 - k^2(ctk - 1)}{(1 - tk)^2} \quad .$$

This looks rather unpromising but in fact simplifies reasonably. Multiplying out the bracketed terms in the numerator,

$$\frac{d}{dt}\left(\frac{k}{1 - tk}\right) = \frac{-ck^2 + ctk^3 - ctk^3 + k^2}{(1 - tk)^2} \quad ,$$

and, canceling ctk^3,

$$\frac{d}{dt}\left(\frac{\Delta Y}{\Delta D}\right) = \frac{k^2(1 - c)}{(1 - tk)^2} \quad . \tag{20}$$

Equation (20) needs interpretation, which is not difficult. Since the squared terms must be positive, and $0 < c < 1$, the whole expression is positive, and this is all we wanted to know: the slope of the relation connecting ΔY and ΔD is increased by an increase in the tax rate. This means that a given increase in the deficit is accompanied by a larger increase in income. Thus we see that the reduction in the income-generating effect of government spending must be less than the reduction in the deficit-generating effect, so that a bigger increase in income goes with a given increase in the deficit. A bigger increase in *expenditure* is, of course, required to produce a given increase in income *or* deficit than formerly.

This is another example of a general qualitative result: we did not require numerical values for the parameters to obtain the sign of (20), but only our familiar conditions that $0 < c < 1$ and $0 < t < 1$. We do, however, find one rather anomalous implication of this result. From the point of view of the individual who dislikes deficits, the increased tax rate is a "good thing": desired income levels can be reached with smaller deficits. Nonetheless, since the increased tax rate reduces the value of k, increased income requires larger injections of government spending than at lower tax rates. Thus the increased tax rate appears, not surprisingly, a "good thing" to the man who wants a higher proportion of GNP to be controlled by the government sector of the economy: it now requires more government expenditure to secure full employment, which means that, from his point of view, the constraint has moved in a favorable direction. This appears curious: we normally think of the "fiscal conservative" as a man who is opposed to government expenditure anyhow, but more so if it is not fully covered by tax yield, and the "Galbraith Man," who is in favor of government spending, as being pretty well indifferent to how it is financed.

How, then, can we have moved a constraint in such a way as to please both parties?

The explanation is that to lump together deficits and expenditure as "much the same" from the point of view of people's attitudes is a fallacy: so long as the ratio $\Delta D/\Delta G$ is constant, it does not matter which we concern ourselves with; but as soon as we consider parameter shifts which alter that ratio, it does. Lumping them together is an admissible simplification as long as they move in fixed proportions (they are strictly complementary), but it will not do when we vary their proportions. Thus by investigating the properties of the constraint, we have learned something about political attitudes: if we are to make rational choices among the possibilities open to society, we must determine separately our views about the desirable fraction of GNP that should be managed by the government, and about the desirable ways of financing it.

5.6 INCOME TAX AND THE INCOME-PAYMENTS TRADE-OFF

Application of our new techniques to the open economy is now fairly routine, involving no new analytical problems, but it is a useful exercise and may increase our understanding of some important policy problems. For an open economy with given marginal propensities to consume and to import and a given marginal rate of tax, we have, from Section 3.12, Eq. (45),

$$k = \frac{1}{1 - (1 - t)(c - m)} \quad . \tag{21}$$

To find the rate of change of the multiplier with respect to tax rate, we employ the substitution trick again, and let

$$z = 1 - c + ct + m - mt$$

[multiplying out the bracketed terms in the denominator of Eq. (21)]. Clearly

$$k = z^{-1}$$

and

$$\frac{dk}{dz} = -z^{-2} \quad ,$$

while

$$\frac{dz}{dt} = c - m \quad .$$

Hence

$$\frac{dk}{dt} = \frac{dk}{dz} \cdot \frac{dz}{dt}$$

$$= -z^{-2}(c - m)$$

$$= -(c - m)k^2 \tag{22}$$

(since $k = 1/z$). This is negative because consumption of imported goods must be less than total consumption, that is, $c > m$, and it is of the same form as (15), merely adjusted to take into account the fact that induced expenditure on home-produced goods and services is given by $c - m$ in the open economy in place of c alone in the closed economy.

The trade-off rate between increased income and balance of trade deficit (which on our present assumption is the balance of payments deficit) was given in Section 3.12, Eq. (47):

$$\frac{\Delta Y}{\Delta B} = \frac{1}{m(1 - t)} \quad . \tag{23}$$

Again, we can easily find the derivative of this with respect to tax rate by putting

$$z = m - mt \quad ,$$

whence

$$\frac{dz}{dt} = -m$$

and

$$\frac{d}{dt}\left(\frac{\Delta Y}{\Delta B}\right) = mz^{-2}$$

$$= \frac{m}{(m - mt)^2}$$

$$= \frac{1}{m(1 - t)^2} \tag{24}$$

which is positive: a higher tax rate allows a larger increase in income for a given increase in balance of payments deficit [although, from (22), it requires more government expenditure to generate the increased income]. It may not be immediately obvious why this should be: the same proportion of disposable income, m, is devoted to imports, whatever the level of income, so why should an increased tax rate improve the income-deficit trade-off? The answer is simply that, with increased taxes, less of any income *is* disposable — more goes in taxes, which, by assumption, are not spent on imports.

We have already seen that the slope of the relation between increments in income and increments in the balance of payments deficit is positive. The question naturally arises, can we apply the result of (24) to the current policy problem facing deficit countries? The answer depends on whether the assumptions of the model are reasonably well satisfied. We assumed unemployment, constant prices, and all investment autonomous. Thus the model may fit fairly well in times of recession, but it would be unwise to apply its conclusions in times of high employment and inflation. We should also remember that, in the real world, capital goods may be imported, and governments may import too (if only by maintaining armies in foreign countries). We shall show briefly how the model may be extended to accommodate imports by investors and government, and leave the complete analysis as an exercise in the questions at the end of the chapter.

For simplicity, assume proportionality. Thus let imported investment goods, M_i, be a constant proportion, i, of investment, and government imports, M_g, be a constant proportion, g, of government expenditure. Letting imported consumption goods $M_c = m(1 - t)Y$, as before, we have

$$M = M_i + M_g + M_c$$
$$= iI + gG + m(1 - t)Y \quad .$$

Substituting into

$$Y = C + I + G + X - M \quad ,$$

we have

$$Y = cY(1 - t) + I + G + X - mY(1 - t) - iI - gG \quad .$$

Collecting the Y-terms and factoring, as usual,

$$Y[1 - c(1 - t) + m(1 - t)] = I(1 - i) + G(1 - g) + X \quad ,$$

whence

$$Y = \frac{1}{1 - (1 - t)(c - m)} [I(1 - i) + G(1 - g) + X] \quad . \tag{25}$$

From (25) we see that our new assumptions affect the *multiplicand*, not the multiplier. But this will affect the trade-off rates between total government spending (on home and foreign goods) and income, and between income and the balance of payments. Does it change the effect of increased taxes on the trade-off rates? You are invited to find out for yourself in Question 6. Notice, by the way, that we might perfectly well have assumed import content in exports while we were about it. This would have introduced no change in form. If the proportion of imported raw materials in exports is a constant, r, then in place of X in (25) we should simply have had $X(1-r)$, which is not a serious complication: again, it merely alters the multiplicand. This prompts a concluding remark about multiplier analysis. It is based on the assumption that we can make a clear distinction between autonomous expenditure, independent of current income levels, and induced expenditure, which is a function of current income levels. Autonomous expenditure always appears in the multiplicand, adjusted if necessary, as we have just seen, to make sure that we multiply only that part which is an injection to the home economy. The multiplier itself, of course, simply depends on the rate of flow of induced expenditure, and is therefore a function, as we have seen, of the parameters of the expenditure functions. Thus we may conclude that, when faced with a problem in multiplier analysis, the first question to ask is "does this affect the multiplier or the multiplicand?" A second question is a serious empirical one that we cannot take up here: "For what time periods can what items properly be treated as autonomous?" If we cannot answer that, we cannot sensibly apply multiplier analysis.

Miscellaneous Application

5.7   MARGINAL COST

The concept of marginal cost familiar from elementary theory is one of many examples of first derivatives going by other names in economics. Total cost is assumed to vary with output, so that the total cost function may be written as

$$C = c(q) \quad , \tag{26}$$

where C is total cost and q output. In elementary textbooks marginal cost is often defined as an incremental ratio $\Delta c/\Delta q$. But such a measure suffers from the ambiguity of all incremental ratios: if the cost function is nonlinear, the incremental cost ratio is not unique.

Indeed marginal cost can be satisfactorily interpreted only as the first derivative of total cost with respect to output:

$$MC = \frac{dC}{dq} = c'(q) \quad . \tag{27}$$

But we may go further. If there is any part of cost that is fixed, then it, by definition, does not vary with output, so we may rewrite (26) as

$$C = k + f(q) \quad , \tag{28}$$

where k is fixed cost and $f(q)$ gives the relationship between total variable cost and output. Since k is not a function of q, the rate of change of C with respect to q is independent of k, that is,

$$\frac{dC}{dq} = f'(q) \quad . \tag{29}$$

Thus marginal total cost equals marginal variable cost and is independent of fixed cost.

Now, with the aid of our more powerful technique, we may consider the case of perfect competition. It is a familiar result that equilibrium for the individual firm in perfect competion is possible only where marginal cost is rising. This suggests that we may find that only some cost functions are compatible with perfectly competitive equilibrium. To investigate this question, we start by considering the cost function

$$C = aq^2 + bq + c \quad . \tag{30}$$

Marginal cost is given by

$$\frac{dC}{dq} = 2aq + b \tag{31}$$

which is linear. Since perfectly competitive equilibrium is possible only where marginal cost is rising, it immediately follows that a must be positive if (30) is to be consistent with perfect competition. But (30) does not give us the marginal cost curve, familiar from textbook illustrations, that slopes down and then rises. To obtain this marginal cost curve, we need a total cost curve that is more complicated than a quadratic. In fact, a suitable cubic will do it. Consider

$$C = aq^3 + bq^2 + cq + d \quad .$$

Marginal cost is given by

$$\frac{dC}{dq} = 3aq^2 + 2bq + c \quad ,$$

itself a quadratic. This will take on the conventional ∪-shape provided that it is "the right way up," and not an inverted ∪, which involves some restrictions on the signs of the coefficients. It proves that working out the required restrictions is rather laborious (we had to do it in order to set Question 8, which might well be done at this point). Furthermore, after we have the technique of maxima and minima, which is the subject of Chapter 6, we can discover very easily what sort of cubic will give the textbook total cost curve, so it is not worth pursuing the matter now.

We may now use our new technique to obtain in an easy and efficient manner many standard propositions of micro theory, some of which are met in a principles course and all of which are used so frequently that it is a good idea to have them properly established. In Section 5.8, we shall derive the marginal revenue function and then prove that a factor's marginal revenue product is equal to its marginal physical product multiplied by marginal revenue, after which we shall establish the relationship between marginal product and marginal cost.

5.8 PRODUCTION, COST, AND REVENUE FUNCTIONS

We already know that marginal product and marginal revenue are derivatives, the former of the production function with respect to an input and the latter of the revenue function with respect to output, or sales. Thus suppose that, for a given capital equipment, total output is given by

$$q = g(l)   , \tag{32}$$

where l is labor measured in man-days. Marginal product is dq/dl or $g'(l)$. We expect positive marginal products, that is, $g'(l) > 0$. Diminishing returns means that the marginal product curve has, at least eventually, a negative slope. When marginal product is decreasing, its derivative must be negative. Its derivative is, however, the second derivative of the output function (32), so the assumption of diminishing returns is simply expressed as $g''(l) < 0$.

We could now construct some possible production functions, as we constructed cost functions in Section 5.7, and consider what restrictions are necessary to generate a conventionally shaped marginal product curve, but we may leave this for the time being. Let us consider the marginal revenue of an individual firm. A firm in nonperfect competition has control over the price of its product: it may set price, whence demand determines sales. Thus we may write $q = q(p)$. But the two variables, price and sales, are related by the demand curve, and it is more convenient to invert the function (which we can do because it is strictly monotonically decreasing) and write it as

$$p = f(q)   , \tag{33}$$

which may be interpreted as saying that the price at which any quantity is demanded is a function of that quantity. Revenue is price times sales:

$$R = pq   . \tag{34}$$

If we substitute (33) into (34), we obtain

$$R = q \cdot f(q) \quad . \tag{35}$$

Eq. (35) expresses total revenue as a function of sales only, which allows us to find its derivative with respect to sales. To do this we need the product rule to obtain

$$\frac{dR}{dq} = q \cdot f'(q) + f(q) \quad , \tag{36}$$

which is the general expression for the marginal revenue function. [Perfect competition is, as we know, the special case in which price is a constant, $\bar{p}$, so that $dR/dq = d(\bar{p}q)/dq = \bar{p}$.]

In the last chapter, marginal revenue was illustrated by a numerical example of a linear demand function. We may complete the illustration in general terms for the linear demand function $p = a + bq$, whence total revenue is given by

$$R = pq = q(a + bq)$$
$$= aq + bq^2 \quad . \tag{37}$$

Equation (37), as we have already seen in Chapter 2, is a quadratic through the origin, and we easily obtain

$$MR = \frac{dR}{dq} = a + 2bq \quad , \tag{38}$$

which shows that a linear demand function gives a linear marginal revenue function.

Let us now try to find an expression for marginal revenue product. This is defined as the rate of change of total revenue with respect to an input, say, labor. We clearly need to express revenue as a function of labor input, and therefore need both the production function, (32), and the revenue function, (35). Substituting (32) into (35) to replace q by $g(l)$ wherever q appears, we have

$$R = g(l) \cdot f[g(l)] \quad . \tag{39}$$

The term $f[g(l)]$ may appear forbidding, but it is only a way of expressing price as a function of the variable input labor: the function f takes q into p and the function g takes l into q, so "f of g of l" takes labor input into prices. Now to find dR/dl we shall have to employ both the product rule and the chain rule. Since the term $p = f[g(l)]$ expresses price as a function of output, which in turn is a function of labor input, the chain rule gives

$$\frac{df[g(l)]}{dl} = \frac{dp}{dl} = \frac{dp}{dq} \cdot \frac{dq}{dl} = f'(q) \cdot g'(l) \quad . \tag{40}$$

We may now apply the product rule to (39) and see that we require

$$\frac{dR}{dl} = g(l)\frac{d}{dl}f[g(l)] + g'(l) \cdot f[g(l)] \quad .$$

Substituting (40) into this, we obtain

$$\frac{dR}{dl} = g(l) \cdot f'(q) \cdot g'(l) + g'(l) \cdot f[g(l)] \quad . \tag{41}$$

Equation (41) looks rather cumbersome, but we may identify individual terms in such a fashion as to yield a straightforward interpretation. Remember that $g'(l)$ is marginal physical product (MPP), that $f'(q)$ is dp/dq, and that $f[g(l)]$ is price, written as a function of demand for the product and labor input. Factoring out $g'(l)$, we have

$$\text{marginal revenue product of labor} = MPP\left\{q \cdot \frac{dp}{dq} + p\right\} \quad .$$

But from (36) we know that the expression in braces is dR/dq, or marginal revenue, so we have proved that

$$MRP = MPP \cdot MR \quad .$$

We shall need this relationship later on.

We can now establish the relationship between marginal product and marginal cost. Assuming fixed capital equipment, and that labor is the only variable input, we use (32) again: $q = g(l)$. Let the wage per man-day be w. Define variable cost simply as

$$V = wl \quad . \tag{42}$$

The marginal cost of another man-day, dV/dl, is obviously equal to the wage, w, but what we want is marginal cost with respect to output, dV/dq. Now, by the chain rule

$$\frac{dV}{dq} = \frac{dV}{dl} \cdot \frac{dl}{dq} \quad , \tag{43}$$

and from (32)

$$\frac{dq}{dl} = g'(l) \quad , \tag{44}$$

whence, since we may assume that $g(l)$ is monotonic increasing, $dl/dq = 1/g'(l)$. So, substituting into (43),

$$\frac{dV}{dq} = \left(\frac{w}{g'(l)}\right) \quad , \tag{45}$$

which is to say that marginal cost of output is equal to the marginal cost of the variable input divided by its marginal product. This result illustrates the power of mathematical notation that we referred to in Chapter 4. To obtain (45), we have not had to specify the actual production function $g(l)$, let alone go through the operation of taking a derivative: it is enough to write $g'(l)$ to indicate that it is the derivative that we are talking about. We can then obtain the general result (45), which can be applied without more ado to any particular case, or employed in any further analysis we may wish to undertake. And, indeed, we have use for it at once.

5.9* THE RELATION BETWEEN MARGINAL PRODUCT AND MARGINAL COST

This section is starred to indicate that it is difficult and may be omitted.

We shall take labor as the factor that is varied in the short run, and we shall prove that, with a constant wage rate, diminishing marginal product of labor is both necessary and sufficient for increasing marginal cost. This is generally taken for granted in the analysis of perfect competition. It is certainly required, since competitive equilibrium is possible only where marginal cost is rising, and the individual firm cannot influence the wage rate. Furthermore, it is intuitively reasonable that diminishing marginal product should give increasing marginal cost, and you may have encountered this proposition in your principles course. It turns out to be quite hard work to prove it, and there is certainly nothing else as difficult in this chapter.

In Eq. (45) we have expressed marginal cost in terms of the wage rate and marginal product. What we now want is the slope of the marginal cost curve, which is given by the derivative of (45), which in turn is the second derivative of (42), total variable cost. Thus we require

$$\frac{d^2V}{dq^2} = \frac{d}{dq}\left(\frac{w}{g'(l)}\right) \quad . \tag{46}$$

This looks a little tricky, because $g'(l)$ is itself dq/dl. Since, however, w is a constant, what we have to find is $d(1/g'(l))/dq$. To evaluate this, it will help to employ again the device of a substitute variable, and to apply the chain rule. If we put

$$z = g'(l) \quad ,$$

then we are seeking

$$\frac{dz^{-1}}{dq} \quad .$$

Since z is a function of l, and l of q, we have to use the chain rule twice to evaluate this:

$$\frac{dz^{-1}}{dq} = \frac{d(z^{-1})}{dz} \cdot \frac{dz}{dl} \cdot \frac{dl}{dq}$$

$$= -z^{-2} \cdot \frac{dz}{dl} \cdot \frac{dl}{dq} \quad .$$

Taking this term by term,

$$-z^{-2} = \frac{-1}{(g'(l))^2} \quad ,$$

$$\frac{dz}{dl} = g''(l) \qquad [\text{see Eq. (44)}],$$

and

$$\frac{dl}{dq} = \frac{1}{g'(l)} = z^{-1} \quad ,$$

so

$$\frac{dz^{-1}}{dq} = \left(\frac{-1}{(g'(l))^2}\right) \cdot (g''(l)) \cdot \left(\frac{1}{g'(l)}\right)$$

or

$$\frac{dz^{-1}}{dq} = \frac{-g''(l)}{(g'(l))^3} \quad ,$$

and, remembering the constant wage rate w, we have

$$\frac{d^2V}{dq^2} = \frac{d}{dq}\left(\frac{w}{g'(l)}\right) = \frac{-wg''(l)}{(g'(l))^3} \quad . \tag{47}$$

Both w and the denominator are positive, so (47) is positive if and only if $g''(l) < 0$, that is, marginal product is diminishing, which is the result we wanted. It is another result that is general, in the sense that we have not had to specify a particular function — and we may take some pride in having completed a difficult proof of an important proposition that often is only asserted.

QUESTIONS

1. Calculate the elasticity of the following.
   a. $q^d = 10p^{-0.75}$
   b. $q^d = 20 + 10p^{-0.75}$
   c. $q^d = a + p^\alpha$
   d. $q^s = 20p$
   e. $q^s = 20p^{1.25}$
   f. $q^s = a + bp^\alpha$

2. Consider the specific demand function $q^d = 5p^{-1.5}$ and the tax yield function $T = tq$.

   a. Determine the effect on the tax yield of a raising of the power term on the demand function from -1.5 to -1.1. [*Hint*: You would be advised to use the function for taxes $T = T(p)$, i.e., $T = 5tp^{-1.5}$.]

   b. Now consider a tax yield equation of $T = tpq$ and answer the same question.

   c. Explain the difference in the two tax yield equations, that is, explain what kind of tax would give rise to each tax yield equation.

3. Evaluate dk/dt, where $k = 1/[1 - c(1 - t)]$ for $c = \frac{3}{4}$ and $t = \frac{1}{5}$.

4. Using the numerical values of Question 17, Chapter 3 (income determination), find (using fractions rather than decimals) the following.

   a. $\dfrac{dk}{dt}$

   b. $\dfrac{d}{dt}\left(\dfrac{\Delta Y}{\Delta D}\right)$

   c. $\dfrac{d}{dt}\left(\dfrac{\Delta Y}{\Delta B}\right)$

5. a. Determine the impact on the multiplier, k, of a change in the marginal propensity to consume, c, given a tax rate of t.

   b. Determine the impact on the marginal deficit/expenditure ratio, $\Delta D/\Delta G$, of the same change.

6. On the assumption that there is import content in investment and government expenditure, find the following.

   a. $\Delta Y/\Delta B$ [*Hint*: Start by finding $\Delta M/\Delta G$. This is the sum of the direct effect, given by g, and the indirect effect due to importing out of increased income, $m(1 - t)\,\Delta Y$. Hence

$$\frac{\Delta M}{\Delta G} = g + m(1 - t)\,\frac{\Delta Y}{\Delta G} \quad,$$

and $\Delta Y/\Delta G$ can be obtained from Eq. (25). Do not forget to adjust the multiplicand for import content.]

   *b. The sign of

$$\frac{d}{dt}\left(\frac{\Delta Y}{\Delta B}\right)$$

7. Consider the following model of an open economy in which exports, X, are exogenous:

$$Y = C + I + G + X - M$$
$$C = a + b(Y - T)$$
$$T = t(Y - I)$$
$$M = mY \quad.$$

   a. Calculate the multiplier.

   b. Determine the effect on income of a change in the tax rate, t.

8. Total cost is given by

$$C = 5000 + 1000q - 500q^2 + \tfrac{2}{3}q^3 \quad.$$

a. Find the marginal cost function.
b. Find the expression for the slope of the marginal cost curve.
c. Find the average total cost function.
d. At what value of q does marginal cost equal average *variable* cost?

9. Use the cost function of Question 8, and add the term $+tq^{4/5}$, where t is a constant.
a. Answer Questions 8a–8c.
b. Can the term t be interpreted as a unit tax?

10. Total cost[2] for a firm in the short run is found by an econometrician to be

$$C = 77.0 + 1.32q - 0.0002q^2 \quad.$$

a. Is it possible that this firm is selling in a perfectly competitive market?
b. Is this cost function consistent with the law of diminishing returns? (Assume that factors are purchased in a perfectly competitive market.)

11. A monopolist's demand curve is given by

$$p = 100 - 2q \quad.$$

a. Find his marginal revenue function.
b. What is the relationship between the slopes of the average and marginal revenue curves?
c. At what price is marginal revenue zero?

12. A demand curve is given by

$$p = aq^\beta \quad.$$

a. Find the marginal revenue function.
b. Find the elasticity of demand.
c. Draw a graph of average and marginal revenue, and interpret your results. What restrictions will you put on the value of β?

13. Output, with fixed equipment, is given by

$$q = al^3 + bl^2 + cl + d \quad.$$

a. Find the marginal product function.
b. Find the average product function.

°14. If demand and output are given by

$$p = a + bq$$

and

$$q = cl + dl^2 \quad,$$

---

[2] Adapted from J. Johnston, *Statistical Cost Analysis*, McGraw-Hill, New York, 1960, p. 65.

show that marginal revenue product is given by

$$\frac{dR}{dl} = ac + 2(ad + bc^2)l + 6bcdl^2 + 4bd^2l^3 \quad .$$

[*Hint*: See Eq. (41).]

15. Output, with fixed equipment, is given by

$$q = 101 + 0.1l^2 - 0.0005l^3 \quad ,$$

and the wage per man-day is constant at 10.
   a. Find marginal cost at $l = 100$.
   °b. At what labor input does marginal cost start to rise? (*Hint*: Find the slope of dq/dl.)

16. Combine the monopolist's demand curve of Question 11 with the output function of Question 13.
   a. Determine the marginal revenue product function.
   b. Calculate $d(MRP)/dl$, and explain. (*Note*: There is no need to reduce the calculation to simplest terms.)

Chapter

Maxima and Minima

It is very commonly assumed that decision-making units, whether firms, households, or governments, seek to maximize something or other, "utility," or "profit," or "social welfare." Hence an acquaintance with the mathematics of maximizing is peculiarly useful to the student of economics, and enables him to tackle a large number of problems, and read a large amount of literature, that would otherwise be inaccessible.

We shall continue to confine ourselves to *functions of a single variable*, but we may nonetheless consider a number of interesting applications in Chapter 7, where we shall be able to analyze far more thoroughly than hitherto the implications of profit maximization. Many important questions require us to deal with functions of more than one variable. We are interested, for example, in the behavior of consumers choosing among many goods, or in the policy makers' decision when faced with the sort of constraints we encountered in Chapter 3. We shall accordingly take up functions of two or more variables in Chapter 8 and substantially extend the range of problems that we can handle. The technique introduced in this chapter is, however, very powerful and enables us to derive the implications of many important hypotheses.

In the first paragraph we referred to firms, households, and governments as "decision-making units." The notion of a "decision maker" is a very useful one. We may refer to any economic unit, faced with a problem of choice, as a *decision maker*, and, as we are interested in the behavior of economic units, we shall formulate hypotheses about their decisions. The familiar hypothesis, or class of hypotheses, is that decision makers maximize "something"; and this has led to a good deal of misunderstanding. It is sometimes said in defense of one or other of the maximization hypotheses that the maximization of the "something" is "rational." The hypothesis of profit maximization is sometimes defended by such argument as "Why else would a man be in business?" or "The object of business is to make money: it would be absurd not to maximize profits." This sort of attempt to settle a priori what is a matter of fact invites the reply that economists still predicate a creature called "economic man," who never existed and never will, merely because it makes the mathematics convenient! Even worse, it provokes—or provides an excuse for—the skeptic to retreat into descriptive institutionalism. "Rationality" is to be understood as the consistent choice of action calculated to achieve what is desired, given the possibilities. The decision to maximize one thing rather than another depends on what is desired, and that is neither rational nor irrational but depends on the tastes and beliefs of the decision makers.

The question of rationality or irrationality is therefore a question of the appropriateness of the means, given the ends, and neither requires nor implies any judgment about the ends. Thus if an entrepreneur decides that he desires some combination of profit and leisure, rather than profit only, with leisure ignored, it is our business to see what follows if he acts rationally, given these ends. Certainly the assumption that something is maximized makes the mathematics convenient, but *any* consistently purposeful action can be seen as maximizing *something:* the question is *what.* We might say that it is the business of the creative theoretician to suggest the hypothesis that the behavior of some decision maker, or *class* of decision makers, will be found comprehensible and predictable if it is assumed that the decision makers endeavor to maximize some particular function; that it is the business of the analyst (probably the same person) to work out just what behavior is predicted by the hypothesis in question; and that it is the business of the empirical worker, or econometrician, to find out just how well the predictions do fit the facts. Whether or not a particular hypothesis, such as profit maximization, should be accepted, at least provisionally, depends, of course, on the correspondence we find between prediction and observation, rather than on any a priori argument about rationality or the objects of modern corporations. Before we can test, however, we must derive the predictions of the theory, and to do this we must develop the necessary mathematical technique. Thus we are in no way committed to the notion that it is peculiarly "rational" to maximize profit instead of power, or leisure time, or some combination of all three. We do, however, recognize the possibility that the profit motive is so strong that a hypothesis that ignores other goals will, nonetheless, prove to fit the facts pretty well; and if we want to explore such a possibility, then we must be equipped to work out the implications of the hypothesis.

6.1 EXTREME VALUES

In many of the examples of Chapter 5 we came very close to looking for a maximum value to some function or other when we asked if its rate of change with respect to some parameter or variable in which we were interested was positive or negative. If the rate of change is always one or the other, the dependent variable is a monotonic increasing, or decreasing, function of the independent variable, as the case may be. But we may encounter cases in which it is first increasing and then decreasing, as we did in Section 5.2. It will be recalled that the case we had there was a competitive market with linear supply and demand curves. We expressed tax yield (tax rate times quantity sold) as a function of tax rate and found it to be a quadratic, so that the yield was an increasing function of the rate for some values of the rate and a decreasing function for other, higher, values. Intuition suggests that, if a function first increases and then decreases, there must be a point at which it has a maximum value. (Indeed, in Chapter 2, we saw that a ∩-shaped quadratic has a maximum at a value of x halfway between its two points of intersection with any horizontal line that does intersect it.)

We now want a method for locating maxima (or minima) of differentiable functions. We must notice that a function may not have a maximum or minimum, except in a trivial sense. Thus consider a monotonic increasing function. As $x \to \infty$, $f(x)$ continuously increases, and there is no maximum value [although there may be some upper bound, or limit, that $f(x)$ approaches]. If we restrict the domain of x to some interval $a \leq x \leq b$, then indeed x has a maximum, at the end point of the interval where $x = b$. We are not interested in this sort of maximum but in a maximum *within* an interval. To make this clear, we define what is called formally a *strict interior maximum* as follows:

The function $y = f(x)$ has a maximum in the interval $a \leq x \leq b$ at $x = \bar{x}$, $\bar{x} \neq a$, $\bar{x} \neq b$, if $f(x)$ for any value of $x \neq \bar{x}$ in the interval is less than $f(\bar{x})$.

This definition may seem a little imposing at first sight, but it really is a very simple concept. We are defining a maximum over some interval of variation of x between a lower limit of a and an upper limit of b. If the function has a maximum within that interval, we denote the value of x at which it occurs as $\bar{x}$. We exclude the possibility of $\bar{x}$ equaling a or b because, for example, any monotonic increasing function will have a maximum at b if the domain is defined to include a

and b. We are looking for the kind of maximum where $f(x)$ decreases in either direction from $\bar{x}$, and to ensure that we find only this kind of maximum it must be possible for x both to diminish and increase from $\bar{x}$ within the defined domain. If when this is done the value of the function is less than its value at $\bar{x}$ for any other x in the interval a to b, we say that the function has a maximum at $x = \bar{x}$.

It may be worth knowing that an interval written $a \leqslant x \leqslant b$ is called "closed" because it includes its own end points. If we meant "all numbers *between* a and b (but *excluding* a and b)," we should write $a < x < b$. The interval is then called "open." You are asked in Question 5 to consider whether a monotonic increasing function can reach a maximum value within an open interval. An interval, if it is understood to be small, is often called a "neighborhood." The $\bar{x}$ of our definition is an *interior point* of a *closed interval*, and we say that $f(\bar{x})$ is a maximum if $f(x) < f(\bar{x})$ for $x \neq \bar{x}$ in the neighborhood of $\bar{x}$.

A minimum is defined analogously.

Before we develop practical methods of locating maxima and minima, let us look at some geometrical illustrations. Consider the two curves and their tangents in Figures 6.1(a) and 6.1(b) (for simplicity, we confine our illustrations here to the positive orthant). Both curves have positive first derivatives: they are monotonic increasing (over the range and domain illustrated). Both lie entirely *on one side of the tangent*. The curve in Figure 6.1(a) is concave to the y-axis, and the curve in Figure 6.1(b) is convex to the y-axis. From our definition of a maximum, the curve of $f(x)$ must lie entirely on one side of its tangent in the neighborhood of $\bar{x}$: it must lie *below* it. This is illustrated in Figure 6.2(a). We see there that the tangent must have a positive slope if $x < \bar{x}$ and a negative slope if $x > \bar{x}$. This means that the first derivative must *change sign*, and this, in turn, is possible only if it equals zero at $x = \bar{x}$. Thus we have found a *necessary condition*

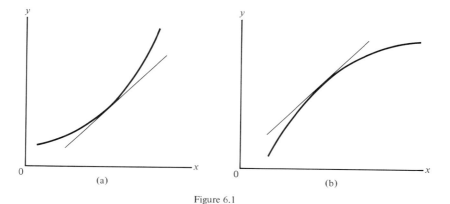

(a)   (b)

Figure 6.1

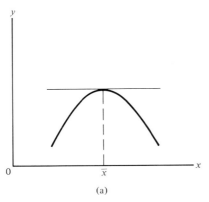
(a)

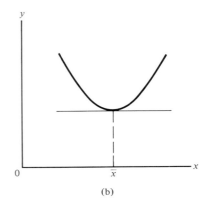
(b)

Figure 6.2

for a maximum: $f'(x) = 0$. [As is clear from Figure 6.2(b), this is a necessary condition for a minimum too: we shall shortly seek methods of distinguishing maxima and minima. Collectively, maxima and minima are known as *extrema*.]

The condition $f'(x) = 0$ is intuitively clear from the geometry. We may, however, obtain it rather more formally by remembering the definition of a derivative from Eq. (11), Section 4.3:

$$\frac{dy}{dx} = \lim_{h \to 0} \frac{f(x+h) - f(x)}{h} \quad .$$

Let us put $x = \bar{x}$, and choose h to be negative. Then, since $f(\bar{x})$ is a maximum, by hypothesis, $f(x+h) - f(x)$ is negative, and dy/dx is positive. Now choose h to be positive, and, by the same argument, dy/dx must be negative. But, if the function is differentiable at $x = \bar{x}$ as we have assumed, dy/dx must have a unique value as h goes to zero. If it is positive for negative h, negative for positive h, this limit can only be zero.[1]

In many practical cases, it will be obvious from inspection whether we have a maximum or a minimum where $f'(x) = 0$. After all, $f(x)$ must lie everywhere below the tangent at $\bar{x}$ if $f(\bar{x})$ is a maximum and everywhere above if $f(\bar{x})$ is a minimum. If the worst came to the

---

[1] The expressions we get with h negative and h positive are sometimes known as the left-hand and right-hand derivatives, respectively, referring to the side from which $\bar{x}$ is approached as h tends toward zero. We shall not use these terms elsewhere in this book, but it is interesting to note that they give us a good definition of differentiability or "smoothness": we may define a function as differentiable, within some interval, if, at any point within that interval, the left-hand and right-hand derivatives tend to the same limit.

worst, we could, after solving the equation $f'(x) = 0$ to find $\bar{x}$, simply plot a few values of $f(x)$ in the neighborhood of $\bar{x}$. There are, however, better methods, which are general in the sense that we do not need arithmetic, and are, in a wide range of cases of interest, extremely simple. Before discussing them, however, we have to consider the fact that, although $f'(x) = 0$ is a *necessary* condition for an extreme value to exist, it is not *sufficient*.

6.2 POINTS OF INFLEXION AND STATIONARY VALUES

Consider Figure 6.3(a), where the curve of $f(x)$ lies below the tangent at $x = \bar{x}$ for $x < \bar{x}$ and above the tangent for $x > \bar{x}$. Where this occurs, the point $\bar{x}$ is called a *point of inflexion*. In this case, the tangent has a positive slope, that is, $f'(x) > 0$. It is also possible to draw a curve that possesses a point of inflexion at a point where the tangent is horizontal: this is illustrated in Figure 6.3(b). Comparing Figures 6.3(b) with 6.2(a) and 6.2(b), which illustrate a maximum and a minimum, respectively, we see that the condition $f'(x) = 0$ is satisfied at $x = \bar{x}$ in all three cases. Where this condition holds we have what is called a *stationary value*. Stationary values occur where $f'(x) = 0$. They include maxima, minima, and values that are not extremal but inflexional.

There is clearly no risk of confusing stationary points with nonstationary inflexional points, since at the latter the first derivative is nonzero. We must, however, find a means of distinguishing maxima, minima, and inflexional stationary values. Our treatment of the problem, though not complete, will be sufficient to solve the problems we shall encounter in our economic applications.

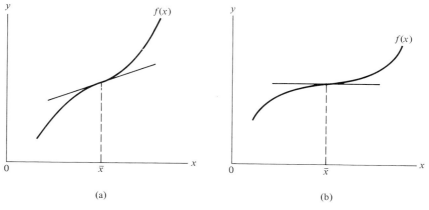

(a) (b)

Figure 6.3

Let us go back to the maximum illustrated in Figure 6.2(a) and consider the function $f'(x)$. We see that its value is decreasing everywhere in the neighborhood of $\bar{x}$: it is positive, then zero, and becomes negative when $x > \bar{x}$. It follows that *its* derivative must be negative in the neighborhood of $\bar{x}$. Its derivative is, of course, the second derivative of the original function, or $f''(x)$. Now consider the minimum illustrated in Figure 6.2(b). Here the first derivative is negative for $x < \bar{x}$, zero at $\bar{x}$, and positive for $x > \bar{x}$. Thus its derivative, $f''(x)$, is positive in the interval. Finally, consider Figure 6.3(b). $f'(x)$ is positive on both sides of $\bar{x}$ and zero at $\bar{x}$. If we go back to our original definition of an extreme value, in Section 6.1, we see that $f'(x)$ must have a minimum at $\bar{x}$. Hence *its* derivative, which is, of course, $f''(x)$, must be zero at $\bar{x}$.

Let us summarize what we now know.

1. A necessary and sufficient condition for there to be a stationary value of $f(x)$ at $\bar{x}$ is that $f'(\bar{x}) = 0$.
2. A sufficient condition for the stationary value at $\bar{x}$ to be a maximum is that $f''(\bar{x}) < 0$; a sufficient condition for the stationary value to be a minimum is $f''(\bar{x}) > 0$ (*first warning:* $f''(\bar{x}) = 0$ is not sufficient to tell us that we have neither a maximum nor a minimum); a necessary condition for the stationary value to be a point of inflexion is $f''(\bar{x}) = 0$ (*second warning:* as we shall see below, and as follows from our first warning, $f''(x) = 0$ is not *sufficient* to guarantee a point of inflexion).

Finally, although there is no danger of confusing a nonstationary inflexional point, such as that illustrated in Figure 6.3(a), with a stationary point, let us see if we can learn to distinguish the former more clearly. We see that the first derivative is positive on both sides of $\bar{x}$ and at $\bar{x}$ itself (this is why we are in no danger of picking such a point when we are looking for an extreme value). We also see that the slope diminishes as x approaches $\bar{x}$ and increases thereafter. It follows that, as in Figure 6.3(b), $f'(x)$ must have a minimum at $x = \bar{x}$. Thus if we find $f''(x) = 0$ where $f'(x) \neq 0$, we know that we have a nonstationary point of inflexion. (You are asked in Question 7 to consider how we might distinguish a nonstationary point of inflexion on a decreasing function.)

6.3 EXAMPLES

The last two sections may have seemed rather heavy going. It is not to be expected that anyone will grasp the whole contents immediately, and, unfortunately, there are yet more complications to worry about. Practice in working a few examples will, however, soon make the subject familiar, and we may defer consideration of complications.

Let us start by finding the extreme value of a quadratic

$$y = ax^2 + bx + c \quad . \tag{1}$$

The first thing to do is to find the first derivative:

$$\frac{dy}{dx} = 2ax + b \quad . \tag{2}$$

We know that a stationary value occurs where this is zero, so we must solve for x the equation

$$2ax + b = 0 \quad . \tag{3}$$

This is solved by

$$x = -\frac{b}{2a} \quad . \tag{4}$$

To find out what kind of stationary value this is, we take the second derivative of (1),

$$\frac{d^2y}{dx^2} = 2a \quad . \tag{5}$$

The sign of (5) depends on the sign of a. If a is positive, the quadratic has a minimum at $x = -b/2a$, that is, it is ∪-shaped, whereas if a is negative, the quadratic has a maximum at $x = -b/2a$, that is, it is ∩-shaped. If a is positive, then for large enough absolute values of x the function must be increasing, hence it must have a minimum at smaller x; and if a is negative the function must decrease for large enough x and correspondingly must have a maximum at a smaller x. (This is a good moment to do Question 1.)

It is clear that a quadratic has one and only one stationary point, which must be either a maximum or a minimum, since (3) can have only one solution, and (5) must be either positive or negative (it cannot be zero, since this would require $a = 0$, in which case (1) would not have been a quadratic but a straight line). If we are interested in finding the extreme value of y inself, we substitute (4) into (1) to obtain

$$y = \frac{b^2}{4a} - \frac{b^2}{2a} + c \quad , \tag{6}$$

which can be either positive or negative. Thus the extreme value of a quadratic, whether a maximum or a minimum, may occur at a positive or a negative value of y.

A numerical example may help. Let

$$y = 10x^2 - 5x + 1 \quad . \tag{7}$$

We find the first derivative and set it equal to zero:

$$\frac{dy}{dx} = 20x - 5 = 0 \quad . \tag{8}$$

The value of x that satisfies (8) is

$$\bar{x} = \tfrac{5}{20} = \tfrac{1}{4} \quad . \tag{9}$$

The next step is to find

$$\frac{d^2y}{dx^2} = 20 \quad , \tag{10}$$

which is positive for any x including, of course, $x = \bar{x}$. Finally, substituting from (9) into (7),

$$y = 10(\tfrac{1}{4})^2 - \tfrac{5}{4} + 1 = \tfrac{3}{8} \quad . \tag{11}$$

We have already seen that the second derivative of a quadratic is everywhere positive or everywhere negative. It follows that a quadratic cannot have a point of inflexion. To illustrate an inflexional point we must therefore choose from some other class of functions; and the simplest example of a point of inflexion of this sort is afforded by a cubic. Let

$$y = x^3 + 3x^2 + 3x \quad , \tag{12}$$

whence

$$\frac{dy}{dx} = 3x^2 + 6x + 3 \tag{13}$$

and

$$\frac{d^2y}{dx^2} = 6x + 6 \quad . \tag{14}$$

If there is a point of inflection, it will occur where $f''(x) = 0$. This is obviously the case if $x = -1$. Also, dividing (13) by 3 and setting it equal to zero, we obtain

$$x^2 + 2x + 1 = 0 \quad ,$$

which is satisfied by $x = -1$ and by no other value of x. Looking at (13) and (14), we see that (13) has a minimum at $x = -1$ and is everywhere positive. It follows that (12) is a nondecreasing function of x, whence y has a stationary value that is not an extreme value at $x = -1$ (where $y = -1$) and has no other stationary values. (It is a good idea to plot the function for a few values of x, and see how it behaves.)

Of course, not all cubics behave like this. Let us find the stationary values of

$$y = \tfrac{1}{3}x^3 + \tfrac{3}{2}x^2 - 4x + 10 \quad . \tag{15}$$

Set the first derivative equal to zero:

$$\frac{dy}{dx} = x^2 + 3x - 4 = 0 \quad , \tag{16}$$

which factors into

$$(x + 4)(x - 1) = 0 \quad , \tag{17}$$

so stationary values occur at $x = -4$ and $x = 1$. To discover what sort of stationary values they are, we look at the second derivative,

$$\frac{d^2y}{dx^2} = 2x + 3 = \begin{cases} -5 & \text{if } x = -4 \\ 5 & \text{if } x = 1 \end{cases} . \tag{18}$$

Thus we have a maximum at $x = -4$, and a minimum at $x = 1$, and no stationary value that is not an extreme value. The function also has a nonstationary point of inflection, which you should find for yourself.

Now let us consider another example:

$$y = \tfrac{1}{3}x^3 + \tfrac{1}{2}x^2 + x + 10 \quad . \tag{19}$$

Evaluating the derivatives,

$$\frac{dy}{dx} = x^2 + x + 1 \tag{20}$$

and

$$\frac{d^2y}{dx^2} = 2x + 1 \quad . \tag{21}$$

If there is a point of inflexion, it will occur where $f''(x) = 0$. This occurs at $x = -\tfrac{1}{2}$. At this value of x

$$\frac{dy}{dx} = \frac{1}{4} - \frac{1}{2} + 1 = \frac{3}{4} > 0 \quad .$$

The curve thus crosses its positively sloped tangent at $x = -\tfrac{1}{2}$. To find out if the function has extreme values, we must solve the equation

$$\frac{dy}{dx} = x^2 + x + 1 = 0 \quad . \tag{22}$$

This does not factor, so we must use the quadratic formula first introduced in Section 2.9:

$$x = \frac{-b \pm \sqrt{b^2 - 4ac}}{2a} \quad .$$

Substituting in,

$$x = \frac{-1 \pm \sqrt{1-4}}{2}$$

$$= \frac{-1 \pm \sqrt{-3}}{2}$$

$$= -\frac{1}{2} \pm \frac{\sqrt{3}}{2}\sqrt{-1} \quad . \tag{23}$$

Here we have the "square root of minus one," usually denoted by i, that we first encountered in Section 2.1. We can rewrite (23) as

$$x = -\frac{1}{2} \pm \frac{\sqrt{3}}{2}i \quad ,$$

which is a complex number. The result is that the equation $dy/dx = 0$ has only "complex roots." This means that there is no real value of x for which the function $y = \frac{1}{3}x^3 + \frac{1}{2}x^2 + x + 10$ has a stationary value. It has, as we have already seen, a nonstationary point of inflexion at $x = -\frac{1}{2}$.

Let us now look at a cubic that does have extreme values. We take

$$y = 4x^3 - 6x^2 - 24x + 120 \quad . \tag{24}$$

Setting the first derivative equal to zero,

$$12x^2 - 12x - 24 = 0 \quad . \tag{25}$$

We can divide through by 12 to obtain

$$x^2 - x - 2 = 0 \quad ,$$

which factors into

$$(x-2)(x+1) = 0 \quad , \tag{26}$$

so there are extreme values at $x = 2$ and $x = -1$. Taking the second derivative, we find

$$\frac{d^2y}{dx^2} = 24x - 12 = 12(2x - 1) \quad . \tag{27}$$

Evidently we need worry only about the sign of $2x - 1$, an expression which we could have obtained directly by taking the derivative of $x^2 - x - 2$. (27) is positive at $x = 2$ and negative at $x = -1$, so we have a minimum and a maximum, respectively. A little thought, or geometrical experiment, suggests, however, that if a maximum point and a minimum point are to be "connected up" by a smooth, continuous function, a point of inflexion in between is called for. It will have to be nonstationary to do the trick; and in any case we have already found all the stationary values of this function. To find the required point of inflexion, put

$$\frac{d^2y}{dx^2} = 24x - 12 = 0 \quad , \tag{28}$$

which is satisfied by $x = \frac{1}{2}$, a value which lies between $x = -1$ and $x = 2$, as we expected. (You now have all the information required to sketch the function. You will necessarily discover, in the process of sketching, where it is convex from above and where concave. Notice that you can check curvature from the third derivative if you wish. Thus at $x = \frac{1}{2}$, the nonstationary point of inflexion, $d^3y/dx^3 = 24 > 0$.)

As a last example, let us consider the function

$$y = \frac{4 + x^2}{x} \quad . \tag{29}$$

A little rearrangement is required: we separate the two terms to obtain

$$y = 4x^{-1} + x \quad .$$

We note that, since division by zero is undefined, this function has a discontinuity at $x = 0$. It has, however, two continuous branches, over the negative and positive halves of the real line, which we may investigate. Setting the first derivative equal to zero, we have

$$\frac{dy}{dx} = -4x^{-2} + 1 = 0$$

or

$$x^2 = 4 \quad ,$$

whence

$$x = \pm 2 \quad .$$

We have two stationary values. Also,

$$\frac{d^2y}{dx^2} = 8x^{-3} \quad .$$

(Note that neither of the derivatives is defined at $x = 0$, which should not surprise us.) If $x = 2$ we have

$$\frac{d^2y}{dx^2} = \frac{8}{8} = 1 > 0 \quad ,$$

whence $x = 2$ is a minimum, whereas if $x = -2$, we have

$$\frac{d^2y}{dx^2} = \frac{8}{-8} = -1 < 0 \quad ,$$

whence $x = -2$ is a maximum.

6.4 CONCLUDING REMARKS

It is time to gather up some loose ends. The first concerns the nature of the maxima or minima we have learned to locate. Our original definition of a maximum of $f(x)$ was defined on an *interval* of the real line. This is deliberate: according to our definition, a function $f(x)$, defined over some domain of x, may have any number of extreme values. Figure 6.4 illustrates some functions with multiple extrema. Let us consider in particular the curve marked (a). The tangent to this curve is horizontal at three points, two of which, x_1 and x_2, are at maximum values of the function. It is obvious by inspection that $f(x_2) > f(x_1)$. Our methods do not, however, discriminate between these values. We appear to have a deficiency.

The answer is that calculus methods are designed to locate *all* such points. If we want to know which "maximum" is the largest, we must substitute the solution values of x_1, x_2, etc., back into the original function, $f(x)$. If the function is specified generally, without numbers, we are unlikely to be able to find out which of $f(x_1)$, $f(x_2)$, etc., is the largest. We say that calculus methods discover "local," or "relative," extreme values, but not necessarily the "most" extreme, or "global" maximum or minimum. Indeed, this is true: in general, all that calculus can do is to discover (all) the local extrema. This is why we were so careful, in our definition, to consider a maximum of $f(x)$ only over an interval of x. For some purposes, this deficiency may be serious, but, as we shall see, for a wide range of applications we have all the tools we need.

The second loose end is easily stated. We have developed meth-

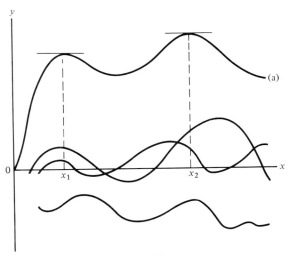

Figure 6.4

ods for locating the extreme values of differentiable functions: it does not follow that nondifferentiable functions do not have extreme values, but only that calculus methods will not serve to locate them. Thus consider the function $y = |x|$ which we considered in Section 2.6 and illustrated in Figure 2.10. This function obviously has an extremal value (minimum) at $x = 0$, but it has no derivative at that point, as we have seen, so that the methods we have developed in this chapter would not serve to locate the minimum. All this means is that if we had to consider nondifferentiable functions, we should have to develop other methods for locating their extrema. We can, however, do so much with differentiable functions that we shall not concern ourselves here with other cases.

We now discuss a third loose end, but shall leave it a little loose, since it will occasion no trouble in any of the economic applications we wish to use. The loose end is suggested by the nondifferentiable function $f(x) = |x|$, which has its minimum at $x = 0$. Let us consider a differentiable function that has a stationary value at $x = 0$. An example is

$$f(x) = ax^4 \quad .$$

The first derivative is

$$f'(x) = 4ax^3 \quad .$$

This can be zero only if $x = 0$. Thus ax^4 has a stationary value at $x = 0$. But what kind? To answer this, we have learned to look at the second derivative,

$$f''(x) = 12ax^2 \quad .$$

At $x = 0$, however, $f''(x) = 0$ whatever the sign of a. We can, in fact, be quite sure that whether the extremum at $x = 0$ is a maximum or a minimum depends solely on the sign of a, since $x^4 > 0$ for any nonzero value of x, but the second derivative is no help. This is a little disconcerting: the derivative is not telling us something that is, in fact, obvious. For luck, if for no other reason, let us try differentiating again. We obtain

$$f'''(x) = 24ax \quad . \tag{30}$$

The sign of (30) still depends on the sign of x, and (30) is, of course, zero where $x = 0$. We differentiate yet again, to obtain

$$f''''(x) = 24a \quad . \tag{31}$$

The sign of this derivative is determined by the sign of a, independent of the value of x. Since $x^4 > 0$ for any x, we are sure that it is only the sign of a that determines whether a maximum or a minimum occurs at $x = 0$. We may at last check this in (31).

Rather than trying to generalize, let us consider the function

$$f(x) = ax^3 \quad . \tag{32}$$

The first derivative is

$$f'(x) = 3ax^2 \quad . \tag{33}$$

Thus, as in (27), a stationary value occurs where $x = 0$ and nowhere else. Differentiating again, we have

$$f''(x) = 6ax \quad . \tag{34}$$

Again, (34) is zero at $x = 0$. We differentiate again:

$$f'''(x) = 6a \quad . \tag{35}$$

This suggests a maximum or minimum, at $x = 0$, depending on the sign of a. From inspection of (32), however, we can see that this is wrong. For $x > 0$, x^3 is monotonic increasing; for $x < 0$, x^3 is negative, but also monotonic increasing (as x increases from larger to smaller negative values, x^3 does the same). It follows that x^3 has no extreme values, whence $x = 0$ must be a point of inflexion of the sort illustrated in Figure 6.3(b) (but with $\bar{x} = 0$ and $f(\bar{x}) = 0$: it would be a good plan to draw the figure for yourself).

All this looks rather messy, and, indeed, it is. Furthermore, we shall not attempt to clear up the mess. What we shall do is restate the rules we may depend on, and which turn out to be all we need for our purposes.

1. $f'(\bar{x}) = 0$ is a *necessary and sufficient* condition for a (local) stationary value at $x = \bar{x}$.
2. $f''(x) \neq 0$ (negative, positive) is a *sufficient* condition for the stationary value to be a (local) extremum (maximum, minimum).
3. If $f''(\bar{x})$ is zero, we have to inquire further [in particular, if $f'(\bar{x})$ is not zero, we have a nonstationary point of inflexion, but if $f'(\bar{x}) = 0$, we must look at higher-order derivatives].

We do not attempt to give a complete rule. The fact is that rules 1 and 2 are all we need to deal with a wide range of important economic applications.

QUESTIONS

1. The quadratic $y = ax^2 + bx + c$ has either a maximum or a minimum at $x = -b/2a$. What determines the quadrant in which this value occurs?

2. Find the values of x that give extreme values of the following functions, and determine whether they are maxima or minima.
   a. $y = 10x - 0.2x^2$
   b. $y = 100 - 2x + 0.01x^2$
   c. $y = 5 + 10x - x^2$
   d. $y = 5 + 10x + x^2$
   e. $y = \frac{1}{2}x^2 + x + 1$

3. Find the maximum and minimum of
$$y = \tfrac{1}{15}x^3 - \tfrac{3}{10}x^2 - 2x + 10 \quad .$$
   Has it a nonstationary inflexional point? Draw a rough sketch of the function.

4. Find the stationary and inflexional value(s) of the following.
   a. $y = \frac{1}{3}x^3 + x^2 + x + 1$
   b. $y = \frac{1}{3}x^3 - x + 10$
   c. $y = \dfrac{x^3 + 4x^2 + 5x + 2}{x + 1}$
   d. $y = (x^2 - 1)^2$
   e. $y = x^3 + 2x^2 - 7x + 1$
   f. $y = \frac{1}{3}x^3 + \frac{1}{2}x^2 - 2x + 10$

5. If a monotonic increasing function of x is defined on an interval $a \leqslant x \leqslant b$, its maximum within the interval is at $x = b$. Does it have a maximum within the open interval $a < x < b$?

6. Construct a proof, analogous to that in Section 6.2, that $f'(x) = 0$ where a local *minimum* of $f(x)$ occurs.

7. How would we proceed to locate a nonstationary point of inflexion on a *decreasing* function?

8. We illustrated [Figure 6.2(a)] a local maximum in the positive orthant only. What part of our definition should we have to alter if the maximum occurred in another orthant?

9. Does a rectangular hyperbola have any extreme values?

10. State both a necessary condition and a sufficient condition for $y = f(x)$ to have
    a. A minimum.
    b. A maximum.
    c. A nonstationary point of inflexion.
    d. Does $f'' < 0$ at a particular value for x, say $x°$, give either a sufficient or a necessary condition for a maximum of the function when $x = x°$?

11. Consider $y = (x^2 + 5)^{1/2}$. Determine if the function has any stationary points, and indicate for each whether it is a maximum, a minimum, or a a point of inflexion. Sketch the curve. Compare that function to $y^2 = x^2 + 5$, and point out the difference between the two.

12. Find the stationary points of $y = ax^2 + bx + c$ in the open interval $0 < x < -b/2a$. Do the same for the closed interval $0 \le x \le -b/2a$. Discuss.

13. Determine the maximum, in the domain $0 < x \le 10$, if it exists, of the following.
   a. $y = 0$
   b. $x = 0$
   c. $y = 5$
   d. $y = 5x$
   e. $y = 5 + 5x$
   f. $y = 5 - 5x$
   g. $y = 1 - 40x + x^2$
   h. $y = 11 - |x - 12|$

14. Consider two functions $z = z(x)$ and $w = w(x)$ and the composite function $y = xz - w$. Determine a necessary condition, and a sufficient condition, for y to achieve a maximum. Notice that $y'' < 0$ at a given value of x, denoted by x°, is not a sufficient condition for y maximum at $x = x^\circ$.

15. Use the rules for differentiating compound expressions to find an extreme value for $y = (x + 1)(x - 1)$, and show that the extreme is at zero and is a minimum.

16. Use the chain rule to find dy/dx for

$$y = \left(\frac{3x + 2}{10}\right)^{1/3} \quad .$$

Chapter 7

Economic Applications of Maxima and Minima

In this chapter we consider applications of maxima and minima. Our applications are mainly from micro-economics since these techniques are not directly relevant to most problems studied in *simple* macro-economic models. We shall find, however, enough micro-examples to keep us very busy!

The Competitive Market

7.1 MAXIMIZING THE YIELD OF AN EXCISE TAX

In Section 5.2 we investigated the effect on tax yield of changes in tax rate (specific excise tax; competitive market; linear demand and supply) and obtained the expression [Eq. (12)]

$$\frac{dT}{dt} = \frac{ad - bc}{d - b} + \frac{2bdt}{d - b} \quad , \tag{1}$$

which we found to be positive for some values of t and negative for others. We can now show that there is indeed a unique tax rate that maximizes yield. Setting $dT/dt = 0$, we obtain

$$\frac{2bdt}{d - b} = -\frac{ad - bc}{d - b} \quad ,$$

whence

$$t = \frac{bc - ad}{d - b} \cdot \frac{d - b}{2bd}$$

$$= \frac{bc - ad}{2bd} \quad . \tag{2}$$

We must make sure that the maximum occurs at a positive value of t and that it is a maximum rather than a minimum. Our standard assumptions are $b < 0$, $d > 0$, $0 < c < a$, which ensure that $t > 0$. [bc is negative, and ad is positive; hence the numerator of (2) is negative, but the denominator is negative because b is negative, so (2) is positive.] Further,

$$\frac{d^2T}{dt^2} = \frac{2bd}{d-b} < 0 \quad , \tag{3}$$

so we do indeed have a maximum.

We get a striking result if we manipulate the expression for the value of t that maximizes T. In our supply and demand functions, we took q as the dependent variable, although in the conventional Marshallian diagram q appears on the horizontal axis. Let us see what happens if we treat p as the dependent variable. We now read the demand equation as showing the price at which consumers will clear the market of each quantity, and the supply equation as showing the price required to induce suppliers to put each quantity on the market. Thus instead of the q^d and q^s of our earlier treatment, we shall have p^d and p^s, which we may call demand price and supply price, respectively. In the linear case, demand price is given by

$$p^d = \alpha + \beta q \tag{4}$$

and supply price by

$$p^s = \gamma + \delta q \quad . \tag{5}$$

We also have the equilibrium condition

$$p^d = p^s + t \quad . \tag{6}$$

Substituting,

$$\alpha + \beta q = \gamma + \delta q + t \quad ,$$

whence

$$q = \frac{\gamma - \alpha}{\beta - \delta} + \frac{t}{\beta - \delta} \tag{7}$$

(notice that, if the demand curve slopes down and the supply curve up, $\beta - \delta < 0$, but we must also have $\alpha > \gamma$, i.e., $\gamma - \alpha < 0$).

Now

$$T = tq = \frac{\gamma - \alpha}{\beta - \delta} t + \frac{t^2}{\beta - \delta} \quad . \tag{8}$$

For maximum yield we put

$$\frac{dT}{dt} = \frac{\gamma - \alpha}{\beta - \delta} + \frac{2t}{\beta - \delta} = 0 \quad ,$$

whence

$$t = \frac{1}{2} \frac{(\alpha - \gamma)}{(\beta - \delta)} (\beta - \delta)$$

$$= \frac{1}{2} (\alpha - \gamma) \quad , \tag{9}$$

or one half of the difference of the intercepts on the price axis: that is, t is independent of the slope coefficients β and δ. We may consider this result rather striking, since relations of this sort usually turn out to depend on elasticities, and since the slope coefficients are absent from (9), this result cannot be expressed in terms of elasticities.

It remains to be shown that we did get the same result earlier in Eq. (2), that is, that

$$\frac{bc - ad}{bd} = \alpha - \gamma \quad .$$

This simply requires rearranging the demand and supply functions:

$$q^d = a + bp$$

or

$$p^d = \frac{-a}{b} + \frac{q}{b} \quad ;$$

$$q^s = c + dp$$

or

$$p^s = \frac{-c}{d} + \frac{q}{d} \quad .$$

So we put

$$\alpha = -\frac{a}{b}$$

$$\beta = \frac{1}{b}$$

$$\gamma = -\frac{c}{d} \tag{10}$$

$$\delta = \frac{1}{d}$$

when we want to work with p as the dependent variable. Checking,

$$\alpha - \gamma = \left(-\frac{a}{b} - \frac{-c}{d}\right)$$

$$= -\left(\frac{a}{b} - \frac{c}{d}\right)$$

$$= \frac{bc - ad}{bd} \quad.$$

The price-axis intercepts, α and γ, depend, as can be seen from (10), on the quantity intercepts, a and c, *and* on the slope coefficients, b and d; but once we have found the price-axis intercepts, we can express the yield-maximizing tax rate directly as half their difference, without further consideration of the slope coefficients.

The Model of Income Determination

7.2 MAXIMIZING THE YIELD OF AN INCOME TAX

We have now followed our regular practice of applying each new piece of technique in turn to the solution of a problem in our linear model of a perfect market. Following the same practice, we should now take up our linear macro-model. We shall, however, find few examples of the application of maxima and minima to elementary macroeconomics. The reason is quite simple. If we are only trying to maximize income or employment, we proceed to the full-employment ceiling, illustrated in Figure 3.5, without requiring the maximization technique: we go as far in one direction as we can. If, on the other hand, we are trying to make an optimal choice given a constraint between, for example, ΔY and ΔB (see Figure 3.6), we are dealing with a more complicated problem than we yet have the technique for, a problem of choice in two variables where the possibilities are limited or constrained by a function of two variables, Y and B. In microeconomics, on the other hand, the assumption that firms try to maximize profits obviously invites us to apply the techniques of Chapter 6. There is, however, one straightforward application of the theory of maxima to macroeconomics that we may take up first.

A plausible-sounding intuitive argument goes as follows: the higher the rate of income tax, the lower is income, given autonomous spending, but the more yield is obtained from taxing any given income; trading one effect off against the other, we should find a rate of income tax that maximizes tax yield. With the analytical tools we now have, we can show that, at least in our simple linear model of income determination, this is a fallacy. For the closed economy, we have

$$T = tY = tkZ \quad , \tag{11}$$

where

$$k = \frac{1}{1 - c(1 - t)}$$

is the multiplier and Z is the sum of autonomous expenditures. Differentiating (11),

$$\frac{dT}{dt} = \left(t\frac{dk}{dt} + k \right)Z \tag{12}$$

by the product rule. We have already found [in Section 5.3, Eq. (15)] that

$$\frac{dk}{dt} = -ck^2 \quad ,$$

so we substitute this into (12). Necessary conditions for a maximum require

$$-ctk^2 + k = 0$$

or

$$k(1 - ctk) = 0 \tag{13}$$

[since Z cannot be zero, (13) must be true if the whole derivative is to be zero]. Equation (13) is satisfied only if either k or $1 - ctk$ is zero; but neither is possible if we assume that $0 < c < 1$ and $0 < t < 1$, as we have done (see Section 3.10). If we put $1 - ctk = 0$, we obtain $t = 1/ck$. What this amounts to is simply that the function $T = tkZ$ does not have a maximum if $0 < c < 1$ and $0 < t < 1$.

It is easy to see that T is in fact a monotonic increasing function of t; that is, dT/dt is everywhere positive (for positive t). From (12) and (13) we may write $dT/dt = k(1 - ckt)Z$, which is positive if $ckt < 1$, which we proved in Section 3.10. If t were exactly unity, then $k = 1/[1 - c(1 - t)] = 1$, and T would equal Z, that is, 100 percent taxation takes all autonomous income (expenditure) and leaves no induced income. Any reduction in taxation below 100 percent reduces yield because the increase in taxable income is more than offset by the reduction in rate. Values of t in excess of unity of course make no economic sense: people do not have unlimited resources out of which to pay taxes in excess of their incomes. Nonetheless, taxes in excess of 100 percent would, if they were possible, actually increase tax yield. T, that is, is monotonic increasing in t for all positive t, not merely for values of t between zero and 1. It follows that T is not maximized by any t short of infinity, which is why we cannot solve Eq. (13), the condition for $dT/dt = 0$, for a finite value of t.

We could have obtained this result directly from Section 5.4 where we examined Eq. (17),

$$\frac{d}{dt}\Delta D = k(ctk - 1) \quad,$$

and showed this to be negative. If the deficit is a monotonic *decreasing* function of the tax rate, tax yield is a monotonic *increasing* function, and obviously

$$\frac{dT}{dt} = -\frac{d}{dt}\Delta D$$

if G is constant.

This result may in fact be a little surprising: the intuitive argument that suggests that there should be a maximum seems convincing. But remember that, if we have two offsetting effects, there is no reason why there should always be an extreme value or point of balance between the two effects — it is perfectly possible that one is always stronger than the other, and we found other examples of this in Chapter 5. We have, of course, a very simple static model here. We have neglected any incentive or disincentive effects of changed tax rates; and by taking all investment to be autonomous we have ignored the direct effects of taxation on investment as well as any accelerator effects via the change in income. We may, however, conclude that, if anyone still believes the intuitive argument that there is a yield-maximizing rate short of infinity, the burden of proof is on him to produce a less simplified model in which this is true. It would not be an easy task.

Miscellaneous Applications

7.3 AVERAGE AND MARGINAL RELATIONS

We now pass on from our basic models to consider some miscellaneous but very important topics in the theory of the firm. In this section we prove one or two very familiar results. We then take up an entirely new topic, profit maximization, and, after deriving the equilibrium conditions, attempt some comparative static analysis. This proves to be easy enough when we take linear examples but ambitious in the general case, so that Section 7.7 is starred.

First, let us demonstrate the well-known textbook relation that the marginal product curve passes through the maximum point of the average product curve. If output is given by

$$q = g(l) \quad, \tag{14}$$

then average product (AP) is given by

$$\frac{q}{l} = \frac{g(l)}{l} \qquad (15)$$

and marginal product by

$$\frac{dq}{dl} = g'(l) \quad . \qquad (16)$$

To find the maximum point on the AP curve, we set

$$\frac{d}{dl}\left(\frac{q}{l}\right) = 0 \quad .$$

Applying the quotient rule to (15), we have

$$\frac{lg'(l) - g(l)}{l^2} = 0 \quad .$$

Multiplying both sides by l^2 we obtain

$$lg'(l) - g(l) = 0 \quad ,$$

or

$$\frac{g(l)}{l} = g'(l) \quad ;$$

i.e.,

$$AP = MP \quad .$$

(The proof that MC passes through the minimum point on AC — if the latter has a minimum — is similar and is left to Question 3.)

As a second exercise we consider the elasticity of demand at the point on the demand function where total revenue is at a maximum. We obtained the derivative of the total revenue function with respect to quantity in Section 5.8. Now to find the maximum, set the derivative equal to zero:

$$\frac{dR(q)}{dq} = q \cdot f'(q) + f(q) = 0 \quad , \qquad (17)$$

whence, at the maximum,

$$f'(q) = -\frac{f(q)}{q} = \frac{-p}{q} \quad . \qquad (18)$$

But the elasticity of demand is defined by

$$\eta = \frac{dq}{dp} \cdot \frac{p}{q} \quad . \qquad (19)$$

Substituting for $f'(q)$ from Eq. (18), we find that at the maximum point on $R(q)$

$$\eta = \frac{-q}{p} \cdot \frac{p}{q} = -1 \quad . \tag{20}$$

This is yet another general result and yet another example of the power of notation. In obtaining (20) we have used the first-order conditions for a maximum, the definition of η, and the assumption that there is a value of q that satisfies (17), i.e., that the revenue function has a maximum. We have demonstrated that (20) will hold for *any* demand function such that the revenue function does have a maximum.

7.4 PROFIT MAXIMIZATION

We may now take up the important topic of profit maximization. We discussed at the beginning of Chapter 6 some methodological aspects of the maximizing hypothesis. We now address ourselves directly to the maximizing conditions as a preparation for the comparative static analysis from which we hope to obtain some testable predictions.

We define profit, Π, as the difference between revenue, R, and costs, C. If we express revenue and costs as functions of quantity, then $\Pi = \Pi(q) = R(q) - C(q)$. This we can do since $R = pq$, and we can take p either as a constant (perfect competition), or as a function of the quantity (nonperfect competition). Thus we are able to reduce the problem to one in a single variable, just as we did in the competitive market example of Section 3.1, where, by substitution, we were able to solve a single equation for equilibrium quantity and then substitute into either the demand or the supply equation to find the corresponding price. Now if

$$\Pi = R(q) - C(q) \quad , \tag{21}$$

to find profit-maximizing output we set the first derivative equal to zero, so we require the q that satisfies

$$\frac{d\Pi}{dq} = \frac{dR}{dq} - \frac{dC}{dq} = 0$$

or

$$MR = \frac{dR}{dq} = \frac{dC}{dq} = MC \quad . \tag{22}$$

[If $p = f(q)$, we have already seen that $dR/dq = qf'(q) + f(q)$.] (22) is the necessary condition, and, if this is satisfied, then a sufficient condition is

$$\frac{d^2\Pi}{dq^2} = \frac{d^2R}{dq^2} - \frac{d^2C}{dq^2} < 0 \quad . \tag{23}$$

These conditions are very familiar. (22) requires equality of marginal cost and marginal revenue; if (23) is satisfied, the marginal cost curve must cut the marginal revenue curve from beneath, that is, $MC > MR$ to the right of the equilibrium value $\bar{q}$. Unless we have the actual cost and revenue functions, however, we cannot find $\bar{q}$ explicitly from Eq. (22). If we have $\bar{q}$, we may also substitute back into the demand function to find price (in cases in which it is not a constant).

Our aim is, of course, to obtain some comparative static predictions but, in the general nonlinear case, this proves to be rather difficult. If, however, we assume that the demand and cost functions are linear, it is quite easy. We shall therefore start by working out two examples, one linear and one nonlinear, in this section and the next. Then, in Section 7.6, we shall subject the linear example to some comparative static analysis. The analysis of the general nonlinear case, in which our knowledge is confined to qualitative restrictions, is left to Section 7.7, which is starred to indicate that it is difficult and may be omitted.

To construct a linear model of a firm in nonperfect competition (a monopolist) we assume that

$$C = k + cq \tag{24}$$

and[1] that

$$p = a - bq \quad , \tag{25}$$

whence

$$R = pq = aq - bq^2 \tag{26}$$

[it is by (26) that we are able to reduce the problem to one in a single variable]. Now

$$\Pi = R - C = aq - bq^2 - k - cq \quad . \tag{27}$$

We set the first derivative equal to zero:

$$\frac{d\Pi}{dq} = a - 2bq - c = 0 \quad ,$$

whence

$$2bq = a - c$$

---

[1] Notice that we now write $-bq$ in the demand function instead of $+bq$. This simply means that the condition for the demand curve to slope down is now that b be a *positive* number.

or

$$q = \frac{a - c}{2b} \quad , \tag{28}$$

and to find p we substitute from (28) into (25),

$$p = a - b\frac{a - c}{2b}$$

or

$$p = \frac{a + c}{2} \quad . \tag{29}$$

Equation (29) gives the surprising result that the profit-maximizing price is independent of the slope of the demand curve. This may remind us of our earlier result in Section 7.1, Eq. (9), that the yield-maximizing excise tax was independent of the slopes of the demand and supply curves. We saw that (9) was the result of taking price as the dependent variable, whereupon the price-axis intercepts actually depend on the slope coefficients. What is the reason for the analogous result in (29)? We have constant marginal cost, c, which must be equal to marginal revenue, so equilibrium requires the same marginal revenue whatever the slope of the demand curve. If, however, $p = a - bq$ and we keep the intercept, a, constant, varying the slope, b, we trace out a family of iso-elastic demand curves,[2] and two demand curves with the same elasticity at a given price give the same marginal revenue at that price. So, in the case of a linear demand curve *and* constant marginal cost, price *is* independent of the slope of the demand curve. (You should illustrate this result geometrically and satisfy yourself that it makes sense.)

It remains to check what seems obvious in the linear case, that we have found a maximum and not a minimum. Differentiating (27),

$$\frac{d^2\Pi}{dq^2} = -2b < 0 \quad , \tag{30}$$

as required.

---

[2] In case the notion of iso-elastic demand curves is unfamiliar, we explain it here: we say that two demand curves are iso-elastic when they have the same elasticity at every common price. To show that a family of linear demand curves with a common intercept is iso-elastic, take an arbitrary price $\bar{p}$. Since $p = a - bq$, we can write $b = (a - \bar{p})/q$. Now $\eta = (dq/dp)(p/q)$ and $dq/dp = 1/(dp/dq) = -1/b$. Since $q = (a - p)/b$, $-1/b = -q/(a - b)$. Thus at $\bar{p}$,

$$\eta = \frac{-q}{a - \bar{p}} \cdot \frac{\bar{p}}{q} = -\frac{\bar{p}}{a - \bar{p}} \quad .$$

This says that if we fix a and $\bar{p}$, η is given independently of the slope coefficient. This is a good moment to work out for yourself, if you do not already happen to know it, that all linear supply curves through the origin have the same elasticity (unity).

7.5 A NONLINEAR EXAMPLE

Before going on to comparative statics, it seems prudent to be sure that we can manage a nonlinear example. This once again involves us in nonlinear cost functions. Construction of a cost function with a prescribed list of characteristics is quite an exacting task.

We have already seen in Section 5.7 that a ∪-shaped marginal cost curve must be of at least second degree (a quadratic). Consideration of the rule for taking the derivative of a power function, $d(ax^n)/dx = anx^{n-1}$, makes it clear that the total cost function must be one degree higher, at least a cubic. If its first derivative is to fall and then rise, however, the total cost function must have a point of inflexion, and we can show that this point occurs where marginal cost is at a minimum. If we want a particular function to serve as an illustration of a possible cost function, however, we require some other characteristics. We certainly expect total cost to be a monotonic increasing function of output, and this means that the function must increase for all (positive) values of q: if it has a point of inflexion, it must not be a stationary value. We also require that marginal cost be everywhere positive. Now, we saw in Chapter 6 that, at a nonstationary point of inflexion, the first derivative is nonzero but that the second is zero, and this is precisely what we require. Where marginal cost is positive but at a minimum, its derivative, which is the second derivative of total cost, is zero, and here is our nonstationary point of inflexion, dividing the region of increasing returns to the variable factor from that of decreasing returns.

A cost function with the required properties is

$$C = \tfrac{1}{3}q^3 - 5q^2 + 30q + 10 \quad , \tag{31}$$

and it is a good exercise to check for yourself that it does have the properties claimed. If you set the first derivative of (31) equal to zero, you will find an equation with no real roots—application of the formula for solving a quadratic will lead to an expression involving $\sqrt{-1}$. This means, of course, that the marginal cost curve does *not* cross the horizontal axis, which is as it should be.

The cost function (31) is consistent with perfect competition, so we may as well complete the illustration for practice, setting $p = \bar{p} = 6$. Now

$$\Pi = 6q - \tfrac{1}{3}q^3 + 5q^2 - 30q - 10 \quad . \tag{32}$$

We require the value of q that satisfies

$$\frac{d\Pi}{dq} = 6 - q^2 + 10q - 30 = 0 \quad , \tag{33}$$

or, rearranging, that satisfies

$$q^2 - 10q + 24 = 0 \quad .$$

This factors into

$$(q - 6)(q - 4) = 0 \quad .$$

Hence (33) is solved by $q = 4$ or 6. We expect that at the smaller value Π is at a minimum and at the larger it is at a maximum. This is confirmed by inspecting

$$\frac{d^2\Pi}{dq^2} = -2q + 10 \quad , \tag{34}$$

which is negative if $q > 5$, as expected. (The profitability of this firm is investigated in the questions at the end of this chapter.)

Comparative Statics

7.6 COMPARATIVE STATICS IN THE LINEAR CASE

In Chapter 3 we first discussed comparative statics and the idea of looking for qualitative predictions, which proved, in general, to mean looking for the signs of the derivatives of endogenous variables with respect to exogenous variables or parameters. To start our comparative static analysis of the profit-maximizing model, we need something that we can use as an exogenous variable, or a "shift parameter" such as the price of an input, or a tax rate. It is easier to introduce a tax rate than an input price, and we shall use this example for the moment. Hence we shall introduce an excise tax—as usual—to the linear-monopoly case of Section 7.4. If a specific tax is imposed at t per unit, we may regard this as an addition to variable costs, so the cost function becomes

$$C = k + cq + tq \tag{35}$$

and

$$\Pi = aq - bq^2 - k - cq - tq \tag{36}$$

if we retain the demand function of (25). We solve the equation

$$\frac{d\Pi}{dq} = a - 2bq - c - t = 0$$

for q, whence

$$q = \frac{a - (c + t)}{2b} \quad . \tag{37}$$

Comparison of (37) with (28) shows that we have merely moved the MC curve up by the amount of the tax. We expect that the effect of the tax is to reduce q, and this is confirmed: differentiating (37), we find $dq/dt = -1/2b < 0$. We also expect to find an increase in price. Substituting (37) into the demand equation (25), we find

$$p = a - b\frac{a - c - t}{2b}$$

$$= \frac{a + c + t}{2} \quad , \tag{38}$$

which is evidently larger than $(a + c)/2$. Equation (38) is what we want: it expresses the endogenous variable, p, as a function of the shift parameter, t. It is a simple linear relationship, and obviously

$$\frac{dp}{dt} = \frac{1}{2} > 0 \quad . \tag{39}$$

(39) is signed, which is a success: we have proved that increasing the tax does indeed increase price. That it does so by half the tax change is due to our choice of linear functions. (Notice that $AR = a - bq$ and $MR = a - 2bq$. This is a good moment to do Question 6.)

7.7* QUALITATIVE COMPARATIVE STATICS AND SECOND-ORDER CONDITIONS

This is an ambitious section, which will stretch our available technique to the limit. What we want to do is to generalize our result by proving $dp/dt > 0$ where we do not have specific functions but only assume qualitative restrictions such as a downward-sloping demand curve. It turns out that we can produce a general proof, and an important one, since it is an example of a class of results that is of great generality.

Suppose we merely have

$$R = qf(q) \tag{40}$$

$$C = g(q) + tq \tag{41}$$

and the qualitative knowledge that the demand curve slopes down and that marginal cost is everywhere positive. Since we require the equilibrium condition for maximizing profits, we start by obtaining

$$\frac{d\Pi}{dq} = qf'(q) + f(q) - g'(q) - t = 0 \quad . \tag{42}$$

This gives

$$q = \frac{g'(q) + t - f(q)}{f'(q)} \quad . \tag{43}$$

It would be tempting to conclude that $dq/dt = 1/f'(q)$ – and quite wrong. The change in tax leads to a change in equilibrium price, so $f(q)$ changes, and with it $f'(q)$; and as q changes so will $g'(q)$. The equilibrium values of price, quantity, marginal revenue, and marginal cost are all interdependent, and if we disturb equilibrium by changing the tax, we have to sort out simultaneously the changes required for a new equilibrium. We have, of course, done this in our linear examples, but the general case is more subtle than anything we have done so far.

It helps to consider the form of the relationship we now have between the endogenous variable q and the shift parameter t. A simple rearrangement of (42) gives

$$q \cdot f'(q) + f(q) - g'(q) = t \quad . \tag{44}$$

The left-hand side of (44) is a function of q, which we may write as $F(q)$. The equilibrium condition is that (42) – or (44) – *must* be satisfied if profits are to be maximized, whatever the value of t, and we can express the equilibrium condition in the form of (44) as

$$F(q) = t \quad . \tag{44a}$$

Solution of (44a) gives the equilibrium value, $\bar{q}$, for any t, and we can look on it as merely another form of the function relating an endogenous to an exogenous variable. In our earlier examples, we have always been able to express the dependent variable as an explicit function of the shift parameter, but the difference between (44) and an earlier example is only the difference between an expression of the form $q = h(t)$ and of the form $F(q) = t$. Evidently we can expect to obtain the explicit form $q = h(t)$ only where we have the actual functions. We have, however, consistently taken as our goal the discovery of general qualitative comparative static predictions; and, in general, we do not have the functions specified and therefore can only get forms such as $F(q) = t$. If, therefore, we can make headway in this case, we have made a big step forward in extending the scope and generality of our comparative static analysis.

It turns out that, given the assumption that equilibrium conditions are satisfied, systematic appeal to the chain rule will do the trick for us. Notice that, if $F(q) = t$ is our equilibrium condition, it must still be satisfied by an appropriate value of q if t is changed to, say, t': for equilibrium, we must still find q such that $F(q) = t'$. But if this is the case, then it must be true that

$$\frac{dF(q)}{dt} = \frac{dt}{dt}$$

or

$$\frac{d}{dt}[qf'(q) + f(q) - g'(q)] = 1 \quad, \tag{45}$$

and all we have to do now is take the derivative indicated in (45). This in fact is not too troublesome, since, by the rule for taking the derivative of a sum of functions, we may proceed term by term.

Consider first the second term, $f(q)$. Now, $f(q) = p$, and, by the chain rule, we must have

$$\frac{dp}{dt} = \frac{dp}{dq} \cdot \frac{dp}{dt} \quad,$$

that is,

$$\frac{df(q)}{dt} = f'(q) \cdot \frac{dq}{dt} \tag{46}$$

whatever dq/dt may turn out to be. This is encouragingly simple, and we go on to $g'(q)$. Now, $g'(q)$ is marginal cost, and, whatever dq/dt may turn out to be, we have, again by the chain rule,

$$\frac{dMC}{dt} = \frac{dMC}{dq} \cdot \frac{dq}{dt} \quad,$$

that is,

$$\frac{dg'(q)}{dt} = g''(q) \frac{dq}{dt} \quad. \tag{47}$$

In case (47) looks like sleight of hand, let us consider the economic interpretation. If the tax changes, output changes; if output changes, MC changes; hence the rate of change of MC with respect to the tax rate is equal to the rate of change of MC with respect to output times the rate of change of output with respect to tax rate, whatever the latter may prove to be.

This leaves the more complicated term, $qf'(q)$, to which we shall have to apply the product rule:

$$\frac{d}{dt} qf'(q) = q \cdot \frac{d}{dt} f'(q) + f'(q) \cdot \frac{dq}{dt} \quad.$$

Using the chain rule again,

$$\frac{d}{dt} f'(q) = \frac{d}{dq} f'(q) \cdot \frac{dq}{dt}$$

$$= f''(q) \cdot \frac{dq}{dt} \quad,$$

so

$$\frac{d}{dt} qf'(q) = q \cdot f''(q) \frac{dq}{dt} + f'(q) \frac{dq}{dt} \quad. \tag{48}$$

We now collect up (46), (47), and (48) and substitute into (45) to obtain

$$q \cdot f''(q) \frac{dq}{dt} + f'(q) \frac{dq}{dt} + f'(q) \frac{dq}{dt} - g''(q) \frac{dq}{dt} = 1 \quad .$$

This simplifies readily:

$$\frac{dq}{dt} [q \cdot f''(q) + 2f'(q) - g''(q)] = 1 \quad . \tag{49}$$

Now dq/dt is what we are looking for, and rearranging (49) we have

$$\frac{dq}{dt} = \frac{1}{q \cdot f''(q) + 2f'(q) - g''(q)} \quad . \tag{50}$$

Comparing (50) with (45), we can see that what we have done is find $dF(q)/dt$, and that, by the chain rule, this is nothing but $F'(q)dq/dt$, which is what we have in (49). Simple rearrangement then gives us

$$\frac{dq}{dt} = \frac{1}{F'(q)} \quad ,$$

which we have in (50).

What this means is that (50) gives us the rate of change of *equilibrium* q, or $\bar{q}$, the value of q that satisfies (42) — or (43), or (44) — with respect to the shift parameter t. We may again compare (45) with some of our earlier exercises in comparative statics, where we expressed some endogenous variable, say, y, as a function of some exogenous variable, say, z, and then found $d\bar{y}/dz$. In our earlier cases we had simple relations of the form $y = h(z)$, whereas this time we have had a rather complicated expression in the form $F(y) = z$, but there is no difference in principle.

We may recall that the object of the exercise was to prove that $dp/dt > 0$. Hence the step required now is obviously to prove that $dq/dt < 0$. Thus we want to show, if we can, that (50) is negative. This looks a little unpromising: (50) is rather complicated. Furthermore, we do not get much encouragement from inspecting it term by term. $f''(q)$ is the rate of change of the slope of the demand curve, and we have made no general assumption about that; and while $f'(q)$ must be negative, $g''(q)$, the slope of the marginal cost curve, can have any sign at equilibrium in nonperfect competition. Nonetheless, we can make progress, and we shall discover an example of one of the most important theorems of comparative statics. The equilibrium value $\bar{q}$ is found by solving for q Eq. (42), the first-order maximum condition. A sufficient condition for $\bar{q}$ to maximize profits is, however, that

$$\frac{d^2\Pi}{dq^2} = q \cdot f''(q) + 2f'(q) - g''(q) < 0 \quad . \tag{51}$$

From now on, to avoid some awkward special cases, we will assume that (51) is satisfied at $\bar{q}$. Inspection now reveals a remarkable circumstance: the right-hand side of (51) is identical to the denominator of (50), hence, if $\bar{q}$ is the profit-maximizing value of q, (50) is negative too, and we have our proof. It is easily completed by remembering that, with $p = f(q)$, we must have

$$\frac{\mathrm{d}\bar{p}}{\mathrm{d}t} = f'(q)\,\frac{\mathrm{d}\bar{q}}{\mathrm{d}t} \tag{52}$$

by the chain rule again, and since both $f'(q)$ and $\mathrm{d}\bar{q}/\mathrm{d}t$ are negative, $\mathrm{d}\bar{p}/\mathrm{d}t > 0$.

We set out to prove $\mathrm{d}\bar{p}/\mathrm{d}t > 0$ in the general case, without specific functions, using only the assumptions that the demand curve slopes down and that marginal cost is positive. It turns out, not surprisingly, that we also have to assume that equilibrium conditions *are* satisfied, just as we did in the linear models of a perfect market or of income determination. In the case of a maximization hypothesis, however, the assumption that equilibrium obtains allows us to assume not only that the necessary, or first-order, conditions are satisfied, but also that a sufficient second-order condition is satisfied. Then the assumption that the values of q and p are such as to satisfy the *sufficient conditions* for a maximum *after* equilibrium has been disturbed is itself sufficient to tell us their direction of change with respect to a shift parameter, that is, to sign (50) and (52), which give the rates of change of *equilibrium* values with respect to the shift parameter. This is an example of one of the most important results in the theory of maximizing models, that the assumption that the solution *is* a maximum can be sufficient, under certain conditions, to yield qualitative comparative static predictions. What we have just done, in deriving (50), and obtaining its sign from (51), is an example of what is called "the qualitative calculus." Much of Professor Paul Samuelson's great book *The Foundations of Economic Analysis*[3] is devoted to the qualitative calculus, that is, to the differentiation of equilibrium conditions with respect to shift parameters, and the search for predictions about directions of change. The book itself requires a good deal more technique, but we now have the principles. It is by the application of the qualitative calculus that we find the predictions, if any, that follow from our model. Indeed, we have applied it frequently in this book already, and many of the best-known results in standard microeconomics are examples of the qualitative calculus, proved by the methods we have just used.

This is a starred section, and it seems appropriate to address a

---

[3] P. A. Samuelson, *The Foundations of Economic Analysis*, Harvard University Press, Cambridge, Mass., 1947.

remark to the reader who has persisted with it. You might reflect upon the extraordinary power of the analystical tools that have allowed us to provide so general a proof: it has, after all, been managed with little more than repeated applications of the chain rule, and the assumption that the conditions for a maximum are satisfied, that is, that we are talking about equilibrium behavior. You might also reflect that, if you have come this far, you have proved what we asserted at the beginning, that if you can do economics, you can do mathematical economics.

It would be nice to be able to generalize further and apply our comparative static analysis in the case of other shift parameters besides our rather overworked excise tax. Thus demand might be shifted by some parameter such as income, or costs might be made to depend on output and the price of an input, such as the wage rate. The appropriate functions would then be

$$p = f(q, \alpha)$$

and

$$C = g(q, w) \quad .$$

Evidently we cannot go further in this direction unless we can handle functions of two or more variables, which are the subject of Chapter 8. Before going on, however, we might wonder why we were able to handle the tax case, since this gives

$$C = C(q, t)$$

as the general cost function. The reason is that the tax is simply to be *added* to the other costs, so that this becomes

$$C = g(q) + qt$$

and C is linear in t. The derivative of C with respect to q is obviously $g'(q)$ *plus* t; and the derivative of C with respect to t is obviously q. We shall now seek more general methods of handling functions of two or more variables that we can use when we do not have these simple additive cases.

QUESTIONS

1. Assume that a firm has the following demand and cost functions,

$$p = 150 - 0.5q$$
$$C = 100 + 3q + 7q^2 \quad ,$$

and that a subsidy is paid of 3 per unit.
a. Find profit-maximizing price and quantity.

b. Would anything be produced in the absence of the subsidy?

c. Find the rates of change of equilibrium price and quantity with respect to the subsidy.

2. In a competitive market, demand and supply are given by

$$q^d = 1200 - 2p$$

$$q^s = 4p \quad .$$

Find the tax rate that maximizes tax yield. (This is the numerical example of Section 3.1.)

3. Prove that $MC = AC$ at the minimum point on the latter (if it exists).

4. Prove that a monopolist who has zero marginal cost maximizes profit by setting the price at which the elasticity of demand is unity. (This is the famous "mineral springs" case, proved by the French mathematical economist Cournot in 1838 in his *Récherches sur les Principes Mathématiques de la Théorie des Richesses.*[4])

5. a. Suppose that an employer's demand for labor is given by

$$l^d = 100 - 2w \quad ,$$

where w is the wage rate. If a union wishes to maximize the total pay of its membership, and is not concerned with unemployment, what wage rate will it ask for? What wage rate will it ask for if the members adopt a work- and wage-sharing scheme? Is this result dependent on the demand curve being linear? Try to generalize.

b. A payroll tax of $0.1w$ is now imposed. Find the wage rate that maximizes total pay to employees. (*Hint:* The union wishes to maximize wl; due to the payroll tax, $w = 0.9\bar{w}$, where $\bar{w}$ is the total price paid by the employer.) Do you regard the answer as freakish or general? Who would you say "bears the tax" in this case?

6. a. Assume that $p = a - bq$, as in the example of Sections 7.4 and 7.6, but that cost is given by

$$C = k + cq + dq^2 \quad .$$

Find the expressions for the profit-maximizing p and q. What restrictions will you put on the value of the coefficient d?

b. Now suppose that an excise tax is levied at rate t. Find $d\bar{p}/dt$, and compare your result with the result of the text, where marginal cost was constant.

7. a. Using $C = C(q)$, write equations for total cost, average cost, and marginal cost.

b. Is the marginal cost function the first derivative of the average cost function?

---

[4] The relevant section is reprinted in the collection of readings *The Theory of the Firm*, edited by G. C. Archibald, Penguin Modern Education, Baltimore, Md., 1971.

c. Using $P = P(q)$, write equations for total revenue, average revenue, and marginal revenue.

d. Write a necessary and a sufficient condition for profit maximization when the firm is (i) a monopolist (ii) a member of a perfectly competitive industry.

8. a. In the example of Section 7.5, find whether an output of 6 actually exceeds the output at which average variable cost is at a minimum, and determine whether it pays better to produce 6 or nothing.

   b. Sketch the average and marginal cost curves, and illustrate your answer to part a.

9. Consider a firm in a perfectly competitive industry facing a market price of $6 per unit. Assume that the government grants a subsidy, for this firm only, of $3 per unit.

   a. Using the cost function of (31), calculate the new equilibrium quantity and compare it with the old equilibrium quantity. Is the firm now profitable?

   b. If the subsidy were to be applied to all firms in the industry, the analysis would not apply. Why not?

10. Consider a firm in a perfectly competitive industry, facing a price of $6 per unit, and having a cost function given by (31), but whose behavior, rather than maximizing profits, is to minimize total cost less six times the quantity. Compare the results of this firm's behavior with that of the profit maximizer. Explain.

11. In Section 7.5 we determined a profit-maximizing quantity of 6 for the profit function given by (32).

    a. Why is this firm no longer in business?

    b. Write out the necessary condition for average cost to be at a minimum, using the total cost function (31). The sufficient condition for this minimum gives us a qualitative restriction on q. What is it?

    c. Does $q = 7.75$ give us the minimum point?

    d. Using the profit function (32) but with price set at 12.56 rather than 6, determine the profit-maximizing quantity and the firm's profit at this point.

12. Does qualitative comparative static analysis necessarily involve maxima and/or minima?

Chapter **8**

Functions of More than One Variable

So far, we have confined ourselves to functions of one variable, but this is in fact very restrictive, as the following examples illustrate. We expect the quantity demanded of a good to depend on income, and on prices of substitutes, as well as on the price of the good in question; cost is a function of such variables as wage rates as well as output; and we do not wish to be confined to assuming always that wages are constant when output and employment change. The value of the multiplier depends on several parameters, any one of which may change. Thus in the multiplier

$$k = \frac{1}{1 - (c - m)(1 - t)} \tag{1}$$

we could ask what happened to k if c or m changed as well as if t changed. Previously we dealt with this (see Section 5.6) by assuming that m and c were constants while we varied only t. We cannot always adopt so simple an approach, and it is now time to investigate a function of more than one variable in which all the variables can change. We shall deal first with functions of two variables $z = z(x, y)$ but the techniques developed extend in an obvious manner to functions of more than two variables.

8.1 PARTIAL DERIVATIVES: THE PROBLEM

Consider the very simple case of a household's demand function containing only two independent variables,

$$q^d = D(p, y) \quad , \tag{2}$$

where q^d is the quantity that the household demands of some commodity, p is the price of the commodity, and y is the household's income. Equation (2) is a function of two variables, and we wish to study its properties. First, we wish to know how demand changes as price changes, income held constant, and how demand changes as income changes, price held constant. Later, we shall wish to ask such questions as "is the reaction of q^d to a change in price itself altered by a change in income?" or "is the reaction of q^d to a change in income itself altered by a change in the price of the commodity?" We need a technique to handle these and other related questions. When we dealt with the multiplier, restated in (1), our method was to assume c and m to be constant while we found the reaction of k to changes in t. We could also (although we did not have occasion to do so) have assumed t and c to be constant in order to find the reaction of k to changes in the value of m, and so on. We can now use this method systematically to attack functions of many variables.

8.2 DEFINITIONS AND AN EXAMPLE

To begin with let us consider the following demand function as a specific example of a function of two variables:

$$q^d = 10y^2 + 2y^4p^{-2} - 3p^3 \quad . \tag{3}$$

For obvious reasons we define this function only in the positive orthant. As we are only going to consider the demand function, there is no risk of confusion between quantity demanded and quantity supplied, and we may accordingly suppress the superscript on q in this chapter. If p is held constant, we can treat it just as we would any constant in a function of one variable, and we can obtain the derivative of q with respect to y in the ordinary way. If you do this, you will find that its value is $20y + 8y^3p^{-2}$. We can also hold y constant, treat it as we would a constant in simple differentiation, and obtain the derivative of q with respect to p. We obtain $-4y^4p^{-3} - 9p^2$.

Now consider what we have done. Notice that we have obtained two different derivatives from (3), and in each case we need to specify the variable with respect to which we have taken the derivative. In the first case we asked how demand changed as income changed, price held constant, and to answer this we found the derivative of q with respect to y. In the second case we asked how q changed as price changed, income held constant, and to answer this we found the derivative of q with respect to p. To remind us that when we take the derivative of a function of two or more variables with respect to one of its arguments, we hold the other arguments constant, we speak of *partial derivatives,* or just partials for short. Partial derivatives are denoted by "curly d's," ∂, in place of ordinary Roman d's. Thus from (3) above we have derived two partial derivatives, which we write as

$$\frac{\partial q}{\partial y} = 20y + 8y^3 p^{-2} \tag{4}$$

and

$$\frac{\partial q}{\partial p} = -4y^4 p^{-3} - 9p^2 \quad . \tag{5}$$

Partials may be denoted in at least three ways. To illustrate the notation we write the partials of $z = f(x, y)$:

$$f_x = \frac{\partial z}{\partial x} = \frac{\partial f(x, y)}{\partial x}\bigg|_{y \text{ constant}} \tag{6}$$

$$f_y = \frac{\partial z}{\partial y} = \frac{\partial f(x, y)}{\partial y}\bigg|_{x \text{ constant}} \tag{7}$$

All three expressions in (6) are read "the partial derivative of z with respect to x," and all three in (7) are read "the partial derivative of z with respect to y." The subscript in f_x or f_y shows the argument with respect to which the function has been differentiated.

Now let us give a formal definition of a partial derivative. Consider the function $z = f(x, y)$. The partial derivatives of z with respect to x and y are defined as

$$\frac{\partial z}{\partial x} = \lim_{h \to 0} \left(\frac{f(x + h, y) - (f(x, y)}{h} \right) \tag{8}$$

and

$$\frac{\partial z}{\partial y} = \lim_{k \to 0} \left(\frac{f(x, y + k) - (f(x, y)}{k} \right) \quad . \tag{9}$$

In both (8) and (9) the change in the value of the function is the result of a change in only one of the independent variables. (8) gives the instantaneous rate of change of the function with respect to x, y constant; (9) gives the instantaneous rate of change of the function with respect to y, x constant.

Notice that you have now learned a new concept in the space of a very few pages and with a minimum of effort. If you recall the problems encountered in learning simple differentiation in Chapter 4, you may wish to remark on the ease with which this new and very important idea has been mastered.[1]

---

[1] The fact that we can define a partial derivative does not guarantee that it exists. The relation of continuity and smoothness to differentiability is more complex in the case of partial derivatives of functions of more than one variable than in the case of derivatives of functions of only one variable. These complications need not concern us because we shall be dealing with functions for which partial derivatives do exist.

Now let us return to the example of the demand function of (3) and to its two partial derivatives in (4) and (5). The partial of the quantity demanded with respect to price was

$$\frac{\partial q}{\partial p} = -4y^4 p^{-3} - 9p^2 \quad . \tag{5}$$

Notice that this expression for the partial of demand with respect to price has income as an argument. Thus $\partial q/\partial p$ is a function not only of p but also of y. This partial derivative can be given a specific value only if a specific value of the other argument (income in this case) is stated. This should not seem too surprising since it is necessary to hold income constant when finding $\partial q/\partial p$. The fact that $\partial q/\partial p$ depends not only on p but also on y suggests that we consider what happens to the reaction of q to p as y changes. We could ask, for example, if the demand for the commodity becomes more or less responsive to a change in its price as the household's income rises. Formally, we are asking what happens to $\partial q/\partial p$ as y varies. We can write this as $\partial(\partial q/\partial p)/\partial y$, which denotes the partial derivative with respect to a change in income of the partial derivative of quantity demanded with respect to a change in price. Although this sounds very complex, it expresses in formal terms a very simple question: "how does the responsiveness of q to a change in p vary as y varies?"

We can easily discover the answer for the demand function in (3) by differentiating (5) with respect to y to give

$$\frac{\partial(\partial q/\partial p)}{\partial y} = \frac{-16y^3}{p^3} \quad . \tag{10}$$

We may notice that for p and y positive (10) is always negative: the response of q to changes in p declines as y rises.

We can also ask how the response of q to y varies as p varies, and to do this we differentiate (4) with respect to p, obtaining

$$\frac{\partial(\partial q/\partial y)}{\partial p} = \frac{-16y^3}{p^3} \quad . \tag{11}$$

This expression tells how the response of demand to a change in income varies as price varies.

The notation on the left-hand side of (10) and (11) is rather clumsy, although descriptive, and the following notation is usual:

$$\frac{\partial(\partial q/\partial p)}{\partial y} = \frac{\partial^2 q}{\partial p \, \partial y} = f_{py} \quad . \tag{12}$$

The first term in (12) has been used already, and it is to be read as directing us to take the partial of q with respect to p [Eq. (5)] and differentiate it with respect to y [Eq. (10)]. The "two" in the numerator of the second expression indicates that the function has been differentiated twice, while the terms in the denominator indicate that the process of partial differentiation has been carried out once with respect to p and once with respect to y. The third expression in (12) is the most compact notation: it indicates that the function f has been differentiated first with respect to p and then with respect to y.

Applying this notation to (11) we have, analogously,

$$\frac{\partial(\partial q/\partial y)}{\partial p} = \frac{\partial^2 q}{\partial y\,\partial p} = f_{py} \quad . \tag{13}$$

These terms are referred to as *second-order cross-partial* derivatives, or "cross-partials" for short. A cross-partial measures the rate of change in a first-order partial as one of the variables originally held constant changes.

A comparison of (10) and (11) shows that $f_{py} = f_{yp}$. Indeed, this is no accident. The order in which we do the differentiation is of no consequence, and it is always true that for any function $f(x, y)$

$$f_{xy} = f_{yx}$$

(assuming, of course, that the function can be differentiated twice, i.e., that both it and its first derivatives are continuous and smooth). We shall not attempt to prove this important result here, but its proof can be found in any standard textbook on mathematics.[2]

It seemed obvious to pose the questions that we have just considered: what happens to $\partial q/\partial p$ as y changes, and what happens to $\partial q/\partial y$ as p changes? There is also another related question we could ask: what happens to $\partial q/\partial p$ as p itself changes? Now we are wondering if the reaction of q to p is different when price is high from what it is when price is low. No student who is familiar with the elementary proposition that demand elasticity varies over the range of most demand curves will be surprised by this question. To answer it we merely differentiate (5) once again with respect to price, and we get

$$\frac{\partial(\partial q/\partial p)}{\partial p} = 12y^4 p^{-4} - 18p \quad . \tag{14}$$

We adopt the following notation:

$$\frac{\partial(\partial q/p)}{\partial p} = \frac{\partial^2 q}{\partial p^2} = f_{pp} \quad . \tag{15}$$

This is called the second-order partial derivative of q with respect to

---

[2] See, for example, R. Courant, *Differential and Integral Calculus*, Blackie & Son, London, 1936, vol. II, pp. 55–57. The proof requires that the function is twice differentiable at the point in question.

price, and it is found by partially differentiating the original function twice with respect to price. What it tells us is how the reaction of q to a change in price, income held constant, is itself changing as we change price. The sign of the second partial f_{pp} tells us if the slope of the demand curve is increasing or diminishing as we move up the curve.

A similar question could be asked about q and y and is answered by differentiating (4) with respect to y to give

$$\frac{\partial(\partial q/\partial y)}{\partial y} = 20 + 24y^2 p^{-2} \quad . \tag{16}$$

The notation in this case is

$$\frac{\partial(\partial q/\partial y)}{\partial y} = \frac{\partial^2 q}{\partial y^2} = f_{yy} \quad . \tag{17}$$

This is called the second-order partial derivative of q with respect to income. It tells us how the response of q to a change in y is itself changing as y changes.

We may now summarize the results obtained so far for the case of a smooth continuous function $z = f(x, y)$.

1. There are two first-order partial derivatives of the function that are written f_x and f_y or $\partial z/\partial x$ and $\partial z/\partial y$. They are obtained by differentiating the function with respect to the relevant variable, holding the other variable constant.

2. There are two direct second-order partial derivatives, f_{xx} and f_{yy}, which are also often written as $\partial^2 z/\partial x^2$ and $\partial^2 z/\partial y^2$. These are obtained by differentiating $f(x, y)$ twice with respect to x in the first case and twice with respect to y in the second case.

3. There are two second-order cross partial derivatives f_{xy} and f_{yx}, which are also often written as $\partial^2 z/\partial x \, \partial y$ and $\partial^2 z/\partial y \, \partial x$. These are obtained by differentiating $f(x, y)$ first with respect to x and then with respect to y in one case, and first with respect to y and then with respect to x in the other case. In fact, the order of differentiation turns out not to matter so that $f_{xy} = f_{yx}$.

Now let us draw together the results for our specific demand function to see what we can learn about its behavior.

$$q^d = 10y^2 + 2y^4 p^{-2} - 3p^3 \tag{3}$$

$$f_y = 20y + 8y^3 p^{-2} \tag{4}$$

$$f_p = -4y^4 p^{-3} - 9p^2 \tag{5}$$

$$f_{yp} = f_{py} = -16y^3 p^{-3} \tag{10 and 11}$$

$$f_{pp} = 12y^4 p^{-4} - 18p \qquad (14)$$

$$f_{yy} = 20 + 24y^2 p^{-2} \quad . \qquad (16)$$

Let us see if we can sign each of the first- and second-order partial derivatives. Inspection reveals the following for y, $p > 0$.

1. $f_y > 0$, which shows that the good is normal at all levels of income.
2. $f_p < 0$, which shows that the demand curve for the commodity slopes downwards at every level of income.
3. $f_{pp} \gtreqless 0$ according to the values of y and p (the symbol $\gtreqless$ is read "greater than, equal to, *or* less than"), which shows that the responsiveness of demand to increases in price itself increases as price increases at some price–income combinations and decreases as price increases for other price–income combinations.
4. $f_{yy} > 0$, which shows that the responsiveness of demand to a change in income increases as income increases.
5. $f_{yp} = f_{py} < 0$, which shows both that the responsiveness of demand to a change in income decreases as price increases and that the responsiveness of demand to a change in price decreases as income increases.

Evidently, although it is a simple matter to take the five first- and second-order partial derivatives of a function of two variables, they reveal a great deal of rather complex information about the behavior of the function.

8.3 SEPARABLE FUNCTIONS

Consider the household demand function

$$q = 4y + 3y^5 - 20p^2 - 100p^{-8} \quad . \qquad (18)$$

This function differs fundamentally from the demand function in (3) in that in (18) there are no terms involving both y and p, whereas in (3) there is such a term, $2y^4 p^{-2}$. We shall see the importance of this if we calculate the first- and second-order partial derivatives for the function in (18):

$$f_y = 4 + 15y^4 \qquad (19)$$

$$f_p = -40p + 800p^{-9} \qquad (20)$$

$$f_{yy} = 60y^3 \qquad (21)$$

$$f_{pp} = -40 - 7200p^{-10} \qquad (22)$$

$$f_{yp} = f_{py} = 0 \quad . \qquad (23)$$

Because there are no terms involving both y and p, it follows that the reaction of demand to price is independent of the level of income and also that the reaction of demand to changes in income is independent of the level of price. Formally, this is shown by the fact that the cross-partials are zero for all values of x and y. Whenever the cross-partials are zero it follows that the value of the function is determined by the sum of the separate effects of the independent variables in question and that there is no "interaction" between the variables. The general case of a function of this sort can be written as

$$F(x_1, \ldots, x_n) = f^1(x_1) + f^2(x_2) + \cdots + f^n(x_n) \quad .$$

The function is known as "linear additive" and is *strongly separable:* all the cross-partial derivatives are zero for all values of the x's. We see now why, in Chapter 7, we were able to handle the cost function $C = C(q, t)$ even though we did not know anything about cross-partial derivatives: our assumptions gave us the strongly separable form $C(q, t) = f(q) + qt$.

8.4 THE CHAIN RULE APPLIED TO PARTIAL DERIVATIVES

In Chapter 4 we developed the chain rule for functions of one variable and showed that if $y = y(x)$ and $x = x(z)$, then $dy/dz = (dy/dx)(dx/dz)$. We may now develop an analogous chain rule for functions of two variables.

Suppose that we have the function $z = f(x, y)$ and suppose that both x and y are functions of yet another variable, t, say. We denote this by writing $x = x(t)$ and $y = y(t)$. Substitution now gives

$$z = f[x(t), y(t)] \quad . \tag{24}$$

In (24), z is a function of one variable, t: it is a function of two functions both of which have the same argument, t. Thus we may write

$$z = F(t) = f[x(t), y(t)] \quad . \tag{25}$$

Assuming that all these functions are differentiable, our problem is, can we find $dz/dt = F'(t)$?

Problems such as this often occur in economics. Consider one example. The function $f(x, y)$ might be a production function relating output z to two inputs, labor, x, and capital, y. The two functions $x(t)$ and $y(t)$ might show how supplies of the two inputs were growing over time. Our problem would then be to discover, assuming full employment of both factors, how output was growing over time.

Now let us proceed to find the derivative dz/dt from (25). From the definition of the derivative we have

$$F' = \lim_{h \to 0} \frac{F(t+h) - F(t)}{h}$$

$$= \lim_{h \to 0} \frac{f[x(t+h), y(t+h)] - f[x(t), y(t)]}{h} \quad . \quad (26)$$

We now manipulate the last expression in (26) in a familiar way, adding and subtracting $f[x(t+h), y(t)]/h$. This gives

$$F' = \lim_{h \to 0} \left\{ \left(\frac{f[x(t+h), y(t)] - f[x(t), y(t)]}{h} \right) \right.$$

$$\left. + \left(\frac{f[x(t+h), y(t+h)] - f[x(t+h), y(t)]}{h} \right) \right\} \quad . \quad (27)$$

Start by considering the first term in parentheses in (27). Here y has the value $y(t)$ and is accordingly constant as h varies. It follows that the term depends only on x, which has the values $x(t+h), x(t)$. Thus x is here a function of h, and the whole term is thus a function of a single variable, h. Since only x varies with h, and hence f with h, we may appeal at once to the chain rule, developed in Section 4.6.

For the first term in (27) we accordingly have

$$\frac{df}{dx} \frac{dx}{dt} \quad . \quad (28)$$

f, however, is a function of two variables, and in (28) we are taking its derivative partially with respect to x, y constant. We must accordingly rewrite (28) as

$$\frac{\partial f}{\partial x} \frac{dx}{dt} \quad . \quad (29)$$

Now consider the second term in parentheses in (27). Here x has the same value, $x(t+h)$, on both sides of the minus sign, whatever the value of h. The two y-values, on the other hand, are $y(t+h)$ and $y(t)$. It follows that the difference between the two y-values, and therefore the value of the whole term, is a function of h. We again appeal to the function-of-a-function rule and see that the limit of the second term as $h \to 0$ is

$$\frac{\partial f}{\partial y} \frac{dy}{dt} \quad . \quad (30)$$

All that remains is to collect (29) and (30):

$$F' = \frac{dz}{dt} = \frac{\partial f}{\partial x} \frac{dx}{dt} + \frac{\partial f}{\partial y} \frac{dy}{dt} \quad ,$$

or, in alternative notations,

$$F' = \frac{\partial z}{\partial x}\frac{dx}{dt} + \frac{\partial z}{\partial y}\frac{dy}{dt}$$

$$= f_x\frac{dx}{dt} + f_y\frac{dy}{dt} \quad . \tag{31}$$

In terms of the simple economic example mentioned earlier in this section the interpretation of (31) is easy. The rate at which output, z, changes over time depends on the rates at which the two inputs change over time, dx/dt and dy/dt, each rate being multiplied by the appropriate marginal product, f_x or f_y.

8.5 ONE INDEPENDENT VARIABLE IS A FUNCTION OF THE OTHER

In Section 8.4 the function $z = f(x, y)$ was reduced to a function of one variable, t, because both x and y were functions of t. A similar situation occurs if one of the independent variables, say, y, is a function of the other, that is, $y = y(x)$. This once again makes z a function of a single variable, x this time, and we ask how z changes as x changes, allowing both for the direct effect of x on z and for the indirect effect of z causing y to change, in turn changing z.

In terms of the illustration used in Section 8.3, $f(x, y)$ might still be a production function but, instead of x and y varying with time, we might have a case in which y, capital, varied systematically with x, labor. The problem is now to discover the overall effect on output of variations in the rate of growth of the labor force.

We have $z = f(x, y)$ and $y = y(x)$. Substitution of the latter into the former yields

$$z = f[x, y(x)] \quad . \tag{32}$$

In (32), z is a function of a single argument, whence we could write instead $z = z(x)$. We want, however, to find dz/dx from (32) in terms of the partial derivatives f_x and f_y and the derivative $y'(x)$. From the definition of a derivative we have

$$\frac{dz}{dx} = \lim_{h\to 0}\frac{f[x+h, y(x+h)] - f[x, y(x)]}{h} \quad . \tag{33}$$

We manipulate this in the usual way by adding and subtracting $f[x, y(x+h)]$. This gives

$$\frac{dz}{dx} = \lim_{h\to 0}\left(\frac{f[x+h, y(x+h)] - f[x, y(x+h)]}{h}\right.$$

$$\left. + \left(\frac{f[x, y(x+h)] - f[x, y(x)]}{h}\right) \quad . \tag{34}\right.$$

The analogy with (27) is obvious. Indeed, having worked out that case, we shall find (34) easier. Looking at the first term in round brackets, we find $y(x + h)$ on both sides of the minus sign but $x + h$ on one side and x on the other. There is no difference between the two y-terms as h varies, whence the limit of this term as $h \to 0$ is f_x. Looking at the second term, we see that x is a constant, whereas y, here equal to $y(x)$, varies as h varies. Appealing again to the chain rule, we see that the limit of this term is $f_y y'$. Collecting results,

$$\frac{dz}{dx} = f_x + f_y \, y'(x)$$

or

$$\frac{dz}{dx} = f_x + f_y \frac{dy}{dx} \quad . \tag{35}$$

In terms of our illustration, (35) tells us that the rate at which output changes as labor changes, given the rule relating changes in capital to changes in labor, is equal to the marginal product of labor, f_x (the direct effect), plus the rate at which capital changes as labor changes, dy/dx, multiplied by the marginal product of capital, f_y (the indirect effect).

8.6 GEOMETRICAL INTERPRETATION OF PARTIAL DERIVATIVES

In Figure 8.1 we have drawn a three-dimensional "surface," in the positive orthant, which is a graphical representation in that orthant of a particular function $z = f(x, y)$. You should try to visualize the surface as being concave to the origin, that is, as bulging out toward you. We may now try to give a geometrical interpretation to the partial derivatives that we have identified in Section 8.2. Consider first $\partial z/\partial x$ evaluated at some point, Q, on the surface (i.e., at some specific values of x and y, say, x_0 and y_0). This partial derivative measures the slope in the x-z-plane of the tangent to the curve at Q. This tangent is the line T_x in Figure 8.1. To see what is meant by the x-z-plane, imagine taking a knife and cutting the surface open along a line perpendicular to the y-axis. This will expose a new surface, which was formerly in the interior, such as the shaded one in Figure 8.2(a), and, if you look at this end on, you will see the curve of its outer edge, which is shown in Figure 8.2(b). The slope of the tangent to the curve in Figure 8.2(b) is the partial derivative $\partial z/\partial x$, measured at the value of y at which we cut open the surface. If we take our knife and again cut the surface open perpendicular to the y-axis but at a different level of y, we will expose a new curve in the x-z-plane, and there is no guarantee that it

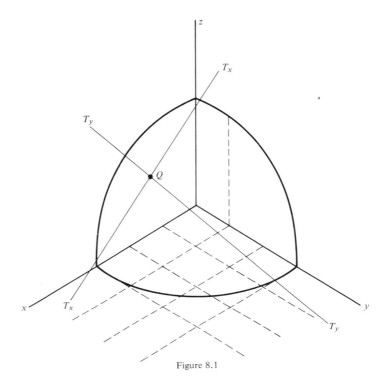

Figure 8.1

will have the same shape, whence there is no guarantee that it will have the same tangent slope at any given value of x as the curve first exposed.

The second-order partial derivative $\partial^2 z/\partial x^2$ indicates what is happening to $\partial z/\partial x$ as we increase x holding y constant. Figure 8.2(b) shows that this second-order partial must be negative throughout because the slope of the tangent (i.e., $\partial z/\partial x$) diminishes as x increases. (The tangent slope is negative, and its algebraic value is decreasing as x increases.)

Next consider the partial derivative $\partial z/\partial y$ evaluated at Q. We are now interested in the tangent slope in the y-z-plane which is the slope of the surface when it is cut open perpendicular to the x-axis. This tangent slope is shown in Figure 8.1 by the line T_y. The surface is shown cut open in Figure 8.3(a), and, when viewed end on as in Figure 8.3(b), the tangent gradient is seen as the slope of the tangent along the cross section that allows y and z to vary with x held constant. The second-order partial, $\partial^2 z/\partial y^2$, measures the rate of change of this tangent slope as we slide it around in the z-y-plane holding x constant. As in the case of $\partial^2 z/\partial x^2$, it is everywhere negative, showing that $\partial z/\partial y$ falls in algebraic value as y increases.

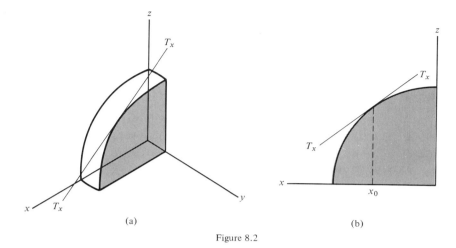

Figure 8.2

It will be evident from inspection of Figures 8.1, 8.2, and 8.3 that employment of the words "the partial derivative *evaluated at Q*" is not idle pedantry. The tangent slopes vary as we move about the surface, and each is changed by a change in the other variable—hence the existence of cross-partial derivatives. Thus $\partial^2 z/\partial x\,\partial y$ measures the rate of change in the slope of the tangent T_x as we slide Q toward y, and similarly $\partial^2 z/\partial y\,\partial x$ measures the rate of change in the slope of the tangent T_y as we slide Q toward x. But recall that we have already asserted that the cross-partials are always equal. What their equality shows is that it does not matter in which order one differentiates. In terms of Figure 8.1 it means that the rate of change of T_x with respect to y is identical with that of T_y with respect to x at any given point Q.

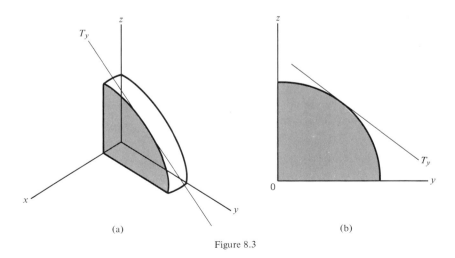

Figure 8.3

8.7 ISO-*F* CURVES

Inspection of Figure 8.1 reveals the existence of a third plane that can be cut out of the function. We can take our knife and cut the function open perpendicularly to the *z*-axis, revealing a surface such as the shaded one in Figure 8.4(a). If you look at this surface straight on, that is, in the *x*-*y*-plane, you will see the curve of its outer edge, which is drawn in Figure 8.4(b). This shows how *x* and *y* vary with each other when *z* is held constant at the value of *z* at which we cut open the surface.

A familiar device in economic analysis is to convert a three-

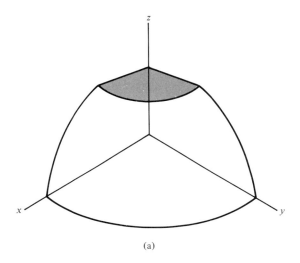

(a)

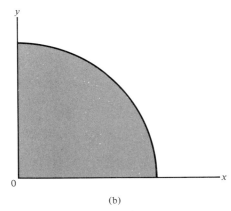

(b)

Figure 8.4

dimensional function to a two-dimensional surface by plotting "iso-bars" each one of which shows all those combinations of the two independent variables that keep the value of the function constant at a particular value. The curve in Figure 8.4(b) is an example. Indifference curves, which show all those combinations of two goods that keep utility constant, and iso-quants, which show all those combinations of two inputs that keep output constant, are examples commonly encountered. We shall refer to these curves by the general name "iso-*f*" curves: any one such curve tells us all the combinations of two independent variables that keep the value of the function constant at some stated level.

A whole function of two variables can be illustrated by a series of iso-*f* curves each one of which is associated with a particular value of the function. Such a representation is called an iso-*f* map. Figure 8.5 shows a particular example for a production function $z = f(x, y)$, where z is output and x and y are two inputs, say labor and capital. The iso-*f* contours (in this case called iso-*quants* for constant *quantity*) are plotted for intervals of output of 10 units. Where the curves are close together, output is increasing rapidly as inputs increase; where the curves are far apart, output is increasing only slowly as inputs increase.

In Figures 8.2 and 8.3 we show that the partial derivatives $\partial z/\partial x$ and $\partial z/\partial y$ measure the tangent gradient in the x-z-plane (with y held constant at a particular value) and in the y-z-plane (with x held constant at a particular value). Figure 8.4 suggests that the tangent to the

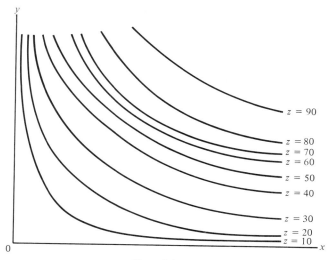

Figure 8.5

iso-*f* curve measures the slope of the function in the *x*-*y*-plane with *z* held constant at some particular value. Thus the slope of an iso-*f* curve [as shown, for example, in Figures 8.4(b) or 8.5] tells us the rate at which *x* must vary with *y* if the value of the function is to be held constant.

Some economic examples are given by the following questions. What is the rate at which one factor must be substituted for another (one factor increased as the other is diminished) if output is to be held constant? What is the rate at which one commodity must be substituted for another (one increased as the other is decreased) if a household's satisfaction (its total utility) is to be held constant? The first question is answered by the slope of the relevant iso-quant and the second by the slope of the relevant indifference curve.

Determining the slope of the iso-*f* curve is an important exercise in economics. Many famous propositions become trivially easy to establish as soon as this has been done. Fortunately, it turns out that we have already established in Sections 8.4 and 8.5 most of what we need to do this.

We now return to the function

$$z = f(x, y) \quad . \tag{36}$$

We note that if *z* is to be held constant at some value z_0, there will be an implied relation between *x* and *y* consistent with $z = z_0$. We write this

$$y = y(x) \quad . \tag{37}$$

Equation (37) is the equation of the iso-*f* curve: it tells us how *x* and *y* must vary with each other if *z* is to be held constant.[3]

We can now substitute $y = y(x)$ into $z = f(x, y)$ to obtain

$$z_0 = f[x, y(x)] \quad . \tag{38}$$

Except for the fact that we have z_0 instead of *z*, this is the same as (32) in Section 8.5. We must write z_0 in this case since the functional relation $y(x)$ is such that variations in *x* will be exactly accompanied by those variations in *y* necessary to hold the value of the function constant. In other words the expression $f[x, y(x)] - z_0$ is identically equal to zero for all values of *x* and *y*.

We can now immediately quote the result in (35), to write, referring to our present equations (36), (37), and (38),

$$\frac{dz}{dx} = f_x + f_y \frac{dy}{dx} \quad . \tag{39}$$

---

[3] The existence of a unique function $y = y(x)$ that describes a contour of the function $z = z(x, y)$ is an important theorem in the theory of functions of two variables. A proof, which we do not attempt here, can be found in Courant, op. cit., p. 114.

This says that the rate of change of z with respect to x in (38) is given by the two partial derivatives from (36) with the one, f_y, multiplied by the derivative dy/dx from (37).

When we obtained (35) our object was to find out how z varied as x varied, given that y was any function of x. In the present case we have, however, chosen $y = y(x)$ such that z does not vary. Thus we have

$$\frac{dz}{dx} \equiv 0 \tag{40}$$

(where the sign $\equiv$, the "identity sign," means that this is true for *all* values of x). This allows us to equate (39) to zero:

$$f_x + f_y \frac{dy}{dx} = 0$$

from which we immediately obtain

$$\frac{dy}{dx} = -\frac{f_x}{f_y} \; . \tag{41}$$

This is an extremely important result. It tells us that if $z = f(x, y)$, the rate of change of y with respect to x that holds z constant is equal to minus one times the ratio of the partial derivatives of the function (evaluated, of course, at the values at which z is held constant).

Consider now a simple example of this important result. Assume that we have the production function

$$z = x^{1/2} y^{1/2}$$

and that we wish to know the equation describing the slopes of the iso-quants. Equation (41) tells us that this is

$$\frac{dy}{dx} = -\frac{f_x}{f_y}$$

$$= -\frac{\frac{1}{2} x^{-1/2} y^{1/2}}{\frac{1}{2} x^{1/2} y^{-1/2}}$$

$$= -\frac{y}{x} \; . \tag{42}$$

8.8 IMPLICIT DIFFERENTIATION

The technique just derived is very valuable in handling functions expressed in implicit form. Consider by way of illustration

$$xy - K = 0 \quad , \tag{43}$$

which is a simple example of an implicit function, $f(x, y) = 0$. In this case we can express x as an explicit function of y,

$$y = \frac{K}{x} \quad , \tag{44}$$

and obtain directly the derivative

$$\frac{dy}{dx} = -\frac{K}{x^2} \quad . \tag{45}$$

But, from (43), $K = xy$, and so, substituting this into (45), we obtain

$$\frac{dy}{dx} = -\frac{xy}{x^2}$$

$$= -\frac{y}{x} \quad .$$

In some circumstances it may be inconvenient, and in other circumstances it is impossible, to obtain the explicit form of the functional relation before differentiating. In either case the result obtained in Section 8.7 allows us to obtain dy/dx from the implicit form of the function. The result in (41) can be applied to the specific implicit form $f(x, y) = xy - K = 0$ to obtain

$$\frac{dy}{dx} = -\frac{f_x}{f_y}$$

$$= -\frac{y}{x} \quad ,$$

which agrees with what we obtained when the function was expressed in explicit form as $y = K/x$. Notice that for positive x and y, $-y/x$ is always negative, indicating that the two independent variables have to change in opposite directions to hold the value of the function constant.

As a further example of implicit differentiation let us consider the demand function given in (3) of Section 8.2:

$$q = f(y, p) = 10y^2 + 2y^4 p^{-2} - 3p^3 \quad .$$

We now ask, if q is to be held constant, how will p and y have to vary with each other?

The simple way to answer this question is to differentiate the implicit function $f(y, p) - \bar{q} = 0$. This gives us

$$\frac{dy}{dp} = -\frac{f_p}{f_y} = \frac{4y^4 p^{-3} + 9p^2}{20y + 8y^3 p^{-2}} \quad . \tag{46}$$

Inspection of (46) shows that for positive values of y and p the expression for dy/dp is always positive. Thus a rise in income (which tends to increase demand) must be offset by a rise in price (which tends to reduce demand) if quantity demanded is to be held constant.

8.9 DIFFERENTIALS

We now come to an important extension in the techniques available to us for handling functions of more than one variable. To begin our study of the concept of differentials it is, however, convenient to return to a brief consideration of functions of one variable.

We recall from Chapter 4 that when we have a function of one variable

$$z = f(x)$$

we can define the derivative of the function as

$$\frac{dz}{dx} = \lim_{h \to 0} \frac{\Delta z}{\Delta x}$$

$$= f'(x) \quad .$$

The value of $f'(x)$ is the slope of the tangent (i.e., the tangent gradient) to the curve $z = f(x)$ at a particular point x_0. This is illustrated in Figure 8.6. If we take the origin as the point (x_0, z_0) — that is, the point of tangency — then the equation of the tangent line can be written as

$$\mathbf{dz} = f'(x) \ \mathbf{dx} \quad . \tag{47}$$

In this equation $\mathbf{dx}$ is an arbitrary increment in x, of positive or

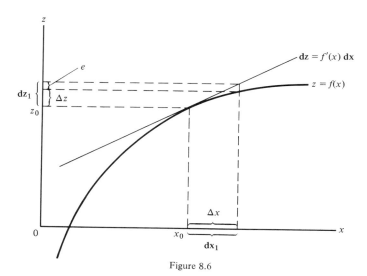

Figure 8.6

negative value, from the point x_0, and **dz** is the associated increment in z calculated from the tangent line at z_0. For example, the increment $\mathbf{dx_1}$ in Figure 8.6 causes an increment in z of $\mathbf{dz_1}$ along the tangent line.

The values **dx** and **dz** in (49) are called *differentials of x and of z*, respectively, and we should note three important properties of these differentials.

1. As defined by (47), the differential **dz** gives the exact value of the change in z for *any* arbitrary change in x, **dx**, calculated from the line tangent to the function at the point at which the differential is evaluated.

2. We can divide both sides of (47) by **dx** to obtain

$$\frac{\mathbf{dz}}{\mathbf{dx}} = f'(x) \quad,$$

which, by the definition of $f'(x)$, means that

$$\frac{\mathbf{dz}}{\mathbf{dx}} = \frac{dz}{dx}$$

$$= \lim_{\Delta x \to 0} \frac{\Delta z}{\Delta x} \quad . \tag{48}$$

This shows that the ratio of the differentials **dz/dx** is exactly equal to the limit of the incremental ratio $\Delta z/\Delta x$ calculated from the function $z = f(x)$ as Δx goes to zero. In other words, by virtue of the dependence of **dz** on **dx**, the ratio of these two differentials has exactly the same value as the derivative dz/dx. *Note, however, that the derivative is a single number obtained as the result of a limiting process, whence* **dx** *and* **dz** *have no independent meanings in the expression* $f'(x) = dz/dx$.

3. Equation (47) gives an approximation, for small changes in x, to the incremental changes in z that could be obtained exactly from the function $z = f(x)$. We can replace the differentials by deltas and write (47) as

$$\Delta z \simeq f'(x) \, \Delta x \quad, \tag{49}$$

where Δx is an arbitrary change in x, $f'(x)$ is the (constant) slope of the tangent line at x_0, and the symbol $\simeq$ means "approximately equal to." Figure 8.6 illustrates. We make an arbitrary, but small, change in x of Δx, and the change in z, according to the function, is Δz. If we use (49) to approximate the change, we will estimate $\Delta z \simeq \mathbf{dz}$ with the error of e shown in the figure.

Consider, for an example, a simple function $z = a + x^{1/2}$. The differential of this function is

$$dz = \frac{1}{2x^{1/2}} \, dx \quad . \tag{50}$$

Using the point $x = 4$ as an example, (50) gives us the following information: (1) the slope of the tangent is exactly $\frac{1}{4}$; (2) if x increases by one unit, then the increase in z is calculated from the tangent line is exactly $\frac{1}{4}$; and (3) if x increases by one unit, then the increase in z to be calculated from the function is approximately $\frac{1}{4}$.[4]

We can now extend the concept of a differential to cover functions of two (or more) variables. Consider once again the function

$$z = f(x, y) \quad .$$

We know that the slopes of the tangent gradients in the x-z- and y-z-planes are given by f_x and f_y, respectively. Assume that we evaluate these partial derivatives at some point. This is a point on a three-dimensional surface that we may denote by (x_0, y_0, z_0). There will be a three-dimensional plane that is tangent to the surface at this point (always assuming, of course, that the function is differentiable). The two partial derivatives, f_x and f_y, give the slopes of the plane in two directions, and this information is, of course, sufficient to determine the position of the whole plane. Taking (x_0, y_0, z_0) as the origin, and letting the differentials dx, dy, and dz stand for arbitrary increments of the dependent variables x and y and the associated increment in the independent variable z along the tangent plane, we can write the equation of the plane as

$$dz = f_x \, dx + f_y \, dy \quad . \tag{51}$$

This equation is called the total differential of the function $z = f(x, y)$. We should note three things about it that are analogous to the points noted for the differential of functions of one variable.

1. Equation (51) is the equation of the plane that is tangent to the function at the values of the variables for which the partials are evaluated. The origin is taken as the point of tangency, and the equation gives the *exact* change in z calculated from the tangent plane that is associated with *any* arbitrary changes in x and y.

2. If we set dx and dy equal to zero alternately and then divide through by the nonzero differential, we obtain

---

[4] The actual increase in z as x goes from 4 to 5 is 0.236, making an error of 0.014 from the increase of 0.250 estimated from (50).

$$\frac{dz}{dx} = f_x$$

and

$$\frac{dz}{dy} = f_y \quad .$$

This shows that the definition of the differentials is such that the ratio of dz/dx is equal to f_x when dy is zero, and such that the ratio dz/dy is equal to f_y when dx is zero. Thus these ratios give the *exact* rate of change of the dependent variable with respect to the independent variable when the other independent variable does not change. It is important that we emphasize once again that dz/dy is *not* the same thing as $\partial z/\partial y = f_y$. The former is the ratio of two distinct quantities; the latter is the result of a limiting process: it is a single number, in which ∂z and ∂x have no separate meanings.

3. Equation (51) can be used to give an approximation to the change in z, Δz, caused by small changes in the independent variables x and y of Δx and Δy. Making the necessary substitutions we can rewrite (51) as

$$\Delta z \simeq f_x\, \Delta x + f_y\, \Delta y \quad . \tag{52}$$

The value of Δz calculated here is an approximation to the change in z that we should have to calculate from $z_1 - z_0 = f(x_0 + \Delta x,\ y_0 + \Delta y) - f(x_0,\ y_0)$.

To illustrate the points we have made about (51) let us again consider a simple example. Assume that we have the production function

$$z = f(x,\ y) = Ax^{1/2}y^{1/2} \quad . \tag{53}$$

Writing the total differential of this function gives

$$dz = f_x\, dx + f_y\, dy$$

$$= \frac{Ay^{1/2}}{2x^{1/2}}\, dx + \frac{Ax^{1/2}}{2y^{1/2}}\, dy \quad .$$

If we take $A = 1$ and evaluate these derivatives at the point $x = 4$, $y = 9$, we obtain

$$dz = \tfrac{3}{4}dx + \tfrac{1}{3}dy \quad . \tag{54}$$

Equation (54) tells us that the *exact* rate of change of z as x changes, y constant, at the point $(x = 4,\ y = 9)$ is $\tfrac{3}{4}$. It also tells us, for example, that the *exact* rate of change of z as x and y are changed in equal amounts (so that $dx = dy$) is $\tfrac{13}{12}$. The equation also allows us to approximate Δz for any Δx and Δy without having to calculate $z_1 - z_0 = f(x_0 +$

Δx, $y_0 + \Delta y) - f(x_0, y_0)$. If, for example, we take $\Delta x = \Delta y = 1$ and substitute $\mathbf{dx} = \mathbf{dy} = 1$ into (54), we obtain an approximate value for Δz of $\frac{13}{12} = 1.083$.[5]

The total differential proves to be an extremely handy concept that is much used in economic applications. It also gives an alternative route to the differentiation of implicit functions that we studied in Section 8.8. Let us say we begin again with the function

$$z = f(x, y) \quad .$$

The total differential is

$$\mathbf{dz} = f_x \, \mathbf{dx} + f_y \, \mathbf{dy} \quad .$$

Now let us assume that y is to be varied as x varies $[y = y(x)]$ in such fashion that the value of z does not change. We accordingly consider the slope of the tangent gradient in the x-y-plane holding z constant. With z constant we have $\mathbf{dz} = 0$, which gives us

$$f_x \, \mathbf{dx} + f_y \, \mathbf{dy} = 0 \quad ,$$

whence

$$\frac{\mathbf{dy}}{\mathbf{dx}} = -\frac{f_x}{f_y} \quad .$$

Now $\mathbf{dy}/\mathbf{dx}$ is the ratio of two finite amounts, but they are defined in such a way that $\mathbf{dy}/\mathbf{dx}$ is equal to dy/dx evaluated from the function $y = y(x)$ at the point x_0, y_0, z_0.

It only requires a slight extension from the case of z constant to handle an implicit function of two variables

$$f(x, y) = 0 \quad .$$

If we could manipulate this function to express y as an explicit function of x, $y = y(x)$, we could then calculate the derivative $dy/dx = y'(x)$. If, however, we cannot or do not wish to do this, we can calculate the total differential

$$f_x \, \mathbf{dx} + f_y \, \mathbf{dy} = 0$$

and manipulate to obtain first the equation of the tangent line

$$\mathbf{dy} = -\frac{f_x}{f_y} \, \mathbf{dx}$$

and second the value of dy/dx as

$$\frac{\mathbf{dy}}{\mathbf{dx}} = -\frac{f_x}{f_y} \quad .$$

This is the slope of the tangent dy/dx.

[5] The correct value is 1.070, giving an error of 0.013.

8.10   COMPOUND FUNCTIONS AND FUNCTIONS OF MORE THAN TWO VARIABLES

The concept of the total differential extends in many ways, and we shall mention only two extensions, both of which we shall require in Chapter 9. First, what if we have a case in which the variables x and y are arguments in two distinct functions? Say, for example, that we have

$$F(x, y) = f(x, y) + g(x, y) = 0 \quad . \tag{55}$$

The total differential of F is quite simply

$$F_x \, \mathbf{dx} + F_y \, \mathbf{dy} = 0$$

from which simple algebraic manipulation produces

$$\mathbf{dy} = -\frac{F_x}{F_y} \, \mathbf{dx} \quad .$$

But what of $f + g$? The answer is quite simply

$$f_x \, \mathbf{dx} + f_y \, \mathbf{dy} + g_x \, \mathbf{dx} + g_y \, \mathbf{dy} = 0 \quad ,$$

which by simple algebraic manipulation produces

$$\mathbf{dy} = \frac{f_x + g_x}{f_y + g_y} \, \mathbf{dx} \tag{56}$$

In other words, because the functions are additive, F_x is merely equal to $f_x + g_x$. If the functions f and g in (55) had been related by a minus sign, then (56) would have contained the differences between the partial derivatives.

This treatment raises one further question: what if instead of (55) we had

$$F(x, y) = f(x, y) + g(x) = 0 \tag{57}$$

in which the second term is a function of only one variable? The total differential is now

$$f_x \, \mathbf{dx} + f_y \, \mathbf{dy} + g'(x) \, \mathbf{dx} \quad , \tag{58}$$

which merely shows that the overall effect F_x of a variation in x is the sum of the effect through the function f, that is, f_x, and the effect through g, that is, $g'(x)$. In such cases, just to keep the notation tidy, it is common to replace $g'(x)$ with g_x even though this is not a partial derivative. Thus we rewrite (58) as

$$f_x \, \mathbf{dx} + f_y \, \mathbf{dy} + g_x \, \mathbf{dx} = 0 \quad , \tag{59}$$

and no confusion is possible because reference to the original equation (57) shows that g_x stands for the derivative of a function of one variable rather than the partial derivative of a function of more than one variable.

As a special case of (57) and (58) we may note that if the function $g(x)$ took the specific form

$$g(x) = x^1 = x \quad , \tag{60}$$

we would proceed as before, except that, since $g'(x) = 1$, the term $g'(x) \, \mathbf{dx}$ reduces to $\mathbf{dx}$.

The final question we ask is, what if we encounter functions of more than two variables? The answer is that the concepts extend quite simply to functions of n variables (providing, of course, that the conditions for differentiability are met). Specifically, for the explicit function

$$z = F(x_1, x_2, \ldots, x_n)$$

we have the total differential

$$\mathbf{dz} = F_{x_1} \, \mathbf{dx}_1 + F_{x_2} \, \mathbf{dx}_2 + \cdots + F_{x_n} \, \mathbf{dx}_n \quad , \tag{61}$$

and for the implicit function

$$G(x_1, x_2, \ldots, x_n) = 0$$

we have the total differential

$$G_{x_1} \, \mathbf{dx}_1 + G_{x_2} \, \mathbf{dx}_2 + \cdots + G_{x_n} \, \mathbf{dx}_n = 0 \quad . \tag{62}$$

This has been a very long chapter, and we delay turning to economic applications of our new tools only for a brief discussion of maximum and minimum values of functions of two or more variables.

8.11 MAXIMUM AND MINIMUM VALUES OF FUNCTIONS OF TWO OR MORE VARIABLES

Our last task in this chapter is to learn how to find stationary values of functions of more than one variable. Of course not all functions of two or more variables will have stationary values. A plane, for example, is the three-dimensional equivalent of a straight line, and just as a linear function has neither a maximum nor a minimum value (it goes on increasing indefinitely in one direction and decreasing in the other) so a plane has neither a maximum nor a minimum. Inspection of Figure 8.1 suggests that the function illustrated there has no stationary value either, at least in the range of positive x, y, and z. But the thimble-shaped function in Figure 8.7 has an obvious maximum at Q, where the two tangents T_x and T_y are both horizontal. We may assert at once that a *necessary condition* for a maximum is that both partial derivatives be zero. This says that we cannot be at a maximum if we

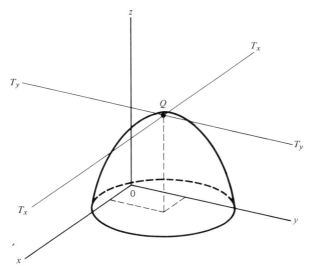

Figure 8.7

can increase the value of the function by changing either of its arguments, the other held constant. We can be quite sure that this condition is not sufficient: if the thimble were turned upside down, we should have a minimum where the slopes of the two tangents were also horizontal. Thus, as with the case of functions of one variable, we require second-order conditions to distinguish maxima from minima. Furthermore, we must expect stationary values that are not extreme values. The possibilities of nonextreme stationary values and nonstationary inflexion points in three dimensions become quite complex. Fortunately, it is not necessary to consider them here.

Second-order conditions for distinguishing minima from maxima in functions of more than one variable are not too difficult. We shall, however, put off considering them until we need them.

QUESTIONS

1. Find the first- and second-order partial derivatives of the following functions and note any points at which the derivatives cannot be evaluated. (*Hint:* Look for points of discontinuity.)
   a. $z = 3x^2 + 4xy + y^2$
   b. $z = x^3 + x^2y + 2y^2x + 2y^3$
   c. $z = ax/y^2$
   d. $z = 1/xy$
   Show that the identity $f_{xy} \equiv f_{yx}$ holds in these cases.

2. If

$$k = \frac{1}{1 - (c - m)(1 - t)} \quad ,$$

find the first- and second-order partial derivatives of k with respect to c, m, and t. (*Hint:* Express the first-order partials in terms of k and calculate the second-order partials without expanding powers of k.)

3. Using limit notation, show that $f_{xy} = f_{yx}$.

4. A consumer has a utility function

$$U = x^\alpha y^\beta \quad ,$$

where x and y are the quantities that he consumes of the only two goods available to him, where $0 < \alpha$, $\beta < 1$, and where U is an index of utility.
   a. Show that there is diminishing marginal utility to increased consumption of either commodity when the consumption of the other is held constant. (*Hint:* This requires both first-order partial derivatives.)
   b. Show that the indifference curves have negative slopes.
   c. What happens to the marginal utility of x as y is increased? (*Hint:* You need a cross-partial here.)
   d. Do you need any further calculation to discover what happens to the marginal utility of y as x is increased?
   e. Does the marginal utility of x or y ever reach zero for finite quantities of x or y?

5. Calculate all the first- and second-order partials of the following.
   a. $q = 500yp$
   b. $z = y^2 + x^2$, where $y = 15x^3$
   c. $q = 500y + 500p$

6. a. Which of the following are "separable"?
      i. $z = x^{1/2}y^{3/4}$
      ii. $z = 35x - 35y$
      iii. $z = 15y$ and $y = \frac{1}{15}x$
      iv. $z = xy - x$
   b. Now taking logs of both sides of Eqs. i–iv, which are "log-separable," that is, which are separable functions when transformed so that $\log z$ is a function of $\log x$ and $\log y$?

7. Find the total differential dz/dt for each of the functions in Question 1 if

$$x = 3t$$

and

$$y = 3t^2 \quad .$$

8. Suppose that labor accepts a lower wage the greater is a firm's safety expenditures, i.e., $W = W(S)$, $W'(S) < 0$. Also assume that a firm's cost function is $C = S + LW$. Taking L, the number of laborers, to be fixed, calculate the responsiveness of cost to safety expenditure.

9. Find an expression for the slope of the iso-z curves for part d in Question 1 and evaluate the slope at $x = 5$, $y = 10$ and at $x = 15$, $y = 30$. What do you conclude about the slopes of the iso-z curves?

10. Using the examples of Question 6, find the equations for the slopes of the iso-z lines.

11. a. Consider $q^d = q(p, y)$. Using differentials, calculate the response in q^d when
    i. price and income are increased in the ratio $dp = 2dy$.
    ii. price and income are increased in the ratio $dp = 0.5dy$.
    iii. any increase in price is matched by a decrease in income of the same absolute magnitude, that is, $dp = -dy$.
    b. Now answer the same question using the specific function given in Eq. (3) (Section 8.1).

12. The implicit function for a sphere with radius 10 is $x^2 + y^2 + z^2 - 100 = 0$. Calculate the following.
    a. The slope dy/dx when z is held constant
    b. The slopes dz/dx and dz/dy when any change in x is matched with twice that change in y

Chapter **9**

Applications of Functions of More than One Variable

We have now added to our array of techniques in a very powerful fashion. Once we can deal with functions of more than one variable, we can deal with functions of n variables whether n be 2 or 2,000,000,000! Most readers will recall many places in their first-year economics course that related some effect, y, to a single cause, x. "Aw, that's too simple: y is affected by lots of x's so what you were told is for the birds"—something like that must have been heard by many of you. What you typically were not told, even by sympathetic first-year teachers, was that the deficiency in handling the problems mentioned by the critics was in you, not in economics (it would be an unpopular thing for an instructor to say). Economics can handle n causal factors. We may not know enough to make sensible hypotheses about the effects of n variables but that is a different point: ignorance afflicts us all but ability to cope with such complexities as we can perceive and understand is not a limitation; the mathematical techniques are available to deal with anything that we do, or wish to assume we could, perceive.

The Competitive Market

9.1 SOME GENERAL RESULTS FOR THE MODEL OF A COMPETITIVE MARKET

In our analysis of the competitive market in earlier chapters, we have made the restrictive assumption of linear demand and supply curves. With the techniques now at our command we can drop this assumption and can obtain results of much more general significance. We now write the behavior equations of our model quite generally:

$$q^d = D(p, \alpha) \tag{1}$$

$$q^s = S(p, \beta) \tag{2}$$

$$q^d = q^s \ . \tag{3}$$

Equations (1) and (2) define demand and supply functions as depending on the price of the product and two *shift parameters*, α and β. There are many other influences besides price that affect demand and supply, such as tastes, income, and taxes. Since a change in any of these factors must shift either the demand or the supply curve (or both), any change can be handled by making an appropriate change in α and/or β. Equation (3) gives the equilibrium condition that quantity demanded equals quantity supplied.

To handle the model, we first substitute the behavioral equations (1) and (2) into the equilibrium condition (3). This gives us

$$D(p, \alpha) = S(p, \beta) \ . \tag{4}$$

The equation

$$D(p, \alpha) - S(p, \beta) = 0 \tag{5}$$

gives, in implicit form, the relation between p, α, and β that will satisfy the equilibrium condition (3). We could write this $F(p, \alpha, \beta) = 0$ and notice that this defines a surface in $(p - \alpha - \beta)$-space such that at every point on the surface equilibrium condition (3) is satisfied. We can call this equation the solution expressed in the solution space $p - \alpha - \beta$.

We may now use the result on total differentiation of functions of two variables given in Section 8.9 to write

$$D_p \ dp + D_\alpha \ d\alpha - S_p \ dp - S_\beta \ d\beta = 0 \ . \tag{6}$$

It is useful to consider (6) term by term. The terms D_p and S_p are the partial derivatives of quantity demanded and quantity supplied with respect to price, and the usual assumptions that demand curves slope downwards and supply curves upwards allow us to sign these as $D_p < 0 < S_p$. The other two partials, D_α and S_β, are the rates of change of demand and supply with respect to change in the shift parameters. They may be assumed to be positive or negative, as is appropriate for the problem at hand. We now assume that $0 < D_\alpha, S_\beta$, which means that demand is increased by an increase in α and supply by an increase in β. The terms dp, $d\alpha$, and $d\beta$ are differentials. In Chapter 8 we wrote these in boldface type so that we would not confuse the ratio of two differentials (e.g., $\mathbf{dy/dx}$) with the corresponding derivative (dy/dx). From here on we follow the standard practice of writing differentials in the same type as derivatives. Since $\mathbf{dy/dx} =$

dy/dx, this cannot cause us to make mechanical errors in our manipulations. (It can, however, cause us to be confused about what we are really doing if we confuse the ratio of two finite differentials **dy/dx** with the derivative of y with respect to x: although the two have the same value, they are not the same thing.)

Now that we have considered (6) term by term, we may manipulate it algebraically to obtain

$$dp = -\frac{D_\alpha}{D_p - S_p}\, d\alpha + \frac{S_\beta}{D_p - S_p}\, d\beta \quad . \tag{7}$$

This is the equation of the tangent plane to (5). It is, of course, linear in the differentials dp, $d\alpha$, and $d\beta$, and the coefficients are ratios of the partial derivatives of the two functions D and S.

Now let us consider the effect on price of shifts in the demand curve with the supply curve held constant. This means that we want $d\beta = 0$. Substituting this into (7) and dividing through by $d\alpha$ yields

$$\frac{dp}{d\alpha} = -\frac{D_\alpha}{D_p - S_p} \quad . \tag{8}$$

Although dp and $d\alpha$ are two differentials, their ratio is, as we know, equal to the derivative $dp/d\alpha$. Thus (8) tells us the derivative of price with respect to α. It is the exact measure of the slope of the tangent to the surface described by (5) in the p-α-plane with β held constant.

Inspection of (8) in the light of the sign restrictions established earlier $(D_p < 0 < S_p, D_\alpha)$ shows that $dp/d\alpha$ is always positive. Thus an increase in demand raises price, and a decrease lowers it.

Next consider the effects of an increase in supply. To do this we substitute $d\alpha = 0$ into (7) and divide through by $d\beta$ to obtain

$$\frac{dp}{d\beta} = \frac{S_\beta}{D_p - S_p} \quad . \tag{9}$$

The sign restrictions on the partial derivatives this time ensure that the value of $dp/d\beta$ is always negative: an increase in supply lowers price, and a decrease raises it.

We have used (7) to determine the exact rates of change of price with respect to α and to β. We can also use it to obtain approximate estimates of the change in p associated with finite changes in a and β. When we do this, we are moving around the tangent plane rather than the function — since (7) is the equation of the tangent plane. We shall not pursue this matter further here because we are mainly interested in the qualitative results on the sign of the change in p associated with shifts in the demand and supply curves.

Note how simply these qualitative results have been attained and how general they are. We are no longer confined to linear demand and supply functions nor to the particular curve that we just happen to draw on a two-dimensional diagram. We are now able to derive the four basic predictions about the effect on price of shifts in the demand and supply curves using only the basic assumptions that q^d and p vary inversely with each other (i.e., $D_p < 0$) and that q^s and p vary directly with each other (i.e., $S_p > 0$). Since α and β stand for anything that shifts the demand and supply curves, we can handle any new case we meet merely by establishing which curve is shifted in which direction. If, for example, the demand curve is shifted to the right, we are interested in the effect on p of an increase in α, that is, in the sign of $dp/d\alpha$. If the demand curve is shifted left, we are interested in the effect of a decrease in α, that is, in the sign of $(-1)dp/d\alpha$. We now have established results of great power and generality.

The Model of Income Determination

9.2 INCOME DETERMINATION

We are also able to drop the restrictive linearity assumption for the relations in our national income model and show how comparative static results can be obtained in the more general case. We shall produce one result as an example and then ask you to derive another in Question 5.

The simplest model of national income is based on the following general relations:

$$C = C(Y, \alpha) \tag{10}$$

$$Z = Z(\beta) \tag{11}$$

$$Y = C + Z \ . \tag{12}$$

Equation (10) gives the behavioral assumption relating to consumption: consumption depends on income and many other influences such as taxes, income distribution, the introduction of new goods, and credit terms. All these other influences are assumed to be constant when we solve the model. We may then investigate the effect on the solution of a change in any one of them by varying the parameter α. Equation (11) refers to autonomous expenditure, by which we mean expenditure that does *not* depend on variables that are endogenous to the model. (The only endogenous variable other than consumption in this model is income.) Equation (11) allows for the fact that current autonomous expenditure may depend on a number of variables, such as the interest rate and the level of taxes, which are exogenous to this model and a change in which can be represented by a change in the parameter β. Equation (12) states the equilibrium condition that current income should equal the sum of the induced component, current consumption expenditure, and the autonomous component, Z.

Substitution of (10) and (11) into (12) produces

$$Y = C(Y, \alpha) + Z(\beta) \quad . \qquad (13)$$

If we rewrite (13) as

$$Y - C(Y, \alpha) - Z(\beta) = 0 \qquad (14)$$

and once again regard α and β as variables, we have, in implicit form, the solution equation in the solution space Y-α-β. So long as we do not have the specific form of the function $C(Y, \alpha)$, we cannot manipulate (14) to obtain Y directly as an explicit function of α and β. We can, however, take the total differential of (14) to obtain the equation for the tangent plane to the surface described by (14):

$$dY - C_y\, dY - C_\alpha\, d\alpha + Z_\beta\, d\beta = 0 \quad . \qquad (15)$$

Looking at the individual terms in (15) we see that dY, dα, and dβ are differentials and that C_α and Z_β show the effects of the shift parameters on C and Z (hence both are positive), whereas C_y represents the effect on consumption of a change in income. C_y, the partial derivative of C with respect to Y, is the magnitude commonly called the marginal propensity to consume. According to standard theory, households always consume a part of any additional income and save the rest. Thus $0 < C_y < 1$.

We now manipulate (15) algebraically to get the equation of the tangent plane in explicit form:

$$dY(1 - C_y) = C_\alpha\, d\alpha - Z_\beta\, d\beta \quad ,$$

whence

$$dY = \frac{C_\alpha}{1 - C_y}\, d\alpha - \frac{Z_\beta}{1 - C_y}\, d\beta \quad . \qquad (16)$$

Let us now consider the case in which the consumption function remains stable while autonomous expenditure increases. If we substitute d$\alpha = 0$ into (16) and divide through by dβ, we obtain

$$\frac{dY}{d\beta} = \frac{Z_\beta}{1 - C_y} \quad . \qquad (17)$$

This gives us the instantaneous rate of change of income with respect to a change in autonomous expenditure. By the restrictions already placed on the partial derivates this derivative is obviously positive. Not only that, but since $1 - C_y$ must be a positive fraction, we have

$$\frac{dY}{d\beta} > Z_\beta \quad , \tag{18}$$

which says that the rate of change in income exceeds that of autonomous expenditure, Z_β, that brought it about. If we divide (18) through by Z_β, we get

$$\frac{dY/d\beta}{Z_\beta} > 1 \quad , \tag{19}$$

which is the famous result that the *multiplier*, defined as the rate of change in income, $dY/d\beta$, *divided by* the rate of change in autonomous expenditure, Z_β, exceeds unity.

All of the above analysis is in terms of instantaneous rates of change. The derivative $dY/d\beta$, for example, measures the tendency for income to change as β changes at a particular level of income. If we wish to assume neither that our behavioral functions are linear (in this model there is only the consumption function) nor that they take on a specific nonlinear form (e.g., $C = 2Y^{1/2} + \alpha$), this is as far as we can go with exact statements. We can go no further since we cannot manipulate (14), the solution equation, to get Y as an explicit function of α and β. But, if we wish, we can use (16), the equation of the tangent plane, to give approximate estimates of finite changes in Y associated with finite changes in α and β. In this case we rewrite (16) as

$$\Delta Y \simeq \frac{C_\alpha}{1 - C_y} \Delta\alpha - \frac{Z_\beta}{1 - C_y} \Delta\beta \quad , \tag{20}$$

where the Δs's refer to movements along the solution surface described by (14) and the $\simeq$ indicates that we are approximating these movements along the tangent plane described by (16).

Clearly, the model can be extended to produce other results, but we shall not bother the reader with them here. Some of them are suggested in the questions at the end of the chapter. We have, however, succeeded, as in the demand-and-supply case, in shedding the assumption of linearity and in deriving general qualitative predictions from the model of national income that depend only on assumptions about qualitative restrictions that can be put on relevant partial derivatives. From (17) it follows, for example, that the change in income exceeds the changes in autonomous expenditure as long as $0 < C_y < 1$.

We have now gone a long way toward producing general results that do not depend on special, and possibly unreal, assumptions such as linearity. We have now illustrated what we asserted in Chapter 1: that, far from forcing our models to be narrow and restrictive, the use of mathematics allows us to shed restrictions that we were forced to employ not because we thought them warranted by our knowledge but only because of the limitations in our verbal and geometrical tools of analysis.

Miscellaneous Applications

9.3 HOMOGENEOUS FUNCTIONS

We now wish to discuss production functions. Before taking up a well-known example, it is convenient to derive some properties of homogeneous functions. A function is said to be homogeneous of degree n if multiplying all the arguments in the function by the same constant, λ, multiplies the value of the function by λ to the power of n, that is, by λ^n.

First consider some examples:

$$q = LK$$

is homogeneous of degree 2 since

$$\lambda L \lambda K = \lambda^2 LK = \lambda^2 q \quad,$$

whereas

$$q = L^{1/4} K^{1/4}$$

is homogeneous of degree $\frac{1}{2}$ since

$$(\lambda L)^{1/4}(\lambda K)^{1/4} = \lambda^{1/2} L^{1/4} K^{1/4} = \lambda^{1/2} q \quad.$$

Indeed, the function

$$y = x^n z^m$$

is homogeneous of degree $n + m$ since

$$(\lambda x)^n (\lambda z)^m = \lambda^{n+m} x^n z^m \quad.$$

Of course not all functions are homogeneous. Any of the previous examples can be rendered nonhomogeneous by giving it an additive constant. For example,

$$q = L^{1/2} K^{1/2} + a \qquad (a \neq 0)$$

is not homogeneous in L and K. If you multiply L and K by λ, you do not multiply q by λ, because the additive constant is unchanged when you change L and K so that doubling L and K is not sufficient to double the value of the function. Thus

$$\lambda L \lambda K + a = \lambda^2 LK + a$$

cannot be derived by multiplying $q = LK + a$ by any power of λ.

In other words, if we have any function $y = \psi(x, z) + a$, where a is a nonzero constant, we cannot obtain the new value of the function resulting from multiplying x and z by λ by multiplying the original value by λ raised to any power: there is no n such that $\lambda^n y = \psi(x\lambda, z\lambda) + a$. Since any additive constant renders a function nonhomogeneous, it follows that homogeneous functions have the property that their value must be zero when all the variables in the function are zero. If y is a homogeneous function of x, then a graph of the function must pass through the origin. Formally we write this as follows: $f(0) = 0$.

We now prove a theorem on homogeneous functions called Euler's theorem (pronounced Oiler's theorem!). This theorem is now well within the technical grasp of the readers of this book. The general statement is as follows. If

$$y = f(x_1, x_2, \ldots, x_n)$$

is a homogeneous function of degree 1, then it is true that

$$y = \frac{\partial y}{\partial x_1} \cdot x_1 + \frac{\partial y}{\partial x_2} \cdot x_2 + \cdots + \frac{\partial y}{\partial x_n} \cdot x_n \quad .$$

We can prove Euler's theorem for the case of two variables quite simply (the proof for many variables is on the same lines but gets cumbersome). Let

$$z = f(x, y)$$

be homogeneous of degree 1. Then

$$\lambda z = f(\lambda x, \lambda y) \quad .$$

Let us choose $\lambda = 1/y$. Then

$$\frac{z}{y} = f\left(\frac{x}{y}, 1\right)$$

or

$$z = yf\left(\frac{x}{y}, 1\right) \quad . \tag{21}$$

Notice now that, in (21), f is a function of a *single argument*, x/y (the distinction between the arguments of a function and the variables contained in it was explained in Section 2.8). We can also write

$$z = yh\left(\frac{x}{y}\right) \quad , \tag{22}$$

where $h(x/y) = f(x/y, 1)$ and h is, of course, a function of a single argument. Now we have the slightly complicated task of taking the partial derivatives of (22). Let us start with x. We obtain

$$\frac{\partial z}{\partial x} = yh'\left(\frac{x}{y}\right)\frac{1}{y} = h'\left(\frac{x}{y}\right) \quad , \tag{23}$$

since, by the chain rule, $d/dx[h(x/y)]$ is $h'(x/y)\cdot d(x/y)/dx = h'(x/y)y^{-1}$. To find the partial of (22) with respect to y we employ the product rule as well as the chain rule. $d[h(x/y)]/dy$ is $h'(x/y)(-xy^{-2})$, so we have

$$\frac{\partial z}{\partial y} = yh'\left(\frac{x}{y}\right)\left(\frac{-x}{y^2}\right) + h\left(\frac{x}{y}\right) = -\frac{x}{y}h'\left(\frac{x}{y}\right) + h\left(\frac{x}{y}\right) \quad . \tag{24}$$

We now multiply (23) by x and (24) by y and add to obtain

$$xh'\left(\frac{x}{y}\right) + y\left[-\frac{x}{y}h'\left(\frac{x}{y}\right) + h\left(\frac{x}{y}\right)\right] = yh\left(\frac{x}{y}\right) = z \quad ,$$

which completes the proof. [We shall make further use of the fact that a constant-returns production function can be written in the form of (21) or (22) when we discuss economic growth in Section 14.4.]

9.4   THE COBB-DOUGLAS PRODUCTION FUNCTION

A great deal of effort has been expended in trying to estimate from empirical data the precise forms of production functions for individual firms, for whole industries, and even for whole countries. One function that has been widely used is the so-called Cobb-Douglas production function,

$$q = Ax_1^{\alpha}x_2^{\beta} \cdots x_m^{\eta} \quad ,$$

where $\alpha + \beta + \cdots + \eta = 1$ and $0 < \alpha, \beta, \ldots, \eta < 1$. This is an example of a homogeneous function.

We do not need to worry here about the problems — which can be formidable — of estimating such functions statistically, nor shall we investigate more complicated functional forms that are now believed to correspond more closely to observation. For purposes of the present exercise we can pretend that the econometricians have told us that the Cobb-Douglas production function does seem to provide a reasonable description of production behavior in many industries, and our job as economic theorists is to discover the implications of this. We ask ourselves the question, if this function does hold, what other things can we expect to hold as well? This is a typical task of the economic theorist. He takes it that certain things are true of the world and seeks to discover what other things must also be true. A good economist will be able to suggest immediately a "shopping list" of relevant questions when presented with a problem such as this one.

In this case our shopping list includes such questions as, what are the shapes of the total, average, and marginal product and cost curves as one factor is varied in the short run? What are the returns to scale when all factors are varied in the long run? What will be the effects on factor earnings of variations in factor supplies? Other interesting questions may suggest themselves as the analysis proceeds, but we start with a list of questions that consideration of standard theory suggests we should ask about any production function that we wish to take seriously.

We shall work with a two-factor production function, identifying the two inputs as labor (L) and capital (K). The argument easily generalizes to any number of factors. The Cobb-Douglas function for two inputs is

$$q = AL^\alpha K^\beta \quad , \tag{25}$$

where $\alpha + \beta = 1$, A is a constant, and L and K are the quantities used of two factors of production, labor and capital.

For a fixed amount of capital, the average product of labor, AP, is given by

$$AP = \frac{q}{L} = AL^{\alpha-1}K^{1-\alpha} \tag{26}$$

(with K a constant and $\beta = 1 - \alpha$). Equation (26) is positive but declines with increasing labor input:

$$\frac{\partial}{\partial L}\left(\frac{q}{L}\right) = (\alpha - 1)AL^{\alpha-2}K^{1-\alpha} \quad .$$

In the same way, the marginal product of labor is everywhere positive but everywhere declining. Thus

$$\frac{\partial q}{\partial L} = \alpha AL^{\alpha-1}K^{1-\alpha}$$

(which must be positive for *all* positive values of L and K), and

$$\frac{\partial^2 q}{\partial L^2} = \alpha(a - 1)AL^{\alpha-2}K^{1-\alpha}$$

(which, since $\alpha - 1 < 0$, is negative for all positive L and K). It is interesting to note the relationship between AP and MP: the latter is α times the former.

The general slopes of these product curves are shown in Figure 9.1. We have now made our first discovery about this production function: marginal and average products decline from the outset. In the production function usually shown in textbooks, the marginal and average products rise at first and only decline eventually. The type of

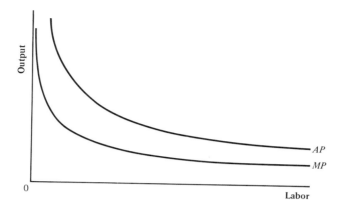

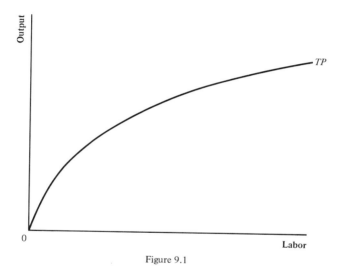

Figure 9.1

curves usually assumed in elementary production theory are illustrated in Figure 9.2.

Now let us consider costs. If we let w stand for the wage rate and r for the price of capital services, we can write total cost (TC) as

$$TC = wL + rK \quad . \tag{27}$$

We want TC as a function of q. We can get total short-run cost very easily by fixing K at $\bar{K}$ so that L varies. Thus q is a function of only one variable, L, and so also is TC. Now write the production function as

$$q = bL^\alpha \quad ,$$

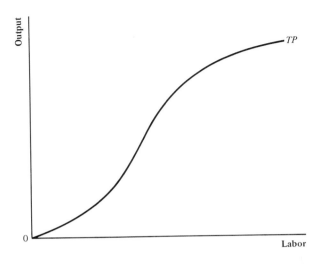

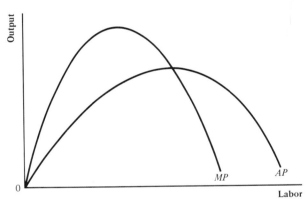

Figure 9.2

where

$$b = A\bar{K}^{1-\alpha} \quad ,$$

and transpose it to obtain

$$L = \frac{q^{1/\alpha}}{b^{1/\alpha}} \quad . \tag{28}$$

We now substitute L from (28) into the total cost expression in (27). This gives

$$TC = \frac{wq^{1/\alpha}}{b^{1/\alpha}} + r\bar{K} \quad . \tag{29}$$

In the short run capital is fixed, and so is the cost of capital services: $r\bar{K} = F$ is fixed costs. If the firm buys its labor in a competitive market, we can assume that the price of labor, w, is a constant. We now have total cost in (29) and can calculate average cost (AC) merely by dividing by q:

$$AC = \frac{TC}{q} = \frac{wq^{1/\alpha}}{b^{1/\alpha}q} + \frac{F}{q}$$

$$= \frac{wq^{1/\alpha - 1}}{b^{1/\alpha}} + \frac{F}{q} \quad . \tag{30}$$

Since $(1/\alpha) - 1 > 0$, the exponent on q is positive, whence average variable cost must rise continuously as output rises. Average fixed cost, however, declines as the fixed capital cost, F, is spread over a larger and larger number of units. The average total cost curve declines at first and then rises.[1]

The marginal cost curve is also easily calculated by differentiating (29):

$$MC = \frac{dTC}{dq} = \frac{wq^{1/\alpha - 1}}{\alpha b^{1/\alpha}} \quad . \tag{31}$$

Since $(1/\alpha) - 1$ is positive, marginal cost rises continuously as output is increased.

The fact that the average and marginal cost curves do not have the textbook U-shape is a consequence of the shape of the average and marginal product curves on which we have already commented. The ATC curve does have the usually assumed "U-shape" because of the influence of fixed costs.

We have already discovered some interesting things. With a production function that is not inconsistent with much observed data, the cost curves do not have the shape they are usually assumed to have in elementary textbooks. This turns out to hold for all twice differentiable constant-returns-to-scale production functions.

Finally we may ask about returns to scale in the Cobb-Douglas function. Since the coefficients sum to unity, it follows that the Cobb-Douglas function is homogeneous of the first degree: multiplying all the independent variables (inputs) by λ multiplies the value of the function (output) by λ. Thus the function displays constant returns to scale.

---

[1] You may wish to gain some practice in differentiation by proving for yourself that the level of output for which the AC curve is a minimum is given by

$$q = \frac{b(F/w)^\alpha}{((1/\alpha) - 1)^\alpha} \quad .$$

9.5 THE DISTRIBUTION OF THE TOTAL PRODUCT

Early classical economists such as Adam Smith and David Ricardo felt that one of the most important problems of political economy was to discover the laws that governed the distribution of the national product between the three classes of society, the laborers, the capitalists, and the landlords. Gradually, toward the latter part of the nineteenth century, the marginal productivity theory gained ascendance. According to this theory, each factor received a payment, per unit of time worked, equal to the value of the marginal product of that factor. Thus if one more laborer added to the existing labor force would add 10 bushels of wheat per month to the product, then the wage rate for *all* workers would be 10 bushels of wheat per month, and the total monthly wage bill would be 10 bushels multiplied by the number of laborers employed—and similarly for each other factor. The marginal productivity theory explained only the demand curve for a factor, and supply had to be explained by other considerations. In equilibrium, however, price and quantity must be at some point on the demand curve (the point where the curve is cut by the supply curve), whence it is a prediction of the theory that in equilibrium the price of every factor will be equal to the value of its marginal product.

The theory posed two major problems. The first was a purely theoretical one and was usually called the *adding-up problem*. The question here was, if each factor is paid at a rate equal to its marginal product, will the total payments to all factors be equal to total production? If total payment exactly exhausts the product, there is no problem, but if these payments are greater than or less than total production, problems must arise. Clearly, it is logically impossible to pay to factors a real amount in excess of what is produced, whereas if less than what is produced is paid out, the problem is, who gets the surplus and how? If payment according to marginal product was impossible because sufficient production would not be available, the marginal productivity theory would be in real trouble. Indeed, it would be refuted on purely logical grounds, since it would be impossible to fulfill the conditions of the theory that each factor should be paid a rate equal to its marginal product.

Now let us consider the adding-up problem in the case of the Cobb-Douglas production function. The function was written as

$$q = AL^\alpha K^\beta \quad . \tag{25}$$

We have seen in Section 9.4 that this function is homogeneous, and if we assume that $\alpha + \beta = 1$, the function is homogeneous of degree 1 (i.e., it has constant returns to scale).

If we wish to study the distribution of the total product, we must first determine the marginal products of the two factors:

$$\frac{\partial q}{\partial L} = A\alpha L^{\alpha-1}K^{\beta} \tag{32}$$

$$\frac{\partial q}{\partial K} = A\beta L^{\alpha}K^{\beta-1} \quad . \tag{33}$$

The total payment to each factor is, of course, the rate of pay per unit *times* the number of units employed. This is

$$Y_L = \frac{\partial q}{\partial L} \cdot L = A\alpha L^{\alpha-1}K^{\beta}L$$

$$= A\alpha L^{\alpha}K^{\beta} \quad , \tag{34}$$

where Y_L stands for the real income of labor.[2] But from (25) we know that $AL^{\alpha}K^{\beta}$ is the total product, q. Therefore we can write (34) as

$$Y_L = \alpha q \quad .$$

Similarly for capital

$$Y_K = \frac{\partial q}{\partial K} \cdot K$$

$$= A\beta L^{\alpha}K^{b-1}K$$

$$= A\beta L^{\alpha}K^{\beta}$$

$$= \beta q \quad . \tag{35}$$

The total income paid to all factors is the sum of the payments to each factor. Thus we have

$$Y = Y_L + Y_K = \alpha q + \beta q$$

$$= (\alpha + \beta)q \quad . \tag{36}$$

Now if $\alpha + \beta = 1$ (36) reduces to $Y = q$, which tells us that the total product is just exhausted by income payments if both factors are paid at a rate equal to the value of their marginal products: this is Euler's theorem.

There are two other cases to be considered. If $\alpha + \beta < 1$, the production function is homogeneous of degree less than 1: there are decreasing returns to scale. According to (36), $Y < q$ when both factors are paid the values of their respective marginal products. In this case

---

[2] Notice that we have expressed the wage in real units. If we wished, we could multiply by the price of the product and obtain the wage in money units. Our problem would then be to discover if the money value of payments to factors equaled the money value of the product. This is, of course, the same as discovering if the real payment to all factors equals real output.

there is a surplus equal to $(1-\alpha-\beta)q$ remaining after all income payments have been made, and there is nothing in our development of the theory here to tell us who gets it, since we are not taking into account the role of the entrepreneur and problems of monopoly.

Consider the case in which $\alpha + \beta > 1$. The production function is homogeneous of degree greater than 1: there are increasing returns to scale since doubling all inputs more than doubles the output. In this case (36) shows $Y > q$, so that it is impossible to pay each factor a wage equal to the value of its marginal product since there is not enough product to go around (whence we suspect that if a firm is in equilibrium at a point where returns are increasing, it must be a monopoly).

Euler's theorem shows that for any linear homogeneous function (constant returns to scale) the value of the function is exactly equal to the sum of the partial derivatives with respect to each variable in the function each multiplied by the value of the variable in question. This shows that the adding-up problem is solved in perfect competition for constant-returns production functions but not for production functions displaying increasing or decreasing returns. Of course, if there is one factor that is hypothesized to earn a rent not related to the value of its marginal product, then the adding-up problem does not occur. In this case $n-1$ factors can be paid the value of their marginal products and the nth merely gets whatever is left over.

The second problem arose when long-run data on distribution were first studied in the interwar period, and the investigators observed what appeared to them to be a remarkable constancy in the distribution of income between labor and capital. What people had expected was never made too clear, but some economists seemed to have felt that the great increase in the capital stock over the previous 100 years should have increased the share of total income going to capital. Others felt that, because of the effect of diminishing returns, the distribution of income should have changed in some direction or another in response to changes in relative factor proportions, and that the persistence of a constancy must mean that, contrary to the prediction of marginal productivity theory, relative factor shares did not respond to relative factor proportions.

Later investigation has raised considerable doubt about the alleged constancy, but let us suppose that we have been presented with the situation outlined by the following two points.

1. We assume that marginal productivity theory holds.
2. We accept that over the last 100 years the total quantity of capital has increased faster than the total quantity of labor (i.e., K/L has risen).

We then ask ourselves the following two questions.

1. Do we have any prediction to offer regarding the relative shares of income going to labor and to capital (i.e., about the ratio Y_K/Y_L)?
2. Specifically, would the observation of a constant Y_K/Y_L over an extended period of time refute any prediction of the marginal productivity theory of distribution?

We already know from (34) and (35) that, for a constant-returns Cobb-Douglas function, $(\beta = 1 - \alpha)$ we have

$$Y_L = \alpha q$$

and

$$Y_K = (1 - \alpha)q \quad ,$$

whence the fraction of total income going to each factor is

$$\frac{Y_L}{Y} = \frac{A\alpha L^\alpha K^{1-\alpha}}{AL^\alpha K^{1-\alpha}} = \alpha \tag{37}$$

$$\frac{Y_K}{Y} = \frac{A(1-\alpha)L^\alpha K^{1-\alpha}}{AL^\alpha K^{1-\alpha}} = 1 - \alpha \quad . \tag{38}$$

Thus the proportion of income going to labor and capital depends only on the coefficient α and is quite independent of the size of the labor force, L, and of the size of the capital stock, K. This is a most remarkable and interesting result, and we would have been unlikely to have discovered it by unaided verbal analysis. Yet the result follows from a routine application of a simple mathematical technique to the production function, and one does not have to be gifted with great theoretical insight to discover it for oneself, once the necessary mathematical technique has been mastered.

We have seen that the combination of marginal productivity theory with the Cobb-Douglas production function predicts that factor shares will remain constant in the face of changing factor supplies. The reason for this is that an increase in the quantity of one factor drives its marginal product and hence its price down *in proportion to the increase in quantity* so that the factor's share remains constant. Investigation of the Cobb-Douglas production function shows that the answer to question 2 above is "no." Indeed, if production functions are Cobb-Douglas, we expect the shares of income going to labor and capital to remain constant, provided, of course, that the parameter α remains constant. If the effect of technological change is only to increase the multiplicative constant A, it is possible for α to be stable in spite of important advances in technology.

The results presented so far assume perfect markets, for only in the case of perfect competition does labor receive the value of its marginal physical product as a wage. Let us now consider very briefly the case in which firms sell their products on nonperfect markets (but are not monopsonists in the labor market). In this case the wage will be equal to the marginal revenue product of labor, which is the change in revenue due to a marginal change in the labor force. This will be less than the value of the marginal product of labor because an increase in output drives the price down (so that a reduction in revenue is suffered on those units already being produced). We may now write

$$w = MRP = MPP \cdot MR \quad , \tag{39}$$

where w is the wage rate. A familiar result allows us to rewrite this as[3]

$$w = MPP\left(1 + \frac{1}{\eta}\right)p \quad .$$

We now consider the total wage bill, W:

$$W = wL = (MRP)L = L \cdot MPP\left(1 + \frac{1}{\eta}\right)p \quad . \tag{40}$$

In the Cobb-Douglas case we already know that

$$L \cdot MPP = \alpha AL^\alpha K^\beta$$
$$= \alpha q \tag{41}$$

where q is total output. Substitution of (41) into (40) gives

$$W = \alpha q\left(1 + \frac{1}{\eta}\right)p \quad .$$

Multiplying both sides by $1/pq$ gives

$$\frac{W}{pq} = \alpha\left(1 + \frac{1}{\eta}\right) \quad , \tag{42}$$

---

[3] In Chapter 5, Eq. (41), we had

$$MRP = MPP\left(q\frac{dp}{dq} + p\right) \quad .$$

We now substitute w for MRP because the wage paid will equal MRP, and we factor out the p to get

$$w = MPP\left(\frac{q}{p} \cdot \frac{dp}{dq} + 1\right)p$$
$$= MPP\left(\frac{1}{\eta} + 1\right)p \quad .$$

where W is already in money units from (39) and pq gives output also in money units. Thus the share of wages will be constant for a given α if η remains constant but will vary if η varies.

We see that, in this case, the share of income going to labor depends partly on the production function and partly also on market conditions. It is worth asking if we can give any meaning to the factor $1/\eta$ that appears in (42). It may be interpreted as showing the degree of monopoly. If a commodity is sold under perfect competition, elasticity to the individual firm is $-\infty$ and, at the limit, $1/\eta = 0$. If there is some product differentiation, but not a great deal (a situation that we might get under monopolistic competition) η is finite but still quite large, and thus $1/\eta$ is still small. As the degree of product differentiation increases each producer becomes more like a monopolist, his own elasticity decreases, and $1/\eta$ increases.

Now this begins to look more interesting. It appears that our marginal productivity theory in a world of nonperfect competition gives rise to a theory that distribution depends on the degree of monopoly in the economy. We shall not pursue this topic further here, but it does seem that there is some interesting material to be explored along these lines.[4]

QUESTIONS

1. Establish the effects on price and quantity of a leftward and a rightward shift in the supply curve in a perfectly competitive market. [See Eq. (8).]

2. A profit-maximizing monopolist has a profit function, $\Pi = p(q, \alpha)q - C(q, \beta)$. Write down the equilibrium condition for this firm. Now using α and β as variables, as well as q, take total differentials, and obtain the equation of the tangent plane to the profit function in explicit form.

3. Consider the effects of an upward shift of the consumption function on the level of national income.

4. The quantity theory determines the price level according to the equilibrium condition

$$kPT = M \quad ,$$

where P is the price level, T is the volume of transactions, k is the fraction of the money value of transactions people desire to hold as balances, and M is the supply of money.
a. Write P as an explicit function of M, T, and k.

---

[4] The interested reader might wish to start with N. Kaldor, "Alternative Theories of Distribution," reprinted as chap. 12 in *Essays on Value and Distribution*, Duckworth, London, 1960.

   b. Investigate the change in P for changes in each of the independent variables, the others held constant.

   c. Write the total differential of this function.

5. Using the simple model of national income given by Eqs. (10), (11), and (12), calculate $dY/d\alpha$ and $dY/d\beta$ when α and β shift equally. The sign of these two slopes depends solely on the relative magnitude of which two derivatives?

6. Calculate $dY/d\alpha$ for $C = 10 + 0.92Y + \alpha$, $Z = 600 + \beta$, and $Y = C + Z$. Now take a finite difference for α, $\Delta\alpha = 30$, and compute an approximation for ΔY.

7. Consider the production function

$$q = K^{2/3}L^{2/3} \quad .$$

   a. Does it display decreasing returns to each factor?

   b. Does it have constant, increasing, or decreasing returns to scale?

   c. Calculate the expression for total payments if both factors get a price equal to the value of their marginal products.

8. Consider the production function

$$q = AK^{\alpha}L^{\alpha} \quad .$$

   a. Can you discover what the value of α would have to be for each factor to have constant returns to that factor (the other held constant)?

   b. Can you give any interpretation of this result?

9. Check that Euler's theorem holds for the function $y = x^2z^{-1}$ at the point $x = 2$, $z = 4$.

10. Write Euler's theorem and the total differential for $Z = f(X, Y, W)$. What restrictions on f must be made for the two equations you have written to be valid?

11. State which of the following functions are homogeneous. For those that are, state of what degree.

   a. $y = \sqrt{x^2y^3}$

   b. $y = 3 + x^{1/3}y^{1/3}$

   c. $y = x^{1/2}y^{1/2}$

   d. $y = xy/\sqrt{xy}$

12. Write down two examples of functions that are

   a. Homogeneous of degree 0.

   b. Homogeneous of degree 2.

Chapter 10

Constrained Maxima and Minima

". . . Economics brings into full view that conflict of choice which is one of the permanent characteristics of human existence. Your economist is a true tragedian."

Robbins

10.1 CHOICE AND ECONOMICS

In Chapter 3 we encountered the notion of a constraint limiting the quantities of two desired variables that might be had in combination. In Chapter 6 we defined rational action as action chosen consistently to get as near to any desired goal as circumstances permit. A constraint, of course, delimits just what circumstances do permit. Going as far as one can in the desired direction, given the circumstances, is known technically as *maximizing subject to a constraint.* The idea of maximizing subject to a constraint is probably the most important single idea in economics. If economics is the "science of choice," then its subject matter is precisely the study of constrained maxima. Just how important constrained maxima are we shall see more clearly in Chapter 11 in which we consider governmental policy making and entrepreneurial decision making as well as household behavior. "But when time and the means for achieving ends are limited *and* capable of alternative application, *and* the ends are capable of being distinguished in order of importance, then behavior necessarily assumes the form of choice."[1]

---

[1] Lionel Robbins (Lord Robbins), *An Essay on the Nature and Significance of Economic Science,* 2nd ed., Macmillan: London, 1935, p. 14.

As in Chapter 6, we confine our discussion to calculus methods, which means that we assume continuity and differentiability.

It is important to distinguish between a constraint that must be *exactly* satisfied and one that need not be, which therefore only imposes a frontier or limit on behavior. If the constraint has to be exactly satisfied, we shall write it as an equality. If it need not be, but is a limit, a rule of the sort "anywhere up to . . . but not beyond," we shall write it as a *weak inequality*, "less than *or* equal to." Thus suppose that we are building a model of consumer behavior that is to account for the disposal of all income, including, besides consumption, saving, transfers, and losses. We shall naturally assume that the budget constraint is exactly satisfied. Consider, on the other hand, the production possibility frontier. This is a constraint that is to be exactly satisfied only if we assume full employment. If we are interested in models in which this assumption is inappropriate, it is a frontier, a "thus far and no further" rule.

We have already remarked that there can exist maxima that cannot be found by calculus methods. These are particularly frequent and important in practical cases that arise in trying to find constrained maxima. In fact, if the constraint is a weak inequality, the methods we are studying here do not work at all. We shall consider some examples, and offer some explanation, in Section 10.8, where we discuss rationing. The modern technique of linear programming is designed to find the maxima in cases in which the frontier is defined by weak inequalities. We might say that linear programming makes the "science of choice" operational. (It is introduced in Chapter 18.) It should also be emphasized now that this chapter will be about the least rigorous of *this* book. We shall show a method of solving the problem, but there will be little by way of proof.

If one "good" is independent of all others, there is no problem of choice: we merely take as much as is available, or as affords satiety, whichever is the less. If there are two goods, but they are positively associated, the situation is not materially altered: we take as much of the combination as is available, or as affords satiety. Thus a problem of choice arises only if there are two or more desired goods which are negatively associated in the real world, so that an increase in one involves some sacrifice of the other. We may say that a problem of choice arises when two or more goods are positively desired but negatively associated. We shall give examples later. For the moment, it does not matter what the "goods" may be, whether income and leisure, present or future consumption, or high employment and price stability.

For a constrained maximum problem to arise, there must be two or more goods. There must also be at least two functions connecting them. One is obviously the constraint. The other is the *maximand,* that which is to be maximized. The essential characteristic of the maximand is that it is an increasing function of both goods. We shall consider other properties later, but for a constrained maximum we require that the two goods both be desired and that all alternative combinations of the two goods can be *ranked* or *ordered* consistently by the decision maker. The function representing this ordering is the function to be maximized, often called the *objective function.* One very familiar objective function is the *utility function* ascribed to the individual consumer. Evidently so long as there *is* a consistently ordered function to be maximized, it is immaterial what we call it. Tradition has it that in the case of the individual consumer the maximand is to be called a utility function and in other cases merely an objective function. What matters is to realize that, whenever we have a choice problem, we have a constraint (or frontier, or boundary), and a maximand (or objective function, or utility function).

10.2   TANGENCY CONDITIONS

Suppose now that we have a maximand, $f(x, y)$, and a constraint, $F(x, y)$. In the interests of easy recognition, we shall use here the lowercase f to denote the objective function and the uppercase F to denote the constraint. Many other notations are used, and will serve. The objective function is often denoted by U or ψ, and the constraint by virtually any functional symbol. We could always turn things round and consider the minimization of loss instead of the maximization of gain. We shall not do this here and shall also confine the discussion of this chapter to the positive orthant.

The easiest case to start with is the familiar one illustrated in Figure 10.1, where the constraint gives a straight-line frontier, *BC.* The iso-*f* curves, which connect pairs of values of x and y that give constant values of the function $f(x, y)$, are assumed to be convex from below and associated with higher values of $f(x, y)$ the farther they are from the origin. (We looked into the properties of iso-*f* curves in Chapter 8.) In the case of the individual consumer, whose objective function is usually called a utility function, the iso-*f* curves are known as indifference curves. Iso-*f* curves, however, exist *whatever* is being maximized and whatever we call it, so long as the maximand is a continuous, differentiable function; and so much confusion and mystery has been occasioned by the notions of utility, indifference, satisfaction, etc., that it seems wiser to use, for the moment at least, the more neutral terminology of objective function and iso-*f* curve.

From inspection of Figure 10.1, it is obvious that the highest attainable level of $f(x, y)$ is reached at A, where an iso-*f* curve is

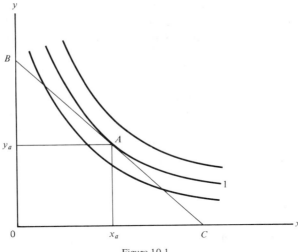

Figure 10.1

tangential to the frontier. At A, the quantities of the goods obtained are $0x_a$ and $0y_a$. We shall henceforth take it for granted, *without proof,* that if there is a tangency it is a maximum. The problem now is to find an algebraic method that will allow us to *calculate* the values of x and y that give tangency when we are given the functions algebraically or numerically: we do not wish to be reduced to trial-and-error approximate methods with ruler and compass, which, incidentally, would be impossible in cases of more than two variables.

First, let us write the constraint as

$$F(x, y) = B - cx - dy = 0 \qquad (1)$$

which turns out to be a convenience. This is just a rearrangement of $B = cx + dy$, where B may be thought of as a constant "income" and c and d are two "prices." A further rearrangement of Eq. (1) gives

$$y = \frac{B}{d} - \frac{c}{d}x \qquad (2)$$

which is the equation of BC in Figure 10.1. The ratio $-c/d$ is the slope of the frontier, or trade-off rate. Clearly we could count in units of y, putting $d = 1$ if we chose, but it is helpful to retain the form of Eq. (1) for the moment. Now, tangency at A means that the slopes of the constraint and the iso-f curve are the same, so let us consider their slopes. We know that the slope of the frontier is $-c/d$, but for the sake of symmetry let us derive this result by the methods of Chapter 8, which we shall have to use to obtain the slope of the objective function. We saw in Section 8.8 that, if

$$F(x, y) = 0 \quad , \tag{3}$$

then

$$\frac{dy}{dx} = -\frac{F_x}{F_y} \quad . \tag{4}$$

We can look on (3) as the equation of an "iso-B" curve if we like. In Eq. (1) we assume that B is a constant, which gives $F(x, y) = 0$ for given B. Different values of B, with c and d unchanged, would give frontiers parallel to BC. Now we merely check that (4) gives the correct slope. Differentiating (1), we have $F_x = -c$ and $F_y = -d$, so the slope of the constraint is $-c/d$. We now apply the same technique to the maximand. We saw in Section 8.8 that for a function

$$f(x, y)$$

the slope of the iso-f curve is

$$\frac{dy}{dx} = -\frac{f_x}{f_y} \quad . \tag{5}$$

But at A, where the two slopes are equal,

$$\frac{dy}{dx} \text{(constraint)} = \frac{dy}{dx} \text{(maximand)} \quad , \tag{6}$$

or, using (4) and (5),

$$-\frac{f_x}{f_y} = -\frac{F_x}{F_y} \quad . \tag{7}$$

We may give (7) a familiar economic interpretation. If $f(x, y)$ is the consumer's utility function, the partial derivatives f_x and f_y are the marginal utilities, and their ratio is the marginal rate of substitution, which is the slope of the indifference curve. Hence (7) is the famous result that the ratio of the marginal utilities, f_x/f_y, must be equal to the price ratio or trade-off rate F_x/F_y, or c/d.

Evidently (7) must be satisfied at a constrained maximum. By rearranging it, we can obtain a clue to the sort of procedure that will solve for equilibrium x and y. Dividing both sides by $-F_x$ and multiplying both sides by f_y, we obtain

$$\frac{f_x}{F_x} = \frac{f_y}{F_y} \quad . \tag{8}$$

(This is the famous result that the ratio of the marginal utility of one good to its price must be equal to the ratio of the marginal utility of the other good to its price.)

What we now require is an algebraic procedure for maximization subject to constraint. We know that it must generate the tangency condition of (7) or (8). We also expect it to have the property that it will extend to functions of more than two variables, which we could not otherwise handle. We shall introduce the procedure without justification, work it out, and discuss it later, but we shall not offer a proof.

We form a new function

$$V = f(x, y) - \lambda F(x, y) \quad . \tag{9}$$

This is called the Lagrangian equation, and λ an "undetermined Lagrangian multiplier," after the French mathematician Joseph Louis Lagrange (1736–1813). It appears that we are only complicating the problem, but first V and then λ will drop out again shortly. Let us try to maximize V. Since the value of F, the constraint, is always zero, maximizing V is the same as maximizing f, the maximand, which is what we want to do. V is a function of three variables, x, y, and λ, so we must set all three partial derivatives simultaneously equal to zero. Differentiating (9) with respect to each in turn, we obtain

$$V_x = f_x - \lambda F_x = 0 \tag{10a}$$

$$V_y = f_y - \lambda F_y = 0 \tag{10b}$$

$$V_\lambda = F(x, y) = 0 \quad . \tag{10c}$$

Now take $-\lambda Fx$ in (10a) and $-\lambda Fy$ in (10b) to the RHS and divide (10a) by (10b) to obtain

$$\frac{f_x}{f_y} = \frac{F_x}{F_y} \quad ,$$

which is (7), or, on cross-multiplying, (8). Thus it turns out that introducing the new unknowns, V and λ, and maximizing V produces the tangency conditions.

We have now produced a method, via V and λ, that gives our tangency requirements in such a form that we can actually find x and y once we are given particular functions. There may be some suggestion of sleight of hand about the whole operation, however, so we shall consider it a little further. Up through Eq. (8) we were only manipulating the tangency requirements, which we said were evident from consideration of Figure 10.1. Then we suddenly introduced V, which turned out, on differentiation, to give (10a), (10b), and (10c); that is, maximizing V gives the tangency requirements for maximizing $f(x, y)$ subject to $F(x, y) = 0$. How can this be? Bear in mind that we write the constraint in such a fashion that $F(x, y)$ *does* equal zero and Eq. (9) becomes

$$V = f(x, y) + \lambda(0) \quad . \tag{11}$$

It does not follow that we can write $V = f(x, y)$, arguing that $\lambda(0) = 0$

and can be dropped, because we have still to *find* values of x and y such that $F(x, y) = 0$. Thus if we maximize V, we are maximizing f and *at the same time* keeping the constraint satisfied, that is, holding $F(x, y) = 0$. The difference between maximizing f alone and maximizing V is that when we maximize V we keep the constraint satisfied since the partial derivative $V_\lambda = F(x, y)$, and we bring in the derivative (the slope of the constraint) that we require for tangency. And this is as far as we can go in justifying this subtle but very powerful procedure. Part of its power lies in the fact that it extends immediately to functions of three or more variables.

10.3 TWO METHODS OF HANDLING A CONSTRAINT

Consider, for example, the problems of profit maximization for the firm that we dealt with in Chapter 7. It would now be easy to set up this problem as one of finding a constrained maximum by taking $\Pi = R - C$ as the objective function and the market demand curve, $p - f(q) = 0$, as the constraint. Substitution from $p = f(q)$ into the Π function, however, so easily turns this into a single-variable problem that Lagrangian techniques are seldom employed. It is perhaps worth doing for yourself as an exercise.

Two points about this example should be noticed. The first is technical. We can often substitute and reduce the number of variables if we wish. Thus if the objective function is $f(x, y)$ and the constraint is $F(x, y) = B - rx - sy = 0$, we can express y by $y = (B - rx)/s$ and substitute into the objective function so that we only have to maximize $f\{x, [(B - rx)/s]\}$ with respect to x. In general, if $F(x, y) = 0$, we expect there to be a corresponding explicit relationship $y = g(x)$, *if* we can discover it by suitable manipulations of F, in which case we can maximize $f\{x, g(x)\}$ using the chain rule. Thus whether we substitute or use our Lagrangian method is a matter of convenience. The second point is that, if you can handle objective functions of two or more variables, you are equipped to handle other hypotheses about the behavior of firms besides simple profit maximization. A good deal of literature on this topic is now accessible to you.[2]

10.4 CONVEXITY

We should now say something about second-order conditions that are needed to distinguish maxima from other stationary points such as minima and stationary points of inflection, but the algebra required

---

[2] Examples may be found in the collection of readings *The Theory of the Firm*, edited by G. C. Archibald, Penguin Modern Education, Baltimore, Md., 1971.

for a full treatment is too much for us here. We can, however, make some headway with a geometrical consideration of a simple and common case. Thus in Figure 10.1, it is obvious that *A is* a maximum. But consider Figure 10.2, where the first-order or tangency conditions are satisfied at *Q*. If the curve labeled 1, the flatter of the two curves, is the constraint, and the curve labeled 2 is an iso-*f* curve, then all is well. Suppose, however, that 1 were an iso-*f* curve and that 2 were the constraint: then higher values of the maximand would be attainable by moving along 2 to higher iso-*f* curves, and *Q* would certainly not be a maximum. In Figure 10.3, the constraint is again

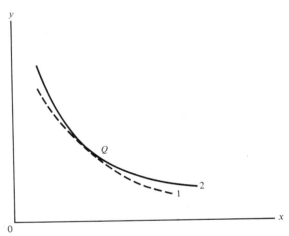

Figure 10.2

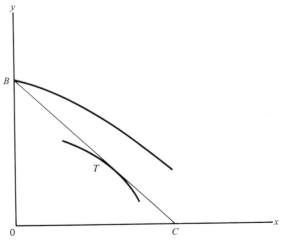

Figure 10.3

the straight line BC, but the objective function is concave toward the origin. Tangency conditions are satisfied at T, but T is a minimum rather than a maximum. The maximum will occur at a "corner solution" such as B (which cannot be discovered by our methods). Comparison of these three figures suggests that, *if* the frontier is a straight line, convexity to the origin of the iso-f curves is sufficient to ensure that if a tangency occurs it is at a maximum; we can see that when the first-order conditions are satisfied the second-order conditions for a maximum must be also. If the frontier is nonlinear, however, there are no shortcuts, and a full-dress treatment of second-order conditions is required.

Since linear constraints are fairly common in economics, we will conclude by working out the conditions for convexity in the iso-f curves. Let the function be $f(x, y)$, and let the slope of its iso-f curve, which we shall denote by r, the *marginal rate of substitution*, be given by

$$r = \frac{dy}{dx} = \frac{-f_x}{f_y} \quad . \tag{12}$$

Convexity means that, as x increases, sliding round a curve, the slope itself becomes less steep, or "less negative." Thus convexity means that the marginal rate of substitution, or tangent slope, r itself, has a rate of change with respect to x that is *positive*. Thus the convexity condition is

$$\frac{dr}{dx} > 0 \quad . \tag{13}$$

Since in general $r = r(x, y)$, we require the total differential

$$dr = \frac{\partial r}{\partial x} dx + \frac{\partial r}{\partial y} dy \quad .$$

Dividing through by dx, this gives

$$\frac{dr}{dx} = \frac{\partial r}{\partial x} + \frac{\partial r}{\partial y} \frac{dy}{dx} \quad ,$$

or from (12)

$$\frac{dr}{dx} = \frac{\partial}{\partial x} \left(\frac{-f_x}{f_y} \right) + \frac{\partial}{\partial y} \left(\frac{-f_x}{f_y} \right) \cdot \left(\frac{-f_x}{f_y} \right) \quad . \tag{14}$$

[Notice that in (14) we have substituted for $dy/dx = r = -f_x/f_y$ in the last term.] Since the ratio of the differentials is equal to the derivative dr/dx, the RHS of Eq. (14) gives us the derivative of the marginal rate of substitution with respect to x, which is what we require. To evaluate the two partial derivatives of r we next apply the quotient rule (see Section 4.6) to each in turn, since f_x and f_y are in general both functions of x and y, to obtain

$$\frac{dr}{dx} = -\left(\frac{f_y f_{xx} - f_x f_{xy}}{f_y^2}\right) - \left(\frac{f_y f_{xy} - f_x f_{yy}}{f_y^2}\right)\left(\frac{-f_x}{f_y}\right)$$

which, with a little manipulation, simplifies to

$$\frac{dr}{dx} = -\frac{f_y^2 f_{xx} - 2f_x f_y f_{xy} + f_x^2 f_{yy}}{f_y^3} \quad .$$

Since f_y and therefore f_y^3 are positive, our convexity condition is

$$f_y^2 f_{xx} - 2f_x f_y f_{xy} + f_x^2 f_{yy} < 0 \quad . \tag{15}$$

Now f_y and f_x and their squares are all positive, so the inequality (15) is satisfied if, for example, f_{xx} and f_{yy} are both negative and f_{xy} is nonnegative (positive or zero). If f_{xy} were negative, then whether or not inequality (15) was satisfied would depend on relative magnitudes, and could not be determined qualitatively. If, however, f_{xx} or f_{yy} were positive, it would still be possible to satisfy (15) if f_{xy} were also positive and sufficiently large. Thus we cannot lay down any very simple conditions for convexity, other than that (15) must be satisfied. In particular, we should notice that our discussion of (15) shows that the condition $f_{xx} < 0$ and $f_{yy} < 0$ is neither necessary *nor* sufficient for convexity, because of the possible effects of the term f_{xy}. This is important because, in the case of a utility function, f_x may be interpreted as marginal utility with respect to x, and $f_{xx} < 0$ as diminishing marginal utility. Since convexity may be interpreted as diminishing marginal substitutability, what we have found is that diminishing marginal utility is neither necessary nor sufficient for diminishing marginal substitutability.[3] You will be asked in Question 1 to check convexity in a particular example, and it might be a good idea to try this question now.

10.5 CONSTRAINED MINIMA

It remains to say something about constrained minima, but they are now straightforward: the first-order conditions are identical with those for a maximum, and only the second-order conditions are different. Second-order conditions are troublesome, but we can clear up a couple of simple cases. First, suppose that it is desired to minimize $f(x, y)$ subject to a linear constraint, that is, to get as near as possible

---

[3] This is very clearly explained by Sir John R. Hicks, *Value and Capital*, 2nd ed., Oxford University Press, London, 1946, pp. 12–16; he gives the economic interpretation, too.

to the origin in Figure 10.4. Then, by an obvious reversal of the convexity argument of Section 10.4, the tangency at *R* gives a minimum
provided that the iso-*f* curve is *concave* from below. Second, suppose that it is desired to minimize a *linear* function $f(x, y)$ subject
to a nonlinear constraint $F(x, y) = 0$. We may use Figure 10.1 to illustrate this if we think of *BC* as an iso-*f* curve, and wish to reach the
iso-*f* curve as near to the origin as possible. Suppose also that one of
the present iso-*f* curves, say that labeled 1, is now the constraint.
Then evidently tangency is sufficient for a minimum provided that
the *constraint* is convex from below.

10.6   ILLUSTRATIONS

A little more illustration of the ideas of this chapter may be helpful. Suppose that we are given an objective function of the (Cobb-
Douglas) form

$$f(x, y) = Ax^\alpha y^\beta \tag{16}$$

which is to be maximized subject to some linear constraint $F(x, y) = 0$.
We continue to confine ourselves to the positive orthant. We ask what
restrictions are to be put on the permissible values of the coefficients
A, α, and β for this to be a reasonable objective function, and to satisfy the conditions for a tangency being a maximum. First, if the function is to be positive, A must be positive. Second, we require that it
be an increasing function of both x and y; that is, we require positive
first derivatives:

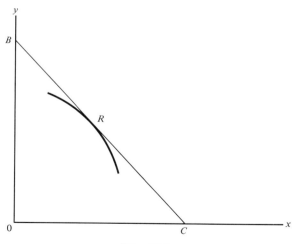

Figure 10.4

$$f_x = \alpha A x^{\alpha-1} y^\beta > 0 \tag{17a}$$

and

$$f_y = \beta A x^\alpha y^{\beta-1} > 0 \quad . \tag{17b}$$

Thus we must have A, α, and β all positive. Now, we have already seen that negative second derivatives are neither necessary nor sufficient for convexity of the iso-f curves, but in many contexts they seem sensible. If we interpret f_x and f_y as marginal utilities, as we suggested in our discussion of convexity in Section 10.4, then f_{xx} and f_{yy} are the rates of change of the marginal utilities. The idea of diminishing marginal utility has considerable intuitive appeal, although it is not strictly necessary for equilibrium positions to exist (because, in its absence, we get convexity from a suitable range of values of the second-order cross-partial derivative f_{xy}). It certainly helps to make sense of the idea of utility and scarcity, that it is not the "absolute" or "total" utility of a good that determines its value, but its marginal utility, which we expect to be smaller the more of the good is taken, that is, the less scarce it is. Now if we want

$$f_{xx} = \alpha(\alpha - 1) A x^{\alpha-2} y^\beta \tag{18a}$$

and

$$f_{yy} = \beta(\beta - 1) A x^\alpha y^{\beta-2} \tag{18b}$$

to be negative, we must have $\alpha < 1$ and $\beta < 1$. The slope of the iso-f curves is given by

$$\frac{dy}{dx} = \frac{-f_x}{f_y} = \frac{-\alpha A x^{\alpha-1} y^\beta}{\beta A x^\alpha y^{\beta-1}}$$

$$= -\frac{\alpha}{\beta} \frac{y}{x} \tag{19}$$

which is obviously negative since both first derivatives are positive. Finally, we require

$$\frac{dr}{dx} > 0 \quad .$$

To find dr/dx, we may substitute into (15) or proceed directly as follows. Take the total differential of

$$r = -\frac{\alpha}{\beta} y x^{-1}$$

to obtain

$$\frac{dr}{dx} = -\frac{\alpha}{\beta} \left[\frac{-y}{x^2} + \frac{1}{x} \frac{dy}{dx} \right] \quad .$$

Substituting for dy/dx, as before, we have

$$\frac{dr}{dx} = -\frac{\alpha}{\beta}\left[\frac{-y}{x^2} - \frac{\alpha}{\beta}\frac{y}{x^2}\right]$$

$$= \frac{y}{x^2}\left(1 + \frac{\alpha}{\beta}\right)\frac{\alpha}{\beta} \tag{20}$$

which is positive, as required.

If we are invited to maximize the objective function (16) subject to

$$F(x, y) = B - rx - sy = 0 \quad , \tag{21}$$

and we use the method of Lagrangian multipliers, we put

$$V = Ax^\alpha y^\beta + \lambda(B - rx - sy) \tag{22}$$

and set the partial derivatives equal to zero:

$$V_x = \alpha Ax^{\alpha-1}y^\beta - \lambda r = 0 \tag{23a}$$

$$V_y = \beta Ax^\alpha y^{\beta-1} - \lambda s = 0 \tag{23b}$$

$$V_\lambda = B - rx - sy = 0 \quad . \tag{23c}$$

To solve these equations we start by eliminating λ. From the first equation

$$\lambda = \frac{\alpha Ax^{\alpha-1}y^\beta}{r} \quad .$$

Substituting into the second,

$$\beta Ax^\alpha y^{\beta-1} = \frac{s}{r}\alpha Ax^{\alpha-1}y^\beta \quad .$$

Canceling A and dividing both sides by $\beta x^{\alpha-1}y^{\beta-1}$,

$$x = \frac{s}{r}\frac{\alpha}{\beta}y \quad ,$$

and substituting this into the third equation,

$$B - s\frac{\alpha}{\beta}y - sy = 0 \quad ,$$

whence

$$B - ys\left(\frac{\alpha}{\beta} + 1\right) = 0$$

or

$$y = \frac{B}{s}\left(\frac{\beta}{\alpha + \beta}\right) \tag{24a}$$

and

$$x = \frac{B}{r}\left(\frac{\alpha}{\alpha + \beta}\right) \cdot \qquad (24b)$$

The solutions in Eqs. (24) are worth attention: they have a number of interesting properties, and we shall quickly find that we have in fact established a great deal. First, the terms B/r and B/s may be interpreted as the purchasing power, or real value, of the budget, expressed in each equation in terms of the price of the relevant good. Thus Eqs. (24) say that equilibrium quantities depend on income and relative prices and on the exponents of the objective function only. Second, notice that if B increases, prices constant, x and y increase in proportion. This means that the *proportion* in which x and y are taken depends on relative prices and is independent of B, as may be confirmed by evaluating

$$\frac{x}{y} = \frac{Br^{-1}}{Bs^{-1}}\left(\frac{\alpha/(\alpha + \beta)}{\beta/(\alpha + \beta)}\right) = \frac{s}{r} \cdot \frac{\alpha}{\beta} \cdot \qquad (25)$$

It follows that the expansion path, or "income-consumption curve," corresponding to changing B with given s/r is a straight line through the origin. This is a property of a *homogeneous* objective function, and we can easily show that (16) is homogeneous of degree $\alpha + \beta$ (see Chapter 9). Finally, notice that if prices and money income (i.e., r, s, and B) all change in proportion, the equilibrium values of x and y given by (24) are unaffected. Thus the demands are *homogeneous of degree zero* in absolute prices and money income. This property is often described by saying that the demands are free of money illusion.

In Chapter 9, we discussed homogeneous functions, and we have considered an example in the Cobb-Douglas production function. The objective function of (16), $Ax^{\alpha}y^{\beta}$, is obviously a close relation to the Cobb-Douglas function. If we make $\alpha + \beta = 1$, we have the first-order homogeneous case; if we do not impose this restriction, we have a homogeneous objective function of order $\alpha + \beta$. If x and y are each increased by some factor μ, which leaves their ratio unchanged, we have $A(\mu x)^{\alpha}(\mu y)^{\beta} = A\mu^{\alpha+\beta}x^{\alpha}y^{\beta} = \mu^{\alpha+\beta}(Ax^{\alpha}y^{\beta})$.

10.7 MANY VARIABLES

We now come to a remarkable demonstration of the power of our calculus methods compared with compass and ruler: we can extend our technique to cases of more than two variables with great ease (although you should note again that we do not offer a proof).

Let us start with the case of three variables, x, y, and z, and a single constraint. If we write the objective function $f(x, y, z)$ and the constraint $F(x, y, z) = 0$, all we need do is form the equation

$$V = f(x, y, z) - \lambda F(x, y, z)$$

and set all four partial derivatives equal to zero:

$$V_x = f_x - \lambda F_x = 0 \qquad (26a)$$

$$V_y = f_y - \lambda F_y = 0 \qquad (26b)$$

$$V_z = f_z - \lambda F_z = 0 \qquad (26c)$$

$$V_\lambda = -F(x, y, z) = 0 \quad . \qquad (26d)$$

Equations (26) give, by analogy with (10), the conditions for tangency between two *surfaces* in three dimensions. If the constraint is linear, and the iso-f surfaces convex, this may be visualized as tangency between an inclined plane (say, the surface of a book suitably tilted) and an iso-f curve shaped like a smooth cup or saucer. Simple rearrangement of (26) gives the usual "marginal equalities" or tangency conditions,

$$\frac{f_x}{F_x} = \frac{f_y}{F_y} = \frac{f_z}{F_z} = \lambda \quad , \qquad (27)$$

perfectly analogous with those in two dimensions. If we know that the constraint is linear and the objective function convex, then the first-order conditions in (26) are sufficient for a maximum. (No proof: but consider for yourself the cup and book analogy.) If we do not know this, then second-order conditions are required, and the mathematics needed to obtain them are beyond the scope of this book.

A useful and simple trick is now to extend this analysis to any number of variables. It is useful because, among the many possible applications of constrained maxima, one is to the case of the individual consumer, facing a large number of consumer goods, and *we do not wish to have to specify, on every separate occasion, how many he faces: we want a general result.* That it is simple we shall now demonstrate: all we need is a little notation.

Let the number of variables be n, where n is any number greater than or equal to 2. Then denote the variables by

$$x_1, x_2, \ldots, x_n \quad .$$

The objective function can accordingly be written as

$$f(x_1, x_2, \ldots, x_n) \quad , \qquad (28)$$

and the constraint as

$$F(x_1, x_2, \ldots, x_n) = 0 \quad . \qquad (29)$$

The common case of interest is that of a linear constraint. This can now be written as

$$B - \sum_i p_i x_i = 0 \qquad (i = 1, \ldots, n) \quad . \tag{30}$$

The very compact notation of (30) is new and requires explanation. The "summation sign" (capital sigma) means "the sum of," so $\sum_i x_i$ means "the sum of all the x's." The marginal note "$i = 1, \ldots, n$" (read "i equals one to n") tells the reader which x's: here $x_1, x_2, \ldots, x_n$. Thus

$$\sum_i x_i (i = 1, \ldots, n) = x_1 + x_2 + x_3 + \cdots + x_n \quad .$$

Instead of using the marginal note with the summation sign, this may be written

$$\sum_{i=1}^{n} x_i \quad ,$$

which is read "the sum from i equals one to n of the x_i," and means the same thing. Equation (30) should now be compared with (21), the linear constraint in the two-variable case, where

$$F(x, y) = B - rx - sy = 0$$
$$= B - (rx + sy) \quad .$$

In (30), where there may be more than two variables, we have written x_i instead of x, y, z, v, w, etc. In the same way, we have put p_i for the coefficients r, s, etc. Imagine trying to write out (30) without this notation in a case in which $n = 100$: there are not enough letters in the alphabet! The notation $\sum_i p_i x_i$ means that, attached to each x_i, there is a coefficient p_i, and that each x is to be multiplied by its co-efficient before the sum is taken. Thus

$$\sum_{i=1}^{n} p_i x_i = p_1 x_1 + p_2 x_2 + \cdots + p_n x_n \quad .$$

As a further simplification of the notation, if there is no room for ambiguity as to the number of x_i to be summed, we may drop the n over the summation sign and the marginal note, writing merely $\sum_i$.

An economic interpretation of (30) is that B is income, the x_i goods, and the p_i their prices: (30) is often known as the "budget equation" or "budget constraint." It is, however, the perfectly general form of an *n-dimensional linear constraint*. And now, indeed, we are in n dimensions, where the geometry of two or three dimensions can aid our intuition but cannot solve our problem.

The solution is, however, quite easy. To maximize (28) subject to (30) we form the usual equation,

$$V = f(x_1, x_2, \ldots, x_n) + \lambda\left(B - \sum_{i=1}^{n} p_i x_i\right) \qquad (31)$$

and set all the partial derivatives equal to zero. To obtain the partial derivatives of the second term in (31), we proceed as follows:

$$\frac{\partial}{\partial x_1}\left(\lambda B - \lambda \sum_{i=1}^{n} p_i x_i\right) = \frac{\partial}{\partial x_1}(\lambda B - \lambda p_1 x_1 - \lambda p_2 x_2 - \cdots - \lambda p_n x_n) = -\lambda p_1$$

and so on for each x_i.

There are altogether $n+1$ partial derivatives of (31), one for each x and one for λ. Writing all these out is cumbersome, and, anyhow, we still do not wish to be committed to a particular number for n. Again, a notational device is what is needed. We present a shorthand which is in common use, and with which one rapidly becomes familiar. We can write

$$\left.\begin{array}{l}
V_{x_1} = f_{x_1} - \lambda p_1 = 0 \\
V_{x_2} = f_{x_2} - \lambda p_2 = 0 \\
\quad \vdots \qquad \vdots \qquad \vdots \qquad \vdots \\
V_{x_i} = f_{x_i} - \lambda p_i = 0 \\
\quad \vdots \qquad \vdots \qquad \vdots \qquad \vdots \\
V_{x_n} = f_{x_n} - \lambda p_n = 0 \\
V_\lambda = B - \sum_{i=1}^{n} p_i x_i = 0
\end{array}\right\} \qquad (32)$$

where the dots indicate that the appropriate number of equations *of identical form* have been omitted and the subscripts x_1, etc., on V indicate as usual the variable with respect to which the partial derivative is taken. An even more compact notation for (32) is

$$\left.\begin{array}{l}
f_{x_i} - \lambda p_i = 0 \qquad (i = 1, \ldots, n) \\
B - \sum_{i=1}^{n} p_i x_i = 0
\end{array}\right\} \qquad (33)$$

where the marginal note $i = 1, \ldots, n$ tells the reader that there are n equations of identical form to the ith, which is the only one written out. From (32) or from (33) we can derive the marginal equalities

$$\frac{f_{x_i}}{f_{x_j}} = \frac{p_i}{p_j} \qquad (i, j = 1, \ldots, n)$$

or

$$\frac{f_{x_i}}{p_i} = \frac{f_{x_j}}{p_j} = \lambda$$

(34)

where the subscripts i and j and the marginal note indicate that we can substitute in whichever we like of $1, 2, \ldots, n$; thus we have shown, in the most compact way, that the equalities (34) must be true for *any pair whatever*. In any practical case, solving the $n + 1$ equations in (32) may be quite a chore, but what is very satisfactory is how easily we may obtain the n-dimensional analogue, in (34), of our tangency condition. Equation (34) is true whatever value n may happen to have; and it says that we must have equality for each pair of goods between the trade-off rate given by our constraint, p_i/p_j, and the marginal rate of substitution, f_{x_i}/f_{x_j}.

10.8 MULTIPLE CONSTRAINTS

We have seen that our Lagrangian technique is easily extended to cases of more than two variables. We may now ask whether it extends to cases of more than one constraint. Cases in which there is more than one constraint do arise in economics, as we may briefly illustrate. If a government imposes some sort of rationing scheme – say, of gasoline during a gas shortage – then the individual household is constrained not only by its budget but also by its ration book. A manning agreement between a firm and a union, which specifies a certain number of men for a task, irrespective of whether technological advance may have reduced the required number, will operate on the firm's investment policy as an additional constraint to that imposed by its budget. It does not require much imagination to go on multiplying examples.

The extension of our technique to the case of more than two constraints is quite straightforward *on certain conditions*. But the whole subject of multiple constraints is vast and difficult, so what we shall do here is, first, show how easily we can set up the problem, and then show how easily we can manufacture a simple and important example in which the technique does not work. We shall also derive a few general lessons from the example of failure.

Suppose, first, that we have an objective function $f(x, y, z)$, and that x, y, and z are related by two constraints, say,

$$H(x, y) = 0$$

and

$$F(y, z) = 0 \quad . \tag{35}$$

Without more information, we cannot be sure that there will be a tangency solution: the constraints might, for example, limit us to certain discrete points. Let us assume, however, that a tangency solution is possible. Then it is easy enough to introduce two Lagrangian multipliers, λ and μ, say, set up the equation

$$V = f(x, y, z) - \lambda H(x, y) - \mu F(y, z) \quad , \tag{36}$$

and set equal to zero the partial derivatives with respect to x, y, z, λ, and μ. On the same lines, we can handle a case of n variables and m constraints ($m < n$). To obtain the equilibrium conditions in this case we would evaluate the $n + m$ partial derivatives and equate each to zero. It turns out, however, that the solution of even a very simple example of the form of (36) rapidly becomes tiresome, so we shall not work an example. It is more important to look at the cases in which the method will not work.

In (36) we have three variables and two constraints. There might, however, be as many constraints as there are variables. We can illustrate this perfectly well in two dimensions. Thus let the objective function be $f(x, y)$; let one constraint be of the ordinary budget type, $B - p_x x - p_y y = 0$; and let a second be a rationing constraint, that the amount of x taken may not exceed some fixed amount, say $0D$ in Figure 10.5, where the budget constraint is AB. Since no points outside $0AB$ and no points to the right of the vertical line QD are attain-

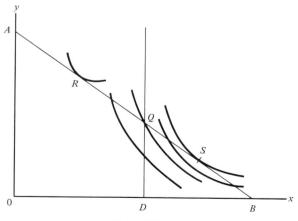

Figure 10.5

able, the effective frontier has become *AQD*. Now there are two possible, and quite distinct, cases.

Suppose, first, that tangency between an iso-*f* curve and *AB* occurs at a point on *AQ* such as *R*. Then the second, or ration, constraint does not affect the chosen position: it is ineffective. Evidently, then, if we tried to maximize $f(x, y)$ subject to the budget and the ration constraints, we should not find *R*, because the rationing constraint is a "weak inequality," written $x \leq 0D$, which is read "*x* less than or equal to $0D$." In plain words, this means that the individual does not have to take up his whole ration if he does not wish to. Thus $0D$ puts a limit or frontier on what is attainable: it is not a constraint that has to be exactly satisfied. There is, however, no place in our present techniques for inequalities. If we want to solve maximizing problems of this sort, we require other methods (linear programming methods can handle some of them). If, of course, we insist that the whole ration is taken, the ration constraint becomes an equality; but now the individual is required to be on *QD*, and, as he must be on *AB*, there is no choice problem: *Q* is the *only* attainable point. In general, if we insist on the *exact* fulfilment of as many constraints as there are variables, we leave the individual with no choice but simply require him to be at a point such as *Q*. Notice that it is impossible for the iso-*f* curve to be tangent to both branches of the frontier at *Q*, and only by a fluke will it be tangent to even one.

Suppose, second, that in the absence of rationing the chosen position is one such as *S* on *QB*. Rationing forces the individual to the left up *SA*, and he evidently goes no further than he must: he goes to *Q*. Here the rationing constraint, even if it is of the weak-inequality variety, is effective because of the individual's objective function. But notice that the iso-*f* curve attainable at *Q* is not tangent to the frontier: if we have tangency at *S*, we cannot have it at *Q*. The solution at *Q* is what is called a corner solution. To find *Q*, we need only to know the ration $0D$ and that the amount of *x* taken would otherwise exceed $0D$. Our calculus methods are no help.

The general lessons of this discussion may be summarized.

1. If there are as many strict constraints as variables, we look directly for the point that satisfies them all — the objective function is irrelevant.
2. If *any* of the constraints are in the form of inequalities, we cannot use the techniques of this chapter.
3. If we know what would be chosen in the absence of a constraint, and add a constraint that allows less, we know that the constraint is effective without further reference to the objective function.

We may conclude that it is extremely fortunate that there are so many interesting and important cases of one constraint and two or more variables. We shall explore some of them in Chapter 11. For important cases of the sort we cannot handle, however, new mathematical techniques that allow for practical computation are available. Some are introduced in Chapter 18.

QUESTIONS

1. a. Determine the values of x and y that maximize the objective function $f(x, y) = 2x^{1/2}y^{1/2}$ subject to the constraint $F(x, y) = 100 - 2x - y = 0$.
   b. Demonstrate that the objective function in part a satisfies the convexity condition $dr/dx > 0$ (where $r = dy/dx$). Interpret this condition in words.
   c. Substitute $F(x, y) = 200 - 2x - y = 0$ for the constraint in part a (i.e., "income" has doubled), and repeat part a. Is any conclusion suggested by a comparison of the new equilibrium values with the old ones?
   d. What difference would it make to equilibrium x and y if $2x^{1/2}y^{1/2}$ were replaced by $10x^{1/2}y^{1/2}$? Or by $2x^{1/2}y^{1/2} + 20$? What conclusion about the form of the maximand does this suggest?

2. a. Find equilibrium x and y if the objective function is

   $$f(x, y) = 20x^{1/2}y^{1/2}$$

   and the constraint is

   $$F(x, y) = 300 - 2x - 5y = 0 \quad.$$

   b. Show that the convexity condition is satisfied.

3. a. Find equilibrium x and y if the objective function is

   $$f(x, y) = 20xy - (x^2 + y^2)$$

   and the constraint is

   $$F(x, y) = 229 - 2x - 5y = 0 \quad.$$

   b. How do the "marginal utilities" behave in the neighborhood of the equilibrium values of x and y?

4. You are given the objective function

   $$f(x, y) = ax + by$$

   defined only over nonnegative x and y, together with the constraint

   $$F(x, y) = C - cx - dy = 0 \quad.$$

   a. It may be obvious to you that the methods of this chapter will not work, but try to apply them anyhow. You will obtain

   $$\lambda = \frac{a}{c}$$

and

$$\lambda = \frac{b}{d} \ .$$

Could both be true simultaneously, save by accident? Can these equations be solved for x and y?

b. Draw a diagram to illustrate the case. Find the best point by inspection. Is there more than one possibility? Consider the answers to part a in the light of your diagram, and interpret.

c. Suggest an economic interpretation.

5. Your answer to Question 1 of this chapter probably employed a function of the form $V = 2x^{1/2}y^{1/2} + \lambda(100 - 2x - y)$. Suppose that you had accidentally used a $-$ instead of a $+$ in front of the λ: How would the results have been affected?

6. a. Consider maximizing an objective function $f(x, y) = xy$ subject to a constraint $y = x$. The objective function is convex and the constraint is linear, but do we have a maximum? Explain why or why not.

b. Can you change a sign in the constraint so that there definitely is a maximum?

7. Using the objective functions given below and the constraint $F(x, y) = 100 - 2x - y = 0$, calculate the equilibrium ratio of x/y analogous to (25).

a. $f(x, y) = xy$
b. $f(x, y) = x/y$
c. $f(x, y) = x^{10}y^{-9}$

8. This question refers to the functions in Question 7. (a) Is the function in part a of the Cobb-Douglas kind? (b) Is b a homogeneous function, and if so, of what degree? (c) Why is c not an appropriate form for a production function even though it is homogeneous of degree 1?

9. Discover the values of x and y that maximize the following functions subject to the given constraints. Consider only nonnegative values of x and y. What is the value of the function when it is at its maximum?

a. $x + y$ subject to $x^2 + y^2 = 1$
b. $x + y$ subject to $xy = 10$
c. $x^2 + y^2$ subject to $x + y = 2/\sqrt{2}$
d. xy subject to $x + y = 2\sqrt{10}$
e. xy^2z^3 subject to $x + y + z = 6$

Chapter 11

Applications of Constrained Maxima and Minima

11.1 THE LEAST-COST COMBINATION

In our chapters of applications, we have developed the analysis of the models of the perfect market and of income determination. In this chapter, we shall not extend the analysis of either model but, rather, supplement it. We shall extend our analysis of production, which lies behind the supply curve. We shall explore the theory of consumers' choice, which lies behind the demand curve. We shall also take up briefly some new topics in general equilibrium theory and welfare economics. We shall discover conditions for an *efficient* allocation of economic resources and show that, at least in certain cases, they will be satisfied in perfect competition.

The first problem is to find the conditions for minimizing the cost of a given output. This is the problem of finding the combination of factors which, with given factor prices, makes a given output most cheaply. It is therefore often referred to as the problem of the "least-cost combination." We looked at production functions in Chapter 9, and, with the tools now at our disposal, we can solve this problem very easily, and we can do it in either of two ways.

Method 1. We seek to minimize the total cost of the inputs, subject to production being at some predetermined level.

Method 2. We seek to maximize production, subject to costs being at some predetermined level.

These two methods are illustrated in Figure 11.1, where one

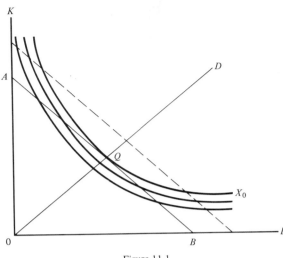

Figure 11.1

input, say capital, K, is measured on the vertical axis, and another, labor, L, on the horizontal axis. Each iso-f curve or iso-quant shows all the combinations of K and L that will produce a given output. Thus we assume that the production function is continuous and twice differentiable (no corners) and, in particular, that we have diminishing marginal substitutability, which gives convexity in the iso-quants. We assume given factor prices, the wage rate being fixed at w and the interest rate at r. The slope of a line such as AB measures the factor price ratio. Now consider what our two methods mean geometrically.

Method 1. We choose an iso-quant, say that corresponding to output X_0, and look for the point on it at which the cost of producing X_0 is minimized. It is pretty obvious geometrically that this occurs where the iso-quant is tangent to a budget line, for example, at Q on AB, and this is the tangency condition that we took for granted in Chapter 10.

Method 2. We choose a budget line, say, AB, and look for the highest attainable output level. This again gives tangency at Q.

It is now quite straightforward to solve the problem analytically, both ways, and to show that the two approaches are completely interchangeable.

Method 1. Since we seek to minimize the cost of a given output, our objective function is total cost, which is simply the sum of the inputs each multiplied by its price:

$$C = wL + rK \quad . \qquad (1)$$

The constraint is that output be at a fixed level, X_0, so, if the production function is

$$X = g(L, K) \quad , \qquad (2)$$

we may write the constraint as

$$X_0 - g(L, K) = 0 \quad . \qquad (3)$$

We now proceed, as we learned in Chapter 10, to write

$$V = wL + rK + \lambda[X_0 - g(L, K)] \quad , \qquad (4)$$

where λ is our undetermined Lagrangian multiplier, and to find an extreme value we set each of the partial derivatives of (4) equal to zero:

$$V_L = w - \lambda g_L = 0 \qquad (5a)$$

$$V_K = r - \lambda g_K = 0 \qquad (5b)$$

$$V_\lambda = X_0 - g(L, K) = 0 \quad . \qquad (5c)$$

The values of L and K that simultaneously satisfy these three equations are those that give the least-cost combination of inputs, given w and r, to produce X_0. A little rearrangement gives our tangency conditions. Thus if the terms containing λ in (5a) and (5b) are taken over to the right-hand side and (5a) is divided by (5b), we have

$$\frac{w}{r} = \frac{g_L}{g_K} \quad , \qquad (6)$$

which is to say that, for cost minimization, the factors must be employed in such quantities as to make the ratio of their marginal products equal to the ratio of the prices: this is the tangency condition. Alternatively, we may rearrange (6) to give

$$\frac{g_L}{w} = \frac{g_K}{r} \quad , \qquad (7)$$

which says that the ratio of the marginal product of one factor to its unit cost must be equal to that of the other factor. This is the common-sense condition that the marginal product of a dollar's worth of factor must be the same for all factors. Thus suppose that it were violated, and we had, for example,

$$\frac{g_L}{w} > \frac{g_K}{r} \quad . \qquad (8)$$

Now w and r are expressed in money units, say \$5 an hour for the wage and 0.20 cents per annum for the use of a unit of capital. The ratios g_L/w and g_K/r tell us marginal product per dollar spent on the factor. Thus the inequality (8) says that a marginal "dose" of extra expenditure on labor adds more to output than the same amount spent on capital. It obviously pays to switch from capital to labor, to adopt, that is, a more labor-intensive method of production. Now if we assume diminishing marginal productivity, the use of more labor reduces g_L and the use of less capital increases g_K, so we move in the direction of equality (7). [Remember that we saw, in Chapter 10, that negative second derivatives, or diminishing marginal products, are neither necessary nor sufficient for convexity of the iso-quants. If we did not assume diminishing marginal productivity, we should still have Eqs. (5), and hence the alternative conditions (6) and (7), and to explain the movement from (8) to (7), we should appeal to diminishing marginal substitutability, or convexity.]

Method 2. Now our objective function is output, so we seek to maximize

$$X = g(L, K) \tag{2}$$

subject to the constraint of a fixed budget,

$$B_0 - wL - rK = 0 \quad . \tag{9}$$

Instead of (4) we write

$$V = g(L, K) + \lambda(B_0 - wL - rK) \tag{10}$$

and set the first derivatives equal to zero:

$$V_L = g_L - \lambda w = 0 \tag{11a}$$

$$V_K = g_K - \lambda r = 0 \tag{11b}$$

$$V_\lambda = B_0 - wL - rK = 0 \quad . \tag{11c}$$

After our geometrical discussion, the similarity between (11) and (5) is hardly surprising. Equations (6) and (7) can be derived from (11) exactly as from (5), and the derivation is left to the reader.

What we have illustrated here is the extraordinary flexibility of the method of constrained maxima or minima. We also learn something about objective functions and "utility." In Method 1 we minimized cost. Now $B = wL + rK$ hardly looks like a "utility" — or "disutility" — function, but all we need do is to assume that the producer would rather achieve any output for less cost than for more and we have an objective function, something that we want to minimize. Similarly, the production function $X = g(L, K)$ is not a utility function, but if we assume that the producer would rather have more output than less, for a given outlay, we have something to maximize. Later on we shall take up the case of the individual consumer, and the objective function will then be a utility function in the ordinary sense; but we may guess now that if "utility" is looked upon merely as an objective function, much of the mystery often attached to it dissolves, and we may also guess that the technique of constrained maxima may be profitably employed *wherever* something can be discovered of which, *ceteris paribus,* either more or less is desired, giving us an objective function, and there is some frontier or constraint limiting the amounts that may be had

The next step in a systematic treatment of production is comparative static analysis. That is, we should ask how the least-cost combination is changed when the factor prices, w and r, change. We should hope to obtain the signs of such expressions as

$$\frac{\partial \bar{L}}{\partial w}, \quad \frac{\partial \bar{L}}{\partial r}, \quad \frac{\partial \bar{K}}{\partial w}, \quad \text{and} \quad \frac{\partial \bar{K}}{\partial r} \quad . \tag{12}$$

(The variables L and K are barred to remind us that the partials are evaluated at the equilibrium values for L and K so that they tell us how these *equilibrium* values for L and K change as w and r change.) Since capital is one of our factors, we are dealing with the long run (by definition) or, as it is sometimes called, the case of "full adjustment." If we had the signs of the expressions in (12), we should have the predicted directions of change of both factors, allowing for full adjustment, in response to a change in either factor price. We have seen in earlier examples in Chapter 7, however, that to obtain directions of change at extremum points we have to make use of second-order conditions; and the derivation of second-order conditions to go with (5) or (11) requires a good deal more technique than we now have. So we shall leave the general case here, and take up again the particular example of the Cobb-Douglas production function that we discussed in Chapter 9. With this example we shall be able to carry out a complete analysis and obtain some remarkable, and famous, results.

11.2 THE ELASTICITY OF SUBSTITUTION

In the present section we first bring some general results developed earlier to bear on the special case of the Cobb-Douglas production function. We then go on to use that production function to introduce and to illustrate a new concept: the elasticity of substitution.

In Section 10.6 we developed some results in the case in which the objective function $f(x, y) = Ax^\alpha y^\beta$ is maximized subject to a linear constraint. The Cobb-Douglas production function first considered in Chapter 9 is a special case of this function in which $\alpha + \beta = 1$. To emphasize this we write the Cobb-Douglas function in the two-input case (dropping the multiplicative constant A) as

$$X = L^\alpha K^{1-\alpha} \quad . \tag{13}$$

The budget constraint is given by

$$B_0 - wL - rL = 0 \quad . \tag{14}$$

Results obtained in Section 10.6 allow us to write the ratio of labor to capital when output is maximized subject to the budget constraint as

$$\frac{L}{K} = \frac{r}{w}\left(\frac{\alpha}{1-\alpha}\right) \quad . \tag{15}$$

[This is Eq. (25) from Section 10.6 with the variables L and K substituted for x and y, the constants w and r substituted for r and s, and the parameter $1 - \alpha$ substituted for β.] This is the familiar result that the least-cost labor: capital ratio, L/K, depends on the factor price ratio, r/w, and the exponents α and $1 - \alpha$, and is independent of the scale of production, since B does not occur in (15).

A second important result is obtained directly from (24a) and (24b) in Section 10.6:

$$L = B_0\frac{\alpha}{w} \tag{16a}$$

and

$$K = B_0\frac{1-\alpha}{r} \quad . \tag{16b}$$

Equations (16) are obtained from the earlier ones by the same changes of symbols as yield (15) above. Equations (16) state that the optimal amount of labor depends on the ratio of the exponent in the production function, α, to the price of labor, w, with total outlay, B, entering as a multiplicative factor only, and similarly that the optimal amount of capital depends on the ratio $(1 - \alpha)/r$, with B again as a multiplicative (scale) factor only.

We saw in Chapter 9 that, in the case of a Cobb-Douglas production function, factor shares (the proportion of total product paid to each factor) depend on the exponents only, and are constant so long as the exponents are unchanged, being independent of actual factor prices or the scale of production. For factor shares, wL/rK, to remain constant if, say, the wage rate increases, it is necessary that the reduced amount of L times increased w exactly cancels increased K.

To see that this is what happens, we introduce a new term, *the elasticity of substitution,* denoted by σ (read "sigma"; we encountered capital sigma, Σ, earlier). The elasticity of substitution is defined as

$$\frac{\text{proportionate change in factor proportions}}{\text{proportionate change in relative factor prices}} ,$$

or

$$\sigma = \frac{d(L/K)}{d(r/w)} \frac{r/w}{L/K} . \tag{17}$$

It is very easy to evaluate this here. We already have (15):

$$\frac{L}{K} = \frac{r}{w} \frac{\alpha}{1 - \alpha} ;$$

hence

$$\frac{d(L/K)}{d(r/w)} = \frac{\alpha}{1 - \alpha} . \tag{18}$$

If we substitute (15) and (18) into (17), we obtain

$$\sigma = \frac{\alpha}{1 - \alpha} \cdot \frac{r/w}{\dfrac{r}{w} \cdot \dfrac{\alpha}{1 - \alpha}}$$

$$= 1 . \tag{19}$$

Thus the elasticity of substitution is equal to unity, and, as relative factor prices alter, we have the exactly offsetting effect that our intuitive argument led us to expect.

It may help to see what σ means in terms of the shape of the iso-quants. Let the budget line AB of Figure 11.1 change slope, and slide it round to preserve tangency with a given iso-quant: we are asking what happens to factor proportions as the slope changes. But as we have tangency, we are really only asking about the shape of the iso-quant: if we move along it, changing its slope, how "far" do we move in terms of K/L for a given change in slope? That is, we can replace r/w with the ratio of the marginal products [refer back, if necessary, to Eq. (6)] and write σ, if we choose, as

$$\sigma = \frac{d(L/K)}{d(MPK/MPL)} \frac{MPK/MPL}{L/K} , \tag{20}$$

where MPL and MPK are the marginal physical products of labor and capital, respectively. The expression $d(MPK/MPL)$ looks forbidding, but remember that it is only the change in the slope of the iso-quant. By assuming tangency, we have simply replaced it with the change in the slope of the constraint, $d(r/w)$, and found

$$\frac{\mathrm{d}(L/K)}{\mathrm{d}(r/w)} = \frac{\mathrm{d}(L/K)}{\mathrm{d}(MPK/MPL)} \quad ,$$

which is the rate of change in factor proportions as one alters the slope of the iso-quant by sliding along it.

11.3 THE EFFICIENT ALLOCATION OF RESOURCES

We can now take up some quite new topics in economics. They are new in the sense that we have not discussed them before, and also in the sense that they are not included in principles courses, or, indeed, in many second-year courses. Thus in terms of its economic content, this section is ambitious. Yet we make such an enormous gain in analytic power by using what is now routine mathematical technique that this section should not be found particularly difficult: it is possible to concentrate on the economic interpretation rather than on the technical difficulties.

We shall prove the famous propositions of welfare economics that, for an efficient allocation of resources, the marginal product of a factor must be the same in all uses and its price the same to all users. This is one of the conditions for allocative efficiency first proved by the great Italian economist Vilfredo Pareto. It may be proved piecemeal by the method of finite differences, or geometrically, or much more generally and powerfully by calculus methods. We shall start with the geometry. This is worthwhile because the construction required is frequently employed in the economic literature, and it is useful to be familiar with it, but we shall shortly see that it is remarkably long-winded and cumbersome compared with our calculus methods.

We assume that society is endowed with limited quantities of two resources, say capital and labor, which can be combined, with given production functions, to produce two goods, A and B. We assume constant returns in the production of both A and B. Now we construct the famous "box diagram."[1] In Figure 11.2 we mark off the endowments $0K$ of capital and $0N$ of labor along the axes in the ordinary way. Now draw in the iso-quants for one of the goods, say A. (Figure 11.2 is drawn complete, but it is helpful to take paper and pencil and construct it step by step for yourself if you have never done it before.) Complete the box by constructing a horizontal line through K, and a vertical one through N, and marking their inter-

---

[1] Since the box diagram is thoroughly explained in most intermediate textbooks, the geometrical treatment here is very condensed. See, for example, G. J. Stigler, *The Theory of Price*, Macmillan, New York, 1972, chap. 4, or K. Boulding, *Economic Analysis*, vol. I, 4th ed., Harper & Row, New York, 1966, chap. 28.

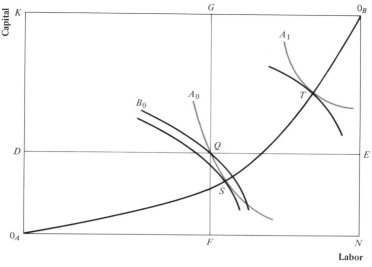

Figure 11.2

section 0_B (correspondingly relabel the southwest origin 0_A). Now consider a point in the box such as Q. At Q, $0_A D$ of capital and $0_A F$ of labor are used in the production of A, hence DK of capital and FN of labor are available for the production of B. But $DK = 0_B E$, and $FN = 0_B G$. Thus measuring along the axes from 0_A we have factor use in the A industry, and measuring from 0_B we have factor use in the B industry: everywhere in the box we have full employment of both factors. We can now draw the B iso-quants with 0_B as origin. Every point in the box now corresponds to a unique allocation of factors between the two industries and a unique pair of outputs. Suppose now that Q lies on the iso-quant B_0. Q is then inefficient because by sliding round A_0, A output constant, to S, one can reach a higher B output. At S we have tangency. But the slope of an iso-quant is the ratio of the marginal products, so when the iso-quants are tangential the ratio of the marginal products must be equal. We will consider this further in a moment.

First, we notice that a point such as S is efficient in the sense that it is impossible to reallocate resources in such a fashion as to increase the output of one good without reducing that of the other. Nothing is said about the relative valuations of the two goods or what combination of the two society wants or "should" want: an "efficient point" is one that is *on the production frontier,* and that is all. Second, we pick any other A iso-quant, say A_1, and then search for a B iso-quant that is tangent to it. Let the tangency occur at T. Then T is an efficient point

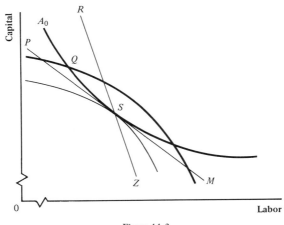

Figure 11.3

in precisely the same sense as S. If we locate all such points of tangency and connect them up, we get the curve 0_A0_B, *the locus of efficient allocations.*

Figure 11.3 shows the curves in the vicinity of S in Figure 11.2 blown up in scale for convenience. If firms in the A industry are to be in equilibrium at S, the iso-quant must there be tangent to the price line, which is the case as we have drawn the price line *PM*. If industry B faces the same relative prices, it will be in equilibrium at S, too, and not at an inefficient point such as Q. Suppose, on the other hand, that the price of labor were higher to industry B, due to some market imperfection or tax. (It is a good exercise now to work out for yourself in which direction this will rotate the relative price line to the B industry.) Consider industry B moving down *PM*. As B moves down, it is increasing its amount of capital — A is giving up capital — and losing labor. Thus a movement upwards and to the right in the box corresponds to a gain of labor to B and loss of capital. Hence a steeper line such as *RZ* indicates that for a given gain in labor B must give up more capital. But if B's price line is *RZ*, B will certainly not be in equilibrium at S, so an efficient allocation cannot be achieved. On the full-employment assumption, however, both industries must be at the same point in the box. The situation will therefore be one such as V in Figure 11.4, where the A iso-quant is tangent to *PM* and the B iso-quant to *RZ*.

To achieve an efficient point if firms in each industry adjust to least-cost factor combinations therefore requires that the factor price ratio be the same for each industry: otherwise the ratios of marginal products will be unequal. But we already know that equilibrium for

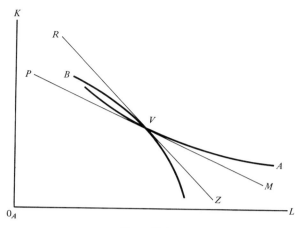

Figure 11.4

the firm requires that marginal products be equal to real factor prices or wages; hence we not only have equality of ratios but of the absolute marginal products themselves as a condition for efficiency. We have something else, too. The marginal-product-equals-real-wage condition, or money-wage-equals-marginal-value-product, holds only in perfect competition: we have in fact assumed that A and B are produced in conditions of perfect competition.

The mathematics of efficient allocation are now familiar and easy. We have two constant-returns production functions, which we write as

$$A = f^A(L_A, K_A) \tag{21a}$$

and

$$B = f^B(L_B, K_B) \quad . \tag{21b}$$

(The notation f^A and f^B reminds us which production function is which and, since we use the subscript notation for partial derivatives, should occasion no confusion. It is not, of course, assumed that $f^A = f^B$.) We pick a value of A, say A_0, and look for the conditions which maximize B subject to $A = A_0$. We also have to take into account the limits on total factor supplies, that is, the size of the box. Thus we have $L_A + L_B = L_0$ and $K_A + K_B = K_0$, where L_0 and K_0 are the total supplies of labor and capital, respectively. To avoid employing three constraints, it is convenient to make the substitutions $L_A = L_0 - L_B$ and $K_A = K_0 - K_B$. The problem now is to maximize $B = f^B(L_B, K_B)$ subject to $A_0 - f^A(L_0 - L_B, K_0 - K_B) = 0$. We write the Lagrangian

$$V = f^B(L_B, K_B) - \lambda[A_0 - f^A(L_0 - L_B, K_0 - K_B)] \tag{22}$$

and equate the partial derivatives of V to zero. (Notice that $\partial f^A/\partial L_B = -f_L^A$ because $L_A = L_0 - L_B$.) This gives

$$f_L^B - \lambda f_L^A = 0 \tag{23a}$$

$$f_K^B - \lambda f_K^A = 0 \tag{23b}$$

$$A_0 - f^A(L_0 - L_B, K_0 - K_B) = 0 \quad . \tag{23c}$$

We may rearrange (23a) and (23b) to give

$$\frac{f_L^B}{f_L^A} = \lambda = \frac{f_K^B}{f_K^A} \tag{24a}$$

or

$$\frac{f_L^B}{f_K^B} = \frac{f_L^A}{f_K^A} \quad . \tag{24b}$$

It is obvious that our conditions for an efficient allocation are independent of the size and shape of the box. The conditions (24) have to be satisfied for an efficient allocation *whatever* the endowments may be, equally in a large country or a small one, one with much labor and little capital, or one with abundant capital and expensive labor. Insofar as the conditions for efficiency are concerned, the absolute size of Figure 11.2 is irrelevant, as is the capital: labor ratio in each industry, and it is clear from inspection of Figure 11.2 that the ratios will in general neither be the same for each industry nor be the same at different points on the curve $0_A 0_B$.

11.4 UTILITY MAXIMIZATION

Now that we have dealt with production, the case of the individual consumer is straightforward and very similar. In Section 10.6 we considered a utility function $f(x, y) = Ax^\alpha y^\beta$ and the properties given it by consumer theory. We now write the general utility function

$$U = U(x, y) \quad . \tag{25}$$

We must consider what assumptions we need to make about the properties of (25). Since we wish to discuss the demand for goods (as opposed to dis-goods or "bads") and to avoid the complications of satiation, we assume that it is strictly increasing in both arguments: U_x, $U_y > 0$. (If an individual were to "satiate" on both goods, we should have $U_x = U_y = 0$ at some values x_0, y_0. It is a good exercise to work out for yourself what the indifference curves would look like in this case.) It was once believed that we should also assume "diminishing marginal utility," U_{xx}, $U_{yy} < 0$. We, in fact, need diminishing marginal substitutability, for which U_{xx}, $U_{yy} < 0$ is neither necessary nor sufficient ("cardinal" and "ordinal" utility are discussed in Section 11.5).

The slope of an indifference curve is the marginal rate of substitution, given by

$$r = -\frac{U_x}{U_y} \quad . \tag{26}$$

Since U_x and U_y are both positive by assumption, this is negative, as required. Convexity means that the slope gets absolutely smaller as x increases. But as the slope is negative, this means that its rate of change must be positive, so our familiar convexity condition is

$$\frac{dr}{dx} > 0 \quad . \tag{27}$$

As in Section 10.4, we require the total differential,

$$\frac{dr}{dx} = \frac{\partial}{\partial x}\left(-\frac{U_x}{U_y}\right) + \frac{\partial}{\partial y}\left(-\frac{U_x}{U_y}\right)\frac{dy}{dx} \quad .$$

Evaluating this, we obtain

$$\frac{dr}{dx} = -\frac{U_y{}^2 U_{xx} - 2U_x U_y U_{xy} + U_x{}^2 U_{yy}}{U_y{}^3} \quad . \tag{28}$$

Since the denominator is positive, (28) is positive if

$$U_y{}^2 U_{xx} - 2U_x U_y U_{xy} + U_x{}^2 U_{yy} < 0 \quad . \tag{29}$$

Examination of (29) shows that "diminishing marginal utility" (U_{xx}, $U_{yy} < 0$) is neither necessary nor sufficient to satisfy the condition $dr/dx > 0$. Even if both U_{xx} and U_{yy} are negative, it is possible that a sufficiently large absolute value of U_{xy} negative might upset the inequality; and if both were "wrongly" signed, the inequality might still be preserved by a sufficiently large positive value of U_{xy}. What this amounts to is that we *assume* that the inequality (29), diminishing marginal substitutability, holds: it cannot be *derived* from other assumptions.[2]

Thus we have effectively assumed a well-behaved objective function, but nothing more. This much we have to do to obtain a mathematically tractable model of consistently purposeful action. Whether it is empirically justified is, of course, an entirely separate question. We may, for example, be able to conceive a world in which consumers' tastes fluctuate so much that no one objective function can

---

[2] If U_{xy} is assumed to be zero, then U_{xx}, $U_{yy} < 0$ is, in fact, sufficient for $dr/dx > 0$, as may be verified from (29). In general, this "cross-effect" U_{xy} is not zero; and the assumption that it is limits us to "cardinal" utility theory: see Section 11.5.

help us to derive a good model. Tastes, too, may be closely related to experience, in which case several of our assumptions will be inappropriate.

1. If experience matters, today's purchases depend on yesterday's, and we require a dynamic instead of a static treatment.
2. Possible experience depends on the budget constraint: if experience matters, tastes will not be independent of past and present budgets and prices.

It is also, of course, possible that there is a large random component in consumer behavior. There are, furthermore, important choice problems in which the assumption of continuity may be inappropriate.

We may speculate on these matters, and speculation certainly helps us to see just what we are assuming, but our assumptions cannot be justified a priori: we require some testable predictions. The first step is of course to find equilibrium conditions.

We seek to maximize the objective function (25) subject to a budget constraint

$$B - p_x x - p_y y = 0 \quad . \tag{30}$$

Procedure is routine. Write

$$V = U(x, y) + \lambda(B - p_x x - p_y y) \tag{31}$$

and set the first-order partial derivatives equal to zero:

$$V_x = U_x - \lambda p_x = 0 \tag{32a}$$

$$V_y = U_y - \lambda p_y = 0 \tag{32b}$$

$$V_\lambda = B - p_x - p_y = 0 \quad . \tag{32c}$$

Rearrangement of Eqs. (32) gives us the famous equilibrium conditions. We find

$$\frac{U_x}{p_x} = \lambda = \frac{U_y}{p_y} \quad , \tag{33}$$

which says that the ratio of the marginal utility of each good to its price must be equal to the common ratio, λ, or, what comes to the same thing, that marginal utility per penny of expenditure must be the same in every line of expenditure. Notice particularly that (33) is formally identical with the least-cost production conditions derived from Eqs. (5) in Section 11.1.

We now come to the obstacle encountered in Section 7.7*: to do comparative statics, and obtain signs, if we can, for dx/dp_x, dy/dp_y, etc., we require the formal second-order conditions for maximizing (31). We shall therefore have to be content with a rather rough, intuitive treatment. Imagine that prices alter so that the budget line changes slope, but that it is slid in or out to preserve tangency with the indifference curve on which the initial equilibrium is located. We in fact conducted a similar experiment with the Cobb-Douglas production function. In the case of the consumer, the sliding in or out of the budget line to preserve constant utility after a price change is referred to as "income compensation." Now, from the assumption of convexity alone we know how demand alters in the case of compensated price changes. Thus suppose that x becomes relatively cheaper: the budget line becomes flatter. Thanks to convexity, a flatter portion of the indifference curve is reached by increasing x. Hence a compensated demand curve has a negative slope: this is the result of the "substitution effect." That is clear and is, in fact, as much as we could prove with the full armory of second-order conditions. The reason it is not sufficient to tell us that all demand curves slope down may be found in any intermediate text: when we do not compensate, but leave the intercept of the budget line unchanged when its slope alters, there is an income effect as well as a substitution effect. To see that there is an income effect, imgaine a two-step procedure. First, by compensating, we discover the chosen point at the new price ratio on the old indifference curve: this allows us to isolate the substitution effect. Next we "uncompensate": we slide the compensated budget line, slope unaltered, until its intercept coincides with that of the old budget line. The whole line in fact now coincides with the new budget line, but the change in the demand for x induced by this parallel shift is the income effect on demand. If the income effect is positive (normal good), all is well, and we predict a downward-sloping demand curve. If the income effect is negative (inferior good), it and the substitution effect pull in opposite directions, and we can derive no general *quali-tative* prediction.

This may be a little disappointing: we do not seem to get much out of consumer theory. We demonstrate that the substitution effect has the "right sign," which we might indicate by

$$\left.\frac{\partial x}{\partial p_x}\right|_{U\text{ constant}} < 0 \quad ,$$

and that is all. We shall see in Section 11.6, however, that we can derive some rather remarkable and interesting results about economic "efficiency," in a very carefully defined sense, with the help of utility functions. First, we may just notice how easily our algebraic treatment can be extended to the case of many goods, to which geometry will not extend. We simply replace the objective function (25) with

$$U = U(x_1, x_2, \ldots, x_n) \quad , \tag{34}$$

where $x_1, x_2, \ldots, x_n$ are the goods consumed. Now employing the summation notation, we can write the budget constraint as

$$B - \sum_i x_i p_i = 0 \quad . \tag{35}$$

$\Sigma_i x_i p_i$ is the sum of the expenditures on each good, quantity of x_1 times its price, plus quantity of x_2 times its price, etc. Now we write

$$V = U(x_1, x_2, \ldots, x_n) + \lambda \left(B - \sum_i p_i x_i \right) \tag{36}$$

and obtain $n + 1$ derivatives — one each for each of the x's, plus λ. This, as we saw in Chapter 10, can be written conveniently and compactly as

$$V_{x_i} = U_{x_i} - \lambda p_i = 0 \qquad (i = 1, \ldots, n) \tag{37a}$$

and

$$V_\lambda = B - \sum_i p_i x_i = 0 \quad . \tag{37b}$$

Equation (37a) says that we have n equations identical in form, one for each x. If we pick out another, say the jth,

$$U_{x_j} - \lambda p_j = 0 \quad ,$$

we can derive the conditions

$$\frac{U_{x_i}}{p_i} = \lambda = \frac{U_{x_j}}{p_j} \tag{38}$$

for *any* pair x_i and x_j. What this demonstrates is the enormous power and convenience of really good notation. We have derived (38) for *any* pair i and j, and we simply do not care about the value of n. Imagine the alternative: we should have to write out 40 equations in the case of $n = 40$, and if a cautious skeptic said "What about the case of 41 goods? You haven't proved that yet," we should have to do it again. We have proved (38) once and for all for any n.

11.5 CARDINAL AND ORDINAL UTILITY

It is now easy and convenient to clear up the sometimes confusing notions of "cardinal" and "ordinal" utility functions. By an *ordinal* utility function, we mean one that indicates the ordering of bundles of goods, *and nothing more*. The function attaches a utility number to each bundle of goods, but the number itself means nothing, only the direction of change of the number as the bundle changes. It follows that *any* function that preserves the ordering is as good a representation of the consumer's tastes as any other. We express this mathematically by saying that utility is determined only *up to a monotonic increasing transformation*. Let us see how this works.

Suppose that an individual's tastes are represented by the utility function

$$U = U(x_1, x_2, \ldots, x_n) \quad . \tag{39}$$

Remember that the U's are numbers, and that if we confine ourselves to situations in which the individual's desire for each commodity is unsatiated, we require U to be strictly increasing in its arguments; i.e., $U_{x_i} > 0$ for all i. By applying a monotonic increasing transformation we mean that we construct a new utility function, say

$$V = \phi(U) \tag{40}$$

with ϕ' strictly positive: V increases whenever U does, whence the ordering of commodity bundles is preserved. ϕ may be *any* function with a positive first derivative. Thus ϕ might represent a string of instructions such as take the original U number and square it, add 10, raise it to the fourth power, take the log, add 100, and raise it to the power $\frac{11}{3}$. As long as the first derivative is positive at each step in the transformation, the new set of utility numbers (the V's) will order the bundles exactly as did the old set (the U's).

The important property of ordinal, as opposed to cardinal, utility is that it preserves marginal rates of substitution but *not* marginal utilities. If we differentiate V with respect to, say, the ith good, we get, by the chain rule,

$$\frac{\partial V}{\partial x_i} = \phi' \frac{\partial U}{\partial x_i} \quad . \tag{41}$$

This obviously depends on ϕ'. But now consider a marginal rate of substitution, as we did in (26). In terms of U, we have, for the goods x_i and x_j,

$$r = -\frac{\partial U/\partial x_i}{\partial U/\partial x_j} \quad . \tag{42}$$

In terms of V we have

$$-\frac{\partial V/\partial x_i}{\partial V/\partial x_j} = -\frac{\phi' \partial U/\partial x_i}{\phi' \partial U/\partial x_j} = -\frac{\partial U/\partial x_i}{\partial U/\partial x_j} \quad : \tag{43}$$

the marginal rate of substitution is unaltered by the transformation. This is a remarkably convenient result. Looking back at (29), we recall that the assumption of diminishing marginal utilities is neither necessary nor sufficient to ensure convexity of the indifference curves: it is something we must assume directly. We now see that a monotonic increasing transformation of a utility function preserves the ordering of bundles and, as a natural consequence, the shape of the indifference map. All it does is attach new utility numbers to each indifference curve.

From the fact that it does not matter what numbers are attached to the indifference curves, provided that they are correctly ordered, we see that we cannot talk of "decreasing marginal utility" if we assume only ordinal utility functions. In view of (29), we know, of course, that it would do us no good if we could. Thus suppose that we consider points on three indifference curves labeled 9, 14, and 15. "Marginal utilities" between these points are 5 and 1 (decreasing). But the labeling 9, 10, 20 would preserve the ordering just as well, while altering the ordering of the "marginal utilities" to 1 and 10. In other words, *monotonic increasing transforms of a function do not necessarily preserve the ordering of its first derivatives, but only their signs.*

Now we can attach meaning to "cardinal utility": a representation of the ordering of bundles such that the first derivatives are ordered, that is, a representation such that it makes sense to talk of "decreasing marginal utility." There is a restricted class of monotonic increasing transforms that preserves the ordering of the first derivatives, the *linear transforms*. Thus suppose that we again start with an ordering represented by $U(x_1, x_2, \ldots, x_n)$. We restrict ourselves to transforms that can be written as

$$W = a + bU \quad , \tag{44}$$

where a and b are constants but b must be positive. Since the first derivatives of U are all to be multiplied by the same positive number, b, ordering is preserved by this restricted class of transforms: it now makes sense to talk of "increasing (or decreasing) marginal utility." Thus consider our example of indifference curves labeled 9, 14, 15. If we restrict ourselves to linear transforms, they can only be relabeled $a + 9b$, $a + 14b$, $a + 15b$, and not, for example, 9, 10, 20. The first differences are

$$(a + 14b) - (a + 9b) = 5b$$

and

$$(a + 15b) - (a + 14b) = b \quad ,$$

which preserve the ranking for *any* positive b.

Let us return for a moment to (29). Suppose that we had a representation of a preference ordering such that $U_{xy} = 0$ (no "cross-effects"). In this case, U_{xx}, $U_{yy} < 0$ does ensure diminishing marginal substitutability as may be verified from (29) (footnote 2, page 281). We now show that the condition $U_{xy} = 0$ *does not survive monotonic transformation of U*, whence this apparent exception to the rule that U_{xx}, $U_{yy} < 0$ does not ensure that diminishing substitutability holds only if cardinality is assumed. Thus let

$$U = U(x, y)$$

with $U_{xy} = 0$. Apply a monotonic transformation, so that we consider the utility index $V = \phi[U(x, y)]$, $\phi' > 0$. For first derivatives we have

$$V_x = \phi' U_x \quad \text{and} \quad V_y = \phi' U_y \quad .$$

We now require $V_{xy} = V_{yx}$. How do we take the derivative with respect to y of $\phi' U_x$ (or with respect to x of $\phi' U_y$)? We have to combine the chain and product rules. We have $\phi'(x, y)$ and $U_x(x, y)$, and their product has to be differentiated with respect to y. Thus we have

$$\frac{\partial}{\partial y} \phi' U_x = \phi' \frac{\partial U_x}{\partial y} + U_x \frac{\partial}{\partial y} \phi' \quad .$$

The first term is zero, from the assumption that $U_{xy} = 0$, but, by the chain rule,

$$\frac{\partial \phi'(U)}{\partial y} = \phi'' U_y \quad ,$$

from which it follows that

$$V_{xy} = \phi'' U_x U_y$$

which is not zero even if U_{xy} is assumed to be zero. The result is that the special case of no cross-effects, $U_{xy} = 0$, requires that we assume cardinal utility, that is, rule out nonlinear transforms of the utility index. (You should check for yourself that, if we limit ourselves to linear transforms, we have $\phi'' = 0$, and $V_{xy} = 0$ if $U_{xy} = 0$.)

Since the work of Sir John R. Hicks, in *Value and Capital,* in the 1930s, it has been recognized that, to represent the consumer's equilibrium and derive demand curves, it is necessary to assume only that the consumer can order his bundles, that is, that utility is determined up to a monotonic transform. The objections to assuming cardinal utility (utility determined up to a linear transform) are not so much empirical (or moral) as that it is *logically unnecessary* (even unhelpful) and that it saddles us with the embarrassing (and unnecessary) task of trying to explain what we might mean by "utils." If, of course, we are philosophical utilitarians, we shall not only assume cardinal utility but believe that it is *interpersonally comparable* (it is obviously logically impossible for ordinal utilities to be interpersonally comparable). This position affords a much stronger basis for welfare economics; but the "new welfare economics," some of which we have discussed in this chapter, follows Hicks in assuming only ordinal utility functions.

It is convenient to end this section by considering the interpretation of the "undetermined Lagrangian multiplier" λ. From the first-order conditions for utility maximization we have

$$U_i = \lambda p_i \quad .$$

The left-hand side is "utils per unit" (for the utility index U). On the right-hand side we have p_i, dollars per unit. Then, to attain consistency in the units, λ must be "utils per dollar," the *marginal utility of (money) income*. It is sometimes called a "shadow price."[3] If we wish to avoid assuming that utility is cardinally measurable, we must check that this interpretation of λ, as utils per dollar, is consistent with ordinality. Let us replace U with $V = \phi(U)$. Then the first-order condition becomes

$$V_i = \phi' U_i = \lambda p_i$$

and

$$\lambda = \frac{\phi' U_i}{p_i} \quad .$$

This means that λ is still "utils per dollar," but the units (or utils) change with ϕ, as we should expect.

11.6 THE CONTRACT CURVE

An important concept in economics is that of an *efficient* or *optimal* allocation. We have already worked out some conditions for an efficient allocation of factors in production (Section 11.3). We can do something very similar for consumers, but we need to be particularly careful about what it means if we are not going to make unwarranted policy inferences. We know, of course, that the conditions for optimal allocations are those given by solution of the appropriate constrained maximum problem. They are therefore optimal from the point of view of the particular objective function chosen, and there is no occasion to interpret optimality in any wider ethical or political sense. The conclusion is the creature of the objective function chosen. If, however, we can work with a fairly general function, our results may be of considerable scope.

---

[3] "Shadow prices" are explained in Sections 18.4 and 18.5.

In our discussion of the box diagram, we found a locus of efficient points in the sense that, when off the locus, more of one good could be produced without sacrifice of the other, whereas, when on it, more of one good could be had only at the cost of the other. We can similarly draw a box for two consumers trading with each other, putting the two goods on the axes, and measuring the amounts enjoyed by consumer *A* from one origin and the amounts enjoyed by consumer *B* from the diagonally opposite origin. If we draw in their indifference maps, we shall find a locus of efficient points in the sense that, once on it, one consumer can be made better off only at the expense of the other, whereas, if off it, one can be made better off *without* making the other worse off. We shall show that if two consumers are faced by different price ratios, they will be off this locus: the welfare of one of them could be increased without loss to the other.

The geometry of the box is similar to that in the case of production. We labored through the construction there, and then saw how much more quickly we could proceed by using calculus methods. Construction of the box for two consumers is left to you. What we shall do is derive the efficiency conditions directly for the case of *three* goods, where the geometry would be impossibly cumbersome. Following the discussion at the end of Section 11.5, you may be able to generalize this to the case of *n* goods for yourself, and it would be worthwhile attempting the exercise. We assume two individuals, *A* and *B*, and three goods, *x*, *y*, *z*. We also have two utility functions,

$$U^A = U^A(x_A, y_A, z_A) \tag{45}$$

$$U^B = U^B(x_B, y_B, z_B) \quad . \tag{46}$$

We already know (from Section 11.3) the two basic tricks to use here: we use the total availabilities constraint to eliminate one of x_A, y_A, z_A or x_B, y_B, z_B, and we maximize the value of one utility index subject to the other being at some predetermined level. Thus we write our Lagrangian as

$$V = U^A(x_A, y_A, z_A) - \lambda[U_0^B - U^B(x - x_A, y - y_A, z - z_A)] \quad , \tag{47}$$

where *x*, *y*, and *z*, without subscripts, are the total quantities of the goods available. [Notice that the only difference between this and (22) is the trivial one that we have three goods instead of two.] Equating the partial derivatives of *V* to zero we have

$$U_x^A - \lambda U_x^B = 0 \tag{48a}$$

$$U_y^A - \lambda U_y^B = 0 \tag{48b}$$

$$U_z^A - \lambda U_z^B = 0 \tag{48c}$$

$$U_0^B - U^B = 0 \quad . \tag{48d}$$

From Eqs. (48) we may obtain the conditions for equality of marginal rates of substitution:

$$\frac{U_x^A}{U_y^A} = \frac{U_x^B}{U_y^B}, \qquad \frac{U_y^A}{U_z^A} = \frac{U_y^B}{U_z^B}, \qquad \frac{U_x^A}{U_z^A} = \frac{U_x^B}{U_z^B}, \tag{49}$$

or

$$\frac{U_x^A}{U_x^B} = \frac{U_y^A}{U_y^B} = \frac{U_z^A}{U_z^B}. \tag{50}$$

Equations (49) and (50) hold at the efficient point consistent with $U^B = U_0^B$, but, since U_0^B was arbitrarily chosen, they hold at any efficient point.

We already know, however, that each individual, facing given prices, will maximize his utility by choosing that combination of goods that makes the ratios of the marginal utilities, or marginal rates of substitution, equal to the price ratios [Eq. (33)]. Hence if the two individuals are to have the same marginal rates of substitution, which by (49) is a condition for their being on the locus of efficient points, they must face a common price ratio. The analogy with the theory of production is very close. You are asked in Question 7 to extend the analysis a little for both cases.

Our analysis makes it very easy to settle a question that much perturbed our ancestors. Some believed that a good must have some definite, inherent value; and they accordingly argued that, if one party to a transaction gains, the other must lose: one party must receive more, or less, than the good is really worth if either is to gain. Probably no one really believes this now save a few flat-earthers, but it was an important idea: it lay behind many schemes for noncommercial utopian communities, and its overthrow, the belief that *both* parties may gain from exchange, was important to the development of the law of free contract. Once we give up the idea of goods having "inherent value," instead of merely utility to individual consumers and relative scarcity, the problem is scarcely likely to bother us; but we can easily demonstrate the gains from trade with our box diagram. In Figure 11.5 we draw a box, and we give each individual an initial arbitrary allocation of the two goods. Suppose that they start at Q where A has $0_A E$ of x and $0_A D$ of y, and B has the remainder. If by trading they move to any point outside the area enclosed by the two indifference curves through Q, someone is worse off than with his initial allocation: these two indifference curves enclose the area of mutually advantageous bargains. Notice that we could construct a locus of efficient points that would contain points outside the area bounded by the two indifference curves that pass through Q. No consumer with an initial endowment represented by Q would wish to go to such a point. The subset

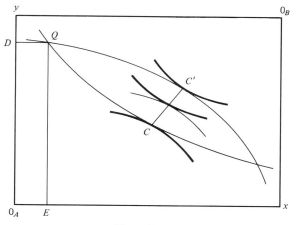

Figure 11.5

of efficient points to which consumers who started at Q would go to voluntarily is called the *contract curve,* and is the curve CC' in Figure 11.5. The contract curve is the locus of points such that one party can only make a further gain at the expense of the other. However, since any point on it is better for both parties than the initial point Q, we see that it is *possible* for both parties to gain from trade, and the old worry, that one man's gain *must* be another's loss, is dispelled.

If the two individuals' marginal rates of substitution had happened to be equal at their initial endowment, there would have been no possibility of gain from trade and no motive for trade. Equality of the marginal rates of substitution means, of course, tangency of the indifference curves. Thus equality of the MRS's at the initial endowment would mean that Q happened to lie on the locus of efficient points. Hence we can look on the possibility of mutual gain from trade as arising from the nonequality of MRS's, and as being exhausted once a bargain has been made that equalizes the MRS's. Once the contract curve is reached, there is no further room for mutual benefit, but only for redistribution.[4]

This is a good moment to emphasize one assumption that we have made throughout this section: that the two utility functions are independent. In the real world, this may well not be the case. A may well

[4] A fascinating account of the benefit from trade, arising from nonequality of individuals' MRS's at an initial arbitrary endowment, is given in R. A. Radford, "The Economic Organization of a Prisoner of War Camp," *Economica,* Aug., 1945. This is an example of purely literary economics that may be read with great profit now that the underlying analysis has been mastered.

respond to B's well-being and vice versa. Both individuals may have feelings of personal benevolence, or opinions about the fairness of the distribution. If they do not, they still may respond to each other's consumptions, for many possible reasons, such as "keeping up with the Joneses" or because they are disturbed by the neighbor's radio. A little imagination suggests a wide variety of attitudes of individuals toward others that occur in the real world and might be allowed for. All we can say is that both parties *can* gain from trade, and that there is a well-defined locus of efficient points *if* the utilities of the two individuals are independent of each other.

11.7 THE PRODUCTION POSSIBILITY FRONTIER

The production possibility, or "guns and butter," frontier is a familiar two-dimensional construct. We have already derived, in Section 11.3, the conditions for an efficient allocation of resources that must be satisfied on the frontier. Let us now consider the production possibility frontier itself. We have all the mathematical technique we need to develop the general case, with n goods and m inputs, but it is laborious, and we shall lose little by confining ourselves to the case of two inputs and two outputs.

We assume that society has two resources available in fixed amounts, q_1 and q_2, say. Each of them is used in the production of two goods, x_1 and x_2, say. Production is given by the two production functions

$$x_1 = f^1(q_{11}, q_{21})$$
$$x_2 = f^2(q_{12}, q_{22}) ,$$

where the two subscripts on the q's indicate, first, the resource, and, second, the industry in which it is employed. We shall assume constant returns to scale and diminishing returns to each factor separately in both production functions.

Now, we have rather a puzzle. What are we going to maximize? We already know how to maximize one of the x's, given an arbitrary value of the other, and derive the efficiency conditions. What we want now is to derive a functional relation between the x's themselves that describes the locus of "best" points, given the production functions and the factor endowments.

Let us start in a seemingly arbitrary way by assuming that we have already been told p_1 and p_2, the prices of the two goods. Now the obvious thing to do is maximize GNP, which is the linear objective function $p_1x_1 + p_2x_2$ ($\Sigma_{i=1}^n p_ix_i$ in the general case for n commodities). Thus we may set up the formal problem: maximize

$$p_1 x_1 + p_2 x_2$$

subject to

$$x_1 = f^1(q_{11}, q_{21})$$
$$x_2 = f^2(q_{12}, q_{22}) \tag{51}$$

and

$$q_{11} + q_{12} = q_1$$
$$q_{21} + q_{22} = q_2 \quad .$$

(51) is a problem in six variables, four q's and two x's. It helps to use the production functions to eliminate the x's, deriving the simpler problem: maximize

$$p_1 f^1(q_{11}, q_{21}) + p_2 f^2(q_{12}, q_{22})$$

subject to

$$q_{11} + q_{12} = q_1$$
$$q_{21} + q_{22} = q_2 \quad . \tag{52}$$

To solve this, we set up the familiar Lagrangian

$$L = p_1 f^1(q_{11}, q_{21}) + p_2 f^2(q_{12}, q_{22}) - \lambda(q_{11} + q_{12} - q_1) - \mu(q_{21} + q_{22} - q_2) \tag{53}$$

where λ and μ are two undetermined multipliers. Next differentiate with respect to q_{11}, q_{21}, q_{12}, and q_{22} (q_1 and q_2 are constants standing for the fixed total supplies of the two factors). This gives us

$$p_1 f_1^1 - \lambda = 0 \tag{54a}$$
$$p_1 f_2^1 - \mu = 0 \tag{54b}$$
$$p_2 f_1^2 - \lambda = 0 \tag{54c}$$
$$p_2 f_2^2 - \mu = 0 \tag{54d}$$

(where f_1^2, say, means the partial derivate of x_2 with respect to q_1, or the marginal productivity of the first factor in the second industry).

The first-order conditions can be manipulated in a revealing manner. Dividing the first equation by the second, and the third by the fourth, we have

$$\frac{f_1^1}{f_2^1} = \frac{\lambda}{\mu} = \frac{f_1^2}{f_2^2} \quad . \tag{55}$$

This is the condition, familiar in welfare economics, that the marginal rate of substitution between the factors (i.e., the ratio of their marginal products) be the same in both industries. An alternative rearrangement gives

$$p_1 f_1^{\,1} = p_2 f_1^{\,2}$$

and

$$p_1 f_2^{\,1} = p_2 f_2^{\,2} \quad : \tag{56}$$

each factor's marginal value product must be the same in each use.

For the given prices, p_1 and p_2, there will be some pair of values of x_1 and x_2 given by the solution to Eqs. (54) and the two constraints. We initially chose p_1 and p_2 arbitrarily. Let us pick another pair of values, and maximize GNP again. We shall obtain another pair of values of x_1 and x_2. If we keep on doing this, we shall trace out the production possibility frontier. Thus the production possibility frontier is the *locus* of solutions to the problem: maximize

$$\text{GNP} \left(= \sum p_i x_i \right)$$

subject to the resource constraints and production functions for *all* (nonnegative) prices.

In may be written in implicit form,

$$g(x_1, x_2) = 0 \quad . \tag{57}$$

It is sometimes helpful to write it

$$g(x_1, x_2; q_1, q_2) = 0 \quad , \tag{58}$$

where the appearance of the q's after the semicolon serves to remind us that the function gives a relation between the x's only for given q's.

If we want the production possibility frontier in explicit form, we may now write

$$x_1 = h(x_2) \quad . \tag{59}$$

Equation (59) says the same thing as (57): there is a relationship between the x's that gives the maximum attainable value of one for each value of the other. We can also, of course, write

$$x_1 = f^1(q_1 - q_{12}, q_2 - q_{22}) \quad . \tag{60}$$

Now that we have the production possibility frontier, let us maximize utility. We assume that there are n people in the community, and that each has a utility function U^i, defined only over consumption of the two goods, so that we can write

$$U^i = U^i(x_1, x_2) \qquad (i = 1, \ldots, n) \quad . \tag{61}$$

What function shall we choose to maximize?

Consider a function that apparently involves cardinal utility,

$$\sum_i c_i U^i \quad , \tag{62}$$

where c_i is the weight attached to the ith individual's utility. Choice of the c_i is a matter of value. You might believe that all the c_i should be equal, or, if you were supremely selfish, you might make your own positive and everyone else's zero. There is no way we can determine what the c_i's ought to be: we can only make our own choices. Nonetheless, we can obtain some interesting and quite general results with remarkable ease.

Let us proceed to maximize $\sum_i c_i U^i$ for any arbitrary set of (nonnegative) weights, c_i, subject to (57), $g(x_1, x_2) = 0$. We denote the ith individual's consumption of each good by x_{1i}, x_{2i}, so that

$$\sum_i x_{1i} = x_1$$

and

$$\sum_i x_{2i} = x_2 \quad . \tag{63}$$

We substitute (63) into the production possibility function, and write the Lagrangian

$$L = \sum_i c_i U^i(x_{1i}, x_{2i}) - \lambda g\left(\sum_i x_{1i}, \sum_i x_{2i}\right) \quad . \tag{64}$$

We shall have, with two goods, n individuals, and one constraint, a total of $2n + 1$ first-order equations. Let us write just four of them:

$$c_i U_1{}^i - \lambda g_1 = 0 \tag{65a}$$

$$c_i U_2{}^i - \lambda g_2 = 0 \tag{65b}$$

$$c_j U_1{}^j - \lambda g_1 = 0 \tag{65c}$$

$$c_j U_2{}^j - \lambda g_2 = 0 \quad . \tag{65d}$$

Again, a little rearrangement is illuminating. Dividing the first equation by the second, and the third by the fourth, we have

$$\frac{U_1{}^i}{U_2{}^i} = \frac{g_1}{g_2} = \frac{U_1{}^j}{U_2{}^j} \quad . \tag{66}$$

This is remarkable. The weights have dropped out, so we have the efficiency condition, for *any* weights, that the marginal rates of substitution between the goods should be equal for any pair of individuals (which we discovered in Section 11.6), *and* that they should be equal to g_1/g_2, which is known as the marginal rate of transformation.

Furthermore, the result in (66) does not require that utility be cardinally measurable: it involves only marginal rates of substitution, which are ratios of marginal utilities.

Let us make sure of what this rate of transformation is. Suppose that we want to find the slope, in the x_1, x_2 plane, of the implicit function $g(x_1, x_2) = 0$. We first take the total differential

$$dg = g_1 \, dx_1 + g_2 \, dx_2 \quad . \tag{67}$$

Next, we notice that if the value of the function g is zero, so also must the change, dg, be zero. Equating (67) to zero, we perform the familiar rearrangement to obtain

$$\frac{dx_1}{dx_2} = -\frac{g_2}{g_1} \tag{68}$$

as the marginal rate of transformation, the slope of the production possibility frontier. Equation (68) shows the rate at which society can, given its technology and its resources, swap one good for another. Equation (66) shows that the efficiency condition is that this rate be equal to the rate at which each individual is willing to make the swap, irrespective of how tastes vary between individuals and how individual utility functions are weighted in the construction of the objective function.

This completes our account of what are called the Paretean optimality conditions. We must end with a warning. We have not justified any attempt to recommend fulfilling these conditions, wherever possible. The reason is that we have omitted many important issues in welfare economics that are beyond the scope of this book. We list them here by way of illustration, and urge that any serious student of welfare economics pay them due attention. The first is the problem of externalities. The second is the second-best problem. And the third is the problem of the distribution of wealth (initial endowments) and income.

11.8   THE UBIQUITY OF CONSTRAINED MAXIMUM PROBLEMS

The Lagrangian method is now routine, although some complicated expressions quickly occur. There are also analytical difficulties requiring a good deal of sophistication if the attack is to be complete, with second-order conditions and a full comparative-static analysis. The important point is that a choice problem is a constrained maximum problem. If an alleged choice problem does not appear to be a constrained maximum problem, either the problem has not been correctly formulated or it is not in fact a choice problem. Where skill, indeed perhaps real insight, may be required is in sorting out what is really the objective function and what the constraint, and in finding out just what the constraint looks like. All political, social, and economic policy is subject to the constraints set by the actual behavior of society, and we might define the task of social science as the discovery and elucidation of those constraints. A policy choice, made by any government, is some sort of attempted solution to some sort of constrained maximum problem. Now, the constraints are objectively given, by the nature of the world. If we disagree about them, we disagree about a positive, scientific question, one that is ultimately to be settled as a matter of fact. Disagreement over the objective function, however, is an ethical matter, one of judgment about values. If we are to judge our rulers fairly and adequately, it is important to understand *their* decisions, and to be able to distinguish their objective function. Thus suppose that less resources are devoted to urban renewal (or any other virtuous activity) than we judge desirable. We conclude that the responsible authorities are hard-hearted vote catchers, indifferent to the sufferings of the unfortunate minority. If we knew the opportunity cost of urban renewal in terms of some other goal, say, economic growth, we might have to agree, however grudgingly, with the decision—or we might conclude that urban renewal had a rating so low in our rulers' objective function as to prove them the monsters we had thought. Unless we know the facts, it is hard to judge.

Decisions are commonly taken in a state of less than certainty about the nature of the world. It will be clear by now that by maximization under constraints we mean nothing more than "making the best of a bad job," which is the common human problem. The contribution of mathematical technique is, on the one hand, to help one to handle hypotheses about how people behave, and, on the other hand, to provide methods for finding "better bests." One fascinating technical innovation is the theory of decision making under uncertainty, or "how to gamble if you must." In fact, in an uncertain world, we cannot help gambling, as we acknowledge when we hold "precautionary balances," take out some insurance, buy shares or bonds, or opt for a monthly or a yearly tenancy on an apartment, but the theory of "statistical decision making" is a recent innovation, in spite of the long history of insurance and even longer history of gambling. Naturally, one needs some acquaintance with probability theory to follow the theory of decision making, or optimizing, under uncertainty, and we can do no more here than recommend it as extremely rewarding.

QUESTIONS

1. Assume that production is given by

$$X = 10L^{3/5}K^{2/5} \quad ,$$

where X is output, L labor, and K capital. Suppose that labor costs 3 per unit and capital services 2. Find the least-cost capital:labor ratio.

2. Using

$$\sigma = \frac{d(L/K)}{L/K} \frac{r/w}{d(r/w)} \quad ,$$

calculate the elasticity of substitution for the production function of Question 1. Now do the same for $X = 100L^{4/5}K^{4/5}$. Are you surprised at either of these results?

3. a. The elasticity of substitution is defined as $\dfrac{d(L/K)}{(L/K)} \dfrac{(r/w)}{d(r/w)}$, but it is also

   sometimes written as $\dfrac{d(L/K)}{(L/K)} \dfrac{(MPK/MPL)}{d(MPK/MPL)}$. Is the second form also a

   definitional relationship, or does it embody an equilibrium condition?
   b. Are the following also valid expressions for the elasticity of substitution?
      i. $\sigma = d \log (L/K)/d \log (r/w)$
      ii. $\sigma = -d \log (L/K)/d \log (w/r)$

4. Assume that an individual's utility function and budget constraint are given by

$$U = xy$$

   and

$$100 - x - y = 0 \quad .$$

   a. Find the consumption of x and y.
   b. Now assume that rationing is imposed, and that the individual is not allowed more than 40 units of x, prices being unchanged. Find, by geometrical or other methods, consumption of x and y. Do you expect the Lagrangian method of this chapter to work here? If not, why not?

5. Determine the general expression for the marginal rate of substitution along the utility function $U = 100x^{1/2}y^{1/2}$. What is the value of the marginal rate of substitution when this utility function is maximized subject to the constraint $y + x - 100 = 0$? Compare this value to the slope of the budget constraint.

6. Consider the repeated transformations of the utility function $U(x, y) = x^{1/4}y^{3/4}$ and indicate the point at which i cardinality and ii ordinality is lost.
   a. $V_1(x, y) = 200U(x, y) = 200x^{1/4}y^{3/4}$
   b. $V_2 = 16 + V_1 = 16 + 200x^{1/4}y^{3/4}$
   c. $V_3 = 14 + V_2 = 30 + 200x^{1/4}y^{3/4}$
   d. $V_4 = 20V_3 = 600 + 4000x^{1/4}y^{3/4}$

e. $V_5 = V_4^2 = 360,000 + 4,800,000x^{1/4}y^{3/4} + 16,000,000x^{1/2}y^{6/4}$

f. $V_6 = -50V_5 = -360,005 - 4,800,000x^{1/4}y^{3/4} - 16,000,000x^{1/2}y^{6/4}$ ·

7. In the discussion of the box diagram in Section 11.3 and the contract curve in Section 11.5, nothing was said about second-order conditions. In Chapter 10 we argued geometrically that, if the constraint is linear and the objective function convex, the first-order conditions are sufficient. Can you extend the geometric and intuitive argument to the case of tangency between two iso-*f* curves?

8. (For discussion.) Suggest examples of constrained examination problems faced by the following:

   a. The Senate or Board of Governors of your university.

   b. Your student union

   c. Your local Congressman

   d. Yourself.

Chapter 12

An Introduction to Dynamics

12.1 STATICS AND DYNAMICS

We have confined outselves so far to the determination of positions of static equilibrium and to a comparison of two positions of equilibrium before and after a parameter shift. This is the method of comparative statics. In using this method we ignore the question of the time path that our variables may follow as they move from one equilibrium position to another, and the associated question of whether or not a system that starts out of equilibrium (because, say, of some parameter shift) will ever move back into equilibrium. We now begin a study of these two questions: (1) the time path of our variables as they move from one position of equilibrium to another, and (2) the stability of adjustment processes.

Dynamic analysis is not to be regarded as just a sophisticated frill added to a fully satisfactory static model. We live in a world in which many magnitudes are changing continually. Productivity, and hence real income, is growing continually, and, as a result, demand and supply curves are shifting continually, and at different rates for different commodities. The process of economic growth thus forces a process of continuous resource reallocation on the economy. We become acutely aware of this problem whenever a particular region of the country is heavily committed to industries the demand for whose products is not expanding fast enough to keep their existing labor force employed, given the increase in productivity that is occurring. In this case people are being discharged from employment at, say, a constant *rate* through time. Economic incentives will then lead to some rate of outflow of the population from the region, and the government may introduce measures designed to change the rate of outflow. (We consider some alternative policies in Section 18.8.) If we wish to analyze this process, we must have a dynamic model capable of handling functional relations in which variables are stated in terms of rates of change, for example, the *rate* of out-migration as a function of the *level* of unemployment. If we try to use a static model to analyze the problem of regional unemployment, we may get completely mistaken predictions from it. In many static models we shall find that a single disturbance that creates unemployment in one region will lead to a chain of adjustments that eventually eliminates the unemployment. It would be quite wrong to conclude from this that the price system will remove regional unemployment. Once the problem is set up as a continuous model incorporating the rates of decline in a region's employment and of out-migration, we might find that the price system will lead to a constant level of regional unemployment, which might be quite a high one. Government policies that affect some of these critical rates may well lower the equilibrium level of unemployment, but, if we are to study the effects of such policies, we require a dynamic model.

Regional unemployment was chosen merely as an example of a problem that could not be studied without a dynamic model. We shall see several others in the next three chapters. In this chapter we begin by considering the problem of stability of equilibrium in the model of the single competitive market whose static properties we have several times studied. We then go on in the rest of the chapter to introduce some basic concepts in dynamics. We could assume that your study of economics had made you familiar with the basic theoretical notions of statics. Dynamic theory, however, is rarely studied in a first-year course. The reason is simple: you can do almost no dynamics without mathematics. For this reason we must devote a chapter to a discussion of some basic concepts and definitions. In Chapter 13 we introduce you to some of the mathematics required for dynamics, and in Chapter 14 we apply these mathematical techniques to the study of some problems in dynamic economics. Dynamics is a vast subject and requires much mathematics well beyond the scope of this book. Nevertheless we hope in this brief three-chapter introduction to give you an idea of the importance of the subject and to show you how some very interesting problems can be handled even with the very limited amount of mathematics that we cover in Chapter 13.

12.2 A COMPETITIVE MARKET WITH AN AUCTIONEER

We are now going to consider the behavior of competitive markets when they are out of equilibrium. We do this in three stages, first considering a model in which no trading occurs out of equilibrium, then considering a model in which trading occurs at prices off the producers' supply curve but in which a type of equilibrium is always established, and finally considering a full dynamic model in which trading may occur at prices off either or both of the demand and supply curves. First, consider the market illustrated in Figure 12.1 in which both the demand and the supply curves have their normal shape. Elementary treatments usually seek to establish the tendency toward equilibrium in such a case by stating something like *"there is an upward pressure on price when quantity demanded exceeds quantity supplied and a downward pressure on price when quantity supplied exceeds quantity demanded."*

But we must wonder who it is that changes price and why. In the theory of perfect competition the individual firm is a price taker, assuming that it can sell all it wants at the going price. There is nothing in this theory to determine the firm's behavior with respect to price or quantity if it is unable to sell all it wants at the going price. (Notice that whenever quantity supplied exceeds quantity demanded at least some firms *cannot* sell all they want at the going price.) Consumers are also assumed to be price takers who buy all they want at the going price. There is nothing in the theory to determine their behavior if they are unable to obtain all they want to buy of some commodities. We have important problems here, and something of a deficiency in contemporary theory. These problems are in fact the subject of much research that is now going on in the pure theory of the behavior of markets in disequilibrium situations.

In the model that we consider first, these problems are handled (it might be better to say, avoided) by the fiction of an auctioneer who varies the price until he has discovered the equilibrium, and who allows no one to conduct actual trades until this has been done. The

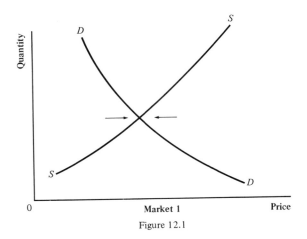

Market 1

Figure 12.1

process works roughly as follows. The auctioneer opens the market by calling out a "trial price" chosen haphazardly. Potential purchasers place orders to buy at that price, and potential suppliers state the quantities they are willing to sell. The auctioneer adds up all the quantities people wish to buy and those that people wish to sell. If the two totals are equal, he has, by incredible luck, chosen the equilibrium price at the first try. He then allows trade to occur in the knowledge that everyone who wishes to buy or to sell will be able to do so. If, however, the quantity offered for sale does not equal the quantity demanded, he does not allow any trading to occur, *but instead he calls out a new trial price.* The rule he follows is to raise price if the quantity demanded is more than the quantity offered for sale and to lower price if quantity demanded is less than the quantity offered for sale. He then repeats, at the new trial price, the process of determining desired sales and purchases of each person in the market, allowing trade only if the total quantity demanded equals the total quantity supplied, or calling out a new price if they do not. He continues until he reaches (if he ever does) an equilibrium price at which total quantity demanded equals total quantity supplied.

This is a model, admittedly artificial but nonetheless instructive, of a disequilibrium adjustment process in a competitive market. We may now ask if the adjustment process is stable in the sense that the price called out by the auctioneer converges on the equilibrium price. If it does not converge on equilibrium, it might oscillate perpetually around equilibrium or diverge ever farther from it.

The rule that governs the auctioneer's behavior is that he raises his "trial price" whenever there is excess demand and he lowers it whenever there is excess supply. Thus consider Market 1, illustrated in Figure 12.1, in which quantity demanded exceeds quantity supplied at all prices below the equilibrium price and quantity supplied exceeds quantity demanded at all prices above the equilibrium price. Here the auctioneer's rule has the effect of raising price whenever price is below its equilibrium value and lowering price whenever price is above its equilibrium value.

We can now see that in this market there will be a tendency for price to be pushed in the direction of equilibrium if we start from any disequilibrium position. Such a tendency for a system to be pushed back in the direction of its equilibrium value should it deviate from it is called *negative feedback.* It is symbolized in the figure by the arrows indicating a pressure in the direction of the equilibrium price.

Now consider the market in Figure 12.2. This market exhibits excess supply at all prices below the equilibrium and excess demand at all prices above it. If we continue to assume that the auctioneer raises price when there is excess demand and lowers price when there

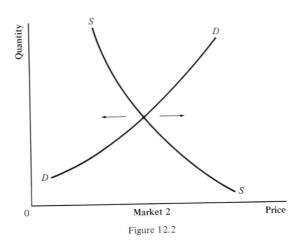

Figure 12.2

is excess supply, then, starting from any disequilibrium position, price will be pushed farther and farther away from its equilibrium level. Such a tendency for a system to be pushed farther and farther away from its equilibrium once it originally deviates from it is called *positive feedback*. It is symbolized in Figure 12.2 by the arrows indicating a pressure away from the equilibrium price.

In the two markets discussed above we had negative feedback when the two curves had the normal shape, that is, the demand curve sloped downward and the supply curve sloped upward, and positive feedback when the slopes of both curves were reversed.

We must now consider exactly what circumstances give rise to negative and to positive feedback. That an abnormal slope to one of the curves is not sufficient to produce positive feedback is shown by the two markets in Figures 12.3 and 12.4. In Market 3 both the supply and the demand curves are upward-sloping, whereas in Market 4 both curves are downward-sloping, and yet both markets display negative feedback since there is excess demand at prices below equilibrium and excess supply at prices above it. To derive necessary and sufficient conditions for negative feedback we must define a new concept, *the excess demand function*.

By excess demand, E, we mean the difference between the quantity demanded and the quantity supplied: $E = q^d - q^s$. Note that excess demand can be positive $(q^d > q^s)$ or negative $(q^d < q^s)$. Negative excess demand is often called excess supply. Since q^d and q^s are both functions of price, it follows that E must be a function of price. We illustrate the excess demand *function*, $E = E(p)$, in Figure 12.5. Since equilibrium occurs where $E = 0$ and $p = \bar{p}$, it follows that any excess demand curve cuts the price axis at $\bar{p}$.

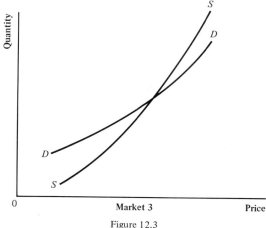

Market 3

Figure 12.3

We shall now find that we can state the conditions for negative feedback in terms of the slope of the excess demand function. If the market price is to move toward its equilibrium value $\bar{p}$, we require that price should rise when it is below equilibrium and fall when it is above equilibrium. (The basic assumption about the behavior of price in a competitive market, with or without a fictional auctioneer, is, however, that price rises when $E > 0$ and falls when $E < 0$.) This gives us the following requirements for negative feedback:

$$E > 0 \quad \text{when} \quad p < \bar{p}$$

and

$$E < 0 \quad \text{when} \quad p > \bar{p} \ .$$

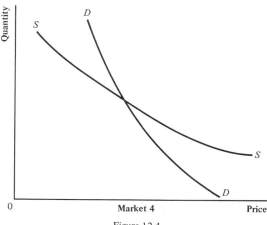

Market 4

Figure 12.4

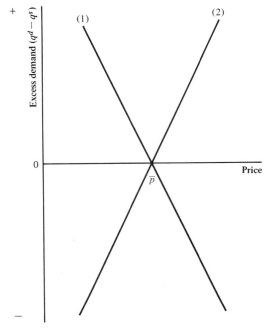

Figure 12.5

Expressed graphically these requirements are that the excess demand function should slope downwards to the right as does curve (1) in Figure 12.5, and not upwards to the right as does curve (2) in Figure 12.5. In other words, we require that there be positive excess demand at prices below the equilibrium and negative excess demand at prices above the equilibrium. A downward-sloping demand curve *and* an upward-sloping supply curve are sufficient to give the right slope to the excess demand function but are not necessary.

Now let us take the simple linear model that we have used several times before and consider the conditions for it to have negative feedback:

$$q^d = a + bp \qquad\qquad (1)$$

$$q^s = c + dp \qquad\qquad (2)$$

$$E = q^d - q^s \qquad\qquad (3)$$

$$= a + bp - c - dp$$

$$= a - c + (b - d)p \quad . \qquad\qquad (4)$$

Equation (4) gives excess demand as a function of price and the four parameters that determine the positions of the demand and supply curves. To discover how excess demand varies as price varies we merely take the derivative of E with respect to price:

$$\frac{dE}{dp} = b - d \quad . \tag{5}$$

We have seen that for negative feedback we require that the excess demand curve be downward-sloping, that is, that $dE/dp < 0$. Equation (5) shows that the condition for this is merely that $b < d$. This condition gives rise to four possible cases distinguished by the signs of b and d. Let us consider each of them.[1]

> **1.** If $b < 0$, $d > 0$, then $b < d$.
> **2.** If $b > 0$, $d < 0$, then $b > d$.
> **3.** If $b < 0$, $d < 0$, then $b < d$ if $|b| > |d|$.
> **4.** If $b > 0$, $d > 0$, then $b < d$ if $|b| < |d|$.

We may state the following conclusions: negative feedback always occurs if the curves have the normal slope (case 1); it never occurs if both curves have the "wrong" slope (case 2); it occurs if both curves slope downwards as long as the demand curve is steeper than the supply curve (case 3); and it occurs if both curves slope upwards as long as the demand curve is flatter than the supply curve (case 4).[2] You should now illustrate graphically those cases that have not already been covered in Figures 12.1 to 12.4.

So far we have studied the conditions for the existence of positive or negative feedback in a competitive market. We now wish to consider the *stability* of the adjustment process in such markets. We say that a market adjustment process is *stable* if it restores equilibrium should the equilibrium be disturbed. We say that a market adjustment process is *unstable* if it does not restore equilibrium. We have seen from studying Market 2 above that positive feedback is sufficient to make a market unstable: if the auctioneer's rules have the effect of increasing price whenever $p > \bar{p}$ and lowering price whenever $p < \bar{p}$, any divergence between p and $\bar{p}$ will get larger and larger as each new trial price is called out (at least until some limit is reached beyond which price cannot rise or fall, and one obvious limit is set by the fact that price cannot normally be negative). Since positive feedback is a sufficient condition for instability, it follows that the absence of positive feedback, that is, the presence of nega-

---

[1] Recall that $|x|$ is the absolute value of x. Thus, for example, $|-2| > |+1|$ even though $-2 < +1$.

[2] "Flatter" and "steeper" refer to the curves when drawn, as we have throughout this book, with price on the x-axis and quantity on the y-axis.

tive feedback, is a necessary condition for stability. The question now arises, is negative feedback a sufficient condition for stability? The answer is "no," even for the model with the fictional auctioneer. To see this, assume that the auctioneer opens the market illustrated in Figure 12.1 and calls out a trial price 5 percent above the equilibrium one. He then discovers that there is excess supply. His rule requires him to call out a lower price; he does, but he calls one 10 percent below the equilibrium price. (He does not, of course, know what the equilibrium price is, for, if he had known it, he would have called it in the first place.) He now discovers that there is excess demand, and, still following his rule, he calls out a price 15 percent above equilibrium. Discovering excess supply at this price, he calls out a price 20 percent below the equilibrium price. Although we might suspect that such an auctioneer was lacking in common sense, this example shows that negative feedback is not sufficient for a convergent adjustment process. The auctioneer's behavior creates negative feedback: every time price is below equilibrium he raises price, *but he raises it too far;* every time price is above equilibrium he lowers price, *but he lowers it too far.* Thus there occurs a series of oscillations of ever-increasing magnitude around the equilibrium price. Unless he changes his behavior, the equilibrium price will never be reached.

We may now pass from the model with a fictional auctioneer to a model closer to at least some real-world behavior. This is the cobweb model, which is familiar to most students of elementary economics, and which provides another counterexample to the proposition that negative feedback is sufficient to cause an adjustment process to converge to equilibrium.

12.3 THE COBWEB MODEL

In the cobweb model supply and demand depend on price, and the usual assumptions of a downward-sloping demand curve and an upward-sloping supply curve are adhered to. The model is distinguished from the ordinary model to which we have devoted much attention throughout this book by the single variation that supply is assumed to react to price with a *lag* of one time period. The common sense of this assumption is that supply decisions take time to implement. If price rises today, firms may wish to increase their rate of production and sales from today, but they may not be able to do so for some time (more labor may have to be employed, more raw materials ordered *and* delivered, and more plant and equipment may even have to be installed). A simple case similar to the cobweb can occur in agriculture. In the case of an annual crop, farmers may look at this year's price when planting crops that will not be harvested until next year, so that *this* year's harvest depends on last year's plantings, which were in turn influenced by last year's prices. The assumption made about demand is the normal one: current demand depends on current price. The market is assumed to be a competitive one in which the price is set so as to equate current demand with the quantity currently being supplied.

We shall study a model of such a market with linear demand and supply curves:

$$q_t^d = a + bp_t \tag{6}$$

$$q_t^s = c + dp_{t-1} \tag{7}$$

$$q_t^d = q_t^s \quad . \tag{8}$$

Note the introduction of time subscripts, which have been made necessary by the introduction of time lags. A subscript t refers to any time "t," while $t - 1$ refers to the time one period prior to "t." Thus Eq. (6) states that quantity demanded at any time t is a linear function of the price ruling at that time. Equation (7) states that quantity supplied at any time t is a linear function of the price ruling one period previously. Equation (8) states that the price will always be such as to equate current demand with current supply.

The first thing to do is to check that in equilibrium the model gives results that are consistent with those given by the linear model without time lags. When we are in equilibrium, the price must repeat itself period after period so that

$$p_{t-1} = p_t = p_{t+1} = \bar{p} \quad . \tag{9}$$

We first substitute (6) and (7) into (8) to obtain an expression for price in period t in terms of price in the previous period:

$$a + bp_t = c + dp_{t-1}$$

whence

$$p_t = \frac{c - a}{b} + \frac{d}{b} p_{t-1} \quad . \tag{10}$$

We now note from (9) that in equilibrium $p_{t-1} = p_t = \bar{p}$, and, substituting this into (10), we get

$$\bar{p} = \frac{c - a}{b} + \frac{d}{b} \bar{p} \quad ,$$

whence

$$\bar{p} = \frac{c - a}{b - d} \quad . \tag{11}$$

This is, as we should expect, the static solution to the linear model that we first obtained in Chapter 3 and that we have used many times since. The equilibrium quantity is found from (11) and either (6) or (7) to be

$$\bar{q} = \frac{cb - ad}{b - d} \quad , \tag{12}$$

which also agrees with the static solution first obtained in Chapter 3.

We now wish to study the model's behavior out of equilibrium. We have assumed that in each period price will be such as to clear the market by equating current demand with current supply. We substitute (6) and (7) into (8) to solve for current quantity in terms of prices now and one period ago:

$$q_t = a + bp_t = c + dp_{t-1} \quad . \tag{13}$$

Now assume that an equilibrium has been established in which price repeats itself period after period: we substitute (9) into (13) to find the equilibrium quantity given by

$$\bar{q} = a + b\bar{p} = c + d\bar{p} \quad . \tag{14}$$

The difference between (14) and (13) is that, once equilibrium is established, the time lag on the supply equation ceases to influence the behavior of the model because the price this period is equal to the price last period so that supply will be the same whether or not it is subject to a time lag.

We have an expression in (14) for the equilibrium quantity and in (13) for the quantity in any particular period (for which $p_t \neq p_{t-1}$). It is now convenient to deal in deviations of the actual values from their equilibrium ones. To obtain these deviations we subtract Eq. (13) from (14) to obtain

$$\bar{q} - q_t = b(\bar{p} - p_t) = d(\bar{p} - p_{t-1}) \quad . \tag{15}$$

We now use a hat on the q's and p's to denote their deviations from their respective equilibrium values and rewrite (15) as

$$\hat{q}_t = b\hat{p}_t = d\hat{p}_{t-1} \quad . \tag{16}$$

The last two terms in (16) allow us to express the deviation of price from equilibrium this period as a function of the deviation from equilibrium last period:

$$\hat{p}_t = \frac{d}{b}\hat{p}_{t-1} \quad . \tag{17}$$

If we denote d/b by A, we have

$$\hat{p}_t = A\hat{p}_{t-1} \quad . \tag{18}$$

This is what is called a *first-order difference equation*, and it expresses this period's $\hat{p}$ as a function of last period's $\hat{p}$. It is called a difference equation because we are explaining differences; and it is a first-order equation because we are explaining the difference between price now and price only one period ago.

The solution to (18) is easily discovered. Start with the first period, which we call t_0, and to get the cobweb process under way assume some initial disequilibrium. The value of $\hat{p}$ at time zero, which we indicate as $\hat{p}_0$, is thus the initial deviation from equilibrium with which we start. Our task is to study how the market reacts to this disequilibrium situation. Once we have chosen a $\hat{p}_0$ (we shall see later how we can interpret it) Eq. (18) tells us how to find $\hat{p}_1$. Once we have $\hat{p}_1$ we again use (18) to find $\hat{p}_2$. Clearly we can continue the process to generate as many values of $\hat{p}$ as we wish. Let us follow out a few steps formally:

$$\hat{p}_1 = A\hat{p}_0$$
$$\hat{p}_2 = A(\hat{p}_1) = A(A\hat{p}_0) = A^2\hat{p}_0$$
$$\hat{p}_3 = A(\hat{p}_2) = A(A^2\hat{p}_0) = A^3\hat{p}_0$$
$$\hat{p}_4 = A(\hat{p}_3) = A(A^3\hat{p}_0) = A^4\hat{p}_0 \quad .$$

It is now obvious by inspection that the solution for $\hat{p}_5$ will contain A^5, that for $\hat{p}_6$ will contain A^6, and so on. We can now write the solution for $\hat{p}$ at any time, t, as

$$\hat{p}_t = A\hat{p}_{t-1} = A^t\hat{p}_0 \quad . \tag{19}$$

Equation (19) gives us the general solution for this linear cobweb model, which allows us to find $\hat{p}_t$ at any time, given the slopes of the demand and the supply curves ($A = d/b$) and $\hat{p}_0$. This value of $\hat{p}_0$ is referred to as the initial arbitrary disturbance. The word *arbitrary* is meant to imply that $\hat{p}_0$ can take on any sign and magnitude that we like to give it. It is not meant to imply that this disturbance is created in any mysterious way. The original $\hat{p}_0 \neq 0$ might have been brought about by some reasons not connected with the demand and supply curves, for example, a price-control policy that is removed at time t_0. It might also have been brought about by a shift in either the demand or the supply curves so that $\hat{p}_0$ represents the difference between the old and the new equilibrium prices, which is the discrepancy that the free market adjustment process is then called on to remove. The important point is that, because the analysis is quite general in this respect, we can always start with some arbitrarily chosen discrepancy between actual and equilibrium values without concerning ourselves further with the cause of the discrepancy.

If the demand curve slopes downward and the supply curve slopes upward, $b < 0$ and $d > 0$ so that A is negative. Thus A^t will alternate in sign, being negative in odd-numbered periods and positive in even-numbered periods. This proves that with normal-shaped demand and supply curves the cobweb will always produce a two-period oscillation with actual price being alternately above and below equilibrium price. It remains to see if these oscillations will converge on to or diverge from $\bar{p}$. If the demand and supply curves have their normal slopes, there are still three cases to consider.

1. The supply curve is steeper than the demand curve so that $|d| > |b|$ and $|A| > 1$. In this case the absolute value of A^t increases as A is raised to higher and higher powers. Thus *the oscillations are explosive*, and, unless they hit limits (as in practice they no doubt will), they get larger and larger indefinitely. The market displays an unstable adjustment process.
2. The demand curve is steeper than the supply curve so that $|d| < |b|$ and $|A| < 1$. In this case the absolute value of A^t diminishes as A is raised to higher and higher powers. *The oscillations are damped:* the market price converges on its equilibrium value. The market displays a stable adjustment process.
3. The slopes of the two curves are equal so that $|d| = |b|$, $|A| = 1$ and $A = -1$. This is the limiting case in which the oscillations neither increase nor decrease. The equation of the system is $\hat{p}_t = \hat{p}_0(-1)^t$ so that the original disequilibrium returns every other period. The system displays *regular oscillations* that are neither damped nor explosive.

This linear cobweb model displays negative feedback: whenever price is above equilibrium it falls in the next period, and whenever price is below equilibrium it rises in the next period, but the adjustment is *always* too much whence the equilibrium price is *always* overshot. In the stable case the overshoot gets smaller and smaller so that the equilibrium price is approached. In the unstable case each overshoot is larger than the previous one so that the actual price diverges from equilibrium more and more as time passes.

Evidently, negative feedback, although a necessary condition for stability, is not a sufficient condition. This is one of the most important propositions in elementary dynamics. For many years economists concentrated on showing that their models displayed negative feedback, thinking that by doing so they had shown them to be stable. We now know that this is not sufficient, and that the behavior of any adjustment mechanism depends critically on the time lags involved and on the magnitude of the adjustment once it occurs.

12.4 A MODEL OF CONTINUOUS ADJUSTMENT

In the cobweb model supply changed in a discrete jump once each period, and it was possible to imagine price changing at the beginning of each period in order to adjust demand to the available supply. In such a model the price changes instantaneously from one short-run equilibrium position (where current demand equals current supply) to another short-run equilibrium position. No price other than the short-run equilibrium price ever rules in the market whence no sales ever take place at a disequilibrium price.

We now take a critical step in moving to a model in which price changes continuously through time, and in which transactions take place — as they do in the real world — during the process of adjustment. At this stage we have to make a fundamental decision about how we should treat time: should we divide it into discrete periods, as we did in the case of the cobweb, where discrete changes in price occurred only at the end of each period, or should we assume time to be a continuous variable with continuous adjustments of price and quantity occurring through time? The choice is often dictated by the problem at hand. If supply suddenly changes when a new harvest appears, and then remains constant until the next harvest, as it did in the cobweb model, a discrete model is most appropriate. In other cases where supply may be varied daily, or even hourly, or where national income is growing continuously, a continuous model may be appropriate. The approach selected will determine the mathematical techniques used to handle the model. In the case of discrete time periods we use difference equations, the simplest case of which occurred in (18), and in the case of continuous time we use differential equations. In the remainder of this book we shall adopt the continuous treatment of time.

We now need to have a precise rule determining the behavior of price when the market is not in equilibrium. For a fully satisfactory theory we should want to have a micro-model that explained the disequilibrium behavior of competitive sellers and purchasers. A great deal of theoretical work is currently being done on such models, but as yet there is no well-developed theory that would allow us to deduce the disequilibrium behavior of a competitive market from a theory of the maximizing behavior of individual buyers and sellers. For this reason we shall investigate only the consequences of some possible rules that might be assumed to govern the behavior of price in disequilibrium situations. We shall accordingly study the influence of these rules on the stability of the adjustment process while leaving unanswered the question of what specific rules might be derived from what particular models of individual maximizing behavior under conditions of disequilibrium.

Since we are going to allow price to change continuously, we need a rule determining *the rate of change of price at any moment of time*. This rate of change is measured by the derivative of price with respect to time, written dp/dt, which gives the rate at which price changes per unit of time. If, as in Figure 12.7, we draw a time-series graph showing the level of price at each point of time, dp/dt then measures the slope of the tangent to the curve at any point. We now introduce, without derivation, a very common assumption, that *the speed with which price is changing depends on the magnitude of the disequilibrium:* the larger is the disequilibrium, the faster will price be changing. If we write this assumption in functional form, we obtain what is called a *reaction function*. In general, a reaction function states the rate of change of the dependent variable as a function of the disequilibrium. In the model of a single competitive market two possible reaction functions obviously are

$$\frac{dp}{dt} = f(q^d - q^s) \tag{20}$$

$$= f(E) \tag{21}$$

and

$$\frac{1}{p}\frac{dp}{dt} = g\left(\frac{q^d - q^s}{q^s}\right) \tag{22}$$

$$= g\left(\frac{E}{q^s}\right) \quad . \tag{23}$$

(Since E is $q^d - q^s$, we can write the functions in terms of either E or $q^d - q^s$.) Equations (20) and (21) give the absolute rate of change of price in terms of the absolute difference between quantity demanded and quantity supplied. Equations (22) and (23) state that the proportional change in price is a function of proportional excess demand. They represent different hypotheses about the way in which price reacts to market disequilibrium. We shall concentrate here on reaction functions in the form of (20) and (21).

To make the reaction function consistent with what we assume in static theory we must place two restriction on it. First, since we assume in our static theory that price rises when $q^d > q^s$ and falls when $q^s < q^d$, we must choose the function so that dp/dt and E vary directly with each other. Second, since we assume in static theory that price does not change when $q^d = q^s$, we want our reaction function to give $dp/dt = 0$ when $E = 0$. This means that the function must not contain an additive constant: the line relating dp/dt to E on a graph must pass through the origin.

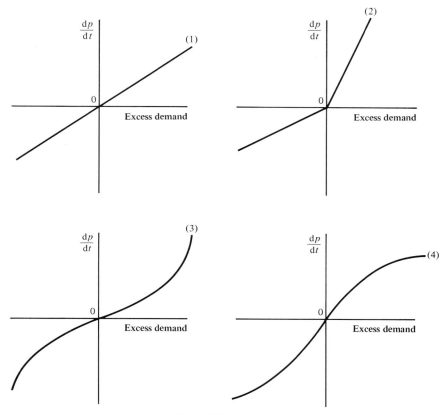

Figure 12.6

We show some possible reaction functions in Figure 12.6. Curve (1) illustrates a case in which dp/dt is simply proportional to excess demand, that is, if you double excess demand, you will double the speed at which price is changing. Curve (2) also illustrates a proportional relation, but one that is different for excess demand and for excess supply. Prices rise faster in response to a given amount of excess demand than they fall in response to the same amount of excess supply. In curves (3) and (4) the relation is nonlinear. In the case of curve (3) the reaction of price to excess demand or supply is greater the larger is the existing amount of excess demand (i.e., $d^2p/dE^2 > 0$). In case (4) the rate of change of price approaches a maximum that it never exceeds no matter how great is the current discrepancy between q^s and q^d (i.e., $d^2p/dE^2 < 0$).

It is very important to note that by specifying an adjustment function we have necessarily introduced a lag into the adjustment of price to its equilibrium value. Whenever we allow the dependent variables

of our system to react to the existence of disequilibrium with any
speed less than infinity, we imply that some time must pass before
a disequilibrium is removed. Of course, the reaction may be very fast
so that the disequilibrium does not persist for long; but persist it
must. Since the system necessarily takes a finite amount of time to
move from one position of static equilibrium to another, states of
disequilibrium must persist through time, and purchases and sales
will take place at prices other than the equilibrium one.

We have seen that the reaction function necessarily introduces
an adjustment lag into the system. There are other ways, however, in
which lags can occur, and we must now consider more systematically
the variety of possible lags in the model of a single competitive
market.

Consider a dynamic version of the model of a single competitive market:

$$q^d = D(p)   ,$$
$$q^s = S(p)   ,$$

and

$$\frac{\mathrm{d}p}{\mathrm{d}t} = f(E)   .$$

There are three variables in this system, q^d, q^s, and p, and each of
them can react to the other variables with a time lag. We now use τ
(the Greek letter tau) to stand for an interval of time. Thus $t - \tau$ means
the time t minus an interval of time, τ. If, for example, τ were two
time periods, $t - \tau$ would refer to time two periods prior to t. We can
now write some possible lags in the competitive model as follows:

$$q_t^d = D(p_{t-\tau_1}) \tag{24}$$
$$q_t^s = S(p_{t-\tau_2}) \tag{25}$$
$$\frac{\mathrm{d}p}{\mathrm{d}t} = f(E_{t-\tau_3})   . \tag{26}$$

The first two equations are the familiar demand and supply equations,
but they now allow for time lags in the adjustment of q^d and q^s to
price: q^d responds now to the price that ruled τ_1 periods in the past,
and q^s reacts to the price that ruled τ_2 periods in the past. Such lags
arise because information only becomes available to decision makers
with a time lag, because the decision process itself takes time, and
because decisions, once taken, take time to implement. The third
equation says that the speed at which price changes depends on the
level of excess demand ruling at some time $t - \tau_3$. Since we have
merely assumed the adjustment function, rather than derived it from

any model of individual behavior, we can only be arbitrary in attributing any lag to this adjustment function.

We already know that a competitive market can have a stable or an unstable adjustment mechanism. To discover how the adjustment mechanism works we must specify the dynamic model completely, and then study its behavior when it starts from a position of disequilibrium. (We say the same thing in different words when we say that we study its behavior in response to an arbitrary disturbance of equilibrium.) Some possible patterns of behavior are illustrated in Figure 12.7.

The figure is a time-series graph of various paths of price through time. The equilibrium price is initially $0c$, and we assume that at time t_0 there is a once-and-for-all discrete change in the equilibrium price from $0c$ to $0d$. This change in $\bar{p}$ could be due to a shift in either the demand or the supply curve. The change is often called a *step change*, for reasons that should be visually obvious from the figure. We now ask how the actual market price might respond to this step change in the equilibrium price. In case (1) the market shows positive feedback. The price shoots away from the equilibrium from the outset. A market that behaves like this has an unstable adjustment mechanism. In all the remaining cases negative feedback exists, that is, price begins by moving in the direction of equilibrium. In case (2) the price moves to its new equilibrium without oscillation. In case (3) the price overshoots and then goes back toward the equi-

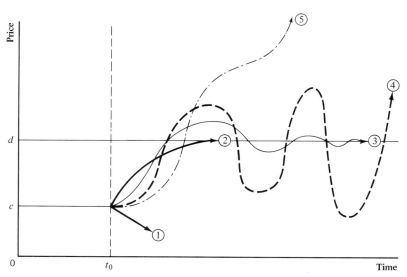

Figure 12.7

librium, overshooting again, but each time the swings diminish, and eventually the equilibrium price is reached. We say that price exhibits *damped oscillations*. In case (4), the oscillations get larger and larger so that the equilibrium is never reached. We say that price exhibits *explosive oscillations*. In case (5) the first overshoot is also the last one: the price overshoots its equilibrium value and continues to rise indefinitely.

We now wish to see which of the paths will be followed by the model of a competitive market set out in Eqs. (24)–(26). To make a start we shall take a very simple case of this dynamic model. We assume that there are no lagged values of the variables in any of the equations ($\tau_1 = \tau_2 = \tau_3 = 0$): the only lag in the system results from the fact that price adjusts to a state of excess demand with a speed of less than infinity. This allows us to concentrate on the effects of the reaction function on the behavior of the model, and it paves the way for more complex models in which any one, or combination, of τ_1, τ_2, and τ_3 are nonzero.

We must now commit ourselves to some assumption about the form of the reaction function. Following our practice of investigating the simplest cases first, we shall make the simple assumption that dp/dt is proportional to excess demand. The reaction function is

$$\frac{dp}{dt} = \alpha E$$

where α is a positive constant. The graph of this function is a straight line through the origin with a slope of α. The line labeled (1) in Figure 12.6 provides an example of such a function.

To begin with we consider the linear form of the competitive model, which is given by

$$q_t^d = a + bp_t \tag{27}$$

$$q_t^s = c + dp_t \tag{28}$$

$$\frac{dp}{dt} = \alpha(q_t^d - q_t^s) \quad , \tag{29}$$

and we ask if a market described by these equations will show a stable or an unstable adjustment process, or if, like the cobweb, it will be either stable or unstable depending on the relative slopes of the demand and the supply curves. To answer this question we need a rule whereby we can find price at any point of time. Our problem is as followed: we know the rule that governs the change in price [Eq. (29)], and we want to know if we can discover what the actual price will be at each moment of time. The answer, and this should not surprise anyone, is "yes, as long as we know from where price started": if we know the initial price and the rule that governs its subsequent change, then we can say where price will be at any moment of time. To do this we need a rule from which we can *deduce p from* dp/dt. To be able to make this step we need more technique. The mathematical technique that solves the problem posed above is called integration. We shall study this in Chapter 13.

12.5 THE SIMPLE MACRO-MODEL

We have many times throughout this book studied the static properties of the simple macro-model

$$C = C(Y) \tag{30}$$

$$Z = \bar{Z} \tag{31}$$

$$Y = C + Z \quad . \tag{32}$$

We now wish to study the behavior of this model out of equilibrium. We arbitrarily assume an adjustment function stating the speed with which income changes in response to a situation of disequilibrium. Before we can write such a function we need to know how we can show a disequilibrium in the above model.

It is well known that, as the magnitudes are defined in national income accounting, expenditure ($C + Z$ in this simple model) is the same thing as gross national output (our Y). If (32) is to be a genuine equilibrium condition, $C + Z$ must be defined so that their sum is not identical with Y but can be equal to Y in equilibrium. The usual way in which this is done is to interpret C and Z as desired expenditure and Y as actual output (which is the same as actual expenditure as defined by national income accountants). There are some problems with this interpretation,[3] but they do not need to concern us here. We say, therefore, that the characteristic of *disequilibrium* in this model is that desired spending, $C + Z$, does not equal actual national income, Y. When this happens we expect Y to be changing, and we assume the simple adjustment rule that the rate of change of Y will be proportional to the disequilibrium: $dY/dt = \alpha[Y - (C + Z)]$. Our dynamic version of the simple income model can now be written

$$C_t = a + cY_t \tag{33}$$

$$Z_t = \bar{Z} \tag{34}$$

$$Y_t = C_t + Z_t \tag{35}$$

$$\frac{dY}{dt} = \alpha(Y - C - Z) \quad . \tag{36}$$

---

[3] See our discussion in note 1 page 81.

This model is analogous to the one we developed in Section 12.4 for the linear competitive model. We wish to know how the model behaves out of equilibrium and whether or not Y will return to its equilibrium value after a disturbance. To answer these questions we need a method of discovering where income is at any time t given its initial starting point and the rule whereby income changes [Eq. (36)]. Again we need to know something of the technique of integration, which is the subject of Chapter 13.

QUESTIONS

1. a. "Negative feedback is a sufficient but *not* a necessary condition for dynamic stability." True or false?
   b. Is the converse true or false?

2. Consider the demand and supply functions $q^d = f(p)$, $q^s = g(p)$.
   a. Derive the expression for the response of excess demand to a price change.
   b. Is the function useful for studying large changes in price?
   c. Compare your function with the adjustment function (5) in the text.

3. Consider the following two competitive markets:

$$\text{Market 1:} \quad \text{(i)} \quad q_t{}^d = 1200 - 6p_t$$
$$\text{(ii)} \quad q_t{}^s = 2p_{t-1} \quad .$$
$$\text{Market 2:} \quad \text{(i)} \quad q_t{}^d = 2700 - 4p_t$$
$$\text{(ii)} \quad q_t{}^s = 5p_{t-1} \quad .$$

   a. Discover the equilibrium price and quantity in both markets.
   b. Consider the stability of the adjustment to a disturbance in each market.
   c. Draw a time series graph for p in the first five periods following a disturbance that moves price 200 units above its equilibrium in Market 1 and 20 units below in Market 2.
   d. The explosive oscillations in one market cannot go on increasing indefinitely. What economic limits to the oscillation are finally reached? Illustrate graphically.

4. a. The cobweb model of Section 12.3 incorporated a supply lag. Change the model to a demand lag, that is, $q_t{}^d = a + bp_{t-1}$ and $q_t{}^s = c + dp_t$, and determine the expression for A [of the difference equation (18)].
   b. Analyze the condition for oscillations assuming "normal" slopes.
   c. Briefly consider the situation in which both q^d and q^s are lagged on prices one period.

5. Consider the following reaction functions: Are they consistent with static theory in the sense outlined in Section 12.4?
   a. $dp/dt = -(q^d - q^s)$
   b. $dp/dt = (q^s - q^d)^2$
   c. $dp/dt = (q^s - q^d)^3$
   d. $\dfrac{1}{p}\dfrac{dp}{dt} = -(q^s - q^d)/(q^s)^{1/2}$

e. $\dfrac{1}{p}\dfrac{dp}{dt} = -(q^s)^{1/2} + (q^s)^{-1/2}q^d$

f. $\dfrac{1}{p}\dfrac{dp}{dt} = (q^d - q^s)(q^s)^{-1/2} + q^s$

6. Consider the simple macro-model in Section 12.5.
   a. What is the sign of α in Eq. (36)?
   b. Draw a graph of the reaction function relating dY/dt to the difference between output and expenditure.
   c. Describe in words the condition for this model to have negative feedback (i.e., we want Y to fall when it is above the equilibrium level and rise when it is below it).
   d. What restriction do we need on the sign of the parameters for there to be negative feedback in this model? (*Hint:* You need a relation analogous to Eq. (5) for the model of the competitive market.)

7. The driver of an automobile becomes sleepy, with the result that his car occasionally wanders out of its lane. When it does this, the driver wakes up and corrects the steering. Describe his behavior in terms of feedback, and consider the possibility of oscillations.

8. There is probably a thermostat in your classroom, connected to a furnace somewhere in the basement. Describe the system of room-temperature, thermostat, and furnace, in terms of feedback. Is it necessarily stable?

9. a. Give some examples of markets to which the cobweb model might apply.
   b. Suppose that speculators enter such a market. Supposing that the product is durable, how might they behave? Could they make money?
   c. Would there be any incentive to set up a "futures" market?
   d. Suppose that producers "caught on" to the cobweb. How might it be necessary to change the model?
   e. Would you in fact expect a cobweb to continue for very long without producers and consumers "catching on" and altering their behavior (perhaps by speculating), or professional speculators entering?

10. Suppose that, whenever registration drops for any reason, a university raises its tuition fee for the following year. Given that the demand curve has a negative slope, will this be a positive or negative feedback system? Can you suggest a more sensible policy (for discussion)?

11. a. If the population of rabbits falls for any reason, the population of foxes (which, for simplicity, we assume to live mainly on rabbits) falls, with some lag. A reduction in the number of foxes allows the population of rabbits to rise at once. Use difference equations to write this model out formally.
   b. Assume that each population reacts with a lag of one period to the size of the other population, and write the model out formally.

12. (For discussion.) Suppose that when the USSR builds more missiles, the USA responds by also building more, with some time-lag, and vice-versa. Speculate on the possible time path of this system.

Integration and Exponential Functions

In Chapter 4 we considered the problem of discovering, at any point on the function

$$y = f(x) \quad , \tag{1}$$

the rate of change of y in response to a change in x. We learned some rules for obtaining the derivative

$$\frac{d}{dx} f(x) = f'(x) \quad . \tag{2}$$

In Chapter 12 we assumed that we knew the rule that determined the *rate of change* of price as a function of excess demand, and we wondered if we could discover the rule for determining price itself. We also assumed that we had the rule determining the *rate of change* of national income as a function of the difference between income and expenditure, and we wondered if we could discover the rule for determining the *level* of national income. In general these problems amount to knowing (2) and trying to derive from it the function in (1). What we need to do, therefore, is to reverse the process of differentiating (1) to get (2). When we do this, we say that we *integrate* (2) in order to get (1).

13.1 THE IDEA OF INTEGRATION

In the case of simple power functions we can integrate by inspection. Consider two examples. First, we know that if $y = x^2$, then $dy/dx = 2x$. Thus if we are given $dy/dx = 2x$, we can immediately say that $y = x^2$

will do as a function that satisfies the condition $dy/dx = 2x$. For a second example, assume that marginal revenue is given by

$$\frac{dR}{dq} = 100 - 10q \quad .$$ (3)

We seek to discover the total revenue function and the demand function. What we need is a function whose first derivative is $100 - 10q$, and, by inspection, $100q - 5q^2$ will do, so we may write

$$R = 100q - 5q^2 \quad ,$$ (4)

and to complete the problem we write

$$p = AR = \frac{R}{q} = 100 - 5q \quad .$$ (5)

In general we say that if

$$\frac{dy}{dx} = f'(x) \quad ,$$ (6)

then

$$y = \int f'(x) \, dx \quad .$$ (7)

Equation (7) reads "y equals the *integral* of $f'(x)$ with respect to x." $\int$ is the integral sign, an elongated S. The expression $\int f'(x) \, dx$ in (7) is called the *indefinite integral* of the function $f'(x)$. The function that is to be integrated, $f'(x)$ in this case, is called the *integrand,* and the variable on which it is defined is called the variable of integration. In this case the integrand is $f'(x)$, but any function that can be integrated may be used in (7). We know that not all functions can be differentiated everywhere and, similarly, that not all functions can be integrated. If, however, the integrand was arrived at by differentiating another function, we may be sure that it can be integrated. Equation (7) says that, if the derivative of y with respect to x is some function of x, then y is found by integrating this function with respect to x.

We immediately start to think of integration as "reverse" or "backward differentiation"; but there is an important complication. Consider

$$\frac{dy}{dx} = 2x$$ (8)

and find

$$y = \int 2x \, dx \quad .$$ (9)

$y = x^2$ is a function that satisfies (8), but so is $y = x^2 + 10$ or $y = x^2 - 200$.

Indeed $y = x^2 + A$ satisfies (8), where A is any constant whatever. Since the constant disappears when we differentiate, all functions of the form $y = x^2 + A$ have the same derivative, that is, $2x$. From this it follows that, when we reverse the process and integrate (8), we must add a constant. This shows that we cannot tell from a derivative alone what constant was contained in the function before it was differentiated.

An economic example is very familiar. Suppose that we have the marginal cost function

$$MC = \frac{dC}{dq} = 10 + 3q \qquad (10)$$

and wish to find the total cost function. We write

$$TC = \int MC \, dq = \int (10 + 3q) \, dq = 10q + 1.5q^2 + A \quad . \qquad (11)$$

The constant A is, of course, fixed cost. It is that part of cost that does not vary with output. Every student knows that fixed cost has no influence on marginal cost, that is, A disappears when we differentiate the total cost function, and the corollary of this is that we cannot tell how big A (fixed cost) is if we have only the marginal cost function.

This discussion suggests that, whenever we integrate a function, we must add an arbitrary constant to show that we cannot discover from the derivative of a function what constant, if any, was contained in the original function. This arbitrary constant is called the constant of integration. It is arbitrary in the sense that it could take on any value whatsoever, but not in the sense of being in any way mysterious: we know exactly why it arises.

13.2   THE INTEGRATION OF POWER FUNCTIONS

We saw in Chapter 4 that if

$$y = ax^n \qquad (12)$$

then

$$\frac{dy}{dx} = nax^{n-1} \quad . \qquad (13)$$

We may now reverse this and write the following: if[1]

$$\frac{dy}{dx} = ax^n \qquad (14)$$

---

[1] This rule works for any value of n except $n = -1$. For this case see the subsequent discussion in Section 13.6.

then

$$y = \int ax^n \, dx$$

$$= \frac{a}{n+1} x^{n+1} + C \quad . \tag{15}$$

In any but the very simplest cases integration becomes a very tiresome and cumbersome business. There are many tricks of the trade to learn, but very few general principles. By and large, facility at integration is developed by learning a few techniques and then working through countless examples until one gains an intuitive feel for the transformation of a function that will allow a particular technique to be applied to it. The student who goes further than this book will have to devote time to mastering the technique of integration. For the economics we wish to do here it is sufficient to know in an intuitive way what integration means, and to be able to integrate two sorts of functions, power functions, which we have just considered, and exponential functions, to which we must soon turn our attention.

Before we go on to exponential functions, however, there are a few elementary cases that we must consider. If we are told that dy/dx is the sum of two functions of x, how do we find y? For example, we might have

$$\frac{dy}{dx} = 2x + 6x^2 \tag{16}$$

and wish to find y. By appealing to the idea of integration as the reverse of differentiation we can immediately write

$$y = \int (2x + 6x^2) \, dx$$

$$= x^2 + 2x^3 + C \quad . \tag{17}$$

You may check that this works by finding dy/dx from (17) and seeing that it does equal the function in (16). We already know that if

$$y = f(x) + g(x) \quad ,$$

then

$$\frac{dy}{dx} = f'(x) + g'(x)$$

From this it follows that

$$\int [f'(x) + g'(x)] \, dx = \int f'(g) \, dx + \int g'(x) \, dx = f(x) + g(x) + C \quad , \tag{18}$$

so that the integral of the sum of two functions is merely the sum of separate integrals of each function.

Differences are easily dealt with in the same fashion as sums. Integration of products is, however, more difficult, and we shall not here derive the rule for finding y when we encounter

$$\frac{dy}{dx} = f(x) \cdot g(x)$$

except to observe[2] that $\int f'(x) \cdot g'(x) \, dx \neq \int f'(x) \, dx \int g'(x) \, dx$ since $(d/dx)[f(x) \cdot g(x)] \neq f'(x) \cdot g'(x)$.

Next consider the case in which the function $f(x)$ is multiplied by a constant, a. It follows from the result

$$\frac{d}{dx}[af(x)] = af'(x)$$

that

$$\int af'(x) \, dx = a \int f'(x) \, dx = af(x) + C \quad . \tag{19}$$

Next consider

$$\frac{dy}{dx} = a \quad .$$

We can write

$$y = \int a \, dx$$

$$= ax + C \quad , \tag{20}$$

which we get just by recalling that $d/dx[ax] = a$. It is worth noticing that since an $x^0 \ (=1)$ is understood when we write $dy/dx = a$, that is, $dy/dx = ax^0$, this result follows the general rule for the integration of power functions stated in (15). It is also worth noting the special case

$$f'(x) = 1$$

in which

---

[2] Manipulation of the derivative

$$\frac{d}{dx}[f(x) \cdot g(x)] = f'(x)g(x) + f(x)g'(x)$$

produces the following rule for integrating the product of two functions of x:

$$\int f(x)g(x) \, dx = f(x) \int g(x) \, dx - \int \left\{ \int g(x) \, dx \right\} f'(x) \, dx \quad .$$

We shall not need this rule here.

$$\int f'(x) \, dx = x + C \quad . \tag{21}$$

We are now able to integrate any polynomial

$$\frac{dy}{dx} = a + bx + cx^2 + dx^3 + \cdots + mx^n \tag{22}$$

to obtain

$$y = ax + \frac{b}{2}x^2 + \frac{c}{3}x^3 + \frac{d}{4}x^4 + \cdots + \frac{m}{n}x^n + C \quad , \tag{23}$$

where C is the constant of integration. Of course any of the coefficients in (22), and thus in (23), can be zero. This allows us to integrate any of the members of this family such as linear expressions $(c, d, \ldots, m = 0)$ and quadratics $(d, \ldots, m = 0)$.

13.3 INTEGRATION AS THE LIMIT OF A PROCESS OF SUMMATION

So far we have relied merely on the idea of integration as being the reverse of differentiation. We can, however, give the process a little more intuitive appeal if we consider the geometrical interpretation of an integral as an area.

Suppose that we have some function $f(x)$ that is continuous and smooth. We suppose, for the moment, that $f(x)$ is also positive over the interval with which we are concerned. An example of such a function is shown in Figure 13.1. Let a and b be particular values of x, and suppose that we wish to find the area bounded by $f(x)$, the x-axis, and the perpendiculars at $x = a$ and $x = b$. This is the shaded area in the figure. Geometrical methods do not allow us to measure directly the area of a figure with any curved side. Something else is required.

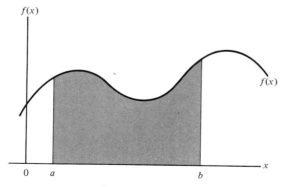

Figure 13.1

First let us subdivide the interval between a and b into n equal subintervals. Erecting a perpendicular at the end point of each subinterval divides the area in which we are interested into n strips of equal width. But the boundary at the top of each strip is curved, so we cannot measure the area of each strip any more than we could measure the whole area. What we can do is to set an upper and a lower limit to the area of each strip, and hence to the sum of their areas. To do this we form for each strip two rectangles whose heights are given by the greatest and the least values of $f(x)$ within the strip. In the strip whose left-hand end point is at a, for example, $f(x)$ increases monotonically, and thus the least value of $f(x)$ is on the left-hand end point, while the greatest value is on the right-hand end point. The two rectangles for each strip are shown in Figure 13.2. The tops of the larger rectangle defined by the largest value of $f(x)$ in each strip are shown by heavy lines, while the tops of the smaller rectangles defined by the least value of $f(x)$ in each strip are shown by the light lines.

There is no difficulty in calculating the area of each of these rectangles and thus the sum of the areas in each of the sets of rectangles. By inspection of the diagram, the sum of the areas of the rectangles defined by the largest $f(x)$ in each interval cannot be less than the area under the curve, which in turn cannot be less than the sum of the areas of the rectangles defined by the least value of $f(x)$ in each strip.

Now increase the number of strips, n, placed within the fixed interval between a and b. Geometrical intuition suggests that as the number of strips is increased the discrepancy between the three areas just defined will diminish. Indeed we will assert, but will not prove, that as the number of strips, n, increases without limit so that the length of each of the n subintervals approaches zero, the areas of both sets of rectangles approach a single limit which we *define* as the area under the curve $f(x)$.

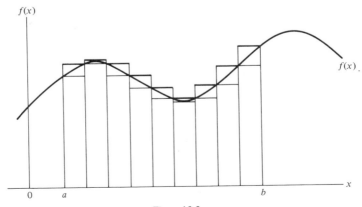

Figure 13.2

Another approach to finding the area under the curve is possible: rather than considering the rectangles defined by the greatest and least values of $f(x)$ in each subinterval we can pick a single arbitrary value of x within each interval and calculate the value of the function $f(x)$ at the arbitrarily chosen value of x. We let ϵ_1 stand for the value of x chosen arbitrarily within the first subinterval, whence $f(\epsilon_1)$ is the value of the function at that point; we let ϵ_2 stand for the value of x chosen within the second subinterval, whence $f(\epsilon_2)$ is the value of $f(x)$ at that point; and so on up to ϵ_n and $f(\epsilon_n)$. This defines n rectangles, each with a width of $1/n$th the interval from a to b, and each with a height of $f(\epsilon_i)$ $(i = 1, \ldots, n)$. This construction is illustrated in Figure 13.3 where $n = 9$.

The sum of the areas of the rectangles in Figure 13.3 can be expressed as

$$\sum_{i=1}^{n} f(\epsilon_i)\, \Delta x \quad , \tag{24}$$

where ϵ_i stands for the value of x arbitrarily chosen within the ith interval and Δx stands for the width of each interval. The area of all n rectangles together is obtained by summation.

If we once again let the number of rectangles, n, increase without limit so that the width of each approaches zero, the sum of their areas can be shown to approach a limit. Indeed the limit is the same as that approached by the sums of the areas of the rectangles defined by the minimum and the maximum values of $f(x)$ within each of the n intervals.

We now define the *definite integral* of the function $f(x)$ within the interval from a to b as the limit, as $n \to \infty$, of the sum of areas of n rectangles each of equal width and each of height given by $f(\epsilon_i)$ for

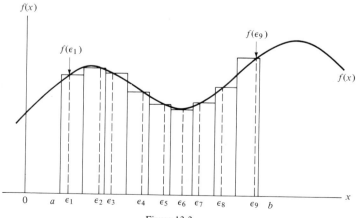

Figure 13.3

an ϵ_i arbitrarily chosen from within each of the n subintervals. We write this

$$\lim_{n \to \infty} \sum_{i=1}^{n} f(\epsilon_i) \, \Delta x = \int_a^b f(x) \, dx \quad , \tag{25}$$

where Δx is the width of each[3] of the n subintervals, that is, $\Delta x = (b - a)/n$.

If the sum on the left-hand side of (25) has a unique finite limit, then the function has an integral: it is said to be integrable. (Finding an analytical expression for the integral is another matter.) If the sum does not have a unique finite limit, the function is said to be non-integrable.

Two restrictions that we have used so far may now be removed. We assumed earlier that $f(x)$ was everywhere positive over the interval in which we were interested. If we make $f(x)$ negative, over the whole interval from a to b, the sides of the rectangle from the x-axis to the curve graphing $f(x)$ are of negative length according to our geometrical convention. The sum of the areas of the rectangles defined in (24) is thus a negative number. Whenever $f(x)$ is negative over some interval, the area defined by integrating $f(x)$ over that interval is also negative. [One must, therefore, be careful in saying that the integral of $f(x)$ measures the area "*under* the curve $f(x)$"; what it measures is the area between the curve and the x-axis with a negative sign attached to areas where $f(x) < 0.$]

In measuring the area between the curves and the x-axis in the interval between a and b we wrote a as the lower end point and b as the upper end point. Finding the definite integral can then be thought of as starting from a in Figure 13.1 and integrating up to b. Instead, however, we may start from b and move to the left on the x-axis until we get to a. We are still measuring the same area but "in the other direction." Areas measured in this way are of opposite sign to those measured from a to b. Thus we write

$$\int_a^b f(x) \, dx = -\int_b^a f(x) \, dx \quad . \tag{26}$$

The definite integral has now been shown as the area under the curve graphing $f(x)$ between the two end points a and b. This area, and hence the integral, has been defined as the limit of a sum. For a particular function $f(x)$, integrated between two end points a and b, the definite integral has a definite single value such as $12, -2/3$, or $\sqrt{2}$.

---

[3] In the above discussion we assumed an equal width for each of the n subintervals. This is not necessary: the same limit can be shown to be approached by the sum of the areas of the n rectangles as $n \to \infty$ even if the rectangles are of uneven width, provided that it is also assumed that as $n \to \infty$ the width of the widest rectangle $\to 0$.

So far we have called a and b the two "end points" in order to stress the geometrical interpretation. We now adopt the more common terminology of referring to a and b as the lower and upper limits of integration.

We may now move from the concept of a definite integral to that of the indefinite integral of which we found examples by inspection of the power function. As a first step we keep the lower limit of integration a as a fixed parameter, but we make the upper limit a variable. To indicate this we replace the b at the top of the integral sign with an x, which reminds us that the upper limit has become a variable. Since, however, we are going to use x to symbolize the variable upper limit of integration, it will be clearer if we do not use x to denote the variable of integration in the function f. To avoid ambiguity we write the integrand as $f(u)$, where f is the same function as before but the symbol u rather than x is used to indicate the value of the independent variable. This procedure is a possible source of confusion, so a little more discussion may be useful. We have a single function f. This function is going to be integrated between a given lower limit, a, at which point the value of the function is $f(a)$, and a variable upper limit x, the value of the function at the upper limit being $f(x)$. The independent variable must, however, be able to take on all values between the lower and upper limits of integration, and we therefore use a new letter, u, which may range between a and x.

We can now write the expression for the integral as

$$\int_a^x f(u)\ du\ .\tag{27}$$

Equation (27) is called the indefinite integral of the function $f(u)$.

For a particular value of x, say $\bar{x}$, the interpretation is just as before: the expression becomes a definite integral evaluated between a and $\bar{x}$ that measures the whole shaded area in Figure 13.4 that lies under the curve in the interval from a to $\bar{x}$. If we take a second value of x, say $\bar{\bar{x}}$, we have a new area between a and $\bar{\bar{x}}$. Thus the area under the curve varies as the upper limit of integration, x, varies: the area is a function of that upper limit, x.

Now consider making a single discrete change from a to c in the parametric value of the lower limit of the indefinite integral. This gives a new indefinite integral

$$\int_c^x f(u)\ du\ .\tag{28}$$

Now compare the two integrals in (27) and (28) for a particular value of x, the upper limit of integration. If, for example, x takes on the value of $\bar{x}$, the areas defined by the two integrals are the whole shaded area for (27) and the shaded area *minus* the darker-toned area between c

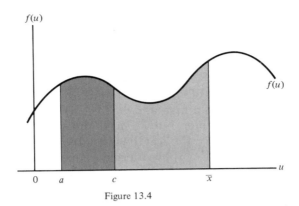

Figure 13.4

and a for (28). As the upper limit of integration, x in (27) and (28), varies, both of the areas defined by (27) and (28) vary. But, since the lower limits are fixed (at a and c), the difference between the two areas remains constant. In Figure 13.4 the constant difference is the darker-toned area between $f(u)$ and the two fixed lower limits a and c. Thus the difference between any two indefinite integrals of the same function, $f(u)$, is a constant.

This important result can be shown without appeal to geometrical intuition. Because the value of each of the indefinite integrals of x varies with the upper limit x, each can be expressed as a function of x. We may therefore write

$$\int_a^x f(u)\ du = \psi(x)$$

and

$$\int_c^x f(u)\ du = \phi(x)\quad.$$

The difference between the two integrals is

$$\psi(x) - \phi(x) = \int_a^c f(u)\ du = C$$

[since, given that the integral of $f(u)$ from a to c exists, it is equal to some definite number which we may denote by C], whence

$$\psi(x) = \phi(x) + C\quad. \tag{29}$$

Because the indefinite integrals of any function $f(u)$ differ from each other by a constant, there is no ambiguity in the common practice of dropping the letters indicating the limits of integration and writing the indefinite integral as

$$\int f(u) \; du = F(u) + C \quad . \tag{30}$$

(Remember that any letter can be used to indicate the independent variable in the functions f and F.) In practice, the arbitrary constant C is often omitted when the integral is written in its general form, $F(u)$, but it is always understood to be present.

We may now relate these results to our initial discussion of integration as the reverse of differentiation by showing the following basic result: the indefinite integral $F(x)$ of the function $f(x)$ always possesses a derivative $F'(x)$; this derivative $F'(x)$ is identical to the function $f(x)$. In other words, if we take a function $f(x)$, integrate it to get $F(x)$, and differentiate $F(x)$ to get $F'(x)$, then $F'(x) = f(x)$. Differentiation reverses the process of integration, and integration reverses the process of differentiation.

The proof of this basic proposition is illustrated in Figure 13.5. The curved line is the graph of the function $f(u)$. The area under the curve between a parametric lower limit of integration a (not shown in the figure) and a variable upper limit x is the integral of $f(u)$ between these limits. Because the value of the integral varies with the value of the variable upper limit of integration, we write it as $F(x)$.

We now wish to find the derivative of $F(x)$. This, by definition, is the limit as h goes to zero of

$$\frac{F(x+h) - F(x)}{h} \quad .$$

The numerator of this ratio can be expressed as

$$\int_a^{x+h} f(u) \; du - \int_a^x f(u) \; du = \int_x^{x+h} f(u) \; du \quad . \tag{31}$$

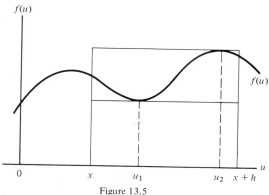

Figure 13.5

The numerator of the ratio is thus the area under the curve between x and $x + h$. Now find the least and greatest value of $f(u)$ within the interval x and $x + h$ and denote the corresponding values of the independent variable as u_1 and u_2. These values are shown in the figure. Since the distance from x to $x + h$ is, of course, h, the areas of the two rectangles defined by these greatest and least values of $f(u)$ in the interval are $hf(u_1)$ and $hf(u_2)$. By the argument given earlier, and by inspection of Figure 13.5, the areas of the two rectangles and the area under the curve must lie in the following relation to each other:

$$hf(u_1) \leq \int_x^{x+h} f(u) \ du \leq hf(u_2) \quad . \tag{32}$$

Rewriting the area under the curve in its analytical form gives

$$hf(u_1) \leq F(x + h) - F(x) \leq hf(u_2) \quad ,$$

and dividing through by h we obtain

$$f(u_1) \leq \frac{F(x + h) - F(x)}{h} \leq f(u_2) \quad . \tag{33}$$

Now let $h \to 0$ and consider the limits of the terms in (33). In Figure 13.5 the upper end point, $x + h$, approaches the lower end point, x, as $h \to 0$. As this happens $[F(x + h) - F(x)]/h \to F'(x)$. Also $f(u_1)$ and $f(u_2) \to f(x)$ (since the function is continuous, it follows that, as $x + h$ approaches x, the values of both $f(u_2)$ and $f(u_1)$ must approach the value of the function *at* x]. Thus we have the result

$$F'(x) = \lim_{h \to 0} \frac{F(x + h) - F(x)}{h} = f(u) \quad . \tag{34}$$

This is the result we require: if $F(x)$ is the integral of $f(u)$, the derivative of $F(x)$ is the original function $f(u)$. This fundamental result establishes the link between the integral as the means of calculating the area under the curve $f(u)$ and the integral as the means of reversing the process of differentiation.

Finally, let us remark on the fact that we have chosen to illustrate our basic result by picking a function, $f(u)$, and an interval, x to $x + h$, such that the former is not monotonic over the latter. This is not a special restriction: indeed, it was done in the interests of increased generality. It is a good exercise to check this for yourself, but we offer a hint. Consider what would happen if, in the interval x to $x + h$, the minimum value of $f(u)$ occurred at the end point x itself. Then u_1 and x would coincide, but nothing above would require alteration except that, as h goes to zero, u_2 approaches x, whereas u_1 is already at x. You should consider what modification is needed in the case in which the maximum value of $f(u)$ in the interval occurs at $x + h$, and, finally, what modifications are needed if the function is monotonic (increasing or decreasing) throughout the interval.

13.4 SOME EXAMPLES

Suppose that we have the function

$$f(x) = 6x \quad .$$

We can integrate this by inspection to obtain the indefinite integral

$$F(x) = \int f(x) \ dx = 3x^2 + C \quad .$$

We may wish to find the definite integral of this function over some interval, say from $x = 2$ to $x = 4$. To do this we merely evaluate the integral at $x = 2$ and at $x = 4$ and subtract the former from the latter. We write this as follows:

$$\int_{x=2}^{x=4} 6x \ dx = [3x^2]_{x=2}^{x=4} = 48 - 12 = 36 \quad . \tag{35}$$

The area under the curve $f(x) = 6x$ in the interval $x = 2$ to $x = 4$ is thus 36. [Since $f(x)$ in this instance is linear, (35) is easily checked by geometrical methods.]

In (35) we first state that we require the definite integral of the function $6x$ between the limits $x = 2$ and $x = 4$; we then enclose the indefinite integral within square brackets with the lower and upper limits of integration at the lower and upper corners of the brackets; we then evaluate the integral of these two values of x; the difference between the values of the integrals is the result we are looking for. The constant C is not needed inside the square brackets since it disappears when the difference between the two integrals is formed.[4]

For a second example consider the function

$$f(x) = 1 + x + 10x^4 \quad ,$$

which has the indefinite integral

$$F(x) = \int f(x) \ dx = x + \tfrac{1}{2}x^2 + 2x^5 + C \quad .$$

The definite integral between $x = -1$ and $x = +1$ is

$$\int_{x=-1}^{x=+1} (1 + x + 10x^4) \ dx = [x + \tfrac{1}{2}x^2 + 2x^5]_{x=-1}^{x=+1} = 3\tfrac{1}{2} - (-2\tfrac{1}{2}) = 6 \quad .$$

[4] The two integrals must have the same lower limit of integration, but it does not matter what it is since it only affects the constant, and the constant in any case disappears in the process of subtraction.

Thus the area under the curve graphing the function $1 + x + 10x^4$ between $x = -1$ and $x + 1$ is 6.

13.5 DIFFERENTIAL EQUATIONS

A differential equation is an equation involving a derivative. The order of the equation is the order of the highest derivative that it contains. Thus the market adjustment equation (29) of Chapter 12,

$$\frac{dp}{dt} = \alpha(q^d - q^s) \quad , \tag{36}$$

is called a *first-order differential equation*. Furthermore, it is a first-order, *linear* differential equation with constant coefficients. A differential equation is linear if the variable and all its derivatives enter in linear combination [e.g., $dy = f'(x)f''(x) \, dx$ is not linear since the first and second derivatives appear as the product of each other]. A differential equation has constant coefficients if the coefficients of the variable and all its derivatives are constants and do not contain the dependent variable in them.

Differential equations occur in any dynamic model that has time as a continuous variable (and difference equations occur if time is broken into discrete intervals). The solution of a differential equation is an equation containing no derivatives of any order. Once such an equation has been obtained the whole model can be solved by ordinary algebraic methods.

Differential equations are solved by integrating an expression for the rate of change of y (or the rate of change of the rate of change of y if second derivatives are involved) to obtain an expression for y. Thus suppose that we are told that marginal cost is $10q + 20$, and we require the total cost function. We can write

$$MC = \frac{dTC}{dq} = 10q + 20$$

$$\int MC \, dq = \int (10q + 20) \, dq$$

$$TC = 5q^2 + 20q + C \quad . \tag{37}$$

If, however, we were given an expression containing only a second derivative, we would have to integrate twice to obtain the "solution." Assume, for example, that we are told only that the second derivative of the cost function is

$$f''(q) = 10 \quad ,$$

and we wish to find the total cost function. We now proceed as follows:

$$f'(q) = \int f''(q) \, dq = \int 10 \, dq = 10q + C_1 \quad ,$$

and again

$$f(q) = \int f'(q) \, dq$$

$$= \int (10q + C_1) \, dq$$

$$= 5q^2 + C_1 q + C_2 \quad . \tag{38}$$

Having only $f''(x)$ does not give us sufficient information to put a numerical value on the parameter attached to q in the way we could when we had the marginal cost function given to us. We are nevertheless able to discover, by integrating the function $f''(q)$ twice, the general shape of the total cost function: in this case it is a quadratic.

13.6   EXPONENTIAL FUNCTIONS

So far in this book we have confined ourselves almost exclusively to power functions. In these functions, the variable x is raised to a fixed exponent, or power (which may, of course, be positive or negative, an integer or a fraction). In (30), Section 2.14, we introduced the exponential function in which the variable x appears as an exponent to a fixed parameter a:

$$y = a^x \quad . \tag{39}$$

This is an important class of functions for economic dynamics. Indeed, we encountered such a function in the cobweb model of Chapter 12. The solution to the model (see (19), Section 12.3) was of the form

$$p_t = A^t p_0 \quad ,$$

where the parameter A is the ratio of the slopes of the demand and the supply curves and the two variables are price and time.

Exponential functions arise in virtually all dynamic problems, and we need to study their properties. Indeed, we have already seen one use of exponential functions, which is to provide the basis of logarithms. If

$$y = a^x \quad ,$$

we *define* the logarithm of y as

$$x = \log_a y \quad .$$

In Chapter 2 we studied some of the uses of logarithms, and since we now intend to build on what was done in that chapter, anyone who then felt, or now feels, at all shaky on the subject of logarithms should reread Section 2.14.

When we use logarithms as a shortcut for accomplishing what would otherwise require laborious calculations (e.g., for finding $(8 \times 17)^{4/3}$) we usually use logs to the base 10. These are called *common logs*, and they show the power to which 10 must be raised to get stated values. In theoretical work it is common to use logarithms to a base other than 10. This base is designated by the letter e. It has the value, correct to four decimal places, of 2.7183. Logarithms to the base e are called *natural logs*. Indeed the number e is a very remarkable number that arises naturally in growth problems. We must now sketch very briefly the derivation of e (which, like π and $\sqrt{2}$, is an irrational number).

Consider the problem of the growth of a sum of money, say \$$P$, invested at a rate of interest of $100r$ percent per year.[5] If the interest is paid once a year, the sum of money available to the investor at the end of the year, called V, will be

$$V = P(1 + r) \quad . \tag{40}$$

Now consider what would happen if interest were paid every 6 months at the rate of $100r$ percent per annum. At the end of 6 months $r/2$ will have been earned, and the sum available will be

$$V_1 = P\left(1 + \frac{r}{2}\right) \quad . \tag{41}$$

But this whole sum V_1, which is more than P, will earn interest for the second 6 months, so, at the end of the year, the whole sum available will be

$$V_2 = V_1\left(1 + \frac{r}{2}\right) \quad ,$$

and if we substitute for V_1 from (41) we get

$$V_2 = P\left(1 + \frac{r}{2}\right)\left(1 + \frac{r}{2}\right)$$
$$= P\left(1 + \frac{r}{2}\right)^2 \quad . \tag{42}$$

Reiteration of the same argument for the case in which $r/3$ is paid 3 times a year will show that the value of the sum available at the end of the year is

---

[5] If the rate of interest is 3 percent, for example, then $r = 0.03$, $100r$ percent $= 3$ percent, and $1 + r = 1.03$.

$$V = P\left(1 + \frac{r}{3}\right)^3 \ , \tag{43}$$

while if interest is paid 4 times a year (still at an annual rate of 100r percent) it will be

$$V = P\left(1 + \frac{r}{4}\right)^4 \ . \tag{44}$$

In general, then, the sum available at the end of the year when interest is paid n times a year at an annual rate of 100r percent on \$$P$ invested is

$$V = P\left(1 + \frac{r}{n}\right)^n \ . \tag{45}$$

As interest is paid and reinvested (which is called compounding) more and more frequently, the sum available at the end of the year increases, because the interest paid during the early part of the year is added to the sum invested and is itself earning interest for the later part of the year. Although V, the sum available at the end of the year, gets larger as interest is paid more and more frequently, it does not grow without limit. A particular limiting value is of great importance. Consider \$1 invested at 100 percent per year, which gives $P = \$1$ and $r = 1$. The value of the sum available at the end of the year is then

$$V = \left(1 + \frac{1}{n}\right)^n \ . \tag{46}$$

We may make a quick check on (46) by assuming that interest is paid only once a year. In this case $n = 1$ and $V = 2$, which checks with what we know: a sum of money invested at 100 percent interest payable at the end of the year will be doubled at the end of the year. If interest is compounded more and more frequently, however, n gets larger and larger. It can be shown that, as n increases, $[1 + (1/n)]^n$ approaches a limit. To four places of decimals the limiting value is 2.7183. This is the value that is designated by the letter e. Thus

$$e = \lim_{n \to \infty} \left(1 + \frac{1}{n}\right)^n \simeq 2.7183 \ . \tag{47}$$

Thus we may regard e as the value at the end of 1 year of \$1 invested at an annual interest rate of 100 percent with continuous compounding (i.e., $n \to \infty$).

We now return to exponential and logarithmic functions and shall very soon find an important use for the number e. Assume that we have the function

$$x = a^y \tag{48}$$

and that we require its inverse. We have this quite simply by the definition of a logarithm:

$$y = \log_a x \quad . \tag{49}$$

From this point we drop the symbol for the base, since the argument refers to any base.

Let us consider first how to find the derivative of the logarithmic function (49). We proceed from first principles in the manner introduced in Chapter 4:

$$\frac{d}{dx} (\log x) = \lim_{h \to 0} \left[\frac{\log (x + h) - \log x}{h} \right] \quad . \tag{50}$$

Now we need to perform a few manipulations on (50) in order to get it into a form from which the derivative is easily discovered. First we write

$$f'(x) = \lim_{h \to 0} \frac{1}{h} [\log (x + h) - \log x] \quad , \tag{51}$$

whence

$$f'(x) = \lim_{h \to 0} \frac{1}{h} \log \left(\frac{x + h}{x} \right)$$

$$= \lim_{h \to 0} \frac{1}{h} \log \left(1 + \frac{h}{x} \right) \quad . \tag{52}$$

We now wish to get this function into a slightly different form so that certain of its characteristics will become more apparent. We have the same problem that we have mentioned many times before: each step in our procedure may seem arbitrary, but it is motivated by the desire to manipulate the expression into a form that will reveal something in which we are interested. In this case, we are going to do something analogous to multiplying and dividing by the same amount, which leaves the value of the expression unchanged. To understand what we are going to do, we need a slight digression. Consider the function

$$C = \log r \quad . \tag{53}$$

We now try to alter the power on r (as written, it is 1) in such a way that the value of the function is unchanged. If we multiply the logarithm by a, this has the effect of raising the original number, r, to the power a:

$$aC = \log (r^a) \quad . \tag{54}$$

If we now divide by a, we get

$$C = \frac{1}{a} \log (r^a) \quad . \tag{55}$$

What (55) says is that if we raise r to the power a, take the logarithm of the result, and divide by a, this will be the same value as the logarithm of r.

Using this result we can now raise the expression inside the brackets in (52) to any power as long as we divide the result by the same number. Let us raise it to the power x/h:

$$f'(x) = \lim_{h \to 0} \frac{h}{x} \frac{1}{h} \log \left(1 + \frac{h}{x}\right)^{x/h}$$

$$= \lim_{h \to 0} \frac{1}{x} \log \left(1 + \frac{h}{x}\right)^{x/h} \quad . \tag{56}$$

Now writing n instead of x/h, we have

$$f'(x) = \lim_{h \to 0} \frac{1}{x} \log \left(1 + \frac{1}{n}\right)^{n} \quad , \tag{57}$$

and at last we are back to something familiar: compare (57) with (47), which defines e! Consider what happens as we let h, our arbitrary increment in x, approach zero. Since $n = x/h$, we have $n \to \infty$ as $h \to 0$. But we know from (47) that, as $n \to \infty$, $(1 + 1/n)^n \to e$. Thus

$$f'(x) = \frac{1}{x} \log e \quad . \tag{58}$$

If we use e as our base (we are beginning to see more reasons for taking e as a base for logarithms), we have $\log_e e = 1$, so we may write

$$\frac{\mathrm{d}}{\mathrm{d}x} (\log x) = \frac{1}{x} \quad . \tag{59}$$

This is an extremely important result: what it says is that as the value of x is changed, the value of the logarithm of x changes by $1/x$.

We have seen how to find the derivative of a logarithmic function, and we can use this to establish another result of fundamental importance. We want to find the derivative of the exponential function $y = e^x$. We can do this merely by reversing the process of logarithmic differentiation. We have seen that if

$$y = \log_e x \quad , \tag{60}$$

then

$$x = e^y \quad . \tag{61}$$

We recall the inverse function rule (see Section 4.10):

$$\frac{\mathrm{d}y}{\mathrm{d}x} = \frac{1}{\mathrm{d}x/\mathrm{d}y} \quad . \tag{62}$$

From (59) we have

$$\frac{\mathrm{d}y}{\mathrm{d}x} = \frac{1}{x} \quad .$$

From (62) we know that the derivative of (61) is

$$\frac{\mathrm{d}x}{\mathrm{d}y} = x \quad ,$$

but from (61) we have $x = e^y$, so we can write the derivative of (61) as

$$\frac{\mathrm{d}x}{\mathrm{d}y} = e^y \quad . \tag{63}$$

This is a very interesting result. Evidently we have found a function whose derivative is itself. We should not regard this as particularly mysterious. Common sense suggests that there must be some function such that

$$f'(x) = f(x)$$

for all values of x, which is to say that *the slope tangent to the curve is at all points equal to the height of the curve.* What we have done is to find this particular function.

Now let us interpret the exponential and the logarithmic functions. Consider first the exponential function. The derivative of this function is the function itself, so the integral of the function must also be the function itself, but, as we have already seen, an arbitrary constant will appear when we integrate. Thus

$$\int e^x \, \mathrm{d}x = e^x + C \quad . \tag{64}$$

Now consider the logarithmic function whose derivative was given in (59). We obviously have

$$\int \frac{1}{x} \, \mathrm{d}x = \log x + C \quad . \tag{65}$$

Since $1/x$ is the derivative of $\log x$, it follows that $\log x + C$ is the integral[6] of $1/x$.

The function e^x is a most remarkable function. It always grows as x changes at a rate equal to its own value. This is of course the verbal translation of the fact that $\mathrm{d}(e^x)/\mathrm{d}x = e^x$.

Having found a function that grows at a rate equal to its own value we must wonder if we can find a function that grows at a rate proportional to its own value. It might be, for example, that national income is growing at a rate of 3 percent per year. This means that the rate of change of national income is 0.03 times the current value of national income whatever the current value may be. To express this we re-

---

[6] As we saw on page 324, footnote 1, x^{-1} cannot be integrated by the power function rule.

quire a function such that $dy/dx = 0.03y$ at all values of y, where x is time measured in years.

The function e^{rx} is the function we require. If r is any constant, we shall find that the function e^{rx} is changing at a rate *proportional* to its own value and that the constant of proportionality is r. Let us check this by finding the derivative of the function $y = e^{rx}$. This is easily done using the function-of-a-function rule. With $z = rx$ we have

$$y = e^z$$

$$\frac{dy}{dz} = e^z$$

$$\frac{dz}{dx} = r$$

$$\frac{dy}{dx} = \frac{dy}{dz} \cdot \frac{dz}{dx} = e^z r \quad,$$

but since $z = rx$, we have

$$\frac{dy}{dx} = re^{rx} \quad.$$

Thus

$$\frac{d}{dx}(e^{rx}) = re^{rx} \quad. \tag{66}$$

If r is 0.03, for example, the rate of growth of this function is 3 percent of the value of the function itself at all times.

If we use this function for growth problems, it is more convenient to denote time by t than by x, whence we shall write e^{rt}, where r is the rate of growth and t is time. The value of the function will grow at the rate of re^{rt} as time passes, and its proportional rate of growth will be $re^{rt}/e^{rt} = r$.

If we wish to express the assumption that national income is growing at a constant rate of $100r$ percent, we write

$$Y_t = Y_0 e^{rt} \quad, \tag{67}$$

where Y_t is national income at time t, Y_0 is the national income at any "base period" from which we begin our measurements, r is the constant rate of growth, and t is time. We assign the value zero to t at the base period and count the passage of time from there. At $t = 0$ the right-hand side becomes simply Y_0, as it should since $e^0 = 1$.

As a final example we consider a relationship that we shall require in Chapter 14. Assume that the labor force is growing at a rate of $100r$ percent per year. We can now write

$$L_t = L_0 e^{rt} \quad , \tag{68}$$

where L_t is the labor force at time t, L_0 is the labor force in the base period, r is the constant rate of growth, and t is time.

We have now discovered the function, e^{rt}, whose rate of growth is proportional to its own value. In Chapter 14 we shall exploit this function in our study of some dynamic models.

13.7   ELASTICITY

Now that we know how to differentiate logarithmic functions, we can obtain a most convenient expression for elasticity. In Section 2.15 we introduced the log–linear function

$$y = ax^\beta \quad . \tag{69}$$

In Chapter 4 we found that, if y denotes quantity and x price, then β is the elasticity of demand. We also took logs, and found that, since the function is linear in the logs,

$$\frac{d \log y}{d \log x} = \beta \quad .$$

But now we know that $d \log y / dy = 1/y$, whence in differential form[7]

$$d \log y = \frac{1}{y} \, dy \quad .$$

Similarly,

$$d \log x = \frac{1}{x} \, dx \quad .$$

By the definition of the elasticity of any dependent variable, y, with respect to an independent variable x,

$$\eta = \frac{dy}{dx} \cdot \frac{x}{y}$$

$$= \frac{1}{y} \, dy \cdot \frac{1}{dx} x$$

$$= \frac{d \log y}{d \log x} \quad . \tag{70}$$

---

[7] Recall from Chapter 8 that the derivative $d \log y / d \log x$ gives the instantaneous rate of change of y with respect to x at the point on the function at which it is evaluated, whereas the differential $d \log y = (1/y) \, dy$ gives the equation of the tangent gradient to the point on the curve at which it is evaluated. The slope of the tangent gradient is of course equal to the instantaneous rate of change at the relevant point on the function.

Now we know that for any function $y = f(x)$, the elasticity of y with respect to x is given by d log y/d log x. In the case of a function of two or more variables we may define a *partial elasticity*, the elasticity of the dependent variable with respect to any one of its arguments all other variables held constant. Thus if $\eta_{y:x_i}$ stands for the elasticity of y with respect to its ith argument,

$$\eta_{y:x_i} = \frac{d \log y}{d \log x_i} \quad . \tag{71}$$

QUESTIONS

1. Integrate the following.
    a. $x^2 + x^2$
    b. x^{60}
    c. e^x
    d. $e^x + x^{-1}$
    e. $35x^3/7x^2$
    f. 3

2. Marginal cost is given by

$$MC = 10 - 0.01x + 0.0009x^2 \quad ,$$

and fixed cost is 100. Find the total cost function.

3. A monopolist has the marginal revenue curve

$$MR = 100 - 10q \quad .$$

    a. Derive his total and average revenue curves.
    b. Can you say what the value of the constant of integration must be in this case?

4. Consider an economy with a constant marginal propensity to import of 0.2 and a constant marginal propensity to spend on domestically produced commodities of 0.7.
    a. Write the expression for dE/dY, where E is expenditure and where the only two classes of expenditure that vary with income are imports and consumption of domestically produced goods.
    b. Derive the equation for aggregate expenditure. What is the economic interpretation of the constant of integration?

5. Solve the following differential equations.
    a. $dy/dx = 3x^2$
    b. $dy/dx = \frac{1}{3}x^3$
    c. $dy/dx = 6x^2 + 3x^3$
    d. $dy/dx = \frac{1}{4}x^{1/2}$
    e. $dy/dx = 3x^{-1/3}$
    f. $dy/dx = x^2 - x$

6. For each of the following,

   i. $dy/dx = 3$
   ii. $d^2y/dx^2 = 3$
   iii. $dy/dx = e^x + x^2$

 a. Express y as a function of x (where the function is not to involve any derivatives).
 b. Determine the value of the constant of integration for i and iii by using the further assumption that when $x = 0$, $y = 10$.
 c. Determine the values of the constants for i and ii if $y = 15$ when $x = 5$ and $y = 30$ when $x = 10$.

7. a. Take the total differential of $z = e^{xy}$.
 b. Does the original function have a maximum? (Recall the necessary conditions for a maximum of a two-variable function.)

8. Differentiate the following with respect to x.

 a. $3e^{0.03x}$
 b. $e^{-x/4}$

9. Solve the following for y.

 a. $dy/dx = 0.1e^{0.1x}$
 b. $dy/dx = 6e^{2x}$

10. The elasticity of substitution has been written heretofore as

$$\sigma = \frac{d(L/K)}{L/K} \frac{r/w}{d(r/w)} \,.$$

Which of the following are equivalent to this expression?

 a. $\sigma = d \log (L/K)/d \log (r/w)$
 b. $\sigma = -d \log (L/K)/d \log (w/r)$
 c. $\sigma = ((d(L/K))/(d(r/w)))(rK/wL)$
 d. $\sigma = (d \log K - d \log L)/(d \log r - d \log w)$

11. a. If y is growing at a constant proportional rate r, from an initial value $y = y_0$, find the equation for y as a function of time.
 b. If $r = 0.01$ and $y_0 = 4$, what is y when $t = 10$?

12. Find the percentage change in quantity produced in response to a 1 percent change in (a) labor input and (b) capital input if production is given by

$$q = L^{2/3}K^{1/3} \,.$$

13. The elasticity of demand for a product is $-\frac{1}{4}$ at all prices. Derive the equation for the demand curve.

14. Determine the indefinite integral for $y = x^{-1}$.

Chapter *14*

Applications of Dynamics

All economic processes operate in *time*, whence the thorough study of any economic problem requires dynamics. We shall find in this chapter that the tools we now have allow us to model simple adjustment processes with a wide range of applications. We complete our study of the competitive market by exploring a simple model of its behavior in disequilibrium. We then, as a further illustration, consider the problem of inflationary expectations. In Section 14.3 we study what is called the "stock adjustment model" (and, incidentally, learn to solve another sort of first-order linear differential equation with constant coefficients). We also see that these simple models, although they take us a long way beyond what we could do earlier, suffer from some serious deficiencies as explanations of disequilibrium behavior. We make, in fact, a great advance in identifying new problems that we need to solve, but that are beyond the scope of this book. Finally, in Section 14.4, we see that the techniques we now have, though limited, are sufficient for us to handle a famous model of economic growth.

14.1 ADJUSTMENT IN A COMPETITIVE MARKET

Our first task is to complete some unfinished business left over from Chapter 12. In that chapter we took the familiar *linear* model of a single competitive market and assumed the existence of a reaction function specifying that the rate of change of market price was proportional to the amount of excess demand (see Section 12.4):

$$q^d = a + bp \tag{1}$$

$$q^s = c + dp \tag{2}$$

$$\frac{\mathrm{d}p}{\mathrm{d}t} = \alpha(q^d - q^s)$$

$$= \alpha(a + bp - c - dp)$$

$$= \alpha[(a - c) + p(b - d)] \quad . \tag{3}$$

We then posed the question of how price would behave if we began from a position of disequilibrium. Some possibilities for the behavior of price were illustrated in Figure 12.7. We are particularly interested to see whether or not the actual price will converge on its equilibrium value. The necessary manipulations are not difficult, but they will take a little time, particularly if we stop at every stage to check that what we have done makes economic sense.

First we check, as we have done previously, that the results of this model conform with those that we have obtained earlier. In particular, we need to check the equilibrium value of p. In equilibrium, price is not changing, so we have

$$\frac{\mathrm{d}p}{\mathrm{d}t} = 0 \quad , \tag{4}$$

which, substituting from (3), gives

$$\alpha[(a - c) + p(b - d)] = 0 \quad .$$

Since $\alpha \neq 0$, the expression in square brackets must be zero, whence equilibrium price is

$$\bar{p} = \frac{a - c}{d - b} \quad . \tag{5}$$

This agrees with the result first obtained in Chapter 3. Note that we designate the equilibrium price by $\bar{p}$, whereas p stands for the price ruling at any time whether equal to $\bar{p}$ or not.

Now let us deal in divergences of price from the equilibrium value just as we did when we studied the cobweb. Thus we define

$$\hat{p}(t) = p(t) - \bar{p} \quad . \tag{6}$$

Thus $\hat{p}$ is just the difference between the equilibrium price, $\bar{p}$, and the actual price, p. We write $\hat{p}$ and p as functions of time to emphasize that, once we have specified our demand and supply curves and the rule that governs the speed of change of price [Eq. (3)], both p and $\hat{p}$ will change in a definite way as time passes, that is, they are functions of time.

Differentiating (6) with respect to time we have

$$\frac{d\hat{p}(t)}{dt} = \frac{dp(t)}{dt} - \frac{d\bar{p}(t)}{dt} \quad . \tag{7}$$

The *equilibrium price* is, of course, determined solely by the demand and supply curves [see (5)] and does not change over time (assuming the curves to be given). Thus we have

$$\frac{d\bar{p}(t)}{dt} = 0 \tag{8}$$

so that (7) becomes

$$\frac{d\hat{p}(t)}{dt} = \frac{dp(t)}{dt} \quad . \tag{9}$$

This says nothing more than that, since $\bar{p}$ is constant, the rate of change of $p - \bar{p}$ is the same as the rate of change of p.

We can now take the expression for dp/dt from (3) and substitute it into (7) to obtain

$$\frac{d\hat{p}(t)}{dt} = \alpha[(a - c) + (b - d)p] - \alpha[(a - c) + (b - d)\bar{p}] \quad . \tag{10}$$

Note that we have not only substituted in the expression for $dp(t)/dt$ into (7), but have also substituted in one for $d\bar{p}(t)/dt$ even though we know this expression has a value of zero.[1] We do this because some of the individual terms can be canceled out with terms from $dp(t)/dt$ to obtain an expression cleared of irrelevant terms. Let us see how this happens:

$$\begin{aligned}
\frac{d\hat{p}(t)}{dt} &= \alpha[(a - c) + (b - d)p] - \alpha[(a - c) + (b - d)\bar{p}] \\
&= \alpha(a - c) - \alpha(a - c) + \alpha p(b - d) - \alpha\bar{p}(b - d) \\
&= \alpha(b - d)(p - \bar{p}) \\
&= \alpha(b - d)\hat{p}(t) \quad . \tag{10}
\end{aligned}$$

Now we have the rate of change of $\hat{p}$ expressed as a function of $\hat{p}$ and the difference between the slopes of the demand and the supply curves. The intercept terms, a and c, have disappeared. Finally let us designate $b - d$ by the Greek letter γ (gamma) so that we have

$$\frac{d\hat{p}(t)}{dt} = \alpha\gamma\hat{p}(t) \quad . \tag{11}$$

---

[1] You can easily check that the term for $d\bar{p}/dt$ in (10) is in fact zero if you substitute the solution for $\bar{p}$ from (5) into it. The term for $d\bar{p}/dt$ in (10) is $\alpha[(a - c) + (b - d)\bar{p}]$. Substituting from (5) for $\bar{p}$, we get $\alpha[(a - c) + (b - d)(c - a)/(b - d)] = 0$.

Next we divide through by $\hat{p}(t)$ to get all terms involving the dependent variable on the left-hand side of the expression:

$$\frac{1}{\hat{p}(t)} \cdot \frac{d\hat{p}(t)}{dt} = \alpha\gamma \quad . \tag{12}$$

Finally, to get it into a convenient form, we replace the derivative $d\hat{p}/dt$ in (12) by the ratio of the two differentials (which has the same value as the derivative) and multiply through by the differential dt to obtain

$$\frac{d\hat{p}(t)}{\hat{p}(t)} = \alpha\gamma \, dt \quad . \tag{13}$$

Now we are getting somewhere. We have managed to derive a first-order linear differential equation of the sort we studied in Chapter 13. Fortunately we know how to solve it by integrating both sides:

$$\int \frac{1}{\hat{p}(t)} \, d\hat{p}(t) = \int \alpha\gamma \, dt \quad . \tag{14}$$

In Chapter 13 we saw that the integral of $(1/x) \, dx$ was the log to the base e of x. This settles the left-hand side. The right-hand integration is even easier since we know that $\alpha\gamma t$ will give $\alpha\gamma$ when differentiated with respect to t so $\alpha\gamma t$ is what we require. Thus we have

$$\log_e \hat{p}(t) = \alpha\gamma t + C \quad , \tag{15}$$

where C is the constant of integration. To find $\hat{p}(t)$ we now take anti-logs to obtain

$$\hat{p}(t) = (e^{\alpha\gamma t}) \, (\text{antilog of } C) \quad . \tag{16}$$

What we are trying to do is to find an expression for $\hat{p}(t)$ that is the divergence of the actual price from the market price given as a function of time. In (15) we are very close to this answer because the right-hand side is the log to the base e of what we want. If $\alpha\gamma t + C$ is the log of our answer, then our answer is the number that corresponds to e raised to the power of $\alpha\gamma t$ (the antilog of $\alpha\gamma t$) multiplied by the antilog of C, which is the number corresponding to e raised to the power C. We do not, however, write e^C as the antilog of C but instead merely designate this value by A. Now write[2]

$$\hat{p}(t) = Ae^{\alpha\gamma t} \quad . \tag{17}$$

[2] If instead of writing A for the antilogarithm of C, we had written e^C, Eq. (17) would have become

$$\hat{p}(t) = (e^{\alpha\gamma t})e^C \tag{17a}$$

This is, of course, the same as (17), but the form in the text happens to be more convenient.

We have now solved our mathematical problem, and it remains only to inspect the solution in (17) to see what we can learn from it. First consider the constant A. This arose in the process of integration and, like all constants of integration, we cannot determine it without further extraneous information. It would be most unsatisfactory if the behavior of our model turned out to depend critically on a constant whose value we could not determine. Fortunately, this is not the case: we can easily give the constant an economic interpretation by considering the value of (17) at the initial time period when the whole process is set in motion. The process begins at time t_0. In (17) we have $t = 0$ at that time, and thus $\alpha\gamma t = 0$ whatever the values of α and γ. We know that any number raised to the power zero is equal to unity, so (17) reduces to

$$\hat{p}(t) = A \qquad \text{(at time } t_0) \ . \qquad\qquad (18)$$

Thus A is the initial value of the divergence of price from equilibrium.[3] This is our starting point: it is the divergence from equilibrium that is needed to put the whole process in motion. It is not surprising that we cannot tell what price will be at any time t unless we know the value from which it started.[4]

Next consider the coefficient $\alpha\gamma t$. t stands for time elapsed since t_0, and it is thus a variable that starts from zero and takes on larger and larger positive values thereafter. α is the adjustment coefficient, and we have already seen (see Section 12.4) that $\alpha > 0$. γ was substituted for $b - d$, the difference between the slopes of the demand and the supply curves. If the curves are of the normal slopes, we have $b < 0$ and $d > 0$, so that $\gamma = b - d < 0$. Thus α and t are positive, whereas γ is negative, so that the sign of the coefficient on e is necessarily negative. (Note that this result is independent of the sign or magnitude of the constant A.) α and γ are constants, and t is a variable, whence it follows that the absolute value of $\alpha\gamma t$ gets larger and larger as t gets larger and larger; in fact $\alpha\gamma t \to -\infty$ as $t \to +\infty$. It is easily seen by inspection that e^{-x} approaches zero as x gets larger and larger.[5] From this we conclude that $\hat{p}(t)$ gets steadily smaller and smaller as t increases.

Finally, consider what would happen if the coefficient $\alpha\gamma t$ were positive (i.e., either both $\alpha, \gamma > 0$, or both $\alpha, \gamma < 0$, which means that one of α or γ must have the "wrong" sign). e^x increases indefinitely

---

[3] For any function of time, the constant of integration A gives the value of the function at t_0.

[4] See Section 12.3 for an analysis of the possible causes of the initial deviation from equilibrium.

[5] The expression e^{-x} is the same thing as $1/e^x$. As x gets larger and larger, e^x gets larger and larger, and thus its reciprocal gets smaller and smaller. Indeed as $x \to \infty$, $e^x \to \infty$, and from this it follows that as $x \to \infty$, $e^{-x} \to 0$.

as x increases as long as x is positive. This means that $\hat{p}$ would increase steadily as t increased: the actual price would get farther and farther from the equilibrium price.

We have now reached a number of conclusions concerning our dynamic model of a competitive market.

1. Assuming that the adjustment coefficient has the correct sign, a necessary condition for stability in this market is that $\gamma = b - d < 0$ (all the possibilities were spelled out in Chapter 12).
2. Assuming that $\gamma < 0$, a necessary condition for stability is that $\alpha > 0$, that is, that price falls when there is excess supply and rises when there is excess demand.
3. There is a combination of two perverse reactions that will produce stable behavior, $\alpha < 0$ and $\gamma > 0$, in which case there is excess supply above the equilibrium price and excess demand below it, but price falls when there is excess demand and rises when there is excess supply.

In the normal case in which $\alpha > 0$ and $\gamma < 0$ we have the following results.

4. The adjustment process is stable in the sense that the actual price converges on the equilibrium one.
5. The approach to equilibrium is a steady one and *not* one of progressively diminishing oscillations around the equilibrium; the path of price is similar to that shown by curve (2) in Figure 12.7.
6. Conclusions 1 and 2 are independent of the size and direction of the initial disturbance.
7. The actual shape of the time path of price is determined by α, the strength of the response of price to excess demand, by γ, and by A, which stands for the original disturbance. The statement that the time path depends on A does not conflict with conclusion 3: the result that the approach to equilibrium is a steady one is independent of A, but the actual position of the path traced out must depend on A — the sign of A determines, for example, whether the approach is from above (initial price too high) or from below (initial price too low).

Result 3, although undoubtedly of little practical interest, does warn us that we need to make an exhaustive study of the behavior of any particular model if we are to be sure that we can identify the special cases — which may or may not be important in practice — in which generalizations derived from the model do not hold.

The model considered above necessarily has a stable adjustment process if the demand and supply curves have their "normal" slope and if price rises in the face of excess demand and falls in the face of excess supply. In the model q^d, q^s, and dp/dt all respond solely to current values of the variables. The time path of price is always of the type shown by curve (2) in Figure 12.7.

We could introduce lags in the models that made q^d and/or q^s respond to past prices (and we have already mentioned examples where this might describe real behavior) or make dp/dt respond to past excess demand (which might or might not emerge from a micro-model of price formation in disequilibrium, once we had one). Once this were done a series of more complex models would be possible. These models are obtained by giving nonzero values to some of the τ's in Eqs. (24)–(26) in Chapter 12. When we had done this we would find that, depending on the lags assumed, the adjustment process might be oscillatory or nonoscillatory and stable or unstable, that is, the actual path of price could follow any of the curves shown in Figure 12.7.

The solution of the dynamic model of income determination set out at the end of Chapter 12 poses no new problems. The solution follows exactly the same steps as those used in the case of the single competitive market, and it is left for the reader to do as an exercise.

14.2 THE STABILITY OF AN INFLATIONARY PROCESS

An important question is: do inflations inevitably explode into hyper-inflations? The "flight from money argument" may appear to suggest that the answer must be "yes."

An intuitive explanation of the flight from money argument goes as follows. Assume for simplicity that people hold money balances for transactions purposes only. If they expect prices to rise, and the value of their money balances to decline accordingly, they will wish to avoid holding wealth in the form of money. This is the notion of flight from money: if a man anticipates a decline in the value of money, we expect him to reduce, if he can, the proportion of his wealth that he holds in the form of money; if he does this by endeavoring to buy goods, he creates inflationary pressure; thus not only is there inflation, as he expected, but more than there would have been had he not expected it. But any continuous inflation will come to be expected, thus lead to flight from money, thus to faster inflation, and so on.

Is this *necessarily* true? In this section, we shall see that it is not: the techniques at our disposal allow us to analyze a simple model incorporating inflationary expectations, and find that whether or not it explodes depends on the values of the parameters, which is, of course,

an empirical question. The fact that flight from money does not necessarily entail explosive inflation of course tells us nothing about the
real world: it is, however, a logical possibility. We are not settling an
empirical question here: we are using our analytic techniques to illustrate, and, in particular, to see what sort of empirical information we
should need to settle the matter.

We may now construct a simple model of an inflation-induced
flight from money. We assume a simple quantity-theory world in
which demand for money is for transactions purposes only and no
speculative balances are held; thus

$$M^d = kPX \quad , \tag{19}$$

where M^d is money demanded, k a constant determined by the behavior of money holders, P the price level, and X real income or output. The implication of assuming that money is held for transactions
purposes only is that we shall ignore other assets such as bonds since,
by assumption, they do not exist or are not substitutes for money. The
money supply is assumed to be a parameter whose value is determined exogenously by the central authorities. Thus

$$M^s = M \quad . \tag{20}$$

In equilibrium

$$M^s = M^d \quad . \tag{21}$$

Substituting into the equilibrium condition (21) and rearranging
terms, we have

$$P = \frac{M}{kX} \quad . \tag{22}$$

If we were interested only in comparative statics, we would merely
note the familiar quantity-theory results, which we may sum up in
two important relations (each of which can be expressed in several
alternative forms):

$$\frac{dP}{dM} = \frac{1}{kX}$$

or

$$dP = \frac{1}{kX} \, dM$$

or

$$\frac{1}{P} \frac{dP}{dM} = \frac{1}{kX} \frac{kX}{M} = \frac{1}{M}$$

or

$$\frac{\mathrm{d}P}{\mathrm{d}M} = \frac{P}{M} \quad .$$

This says that, with output constant, the change in the price level is directly proportional to the change in the quantity of money (the constant multiple being $1/kX$). The final version of the relation above says that the ratio of any *change* in the price level to a *change* in the money supply is the same as the ratio of the price level itself to the total money supply.

To derive the second relation we now regard X as something that can vary as well as M and P, and we write

$$dP = \frac{\partial P}{\partial M} \, dM + \frac{\partial P}{\partial X} \, dX$$

$$= \frac{1}{kX} \, dM - \frac{M}{kX^2} \, dX \quad ,$$

or by the method of Section 8.4

$$\frac{\mathrm{d}P}{\mathrm{d}t} = \frac{1}{kX} \frac{\mathrm{d}M}{\mathrm{d}t} - \frac{M}{kX^2} \frac{\mathrm{d}X}{\mathrm{d}t}$$

or

$$\frac{1}{P} \frac{\mathrm{d}P}{\mathrm{d}t} = \frac{1}{M} \frac{\mathrm{d}M}{\mathrm{d}t} - \frac{1}{X} \frac{\mathrm{d}X}{\mathrm{d}t} \quad .$$

This second main result states that the rate of change of prices is proportional to the rate of increase in the money supply minus the rate of increase in real income.

We are interested, however, in disequilibrium behavior, the adjustment of the system when $M^d \neq M^s$. Before introducing flight from money, let us set up the simplest hypothesis about adjustment, assuming again that the rate of change of the equilibrating variable is proportional to excess demand. An inflationary situation, in this model, is one in which there is an excess supply of money: this is the necessary and sufficient condition for inflation. The basic assumption, of course, is that an excess supply of money means an excess demand for goods: if people find themselves holding more money than they require, they spend it on goods. Notice that this is the adjustment mechanism without any flight: it is the spending out of excess money balances that drives the price level up until the balances are no longer found excessive, that is, the price level satisfies Eq. (22) again. Thus we take excess demand for goods to be identical to excess supply of money (this is often called Walras' law), and, on the assumption that the rate of change of prices is proportional to excess demand, we have

$$\frac{dP(t)}{dt} = \alpha(M^s - M^d)$$

$$= \alpha M^s - \alpha k X P(t) \quad , \tag{23}$$

where $P(t)$ denotes price at time t and we assume real income, X, to be constant. We now recall all the tricks of Section 14.1. Define the discrepancy in the price level by

$$\hat{p} = P(t) - \bar{P} \quad , \tag{24}$$

where $\bar{P}$ is the equilibrium price level from Eq. (22). Following the procedure of Section 14.1 again, we differentiate $\hat{p}$ with respect to time:

$$\frac{d\hat{p}}{dt} = \frac{dP(t)}{dt} - \frac{d\bar{P}}{dt} \quad .$$

We note that $d\bar{P}/dt$ is zero and substitute for $dP(t)/dt$ from (23):

$$\frac{d\hat{p}}{dt} = \alpha M^s - \alpha k X P(t) - 0 \quad . \tag{25}$$

We want to express the right-hand side of (25) in terms of $\hat{p}$ again, so we exploit the fact that $M^s - kX\bar{P} = 0$, and so, therefore, does $\alpha M^s - \alpha k X \bar{P}$. Inserting this in (25) we have

$$\frac{d\hat{p}}{dt} = \alpha M^s - \alpha k X P(t) - \alpha M^s + \alpha k X \bar{P}$$

$$= -\alpha k X (P(t) - \bar{P})$$

$$= -\alpha k X \hat{p} \quad , \tag{26}$$

which is a differential equation that we know how to solve. We re-arrange (26) to get

$$\frac{1}{\hat{p}} \, d\hat{p} = -\alpha k X \, dt \tag{27}$$

and recall that the derivative of $\log_e x$ is $1/x$. We now integrate both sides of (27) to get

$$\log_e \hat{p} = -\alpha k X t + C$$

and, taking antilogs,

$$\hat{p} = A e^{-\alpha k X t} \quad . \tag{28}$$

We can continue by finding A so that $\hat{p} = 0$ when $P(t) = \bar{P}$ in the man-ner of Section 14.1, but this introduces nothing new. Equation (28) is what we are really interested in: the economy is stable if and only if $\hat{p}$ goes to zero as t goes to infinity, which requires that the exponent be negative. This it clearly is, since α, k, and X are all positive: there is no difficulty here.

We now want to introduce the idea of flight from money into this otherwise stable model. The idea is that experience of inflation causes people to expect inflation and therefore to hold less money—demand more goods—than they otherwise would, which in turn causes the inflation to be faster than it otherwise would be. We want the simplest possible case of this behavior. Let us assume that the expected change in prices is simply proportional to the current rate of change,

$$\left(\frac{dP(t)}{dt}\right)_E = \beta \frac{dP(t)}{dt} \quad , \tag{29}$$

where $(dP(t)/dt)_E$ is the expected change in the price level and β is a constant relating expected changes to observed changes in the price level. If $\beta > 0$, the observation of inflation leads people to expect further inflation; if $\beta = 1$, people expect inflation to continue at whatever rate is currently observed; if $\beta > 1$, people expect the rate of inflation to accelerate. This last case must be the most unfavorable case for stability, but we shall find that even this is not sufficient to produce instability.

To proceed we now need a new demand for money equation to take into account the effects on the demand for money of expectations about the future course of prices. A simple one is

$$M^d = kP(t)X - \gamma\left(\frac{dP(t)}{dt}\right)_E \quad . \tag{30}$$

The first term in (30) gives the "static" demand for money, which is the complete demand if the expected change in the price level is zero. In this case the demand for money is simply a fraction, k, of the money value of national income. When prices are expected to rise, however, people hold less money than they would if prices were expected to remain stable.[6] The coefficient γ determines the amount by which a

---

[6] An expected inflation raises the opportunity cost of holding money. If the price level is expected to remain constant, the opportunity cost of holding money is given by the interest rate. If the interest rate is 5 percent per year, the opportunity cost of holding $100 for 1 year is $5 or 5 percent. If the price level is also expected to rise by 5 percent, the opportunity cost of holding $100 cash, rather than an *equity* that will earn $5 and whose capital value will be $105 at the end of the year, is 10 percent because the holder ends up with $100 instead of $110. Thus an expected inflation has the same effect on the opportunity cost of holding cash as has a rise in the rate of interest. Just as we expect a rise in interest rates to cause the demand for money to fall, but not to zero, so we expect an expected rate of inflation to cause the demand for money to fall, but not to zero.

given expected inflation reduces the demand for money. There are some implications of (30) to which we shall refer shortly. First, let us substitute (29) into (30):

$$M^d = kP(t)X - \gamma\beta\frac{dP(t)}{dt} \quad . \tag{31}$$

It would be hard to tell γ, the demand coefficient, from β, the expectations coefficient, from any empirical observations, so we combine them into one *reaction coefficient*, $\delta = \beta\gamma$, for simplicity. We interpret δ as follows: it tells us the amount by which the demand for money is less than it otherwise would be at any given absolute price level because of the observed rate of change of the price level.[7]

We retain the assumption that the rate of change of prices is proportional to the excess supply of money, $M^s - M^d$. We substitute into (31) to replace $\gamma\beta$ by δ and then substitute (31) into our dynamic adjustment equation (23) to obtain

$$\frac{dP(t)}{dt} = \alpha M^s - \alpha\left(kP(t)X - \delta\frac{dP(t)}{dt}\right) \quad . \tag{32}$$

We retain the same definition of $\hat{p}$, Eq. (24), and again use the trick that $\alpha M^s - \alpha k\bar{P}X = 0$, so

$$\frac{d\hat{p}}{dt} = \alpha M^s - \alpha kP(t)X + \alpha\delta\frac{d\hat{p}}{dt} - \alpha M^s + \alpha k\bar{P}X$$

$$= -\alpha kX[P(t) - \bar{P}] + \alpha\delta\frac{d\hat{p}}{dt} \quad . \tag{33}$$

One additional trick has been employed here: since $d\hat{p}/dt = (dP(t)/dt) - 0$, $d\hat{p}/dt$ has been substituted for $dP(t)/dt$ in the flight from money term in M^d.

We proceed with (33) in the usual way, by taking the $d\hat{p}/dt$ term to the left-hand side:

[7] We might wish to ask in what circumstances, if any, demand for money can fall to zero. Put

$$kP(t)X - \delta\frac{dP(t)}{dt} = 0 \quad ,$$

and we have a set of pairs of values of $P(t)$ and $dP(t)/dt$, positively associated: the higher the price level, the larger must $dP(t)/dt$ be to reduce desired money holdings to zero. In fact, the relationship is homogeneous: from the above equations we have

$$\frac{1}{P(t)}\frac{dP(t)}{dt} = \frac{kX}{\delta} \quad ,$$

which defines the proportional rate of inflation at which $M^d = 0$. Evidently the larger the reaction coefficient δ, the lower this will be. But observe that it can occur at finite positive price levels, that is, "inside" the values 0 and ∞.

$$\frac{d\hat{p}}{dt}(1 - \alpha\delta) = -\alpha kX\hat{p} \quad,$$

so

$$\frac{1}{\hat{p}} d\hat{p} = -\frac{\alpha kX}{1 - \alpha\delta} dt \quad. \tag{34}$$

We can now integrate both sides of (34) and write the solution straightaway as a routine matter:

$$P(t) = Ae^{-\alpha kXt/(1-\alpha\delta)} \quad. \tag{35}$$

As before, we are not particularly interested in finding the value of A to conform with the equilibrium condition $\hat{p} = 0$: we are interested only in stability, or convergence of actual $P(t)$ on equilibrium $\bar{P}$. This depends on the sign of the exponent in (35). Since α, k, and X are still positive, this is *negative* if and only if

or

i.e.

$$\left.\begin{array}{c} 1 - \alpha\delta > 0 \\ \alpha\delta < 1 \\ \alpha\beta\gamma < 1 \end{array}\right\} \tag{36}$$

Thus the system is stable if the *product* of α (the goods-market reaction coefficient) β (the expectations coefficient), and γ (the flight coefficient) is less than 1. Evidently flight is *not* sufficient to make the system explosive. Even if the expectations coefficient, β, exceeds unity, it may be "damped" by a weak market coefficient and/or a weak flight coefficient; similarly, a large flight coefficient may be outweighed by small values of the other coefficients.[8]

We now know that the intuitive argument that any continuous inflation will accelerate because of a flight from money is inadequate. Whether or not the system we have studied is explosive depends on

---

[8] We have conducted the analysis in absolute rather than proportional terms, that is, we have $dp/dt = f(M^d - M^s)$ rather than $(dp/dt)(1/p) = f([M^d - M^s]/M^s)$ for reasons of mathematical simplicity. When the analysis is conducted in these terms we cannot give any simple interpretation to the coefficients α and γ. If we did deal in relations such as

$$\frac{dp}{dt} \cdot \frac{1}{p} = \alpha\left(\frac{M^d - M^s}{M^s}\right) \quad,$$

we could give a simple interpretation to α and could have some idea of the likelihood of α being greater than or less than unity. Our present model is not the best one to use for more sophisticated attacks on the basic problem (because it is hard to interpret α and γ), but it is quite enough to show that there is no general theoretical presumption that *any* flight from money necessarily causes inflation to be explosive.

parameter values. It is obvious, however, that the model we have analyzed is extremely naive: the real world is considerably more complicated. A serious study of an inflationary process would require far more care than we have given it, and far more technique than we have developed in this book.

14.3 THE STOCK ADJUSTMENT MODEL

In Section 14.2 we investigated the behavior of prices, assuming that the demand for money depended on the current level of prices and their expected rate of change. We now investigate the behavior of an individual who is not satisfied with the level of his money balances.

We may assume that an individual's demand for money balances is proportional to his money income, i.e., $M^d = kY$, where the M^d and Y now refer to a single individual. We might instead assume something more complicated: M^d may depend on the interest rate as well as money income and perhaps on other variables. In any case we can assume that, at any moment, an individual wishes to hold a definite level of money balances, which we write $M^*(t)$ (where there is no room for ambiguity, we shall omit the t). At any moment in time, he holds some money balances, $M(t)$. Desired balances M^* may be changed by factors quite exogenous to the individual, such as changes in the general level of prices and incomes (or interest rates), or by changes in his own plans or expectations. Unless actual balances $M(t)$ adjust *instantaneously* to changes in M^* we must expect that actual balances will not always be equal to desired balances. Without troubling ourselves further about the reason for the discrepancy, let us see what might happen if $M(t) \neq M^*$. In particular, let us take the case $M(t) < M^*$.

Consider the case in which an individual finds, for whatever reason, that he has too little in his checking account. Toward the end of the month, he is anxiously checking his bankbook, wondering what payments he can postpone, or from whom he might raise a short-term loan. He would be much happier if he could make a once-and-for-all change in his liquidity position and start each month, on the average, with more in his account. Given that his *income* is fixed, how can he achieve this? There are two obvious ways. The first way is to save. If he can reduce his rate of expenditure for a while, he can build up his bank balance. It need only be for a while: when $M(t)$ has been built up to M^*, he can resume his former level of consumption while enjoying the freedom from anxiety afforded by his increased liquidity. Nonetheless, he does have to give up some consumption, with attendant loss of utility. The second way to increase liquidity is to sell financial assets such as stocks or bonds. This inevitably involves brokerage costs and may also involve selling at prices that do not seem to him to be favorable in view of the long-term trends in the markets for these assets.[9]

Whichever way he proceeds, the adjustment process itself is costly. This is a new and extremely important step in our economic analysis: *the process of reaching a preferred position itself imposes costs.* Further, as we have already suggested, the adjustment is likely to take *time.* A man who wishes to increase his total wealth holdings by increasing his average bank balance by a significant amount is unlikely to wish to (or even be able to) achieve the necessary saving over a day or a week: it will probably be better to spread the loss of consumption over weeks or months. With the tools we now have, we can investigate one simple model of an adjustment process (although a full treatment is still out of reach).

We introduce the simple hypothesis that the rate of adjustment itself is a function of the discrepancy between the desired and actual levels of the stock of balances. Indeed, we assume that it is proportional to the discrepancy, whence we write

$$\dot{M} = \alpha(M^* - M(t)) \quad , \tag{37}$$

where $\dot{M}$ ($= dM/dt$) is the rate of change in the individual's money stock, M^* the desired level, and $M(t)$ the actual level at any time t. The similarity of (37) to (3) will be noticed. Here α is an adjustment coefficient *chosen by the individual* to achieve a balance between the drawbacks of *not* having $M(t) = M^*$ and the costs of achieving M^*. (A full treatment of the problem would derive, from utility maximization, the simultaneous determination of M^* and α.)

Our task now is to solve the differential equation (37). It is slightly different from the differential equations we have encountered so far, but we can solve it very easily. For our purposes, we may treat M^* as a constant,[10] but $M(t)$ is not, and, indeed, it is the time path of M that we want to discover. To concentrate for a moment on the mathematics, let us consider the equation

$$\frac{dx}{dt} + \alpha x = C \quad . \tag{38}$$

---

[9] There is a third possible method: to sell some of his durable consumer goods, for example, radios, cars, etc. This is a particularly costly method because these assets usually command a rather poor secondhand price, and, of course, when the balances have been built up, the individual will have to replace the durables if he is to enjoy his former flow of consumption services.

[10] M^* is a function of all of those variables that determine the demand for money. M^* is constant because these variables are assumed constant.

Now, the derivative with respect to t of $xe^{\alpha t}$ is

$$\frac{d}{dt} xe^{\alpha t} = e^{\alpha t} \frac{dx}{dt} + \alpha xe^{\alpha t} \tag{39}$$

(by the application of the product rule and the rules for differentiating exponential functions that we learned in Section 13.6). We see at once that the left-hand side of (38) is $(d/dt)xe^{\alpha t}$ divided by $e^{\alpha t}$. We therefore have

$$\frac{d}{dt} xe^{\alpha t} = Ce^{\alpha t} \tag{40}$$

(multiplying both sides by $e^{\alpha t}$). We can integrate both sides of (40) in the usual way to obtain

$$xe^{\alpha t} = \frac{1}{\alpha} Ce^{\alpha t} + A \quad,$$

and then

$$x = \frac{1}{\alpha} C + Ae^{-\alpha t} \quad, \tag{41}$$

where x is, of course, understood to be $x(t)$ and A is the constant of integration.

This has been so easy that, before we return to the demand for money, let us see if we can generalize it. Suppose that we had the differential equation

$$a_0 \frac{dy}{dx} + a_1 y = B \quad.$$

We should recognize this as an equation of the same form as (38) and rearrange it to give

$$\frac{dy}{dx} + by = C \tag{42}$$

(where, of course, $b = a_1/a_0$ and $C = B/a_0$). Multiply the left-hand side by e^{bx} to give

$$e^{bx} \frac{dy}{dx} + be^{bx}y \quad.$$

It is easy to verify that this is nothing but the derivative with respect to x of

$$e^{bx}y \quad.$$

The term e^{bx} is sometimes known as the "fudge factor." The *procedure* is to divide through by the coefficient of dy/dx (if it is not already unity), and then to multiply by e raised to the power bx. One then sees that one has *exactly* the derivative $d(e^{bx}y)/dx$. The solution is

$$e^{bx}y = \int Ce^{bx}\,dx = C\int e^{bx}\,dx$$

$$= \frac{1}{b}Ce^{bx} + D \tag{43}$$

(where D is the constant of integration), whence

$$y = \frac{1}{b}C + De^{-bx} \quad .$$

We can now compare (37) with (41) and write the solution of the former directly:

$$M(t) = \frac{1}{\alpha}(\alpha M^*) + Ae^{-\alpha t} \quad . \tag{44}$$

The first term is simply M^*: in equilibrium, $M(t) = M^*$. The second term is the so-called "transient," or path of adjustment to M^*. We have to satisfy ourselves that it eventually disappears, that is, goes to zero as t increases without limit, and we have to interpret A. The first is easy: for $\alpha > 0$, $e^{-\alpha t} \to 0$ as $t \to \infty$. As for A, we interpret it as usual as the initial disturbance at "time zero":

$$A = (M(0) - M^*) \quad .$$

Collecting up our results, we now have

$$M(t) = M^* + (M(0) - M^*)e^{-\alpha t} \quad . \tag{45}$$

Let us check this. First, we differentiate to obtain

$$\dot{M} = \alpha(M^* - M(0))e^{-\alpha t}$$

in which we see that $\dot{M} = 0$ if $M^* - M(0) = 0$, as it should, and that, for an initial discrepancy of given size, the rate of change declines with time. We also notice that, in a model of this sort, $\dot{M}$ approaches zero as t increases without limit but does not reach zero in any finite time period. To the question "how long does it take to complete the adjustment?" the correct answer is therefore "never;" but M can be brought arbitrarily close to M^* in a finite period of time. It is obvious, however, that adjustment will be faster the greater α, so we must find an appropriate way of measuring it.

The constant α indicates the speed of response, and its reciprocal, $1/\alpha$, is called the *time constant* of the lagged adjustment process. In Figure 14.1 the exponential path of M is illustrated for $\alpha = 4$, and units have been chosen such that the original discrepancy, $M^* - M(0)$, is

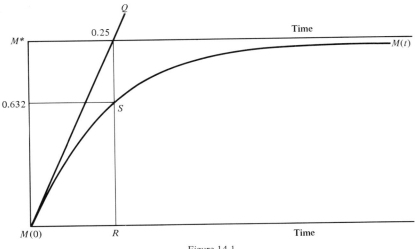

Figure 14.1

unity. The line $M(0)Q$ is tangent to the curve $M(t)$ at the origin $M(0)$. Its slope is the speed of response, α, equal here to 4. This follows from the fact that, if $M^* - M(0) = 1$, and $t = 0$, $\dot{M} = \alpha(1)e^0 = \alpha = 4$. The distance $M(0)R$ is $\frac{1}{4}$, the time constant of the lag. The time constant can also be measured by the time required (one quarter of a unit) to remove 0.632 of the original discrepancy. This is the distance RS in the figure. The number is chosen because it is equal to $1 - e^{-1}$. We can see from (45) why this is a convenient unit to work with by choosing units such that the original discrepancy is unity. But it should be clear that we can take *any* proportion of the original discrepancy, 0.9, or 0.99, and measure off the time required to remove it.

This completes our discussion of the stock adjustment model applied to money balances. We chose money balances for our first application simply because we discussed money in Section 14.2. The choice of illustration is not, however, restrictive: we now know how to handle the stock adjustment model. It is therefore easy to consider a wide range of applications, which we may do very briefly.

Consider first the investment plans of a firm. In earlier chapters we have discussed the determination of the profit-maximizing levels of capital and labor. The optimal level of capital was determined in the static model as a function of the rental rate on capital and the wage rate, together with desired output or the price of the product. Let us call the desired capital stock K^*. At any moment in time there is an actual capital stock, $K(t)$, which is not necessarily equal to K^*. Suppose that it is less. Investment, denoted by I or $\dot{K}$, takes time. Furthermore, the *process of investing*, or adjusting K to K^*, is not itself costless. By this we do not mean that the firm must pay for its capital goods: their price is already reflected in the rental rate, which is a determinant of K^*. We mean that it takes time and money to plan the new investment, place orders, install equipment, and get new production lines started up. Thus the investment process might be described by the differential equation

$$\dot{K} = \alpha(K^* - K(t)) \quad . \tag{46}$$

We have already discussed the solution of this equation, and its properties, and need not repeat our discussion. We note that the constant of adjustment, α, must be determined by consideration of the losses imposed, on the one hand, by not having K^*, and, on the other, by speeding up the rate of investment, $\dot{K}$. In a full treatment, we should determine α simultaneously with K^*.

Although in static analysis we define the long run as the period in which all factors are variable, and the short run as the period in which some (usually capital) are not freely variable, whereas others (labor) are, we should recognize that there are also costs to altering a labor force. It may be necessary to advertise vacancies. Applicants must be interviewed and perhaps tested, documents processed, and records made. It may be necessary to train new workers, or at least to go to some trouble to integrate them into the work force. Vice versa, layoffs may be expensive or difficult, and a firm may well be deterred from laying off workers in the face of falling demand if rehiring is costly and demand is expected to increase again. All this suggests that the stock adjustment model might apply here too: $\dot{L} = \alpha(L^* - L(t))$ (where $\dot{L}$ is the rate of change of the work force over time). Again, in a full treatment, we should simultaneously determine α and L^*. We may conjecture that the model may be a first approximation, if only for one reason: the asymmetry of upward and downward adjustment. Thus the way capital can be reduced (by sale or by waiting for it to depreciate) is very different from the way it can be acquired; and there is obviously a similar asymmetry between the costs of increases and decreases of the work force.

Now let us consider a macro-application. Let C, I, and G be the demands of households, investors, and government. They will be satisfied by an equilibrium level of output, which we denote by $\bar{Y}$. At any moment in time, output is $Y(t)$, not necessarily equal to $\bar{Y}$. Once again, it will take time to adjust output. Materials must be ordered (or orders canceled and inventories run down). Workers must be hired, and perhaps trained (or laid off). All this takes time and imposes costs. It is quite possible that we should find that the adjustment process in the real world could be approximated by

$$\dot{Y} = \alpha(\bar{Y} - Y(t)) \quad , \tag{47}$$

where $\dot{Y}$ is the rate of change of output. In this case, of course, no one decision maker determines α. Its value depends on the speed of adjustment of the entire economy, that is, on literally millions of individual decisions. Again, we should not be surprised if the model were only a first approximation: it is unlikely that the speeds of adjustment in upswings and downswings will be the same.

In Section 14.2 we introduced the idea of expected inflation. To keep the analysis simple, we assumed rather crudely that, whatever the instantaneous rate of change, people expected it to continue. It is clear that the formation of expectations is of great importance to dynamic behavior. Not enough is known about it, but in this section we may go a little further than we did above.

Assume that an individual wishes to forecast the behavior of a variable, y, that changes over time. If we write y^e for the value expected, then at any moment we have the actual value, $y(t)$, and the expected value, $y^e(t)$. What happens when the individual is wrong, as he doubtless often will be? We should expect him to revise his expectations. A very simple revision rule is provided by the *adaptive expectations model*. The rule is that the individual revises his expectations at a rate proportional to his error. Thus we should have

$$\dot{y}^e = \alpha(y(t) - y^e(t)) \qquad (\alpha > 0) \quad , \tag{48}$$

where $\dot{y}^e$ is the rate of change of the individual's forecast value of the variable y. This is really just the stock adjustment model in another guise, so we need say no more about its formal properties.

In (48) we assumed that the individual was attempting to forecast the level of y. He might instead have occasion to forecast its rate of change. The notion that the rule of revision is proportional to the error would have to be expressed as

$$\ddot{y}^e = \beta(\dot{y} - \dot{y}^e) \qquad (\beta > 0) \quad , \tag{49}$$

where $\ddot{y}^e = d^2y^e/dt^2$, the rate of change of the expected rate of change. This introduces second-order differential equations, which we shall not pursue; but the idea underlying (49) is a simple extension of that underlying (48).

This is as far as we shall take the analysis of adjustment processes in this book. We conclude with a warning: the adjustment models discussed here are not merely elementary; they are ad hoc. Let us see why this is so.

Consider first the price adjustment model of Section 14.1, where we assumed that the rate of change of price in a competitive market was proportional to excess demand. We might have assumed a non-linear reaction function, at the cost of complicating the mathematics, but this is not the point at issue. The point is that the assumed behavior is not derived from any notions of the actual behavior of any traders in the market. When excess demand is not zero, the market is in *disequilibrium*. How do people *behave* when a market is not in equilibrium? After all, some people must be disappointed: they cannot carry out their plans because, for example, a dealer has sold out, or prices are not what they expected. We need a model that will explain what they then do. Indeed, are we even entitled to assume that, in a market in disequilibrium, a single price rules? It seems highly unlikely. No trader can know what the equilibrium price is, so sellers must guess at the profit-maximizing price at each moment of time. If individual sellers set different prices during the process of adjustment, as they doubtless will, buyers will want to check more than one seller. But "searching" a market is not costless, so we need *decision rules for buyers who are not perfectly informed*: given what they know or expect, and the costs of search, how persistent does it pay to be?

Models that try to answer these questions, and to derive the behavior of market phenomena from the behavior of individual traders reacting intelligently to the disequilibrium, are currently being developed. These models are at one of the most exciting frontiers of contemporary economic research. They are, for example, likely to shed important new light on the behavior of labor markets as we come to understand better the behavior of imperfectly informed workers searching for jobs (and of imperfectly informed firms searching for workers). The handling of models of this sort requires a substantial investment in technique, particularly probability theory, that is beyond the scope of this book.

That our model of an inflationary process in Section 14.2 was ad hoc needs no emphasis. Its intention was purely illustrative.

Consider next the stock adjustment model. We have, for example, $\dot{K} = \alpha(K^* - K(t))$. Now, K^* is, as we have noted, a function of the rental rate and the wage rate. α itself must depend on the costs of adjustment and on the discounted present value of the profits foregone by not having K^*. It follows that K^* and α, *and therefore $\dot{K}$*, should be determined simultaneously in a model of profit maximization that explicitly includes time and adjustment costs. Such a model is called a model of *intertemporal optimization*. Intertemporal optimization models are increasingly common in economic theory. Unfortunately, they require yet another step in technique, to what is called the calculus of variations, or "optimal control theory."

That the adaptive expectations model is ad hoc must be obvious. It may be a useful approximation for some purposes; but it is certainly not derived from any systematic answer to the question "how might an intelligent individual, with such-and-such information, best predict the value of a variable?" Indeed, this question urgently needs answering, and much current research is being devoted to it.

In Section 14.4 we present a dynamic model of a sort very different from those we have considered so far. It is a model of economic growth, designed to investigate the possibility of stable (equilibrium) growth *paths*. It is not intended as a model of disequilibrium adjustment behavior. Thus, although its assumptions are necessarily restrictive, it is not ad hoc in the sense discussed above.

14.4 A SIMPLE MODEL OF ECONOMIC GROWTH

In 1956, when the modern theory of economic growth was still in its early stages of development, Professor Robert Solow published a growth model[11] in which he studied some of the problems related to equilibrium growth paths with full employment of all resources. In the past, particularly in the 1930s, there had been much concern with the problem of secular unemployment. The worry was often expressed that a rapidly growing capitalist economy might either display unstable cyclical behavior, rocketing off alternatively into uncontrollable booms and ever worsening slumps, or, if it settled down into a stable growth path, necessarily suffer serious permanent unemployment of some factors of production (labor, in particular).

Solow was interested in such questions as whether or not a growing economy could ever produce full employment of all factors, whether or not there was a full-employment natural-rate growth path, and whether a growing economy would converge to this path, or oscillate perpetually around it, or even diverge continuously farther and farther from it.

These are difficult questions, and Solow could not answer all of them even within the context of his own very simplified model. Furthermore, his own model contained assumptions that were a long way from capturing the conditions giving rise to the general worries about growth already mentioned. Nonetheless, he did deal with some questions of general concern, and his model was an important landmark. As is often the case, it is a good idea to be sure we understand some simple models before we go on to more complex ones that capture more of the complexities of the problem with which we are actually concerned. Since we have enough mathematics at our command to understand Solow's basic model, we can use it as an introduction to growth models.

In Solow's model we have only one production function for the

[11] R. M. Solow, "A Contribution to the Theory of Economic Growth," *Quarterly Journal of Economics*, vol. 70, 1956, pp. 65–94.

entire economy. This is usually called an "aggregate" production function: homogeneous capital and labor are the inputs, and are transformed into a single homogeneous output. There is in fact strong evidence that production functions differ among industries, and in the face of this evidence the aggregate production function is a heroic assumption. Nonetheless, it is a simplification well worth trying in the hope that it will help us to increase our understanding without making the model seriously misleading. We therefore assume that total output is a function of two continuously substitutable inputs, labor and capital. Notice particularly that the model does not include any fixed natural resource such as land. Thus the problem of growing population pressing against a fixed supply of land and other resources, that worried the classical economists when they theorized about long-run growth, is absent from Solow's model. Furthermore, the production function remains fixed throughout the whole exercise, and growth in output occurs solely because of an increase in the supply of one or both of the two inputs. Solow is thus talking about growth in a very special sense: the growth of output due to the growth of labor and capital in the context of fixed technology. This is a problem that did concern the classical economists when they worried about stationary economies in which all possible technical advances had already been exploited. It is different from the problem that concerns many of the modern writers on structural unemployment who are concerned rather that the very nature of technical progress—and hence of changes in "the" production function—will create secular unemployment of (at least some types of) labor. A further point to note here is that the model has no monetary sector. Thus the important problems of possible instabilities caused by the behavior of the demand for and/or the supply of money cannot be handled in the model. In spite of these, and other, limitations, something may be learned by studying the behavior of a simple model that captures at least some aspects of growth.

Most growth models pose extremely difficult stability problems. It may, for example, be relatively easy to establish that a particular model has an equilibrium growth path, but very difficult to establish the conditions under which the economy will converge on this path. Solow dealt only with equilibrium growth paths, and he *assumed* that full employment of resources existed. He tried to show that these paths converged to a unique growth path that displayed full employment of all resources *and* a rate of growth of total income equal to the rate of growth of the labor force—the so-called full-employment, natural-rate growth path. This growth path is one in which, although total output grows, output per head remains constant. Thus "growth" in this model is not the kind of growth we refer to in popular discussion (growth in per capita GNP), but this should not surprise us since there is no technical progress in the model.

Let us now consider in more detail the workings of Solow's model. To facilitate comparison of our treatment with Solow's original article we use his notation. (Warning: as a result, the symbols used in this section sometimes have a different meaning from those attached to them in the rest of the book.) There is a single commodity in the economy, and its annual rate of output is given by $Y(t)$. A fraction, s, of this output is saved and the rest, $1 - s$, is consumed. The society's stock of capital, K, is merely the accumulated stock of the single commodity that has been saved in the past. This behavioral assumption ensures that what is saved is exactly what is invested. This allows us to say that current saving determines the rate of growth of society's capital. We write this as

$$\dot{K} = sY \quad , \tag{50}$$

where $\dot{K}$ stands for dK/dt. There are two factors of production, capital, K, and labor, L. Production is given by a production function

$$Y = F(K, L) \tag{51}$$

that displays constant returns to scale.

We are now going to engage in some manipulations that, as we have so often observed before, may seem arbitrary at first sight. When you have some experience with growth theory you will begin to develop a feel for the tactics required to manipulate such models. In the meantime you will be able to follow what is done step by step even though the reason for taking a particular step may not be readily apparent until you have completed all the steps.

As a first step in these manipulations we substitute (51) into (50) and we obtain

$$\dot{K} = sF(K, L) \quad . \tag{52}$$

We now assume that the labor force is growing at a constant rate, n. Thus labor supply is a function of time, t, and we can write

$$L(t) = L_o e^{nt} \quad , \tag{53}$$

where $L(t)$ is the labor force at time t, L_0 is the initial labor force at time t_0, and n is its rate of growth. We want to find out if the capital:labor ratio can always be such as to ensure full employment no matter how fast the labor force may be growing. We also wish to know if this ratio will approach some stable equilibrium level. To investigate further we *assume* that the labor force is fully employed. Given this assumption we can identify $L(t)$ with the amount of labor input in the production function. This allows us to substitute (53) into (52) to obtain

$$\dot{K} = sF(K, L_0 e^{nt}) \quad . \tag{54}$$

This equation tells us the time path that capital accumulation, $\dot{K}$, must follow if labor is to remain fully employed. If we were to solve the equation for K, we would get the time path that the community's stock of capital ($K = \int \dot{K}\, dt$) must follow if full employment is to be maintained.

We wish to know if there is always a time path for capital accumulation, $\dot{K}$, that will ensure full employment whatever the rate of growth of the labor force, n, might be. Equation (54) tells us what $\dot{K}$ *must* be if full employment is to be maintained. It now helps to study the behavior of the capital:labor ratio. To do this we introduce a new variable, r, to stand for the ratio of capital to labor. Thus $r = K/L$ or $K = rL$, and substituting (53) into this expression, we have

$$K = rL_0 e^{nt} \quad . \tag{55}$$

We now need to differentiate (55) with respect to time to get an equation for the rate of change of the capital stock (i.e., investment). Although this may look like a formidable task, it proves to be easily accomplished by a straightforward application of the product rule. There are two arguments that can vary with time, so we set $v = r$ and $u = L_0 e^{nt}$. The product rule gives us

$$\frac{dK}{dt} = u\frac{dv}{dt} + v\frac{du}{dt} \quad .$$

We know from Section 13.6 that $d(L_0 e^{nt})/dt = nL_0 e^{nt}$. Thus the time derivative of (55) is given by

$$\dot{K} = \dot{r}L_0 e^{nt} + nrL_0 e^{nt}$$
$$= (\dot{r} + nr)L_0 e^{nt} \quad . \tag{56}$$

We can infer from (56) what happens to the capital:labor ratio, r, as labor grows at its given rate n. We now take the crucial step of substituting (56) into (54), which tells us how capital is growing given that labor is fully employed and a fraction, s, of full employment output is saved each period. Thus we obtain

$$(\dot{r} + nr)L_0 e^{nt} = sF(K, L_0 e^{nt}) \quad . \tag{57}$$

To manipulate (57) into a more meaningful form we make use of the assumption of constant returns to scale. This assumption means that the production function is homogeneous of degree 1, and, as we saw in Chapter 9, if we multiply all the variables in such a function by λ, we multiply the value of the function by λ. Thus we can *divide* all the *variables* by λ and *multiply* the whole *function* by λ and leave the whole unchanged. We now perform this operation, taking $L_0 e^{nt}$ as our λ. This gives us

$$(\dot{r} + nr)L_0 e^{nt} = sL_0 e^{nt} F\left(\frac{K}{L_0 e^{nt}}, 1\right) \quad . \tag{58}$$

Next divide both sides of (58) by $L_0 e^{nt}$ to give

$$\dot{r} + nr = sF\left(\frac{K}{L_0 e^{nt}}, 1\right) \quad .$$

Now subtract nr from both sides:

$$\dot{r} = sF\left(\frac{K}{L_0 e^{nt}}, 1\right) - nr \quad .$$

Finally write r for the capital:labor ratio, $K/L_0 e^{nt}$, to give

$$\dot{r} = sF(r, 1) - nr \quad . \tag{59}$$

This is a differential equation with the capital:labor ratio, r, as its only variable.

First consider the condition for the capital:labor ratio to be constant over time. This means that $\dot{r} = 0$, and, for this to be so, capital must be growing at the same rate, n, as labor. In this situation we see from (59) that

$$nr = sF(r, 1) \quad . \tag{60}$$

Next consider the behavior of the economy when the capital:labor ratio is changing, that is, $nr \neq sF(r, 1)$. We first consider two limiting cases. If $s = 0$, there is no capital accumulation, and (59) reduces to $\dot{r} = -nr$ or

$$\frac{\dot{r}}{r} = -n \quad . \tag{61}$$

This says that the proportionate change in the capital:labor ratio is *minus* the proportionate rate of change in the labor force. If the labor force is growing at 3 percent per annum, for example, then the capital:labor ratio is declining at 3 percent per annum. To obtain the second limiting case assume that $n = 0$, that is, the labor force is constant over time. Now (59) reduces to $\dot{r} = sF(r, 1)$. This has more intuitive appeal if we express $\dot{r}$ in proportionate terms, which requires some manipulation. First, we divide both sides of $\dot{r} = sF(r, 1)$ by r:

$$\frac{\dot{r}}{r} = \frac{s}{r} F(r, 1) \quad .$$

r is the capital:labor ratio, and it is more convenient to replace r by K/L:

$$\frac{\dot{r}}{r} = s\frac{L}{K}F\left(\frac{K}{L}, 1\right) \quad .$$

Finally we multiply both the inputs by L and divide the value of the function by the same amount [a procedure we justified in connection with (58)]. This gives us

$$\frac{\dot{r}}{r} = \frac{sF(K, L)}{K} \quad . \tag{62}$$

(62) says that the proportionate change in the capital:labor ratio is equal (in this case in which $n = 0$) to the proportionate change in the capital stock (which is in turn equal to the amount of total production saved divided by the existing capital stock).

Equations (61) and (62) show that $\dot{r}$ in (59) is the sum of two components, the first related to the change in labor, (61), and the second related to the change in capital, (62). The equation itself is difficult to interpret because it shows $\dot{r}$ instead of $\dot{r}/r$ as the dependent variable, but, as we have seen, both terms on the right-hand side of the expression are easily interpreted when the dependent variable is made $\dot{r}/r$.

We are now able to see how the economy behaves when the capital:labor ratio is changing. In this case we have $\dot{r} \neq 0$, and (60) tells us that $nr \neq sF(r, 1)$. To see what happens in such cases we plot both nr and $sF(r, 1)$ in Figure 14.2 (copied from Solow), where r is plotted

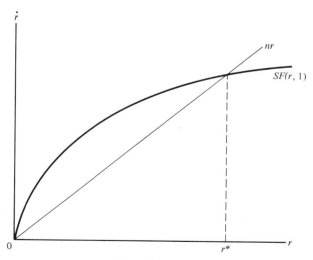

Figure 14.2

on the x-axis and $\dot{r}$ on the y-axis. We have not so far encountered diagrams of this sort, and we must explain carefully how the lines are obtained. To obtain the line nr we set $sF(r, 1) = 0$ and plot the relation between $\dot{r}$ and r, ignoring the negative sign. This line, which has a slope of n, tells us how fast the capital:output ratio would be declining for a given rate of growth of the labor force if savings were zero. To obtain the line $sF(r, 1)$ we let nr be zero and plot the relation between $\dot{r}$ and r given by $\dot{r} = sF(r, 1)$. This line tells us how fast the capital:output ratio would be growing as a result of capital accumulation if the labor force were not growing. If both s and n are nonzero, then the actual value of $\dot{r}$ will be the *difference* between nr and $sF(r, 1)$. This difference is represented by the vertical distance between the two lines. When the line $sF(r, 1)$ is above nr the effect of capital accumulation outweighs that of population growth, and $\dot{r}$ will be positive. When nr lies above $sF(r, 1)$ the reverse is true, and $\dot{r}$ will be negative. Where the two curves intersect, the negative effect on r of population growth exactly balances the positive effect of capital accumulation, and r will be constant at the value r^* with $\dot{r} = 0$.

It remains to consider the shape of the curve $sF(r, 1)$. The expression $F(r, 1)$ may be interpreted as the total product curve with labor input held constant at one unit and capital as the variable factor. In this case r equals K, since $K/1 = K$. The whole term $sF(r, 1)$ shows the amount of this total output that is saved and invested per worker. The assumption of diminishing returns to one factor is sufficient to ensure that the slope of $F(r, 1)$ and therefore of $sF(r, 1)$ must be declining as r is increased. The curve drawn in Figure 14.2 is consistent with the Cobb-Douglas production function. We saw in Chapter 9 that with the Cobb-Douglas function diminishing returns occur over all ranges of r, so that the slope of $sF(r, 1)$ must decline from the outset.

If the economy is at r^* in Figure 14.2, then $nr = sF(r, 1)$, and, from (59), $\dot{r} = 0$, which says that the capital:output ratio is not changing. This is an equilibrium growth situation in which capital and labor are growing at the same proportionate rate so that r remains constant. Because of the constant returns to scale assumption, the rate of growth of output is exactly equal to the rates of growth of capital and labor, and income per head will be constant.[12] Now consider what will happen if the economy is at a point where $r \neq r^*$. To the right of r^*, $r > r^*$, $nr > sF(r, 1)$, and from (59) we know that $\dot{r} < 0$. Thus actual r will decrease toward r^*. To the left of r^*, $sF(r, 1) > nr$, and from (59) we know that $\dot{r} > 0$. Actual r will increase toward r^*. Thus the model dis-

---

[12] Don't forget that there is no technical progress in this model, that is, the function F is constant with respect to time.

plays negative feedback: the capital:output ratio r will move toward r^*, where the rate of growth of capital is equal to the rate of growth of labor and there is full employment at a constant level of per capita output.

The equilibrium shown in Figure 14.2 necessarily exists if the production function is Cobb-Douglas[13] because the slope of $sF(r, 1)$ is infinite at the origin and falls steadily as r is increased. Other production functions can give different results, but the restriction usually placed on production functions, that the marginal product of capital eventually approaches zero as capital approaches infinity, labor held constant $(F_K \to 0$ as $K \to \infty)$, is sufficient to guarantee that if $sF(r, 1)$ cuts nr at all, it will eventually cut it from above and produce a stable equilibrium growth path.[14]

This is as far as we shall take Solow's model, although there is more to it than we have presented here. What the model does establish, among other things, is that full employment of resources is not necessarily inconsistent with growth that is caused by increases in the supplies of labor and capital and which occurs at a rate such that real income per head remains constant (provided, among other things, that there are no resources in fixed supply).

QUESTIONS

1. a. Analyze the following market model for stability:

$$q^d = 10 - 15p$$
$$q^s = 15p - 10$$
$$\frac{dp}{dt} = 5E \qquad (E \text{ is excess demand}) \quad .$$

b. Do the same for the following:

---

[13] With Cobb-Douglas we have

$$\frac{\partial q}{\partial K} = \alpha K^{\alpha-1} L^\beta$$

$$= \frac{\alpha L^\beta}{K^{1-\alpha}} \quad .$$

With labor held constant at unity, this gives

$$\frac{\partial q}{\partial K} = \frac{\alpha}{K^{1-\alpha}} \quad .$$

By inspection the value of this marginal productivity function approaches infinity as K approaches zero and approaches zero as K approaches infinity.

[14] If the function $sF(r, 1)$ were not Cobb-Douglas, it might have a slope less than nr at the origin that declined continuously as r increased: there would be no equilibrium at all. Although this is a possibility it is not one in which we are presently interested.

$$q^d = 15p - 10$$
$$q^s = 10 - 15p$$
$$\frac{dp}{dt} = 5E \quad.$$

2. Consider the macro-model in Eqs. (33)–(36) of Chapter 12. Investigate the stability of the adjustment process using the same technique as was used in the text of Chapter 14 to handle the model of the single competitive market. (This is an important question and it will be worth your while to spend quite a lot of time in working it out.)

3. Consider a Cobb-Douglas production function in which technical progress is introduced by making A a function of time rather than a constant. Make the simple assumption that technical progress occurs at a constant rate so that

$$A(t) = A_0 e^{rt}$$

and production at time t is given by

$$q(t) = A_0 e^{rt} L_{(t)}^{\alpha} K_{(t)}^{1-\alpha}$$

where α is not changed by technical progress.
   a. How do the marginal products of labor and capital change over time if the inputs are constant?
   b. How does the marginal rate of substitution change over time?
   c. How are relative shares affected by the passage of time?
   d. What is the rate of growth of output if labor and capital are constant?
   e. Write the total differential of the function.
   f. Find the rate of growth of output if capital grows at the rate n and labor at the rate m.

4. National income in two economies is growing at the constant rates n in economy 1 and r in economy 2, where $n > r$. In year zero national income was A in economy 1 and B in economy 2.
   a. If $B > A$, at what time will economy 1 overtake economy 2?
   b. Show that if $r > n$ (and with $B > A$) the ratio of the two economies' incomes diverges constantly over time.
   c. If $n = r$ but $A > B$, (i) show the relations between the percentage rates of growth in 1 and 2, (ii) show the ratios of income in 1 and 2, and (iii) show what happens to the absolute difference between the incomes of countries 1 and 2.

5. A Ruritanian National Plan plumped for a target rate of growth in GNP: Call it r percent. Subsequent exercises suggested that this rate of growth would require the labor force to grow at, say, n percent, $n > 0$.
   a. What would be the rate of growth in income per capita?
   b. What can you infer about the objective function of the planners?

6. a. Are the following equivalent to each other: $d \log Y$, dY/Y, % change in Y?

b. Is it true that if there is no change in Y then both d log Y and dY are zero?

c. Take logs and derivatives of $M = kPX$ and show that money balances and prices change in equal proportions, *ceteris paribus*.

7. a. Which of the following two statements characterizes the "flight from money" model of inflation:

   i. Excess demand for goods gives rise to an excess supply of money, and the subsequent attempt to reduce money holdings causes prices to rise.

   ii. The expectation of rising prices makes money balances less attractive relative to consumption. As a result, money balances are reduced, which in turn causes prices to rise even more than would have been the case if the price change had not been anticipated.

   b. Review the monetary model given in this chapter and indicate behavioral equations.

8. a. What is the nature of a solution to a differential equation such as $dy/dx - 60y - 20 = 0$?

   b. Assuming that $y = y_0$ when $x = 0$, would $y = (y_0 + \frac{1}{3})e^{60x} - \frac{1}{3}$ be a solution to the equation in part a?

9. Solve the following differential equations.
   a. $2dy/dx + 4y - 10 = 0$
   b. $ady/dx + by = c$
   c. $y = 3dy/dx$

10. a. If $dy/dt = \frac{1}{4}(y^\circ - y(t))$, what is the "time constant?" (Hint: See Section 16.3).

    b. Suppose that the initial disturbance is one unit of y, that is, $y^\circ - y(0) = 1$. How long would it take to remove 0.632 units of the discrepancy?

11. Outline a stock adjustment model of your own studying or learning behavior.

12. Let K represent the stock of capital in the economy.
    a. In the model $K = \alpha(K^\circ - K(t))$, why might α be a variable rather than a constant?

    b. Supposing α is a variable, suggest at least one economic variable of which it might be a function.

13. a. In the Solow model, does a stable equilibrium growth path imply that output attains a particular level and then remains at that level indefinitely?

    b. If population growth is zero, does output attain a fixed level?

Introduction to Matrix Algebra

Matrix algebra involves a new notation and many definitions and rules, seemingly arbitrary, and all needing to be memorized. It is, however, well worth persevering, since the methods we are about to develop are extremely powerful and will allow us to tackle a wide range of economic problems previously beyond us. This is essentially because matrix algebra provides methods for dealing with sets of *simultaneous* relationships involving many variables. With the tools of this chapter, we shall no longer be restricted to partial equilibrium analysis and macro-models that can be reduced to a single equation or handled graphically. Thus we shall be able to discuss input–output analysis, and to investigate more sophisticated Keynesian models in which the price level is a variable as well as income and employment. We note here that matrix algebra has important uses in statistics, which are beyond the scope of this book,[1] and permits a thorough and rigorous development of demand theory and the theory of the firm in the n-variable case.[2] This last application allows the full comparative static exploitation of the maximization hypothesis. We shall not take it up since it requires theorems on what are called "quadratic forms," and these we regard as too ambitious for a first course. Finally, some

---

[1] They will be found, for example, in two well-known texts on econometrics. See J. Johnston, *Econometric Methods*, McGraw-Hill, New York, 1963, and Arthur S. Goldberger, *Econometric Theory*, Wiley, New York, 1964.

[2] See Sir John Hicks, *Value and Capital*, 2nd ed., Oxford University Press, London, 1946. For a textbook treatment, see J. M. Henderson and R. E. Quandt, *Microeconomic Theory: A Mathematical Approach*, 2nd ed., McGraw-Hill, New York, 1971.

encouragement: as familiarity with matrix algebra grows, so does perception of its logical structure, and, as is always the case, the understanding of a structure relieves the tax on the memory required to store what seem to be arbitrary and unrelated bits. Nonetheless, it is essential to become familiar with the rules and operations. Familiarity comes only with practice. To facilitate practice, we have divided the questions at the end of this chapter by sections. We strongly recommend that the questions be done, section by section, before going on. Some theorems that we do not use, and hence do not prove in the text, are also illustrated in the questions.

15.1 DEFINITION OF A MATRIX

We now define a matrix as a *rectangular array of numbers* and indicate that the array is a matrix by enclosing it in square brackets. Thus

$$\mathbf{A} = \begin{bmatrix} 2 & 3 \\ 7 & 4 \end{bmatrix} \quad \text{and} \quad \mathbf{B} = \begin{bmatrix} 1 & 3 \\ 0 & 5 \\ -1 & 1 \end{bmatrix}$$

are both matrices, whereas

$$\begin{matrix} 1 & 2 & 3 \\ 2 & 7 & \\ 1 & & \end{matrix}$$

is not a matrix, not being rectangular. We shall shortly learn to *operate* on and with matrices, but first we require some rules and notation.

First, we notice that the *elements* of a matrix are numbers, and that a matrix consists of an array or set of numbers, each allocated to a particular position in the array. (They might be real numbers or imaginary numbers, but we shall be concerned here only with matrices whose elements are all real.) Taking advantage of the generality of algebraic notation, we may write a matrix as, for instance,

$$\mathbf{A} = \begin{bmatrix} a_{11} & a_{12} & a_{13} \\ a_{21} & a_{22} & a_{23} \\ a_{31} & a_{32} & a_{33} \end{bmatrix}.$$

Here the location of each element in the array is indicated by its subscripts. Thus we can see that a_{23} is in the second row and third column. The rule is that *the first subscript gives the row and the second the column*. In general, the element a_{ij} is in the ith row and the jth column. Notice that a subscript, such as 23 or ij, is to be read in *order* as "two-three" or "eye-jay": it does *not* mean 23, or 2 times 3. The elements of the subscript might be divided by a comma, as 2, 3, or i, j, but as long as these ordered pairs of numbers appear only in subscripts there is no room for ambiguity, and the comma is omitted.

We have already used boldface capital letters ($\mathbf{A}$, $\mathbf{B}$) to denote matrices, and, when we have written out all of the elements of a matrix we have enclosed the whole array in square brackets. This is standard practice, and we shall adhere to it. It is obviously convenient to be able to refer to a matrix compactly, by a single symbol; and the square bracket notation serves to distinguish matrices from *determinants*, which we shall soon meet. It is also sometimes convenient to denote a matrix by

$$\mathbf{A} = [a_{ij}] \quad,$$

which simply says that a_{ij} is the characteristic element of an otherwise unspecified matrix, $\mathbf{A}$.

To describe the size of a matrix, we define its *order*. A matrix is said to be of *order n by m (written $n \times m$) if it has n rows and m columns* (note again the convention that we refer to rows first, then columns). We may write an $n \times m$ matrix as follows:

$$\mathbf{A} = \begin{bmatrix} a_{11} & a_{12} & \cdots & a_{1m} \\ a_{21} & & & a_{2m} \\ \vdots & & & \vdots \\ a_{n1} & & \cdots & a_{nm} \end{bmatrix} \quad.$$

The notation embodied here is worth careful study. Since there are n rows, the subscripts in the first column run from 11 to $n1$, those in the second from 12 to $n2$, etc. Similarly, along the rows the subscripts run from 11 to $1m$, from 21 to $2m$, and finally from $n1$ to nm. An element that is in the same row *and* column, say the ith, has identical subscripts, such as 11, 22, or ii. If a matrix has the same number of rows and columns, say n, it is said to be *square, of order $n \times n$*. Then the elements with identical subscripts, $a_{11}, a_{22}, \ldots, a_{ii}, \ldots,$ a_{nn}, connect the "corners" of the matrix. These elements compose what is called the *principal diagonal* of the matrix.

So much (for the moment) for notation. At this stage it is natural to ask, perhaps with some impatience, "But what *is* a matrix?" The correct, and infuriating, reply is that it is a rectangular array of numbers. As for what we can do with it, we shall just have to develop some operational rules and see. But it may help to consider two natural ways in which matrices arise. Suppose first that we have observations on a number of economic variables, over time. The variables might be national income, consumption, imports, etc. Say that there are K variables. They have been recorded, perhaps annually or quarterly, so that we have observations over, say, T periods of time. It would be natural to lay out these observations as a *data matrix*, with T rows and K columns. We should tabulate the data as

$$\mathbf{X} = [x_{tk}] \quad ,$$

noting that t runs from 1 to T, and that k runs from 1 to K. National income accounts, and similar statistical sources, are largely laid out in the form of *data matrices*.

A second sort of matrix is a *coefficient matrix*. Since we are chiefly interested in developing useful operations for coefficient matrices, we shall only give an example now. Suppose that we have two simultaneous equations in which x_1 and x_2 are multiplied by *constant* coefficients:

$$4x_1 + 7x_2 = 11$$
$$2x_1 + x_2 = 3 \quad .$$

We write the coefficient matrix as

$$\begin{bmatrix} 4 & 7 \\ 2 & 1 \end{bmatrix} \quad .$$

We shall see shortly that matrix notation affords a compact way of writing simultaneous equations, and that matrix operations afford convenient ways of solving them. If you care to turn back to the simultaneous equations we encountered in Eqs. (32 and 33) of Section 10.7 (constrained maximization in the n-variable case), you will probably agree that some help would be welcome.

15.2 ADDITION AND MULTIPLICATION

The matrix $\mathbf{B}$ is equal to matrix $\mathbf{A}$ only *if every element of $\mathbf{B}$ is equal to the corresponding element of* $\mathbf{A}$. We may express this as the condition

$$b_{ij} = a_{ij} \qquad (\text{all } i, j) \quad .$$

It is obvious that two matrices can be equal only if they are of the same order. Thus

$$\mathbf{A} = \begin{bmatrix} 1 & 0 & 7 \\ 2 & 11 & -1 \\ -5 & 1 & 0 \end{bmatrix} = \begin{bmatrix} 1 & 0 & 7 \\ 2 & 11 & -1 \\ -5 & 1 & 0 \end{bmatrix} = \mathbf{B} \quad ,$$

but neither **C** nor **D** equals **A** where

$$\mathbf{C} = \begin{bmatrix} 1 & 0 & 7 \\ 2 & 11 & -1 \\ -5 & 1 & 0 \\ 2 & 1 & 2 \end{bmatrix} \quad \text{and} \quad \mathbf{D} = \begin{bmatrix} 2 & 11 & -1 \\ 1 & 0 & 7 \\ -5 & 1 & 0 \end{bmatrix}.$$

(**C** has an extra row; in **D**, the first two rows have been interchanged.)

We now define the *operation of scalar multiplication*. We must first, however, define a scalar. A scalar is simply a number, such as 3 or λ. We can, if we like, define a scalar as a one-by-one matrix. All the algebra we have done in previous chapters may now be referred to as ordinary, or scalar, algebra. It may seem unnecessary and pretentious to introduce a new and exotic word to refer to a common-orgarden number. The usage is, however, justified by its convenience: we want to have an unmistakable way of indicating that we are *not* referring to a matrix. Multiplication of a matrix **A** by a scalar λ is written

$$\lambda \mathbf{A} .$$

The rule is that *each element of* **A** *is to be multiplied by* λ. Thus

$$\lambda \mathbf{A} = \begin{bmatrix} \lambda a_{11} & \lambda a_{12} & \cdots & \lambda a_{1m} \\ \vdots & & & \vdots \\ \lambda a_{n1} & & \cdots & \lambda a_{nm} \end{bmatrix}.$$

If $\lambda = 2$ and

$$\mathbf{A} = \begin{bmatrix} 0 & 0.1 \\ -2 & 7 \end{bmatrix},$$

then

$$\lambda \mathbf{A} = \begin{bmatrix} 0 & 0.2 \\ -4 & 14 \end{bmatrix}.$$

The next operation to define is *matrix addition*. As might be expected from the definition of equality and the operation of scalar multiplication the rule is to *add corresponding elements*. Thus if

$$\mathbf{C} = \mathbf{A} + \mathbf{B}$$

$$c_{ij} = a_{ij} + b_{ij} .$$

As an example, if

$$\mathbf{A} = \begin{bmatrix} 0 & 0.2 \\ -4 & 14 \end{bmatrix} \quad \text{and} \quad \mathbf{B} = \begin{bmatrix} -1 & 2 \\ 4 & -4 \end{bmatrix},$$

then

$$C = \begin{bmatrix} -1 & 2.2 \\ 0 & 10 \end{bmatrix} .$$

It will be evident that, whereas we can multiply any matrix by a scalar, *we can only add matrices of the same order.* Thus if

$$A = \begin{bmatrix} 0 & 0.2 \\ -4 & 14 \end{bmatrix} \quad \text{and} \quad D = \begin{bmatrix} -1 & 2 \\ 4 & -4 \\ 2 & 1 \end{bmatrix} ,$$

$A + D$ is *not defined.*

It will now appear that we have a program: to find the matrix equivalents of all the familiar operations of scalar algebra. This indeed is the program, and we shall see that we can complete most of it. Following this program it appears that we should next define *matrix subtraction.* We shall find a rule for the operation, but a new definition is redundant, as we may easily see. Suppose that we want to subtract B from A. All we have to do is apply successively the operations of scalar multiplication and addition. Thus

$$A - B = A + (\lambda B) \qquad \text{where } \lambda = -1 .$$

The *procedure* is, of course, to subtract each element of B from the corresponding element of A.

The next item on the agenda is obviously *matrix multiplication.* This is at first sight arbitrary, nonintuitive, and complicated. The best thing to do is to lay out the rules, and then to see that they produce something usable and something that corresponds with intuition in familiar cases. Let us start by explaining an example. When we multiply two matrices A and B to get C each element of C is the sum of a series of products obtained by multiplying one element of A with one element of B. The element c_{11} of C is the element in the first row and the first column of C. It is obtained by taking the first *row* of A and the first *column* of B, multiplying together "corresponding" elements, and then summing them. When we say "corresponding" elements we mean: read from left to right across A's row and from top to bottom down B's first column and multiply the first element in each; then multiply the second pair; continue to the end of the row (column); finally, add up. The element c_{21} is in the second row and first column of C. It is obtained by taking the second row of A and the first column of B and repeating the procedure described above. Thus the element c_{ij} of C is in the ith row and the jth column of C, and it is found by multiplying corresponding elements from the ith row of A and the jth column of B and summing.

Let us now consider an example. If

$$\mathbf{A} = \begin{bmatrix} 2 & 3 \\ 1 & -4 \end{bmatrix} \quad \text{and} \quad \mathbf{B} = \begin{bmatrix} 1 & 10 \\ -2 & 5 \end{bmatrix} \ ,$$

then

$$\mathbf{AB} = \mathbf{C} = \begin{bmatrix} -4 & 35 \\ 9 & -10 \end{bmatrix} \ .$$

The element $c_{11} = -4$ was obtained from $(2)(1) + (3)(-2)$. It follows immediately that to multiply $\mathbf{A}$ and $\mathbf{B}$ together, $\mathbf{A}$ must have the same number of columns (i.e., the number of elements across any row) as $\mathbf{B}$ has rows (i.e., the number of elements down any column). If this is not so, we cannot apply our rule for multiplication. We shall say more about this below.

Now let us express our "row-by-column" rule more formally. If

$$\mathbf{C} = \mathbf{AB} \ ,$$

then

$$c_{ij} = \sum_k a_{ik} b_{kj} \ .$$

Notice that i and j are fixed, while k varies: it may be called the "free index." Thus

$$\sum_k a_{ik} b_{kj} = a_{i1} b_{1j} + a_{i2} b_{2j} + a_{i3} b_{3j} + \cdots \ .$$

The formal expression $\sum_k a_{ik} b_{kj}$ is therefore a compact way of writing the directions for obtaining an element of $\mathbf{C}$. To obtain the ijth element of the product matrix, $\mathbf{C}$, we are directed to run along the ith *row* of $\mathbf{A}$, multiplying each element by the corresponding element of the jth *column* of $\mathbf{B}$, and to add up. See Figure 15.1.

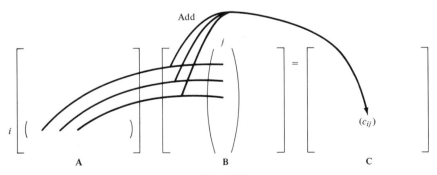

Figure 15.1

This is not as complicated as it looks, and a little practice will make it seem perfectly routine. There are, however, a few more points to make about matrix multiplication. Before we make them, let us apply the formal rule to another example. Suppose that we want to find the product, **AB**, where

$$\mathbf{A} = \begin{bmatrix} 1 & 4 & 1 \\ 3 & 2 & 2 \end{bmatrix} \quad \text{and} \quad \mathbf{B} = \begin{bmatrix} 2 & 3 \\ 2 & 4 \\ 0 & 1 \end{bmatrix}.$$

To find the first element, c_{11}, of **C**, we simply perform the operation indicated by

$$\sum_{k=1}^{3} a_{1k} b_{k1}$$

$$= a_{11} b_{11} + a_{12} b_{21} + a_{13} b_{31}$$

$$= 1 \cdot 2 + 4 \cdot 2 + 1 \cdot 0 = 10 .$$

Similarly,

$$c_{12} = \sum_{k=1}^{3} a_{1k} b_{k2}$$

$$= a_{11} b_{12} + a_{12} b_{22} + a_{13} b_{32}$$

$$= 1 \cdot 3 + 4 \cdot 4 + 1 \cdot 1 = 20 .$$

We thus obtain

$$\mathbf{C} = \begin{bmatrix} 10 & 20 \\ 10 & 10 \end{bmatrix} .$$

(We have not spelled out the derivation of c_{21} and c_{22}: it is a good exercise to check now for yourself.)

The rule for multiplication is "row by column" where the elements in a row of **A** are multiplied into the elements of a column of **B** and the product of each pair of numbers is summed; the resulting number becomes an element of **C** with its row determined by the row of **A** and its column by the column of **B** that went to make it up. We see again a restriction on the *possibility* of matrix multiplication: there must be the same number of elements in a *row* of **A** and a *column* of **B**. But the number of elements in a row of **A** is the number of columns in **A**, and the number of elements in a column of **B** is the number of rows in **B**. Hence the operation of multiplication, denoted by **AB**, is possible only if **A** has the same number of columns as **B** has rows. If this condition is satisfied, **A** and **B** are said to *conform* for multiplication. Formally, if **A** is $n \times k$ and **B** is $k \times m$, **A** and **B** conform. An obvious and useful exercise, to check that the rules are clear, is to work out the order of $C = AB$. We construct a row of **C** by multiplying the corresponding row of **A** by a column of **B**, and adding, column by column, whence **C** has an many elements in a row (as many columns) as **B** has columns. Hence **C** is $? \times m$. But we also construct a column of **C** by multiplying each row of **A** by a column of **B**, and adding, in turn, whence a column of **C** has as many elements as **A** has rows, whence **C** has as many rows as **A**, that is, **C** is $n \times m$. (You should compare this result with the order of **C** in our last example.) To summarize, if

$$\text{\textbf{A} is } n \times k \quad \text{and} \quad \text{\textbf{B} is } k \times m \quad ,$$

$$\text{\textbf{A} and \textbf{B} } conform \quad ,$$

and if

$$C = AB \quad ,$$

$$\text{\textbf{C} is } n \times m \quad .$$

We now discover something that has no analogy in scalar algebra. Suppose that **A** is $n \times k$ and **B** is $k \times m$. Then $C = AB$ exists, and **C** is $n \times m$. What about **BA**? In scalar algebra, $ab = ba$. This is called the law of commutation. But consider **BA**. **B** is $k \times m$ and **A** is $n \times k$. If m and n are unequal, the number of columns in the first matrix is not equal to the number of rows in the second. Thus the product **BA** is not defined. We say that **B** and **A** do *not* conform for multiplication. Thus it is not true of matrix multiplication that it follows the commutative law of scalar multiplication: if **AB** exists, it does not necessarily follow that **BA** does, and vice versa. We also note the following: whereas a scalar may be defined as a one-by-one matrix, scalar and matrix *multiplication* are differently defined.

It is now useful to try the following problem: what conditions must we impose on **A** and **B** to ensure that both **AB** and **BA** exist? The answer should be fairly obvious. Suppose that **A** is $r \times s$ and **B** is $j \times k$; then for **AB** to exist, we require that $s = j$. Let us put $n = s = j$. The two matrices are now $r \times n$ and $n \times k$. The product **BA** involves the multiplication of an $n \times k$ matrix by an $r \times n$ matrix. If this is to be defined, we must have $k = r$. Let us put $m = k = r$. Then **A** is $m \times n$ and **B** is $n \times m$, whence **AB** is $m \times m$ and **BA** is $n \times n$. Now both products exist, but it is clear that **AB** and **BA** are of the same order only if $n = m$. This in turn requires that they both be *square matrices of the same order*, in which case both **AB** and **BA** are of the same order.

Let us illustrate the case in which **AB** and **BA** both exist but are not of the same order. Suppose that **A** is 3×2 and **B** is 2×3. Then **AB** is the product of 3×2 and 2×3: it is 3×3. **BA** is the product of 2×3 and 3×2: it is 2×2. Diagrammatically,

$$3\begin{bmatrix} \cdot & \cdot \\ \cdot & \cdot \\ \cdot & \cdot \end{bmatrix}_{2} \quad 2\begin{bmatrix} \cdot & \cdot & \cdot \\ \cdot & \cdot & \cdot \end{bmatrix}_{3} = 3\begin{bmatrix} \cdot & \cdot & \cdot \\ \cdot & \cdot & \cdot \\ \cdot & \cdot & \cdot \end{bmatrix}_{3}$$

and

$$2\begin{bmatrix} \cdot & \cdot & \cdot \\ \cdot & \cdot & \cdot \end{bmatrix}_{3} \quad 3\begin{bmatrix} \cdot & \cdot \\ \cdot & \cdot \\ \cdot & \cdot \end{bmatrix}_{2} = 2\begin{bmatrix} \cdot & \cdot \\ \cdot & \cdot \end{bmatrix}_{2} .$$

Since **AB** and **BA** are not necessarily equal, even if both exist, the *order of multiplication* is important (which it is not in scalar algebra), and it is convenient to have some terminology. The product **AB** is said to be **A** *postmultiplied* by **B**, or **B** *premultiplied* by **A**. Similarly, **BA** is **B** postmultiplied by **A**, or **A** premultiplied by **B**.

Finally, we notice that, even if **BA** and **AB** both exist and are of the same order (i.e., **A** and **B** are both $n \times n$) it is not necessarily the case that **AB** = **BA**. You should evaluate for yourself **AB** and **BA** where

$$\mathbf{A} = \begin{bmatrix} 2 & 3 \\ 1 & 1 \end{bmatrix} \quad \text{and} \quad \mathbf{B} = \begin{bmatrix} 1 & 1 \\ 2 & 1 \end{bmatrix} .$$

For our purposes, the conditions on which **AB** = **BA** (**A** and **B** *commute*, like scalars) are not important. What matters is that the matrix product is defined if and only if the matrices conform for the required order of multiplication.

15.3 VECTORS

To complete the program, we should now develop the matrix analogy of division in scalar algebra. We are accustomed to defining $1/a$, or a^{-1}, so that $a \cdot a^{-1} = 1$. The matrix analogy is the matrix $\mathbf{A}^{-1}$ such that $\mathbf{A} \cdot \mathbf{A}^{-1} = \mathbf{I}$. But what is **I**? The analogy suggests that **I** will be the matrix equivalent of 1. The relevant characteristic of the scalar 1 is that $1 \cdot a = a \cdot 1 = a$. Thus we seek a matrix **I** such that

$$\mathbf{IA} = \mathbf{AI} = \mathbf{A} .$$

It is easily verified that **I** is the square matrix, of appropriate order, with 1's down the principal diagonal and zeros elsewhere. It is, for example, easily checked that

$$\begin{bmatrix} 2 & 1 \\ 3 & 1 \end{bmatrix} \begin{bmatrix} 1 & 0 \\ 0 & 1 \end{bmatrix} = \begin{bmatrix} 2 & 1 \\ 3 & 1 \end{bmatrix} \quad .$$

I is appropriately called the *unit matrix*, or the *identity* matrix (where a reminder is helpful, it may be written $\mathbf{I}_n$, *the unit matrix of order n*). This is simple enough. Unfortunately, $\mathbf{A}^{-1}$, called the *inverse matrix*, the analogy of the scalar reciprocal a^{-1}, is a good deal more complicated to derive. A substantial digression will be helpful.

First, we introduce *vectors*. A row vector is a row of numbers, and a column vector a column of numbers. Thus if **x** is a row vector,

$$\mathbf{x} = [x_1, x_2, \ldots, x_n] \quad ,$$

whereas if **x** is a column vector,

$$\mathbf{x} = \begin{bmatrix} x_1 \\ x_2 \\ \cdot \\ \cdot \\ \cdot \\ x_n \end{bmatrix} \quad .$$

As with matrices, we see that *order* matters: a vector is a row or column of numbers, written in a certain order, but is not itself a number. We may also see that a convenient notation is useful. We write **x**, in boldface type, for a vector, and x_i for the element. We also use square brackets to denote a row vector, and curly brackets, or braces, to denote a column vector. Thus $\{x_1, \ldots, x_n\}$ indicates a column vector.

More notation: if **x** is a column vector, then we call the row formed of the elements of **x**, in the same order, the *transpose* of **x**, denoted by **x'**. Thus if

$$\mathbf{x} = \begin{bmatrix} x_1 \\ x_2 \\ x_3 \end{bmatrix} \quad , \quad \mathbf{x}' = [x_1, x_2, x_3] \quad .$$

We may take advantage of the bracket-and-brace notation to write this more compactly as

$$\mathbf{x} = \{x_1, x_2, x_3\}, \quad \mathbf{x}' = [x_1, x_2, x_3] \quad .$$

This suggests that we define the *transpose of a matrix* while we are about it. The transpose of **A**, written **A'**, is the matrix formed by turning the rows of **A** into the columns of **A'**. Thus if

$$\mathbf{A} = [a_{ij}] \quad ,$$

then

$$\mathbf{A}' = [a_{ji}] \quad .$$

The elements on the principal diagonal (of a square matrix) are left undisturbed by this operation, as can be seen from the fact that the *ij*th element of $\mathbf{A}'$ is the *ji*th of $\mathbf{A}$: nothing happens to *ii* elements. If a matrix is equal to its own transpose, that is, if $\mathbf{A} = \mathbf{A}'$, the matrix is said to be *symmetric*. It must be the case that $a_{ij} = a_{ji}$.

We may look on a vector as a special sort of matrix. A row vector of, say, k elements, is a $1 \times k$ matrix; a column vector of n elements is an $n \times 1$ matrix. Also, of course, we can look on a matrix as being composed of vectors: it is a column of row vectors, or a row of column vectors, whichever way we care to put it. This suggests that we can apply our rules for matrix operations directly to vectors, which is indeed the case. It also suggests that we could have developed the whole subject differently, starting with vectors, and then combining them to form matrices and generalizing the rules of operation. Many good books do this,[3] but for our purposes it is not the quickest approach.

The rules for equality, scalar multiplication, addition, and subtraction of vectors are precisely those for matrices, since vectors are $1 \times k$ or $k \times 1$ matrices. Let us proceed directly to multiplication. Suppose that we have a $k \times 1$ column vector. This can be premultiplied by any matrix of order $n \times k$, whatever the value of n, to produce a matrix of order $n \times 1$, that is, a column vector. Let us look at this more closely. Let $\mathbf{A}$ be an $n \times k$ matrix, and $\mathbf{x}$ a column vector of k elements. Then

$$\mathbf{Ax} = \begin{bmatrix} a_{11} & \cdots & a_{1k} \\ \vdots & & \vdots \\ a_{n1} & \cdots & a_{nk} \end{bmatrix} \begin{bmatrix} x_1 \\ \vdots \\ x_k \end{bmatrix} = \begin{bmatrix} y_1 \\ \vdots \\ y_n \end{bmatrix} ,$$

where $\mathbf{y}$ is a column vector. Following the "row-by-column" rule, we see that

$$y_1 = \sum_{j=1}^{k} a_{1j}x_j$$

$$y_2 = \sum_{j=1}^{k} a_{2j}x_j, \qquad \text{etc.}$$

If we write these operations out in full, we have

[3] See, for instance, G. Hadley, *Linear Algebra*, Addison-Wesley, Reading, Mass., 1961.

$$a_{11}x_1 + a_{12}x_2 + \cdots + a_{1k}x_k = y_1$$
$$a_{21}x_1 + a_{22}x_2 + \cdots + a_{2k}x_k = y_2$$
$$\vdots \qquad\qquad \vdots \quad \vdots$$
$$a_{n1}x_1 + \qquad \cdots \qquad + a_{nk}x_k = y_n \quad .$$

Thus we have discovered the appropriate compact notation for a set of simultaneous linear equations:

$$\mathbf{Ax} = \mathbf{y} \quad ,$$

where $\mathbf{x}$ is a column vector, $\mathbf{A}$ a matrix of coefficients, and $\mathbf{y}$ a column vector. If $\mathbf{x}$ is $n \times 1$, $\mathbf{A}$ must be $m \times n$, if $\mathbf{Ax}$ is to conform for multiplication. It follows that $\mathbf{y}$ must be $m \times 1$.

If the problem is to find $\mathbf{y}$, given $\mathbf{A}$ and $\mathbf{x}$, then the rules for matrix multiplication, which we have already learned, are all we need. Another problem arises if $\mathbf{A}$ and $\mathbf{y}$ are known, and the problem is to find $\mathbf{x}$. It is the solution of this problem that we are seeking, but we are not yet ready for a direct attack.

Let us use as illustration the familiar case of two simultaneous linear equations. Suppose that, as in Section 15.2, we have

$$4x_1 + 7x_2 = 11$$
$$2x_1 + x_2 = 3 \quad .$$

We can write this as

$$\begin{bmatrix} 4 & 7 \\ 2 & 1 \end{bmatrix} \begin{bmatrix} x_1 \\ x_2 \end{bmatrix} = \begin{bmatrix} 11 \\ 3 \end{bmatrix} \quad ,$$

or, using $\mathbf{A}$, $\mathbf{x}$, and $\mathbf{y}$ to denote the matrix and the two vectors, as $\mathbf{Ax} = \mathbf{y}$ again. If we are given numerical values for $\mathbf{A}$ and $\mathbf{x}$, instead of $\mathbf{A}$ and $\mathbf{y}$, we already know how to find $\mathbf{y}$. Thus

$$\begin{bmatrix} 4 & 7 \\ 2 & 1 \end{bmatrix} \begin{bmatrix} 100 \\ 200 \end{bmatrix} = \begin{bmatrix} 1800 \\ 400 \end{bmatrix} \quad .$$

(You should verify this for practice.) The more difficult problem is to find $\mathbf{x}$, given $\mathbf{A}$ and $\mathbf{y}$, and we have yet to find a method for doing this. We must now complete our account of the rules for operating with vectors.

We may *premultiply* a column vector by a matrix with as many columns as the vector has rows (elements). What about *postmultiplication* of a vector by a matrix? Suppose that the matrix is $k \times n$. If the vector and the matrix are to *conform* for multiplication, the vector must be $1 \times k$. Thus we can postmultiply a *row* vector by a matrix with as many rows as the vector has elements, obtaining a

$1 \times n$ row vector. Thus

$$[\qquad] = \begin{bmatrix} & & \\ & & \\ & & \end{bmatrix} = [\qquad] \,.$$

$$1 \times k \qquad\qquad k \times n \qquad\qquad 1 \times n$$

It is now very easy to handle the multiplication of vectors. $1 \times k$ and $k \times 1$ conform, and so do $k \times 1$ and $1 \times k$. *Nothing else does.* The product of the former will be 1×1, and of the latter $k \times k$. Thus

$$[\qquad] \begin{bmatrix} \\ \\ \end{bmatrix} = [\ ]$$

$$1 \times k \qquad k \times 1 \qquad 1 \times 1$$

and

$$\begin{bmatrix} \\ \\ \end{bmatrix} [\qquad] = \begin{bmatrix} & & \\ & & \\ & & \end{bmatrix} \,.$$

$$k \times 1 \qquad 1 \times k \qquad\qquad k \times k$$

The first multiplication, of a row vector by a column vector, produces a single number as a product. It is therefore referred to as the *scalar product,* or *inner product,* of the vectors. It may seem odd that multiplication of two vectors should produce a scalar, but in fact it is an everyday operation that we perform without thought. What, after all, is national income but the scalar product of a vector of outputs and a vector of prices? A weighted average, such as $\Sigma_i\, c_i x_i$, where the c_i's are the weights, is precisely the scalar product of the vector of weights and the vector of x's. The rules for matrix multiplication may now also seem less arbitrary. The "row-by-column" rule can now be expressed: to find the ijth element of **AB**, take the scalar product of the ith row of **A** and the jth column of **B**. Thus matrix multiplication may be viewed as an extension of the natural rules of vector multiplication.

15.4 DETERMINANTS

We have seen that we can write a system of simultaneous linear equations in the compact form $\mathbf{Ax} = \mathbf{y}$. We still seek a method of solution, if **y** is known and **x** unknown, for which we require the *matrix in-*

verse, $\mathbf{A}^{-1}$. (We defined the matrix inverse in Section 15.4: it is the matrix, denoted by $\mathbf{A}^{-1}$, such that $\mathbf{A}\mathbf{A}^{-1} = \mathbf{A}^{-1}\mathbf{A} = \mathbf{I}$.) We still need, however, one more piece of equipment before we can proceed. We need some familiarity with determinants and their properties. A determinant is a number (scalar), although at first sight it does not look like one.

Consider a set of operations on a 2×2 matrix

$$\mathbf{A} = \begin{bmatrix} a & b \\ c & d \end{bmatrix} .$$

We define the *determinant* of $\mathbf{A}$, written det $\mathbf{A}$ or $|\mathbf{A}|$, as $ad - bc$ (we use the arrows to indicate the pairs of elements that are to be multiplied). *A matrix does not have a value. The determinant, composed of the same elements, and evaluated in this way, is a scalar.* We use parallel lines in place of square brackets to denote a determinant. Thus

$$|\mathbf{A}| = \begin{vmatrix} a & b \\ c & d \end{vmatrix} = ad - bc .$$

Now let us consider a 3×3 matrix:

$$\begin{bmatrix} a_{11} & a_{12} & a_{13} \\ a_{21} & a_{22} & a_{23} \\ a_{31} & a_{32} & a_{33} \end{bmatrix} .$$

Take any element of this matrix, say a_{23}, and eliminate the row and column in which this element appears. Thus

$$\begin{bmatrix} a_{11} & a_{12} & a_{13} \\ a_{21} & a_{22} & a_{23} \\ a_{31} & a_{32} & a_{33} \end{bmatrix} .$$

This leaves us with

$$\begin{bmatrix} a_{11} & a_{12} \\ a_{31} & a_{32} \end{bmatrix} .$$

We may evaluate the determinant of this matrix as we did above:

$$\begin{vmatrix} a_{11} & a_{12} \\ a_{31} & a_{32} \end{vmatrix} = a_{11}a_{32} - a_{12}a_{31} .$$

The determinant

$$\begin{vmatrix} a_{11} & a_{12} \\ a_{31} & a_{32} \end{vmatrix}$$

is called the *minor* of the element a_{23}. Every element in the matrix has a minor, which is the determinant formed by striking out the row and column in which that element appears.

We now introduce another number called a *cofactor. The cofactor of an element is its minor, with a sign attached* according to the pattern

$$\begin{vmatrix} + & - & + \\ - & + & - \\ + & - & + \end{vmatrix} \; .$$

Thus the cofactor of a_{23} is $-a_{11}a_{32} + a_{12}a_{31}$, and the cofactor of a_{11} is $a_{22}a_{33} - a_{23}a_{32}$.

The rule of signs can be expressed more formally and compactly, and in a fashion that holds for any determinant. Looking at the pattern of signs, we see that the pluses are attached to elements whose *subscripts add to an even number:* a_{11}, a_{22}, a_{33}, a_{31}, and a_{13}. The minuses are attached to the elements whose subscripts add to an odd number: a_{12}, a_{21}, a_{23}, and a_{32}. Hence we can determine the sign of the cofactor of any element, say the *ij*th, merely by looking at $i + j$. A compact way of writing the rule is as follows: the cofactor of the *ij*th element $= (-1)^{i+j} \times$ the minor of the *ij*th element. Clearly -1 raised to an even power is plus one, and raised to an odd power it is minus one.

We can now define the determinant of a 3×3 matrix. If

$$\mathbf{A} = \begin{bmatrix} a_{11} & a_{12} & a_{13} \\ a_{21} & a_{22} & a_{23} \\ a_{31} & a_{32} & a_{33} \end{bmatrix}$$

$$|\mathbf{A}| = a_{11} \begin{vmatrix} a_{22} & a_{23} \\ a_{32} & a_{33} \end{vmatrix} - a_{12} \begin{vmatrix} a_{21} & a_{23} \\ a_{31} & a_{33} \end{vmatrix} + a_{13} \begin{vmatrix} a_{21} & a_{22} \\ a_{31} & a_{32} \end{vmatrix}$$

$$= a_{11}a_{22}a_{33} - a_{11}a_{23}a_{32} - a_{12}a_{21}a_{33} + a_{12}a_{23}a_{31} + a_{13}a_{21}a_{32} - a_{13}a_{22}a_{31} \; .$$

The steps in the procedure may be set out in words.

1. Take the first row of **A**.
2. Multiply each element by its cofactor.

3. Add.
4. "Expand" each cofactor by the rule for evaluating an ordinary 2×2 determinant.

Although a determinant is a scalar, it is natural to speak of the *order* of a determinant, by obvious analogy with the order of a matrix. The determinant of a 3×3 matrix is referred to as a third-order determinant, of a 4×4 matrix as a fourth-order determinant, and so on. It should be noted that the cofactors of the elements of an nth-order determinant are determinants of order $n - 1$. Thus the cofactors of the 3×3 determinant are 2×2 determinants.

In defining a 3×3 determinant, we "expanded" it by the first row. It in fact makes no difference if we take a different row of **A**, the second or third, or any one of the columns, provided that each element of the row or column chosen is multiplied by its cofactor and the rule of signs is not forgotten. We are not going to prove this, but it is easy and worthwhile to check it for yourself by expanding the 3×3 determinant above in several ways. Examination of the expansion of the 3×3 determinant above will suggest something about the structure of a determinant. You may notice that the element a_{11} is found multiplied by $(a_{22}a_{23})$ and $(a_{23}a_{32})$. Similarly, a_{23} is found multiplied by $(a_{11}a_{32})$ and $(a_{12}a_{33})$. In fact, an $n \times n$ determinant consists of the sum (with the rule of signs obeyed) of every term that can be composed by multiplying an element by the product of the $n - 1$ elements from the rows and columns to which that element does not belong. This gives us another, more formal, and more systematic definition of a determinant than we are using here. We shall not use this definition. What matters is to realize that this sum (a scalar) *is* the determinant, and that it therefore does not matter which rule of thumb we use to compute it. We only mention this here to lend some justification to our simple rule-of-thumb approach.

It is now easy to handle fourth- and higher-order determinants. The procedure for evaluating determinants of any order may be set out in four steps.

1. Pick any row or column, and form the sum of its elements each multiplied by its cofactor.
2. If the cofactors are of an order higher than 2×2, expand each of them by the same rule.
3. Go on doing this until 2×2 cofactors are reached.
4. Multiply out, and perform the required additions and subtractions.

Let us work through a 4×4 arithmetic example to see how these rules work. Suppose that

$$\mathbf{A} = \begin{bmatrix} 1 & 2 & 1 & 2 \\ 0 & \frac{1}{2} & 3 & 1 \\ 5 & 1 & 0 & 4 \\ 2 & 3 & 0 & \frac{1}{2} \end{bmatrix}$$

In evaluating $|\mathbf{A}|$, it obviously saves labor if we expand by the row or column with the most zeros (if there are any), so let us expand by the third column. Then

$$|\mathbf{A}| = 1 \begin{vmatrix} 0 & \frac{1}{2} & 1 \\ 5 & 1 & 4 \\ 2 & 3 & \frac{1}{2} \end{vmatrix} - 3 \begin{vmatrix} 1 & 2 & 2 \\ 5 & 1 & 4 \\ 2 & 3 & \frac{1}{2} \end{vmatrix} .$$

The cofactors here are 3×3, so we expand again, using the first columns this time to take advantage of the zero. Thus

$$|\mathbf{A}| = -5 \begin{vmatrix} \frac{1}{2} & 1 \\ 3 & \frac{1}{2} \end{vmatrix} + 2 \begin{vmatrix} \frac{1}{2} & 1 \\ 1 & 4 \end{vmatrix} - 3 \begin{vmatrix} 1 & 4 \\ 3 & \frac{1}{2} \end{vmatrix}$$
$$+ 15 \begin{vmatrix} 2 & 2 \\ 3 & \frac{1}{2} \end{vmatrix} - 6 \begin{vmatrix} 2 & 2 \\ 1 & 4 \end{vmatrix} .$$

Now all we have to do is cross-multiply and add up:

$$|\mathbf{A}| = -5(\tfrac{1}{4} - 3) + 2(2 - 1) - 3(\tfrac{1}{2} - 12) + 15(1 - 6) - 6(8 - 2)$$
$$= -87\tfrac{3}{4} .$$

It is clear that evaluation of higher-order determinants rapidly becomes laborious, at least without some calculating equipment. We shall have to try to avoid doing too much of this. We notice that the scalar $|\mathbf{A}|$ can exist only if the matrix $\mathbf{A}$ is square. If the matrix $\mathbf{A}$ is $m \times n$, where $m \neq n$, then $|\mathbf{A}|$ does not exist.

For the cofactor of the ijth element in a square matrix $\mathbf{A}$ let us now write $\mathbf{A}_{ij}$. Then the expansion of $\mathbf{A}$ by its first row can be written

$$|\mathbf{A}| = \sum_i a_{1i} \mathbf{A}_{1i} .$$

Similarly, the expansion by, say, the rth row is

$$|\mathbf{A}| = \sum_i a_{ri} \mathbf{A}_{ri}$$

and by the sth column

$$|\mathbf{A}| = \sum_j a_{js}\mathbf{A}_{js} \quad .$$

This notation for cofactors will shortly prove most convenient.

15.5 SOME PROPERTIES OF DETERMINANTS

We now require a few theorems on determinants. We shall introduce no more than are absolutely essential to obtain the matrix inverse. What we are after is "expansion by alien cofactors." We know that a determinant is evaluated by multiplying the elements of a row (or column) by their cofactors and adding. If we multiply instead by the cofactors of the elements in another, or "alien," row and add, the result is zero. We shall take this in three steps.

1. *Interchange of two rows (or columns) in a determinant only changes the sign of the determinant.* Thus if $\mathbf{B}$ is the matrix formed by interchanging two rows in $\mathbf{A}$,

$$|\mathbf{B}| = -|\mathbf{A}| \quad .$$

We shall give a stepwise demonstration. We start by showing that the interchange of two *adjacent* rows, the ith and the jth say, changes the sign of the determinant. First, expand the determinant by the ith row in its old position, and then by the ith row in its new position. Obviously the minors are identical, but each cofactor has changed sign. The following may help to make this clear:

$$
\begin{vmatrix}
a_{11} & \cdot & \cdot & \cdot & \cdot & a_{1n} \\
\cdot & \cdot & \cdot & \cdot & \cdot & \cdot \\
\cdot & \cdot & \cdot & \cdot & \cdot & \cdot \\
a_{h1} & a_{h2} & \cdot & \cdot & \cdot & a_{hn} \\
a_{i1} & a_{i2} & \cdot & \cdot & \cdot & a_{in} \\
a_{j1} & a_{j2} & \cdot & \cdot & \cdot & a_{jn} \\
a_{k1} & a_{k2} & \cdot & \cdot & \cdot & a_{kn} \\
\cdot & \cdot & \cdot & \cdot & \cdot & \cdot \\
a_{n1} & a_{n2} & \cdot & \cdot & \cdot & a_{nn}
\end{vmatrix}
\qquad
\begin{vmatrix}
a_{11} & \cdot & \cdot & \cdot & \cdot & a_{1n} \\
\cdot & \cdot & \cdot & \cdot & \cdot & \cdot \\
\cdot & \cdot & \cdot & \cdot & \cdot & \cdot \\
a_{h1} & a_{h2} & \cdot & \cdot & \cdot & a_{hn} \\
a_{j1} & a_{j2} & \cdot & \cdot & \cdot & a_{jn} \\
a_{i1} & a_{i2} & \cdot & \cdot & \cdot & a_{in} \\
a_{k1} & a_{k2} & \cdot & \cdot & \cdot & a_{kn} \\
\cdot & \cdot & \cdot & \cdot & \cdot & \cdot \\
a_{n1} & a_{n2} & \cdot & \cdot & \cdot & a_{nn}
\end{vmatrix}
$$

When we move the ith row to the jth place and expand, all we do is switch signs: the elements of the cofactors remain in the identical positions relative to one another, but the change in the position of the elements whose cofactors we are taking alters all their signs.

Thus we see that interchanging rows i and j indeed changes the sign but not the absolute value of the determinant. What if we now interchange two rows that are not adjacent, say row i and row k? We shall construct the interchange as a sequence of interchanges of adjacent rows. To interchange i and k, we first interchange i and j (one change of signs). We next interchange i and k, which are now adjacent (second change of signs). We finally interchange k and j (third, *odd*, change of signs). The following scheme may help to make this clear:

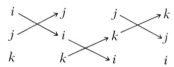

first   second   third
inter-   inter-   interchange change change

We can see that the theorem depends on the fact that interchanging *any* two rows requires an *odd* number of interchanges of *adjacent rows*. This is easily confirmed. The second interchange in the scheme above restores the original sign of the determinant, but it produces the row sequence j, k, i. Comparing this with i, j, k, we see that this is not the direct interchange of two rows. To achieve this, we must interchange two adjacent rows once more, to obtain k, j, i, and change the sign once more. We also notice that a fourth adjacent row interchange, restoring the original sign, would not give us a direct two-row interchange. Either it would "undo" the third interchange, or it would involve a fourth row. Thus suppose that we wish to interchange rows i and l. This is achieved by a sequence of adjacent-row changes as follows:

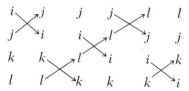

odd even odd even odd

Notice that the "even" step always leaves more than two rows out of position. (The sequence of adjacent-row interchanges that produces l, j, k, i is not unique. You might experiment with some other sequences.)

We shall not repeat the argument for the interchange of columns. It is easily developed in parallel with the demonstration for rows that we have just given.

Let us now collect what we have done. Clearly, if we interchange two identical rows in a determinant, we have in no way altered it, whence its value must be unchanged. We have, however, just seen that a direct interchange alters the sign of the determinant. Taking both together, we require

$$|\mathbf{A}| = -|\mathbf{A}| \quad .$$

This can be true only if

$$|\mathbf{A}| = 0 \quad .$$

We may now write out the last two steps.

2. *A determinant with two identical rows or columns is zero.*

3. *Expansion by alien cofactors vanishes identically.* Consider the sum found from the elements of row i times the cofactor of the corresponding elements of row j. This is exactly what we should get if we correctly expanded a determinant in which rows i and j were identical. But, by step 2, this determinant is zero.

15.6 THE INVERSE MATRIX

Now we can at last set out a procedure for finding the inverse matrix $\mathbf{A}^{-1}$ such that

$$\mathbf{A}^{-1}\mathbf{A} = \mathbf{A}\mathbf{A}^{-1} = \mathbf{I} \quad .$$

1. From the matrix $\mathbf{A} = [a_{ij}]$ form the matrix of cofactors

$$[\mathbf{A}_{ij}] = \begin{bmatrix} \mathbf{A}_{11} & \mathbf{A}_{12} & \cdots & \mathbf{A}_{1n} \\ \mathbf{A}_{21} & & & \vdots \\ \vdots & & & \\ \mathbf{A}_{n1} & & \cdots & \mathbf{A}_{nn} \end{bmatrix} \quad ,$$

where $\mathbf{A}_{ij}$ stands for the cofactor of the *ij*th element in $\mathbf{A}$. Thus each element in $\mathbf{A}$ is replaced by its cofactor (remember that cofactors are determinants, that is, scalars).

2. Transpose $[\mathbf{A}_{ij}]$. The resulting matrix,

$$[\mathbf{A}_{ij}]' = \begin{bmatrix} \mathbf{A}_{11} & \mathbf{A}_{21} & \cdots & \mathbf{A}_{n1} \\ \mathbf{A}_{12} & \mathbf{A}_{22} & \cdots & \vdots \\ \vdots & & & \vdots \\ \mathbf{A}_{1n} & \mathbf{A}_{2n} & \cdots & \mathbf{A}_{nn} \end{bmatrix} \quad ,$$

is called the *adjoint matrix* of $\mathbf{A}$.

3. Divide each element of $[\mathbf{A}_{ij}]'$ by $|\mathbf{A}|$ to obtain

$$A^{-1} = \frac{[A_{ij}]'}{|A|} \quad .$$

Clearly, only a square matrix can have an inverse, since the determinant is defined only for a square matrix. Further, it is necessary that the determinant does not vanish (is not equal to zero). If $|A|$ is zero, A^{-1} is not defined, and A is said to be *singular*. If the inverse of a matrix B exists, $|B| \neq 0$, and B is said to be *nonsingular*. Notice also that we divide *each* element of $[A_{ij}]'$ by $|A|$, which we may factor out following the rules for *scalar multiplication* of matrices given in Section 15.2. (It is not necessary to give a separate rule for scalar division since we merely multiply by λ, where $\lambda = 1/|A|$.)

It remains to check that the formula given is the inverse, that is, that

$$AA^{-1} = I = A^{-1}A \quad .$$

Substituting,

$$AA^{-1} = \frac{A}{|A|} [A_{ij}]'$$

$$= \frac{A}{|A|} \begin{bmatrix} A_{11} & A_{21} & \cdots & A_{n1} \\ A_{12} & A_{22} & & \\ \vdots & & & \vdots \\ A_{1n} & & \cdots & A_{nn} \end{bmatrix}$$

$$= \frac{1}{|A|} \begin{bmatrix} a_{11} & a_{12} & \cdots & a_{1n} \\ a_{21} & & & \\ \vdots & & & \vdots \\ a_{n1} & & \cdots & a_{nn} \end{bmatrix} \begin{bmatrix} A_{11} & A_{21} & \cdots & A_{n1} \\ A_{12} & & & \\ \vdots & & & \vdots \\ A_{1n} & & \cdots & A_{nn} \end{bmatrix} \quad .$$

Now remember the rule for matrix multiplication. If $C = AB$,

$$c_{ij} = \sum_{k=1}^{n} a_{ik}b_{kj} \quad .$$

We shall perform the required multiplication in steps.

1. Consider a diagonal element of AA^{-1}, that is, put $i = j$. We find that

$$(AA^{-1})_{ii} = \frac{1}{|A|} \sum_{k=1}^{n} a_{ik}A_{ki} \quad .$$

Within the summation, we have a row of A and the corresponding column of the adjoint matrix. That column is, however, composed of the cofactors of the *row* of **A**. (The purpose of transposing the matrix of cofactors now appears.) Hence, from the rules for expanding a determinant, we see that

$$\sum_{k=1}^{n} a_{ik}\mathbf{A}_{ki} = |\mathbf{A}| \quad .$$

2. Now consider an off-diagonal element of $\mathbf{AA}^{-1}$, say the *ij*th element:

$$(\mathbf{AA}^{-1})_{ij} = \frac{1}{|\mathbf{A}|} \sum_{k=1}^{n} a_{ik}\mathbf{A}_{kj} \quad .$$

The expression in the summation is precisely the expansion of **A** by alien cofactors, so

$$\sum_{k=1}^{n} a_{ik}\mathbf{A}_{kj} = 0 \quad .$$

3. Combining steps 1 and 2, we see that

$$\mathbf{AA}^{-1} = \frac{1}{|\mathbf{A}|} \begin{bmatrix} |\mathbf{A}| & 0 & \cdots & 0 \\ 0 & |\mathbf{A}| & & \vdots \\ \vdots & & \ddots & \\ 0 & & 0 & |\mathbf{A}| \end{bmatrix}$$

$$= \begin{bmatrix} 1 & 0 & 0 & \cdots & 0 \\ 0 & 1 & & & \vdots \\ \vdots & & \ddots & & 0 \\ 0 & & \cdots & & 1 \end{bmatrix} = \mathbf{I} \quad ,$$

as required.

There are two last points to check, that the matrices commute, and that the inverse is unique. The first, that $\mathbf{AA}^{-1} = \mathbf{A}^{-1}\mathbf{A}$, is simply checked by the procedure above: it is left to you. The second needs to be established: it would be embarrassing if there were more than one inverse to a matrix. A little very straightforward manipulation is sufficient to show that the inverse (if it exists) is *unique*. Suppose that $\mathbf{A}^{-1}$ exists, and that there is a second matrix **B** such that

$$\mathbf{AB} = \mathbf{I} \quad ,$$

which is the equation that defines the inverse. Now, since

$$\mathbf{AA}^{-1} = \mathbf{I}$$

too, we have

$$AA^{-1} = AB \quad.$$

Premultiply each side by A^{-1}:

$$A^{-1}AA^{-1} = A^{-1}AB \quad,$$

that is,

$$IA^{-1} = IB \quad,$$

so

$$A^{-1} = B \quad.$$

In other words, any matrix B that satisfies $AB = I$ is identical to A^{-1}, whence the inverse is unique.

15.7   CRAMER'S RULE

We now have a method for handling *simultaneous linear equations*. If A is an $n \times n$ matrix of *constant coefficients*,[4] and b is an $n \times 1$ vector of constants, and we are asked to find a vector x such that

$$Ax = b \quad,$$

we premultiply both sides by A^{-1} to obtain

$$A^{-1}Ax = A^{-1}b \quad,$$

that is,

$$Ix = A^{-1}b \quad,$$

or

$$x = A^{-1}b \quad.$$

Since we have a procedure for obtaining A^{-1}, we are home. The only trouble is that obtaining A^{-1} by the method developed above can clearly be very laborious. As a practical matter, we shall therefore seek methods of obtaining solutions, at least for special cases of interest, that are less tedious. In fact, computer programs for inverting matrices do not use the procedure we have given, but numerical approximation methods. We shall consider one such method in Chapter 17. What we are going to do now is introduce one famous trick, called Cramer's rule. It enormously simplifies the task of doing comparative statics in economic models requiring simultaneous equations, and we shall use it extensively in Chapter 16.

---

[4] See the discussion of constant coefficients in Section 15.1.

Suppose that we wish to solve for **x** the set of simultaneous equations

$$\mathbf{Ax} = \mathbf{c} \quad,$$

which are solved by

$$\mathbf{x} = \mathbf{A}^{-1}\mathbf{c} \quad.$$

If we write this out in full, we have

$$
\begin{bmatrix} x_1 \\ x_2 \\ \vdots \\ x_n \end{bmatrix}
= \frac{1}{|\mathbf{A}|}
\begin{bmatrix}
\mathbf{A}_{11} & \mathbf{A}_{21} & \cdots & \mathbf{A}_{n1} \\
\mathbf{A}_{12} & & & \vdots \\
\vdots & & & \\
\mathbf{A}_{1n} & & \cdots & \mathbf{A}_{nn}
\end{bmatrix}
\begin{bmatrix} c_1 \\ c_2 \\ \vdots \\ c_n \end{bmatrix} \quad.
$$

Now we apply the row-by-column rule to the multiplication required on the right. Starting with the first row, we have

$$x_1 = \frac{1}{|\mathbf{A}|} \left[\mathbf{A}_{11}c_1 + \mathbf{A}_{21}c_2 + \cdots + \mathbf{A}_{n1}c_n \right]$$

$$= \frac{1}{|\mathbf{A}|} \sum_{i=1}^{n} \mathbf{A}_{i1}c_i \quad,$$

which, of course, is a scalar. Similarly, for any x, say the jth, we have

$$x_j = \frac{1}{|\mathbf{A}|} \sum_{i=1}^{n} \mathbf{A}_{ij}c_i \quad.$$

Now let us look at the expression within the summation sign for x_1. The terms $\mathbf{A}_{11}$, $\mathbf{A}_{21}$, etc., are the cofactors of the elements in the first *column* of **A**. Since each is multiplied by the corresponding c_i, we see that

$$
\sum_{i=1}^{n} \mathbf{A}_{i1}c_i =
\begin{vmatrix}
c_1 & a_{12} & \cdots & a_{1n} \\
c_2 & a_{22} & \cdots & a_{2n} \\
\vdots & \vdots & & \vdots \\
c_n & a_{n2} & \cdots & a_{nn}
\end{vmatrix} \quad.
$$

This is $|\mathbf{A}|$ with the first column replaced by the column vector **c**. Let us denote it by Δ_1. Then x_1 is simply the ratio of two determinants:

$$x_1 = \frac{\Delta_1}{|\mathbf{A}|} \quad.$$

Similarly, we see that for x_j, the expression within the summation sign consists of the cofactors of the elements of the jth column of **A**, each multiplied by the corresponding c_i. Thus

$$\sum_{i=1}^{n} A_{ij} c_i = \begin{vmatrix} a_{11} & a_{12} & \cdots & a_{1,j-1} & c_1 & a_{1,j+1} & \cdots & a_{1n} \\ \vdots & & & & & & & \vdots \\ a_{n1} & \cdots & & a_{n,j-1} & c_n & a_{n,j+1} & \cdots & a_{nn} \end{vmatrix} ,$$

which we denote by Δ_j. This is simply $|A|$ with the jth column re-replaced by the vector **c**. Thus

$$x_j = \frac{\Delta_j}{|A|} .$$

Now we have a straightforward computational procedure which we may write out in four steps.

1. Evaluate $|A|$.
2. To find any x_j, form the determinant Δ_j by replacing the jth column of $|A|$ with the vector **c**.
3. Evaluate Δ_j.
4. Find the ratio $\Delta_j/|A|$.

In many cases of interest, this is much less trouble than having to evaluate all the cofactors of **A**. Its limitation, of course, is that it only provides solutions for a *given* vector **c**, whereas, once one has A^{-1}, only multiplication is required to find **x** for *any* vector **c**. (It is a nice test of ingenuity to work out how one might use Cramer's rule to find the inverse itself. This is explored in Question 3, and another method of building up the inverse is discussed in Chapter 17.)

15.8 LINEAR OPERATORS

In the question for the preceding sections we have developed some properties of matrices and determinants besides those explained in the text. This is not because they are unimportant, but because we do not plan to use them in application. There are many more topics in linear algebra, of importance in economics, that we shall not introduce at all. In particular, we shall not discuss what are called *homogeneous equations* of the form $Ax = 0$, nor shall we be concerned until Chapter 18 with problems in which the number of equations and the number of variables is not equal, so that the matrix **A** is not square and has no inverse. There is, however, one further point that we want to take up. Consider the expression

$$y = Ax .$$

This says that a vector **y** is composed of elements each of which is the scalar product of a row of **A** with the column vector **x**. Thus

$$y_i = \sum_k a_{ik} x_k \quad .$$

We have discussed operations with vectors and matrices. We now suggest that we can consider a matrix itself as an *operator*. Thus in **y** = **Ax**, **A** *operates on* **x** *to give* **y**. Recall our original definition of a function (Section 2.4): for scalars, if $y = f(x)$, f is a rule telling us how to operate on x to obtain y. Clearly, the matrix **A** can be similarly regarded as a rule for vectors. For fairly obvious reasons, the matrix **A** may be called a *linear operator*. Had we developed the geometric approach to linear algebra, we should now consider the orders of **y**, **A**, and **x** in terms of the dimensions of vector space, but we are not concerned with this here.

Let us just reconsider the problem of finding the vector **x** that satisfies

$$\mathbf{Ax} = \mathbf{c} \quad .$$

A is a rule for operating on **x** to give **c**; we know **A** and **c** but not **x**. Our solution is

$$\mathbf{x} = \mathbf{A}^{-1}\mathbf{c} \quad .$$

$\mathbf{A}^{-1}$ itself is, of course, a linear operator just as **A** is. Thus the problem of solving simultaneous linear equations can be stated as that of finding the required linear operator to take **c** into **x**. It is, of course, the inverse, or reciprocal, operation to that which takes **x** into **c**. As we have seen in the questions, if we solve by elimination, we find **x** for the given **c** but not the operator that can be applied to *any* **c**. The advantage of finding the inverse is that linear operators obey some handy rules. Thus if

$$\mathbf{x} = \mathbf{Bc}$$

and

$$\mathbf{z} = \mathbf{Bd} \quad ,$$

then

$$\mathbf{x} + \mathbf{z} = \mathbf{B}(\mathbf{c} + \mathbf{d})$$

and

$$\mathbf{B}\lambda\mathbf{c} = \lambda\mathbf{x} \quad ,$$

and so on. These rules were used in Question 15.7.3 where we used Cramer's rule to build up the inverse matrix a step at a time. We shall exploit them again in Chapter 17.

QUESTIONS

Section 15.1

1. Which of the following are matrices? Of what order?

a. 5 3

   10 9

b. 5 3 2 1 0

   10 9 7 11 −1

c. 2

   3 1

d. 2

Section 15.2

1. Add those of the following matrices that can be added.

a. $\mathbf{A} = \begin{bmatrix} 2 & 3 \\ 4 & 5 \end{bmatrix}$ and $\mathbf{B} = \begin{bmatrix} 1 & 8 \\ -2 & 4 \end{bmatrix}$

b. $\mathbf{A} = \begin{bmatrix} 14 & 15 & 18 & 0 \\ 2 & 3 & -15 & 4 \end{bmatrix}$ and $\mathbf{B} = \begin{bmatrix} 2 & 3 & 4 & -5 \\ 1 & 18 & 19 & 20 \end{bmatrix}$

c. $\mathbf{A} = \begin{bmatrix} 2 & 3 \\ 4 & 5 \end{bmatrix}$ and $\mathbf{B} = \begin{bmatrix} 2 & 3 & 1 \\ 4 & 5 & 2 \end{bmatrix}$

d. $\mathbf{A} = \begin{bmatrix} 2 & 3 \\ 4 & 5 \end{bmatrix}$ and $\mathbf{B} = \begin{bmatrix} 0 & 0 \\ 0 & 0 \end{bmatrix}$

2. Find $\mathbf{A} - \mathbf{B}$ for the matrices in Question 1 (where $\mathbf{A} - \mathbf{B}$ exists).

3. a. Find $\lambda\mathbf{A}$ if $\lambda = 2$ and $\mathbf{A} = \begin{bmatrix} 2 & 3 \\ 4 & 5 \end{bmatrix}$.

b. Find $\lambda\mathbf{I}_n$ where $n = 3$, that is, $\mathbf{I} = \begin{bmatrix} 1 & 0 & 0 \\ 0 & 1 & 0 \\ 0 & 0 & 1 \end{bmatrix}$.

4. If $\mathbf{A} + \mathbf{B}$ exists, does $\mathbf{B} + \mathbf{A} = \mathbf{A} + \mathbf{B}$?

5. Check, by writing out the expression for a characteristic element, that

$$\lambda(\mathbf{A} + \mathbf{B}) = \lambda\mathbf{A} + \lambda\mathbf{B} \quad .$$

6. Check, by the same method, that

$$(\mathbf{A} + \mathbf{B}) + \mathbf{C} = \mathbf{A} + (\mathbf{B} + \mathbf{C}) = \mathbf{A} + \mathbf{C} + \mathbf{B} = \mathbf{C} + \mathbf{A} + \mathbf{B} = \mathbf{C} + \mathbf{B} + \mathbf{A} \quad .$$

7. a. Find **AB** when

$$A = \begin{bmatrix} 2 & 3 \\ 4 & 5 \end{bmatrix} \quad \text{and} \quad B = \begin{bmatrix} 8 & 12 & 16 \\ 10 & 14 & 18 \end{bmatrix}.$$

b. Can you find **BA**?

8. Find **AB** and **BA** where

a. $A = \begin{bmatrix} 1 & 2 \\ 3 & 4 \end{bmatrix}$ and $B = \begin{bmatrix} 2 & 3 \\ 7 & 3 \end{bmatrix}$

b. $A = \begin{bmatrix} 2 & 1 \\ 1 & 0 \end{bmatrix}$ and $B = \begin{bmatrix} 3 & 2 \\ 2 & 1 \end{bmatrix}$

9. If

$$A = \begin{bmatrix} 1 & 2 \\ 3 & 4 \end{bmatrix}, \quad B = \begin{bmatrix} 1 & 1 \\ 2 & 1 \end{bmatrix}, \quad \text{and} \quad C = \begin{bmatrix} 2 & 3 \\ 2 & 1 \end{bmatrix},$$

find **AB**, **(AB)C**, **BC**, and **A(BC)**. Can you make any general statement about repeated multiplication such as **ABC**?

10. The matrices indicated by **A** and **B** in the following have their dimensions indicated in the parentheses.
a. In which cases is **A** conformable with **B**?

    i. **A**(n, k) **B**(k, m)
   ii. **A**$(1, k)$ **B**(k, m)
  iii. **A**$(1, k)$ **B**$(k, 1)$
   iv. **A**$(1, 1)$ **B**(k, m)
    v. **A**(m, m) **B**(m, m)
   vi. **A**$(m, 1)$ **B**$(1, m)$

Indicate the dimension of the product when, if the operation is possible, **A** is postmultiplied by **B**.
b. In which cases can **A** and **B** be summed?

11. Determine the products of the following.

a. $[-1, 1, 1, 1] \begin{bmatrix} 1 \\ 1 \\ 1 \\ -1 \end{bmatrix}$ b. $[-1, 1, 1, 1] \begin{bmatrix} -1 \\ 1 \\ 1 \\ 1 \end{bmatrix}$

c. $\begin{bmatrix} -1 \\ 1 \\ 1 \\ 1 \end{bmatrix} [-1, 1, 1, 1]$

Section 15.3

1. Find **AI** and **IA** if

$$\mathbf{A} = \begin{bmatrix} 2 & 8 \\ 10 & -12 \end{bmatrix} \quad \text{and} \quad \mathbf{I} = \begin{bmatrix} 1 & 0 \\ 0 & 1 \end{bmatrix}.$$

2. If

$$\mathbf{C} = \begin{bmatrix} 20 & 1 \\ 30 & 2 \\ 40 & 3 \end{bmatrix},$$

what order must **I** be for **IC** to exist? For **CI** to exist? Can you make a general statement about the effect of multiplication by a square matrix with 1's down the principal diagonal and zeros elsewhere?

3. a. Check that $\mathbf{I}^2 = \mathbf{I}$ (we might just as well use the exponent notation of scalar algebra; thus we shall write $\mathbf{A}^2$ for **AA**, etc.).
  b. Prove that $\mathbf{I}^n = \mathbf{I}$, for any n, given that $\mathbf{I}^2 = \mathbf{I}$.

4. If **O** is a matrix of appropriate order all of whose elements are zero (called the *null* matrix), check, by writing out in full the expression for a characteristic element, that

$$\mathbf{B} + \mathbf{O} = \mathbf{B} - \mathbf{O} = \mathbf{B}$$

and that $\mathbf{OB} = \mathbf{BO} = \mathbf{O}$.

5. The matrix $\lambda\mathbf{I}$ is called a *scalar matrix*. What will it look like?

6. If $\mathbf{x} = [1, 3, 0, 2]$ (row vector) and $\mathbf{y} = \{2, 0, 7, 1\}$ (column vector), find the *scalar product* of **x** and **y**.

7. a. Suppose that $\mathbf{x} = \{x_1, x_2, x_3\}$. What is $\mathbf{x}'\mathbf{x}$?
  b. What is $\mathbf{xx}'$?
  c. Evaluate $\mathbf{y}'\mathbf{y}$ for the **y** of Question 6.

8. If we are given $\mathbf{Ax} = \mathbf{y}$ for some unspecified **x** and **y** and **A** of order $n \times m$, what must be the orders of **x** and **y**?

9. Write the equations

$$x_1 + 2x_2 + 3x_3 = 1$$
$$2x_1 \qquad + x_3 = 0$$
$$2x_1 - x_2 + 4x_3 = 7$$

in matrix notation, writing out each term in full. (*Hint:* What is the value of the coefficient a_{22}?)

10. If

$$\mathbf{A} = \begin{bmatrix} 1 & 2 & 1 \\ 3 & 0 & 2 \end{bmatrix},$$

what is $\mathbf{A}'$?

11. a. For the matrix **A** of Question 10, find **A′A** and **AA′** and note their order.

b. Does $\mathbf{A}^2 = \mathbf{A} \cdot \mathbf{A}$ exist in this case?

12. If

$$\mathbf{A} = \begin{bmatrix} 1 & 2 & 0 \\ 2 & 3 & 1 \\ 0 & 1 & 1 \end{bmatrix},$$

evaluate **AA′**, **A′A**, and $\mathbf{A}^2$. Can you suggest any general statement?

13. Find $(\mathbf{A} + \mathbf{B})'$.

14. Find $(\mathbf{AB})'$. (This is a difficult one. It pays to try a 2×2 example and to experiment with the characteristic element of the product.)

15. Find **AB** if

$$\mathbf{A} = \begin{bmatrix} 1 & 2 \\ 3 & 4 \end{bmatrix} \quad \text{and} \quad \mathbf{B} = \begin{bmatrix} -2 & 1 \\ \frac{3}{2} & -\frac{1}{2} \end{bmatrix}.$$

16. Given that $\mathbf{AX} = \mathbf{Y}$, does $\mathbf{X'A} = \mathbf{Y}$?

Sections 15.4 and 15.5

1. Evaluate the following determinants.

a. $\begin{vmatrix} 1 & 2 \\ 3 & 4 \end{vmatrix}$

b. $\begin{vmatrix} 3 & 4 \\ 1 & 2 \end{vmatrix}$

c. $\begin{vmatrix} 1 & 0 & 3 \\ 2 & 1 & 3 \\ 2 & 0 & 1 \end{vmatrix}$

d. $\begin{vmatrix} 1 & 0 & 0 \\ 0 & 1 & 0 \\ 0 & 0 & 1 \end{vmatrix}$

e. $\begin{vmatrix} \lambda & 0 & 0 \\ 0 & \lambda & 0 \\ 0 & 0 & \lambda \end{vmatrix}$

f. $\begin{vmatrix} 0 & \lambda & 0 \\ \lambda & 0 & 0 \\ 0 & 0 & \lambda \end{vmatrix}$

g. $\begin{vmatrix} 2 & 1 & 3 \\ 1 & 0 & 3 \\ 2 & 0 & 1 \end{vmatrix}$

h. $\begin{vmatrix} 1 & 2 & 1 \\ 3 & 5 & 3 \\ 1 & 0 & 1 \end{vmatrix}$

i. $\begin{vmatrix} 1 & 2 & 0 \\ 3 & 6 & 1 \\ 1 & 2 & 0 \end{vmatrix}$

j. $\begin{vmatrix} 1 & 2 & 0 \\ 3 & 7 & 1 \\ 1 & 3 & 1 \end{vmatrix}$

k. $\begin{vmatrix} 2 & 1 & 2 \\ 1 & 0 & 0 \\ 3 & 3 & 1 \end{vmatrix}$

2. Prove that adding a multiple of one row of a determinant to another row does not alter the value of the determinant. (*Hint:* Write out the formula for expansion in terms of cofactors by the row to which the addition is to be made.)

3. For each of the determinants i and j in Question 1, show how the second column may be expressed as a linear combination of the other column or columns.

4. Calculate the determinant, if possible, of the following, and indicate the order of the determinant.

a. $\begin{vmatrix} 1 & 0 & 1 & 1 \\ 0 & 1 & 1 & 1 \\ 1 & 1 & 1 & 0 \\ 1 & 1 & 0 & 1 \end{vmatrix}$
b. $\begin{bmatrix} 1 & -1 & 1 \\ 1 & 1 & 1 \end{bmatrix}$

c. $[1, 1, 1]\begin{bmatrix} 1 \\ 1 \\ 1 \end{bmatrix}$
d. $\begin{bmatrix} 1 \\ 1 \\ 1 \end{bmatrix}[1, 1, 1]$

e. $\begin{bmatrix} a & b & c \\ e & f & g \\ d & e & f \\ e & f & g \end{bmatrix}$

Section 15.6

1. a. Find the inverse of the unit matrix **I**.
  b. Find the inverse of the scalar matrix $\lambda\mathbf{I}$.
  c. Find the inverse of $\begin{bmatrix} 2 & 1 \\ 1 & 3 \end{bmatrix}$.
  d. Find the inverse of $\begin{bmatrix} 1 & 0 & 0 \\ 1 & 1 & 0 \\ 1 & 1 & 1 \end{bmatrix}$ (a *triangular* matrix).

2. Which of the following matrices do not have inverses? Why not?

a. $\begin{bmatrix} 6 & 3 \\ 2 & 1 \end{bmatrix}$
b. $\begin{bmatrix} 1 & 0 & 0 \\ 0 & 6 & 3 \\ 0 & 2 & 1 \end{bmatrix}$

c. $\begin{bmatrix} 1 & 0 & 1 \\ 1 & 6 & 3 \\ 0 & 2 & 1 \end{bmatrix}$
d. $\begin{bmatrix} 1 & 0 \\ 1 & 6 \\ 1 & 2 \end{bmatrix}$

e.
$$\begin{array}{cccc} 1 & 1 & 1 & 1 \\ 1 & 1 & 6 & 3 \\ 1 & 1 & 2 & 1 \\ 1 & 1 & 1 & 1 \end{array}$$

f.
$$\begin{array}{cccc} 1 & 1 & 1 & 1 \\ 1 & 1 & 6 & 3 \\ 1 & 1 & 2 & 1 \\ 0 & 1 & 1 & 1 \end{array}$$

3. Find the inverse of the matrix in Question 2c.

4. a. Find the inverse of the triangular matrix

$$\mathbf{A} = \begin{bmatrix} a_{11} & 0 & 0 \\ a_{21} & a_{22} & 0 \\ a_{31} & a_{32} & a_{33} \end{bmatrix}.$$

b. Suppose that we have $\mathbf{Ax} = \mathbf{c}$, where $\mathbf{A}$ is as above and $\mathbf{c}$ is a vector of constants. Can you think of an easier way of solving for $\mathbf{x}$ than by applying our inversion procedure to $\mathbf{A}$?

5. Suppose that $\mathbf{Ax} = \mathbf{c}$, where $\mathbf{A}$ is the matrix of Question 2c and $\mathbf{c} = \{1 \quad 0 \quad 0\}$. Can you find a quicker way of solving for $\mathbf{x}$ than going through the inversion routine?

Section 15.7

1. Use Cramer's rule to solve the equations in Questions 4b and 5 of Section 15.6.

2. Use Cramer's rule to solve $\mathbf{Ax} = \mathbf{c}$ where $\mathbf{A} = [a_{ij}]$ is 3×3, $\mathbf{x}$ is 3×1, and $\mathbf{c} = \{0 \quad 1 \quad 0\}$.

3. Suppose that $\mathbf{Ax} = \mathbf{c}$, where

$$\mathbf{A} = \begin{bmatrix} 1 & 0 & 1 \\ 1 & 6 & 3 \\ 0 & 2 & 1 \end{bmatrix}$$

(which we inverted in Question 3 of Section 15.6). Use Cramer's rule to solve for $\mathbf{x}$ when $\mathbf{c} = \{1 \quad 0 \quad 0\}$, $\{0 \quad 1 \quad 0\}$, and $\{0 \quad 0 \quad 1\}$. Can you make any general remark?

4. Solve for x, by using Cramer's rule, in the following.

a. $3x + 7y = 20$
$2x + 7y = 20$

b. $y + z + x = 10$
$2y + 2z + x = 20$
$2y + z + 2x = 30$

c. $x + y = 10$
$2x + 2y = 50$

Chapter **16**

Chapter

Applications of Linear Algebra

In this chapter, we depart from our usual practice of giving micro-applications followed by macro-applications of new techniques. The reason is that, to extend our treatment of maximizing models, we should need yet more tools. What we can do with the tools we now have is to make a considerable extension of our discussion of macro-models. In the process we make the possibly surprising discovery that our new techniques for solving simultaneous linear equations can be used to deal with nonlinear models also. We can also take up a special case of general equilibrium theory. We devote Chapter 17 to this case, input–output analysis. It is allotted a chapter to itself because, unlike most of the other economic subject matter in this book, we do not assume that you are already familiar with much of it and we accordingly offer a self-contained discussion. The arrangement is therefore such that Chapter 17 could be skipped. It does, however, contain answers to some problems encountered, but not solved, in this chapter.

16.1 THE KEYNESIAN MODEL WITH MONEY ONCE AGAIN

In Chapter 3 we considered several Keynesian macro-models all of which used linear behavioral equations. We solved these models by the simple, and sometimes tedious, method of algebraic substitution. We now have sufficient tools at our command to enable us to handle with comparative ease very much more complex models than those studied so far.

We shall begin by applying our new technique to the last model that we studied in Chapter 3. In subsequent sections we go on to show how easily these techniques allow us to handle more complex models. The equations of the model studied in Section 3.13 are repeated below.

BEHAVIOR EQUATIONS

$$C = cY \qquad (1)$$

$$I = b + gr \qquad (2)$$

$$M^d = d + eY + fr \qquad (3)$$

$$M^s = M_0 \qquad (4)$$

EQUILIBRIUM CONDITIONS

$$Y = C + I \qquad (5)$$

$$M^d = M^s \qquad (6)$$

SIGN RESTRICTIONS ON PARAMETERS

$$0 < c < 1$$

$$g < 0 < b$$

$$f < 0 < d, e$$

The model has four (linear) behavioral equations the parameters of which are given predicted signs by economic theory. There are two equilibrium conditions ensuring that desired expenditure equals actual income and that the demand for money equals the supply. There are five endogenous variables, C, Y, M^d, r, and I, and three exogenous constants, the constant in the investment function, b, the constant in the money demand function, d, and the supply of money, M_0.

In Chapter 3 we solved the model by substituting down to one equation that expressed Y as a function of all the exogenous variables and parameters of the system and to another equation that expressed r as a function of the same exogenous variables and parameters. Such equations are called *reduced form equations*. A single such equation gives the solution for one endogenous variable in terms of the exogenous variables and parameters.[1]

The methods that we studied in Chapter 15 provide us with an

---

[1] In more complex models a reduced form equation gives one endogenous variable as a function of all *predetermined variables*. The concept of predetermined variables need not bother us here, since it is only exogenous variables and parameters that appear on the RHS of any of the reduced form equations encountered in this book.

alternative way of obtaining the reduced form equations. We first substitute the behavior equations into the equilibrium conditions to obtain equations that we write with the endogenous variables on the LHS and the exogenous variables on the RHS. In the present model this yields two equations:

$$(1 - c)Y - gr = b \tag{7a}$$

$$eY + fr = M_0 - d \quad . \tag{7b}$$

From what we learned in Chapter 15 we should immediately recognize the form of Eqs. (7) and see that they can be rewritten as

$$\begin{bmatrix} 1 - c & -g \\ e & f \end{bmatrix} \begin{bmatrix} Y \\ r \end{bmatrix} = \begin{bmatrix} b \\ M_0 - d \end{bmatrix} \quad . \tag{8}$$

In even more compact matrix notation we can write Eq. (8) as

$$\mathbf{Ay} = \mathbf{z} \quad ,$$

where $\mathbf{A}$ is the matrix of coefficients, $\mathbf{y}$ the vector of endogenous variables, and $\mathbf{z}$ the vector of exogenous variables. The solution is given by

$$\mathbf{y} = \mathbf{A}^{-1}\mathbf{z} \quad .$$

In the questions we shall encounter in this chapter, it is usually easier to use Cramer's rule than to invert the matrix directly, so we shall use it here. Let us write Δ for $|\mathbf{A}|$, Δ_Y for the determinant obtained by substituting the $\mathbf{z}$ vector into the first column of $\mathbf{A}$, and Δ_r for that obtained by substituting the $\mathbf{z}$ vector into the second column of $\mathbf{A}$. Then, by Cramer's rule, the solution is

$$Y = \frac{\Delta_Y}{\Delta}$$

and

$$r = \frac{\Delta_r}{\Delta} \quad .$$

All we have to do now is evaluate the determinants. We have

$$\Delta = f(1 - c) + eg$$

$$\Delta_Y = \begin{vmatrix} b & -g \\ (M_0 - d) & f \end{vmatrix} = bf + g(M_0 - d)$$

$$\Delta_r = \begin{vmatrix} 1 - c & b \\ e & (M_0 - d) \end{vmatrix} = (1 - c)(M_0 - d) - eb \quad .$$

We solve for Y as Δ_Y/Δ and separate out the exogenous expenditure and money terms to obtain

$$Y = \frac{b}{(1-c) + eg/f} + \frac{M_0 - d}{(1-c)f/g + e} \quad , \tag{9a}$$

which is Eq. (59) of Chapter 3. The rate of interest solves as

$$r = \frac{(1-c)(M_0 - d)}{f(1-c) + eg} - \frac{eb}{f(1-c) + eg} \quad , \tag{9b}$$

which is Eq. (60) in Chapter 3. Notice that the denominators of (9a) and (9b) are the same (both equal to Δ). This, of course, follows from the fact that

$$\mathbf{A}^{-1} = \frac{1}{|\mathbf{A}|} [\mathbf{A}_{ij}]' \quad .$$

In Chapter 3 we relied on inspection to determine the change in Y associated with a change in each of the exogenous variables. The equations are simple enough so that this crude method works, but we should now note that what we formally require is the partial derivative of each of the endogenous variables with respect to the exogenous variables taken one at a time. For example, we have

$$\frac{\partial Y}{\partial b} = \frac{1}{(1-c) + eg/f} \quad .$$

Analogous expressions can easily be calculated for $\partial Y/\partial d$, $\partial Y/\partial M_0$, $\partial r/\partial b$, $\partial r/\partial d$, and $\partial r/\partial M_0$. It is a common, and good, practice to put bars over variables when one wishes to indicate that it is equilibrium values that are intended. Thus we should write $\partial \bar{Y}/\partial b$, etc., to show that it is the partial derivative of the *equilibrium* value of Y with respect to b. In most of this chapter, we are so obviously discussing changes in equilibrium values that, to avoid notational clutter, we have suppressed the bars.

So far we have shown that we can use Cramer's rule to derive reduced form equations for each of our autonomous variables. We have also shown that we can then differentiate these equations to find the rate of change of the endogenous variable with respect to each of the exogenous variables. We can, however, take an alternative route that allows us to discover these rates of change without going through the intermediate step of deriving reduced form equations. This is a mere convenience with the present linear model, but it is, as we shall see, crucial for nonlinear models.

To proceed in this second way we return to Eqs. (7a) and (7b) and totally differentiate them to obtain

$$(1 - c)\ \mathrm{d}Y - g\ \mathrm{d}r = \mathrm{d}b \qquad\qquad (10a)$$

$$e\ \mathrm{d}Y + f\ \mathrm{d}r = \mathrm{d}M_0 - \mathrm{d}d\ . \qquad\qquad (10b)$$

These equations tell us the changes in Y and r that must be associated with a change in any of the three exogenous variables if the equilibrium conditions are to continue to hold. Since the behavioral equations are all linear, the coefficients of (10) are all constants. If we express these equations in matrix form, we obtain

$$\begin{bmatrix} 1-c & -g \\ e & f \end{bmatrix}\begin{bmatrix} \mathrm{d}Y \\ \mathrm{d}r \end{bmatrix} = \begin{bmatrix} \mathrm{d}b \\ \mathrm{d}M_0 - \mathrm{d}d \end{bmatrix}\ . \qquad\qquad (11)$$

Here we have exactly the form of (8), with the vectors of endogenous and exogenous variables replaced by their differentials.

Let us take further advantage of the compactness of vector notation. If $\mathbf{x}$ is a vector, $[x_1, \ldots, x_i, \ldots, x_n]$, say, we write $\mathbf{dx}$ for the vector $[\mathrm{d}x_1, \ldots, \mathrm{d}x_i, \ldots, \mathrm{d}x_n]$. We may now write (10a) and (10b) as

$$\mathbf{A}\ \mathbf{dy} = \mathbf{dz}$$

and obtain

$$\mathbf{dy} = \mathbf{A}^{-1}\ \mathbf{dz}\ .$$

This should hardly surprise us, since if $ay = z$, then $a\ \mathrm{d}y = \mathrm{d}z$, and $\mathbf{A}$ is the matrix analogy of the scalar coefficient a.

We can again use Cramer's rule to solve these equations for changes in Y and r that are associated with changes in the exogenous variables. The solution for Y is

$$\mathrm{d}Y = \frac{\Delta_Y}{\Delta} = \frac{\mathrm{d}b}{(1-c) + eg/f} + \frac{\mathrm{d}M_0 - \mathrm{d}d}{(1-c)f/g + e}\ .$$

If we let $\mathrm{d}M_0 = \mathrm{d}d = 0$ and divide through by $\mathrm{d}b$, we obtain the familiar

$$\frac{\mathrm{d}Y}{\mathrm{d}b} = \frac{1}{(1-c) + eg/f}\ .$$

We know from Chapter 8 that although $\mathrm{d}Y/\mathrm{d}b$ is the ratio of two finite differentials, they are so defined that their ratio is equal to the slope of the tangent line *at the point at which the partial derivatives are evaluated.*[2] Since in this case we are determining how Y varies

---

[2] In a linear system the italicized qualification is unnecessary since the slope of the tangent is everywhere the same and equal to the slope of the function.

with b, holding M_0 and d constant $(dM_0 = dd = 0)$, we have determined the value of the partial derivative

$$\frac{\partial Y}{\partial b} = \frac{1}{(1 - c) + eg/f} \quad.$$

As long as we remember that, whenever there is more than one exogenous variable, the rate of change of an endogenous variable with respect to a single exogenous variable is a partial derivative (because the other exogenous variables are being held constant) no harm is done by leaving them written in the form dY/db, as is a common practice.

We have now found an alternative method of doing our comparative statics (at least for the linear models): we substitute our behavioral equations into the equilibrium conditions; we totally differentiate the equilibrium conditions and express the resulting equations in matrix form as $\mathbf{A}\,\mathbf{dy} = \mathbf{dz}$; we use Cramer's rule to solve for $\mathbf{dy}$; by letting the elements of $\mathbf{dz}$ take on nonzero values one at a time, we calculate dy_i/dz_j for any pair of endogenous and exogenous variables, i and j, in which we are interested; the expressions obtained for dy_i/dz_j are equal to $\partial y_i/\partial z_j$, which is what we require.

16.2 GOVERNMENT AND FOREIGN TRADE

In Chapter 3 we added foreign trade, the government, and money to the simple Keynesian model one at a time but never simultaneously. For completeness we shall now add both a government and a foreign trade sector to the model of Section 16.1, which already contains money.

We first add a government, which spends at rate G and imposes a proportional income tax at rate t (just as in Section 3.10). We shall not repeat the argument by which we derived

$$C = c(1 - t)Y \quad. \tag{12}$$

Equation (12) now replaces (1) in the model above. The equilibrium condition (5) must be altered to allow for government expenditure:

$$Y = C + I + G \quad. \tag{13}$$

Making the usual substitutions of behavioral equations into equilibrium conditions and gathering independent variables on the LHS and dependent variables on the RHS yields

$$Y - c(1 - t)Y - gr = G + b$$
$$eY + fr = M_0 - d \quad.$$

We can improve on this by factoring the term Y to obtain

$$\{1 - c(1 - t)\}Y - gr = G + b \tag{14a}$$

$$eY + fr = M_0 - d \quad . \tag{14b}$$

We should immediately recognize the form of Eqs. (14) and see that they can be rewritten as

$$\begin{bmatrix} 1 - c(1 - t) & -g \\ e & f \end{bmatrix} \begin{bmatrix} Y \\ r \end{bmatrix} = \begin{bmatrix} G + b \\ M_0 - d \end{bmatrix} \tag{15}$$

Comparing (15) with (11) we see that the only changes are in the element a_{11} in the **A** matrix, which goes from $1 - c$ to $1 - c(1 - t)$, and in the addition of G to the vector of exogenous variables (where it is added to the exogenous constant in the investment expenditure function). The old a_{11} element had the sign restriction $0 < (1 - c) < 1$ and so does the new element: $0 < 1 - c(1 - t) < 1$ (since $0 < c, t < 1$).

We have now made a major change as far as economics is concerned: adding a government to an economy is no trivial matter. As far as the mathematics is concerned, however, the changes *are* trivial. Indeed there is no need to rework all the analysis of Section 16.1. Instead we need only go to any result in which we are interested, dY/dM_0, say, and wherever the term $1 - c$ occurs replace it with $1 - c(1 - t)$.

Now let us allow for foreign trade and see if it can be handled as simply as was government. We use the same simple assumptions about the foreign sector used in Chapter 3. In some ways, this is perhaps not a very good model, since, if we are to introduce the domestic interest rate, we might well want to consider foreign interest rates, exchange rates, price levels, and capital movements. The required analysis is far too ambitious for an elementary book, so we shall content ourselves with the assembly and solution of the model of Chapter 3.

From Section 16.1 we retain Eqs. (2) and (3). From Section 3.12 we have

$$M = mY(1 - t) \quad . \tag{16}$$

(We are running out of symbols: M represents both money and imports. Confusion is, however, avoided, since the money supply always appears as M_0 in the present section.) Our equilibrium condition in the goods market now becomes

$$Y = C + I + G + X - M \quad , \tag{17}$$

which was Eq. (43) of Section 3.12.

Our now-familiar practice of substituting into the equilibrium conditions and arranging the terms suitably yields

$$Y - c(1 - t)Y - m(1 - t)Y - gr = G + X + b$$

and

$$eY + fr = M_0 - d \quad .$$

Factoring out the Y and arranging in matrix form, we have

$$\begin{bmatrix} 1 - (1 - t)(c - m) & -g \\ e & f \end{bmatrix} \begin{bmatrix} Y \\ r \end{bmatrix} = \begin{bmatrix} G + X + b \\ M_0 - d \end{bmatrix} \quad .$$

Again the only changes are in the addition of a new term, X, to the vector of exogenous variables and in the coefficient a_{11} in the $\mathbf{A}$ matrix. It is only necessary to show that the new coefficient, like the old, is a positive fraction. All the parameters t, c, and m are positive fractions, and $m < c$ (since it is impossible that imports of consumer goods should exceed total consumption). It follows that $(1 - t)(c - m)$, the product of two positive fractions, is itself a positive fraction, whence $0 < 1 - (1 - t)(c - m) < 1$. Once again, we do not need to redo all our comparative statics from Section 16.1: we can use the results derived there and replace $1 - c$ wherever it occurs with the new term $1 - (1 - t)(c - m)$. Just as a check you will be asked to do some of the comparative statics of this model in the questions.

16.3 A NONLINEAR KEYNESIAN MODEL WITH MONEY

So far we have confined ourselves to linear versions of the Keynesian models. We are now able to take the decisive step of dropping the highly restrictive assumption that all our behavioral equations are linear. We have seen that the introduction of both a government and a foreign trade sector does not change the model in any basic way, and it is convenient now to revert to the simpler model of Section 16.1. Once we have studied this model in nonlinear form, it is a trivial matter to allow for trade and government, just as it was a trivial matter when we went from Section 16.1 to Section 16.2 in the linear version of the model.

We give below a nonlinear version of the model of Section 16.1 and repeat the linear version beside it for the purposes of comparison.[3]

---

[3] Recall the notation of Chapter 8 whereby C_Y means $\partial C/\partial Y$, I_r means $\partial I/\partial r$, etc.

LINEAR VERSION		NONLINEAR VERSION	
BEHAVIORAL EQUATIONS			
$C = cY$	$(18a)$	$C = C(Y)$	$(18b)$
$I = b + gr$	$(19a)$	$I = I(r)$	$(19b)$
$M^d = d + eY + fr$	$(20a)$	$M^d = L(Y, r)$	$(20b)$
$M^s = M_0$	$(21a)$	$M^s = M_0$	$(21b)$
EQUILIBRIUM CONDITIONS			
$Y = C + I$	$(22a)$	$Y = C + I + Z$	$(22b)$
$M^d = M^s$	$(23a)$	$M^d = M^s$	$(23b)$

SIGN RESTRICTIONS ON PARAMETERS

$0 < c < 1$	$0 < C_Y < 1$
$g < 0 < b$	$I_r < 0$
$f < 0 < d, e$	$L_r < 0 < L_Y$

The model is an obvious nonlinear extension of the already familiar linear model. One or two points, however, require comment. The equilibrium conditions (22a) and (22b) differ only in that (22b) explicitly includes exogenous expenditure, Z, since, with I given by $I(r)$, there would otherwise be no exogenous term in the equation. In the linear model, any constant in any expenditure function (b is the only one in this case) acts as exogenous expenditure, doing the same job as is done by Z in the nonlinear model. The behavior predicted by economic theory is summarized by the signs of the partial derivatives in the nonlinear model. The sign restrictions are exactly the same as those on the corresponding parameters in the linear model, the major difference being that the *magnitudes* of the partial derivatives in the nonlinear case depend on where on the relevant functions they are evaluated, whereas the magnitudes of the linear coefficients are the same everywhere. (The constants in the linear model are, of course, partial derivatives.)

Can we do comparative static exercises with this nonlinear model to obtain results comparable with those obtained for the linear model in Section 16.1? It is clear that we cannot follow the first method used in Section 16.1 of finding a reduced form equation for each of the endogenous variables and then differentiating each equation with respect to each of the exogenous variables. If we substitute the nonlinear behavioral relations into the equilibrium conditions, we obtain

$$Y = C(Y) + I(r) + Z \tag{24a}$$

and

$$L(Y, r) = M_0 \quad , \tag{24b}$$

but there is no way that we can substitute either (24a) or (24b) into the other to eliminate one of the two remaining endogenous variables. We cannot, therefore, obtain a reduced form equation for either Y or r.

We must now try the second method: we totally differentiate (24) and gather all the endogenous variables on the LHS and the exogenous variables on the RHS. This yields

$$dY - C_Y \, dY - I_r \, dr = dZ \tag{25a}$$

and

$$L_Y \, dY + C_r \, dr = dM_0 \quad . \tag{25b}$$

We now have an obvious and urgent question: do Eqs. (25) constitute a pair of linear simultaneous equations? If they do, they can be easily handled: we have only to apply our matrix methods. The coefficients on these equations are the derivatives C_Y, I_r, L_Y, and L_r. Certainly as we alter the values of the variables the coefficients of (25) can be expected to change. (If they did not, we would be back to the linear model, whose restrictions we are seeking to avoid.) But Eqs. (25) are the (linear) equations of the tangent planes to (24) evaluated at a particular point. Indeed, since they must be evaluated at the point where they both hold simultaneously, they must be evaluated at the equilibrium values of Y and r. They therefore measure exact rates of change at that point. Thus we can handle these linear equations by the linear methods of Chapter 15, and use them to obtain rates of change of a nonlinear system at the point at which the (linear) tangent plane touches it.

Recalling the methods of Chapter 15, we can rewrite (25) in matrix form as

$$\begin{bmatrix} 1 - C_Y & -I_r \\ L_Y & L_r \end{bmatrix} \begin{bmatrix} dY \\ dr \end{bmatrix} = \begin{bmatrix} dZ \\ dM_0 \end{bmatrix} . \tag{26}$$

Using a still more compact notation we can rewrite (26) as

$$\mathbf{A} \, \mathbf{dy} = \mathbf{dz} \quad , \tag{27}$$

where $\mathbf{A}$ is the matrix of coefficients, $\mathbf{dy}$ is the vector of differentials of the endogenous variables, and $\mathbf{dz}$ is the vector of differentials of the exogenous variables. We wish to express the changes in the endogenous variables y as functions of changes in the exogenous variables z, whence we require the solution to (26) for dy, which is

$$dy = A^{-1} dz \quad .$$

As in Section 16.1, it is easier to use Cramer's rule than to invert the matrix directly. Again we write Δ for $|A|$, Δ_Y for the determinant obtained by substituting the dz vector into the first column of A, and Δ_r for the determinant obtained by substituting the dz vector into the second column of A. Then, by Cramer's rule, the solution is

$$dY = \frac{\Delta_Y}{\Delta} \tag{28}$$

$$dr = \frac{\Delta_r}{\Delta} \quad . \tag{29}$$

All we have to do now is to evaluate the determinants. From (26) we have

$$\Delta = \begin{vmatrix} 1 - C_Y & -I_r \\ L_Y & L_r \end{vmatrix}$$

$$= (1 - C_Y)L_r + L_Y I_r \quad , \tag{30}$$

$$\Delta_Y = \begin{vmatrix} dZ & -I_r \\ dM_0 & L_r \end{vmatrix}$$

$$= L_r \, dZ + I_r \, dM_0 \quad , \tag{31}$$

and

$$\Delta_r = \begin{vmatrix} 1 - C_Y & dZ \\ L_Y & dM_0 \end{vmatrix}$$

$$= (1 - C_Y) \, dM_0 - L_Y \, dZ \quad . \tag{32}$$

We shall concentrate here on changes in Y, but you will be asked to check changes in r in some of the end-of-chapter questions. We immediately solve for dY by substituting (30) and (31) into (28), whence

$$dY = \frac{L_r}{(1 - C_Y)L_r + L_Y I_r} \, dZ + \frac{I_r}{(1 - C_Y)L_r + L_Y I_r} \, dM_0 \quad . \tag{33}$$

If we let $dM_0 = 0$, we obtain the equation for the tangent line in Y-Z-space evaluated at the point of equilibrium:

$$dY = \frac{1}{(1 - C_Y) + (L_Y I_r)/L_r} \, dZ \quad . \tag{34}$$

Dividing through by dZ gives

$$\frac{dY}{dZ} = \frac{1}{(1 - C_Y) + (L_Y I_r)/L_r} \quad . \tag{35}$$

The sign restrictions on the derivatives allow us to sign (35) as unambiguously positive. This is exactly the same as the multiplier obtained for the linear model in Eq. (61) in Chapter 3 with the exception that the derivatives were there the constant parameters in the linear behavior functions.

To discover the effect of changes in the quantity of money, with autonomous expenditure held constant, we substitute $dZ = 0$ into (33) and manipulate it to obtain

$$dY = \frac{1}{(1 - C_Y)(L_r/I_r) + L_Y} \, dM_0 \quad . \tag{36}$$

This is the equation of the tangent line, and division by dM_0 allows us to determine the value of the partial derivative dY/dM_0 as

$$\frac{dY}{dM_0} = \frac{1}{(1 - C_Y)(L_r/I_r) + L_Y} \quad . \tag{37}$$

Again, except that the constant parameters are replaced by derivatives, this money multiplier is the same as that derived in (62) in Chapter 3.

Evidently we can now dispense with the restrictive assumption that all behavioral relations are linear and yet derive similar results from our more general model. This is a great increase in generality and yet no increase in difficulty of calculation once the necessary techniques have been mastered.

16.4 THE QUALITATIVE CALCULUS

Before going on to consider more complicated models, let us review our method. We start with a set of behavior equations involving endogenous and exogenous variables and a set of equilibrium conditions, and we substitute the former into the latter to "solve" the system. If the equations are linear, we can indeed solve explicitly to obtain the reduced form of the system: a set of equations in which each endogenous variable depends only on the exogenous variables and parameters of the system. Examples of reduced form equations are provided by (9a) and (9b). Comparative statics, as we have seen, is then extremely easy. If, however, we are given only functional relations in general form, such as $q^d = D(p, \alpha)$ or $M^d = L(Y, r)$, we cannot solve explicitly. We can say, however, that if the model has a solution at all, it must in fact be solved by a set of equations of the form

$$y_i = \phi^i(\mathbf{z}) \quad,$$

where we write y_i for the ith endogenous variable, $\mathbf{z}$ for the vector of exogenous variables, and ϕ^i for the specific relation between the endogenous variable and all the exogenous variables. If we had the functions ϕ^i, we should partially differentiate them to obtain

$$\frac{\partial y_i}{\partial z_j} = \phi_j{}^i$$

for all the y_i and all elements of the vector $\mathbf{z}$. The partial derivatives $\phi_j{}^i$ are, of course, the instantaneous rates of change of the endogenous variables with respect to the exogenous variables. If we are successful, we have qualitative predictions (directions of change) that, in principle at least, are testable.

In general, however, we cannot solve explicitly for the functions ϕ^i, so we must proceed otherwise.[4] We introduced the general method in Section 7.7 (which was starred: if you did not read it then, a reference back might be helpful now). There are two differences between what we are now doing and what we did there. The first is that we now have more than one equilibrium equation to deal with (which, thanks to matrix methods, presents no real difficulty). The second is that in Section 7.7 we were dealing with a maximizing model, and could appeal to second-order conditions for help with signs. We are now dealing with market-clearing conditions and have no second-order conditions: as we have seen above, we have to find the sign of each determinant using such restrictions on the signs of partial derivatives as are provided by economic theory. (In Section 16.9 we shall consider some cases in which we cannot do this.) Nonetheless, there is, as we shall see, a fundamental symmetry.

Consider the equilibrium equations (24). We cannot explicitly solve them to obtain the functions ϕ^i. Taking all the endogenous variables to the LHS, however, we may rewrite them, as we did in Section 7.7, as

$$F(Y, r) = Z$$

$$G(Y, r) = M_0 \quad.$$

---

[4] It may help to recall the utility maximization model. We maximize a function $V = U(\mathbf{x}) - \lambda[\mathbf{p'x} - B]$ (using vector notation) to obtain the first-order conditions $U_i - \lambda p_i = 0$ and the budget constraint. These equations are to be solved for the *demand* functions $x^i = \phi^i(\mathbf{p'}, B)$. If we do not have the actual form of U, we cannot, of course, write out the functions ϕ^i algebraically, but we certainly assume that they exist. The partial derivative $\phi_i{}^i$ is simply the slope of the demand curve for the ith good with respect to its own price.

We totally differentiated these equations to obtain (25), which we may now write as

$$F_Y \, dY + F_r \, dr = dZ$$

$$G_Y \, dY + G_r \, dr = dM_0 \quad .$$

Application of our matrix methods provided "solutions" in Eqs. (35) and (37).

Let us consider the nature of these solutions. If we vary the exogenous variables one at a time, we obtain partial derivatives. Thus from (33) we have, holding M_0 constant,

$$\frac{\partial Y}{\partial Z} = \frac{L_r}{\Delta} \quad ,$$

which we may rewrite as

$$\frac{G_r}{G_Y G_r - G_Y F_r} \quad .$$

This, however, is an expression purely in instantaneous (partial) rates of change: it gives the instantaneous rate of change of Y with respect to Z. It is therefore $\phi_Z{}^Y$, the partial derivative with respect to Z of the unknown solution function ϕ^Y. We have, in fact, found the general method for finding the partial derivatives of these functions, evaluated in terms of the partial derivatives of our behavior equations, in spite of the fact that we cannot solve explicitly for the functions ϕ.

We now see that, from (35) and (37), varying the exogenous variables one at a time, we obtain the four partial derivatives

$$\phi_Z{}^Y \qquad \phi_M{}^Y$$

$$\phi_Z{}^r \qquad \phi_M{}^r \quad .$$

These are the exact rates of change.

We may now rewrite (35) and (37) in differential form as

$$dY = \phi_Z{}^Y \, dZ + \phi_M{}^Y \, dM$$

$$dr = \phi_Z{}^r \, dZ + \phi_M{}^r \, dM$$

(and, clearly, we should write $\partial Y/\partial Z = L_r/\Delta$, instead of dY/dZ).

The qualitative calculus is concerned with finding the signs of changes in endogenous variables that are associated with changes in exogenous variables, that is, with instantaneous rates of change. When we come to real-world applications, of course, we find that, even if exogenous variables such as Z and M_0 vary one at a time, they commonly vary by discrete jumps. If, let us say, there is a finite increment in Z, M constant, we predict the changes in the endogenous variables from

$$dY = \phi_z{}^Y \, dZ$$

and

$$dr = \phi_z{}^r \, dZ \quad .$$

In these two differentials, the partial derivatives $\phi_z{}^Y$ and $\phi_z{}^r$ are, of course, the instantaneous rates of change L_r/Δ and $-L_y/\Delta$. In applying them to a discrete jump in Z, however, we obviously introduce error: we are, in effect, using tangents (instantaneous rates of change) to predict the change in the value of a function consequent upon a discrete change in the independent variable. Clearly the bigger the change in Z, and the more nonlinear the functions ϕ^i, the bigger the scope for error. Using the differentials $dY = (L_r/\Delta) \, dZ$ and $dr = (-L_y/\Delta) \, dZ$ is often called "linearizing in the neighborhood of equilibrium," which means treating the partial derivatives of the functions ϕ^i as constants in dealing with discrete changes in the independent variables.

16.5   TWO EXTREME CASES

As a first exercise, let us consider the extreme cases of the "Keynesian" and "classical" models. In the classical model the demand for money is assumed to depend only on income: $M^d = L(Y)$. This means that $L_r = 0$. Inspection of (35) shows that, with $L_r = 0$ and taking changes in exogenous variables one at a time, $dY/dZ = 0$, while $dY/dM = 1/L_y$. Similar inspection of Eq. (37) shows that $dr/dM = (1 - C_y)/I_r L_y < 0$ and $dr/dZ = -1/I_r > 0$. Thus in this extreme classical case a rise in exogenous expenditure leaves national income unchanged but does raise the rate of interest. For this classical world (really a pseudoclassical one), fiscal policy that influences exogenous expenditure does not affect national income but only the division between its various components: only monetary policy has any effect on national income. If the price level is fixed, as in the simple Keynesian model, this means that monetary policy influences real income and employment, while if real income is fixed at its full employment level and the price level is variable, monetary policy influences prices and hence money national income.

Consider next a Keynesian special case in which monetary policy has no effect on national income but fiscal policy does. This case can be produced by either of two extreme situations. For the first, investment is assumed to be completely unresponsive to the interest rate. Formally, this gives $I_r = 0$, and inspection of (35) shows that $dY/dZ =$

$L_r/[(1 - C_y)L_r] > 0$, whereas $dY/dM = 0$. Equation (37) shows that $dr/dM = 1/L_r < 0$ and $dr/dZ = -\{L_y/[(1 - C_y)L_r]\} < 0$. In this case raising the quantity of money lowers the interest rate (because people try to invest their extra money, and this raises the price of bonds), but since no expenditure responds to changes in the interest rate, national income is unaffected. A second extreme Keynesian case occurs if the demand for money becomes infinitely elastic against the interest rate. Keynes envisaged this possibility arising during a depression when the price of bonds was so high—the interest rate so low—that no one would want to invest further money in bonds for fear of capital losses when their price fell in the near future. When the interest rate became so low everyone would want to hold money—possibly in the expectation of investing some of it in bonds after their prices fell—or, in Keynes' terminology, liquidity preference would become absolute. Formally this means $L_r \rightarrow \infty$. Inspection of (35) shows that as $L_r \rightarrow \infty$ then $dY/dM \rightarrow 0$. To establish dY/dZ it is simplest to express the first term of (35) (letting $dM = 0$) as

$$dY = \frac{1}{(1 - C_y) + (I_r L_y)/L_r} \, dZ \quad .$$

Now as $L_r \rightarrow \infty$ it is clear that $dY/dZ \rightarrow 1/(1 - C_y) > 0$, which is the multiplier for a "real" Keynesian model without a monetary sector. Inspection of (35) also shows that as $L_r \rightarrow \infty$, $dY/dM \rightarrow 0$ because the L_r-term in the denominator dominates the whole expression as it increases without limit. For this extreme Keynesian case monetary policy has no effect either on Y or r since any new money created by the central bank merely disappears into idle hoards held against the expectation of an imminent fall in the price of bonds. On the other hand, fiscal policy that increases autonomous expenditure has its maximum expansionary effect since there is no induced rise in interest rates to dampen down investment.

It is now believed by most economists that these two extreme cases are at most rare occurrences, but the analysis shows that the combination of low L_r and high I_r increases the effectiveness of monetary policy relative to fiscal policy, whereas high L_r and low I_r makes fiscal policy more effective relative to monetary policy. One of the major differences between the monetarists and the neo-Keynesians is over the empirical magnitudes of these partial derivatives. Monetarists believe that the rate of interest has a small effect on the demand for money and a large effect on aggregate expenditure, that is, $|L_r|$ is low and $|I_r|$ is high, whereas neo-Keynesians tend to believe that the rate of interest has a large influence on the demand for money and a small influence on aggregate expenditure, that is, $|L_r|$ is high and $|I_r|$ is low.

16.6 CHANGES IN THE STRUCTURE OF THE MODEL

We now have a technique for handling macro-models and discovering their comparative static properties with relative ease. We shall illustrate the use of this technique by ringing some changes on our basic macro-model and seeing what differences they make to the results. Deciding what models are the most interesting theoretically, and the most useful empirically, is one of the major problems usually dealt with in an intermediate macro-course. We cannot attempt so ambitious a task here, so the choice of particular variations and the omission of others is not meant to imply anything about the authors' opinions of the relative merits of the models. Debate about the implications of alternative models is common, and since we now have available an engine for settling many such debates, it seems sensible to illustrate its use.

In the Keynesian model studied so far in macro sections of this book the price level is held constant, whence money and real expenditure vary in proportion to each other. It is a common extension of this model to make the price level a variable by making the real wage rate, W/P, a function of the level of employment. If the money wage, W, is held constant, then the real wage is altered by changes in the price level, P. There are many doubts about the empirical relevance of this model, but, following our present agenda, let us at least try to discover what difference such a change makes in the behavior of the model.

The volume of output depends on the quantity of all factors used, and in the short run with land and capital constant we can write

$$Y = g(N) \quad , \tag{38}$$

where N is the quantity of labor and Y is now the real quantity of output. The marginal product of labor is the derivative of output with respect to labor:

$$MP_L = g'(N) \quad .$$

If profit-maximizing firms sell their products in competitive markets, they will equate the real wage rate to the marginal product of labor:

$$\frac{W}{P} = g'(N) \quad . \tag{39}$$

It would be possible to add Eqs. (38) and (39) directly to our model and proceed as before, but it turns out to be simpler in the long haul to eliminate N first and so express the wage rate as a function of Y.

What we need to do is to invert the function in (38) to obtain

$$N = g^{-1}(Y) \quad , \tag{40}$$

which we can do because Y is a monotonically increasing function of N in (38). Now we substitute (40) into (39) and obtain

$$\frac{W}{P} = (g^{-1})' \quad . \tag{41}$$

From (40), g^{-1} is a function of Y, and (41) is the first derivative of that function. It is convenient to rewrite (41) as

$$\frac{W}{P} = f(Y) \quad , \tag{42}$$

where $f = (g^{-1})'$, and, if we keep W fixed but allow P to vary, we have increased the number of both equations and variables by one.

Before we can proceed, however, there is one further problem that needs attention. As long as the price level was fixed, as in all previous models, there was no distinction needed between real and money expenditures. Once, however, we let the price level change, we must make such a distinction. Some subtle problems are involved, but the easiest method of making this distinction is to define Y, C, I, and Z in real terms. They refer, in other words, to physical units of output.[5] The demand for and the supply of money, on the other hand, are defined in terms of nominal units of money. We then have to change the behavioral equation for the demand for money to allow the quantity of money demanded not only to rise as real income rises and as the rate of interest falls but also to rise as the price level rises. Thus if, for example, real Y and r are constant but the price level doubles, we expect more units of money to be demanded both for transactions purposes and because the speculative demand is likely to require a given amount of real purchasing power held rather than a given amount of nominal monetary units. This makes the demand for money[6]

$$M^D = L(Y, r, P) \qquad (L_P > 0) \quad . \tag{43}$$

If this equation is substituted for (20b) and Eq. (42) is added, we obtain our new model with the price level endogenous and real and

---

[5] In a one-product economy we could measure real output in simple physical units, say bushels of wheat or tons of steel. In a many-product economy "real" output will have to be measured by index numbers using constant price weights.

[6] The demand for money is commonly assumed to be homogeneous of degree 1 in absolute prices. This assumption allows us to be more explicit about (43) and write

$$M^D = PL(Y, r) \quad .$$

In the text we work with the weaker assumption that the demand for money is merely an increasing function of the price level, that is, $L_P > 0$.

money variables distinguished. The full model is now

$$C = C(Y) \tag{18b}$$

$$I = I(r) \tag{19b}$$

$$Y = C + I + Z \tag{22b}$$

$$M^D = L(Y, r, P) \tag{43}$$

$$M^S = M_0 \tag{21b}$$

$$M^D = M^S \tag{23b}$$

$$\frac{W}{P} = f(Y) \quad \text{or} \quad W = Pf(Y) \quad . \tag{42}$$

To keep the model "Keynesian" in character we are still assuming that the money wage, W, is exogenous, but the price level is now an additional variable, and we have added an additional equation (42). (We have also modified the demand-for-money equation.)

We can proceed to discover the comparative static properties of our new model. First substitute behavioral relations into the three equilibrium conditions to obtain

$$Y - C(Y) - I(r) = Z$$

$$L(Y, r, P) = M$$

$$Pf(Y) = W \quad .$$

Totally differentiating these three equations and writing them in matrix form, we have

$$\begin{bmatrix} 1 - C_Y & -I_r & 0 \\ L_Y & L_r & L_P \\ Pf_Y & 0 & f(Y) \end{bmatrix} \begin{bmatrix} dY \\ dr \\ dP \end{bmatrix} = \begin{bmatrix} dZ \\ dM \\ dW \end{bmatrix} \quad . \tag{44}$$

We denote the coefficient matrix of (44) by $\mathbf{A}$ and expand $|\mathbf{A}| = \Delta$ along the first row to get

$$\Delta = (1 - C_Y)L_r f(Y) + I_r L_Y f(Y) - I_r Pf_Y L_P < 0 \quad .$$
$$(+ - +) \qquad + (- + +) - (- - +)$$

As a reminder, the sign of each element is printed below it. [Don't forget that, from (42), $f(Y)$ is the marginal product of labor, which is assumed positive, whereas f_Y is the change in the marginal product with respect to a change in output, which must be negative by the assumption of diminishing marginal productivity.] We next evaluate

$$\Delta_Y = \begin{vmatrix} dZ & -I_r & 0 \\ dM & L_r & L_P \\ dW & 0 & f(Y) \end{vmatrix}$$

$$= f(Y)L_r\, dZ + I_r f(Y)\, dM - I_r L_P\, dW \quad . \qquad (45)$$
$$ (+-) \quad + \quad (-+) \quad - \quad (-+)$$

According to Cramer's rule we have $dY = \Delta_Y/\Delta$, which is

$$dY = \frac{f(Y)L_r}{\Delta}\, dZ + \frac{I_r f(Y)}{\Delta}\, dM - \frac{I_r L_P}{\Delta}\, dW \quad .$$

We can use this equation of the tangent plane in Y-Z-M-W-space to evaluate the slope of the tangent lines, allowing the exogenous variables to change one at a time. Letting dZ, dM, and dW be nonzero one at a time, and using the signs from (45) and the result already established that $\Delta < 0$, we obtain $dY/dZ > 0$, $dY/M > 0$, and $dY/dW < 0$.

Thus, just as in the simpler Keynesian model, Y is increased by an increase in either M or Z. The additional result that we have obtained from this model is

$$\frac{dY}{dW} = -\frac{I_r L_P}{\Delta} < 0 \quad ,$$

which tells us that (assuming unemployment) lowering wages raises employment and vice versa. This is a result that Keynes thought unrealistic. Why do we get it in this model? Consider the model in equilibrium and then impose on it an exogenous reduction in W. According to (42), the only way in which output could be left unaffected would be if P fell in proportion to W so that the real wage were unchanged. But, if this were to happen, less money would be demanded, because the same real transactions would occur at a *lower* price level, and in order to equate the unchanged supply of money to the demand for it the interest rate would have to fall. But this would increase investment and therefore income. Thus a cut in money wages must be associated with a rise in equilibrium income and output in this model, given that the initial equilibrium is at less-than-full employment.

We now wish to know the effect on r and P of changes in our exogenous variables. You are left to expand the appropriate determinants to verify that

$$\Delta_r = (1 - C_Y)f(Y)\, dM - (1 - C_Y)L_P\, dW + (Pf_Y L_P - L_Y f(Y))\, dZ \quad .$$
$$ (\ + \quad + \ ) - (\ + \quad + \ ) + [(-+) - (++)]$$

Since $\Delta < 0$, we have $dr/dM < 0$, $dr/dW > 0$, and $dr/dZ > 0$. Finally you should verify that

$$\Delta_P = -Pf_Y I_r \, dM - Pf_Y L_r \, dZ + [(1 - C_Y)L_r + L_Y I_r] \, dW \quad ,$$
$$- \; (+ \; - \; -) \; -(+ \; - \; -) \; +[(+ \; -) \qquad + \quad (+ \; -)]$$

whence dP/dM, dP/dZ, and dP/dW are all positive. Expansions in Y due to increases either in exogenous expenditure or the money supply are accompanied by increases in the price level.

16.7 ADDING AN ARGUMENT TO ONE OR MORE FUNCTIONS

As an example of a change less radical than adding new variables and equations to a model we will consider a change that has the effect of putting some of the endogenous variables into behavioral equations from which they were formerly absent.

It is sometimes argued that the model we have just been considering is too simple because the rate of interest does, in fact, influence savings decisions, and should thus be an argument of the consumption function, while the level of income influences investment decisions and should accordingly be an argument of the investment function. Let us see if either of these amendments affects the qualitative behavior of the model. The equations of the new model are

$$C = C(Y, r)$$
$$I = I(Y, r)$$
$$Y = C + I + Z$$
$$M^D = L(Y, r, P)$$
$$M^S = M_0$$
$$M^D = M^S$$
$$W = Pf(Y) \quad .$$

Substitution into the three equilibrium conditions now produces

$$Y - C(Y, r) - I(Y, r) = Z$$
$$L(Y, r, P) = M_0$$
$$Pf(Y) = W \quad .$$

Totally differentiating and expressing the results in matrix form gives

$$\begin{bmatrix} 1 - C_Y - I_Y & -(C_r + I_r) & 0 \\ L_Y & L_r & L_P \\ Pf_Y & 0 & f(Y) \end{bmatrix} \begin{bmatrix} dY \\ dr \\ dP \end{bmatrix} = \begin{bmatrix} dZ \\ dM \\ dW \end{bmatrix} \qquad (46)$$

Now compare (46) with (44). Only two elements in the matrix of coefficients have been changed as a result of our new behavioral assumptions: the element a_{11} is now $1 - C_Y - I_Y$ instead of $1 - C_Y$, and the element a_{12} is $-(C_r + I_r)$ instead of $-I_r$. When income changes we must now allow for the effect on I as well as on C, while when the rate of interest changes we must allow for the effect on C as well as on I.

We must first attempt to attach signs to these two new elements.

The element $C_r + I_r$ causes no trouble provided that we assume that a rise in the interest rate lowers both investment and consumption (saving rises). $1 - C_Y - I_Y$ may, however, be positive or negative. If it is negative, this means that the sum of the marginal propensities to spend on consumption and investment exceed unity and the whole model may be unstable. If, for example, expenditure exceeds income, income will rise, but expenditure will rise by even more, and an equilibrium may never be reached. To eliminate this potentially unstable case, we assume that $C_y + I_y < 1$ so that the element $1 - C_Y - I_Y$ is positive.

Having signed these two new elements we may proceed as before. But, before we do, notice that the problem can be stated slightly more generally as

$$\begin{bmatrix} a_{11} & a_{12} & a_{13} \\ a_{21} & a_{22} & a_{23} \\ a_{31} & a_{32} & a_{33} \end{bmatrix} \begin{bmatrix} dY \\ dr \\ dZ \end{bmatrix} = \begin{bmatrix} dZ \\ dM \\ dW \end{bmatrix} \qquad (47)$$

No matter what particular partials go to make up one of the elements, a_{ij}, as long as no previously nonzero element becomes zero, and as long as elements that were zero remain so, then these elements will appear in all the same combinations in the solution. In the present case all we have done is to change the partials that make up two of the elements in the matrix, and it should be intuitively obvious that we can take the solution to the previous case, and, wherever we had $1 - C_Y$, merely write $1 - C_Y - I_Y$ and, wherever we had $-I_r$ now write $-(I_r + C_r)$ and then determine signs. The reader should, however, start from first principles and use (47) to show that

$$\Delta = (1 - C_Y - I_Y) L_r f(Y) + (I_r + C_r) L_Y f(Y) - (I_r + C_r) P f_Y L_p < 0 \quad ,$$

assuming $1 - C_Y - I_Y > 0$ and $I_r + C_r < 0$. We will proceed directly to calculate

$$dY = \frac{\Delta_Y}{\Delta}$$

$$= \frac{f(Y) L_r}{\Delta} dZ + \frac{(I_r + C_r) f(Y)}{\Delta} dM - \frac{(I_r + C_r) L_p}{\Delta} dW \quad . \qquad (48)$$

This gives us $dY/dZ > 0$, $dY/dM > 0$, and $dY/dW < 0$. Indeed, none of the qualitative results of the model are changed as long as we stick to the assumptions that the signs of $1 - C_Y - I_y$ and $-(I_r + C_r)$ are the same as those of $1 - C_Y$ and $-I_r$, respectively.

In this model we avoided a suspected possibility of instability by assuming that $1 - C_Y - I_Y < 0$, that is, that the sum of the marginal propensities to spend on consumption and investment is less than unity. Let us briefly consider what happens if we relax this assumption. From (48) we have

$$\frac{dY}{dZ} = \frac{f(Y)L_r}{(1 - C_Y - I_y)L_r f(Y) + (I_r + C_r)L_Y f(Y) - (I_r + C_r)Pf_Y L_P} \, .$$

If we let $C_Y + I_Y$ increase toward unity, $1 - C_Y - I_Y$ approaches zero. When this term becomes zero the first term in the denominator disappears, but the sign of dY/dZ is unaffected. Apparently $C_Y + I_Y$ can be made greater than unity without affecting any of the qualitative results of the model. Of course, as $C_Y + I_Y$ increases, the magnitude of dY/dZ increases as well. The critical value of $C_Y + I_Y$ is not unity, but that for which the value of the whole expression Δ reaches zero. This value is reached when

$$(1 - C_Y - I_Y)L_r f(Y) = (I_r + C_r)L_Y f(Y) - (I_r + C_r)Pf_Y L_P$$

or

$$1 - C_Y - I_y = \frac{(I_r + C_r)L_Y f(Y) - (I_r + C_r)Pf_Y L_P}{L_r f(Y)} \, .$$

How is it that the sum of the propensities to spend can exceed unity and yet perfectly reasonable comparative static results emerge from the model? The answer lies in the monetary sector. As income rises more money is absorbed into transactions balances, and this raises the interest rate (the public tries to restore balances by selling bonds; this lowers their price and raises the interest rate until there is a reduction in the cash held for speculative and precautionary purposes sufficient to free the amount needed for transactions purposes). The rise in the interest rate lowers $C + I$. Thus there are two offsetting tendencies: the increase in Y tends to increase $C + I$ by more than the increase in Y, but the increase in r tends to reduce $C + I$. As long as the latter tendency is stronger than the former, the model will behave qualitatively just as it did when the sum of the marginal propensities was less than unity.

16.8 A FORMERLY EXOGENOUS VARIABLE BECOMES ENDOGENOUS

In elementary economics the money supply is usually treated as an exogenous variable that can be set at any predetermined level by the central authorities. Recent controversy has suggested that this may be an incorrect assumption. In many countries today the commercial banks hold excess cash reserves above the legal required minimum. When there are opportunities for good loans at high interest rates, banks reduce their excess reserves to a minimum. When lending opportunities dwindle and interest rates fall, banks build up excess reserves. A behavioral equation that caught all the subtleties of this bank action would be complex, and its form is still subject to debate. There is no doubt, however, that this bank behavior makes the money supply at least partially endogenous, and we may assume as a first approximation that it has the effect of making M a function of r, plus a constant.

Let us investigate the qualitative effects of making the money supply endogenous in our model. Instead of having $M^S = M_0$ as before, we now have

$$M^S = S(r) + \bar{M} \qquad (S_r > 0) \quad . \qquad (49)$$

Substituting into equilibrium conditions changes only one of them: instead of

$$L(Y, r, P) = M_0 \quad ,$$

we have

$$L(Y, r, P) - S(r) = \bar{M} \quad .$$

Differentiating all three behavior equations and expressing them in matrix form gives

$$\begin{bmatrix} 1 - C_Y - I_Y & -(C_r + I_r) & 0 \\ L_Y & L_r - S_r & L_p \\ Pf_Y & 0 & f(Y) \end{bmatrix} \begin{bmatrix} dY \\ dr \\ dP \end{bmatrix} = \begin{bmatrix} dZ \\ d\bar{M} \\ dW \end{bmatrix} \qquad (50)$$

Compare this with Eq. (46). All that has changed in the model is that the element a_{22} is $L_r - S_r$ instead of just L_r, as previously. L_r is negative since a rise in the interest rate lowers the demand for money. S_r is positive since, on the behavior outlined at the beginning of this section, a rise in the interest rate increases the quantity of money. But since S_r enters with a minus sign, the sign of the element a_{22} does not change: a_{22} merely takes on a larger absolute value.

One can go through all the comparative statics again if one wishes. Alternatively one can go back to the solutions of the previous model and, whenever L_r appears, replace it by $L_r - S_r$. Also, if one is interested only in qualitative results, it is possible to infer from the fact that L_r and $L_r - S_r$ are both negative that replacing one by the other is not going to change the signs of any of the results such as dY/dZ or $dr/d\bar{M}$. Finally, since $L_r - S_r$ has a larger absolute value than

L_r, we should suspect that the change will affect some of our results *quantitatively.*

The reader is left with the exercise of proving a point that is very important in current policy discussions: that making the money supply an increasing function of r has the effect of increasing the swings in Y in response to exogenous changes in expenditure (i.e., it increases dY/dZ). These swings get larger, the greater is the interest elasticity of the money supply (i.e., the larger the absolute value of S_r). Finally, it can be easily shown that as $S_r \to \infty$ the value of the multiplier dY/dZ approaches the value of the "real" multiplier for the simple Keynesian model without a monetary sector. This last result appeals to common sense: if the money supply expands or contracts as required, there are no rises in the interest rate to curtail booms by discouraging interest-sensitive expenditure and no falls in interest to mitigate slumps by encouraging interest-sensitive expenditure.

We see in this example that some very important economic changes may be trivially easy to handle once the model is fully spelled out at a formal level.

16.9   A CHANGE THAT MAKES IT IMPOSSIBLE TO DETERMINE THE QUALITATIVE EFFECTS OF CHANGES IN SOME OF THE EXOGENOUS VARIABLES

We now assume that the price level influences real consumption in such a way that a rise in P lowers C. There is nothing in economic theory to suggest this as a long-run, full-equilibrium consequence of changes in the price level, but there are many reasons why it might be a consequence for quite a while, such as underreaction of people to price rises and redistribution effects. Following our present agenda, we will merely ask, if this effect were present (for whatever reasons), would it change the qualitative properties of the model? The previous set of equations needs to be amended in only one respect. We now have a new consumption function,

$$C = C(Y, r, P) \qquad (C_p < 0) \quad . \tag{51}$$

Totally differentiating the equilibrium conditions and expressing the results in matrix notation gives us

$$\begin{bmatrix} 1 - C_Y - I_Y & -(C_r + I_r) & C_p \\ L_Y & L_r - S_r & L_P \\ Pf_Y & 0 & f(Y) \end{bmatrix} \begin{bmatrix} dY \\ dr \\ dP \end{bmatrix} = \begin{bmatrix} dZ \\ dM \\ dW \end{bmatrix} \tag{52}$$

This differs from the last two amendments to our model in that a previously zero element has now become nonzero and some wholly new terms will appear in the expansions of the relevant determinants. Evidently, we must solve this new model from the beginning. First, we calculate the determinant of the matrix of coefficients by expanding along the third row:

$$\Delta = Pf_Y \begin{vmatrix} -(C_r + I_r) & C_P \\ L_r - S_r & L_P \end{vmatrix} + f(Y) \begin{vmatrix} 1 - C_Y - I_Y & -(C_r + I_r) \\ L_Y & L_r - S_r \end{vmatrix}$$

$$= - Pf_Y(C_r + I_r)L_P - Pf_Y(L_r - S_r)C_P$$
$$ -(+ - \quad - \quad +) - (+ - \quad - \quad -)$$

$$+ f(Y)(1 - C_Y - I_Y)(L_r - S_r) + f(Y)L_Y(C_r + I_r) \quad .$$
$$+(+ \quad + \quad - \quad) + (+ + \quad - \quad)$$

Now we encounter a wholly new difficulty: the first term in the expansion of Δ, $-Pf_Y(C_r + I_r)L_P$, has the opposite sign to the second term, $-Pf_Y(L_r - S_r)C_P$, so their sum will be positive or negative depending on their relative absolute values. Evidently we are unable to sign Δ even though we know the signs of the partial derivatives.

If we are unable to sign Δ in a model of this sort, we will be unable to sign the derivative of any of the endogenous variables with respect to a shift in any of the exogenous variables since Δ appears in the denominator of each expression:

$$\frac{dx_i}{d\beta_j} = \frac{\Delta_i}{\Delta}$$

where x_i is the ith endogenous variable and β_j the jth exogenous variable.

Our inability to sign Δ makes it impossible to get any unambiguous qualitative results from this model. Another possibility suggests itself: we might be able to sign Δ but not sign some of the terms in the Δ_i's so that we could get *some* but not a full set of qualitative results. This possibility can be illustrated without building another complete economic model. Assume that we have a model whose three equilibrium conditions give the following equations:

$$\begin{bmatrix} a_{11} & a_{12} & a_{13} \\ 0 & a_{22} & a_{23} \\ 0 & -a_{32} & a_{33} \end{bmatrix} \begin{bmatrix} dx_1 \\ dx_2 \\ dx_3 \end{bmatrix} = \begin{bmatrix} d\beta_1 \\ d\beta_2 \\ d\beta_3 \end{bmatrix} ,$$

where the a's are the elements in the matrix of coefficients (the partial derivatives whose signs are known to us and all of which are nonnegative except a_{32}), the x's are the dependent variables, and the β's are the independent variables. Expanding down the first column we get

$$\Delta = a_{11} \begin{vmatrix} a_{22} & a_{23} \\ -a_{32} & a_{33} \end{vmatrix} = (a_{11}a_{22}a_{33}) - [a_{11}(-a_{32})a_{23}] > 0 \quad .$$

But now consider the reaction of x_1 to a change in each of the β's:

$$dx_1 = \begin{vmatrix} d\beta_1 & a_{12} & a_{13} \\ d\beta_2 & a_{22} & a_{23} \\ d\beta_3 & -a_{32} & a_{33} \end{vmatrix} \div \Delta$$

$$= \frac{[(a_{22}a_{33}) - (-a_{32}a_{23})]}{\Delta} d\beta_1 - \frac{[a_{12}a_{33} - (-a_{32}a_{13})]}{\Delta} d\beta_2$$

$$+ \frac{[a_{12}a_{33} - a_{22}a_{13}]}{\Delta} d\beta_3 \quad .$$

This gives us $dx_1/d\beta_1 > 0$ and $dx_1/d\beta_2 < 0$, but $dx_1/d\beta_3$ cannot be signed since the numerator of the term attached to β_3 is positive or negative depending on the relative absolute values of the two positive products $a_{12}a_{33}$ and $a_{22}a_{13}$.

16.10 THE SCOPE OF QUALITATIVE ECONOMICS

All the models we have examined, with the exception of the last one, give unambiguous qualitative results: we can determine the direction of change of the endogenous variables in response to a change in any one of the exogenous variables solely from a knowledge of the signs of the partial derivatives in the coefficient matrix. For more complicated models the existence of unambiguous qualitative results may be more the exception than the rule.

Just what are the necessary and sufficient conditions for the existence of qualitative results is still a subject of discussion in economic theory. It should be clear, however, that all that matters is the pattern of signs (pluses, minuses, and zeros) in the model. Indeed in an earlier model (see Section 16.8) we made an assumption to reflect a major change in the behavior of the monetary sector—the money supply becoming endogenous rather than exogenous—and found that, since it left unchanged the signs of all the elements in the coefficient matrix, it did not change any of the qualitative predictions of the model. This is potentially a very powerful result, for we could assert the absence of qualitative changes without solving the new model. Indeed the qualitative results of macro-models depend only on the pattern of signs of the matrix of coefficients.

Let us see what is involved. Consider, for example, the version of the model laid out in Eq. 50 of Section 16.8. If we replace the elements in the coefficient matrix by their appropriate signs, we have the sign pattern of the matrix

$$\begin{bmatrix} + & + & 0 \\ + & - & + \\ - & 0 & + \end{bmatrix} .$$

The determinant of any matrix with this sign pattern is unambiguously signed whatever the magnitude or interpretation of the individual elements. Expanding along the top row gives

$$+(-\,+) - (0\,+) - (+\,+) + (-\,+) < 0 \quad .$$

The first term is negative, the second term is zero, and the third and fourth terms are negative. If we again let x's and β's stand for the endogenous and exogenous variables, respectively, the equations of the system are

$$\begin{bmatrix} + & + & 0 \\ + & - & + \\ - & 0 & + \end{bmatrix} \begin{bmatrix} dx_1 \\ dx_2 \\ dx_3 \end{bmatrix} = \begin{bmatrix} d\beta_1 \\ d\beta_2 \\ d\beta_3 \end{bmatrix} .$$

To solve for the effects of the β's on dx_1 we need

$$\Delta_1 = \begin{vmatrix} d\beta_1 & + & 0 \\ d\beta_2 & - & + \\ d\beta_3 & 0 & + \end{vmatrix} .$$

Thus $dx_1/d\beta_1 = (-\,+)/|\mathbf{A}| > 0$, $dx_1/d\beta_2 = -(+\,+)/|\mathbf{A}| > 0$, and $dx_3/d\beta_3 = (+\,+)/|\mathbf{A}| < 0$. (Recall that Δ and $|\mathbf{A}|$ are alternative symbols for the determinant of the $\mathbf{A}$ matrix.) Having signed $|\mathbf{A}|$, we can sign $dx_i/d\beta_j$ if and only if we can determine the sign of the principal minor of β_j in the determinant Δ_i. Necessary and sufficient conditions for being able to do this are not easy to establish. But one or two obvious points may be made here.

Any model with the same pattern of signs will have the same qualitative properties. Furthermore, models with apparently different sign patterns can often be shown to be equivalent by manipulating them in ways that do not upset their basic properties. To take the simplest example, rows can be transposed because this is only the equivalent of altering the order in which the equations are written down (and it would be a scandal if this affected the solution of the equations). Also columns can be transposed since this is only the equivalent of altering the order in which the variables occur in the equations.

We have concentrated on simple models with unambiguous qualitative predictions. Many models do not give such clear results.

A study of nothing more than their pattern of signs can often tell us whether or not such qualitative results do exist. But this discussion takes us well beyond the scope of this book and near to one of the frontiers of modern theoretical research. The interested reader will need more mathematics than is contained in this book before he can follow this lead into a very exciting field of study.

16.11 AN OPEN ECONOMY WITH FOREIGN REPERCUSSIONS

In all the models with a foreign trade sector considered so far in this book we have implicitly assumed that we were dealing with *small* open economies. By a small open economy we mean one whose demand in the international market is not large enough to have significant effects on the national incomes of the countries with which it trades. We can safely consider such economies in isolation. We now ask what would happen if the open economy were large enough so that its behavior exerted a significant influence on the national incomes of its trading partners. The major change that this introduces is to make exports an endogenous variable, rather than an exogenous one. Consider a shift in autonomous expenditure in our country that will both raise national income and raise imports according to the relation $M = M(Y)$. But our country's imports are the exports of its trading partners, and the increase in their exports acts in the same way as an increase in any element of aggregate expenditure: it raises their national incomes. When their national incomes rise they will increase their imports, and this will in turn raise our exports and hence our national income.

Thus we have a true general equilibrium situation: a change in our economy has repercussions on the economies of our trading partners, and this in turn causes changes that reflect back on our own economy. We must wonder if we can get very far in analyzing so complex a system.

To concentrate on foreign repercussions we will simplify our model greatly from those we have considered in previous sections: (1) we ignore the government; (2) we ignore the financial sector, holding interest rates constant; and (3) we linearize all our behavioral relations. The first two simplifications are only to allow us to concentrate on the interrelations that interest us. In the light of the results in Section 16.10 you should not be too surprised to learn that, when these simplifications are removed, no qualitative results are changed. The reason for linearizing the system is that we want to develop a new structure, with which we shall deal further in Chapter 17. In any case, we can move with no difficulty from systems of linear behavioral equations with constant coefficients to systems of nonlinear equations where we get exact results for instantaneous rates of change and approximations for small changes.

We begin our analysis of this very simple general equilibrium model by assuming that there are only two countries A and B (A is the home country, and B is the rest of the world). In this very simple model, aggregate expenditure is composed only of consumption C, autonomous expenditure Z, and net exports $X - M$. We must now distinguish expenditures in the two countries, which we do by using subscripts A and B.

The model can be expressed in the following equations:

Country A	*Country B*	
$C_A = c_A Y_A$	$C_B = c_B Y_B$	(53)
$M_A = m_A Y_A$	$M_B = m_B Y_B$	(54)
$Y_A = C_A + Z_A + (X_A - M_A)$	$Y_B = C_B + Z_B + (X_B - M_B)$	(55)

Definitions

$$X_A = M_B \tag{56}$$

$$X_B = M_A \tag{57}$$

The lowercase c's and m's refer to constant marginal propensities to consume and to import. Z is, of course, all autonomous expenditure, and $X - M$ is net imports.[7] Since the world is divided into only two "countries," it follows that the exports of one must be the imports of the other. This is expressed in (56) and (57). Since, from (54), imports are endogenous, and, from (56) and (57), exports are not independent of imports, it follows that the only exogenous variables in the model are Z_A and Z_B.

Given Z_A and Z_B we now wish to solve for the endogenous variables. If we substitute the behavioral equations and the definitions into the equilibrium conditions, we obtain

$$Y_A - c_A Y_A + m_A Y_A - m_B Y_B = Z_A$$
$$Y_B - c_B Y_B + m_B Y_B - m_A Y_A = Z_B$$

or

$$\begin{bmatrix} 1 - (c_A - m_A) & -m_B \\ -m_A & 1 - (c_B - m_B) \end{bmatrix} \begin{bmatrix} Y_A \\ Y_B \end{bmatrix} = \begin{bmatrix} Z_A \\ Z_B \end{bmatrix}. \tag{58}$$

We have a coefficient matrix, postmultiplied by a vector of endogenous variables, and set equal to a vector of exogenous variables.

[7] As in all our previous treatments of open economies we ignore capital movements so that the balance of payments is equal to the balance of trade $(X - M)$.

This is now a familiar form whose solution requires only the matrix inverse.

In case this starts to look trivial, let us consider a three-country problem. We immediately write the equilibrium conditions

$$Y_A = c_A Y_A - m_A Y_A + Z_A + X_A$$
$$Y_B = c_B Y_B - m_B Y_B + Z_B + X_B$$
$$Y_C = c_C Y_C - m_C Y_C + Z_C + X_C \qquad (59)$$

in an obvious extension of the notation we have been employing. In (59), however, we have not allocated any country's demand for imports between the supplying countries. This allocation is essential information. We might assume, for example, that

$$M_A = m_{AB} Y_A + m_{AC} Y_A$$
$$M_B = m_{BA} Y_B + m_{BC} Y_B$$
$$M_C = m_{CA} Y_C + m_{CB} Y_C \quad , \qquad (60)$$

where m_{ij} is the ith country's propensity to import from the jth country (e.g., m_{AB} is country A's propensity to import from country B). We also extend our definitions in an obvious way to cover the three-country world:

Definitions

$$X_A = M_B + M_C$$
$$X_B = M_A + M_C$$
$$X_C = M_A + M_B \quad . \qquad (61)$$

If we substitute (60) and (61) into the equilibrium conditions (59), we obtain

$$Y_A = c_A Y_A - m_{AB} Y_A - m_{AC} Y_A + Z_A + m_{BA} Y_B + m_{CA} Y_C$$
$$Y_B = c_B Y_B - m_{BA} Y_B - m_{BC} Y_C + Z_B + m_{AB} Y_A + m_{CB} Y_C$$
$$Y_C = c_C Y_C - m_{CA} Y_C - m_{CB} Y_C + Z_C + m_{AC} Y_A + m_{BC} Y_B \quad . \qquad (62)$$

We can write (62) more simply:

$$\begin{bmatrix} Y_A \\ Y_B \\ Y_C \end{bmatrix} = \begin{bmatrix} c_A - m_{AB} - m_{AC} & m_{BA} & m_{CA} \\ m_{AB} & c_B - m_{BA} - m_{BC} & m_{CB} \\ m_{AC} & m_{BC} & c_C - m_{CA} - m_{CB} \end{bmatrix} \begin{bmatrix} Y_A \\ Y_B \\ Y_C \end{bmatrix} + \begin{bmatrix} Z_A \\ Z_B \\ Z_C \end{bmatrix} \quad . \qquad (63)$$

We may rewrite this yet again as

$$\mathbf{Y} = \mathbf{DY} + \mathbf{Z} \quad . \tag{64}$$

We write $\mathbf{D}$ now for the coefficient matrix of (63) to avoid confusion with country A and the coefficient matrix $\mathbf{A}$ used in the previous sections. (We also depart from our usual practice and denote the two vectors by capital letters.) We see that (64) looks very different from our earlier results: $\mathbf{Ay} = \mathbf{z}$. How do we now proceed to get a solution, and what is the difference?

To solve (64), we subtract $\mathbf{DY}$ from both sides, obtaining $\mathbf{Y} - \mathbf{DY} = \mathbf{Z}$. We now factor the left-hand side, remembering to use the unit matrix $\mathbf{I}$, of appropriate order, in place of the 1 we should have in scalar algebra. This gives

$$(\mathbf{I} - \mathbf{D})\mathbf{Y} = \mathbf{Z} \quad . \tag{65}$$

Now, $\mathbf{I} - \mathbf{D}$ is *one* matrix, not two. It is, in fact, exactly the coefficient matrix of Eq. (58), in the two-by-two case, or of (63) rearranged as (58) in the three-by-three case. Then, provided that $|\mathbf{I} - \mathbf{D}|$ is not zero, the solution is given by

$$\mathbf{Y} = (\mathbf{I} - \mathbf{D})^{-1}\mathbf{Z} \quad . \tag{66}$$

We now see that the forms of (58) and (65) are identical. It is, however, easier to rearrange equations in matrix notation, proceeding from (63) to (66). If, however, we turn back to (15), we see that it could not be written in the form of (64) due to the asymmetry of the equations. We shall take advantage of the symmetry of a system like (58) or (63) wherever we find it to use the form of (64).

The matrix $\mathbf{D}$ is written out in full in (63). Let us consider some of its terms. We have, for example,

$$d_{11} = c_A - m_{AB} - m_{AC} \quad .$$

This is the proportion of A's income that is spent on A's output: it is A's propensity to consume minus the sum of the import propensities. Similarly

$$d_{22} = c_B - m_{BA} - m_{AC} \quad .$$

We therefore note that the diagonal elements are to be interpreted as the propensities to consume domestically produced output. Now let us consider an off-diagonal element such as $d_{12} = m_{BA}$. This is the demand by country B for A's output per unit of B's income. The interpretation is obvious. We need merely note the identification $1 = A$, $2 = B$, $3 = C$. Evidently we can extend this to as many countries as we choose without altering the mathematical form of the problem.

The general method of procedure is now clear: we substitute and rearrange until, on the left, we have the coefficient matrix (of either form) postmultiplied by the vector of endogenous variables, with the exogenous variables on the right. It is only necessary to add that the "original" behavior equations, in which endogenous variables are dependent on other endogenous variables (e.g., C_A on Y_A), are known as *structural* equations, and that the set of solution equations is known as the *reduced form* of the system. In a reduced form, we are left with only exogenous variables on the right-hand side. Interrelations between endogenous variables have been eliminated by substitution, and the vector of endogenous variables is obtained directly from the vector of exogenous variables.

We shall now consider comparative static analysis, but in general form: examples are given in the questions. We have already seen that we can write

$$dy = A^{-1} dz \quad .$$

If we have the solution in the form of (66), we shall similarly write

$$dY = (I - D)^{-1} dZ \quad .$$

In a *linear system*, the coefficient matrix and the matrix of derivatives are identical. We should notice here the remarkable analogy between $(I - D)^{-1}$ and the scalar multiplier $(1 - c)^{-1}$ (or more complicated single-equation multipliers). $(I - D)^{-1}$ may be called, with reason, a *matrix multiplier*. It is the appropriate form of multiplier for cases in which there are several equilibrium conditions to satisfy simultaneously, and the equations are symmetrical in the sense of (64). We may simply assert what we have now amply illustrated: changing a behavior equation (by, say, substituting $C = c(1 - t)Y$ for $C = cY$) simply alters a *coefficient* in D, whereas introducing another country (or sector) increases the *order* of D. Introducing the government sector did not require us to increase the order of D, because taxes can be handled merely by altering behavior equations and adding G to the appropriate element of the Z vector. Introducing money is another matter.

It is only necessary to be a little careful about what the terms dy, etc., mean. The vector dy (or dY) is the vector of increments in the endogenous variables, whose values we seek. The vector dZ is the vector of increments in the exogenous variables, whose values we assume given. We usually find it more illuminating to alter the exogenous variables one at a time rather than simultaneously. If, for example, we want to examine the effects of an increase in investment in country B, we shall write $dZ = \{0, dZ_B, 0\}$. Solution by Cramer's rule is then routine.

So far, we have simply assumed that the matrices A or $I - D$ are nonsingular. In fact, we want more than the existence of an inverse: we want all the elements of $(\mathbf{I} - \mathbf{D})^{-1}$ to be positive, since all the elements of the $\mathbf{Z}$ vector are positive, and we should be able to guarantee that the model will not generate negative values for imports, income, etc. On the economic assumptions we have made here, the elements of $(\mathbf{I} - \mathbf{D})^{-1}$ will, in fact, all be positive, but we shall not prove this now (it is proved in Section 17.6).

There is another problem. If we refer back to the two-country model, we see that there was no particular reason why, at the given exchange rate and with an arbitrary vector of exogenous expenditures, the two countries should have been in balance of payments equilibrium (or at full employment, either). Suppose that A has a balance of payments deficit, which can be reduced by a reduction in Z_A. It is easily seen that, for a given change in Z_A, the improvement in the balance of payments is less than it was in the case in which we assumed that there were no repercussions from the rest of the world. Here, the reduction in Z_A reduces A's income and its imports from B. This in turn, however, reduces B's income and imports from A. There is now an urgent question: will the reduction in Z_A actually improve A's balance of payments? Is it not possible that the repercussions, via B's income and expenditure, more than offset the saving via A's income and expenditure? We want, if we can, to rule out perverse results of this kind. We can immediately reassure ouselves if we assume (still without proof) that all the elements of $(\mathbf{I} - \mathbf{D})^{-1}$ are positive. This means that there is a positive solution vector for *every* $\mathbf{Z}$ vector, whence changing from $\mathbf{Z}$ to $\mathbf{Z} + \mathbf{dZ}$ cannot produce crazy results: the model cannot "blow up." To exclude the particular perversity we have mentioned, however, we need a little more than this. We can be sure that dY_A/dZ_A is positive, whence dM_A/dZ_A is positive, and that dY_B/dZ_A is positive, whence dM_B/dZ_A is positive also. Thus A's imports and exports change in the same direction, but which changes more?

To answer this, let us return to (58), replacing the $\mathbf{Y}$ vector by $\{dY_A, dY_B\}$ and the $\mathbf{Z}$ vector by $\{dZ_A, 0\}$. We shall have

$$dM_A = m_A \, dY_A = m_A \frac{\Delta_{Y_A}}{\Delta}$$

and

$$dX_A = dM_B = m_B \, dY_B = m_B \frac{\Delta_{Y_B}}{\Delta} \quad ,$$

using the convenient Δ notation introduced earlier. We notice that both expressions have the same denominator, so, since we only want to compare their magnitudes, we need not evaluate Δ. For the numerators, we obtain

$$m_A \Delta_{Y_A} = m_A \begin{vmatrix} dZ_A & -m_B \\ 0 & 1 - (c_B - m_B) \end{vmatrix}$$
$$= m_A \{1 - (c_B - m_B)\} \, dZ_A$$

and

$$m_B Y_B = m_B \begin{vmatrix} 1 - (c_A - m_A) & dZ_A \\ -m_A & 0 \end{vmatrix}$$
$$= m_B m_A \, dZ_A \quad .$$

We want to assure ourselves that

$$m_A \{1 - (c_B - m_B)\} > m_A m_B \quad .$$

Dividing both sides by m_A, a positive fraction, does not reverse the direction of the inequality, which therefore holds if

$$1 - c_B + m_B > m_B \quad .$$

Subtracting m_B from both sides, we see that the condition $1 - c_B > 0$ is sufficient to rule out the perverse results. By a similar argument, we could show that $1 - c_A > 0$ rules out a perverse response to dZ_B, and that similar results obtain in the multicountry model.

In Chapter 3, we made much of frontiers, or trade-offs, for policy makers. There is now no need to rehearse this material. Once one has obtained $\mathbf{I} - \mathbf{D}$, the trade-offs can be directly computed from $(\mathbf{I} - \mathbf{D})^{-1}$, or by Cramer's rule, in any linear system.

Interestingly enough, we shall encounter further examples of matrices of the form $\mathbf{I} - \mathbf{D}$ in Chapter 17 on an apparently quite different subject (input–output analysis), and in Section 17.6 we shall learn practical methods of computing their inverses for some important cases. It should, indeed, come as no surprise that, if we can set up an economic problem as a linear system, its mathematical structure will be the same, whether the subject matter is international trade or interindustry trade.

QUESTIONS

1. In Eq. (15) (Section 16.2), find the directions of change of all the endogenous variables in response to an increase in the propensity to invest.

2. a. In the model of the open economy with government presented in the last half of Section 16.2, find the directions of change of all the endogenous variables in response to

i. an increase in the money supply and

ii. an autonomous increase in exports.

b. What is the income balance of payments trade-off in response to an increase in G?

3. It is well known that, if investment depends on income ($I = d + eY$, say), the expenditure function may cross the 45° line from below. We will investigate the simplest form of such a model:

$$C = a + bY$$
$$I = d + eY$$
$$Y = I + C \quad .$$

a. Write this three-equation system in matrix form.

b. Solve for the endogenous variables. Find a check on your answer.

c. What is the necessary condition for obtaining a positive, finite, solution for Y?

4. We may divide a closed economy into two sectors, firms and households. All household expenditure is received by firms, which spend a proportion r of total receipts on wages and dividends, retaining a proportion $1 - r$ as saving. The firms also invest a fixed amount. Household expenditure is given by the usual linear consumption function.

a. Write the equations of the model.

b. Solve for the endogenous variables.

c. Introduce a government which spends a fixed amount and taxes households by a proportional income tax, and solve again.

d. Without the government, now open the economy. Assume that exports are exogenous, that firms spend a constant proportion of receipts on imported raw materials, and that households spend a constant proportion of income on imported consumer goods. Solve again.

5. Write down the equations of a model in which

i. Consumption (and hence saving) depends on income.

ii. Investment depends solely on the rate of interest.

iii. All other expenditure is exogenous.

iv. The demand for money depends solely on the level of national income.

v. The supply of money is an exogenously determined constant.

Determine the comparative static properties of this model by signing dY/dZ, dY/dM, dr/dZ, and dr/dM. Why does dY/dZ differ from what it was in the model of Section 16.3 in the text?

6. Alter the model of Question 5 to make I depend solely on Y. Explain the change in the comparative static properties of the model.

7. Alter the model of Question 6 to make the demand for money depend on the rate of interest as well as the level of income. Interpret the comparative static properties of this model. (Assume that $C_Y + I_Y < 1$.)

8. a. Examine the behavior of the model in Question 5 if C, I, M^D, and M^S all depend on both Y and r (and there is also a constant component in the demand for money).

   b. Would it make any difference if there were no constant component in M^S?

9. First check your answer to Question 8 and then ask what would happen if (a) $L_Y = S_Y$ and (b) $L_Y < S_Y$.

10. In a two-country world, assume that

$$C_A = 100 + 0.8Y_A$$
$$M_A = 0.1Y_A$$
$$C_B = 50 + 0.6Y_B$$
$$M_B = 0.2Y_B \quad .$$

   a. Given that $I_A = 200$ and $I_B = 100$, find Y_A and Y_B and the balance of payments.

   b. What assurance have we that the coefficient matrix of the two-country problem will have an inverse?

   c. What will be the effect on Y_A and Y_B of a unit change in I_A?

   d. The government of A wishes to restore balance of payments equilibrium. To what level must it reduce I_A?

The following two questions are rather ambitious and take the reader well beyond the content of an introductory economics course.

11.* An interesting case occurs if a classical labor market is grafted onto a Keynesian expenditure model. To do this we add a demand and supply equation for labor both based on the real wage rate and an equilibrium condition to equate demand for and supply of labor. Also we need to relate real income to employment, which is done through the production function. The equations of the model are $C = C(Y)$, $I = I(r)$, $Y = C + I + Z$, $M^D = L(Y, r, P)$, $M^S = M_0$, $M^D = M^S$, $N^D = D(W/P)$, $N^S = S(W/P)$, $N^D = N^S$, and $Y = f(N)$. Note that W/P is a single argument in the labor demand (N^D) and supply (N^S) equations [they are *not* written (W, P)]. Because we are considering only equilibrium situations, it does not matter whether we relate Y to N^D or N^S, and we have used N to stand for the equilibrium quantity of employment. Substitute down to four equations – the three equilibrium conditions and the equation relating Y to N; totally differentiate and express the equations in matrix form. Determine the comparative static properties of the model.

12.* In some Keynesian theories of distribution the level of aggregate consumption is influenced by the real wage rate. Will inserting W/P into the consumption function affect any of the comparative static results of the model of Question 11?

Chapter 17

Input–Output Analysis

The models we have explored so far have, with few exceptions, been either highly aggregated macro-models or partial equilibrium micro-models. We now have the equipment to consider a general equilibrium model. We shall in fact consider a somewhat special example of general equilibrium models, which, at the expense of some very restrictive assumptions, can be applied quantitatively to some important practical questions. We do not assume any previous introduction to input–output analysis, and therefore discuss here not merely the formal model and its solution but also the assumptions and possible applications of the model.

17.1 THE PROBLEM

Suppose that we wished to predict the probable effects of a major cutback in, say, defense expenditure. From our simple macro-models, we know that, if this were accompanied by no other change in government policy, the result would be a reduction in income and employment. The simple macro-model also predicts that this reduction could be avoided by an offsetting increase in some other item of government expenditure (thus keeping G constant), or an appropriate reduction in tax rates (increasing C) or, perhaps, a reduction in interest rates (increasing I). Do we in fact expect a reduction of $\$x$ million in expenditure on aircraft, electronic equipment, etc., matched by an increase of $\$x$ million on school and hospital building, to leave equilibrium happily undisturbed? We do not, for the simple reason that resources are not perfectly mobile. If we start from (more or less) full employment, we expect a bottleneck in the building industry and unemployment among aeronautical and electronics engineers, in the short run, at least. We should therefore notice that, in our simple macro-models, we have been implicitly assuming the existence of only one good.

Input–output analysis recognizes the existence of many goods, and, furthermore, takes into account the fact that some goods are used to produce others. Thus our defense–school-building problem is complicated by the fact that a reduction in aircraft building will lead to lower demand for aluminum and jet engines, while increased school and hospital building will lead to increased demand for timber, cement, and plumbing materials. The increased demand for plumbing materials will, in turn, lead to increased demand for lead, copper, plastics, and so on. Input–output analysis is designed for the quantitative study of these *interindustry relations*. It is thus designed to answer practical questions about, for example, the effects of a switch in government spending of the sort we have been discussing, or the feasibility of a spending program (where will the bottlenecks occur?), or the specific implications for industry of a projected plan. The answers all depend, however, on certain critical assumptions. The required data are also very expensive to collect. We shall return to these matters below. Let us now lay out the model.

17.2   INTERINDUSTRY ACCOUNTS

Let us start by assuming a closed economy, and also suppose that the economy has been divided, perhaps by civil servants organizing a census of production, into four productive sectors: Services; Agriculture, Mining, etc.; Public Utilities; and Manufacturing. (We shall see how to open the economy in Section 17.9, and consider the "best" number of sectors into which to divide it in Section 17.5.) We also assume that, from some source such as a census of production, we have the following information for some time period such as a year: for each industry, the value of its sales *to* each industry (sales of intermediate products) and to final consumption; and, for each industry, the value of its purchases *from* each industry (intermediate products) and its value added. We may arrange this information in a transactions matrix such as Table 17.1.

In the transactions matrix, the row for each industry gives the amounts it *supplies* to other industries and the column its *inputs* purchased from other industries. The characteristic element, which we might write X_{ij}, is thus the value of the output of the ith industry used up as an intermediate input by the jth industry. Let us look at some of these elements. X_{12} is the value of purchases *from* the Services

Table 17.1
A four-sector transactions matrix (in $'s)

	1	2	3	4	$Z_i = \sum_j X_{ij}$	Y_i	$X_i = Z_i + Y_i$
1. Services	X_{11}	X_{12}	X_{13}	X_{14}	Z_1	Y_1	X_1
2. Agriculture, Mining, etc.	X_{21}	X_{22}	X_{23}	X_{24}	Z_2	Y_2	X_2
3. Public Utilities	X_{31}	X_{32}	X_{33}	X_{34}	Z_3	Y_3	X_3
4. Manufacturing	X_{41}	X_{42}	X_{43}	X_{44}	Z_4	Y_4	X_4
$V_i = W_i + R_i$	V_1	V_2	V_3	V_4		$V = Y$	

industry by Agriculture, etc. It is thus composed of items such as insurance premiums, banking and legal charges, consulting fees, and the like. X_{13} and X_{14} carry the same interpretation. What about the elements on the principal diagonal, such as X_{11}, X_{22}? X_{11} is the value of the output of the Services industry used up by the Services industry itself. It is thus composed of items such as insurance premiums and legal fees paid by banks, bank charges and legal fees paid by insurance companies, etc. Similarly, X_{22} is composed of items such as the value of grain and root crops fed to animals (after all, pigs, not humans, are the largest consumers of corn). The elements on the principal diagonal thus give the values of the sector's consumption of its own output. We could, in fact, net out this consumption before presenting the transactions matrix (and they are sometimes built net), but we shall continue to use the gross form.

There are many matters here requiring comment, but let us first tidy up the accounts. Suppose that we add up the elements of a row, forming the sum

$$Z_i = \sum_j X_{ij} \quad . \tag{1}$$

Z_i is the total value of the output of the ith industry used up in the productive process, that is, not available for final demand. We denote final demand by Y_i, and we write Y for the sum, $\Sigma_i \, Y_i$. In our one-good macro-models, we have

$$Y = C + I + G \quad . \tag{2}$$

This gives us our *definition* of final demand: the value of output that goes to households, to expanding productive capacity, and to the public sector. It is the business of the macro-models to explain the determination of the total, Y. Here, we are interested in its industrial composition. If we assume that this is known, we have the column Y_i. We now form the sums

$$X_i = Z_i + Y_i \qquad \text{(for all } i) \quad, \tag{3}$$

and X_i is obviously the total value of output of the ith industry. Equations (3) (there are as many of them as there are sectors) are accounting identities, sometimes known as *balance equations*.

Let us write beneath each column of the matrix the value added in each industry. This is composed of the wage bill, W_i, and the return to capital, R_i. If we take the sum

$$V = \sum_i V_i = \sum_i (W_i + R_i) \tag{4}$$

we have national income, whence $V = Y$. (Remember that R is a residual, so the books must balance.) Finally, suppose that we sum the elements of a column, and add the value added as well. We must have

$$\sum_i X_{ij} + V_j = X_j \quad. \tag{5}$$

In other words, the total value of the output of the jth industry must be equal to the value of its intermediate inputs, its wages bill, and what is left over (R), if anything. We note here that it is only possible to sum the columns if we work in value terms. If we drew up a transactions matrix in physical units, row sums would make sense. If, however, we then attempted to sum columns, we should be trying to add, for example, units of banking services to bushels of wheat, which is impossible. A column sum, incidentally, can be regarded as the scalar product of two vectors, one of physical units and one of their prices.

What we now have is a comprehensive set of interindustry accounts, which may be of descriptive interest but serves no analytic purpose. There is, indeed, a good deal of a descriptive nature that is worth discussion, and to which we return in Section 17.5, but, first, let us introduce the behavioral assumptions with which we can now construct a model.

17.3 THE MODEL

It is natural to assume that X_{ij}, the value of the ith industry's output required by the jth industry, is a function of X_j, the output of the jth industry. The very strong assumptions we introduce here are

    i. that X_{ij} is a function of X_j *and nothing else*,
   ii. that the function is linear, and
  iii. that the function is homogeneous (no constant term).

Thus we assume that

$$X_{ij} = a_{ij}X_j \quad .$$ (6)

We thus assume a constant technology, described by fixed coefficients, in value as well as physical terms. This is a very strong no-substitution assumption: it says, for example, that *every* dollar's worth of manufacturing output requires 5 cents worth of input from services, independent both of prices and of the scale of operations. If, of course, we assume that Eq. (6) correctly describes the economy, then we can derive the coefficients a_{ij} very simply from the transactions matrix, merely by computing

$$a_{ij} = \frac{X_{ij}}{X_j} \quad .$$

This, again, will have to be discussed further below. We should notice here, however, that (6) says nothing about the requirements of capital and labor. It is not, therefore, inconsistent with our earlier discussions of production functions in which we assumed the possibility of continuous substitution between capital and labor (Sections 9.4, 11.1, and 11.2). We can see, indeed, that in those discussions we were implicitly considering the production functions in value-added terms only: intermediate inputs had been netted out.

If all requirements are strictly proportional to outputs, as in Eq. (6), then our four-sector economy is described by the following four equations:

$$X_1 = a_{11}X_1 + a_{12}X_2 + a_{13}X_3 + a_{14}X_4 + Y_1$$
$$X_2 = a_{21}X_1 + a_{22}X_2 + a_{23}X_3 + a_{24}X_4 + Y_2$$
$$X_3 = a_{31}X_1 + a_{32}X_2 + a_{33}X_3 + a_{34}X_4 + Y_3$$
$$X_4 = a_{41}X_1 + a_{42}X_2 + a_{43}X_3 + a_{44}X_4 + Y_4 \quad .$$ (7)

Equations (7) say that the total output of each good must be equal to the total amount of it used up in the production of other goods *plus* the total amount going to final demand. They are therefore again balance equations, but balance equations into which our behavioral assumptions (fixed coefficients) have been substituted.

We now take advantage of our compact matrix notation to write (7) as

$$\mathbf{X} = \mathbf{AX} + \mathbf{Y}$$ (8)

where $\mathbf{X}$ is the column vector $\{X_1, X_2, X_3, X_4\}$, $\mathbf{Y}$ is the column vector $\{Y_1, Y_2, Y_3, Y_4\}$, and the coefficient matrix is

$$A = \begin{bmatrix} a_{11} & a_{12} & a_{13} & a_{14} \\ a_{21} & a_{22} & a_{23} & a_{24} \\ a_{31} & a_{32} & a_{33} & a_{34} \\ a_{41} & a_{42} & a_{43} & a_{44} \end{bmatrix} .$$

A is often known as the "technology matrix." Let us take stock of what we know about it.

1. Each element must be positive: we rule out negative inputs.
2. No element can exceed unity: we rule out negative outputs. If some element exceeded unity, it would mean, for example, that the value of the coke used in making a ton of steel exceeded the value of the steel. We assume that such an activity would not be pursued.
3. The sum of the elements in each column must be less than unity. If this were not true, it would mean that the total value of intermediate products used by an industry exceeded the value of its output. This, in turn, would mean that the value added by that industry was negative. Now, this is not impossible, but, if we assume that the wage bill cannot be negative, it means that the industry must be making losses (indeed, losses greater in absolute value than its wages bill). An industry in which value added is negative is not covering variable costs (intermediate inputs plus the wages bill), and we know from elementary micro theory that in such a case losses will be reduced by closing down. Thus we do not want to describe such an industry in our technology matrix at all.
4. We have already noticed that we have built in the assumption of constant returns to scale: otherwise, we could not describe the technology by a constant-coefficient matrix.
5. We should notice that we have also built in the assumption that there are no externalities. An externality in production would exist if, for example, a factory discharged waste into a river so that a factory farther downstream had to use resources to clean the water before it could use it. In this case, the resource requirements of the second factory would not depend solely on its outputs but would also depend on the activity of the first factory. If we denote the two outputs by q_1 and q_2, we should have to write the production function for q_2 in the form

$$q_2 = f(q_1, X_1, X_2, \ldots, X_n)$$

(where the X's are the inputs). The presence of q_1 as an argument of this function would be sufficient to prevent us describing resource requirements by Eq. (7).

17.4 THE "LEONTIEF MATRIX"

Let us rearrange Eq. (8). Subtracting $\mathbf{AX}$ from both sides, we have

$$\mathbf{X} - \mathbf{AX} = \mathbf{Y} \quad . \tag{9}$$

We now factor out $\mathbf{X}$ to obtain

$$(\mathbf{I} - \mathbf{A})\mathbf{X} = \mathbf{Y} \tag{10}$$

(where $\mathbf{I}$ is the 4×4 unit matrix). The matrix $\mathbf{I} - \mathbf{A}$ is often known as the "Leontief matrix," after Wassily Leontief, the originator of input–output analysis.[1]

We should see what it looks like:

$$\mathbf{I} - \mathbf{A} = \begin{bmatrix} 1 - a_{11} & -a_{12} & -a_{13} & -a_{14} \\ -a_{21} & 1 - a_{22} & -a_{23} & -a_{24} \\ -a_{31} & -a_{32} & 1 - a_{33} & -a_{34} \\ -a_{41} & -a_{42} & -a_{43} & 1 - a_{44} \end{bmatrix} \tag{11}$$

It is thus a matrix with positive numbers (fractions) along the principal diagonal and negative fractions elsewhere. We can see that it is identical in form to the matrix $\mathbf{I} - \mathbf{D}$ that we encountered in Section 16.11. As we explore the properties of $\mathbf{I} - \mathbf{A}$, our results will hold for $\mathbf{I} - \mathbf{D}$, too.

Finally, we suppose that we are given the components of the vector $\mathbf{Y}$, final demand. That is, we have the industrial composition of $C + I + G$, often known as the "final bill of goods." This is the list of required hospitals, airplanes, etc., that we discussed in Section 17.1, plus the commodity breakdown of planned or expected consumption and investment. Thus the problem is, *given* the coefficient matrix $\mathbf{A}$, *and* the final bill of goods, $\mathbf{Y}$, find the outputs required of each industry, that is, the vector $\mathbf{X}$. From (10), we see that the problem is solved by

$$\mathbf{X} = (\mathbf{I} - \mathbf{A})^{-1}\mathbf{Y} \quad . \tag{12}$$

Thus, given $\mathbf{A}$, all we have to do is form the Leontief matrix $\mathbf{I} - \mathbf{A}$ and obtain its inverse. We can then find required outputs for *any*

---

[1] See W. Leontief, *The Structure of the American Economy, 1919–1939; an empirical application of equilibrium analysis*, 2nd ed., Oxford University Press, London, 1951. Professor Leontief was awarded the Nobel Prize in 1973 largely for his work in this field.

final bill of goods merely by multiplying **Y** by $(I - A)^{-1}$. If, in addition, we know each industry's requirements of labor, then we can find the vector of jobs that goes with a final bill of goods. It turns out, in fact, that finding the inverse may be more conveniently done by approximation methods than by the method of the adjoint matrix described in Section 15.6. These methods are of considerable interest, and help us to gain more insight into the model. We shall therefore consider them in Section 17.6, where we shall also consider what we shall now take for granted, that all the elements of $(I - A)^{-1}$ are positive, as common sense requires. Let us, however, first discuss the **A** matrix itself a little further.

17.5 HOW MANY SECTORS? THE TECHNOLOGY MATRIX

The first question is, how far does it pay to disaggregate, or, into how many sectors should we divide the economy? Even if we leave aside costs of data processing and computation, there is no simple answer to this question. Suppose that we use a few very broad sectors, such as manufacturing. Now, manufacturing is a collection of heterogeneous activities, producing a diversity of products. Suppose that we could divide it into a set of subsectors for each of which resource requirements were given by equations of the form of (6). We should not expect all the coefficients to be equal. Thus we see that "the" manufacturing coefficients must be some sort of weighted averages of the subsector coefficients. Now, in practical problems, we are bound to deal with final bills of goods for manufacturing that differ in their internal composition, that is, in the demands on the subsectors. Thus in using a unique set of constant coefficients for "all manufacturing," we shall obviously make errors. Thus it appears that accuracy can be increased by dividing the economy more finely, trying to get our sectors to correspond to homogeneous industrial activities each of which can be described by its own unique coefficient vector.

There is, however, a trade-off. Suppose that we have a really fine classification. Then we will have listed as separate sectors the producers of goods that are, as inputs, close substitutes. Thus manufacturing outputs and service outputs are, as inputs, obviously bad substitutes, whereas steel and nonferrous metals may be quite close substitutes in some industries, and copper, zinc, aluminum, and their various alloys even closer. The trouble with separating outputs that are close substitutes as inputs is that they *will* be substituted in response to changes in relative prices, that is, input coefficients will vary. For theoretical purposes we may assume constant prices, if we wish, but in practical problems too fine a disaggregation will introduce a new source of error. There does not seem to be much we can say theoretically about the trade-off, and the level of disaggregation in practice is determined by data availability, costs, and "feel."

A discussion of practical methods of constructing input–output tables is beyond the scope of this book. It is, nonetheless, worth re-marking that they are expensive articles. They usually have to be built up from the micro-data, and therefore require a full census of production. In the absence of a census, it is largely a matter of in-genuity in finding other data from which coefficients may be inferred —always remembering that the balance equations (3) above have to be satisfied.[2]

We next must recognize that technological change takes place. Thus coefficients change, and, whatever the initial accuracy of our matrix, it must diminish over time. We may appropriately speak of a matrix decaying. Methods for updating the matrices without complete reconstruction have, in fact, been proposed, but are beyond our scope. One last practical matter. Transport costs (and indirect taxes and sub-sidies, if any) cause prices to purchasers to differ from net prices to sellers. We therefore have to decide whether to work in seller's prices or purchaser's prices. Usually the latter are used.

We have referred to the **A** matrix as the technology matrix, and it clearly tells us something about the structure of the economy. What should we look for? First, we might expect some elements to be zero, or, if not zero, negligible. Thus, although we might expect all indus-tries to require some service input, it is hard to imagine the service industry requiring much intermediate input from other industries (heat and light, and some spare parts, perhaps). Thus service inputs should be mostly value added, whereas, at the other end, manufac-turing should have heavy intermediate inputs and relatively little value added. We might also guess that a more developed and sophis-ticated economy would have fewer zeros in its **A** matrix than a less developed and more fragmented one. The extreme case of fragmen-tation would occur if industries used no intermediate inputs from each other. Then the **A** matrix would simply be diagonal, and inputs would consist of the "own washing" item plus value added. Such an economy would be called "decomposable": each sector would be en-tirely independent of the others.

It may be hard to imagine such an extreme case, but it is sugges-tive. First, we can extend our comparison of the structures of devel-

---

[2] For two fascinating accounts of the construction of input–output (I–O) tables *without* the complete micro-data, see Hollis B. Chenery, "Regional Analysis," in *The Structure and Growth of the Italian Economy*, H. B. Chenery, P. G. Clark, and V. Cao-Pinna, eds., U.S. Mutual Security Agency, Special Mission to Italy for Economic Co-operation, Rome, 1953, and W. L. Hansen and C. M. Thiebault, "An Inter-Sectoral Flows Analysis of the California Economy," *Review of Economics and Statistics*, vol. 45, 1963.

oped and less-developed economies. We guess that the more-developed economy not only displays fewer zeros in its **A** matrix but altogether has a higher ratio of intermediate inputs to final output. (In this case the transactions:income ratio will be an increasing function of GNP.) Second, we may be able to find some intermediate cases of interest. Thus consider the coefficient matrix

$$\mathbf{A} = \begin{bmatrix} a_{11} & 0 & a_{13} & a_{14} \\ a_{21} & a_{22} & a_{23} & a_{24} \\ 0 & 0 & a_{33} & 0 \\ 0 & 0 & a_{43} & a_{44} \end{bmatrix} \tag{13}$$

There is nothing to say that the order in which we place the industries is sacred, so let us try swapping them about. Let us change the positions of the industries as follows: swap the first with the third, and the second with the fourth. Then we have

$$\begin{bmatrix} a_{33} & 0 & 0 & 0 \\ a_{43} & a_{44} & 0 & 0 \\ a_{13} & a_{14} & a_{11} & 0 \\ a_{23} & a_{24} & a_{21} & a_{22} \end{bmatrix}$$

(It is easy to check that the swapping has been done correctly by noticing that the first subscript is constant along each row and that the second is constant down each column.) It is now easier to renumber our industries consistent with the change in positions (3 with 1, 2 with 4), whence we have simply

$$\begin{bmatrix} a_{11} & 0 & 0 & 0 \\ a_{21} & a_{22} & 0 & 0 \\ a_{31} & a_{32} & a_{33} & 0 \\ a_{41} & a_{42} & a_{43} & a_{44} \end{bmatrix} \tag{14}$$

For many economies, the **A** matrix is not too unlike the simple triangular form of (14). The equations in this case are said to be *recursive* (see Question 15.6.4). In most practical cases it will not be possible to avoid having some nonzero elements above the diagonal but, with luck and cunning, we may rearrange in such a fashion as to leave only unimportant elements there. We shall see shortly how easy it is to obtain solutions in the triangular case.[3]

---

[3] There are other, more complex, special cases of theoretical and practical interest that we shall not consider. They arise essentially from being able to group industries to take advantage of diagonal and/or triangular relations between the groups.

17.6   SOME SOLUTION METHODS FOR THE A MATRIX

We now discuss some methods of solution. Suppose first that the **A** matrix is diagonal, so that we have

$$\begin{bmatrix} 1 - a_{11} & 0 & 0 & 0 \\ 0 & 1 - a_{22} & 0 & 0 \\ 0 & 0 & 1 - a_{33} & 0 \\ 0 & 0 & 0 & 1 - a_{44} \end{bmatrix} \begin{bmatrix} X_1 \\ X_2 \\ X_3 \\ X_4 \end{bmatrix} = \begin{bmatrix} Y_1 \\ Y_2 \\ Y_3 \\ Y_4 \end{bmatrix} . \tag{15}$$

Each output requirement depends only on the corresponding element of final demand. Thus for X_1 we may simply write

$$(1 - a_{11})X_1 = Y_1$$

or

$$X_1 = \frac{1}{1 - a_{11}} Y_1 = (1 - a_{11})^{-1} Y_1 \quad , \tag{16}$$

and similarly for the remaining X's. Thus the inverse is simply the diagonal matrix with elements $(1 - a_{ii})^{-1}$ down the principal diagonal and zeros elsewhere (see Question 15.6.1).

Now let us consider the case of a triangular **A** matrix, as in (14). The whole net output of the first industry goes to final demand, so in this case, too,

$$X_1 = (1 - a_{11})^{-1} Y_1 \quad . \tag{17}$$

Now the second industry's output goes to the first industry as well as to final demand. Its supply to the first industry is given by

$$a_{21} X_1 = a_{21} (1 - a_{11})^{-1} Y_1 \quad . \tag{18}$$

To this, we have to add the output requirement Y_2. But the nonzero coefficient a_{22} reminds us that this industry, too, uses up some of its own product in its own process. Thus X_2 is given by

$$X_2 = (1 - a_{22})^{-1}(a_{21} X_1 + Y_2) \quad . \tag{19}$$

In the same way,

$$X_3 = (1 - a_{33})^{-1}(a_{31} X_1 + a_{32} X_2 + Y_3) \tag{20}$$

and

$$X_4 = (1 - a_{44})^{-1}(a_{41} X_1 + a_{42} X_2 + a_{43} X_3 + Y_4) \quad . \tag{21}$$

We found the inverse of a triangular matrix in Question 15.6.4a.

Now what about the more general case in which the **A** matrix is not triangular (but perhaps has some zeros, which we shall try to put in the top right-hand corner by our arrangement)? For a given **Y** vector, we could use Cramer's rule. This, however, is unsatisfactory, since we are likely to be interested in the implications of alternative final bills of goods, and we shall have to repeat the whole labor of solution for each bill. We saw, however, in the Questions, that we could build up the inverse by using Cramer's rule to solve in the case **Y** = {1, 0, 0, 0}, then in the case **Y** = {0, 1, 0, 0}, and so on. Even this is tiresome, however, since we shall have to go through the process as many times as there are sectors (although at least det **A** need be evaluated only once). We now ask if there is not some method for finding at least an approximation of $(\mathbf{I} - \mathbf{A})^{-1}$ in one operation. The answer is that it cannot be done in one operation, but we can design an operation successive applications (or "iterations") of which will get us closer and closer approximations.

Let us take **Y** to be the unit vector. A first approximation for **X** is that it, too, is simply the unit vector. But now let us look at the **A** matrix. If we want one unit of an output, the corresponding column tells us the required additional outputs of all other industries. Thus the additional output requirements are simply **A** times the unit vector. We now have as a second approximation

$$\mathbf{X}^{(2)} = (\mathbf{I} + \mathbf{A})\mathbf{Y} \tag{22}$$

[where the superscript (2) on the **X** indicates that it is our second approximation]. Let us just check this. Writing out (22) in the four-sector case, with **Y** as the unit vector, we have

$$\begin{bmatrix} X_1^{(2)} \\ X_2^{(2)} \\ X_3^{(2)} \\ X_4^{(2)} \end{bmatrix} = \left\{ \begin{bmatrix} 1 & 0 & 0 & 0 \\ 0 & 1 & 0 & 0 \\ 0 & 0 & 1 & 0 \\ 0 & 0 & 0 & 1 \end{bmatrix} + \begin{bmatrix} a_{11} & a_{12} & a_{13} & a_{14} \\ a_{21} & a_{22} & a_{23} & a_{24} \\ a_{31} & a_{32} & a_{33} & a_{34} \\ a_{41} & a_{42} & a_{43} & a_{44} \end{bmatrix} \right\} \begin{bmatrix} 1 \\ 1 \\ 1 \\ 1 \end{bmatrix} . \tag{23}$$

Performing the indicated addition and multiplication, we obtain

$$X_1^{(2)} = 1 + a_{11} + a_{12} + a_{13} + a_{14} \quad , \tag{24}$$

and so on. Now, comparing $X_1^{(2)}$ with $X_1^{(1)}$, we see that we have increased it by the sum of the elements of the first row of **A**, and similarly for the other X's. Let us write

$$\Delta \mathbf{X} = \mathbf{X}^{(2)} - \mathbf{X}^{(1)} = \mathbf{A}\mathbf{Y} \quad . \tag{25}$$

But $\Delta \mathbf{X}$ is a new vector of outputs for which inputs are required. These inputs are again given by **A**, so to obtain $\mathbf{X}^{(3)}$ we must add to $\mathbf{X}^{(2)}$ the amounts

$$\mathbf{A}\Delta \mathbf{X} = \mathbf{A}(\mathbf{X}^{(2)} - \mathbf{X}^{(1)})\mathbf{Y} = \mathbf{A}\mathbf{A}\mathbf{Y} \quad . \tag{26}$$

We thus have

$$X^{(3)} = (I + A + A^2)Y \quad . \tag{27}$$

If we keep going "round and round," or iterating, in this fashion, we shall get

$$X^{(4)} = (I + A + A^2 + A^3)Y \tag{28}$$

and, in general,

$$X^{(n)} = (I + A + A^2 + \cdots + A^{n-1})Y \quad . \tag{29}$$

We now must ask whether the successive increments A^n get smaller as n gets larger: if not, we are getting worse approximations instead of better. We similarly want to know if the series in (29) does indeed converge to a definite limit. Given that the answers to these questions are favorable, we also want to know if the powers of A get smaller fast, so that we get a reasonable approximation for the cost of just a few matrix multiplications. Thus we are interested in the formal question, does A^n go to zero, and, if so, does the series $I + A + A^2 + \cdots$ converge, and the purely practical one, if so, how fast? We shall say a little, rather informally, about these formal questions.[4]

In ordinary multiplier analysis, we become familiar with the notion that

$$1 + c + c^2 + c^3 + \cdots = \frac{1}{1 - c} \tag{30}$$

provided that c is less than 1. Alternatively, we say that the series

$$1 + c + c^2 + c^3 + \cdots + c^K \tag{31}$$

approaches the *limit* $(1 - c)^{-1}$ if c^K approaches zero as K goes to infinity: in this case (31) is a *convergent series*. If $0 < c < 1$, then (31) is a convergent series. Our problem now is to consider the matrix analogue of this familiar result in scalar algebra. Thus (29) suggests that

$$I + A + A^2 + \cdots + A^n$$

is a *convergent series*, with limit $(I + A)^{-1}$. The scalar analogy also suggests that this will be true only if A satisfies certain conditions. We

---

[4] This is, in fact, a practical way of obtaining the inverse, particularly if there are some zeros to speed up the multiplication. $X^{(4)}$ may be quite a good approximation. Further, there are some extrapolation formulas available to save time in case convergence is slow. For practical methods, see the discussion in Hollis B. Chenery and Paul G. Clarke, *Interindustry Economics*, Wiley, New York, 1959. For a formal proof that the series converges, see G. Hadley, *Linear Algebra*, Addison-Wesley, Reading, Mass., 1961, chap. 3.22.

also have to consider what we mean by a matrix series converging. The fact that we are trying to approximate to the required **X**, however, suggests the answer. We want the adjustment

$$A\Delta X = A(X^{(n)} - X^{(n-1)})Y \tag{32}$$

to diminish for successively higher values of n. But (32) is also

$$A\Delta X = A^n Y \tag{33}$$

[see (26)]. Thus what we want is that *each element* of A^n approach zero in the limit.

For our purposes, the easiest way to express the conditions on which this occurs are (without proof)

and

$$\left. \begin{array}{ll} 0 \leqslant a_{ij} < 1 & \text{(all } i, j) \\[2mm] \sum_i a_{ij} < 1 & \text{(all } j) \end{array} \right\} \tag{34}$$

Condition (34) is thus the matrix analogue of the scalar condition $0 < c < 1$. It says that each element in **A** must be a nonnegative fraction, and that the column sums must not exceed unity. We saw in Section 17.3 that these are precisely the conditions that the **A** matrix must satisfy. We are therefore assured that we may use this method to obtain the inverse.

We may now settle the question we raised in connection with the matrix multiplier in Section 16.11. As long as all the elements of the matrix **D** are nonnegative fractions, and the column sums are less than unity, we can use the series approximation to $(I - D)^{-1}$. These conditions are satisfied by standard economic assumptions (no negative spending propensities; no dissaving). Further, let us consider the series $A, A^2, A^3, \ldots, A^n$, or $D, D^2, D^3, \ldots, D^n$. As A^n, D^n approach zero only as n goes to infinity, and A, A^2, D, D^2 are nonzero, the inverse must exist. Furthermore, since all the elements in A, D are positive, so are all the elements in their powers. It follows that all the elements in $(I - A)^{-1}$ and $(I - D)^{-1}$ are positive: the usual economic assumptions guarantee that the matrix multiplier will not "blow up."

17.7* CONVERGENCE OF THE MATRIX SERIES

In this section, we show why the conditions (34) are sufficient.

Let us consider the characteristic element of the matrix A^2, which we shall denote by $a_{ij}^{(2)}$. By the ordinary rules of matrix multiplication,

$$a_{ij}^{(2)} = \sum_k a_{ik} a_{kj} \tag{35}$$

Now we take a column sum in $\mathbf{A}^2$:

$$\sum_i a_{ij}^{(2)} = \sum_i \sum_k a_{ik} a_{kj} \quad . \tag{36}$$

Since each element in the jth column of $\mathbf{A}^2$ is obtained by multiplying the jth column of $\mathbf{A}$ by a row of $\mathbf{A}$, (36) is the sum of the scalar products of every row in $\mathbf{A}$ by its jth column. It is thus the sum of every column in $\mathbf{A}$ by the jth column, whence (36) can also be written

$$\sum_i a_{ij}^{(2)} = \sum_k \left(\sum_i a_{ik}\right) a_{kj} \quad . \tag{37}$$

Let us just check (37). First, put $k = 1$. Then the interior summation sign tells us to multiply the first element in the jth column by every element in the first column, and add. The outer summation sign now tells us to repeat the procedure for the second column and the jth column, and to add again. Thus (37) is the same as (36).

Now, from (34), every column sum in $\mathbf{A}$ is less than 1. Thus if the largest column sum is equal to some number, r, we know that r is less than 1 and also that

$$\sum_i a_{ij} \leqslant r < 1 \qquad \text{(for } all \text{ } j) \quad .$$

But the interior summation in (37) is a column sum, whence

$$\sum_i a_{ij}^{(2)} \leqslant r \sum_k a_{kj} \quad . \tag{38}$$

The remaining summation is again over a column, whence

$$\sum_i a_{ij}^{(2)} \leqslant r^2 \qquad \text{(for } all \text{ } j) \quad . \tag{39}$$

If, however, a column sum in $\mathbf{A}^2$ is less than r^2 (which is less than r), then each of its elements must be less than r^2 [guaranteed by (34), since none of them is allowed to be negative]. We can repeat the argument for $\mathbf{A}^3$, $\mathbf{A}^4$, . . . , $\mathbf{A}^n$, and find that all the elements of the successive matrices must be less than r^3, r^4, . . . , r^n. Then, since r is a fraction and r^n goes to zero as n goes to infinity, we know that each element of $\mathbf{A}^n$ indeed goes to zero, and we may be sure that the matrix series converges.

17.8 POSSIBLE TESTS FOR AN INPUT–OUTPUT MODEL

We know that an input–output model is built on strong and restrictive behavioral assumptions, discussed in Sections 17.3 and 17.5. How might we test such a model? Suppose that we had an $\mathbf{A}$ matrix derived from a *census of production* conducted in 1975, say. One procedure would be to obtain the actual outputs and final demands for a later year, 1976, say, and to obtain predicted outputs by postmultiplying $(\mathbf{I} - \mathbf{A})^{-1}$ by the final demand vector. We should then look for discrepancies between predicted and actual outputs. The trouble is that, although we can be sure to find discrepancies, it is far from clear how we should judge them. What is a "big" discrepancy? In particular, how big do discrepancies have to be before we judge that, as a structural model of the economy, input–output is a failure, that is, that the constant-coefficients-constant-prices rules will not do, even in the short run?

The answers are still not clear, but the problem has led to a very important procedure, the deliberate construction of "naïve models" with which input–output results can be compared.[5] The most naïve "model" would simply be the assertion that outputs in 1976 would be the same as those of 1975. This "model" is not hard to beat. Indeed, it is so easily beaten as to provoke the construction of slightly less naïve models. Thus one might try calculating the change (absolute or proportional) in the $\mathbf{X}$ vector from 1975 to 1976, and the assertion that the rate of change from 1975 to 1976 would be the same. And so on. One can produce a whole generation of naïve models to run against the input–output model (and some of the more sophisticated ones will probably beat it). This is an interesting game. Two points about it are particularly worth emphasizing. The first is that *comparison* is a good game to play. We have no absolute standards of "accuracy," only better and worse conformity between prediction and observation. The second is that, although naïve models may be of complicated construction, they are noncausal. Essentially, they say that the future will be like the past, not because of some unchanged structural system, but "just because." They differ only in the ingenuity used to extrapolate (constants, constant rates of change, and so on). Comparison is much more exciting in cases in which we have rival *theories* to run against one another, that is, models that offer alternative explanations of the structural working of the economy. At the moment there is, for many practical purposes, no serious rival to input–output analysis, crude as it is.

17.9 FINAL POINTS

We might now consider some practical problems for which input–output analysis may be an appropriate tool. Instead, since several of the questions are illustrative, we shall consider some final points. In Sec-

---

[5] For a clear and fascinating account, see the third of T. Koopman's *Three Essays on the State of Economic Science*, McGraw-Hill, New York, 1957.

tion 17.2, we assumed a closed economy. Formally speaking, it is extremely easy to "open" the economy. All we need do is add export demand to the final bill of goods, assuming that its commodity composition is determined, and add a vector of import coefficients. We may also hesitate a little. International trade is a resource-saving process: commodities in which a country has a comparative disadvantage are acquired more cheaply by the roundabout method of producing commodities in which the country has a comparative advantage, and trading, than by the direct method of home production. Geography is fairly stable, and so are the broad patterns of trade. But changing levels of demand and resource use change local availabilities, and therefore relative prices, quite quickly. This in turn induces substitution (between *sources* of an input, if not between inputs), whence the notion of a constant vector of import coefficients appears particularly dubious. (There are methods for handling discrete changes in import coefficients, but we shall not discuss them.)

It is as easy, formally, to "close" the model with respect to households as it is to open it with respect to international trade. We have already suggested that one might have an additional vector of labor inputs. In this case a full solution would provide the wage component of household income. We might now add a vector of consumption coefficients: each coefficient would give the proportion of household expenditure devoted to the output of each sector. Then C (or much of it) would disappear from the final bill of goods and become endogenous. The model would then be said to be "closed with respect to households." An even more ambitious program would be to make investment endogenous, remove I from the final bill of goods, and thus close the model with respect to investment. We shall not investigate these closed models further, since there is a more urgent matter.

Whether the model be more or less open or closed, there is a final bill of goods. Question 4 asks you to work out problems for a variety of bills. Exercises of this sort may reveal a great deal about what is *possible* (in real-world applications, too). In looking at the output requirements corresponding to alternative final bills, we reveal all sorts of interesting things, particularly the *feasibility* of the bills. If there are capacity limitations on the outputs of the sectors, we may, by repeated solution for alternative final bills, trace out the *production possibility frontier*, or at least part of it. This is important practical information, which, in much economic analysis, we assume is freely bestowed (we now know that it is, in fact, expensive). It is clear, however, that we have only done part of the job: solving for alternative arbitrary final bills is a method of locating part of the frontier, but tells us nothing about where *on* the frontier the economy should go, that is, which final bills are better than others.

We may now state the obvious: we have not, so far, been dealing with a *choice* (or optimizing) problem at all. Indeed, we have only been describing, and, until we introduce capacity constraints [in Question 4(b)] and therefore start to describe what is feasible, we are only doing illustrative exercises. So the question now is, can we analyze the problem of choice when the technology is described by a matrix of constant coefficients, and resources are in limited supply? This is the subject matter of Chapter 18.

QUESTIONS

1. a. You are called in as a planning consultant by the government of Ruritania. (If you are unfamiliar with Ruritania, you might enjoy *The Prisoner of Zenda* by Anthony Hope, Dutton, New York, 1955. It was made into a movie with Ronald Colman in the late 1930s. It will shed *no* light on these exercises!) On arrival, you are proudly handed a new input–output matrix just produced by the Ruritarian Office of Central Planning. It is

$$\mathbf{A} = \begin{bmatrix} 0.2 & 0 & 0 & 0.2 \\ 0.5 & 0.01 & 0.015 & 0.13 \\ 0.25 & 0.2 & 0.3 & 0.07 \\ 0.1 & 0.01 & 0.015 & 0.19 \end{bmatrix}.$$

The industries are identified in Ruritanian, which you cannot read. You, so far, know nothing whatever about the Ruritarian economy anyhow. Nonetheless, you explain immediately to the local officials that something has gone catastrophically wrong. What?

b. The Ruritanian planners discover what they claim were typographical errors and come up with

$$\mathbf{A} = \begin{bmatrix} 0.2 & 0 & 0 & 0.2 \\ 0.05 & 0.01 & 0.015 & 0.13 \\ 0.25 & 0.2 & 0.03 & 0.07 \\ 0.1 & 0.01 & 0.15 & 0.19 \end{bmatrix}.$$

You cannot reject this one a priori, but you have become very suspicious. What information might you ask for to help you check?

c. You decide to invert the matrix by successive applications of Cramer's rule, using $\mathbf{Y} = \{1, 0, 0, 0\}$, then $\mathbf{Y} = \{0, 1, 0, 0\}$, etc. The Ruritanians wonder how the results of this process can be used to find $\mathbf{X}$ when $\mathbf{Y} = \{10, 5, 7, 11\}$. Explain.

2. The planners tell you that the Ruritanian technology matrix 20 years ago was

$$\begin{bmatrix} a_{11} & a_{12} & a_{13} & 0 \\ 0 & a_{22} & a_{23} & 0 \\ 0 & 0 & a_{33} & 0 \\ a_{41} & a_{42} & a_{43} & a_{44} \end{bmatrix}.$$

a. One industry bought no intermediate products from other industries; it was "all value-added." Which was it?
b. One industry used inputs from all other industries but provided no intermediate inputs to them. Which was it?
c. What is the simplest method of solving for required outputs, given a final bill of goods, in this case?

3. a. Find an approximation for $(\mathbf{I} - \mathbf{A})^{-1}$ if

$$\mathbf{A} = \begin{bmatrix} 0.1 & 0 & 0 & 0.2 \\ 0.05 & 0.01 & 0.05 & 0 \\ 0.1 & 0.2 & 0.1 & 0.05 \\ 0.2 & 0.01 & 0.2 & 0.2 \end{bmatrix} .$$

b. How might you check your result?
c. Suppose that you made an arithmetic error at some point, say in computing $a_{ij}^{(k)}$. Would this necessarily lead to a wrong answer?

4. You at last agree with the planners that $(\mathbf{I} - \mathbf{A})^{-1}$ for Ruritania is approximately

$$\begin{bmatrix} 1.17 & 0.01 & 0.06 & 0.28 \\ 0.06 & 1.02 & 0.06 & 0.02 \\ 0.16 & 0.23 & 1.14 & 0.10 \\ 0.31 & 0.06 & 0.29 & 1.33 \end{bmatrix} .$$

(This is, in fact, the inverse of the matrix in Question 3, computed as a series $\mathbf{I} + \mathbf{A} + \mathbf{A}^2 + \mathbf{A}^3$, and rounded.)
a. If final demand is given by $\mathbf{Y} = \{7, 10, 5, 20\}$, what are required outputs?
b. You discover that there are capacity limits to output, given by $\mathbf{C} = \{15, 12, 12, 25\}$. What do you think might happen, given the $\mathbf{Y}$ of part a?
c. Suppose now that Ruritania is an open economy, with the inverse technology matrix given above, but with, in addition, a vector of intermediate import requirements given by

$$\mathbf{M} = \{0, 0, 0.01, 0.1\} .$$

Given the final demand vector of a, what would be the value of imports? What would be the balance of payments?

Linear Programming

Linear programming is a technique for solving a class of constrained maximization problems that cannot be handled by the calculus methods used so far in this book. This class of problems is characterized by inequalities instead of equalities in the constraints and, as we shall see, attainable frontiers that are not everywhere differentiable.

18.1 A LINEAR PROGRAM

The essential ingredients in a linear program are a *maximand,* or objective function, a constant-coefficient technology matrix, and a vector of scarce resources at least some of which can be used for more than one purpose or activity. Let us consider these ingredients in turn.

Looking at the input–output structure of Chapter 17, it would be natural to choose GNP as the objective, and try to maximize that. We can write GNP as $\Sigma_i\, p_i x_i$, where the p_i's are prices and the x_i's the outputs. This is a *linear* objective function. The problem is to maximize the scalar product of a vector of outputs and a vector of weights or prices. This is clearly restrictive, but is as far as linear programming will take us (techniques exist for handling nonlinear programming problems, but they are beyond the scope of this book). In our examples below, we shall consider profit maximization by a firm that can use its scarce resources to produce more than one good. Given constant prices, revenue is the scalar product of the output and price vectors. Profit, of course, is revenue minus costs, and we shall introduce assumptions such that the variable cost function is linear too, whence profit (the maximand) will be a linear function of the outputs.

The notion of a constant-coefficient technology matrix, which we denote by $\mathbf{A}$, is familiar from Chapter 17. We merely remark now that it implies constant returns to scale and no interactions between the alternative production activities.

We also assume that the firm possesses some resources that are limited in supply (i.e., we have a short-run problem) and have the property that at least some of them can be used to produce more than one good. This is an essential assumption if there is to be a choice problem. If each scarce resource was used for only one good, each would be used to the limit (or not at all if production of the particular good was not profitable), and there would be no allocation problem. Notice that in this trivial case we could always arrange the $\mathbf{A}$ matrix to make it diagonal.

To illustrate, let us now set up the linear programming problem of a firm that can make two goods q_1 and q_2. To construct a linear objective function, we need weights that can be applied to q_1 and q_2. We naturally use the output prices, π_1 and π_2, say, to obtain the profit function

$$\Pi = \pi_1 q_1 + \pi_2 q_2 - \text{costs} \quad,$$

which is to be maximized subject to the technology and resource constraints.

It is now necessary to assume perfect markets so that both q_1 and q_2 are sold at constant prices, and to assume that variable inputs (labor and raw materials) are bought at constant prices. We further assume that the quantity of labor and raw material required per unit of each output is fixed (constant coefficients). This allows us to define "net" prices,

$$p_1 = \pi_1 - \text{variable cost per unit of } q_1$$

and

$$p_2 = \pi_2 - \text{variable cost per unit of } q_2 \quad,$$

whence

$$\Pi = p_1 q_1 + p_2 q_2 \quad.$$

We also assume that the firm possesses three sorts of fixed equipment, R_1, R_2, and R_3, in given amounts, each of which may be used in the production of both q_1 and q_2. We may now write the problem:

$$\text{maximize } p_1 q_1 + p_2 q_2$$

subject to

$$a_{11} q_1 + a_{12} q_2 \leq R_1$$
$$a_{21} q_1 + a_{22} q_2 \leq R_2$$
$$a_{31} q_1 + a_{32} q_2 \leq R_3$$

and

$$q_1 \geq 0, \qquad q_2 \geq 0 \quad .$$

This is a *linear program*. In vector notation, it is easily generalized to

$$\text{maximize } \mathbf{p'q}$$

subject to

$$\mathbf{Aq} \leq \mathbf{R}$$

and

$$\mathbf{q} \geq 0$$

(where a prime indicates a row vector).

The discovery of numerical methods for solving linear programs was a breakthrough of great practical importance, to be discussed in Section 18.6. Even without knowing solution methods, however, an economist can learn a great deal of interest from and about linear programming. Indeed, we are able to leave solution methods to an appendix since knowledge of the methods is not required to understand the material in this chapter.

We shall shortly look at (and solve) a simple numerical example, but first let us look at some properties of our algebraic example.

The technology, or **A** matrix, is, in general, not square. If the number of fixed resources *happened* to be equal to the number of goods the firm could produce with them, it of course would be square, but we should not, in general, expect it to be. (*If* the **A** matrix were square, solution would be easy, as we shall see.) We have weak inequalities before the resource constraints, because, although it is impossible to use more than one has, it might not always pay to use all that one had. Similarly, we have weak inequalities on q_1 and q_2 since it might pay to produce as much as possible of one good only, and none of the other, whereas it is impossible to produce negative quantities. We want to know how much of each to produce, that is, how to allocate the R's. We want to know how much the profit is. And finally, since it might pay to alter the quantity of one of the fixed resources (by investment, or perhaps scrapping), we must find out how much each contributed to the profit, that is, we must *impute* values to them.

18.2 AN ARITHMETIC EXAMPLE

Let us choose numbers and write the program directly in numerical form:

$$\text{maximize } 2q_1 + 3q_2$$

subject to

$$q_1 + 2q_2 \leq 100$$

$$q_1 + q_2 \leq 75$$

$$\tfrac{1}{2}q_2 \leq 50$$

and

$$q_1 \geq 0, \qquad q_2 \geq 0 \; .$$

(Notice that we have chosen $a_{11} = a_{21} = a_{22} = 1$ and $a_{31} = 0$. The net price of q_1 is 2 per unit and of q_2 is 3 per unit.)

Since there are only two outputs, we can illustrate this program in two dimensions, and find out easily how to solve it. In Figure 18.1 we measure q_1 on the vertical axis and q_2 on the horizontal axis. We shall plot one at a time the limits to output imposed by each resource constraint, and then consider what is possible when they are all taken into account at once. Thus we start by looking at the first constraint as though no other constraint operated. If we devoted all of R_1 to q_1, output would be 100. If we devoted it all to q_2, output would be 50. If we were to allocate 99 of it to q_1 and 1 to q_2, we should get 99 units of q_1 and a half unit of q_2. *This* constraint is therefore illustrated in Figure 18.1 by a line of slope minus two from 100 on the vertical axis to 50 on the horizontal axis.

Similarly, the second constraint is illustrated by a line of slope minus one joining the two intercepts at 75 and 75. Finally, the effect of the third constraint is simply to limit output of q_2 to 100, irrespective of anything else, and to impose no limitation on the output of q_1.

The limits to possible outputs imposed by the three constraints are illustrated in the figure, and labeled R_1, R_2, and R_3.

Now let us see what outputs are *possible*, given all three constraints. All points on R_1 and R_2 are *inside* R_3, so it is evident that they are the constraints that matter: we can forget about R_3. To the left of point B, R_2 lies inside R_1: points on R_1 are therefore unattainable, and possible outputs are limited by R_2. Similarly, to the right of B, R_1 lies inside R_2, which is unattainable, and R_1 limits outputs. The limit to what is attainable is therefore given by the line 75-B-50, which is the *frontier of the feasible set*: all points on and within it are attainable, but no points beyond it. The frontier is, in this case, determined entirely by R_1 and R_2.

Once one has discovered the location of the frontier to the feasible set one has done most of the work in solving a linear program. (Obviously if there are n possible outputs, and m constraints, n and m large, this is not an easy task. Our geometrical methods work only where $n = 2$.) To complete the solution, we turn back to the objective

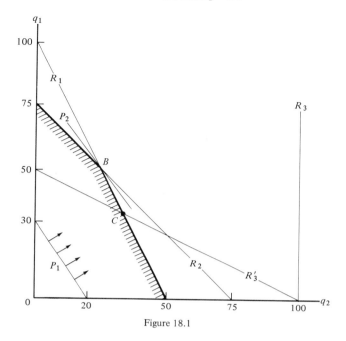

Figure 18.1

functions, $2q_1 + 3q_2$. One dollar of profit can be obtained by producing half a unit of q_1 or one third of a unit of q_2. Similarly, \$2 of profit can be obtained by producing one unit of q_1 or two thirds of a unit of q_2. In general, an iso-profit line is given by

$$2dq_1 + 3dq_2 = 0 \quad ,$$

with slope $dq_1/dq_2 = -\frac{3}{2}$. An iso-profit line is illustrated by the line labeled P_1 in Figure 18.1 with intercepts $q_1 = 30$, $q_2 = 20$ (corresponding to a profit of 60). The farther out this line can be moved (with constant slope), the greater the profit. Thus, as the arrows indicate, we move it out, parallel to itself, as far as we possibly can. We therefore move it out *until it reaches the point on the frontier of the feasible set farthest from the origin.* This can be seen to occur at B, on the iso-profit line labeled P_2. (Notice that, in this example, the slope of the iso-profit line, $-\frac{3}{2}$, lies *between* the slopes of the two binding constraints, -1 and -2. We shall see in Section 18.3 what happens if this condition is not met.)

Now that we know that the profit-maximizing outputs are given by B, the rest of the solution is simple. The first two constraints hold as equalities, and the third is irrelevant (the first two are said to "bind" at the optimum point and the third to be "slack"). Since the first two hold as equalities, we only have to solve

$$q_1 + 2q_2 = 100$$

$$q_1 + q_2 = 75$$

(i.e., we replace the inequalities by equalities for the constraints that bind, and drop the constraint that does not bind). By simple substitution we find that the answer is $q_1 = 50$, $q_2 = 25$. Substituting these values into the objective function, we see that the total profit is 175. This is called *the value of the program.*

18.3   SOME EXTENSIONS

In the program we have just solved, the third resource was not used in the production of the first good (a_{31} was zero). Let us change this assumption and see what happens.

Suppose, first, that the third row of the technology matrix is replaced by

$$\tfrac{5}{8}q_1 + \tfrac{1}{2}q_2 \leq 50 \quad .$$

You should be able to work out for yourself that this leaves the feasible set, and therefore the solution to the program, unaltered. (If the whole of R_3 were devoted to q_1, the intercept would be 80. R_3 therefore still lies entirely outside R_1 and R_2.)

Suppose, second, that the third row is replaced by

$$0.7q_1 + 0.5q_2 \leq 50 \quad .$$

It is easy to calculate that this does alter the feasible set. The new intercept is less than 75 (approximately 71). On the other hand, R_3 is outside R_1 and R_2 at B. (Remember that, at B, q_2 is 25. This leaves $37.5 = 50 - (0.5)(25)$ of R_3 for q_1, so that q_1 would be $37.5 \div 0.7 > 50$ in the absence of the other constraints.) This case is illustrated in Figure 18.2.

Looking at Figure 18.2, we see that our new constraint, although it alters the feasible set, does not in fact bind: it does not alter the solution of the program given the prevailing prices. It is clear that we can add more constraints that alter the feasible set—two more are illustrated by the dashed lines in Figure 18.2. Indeed, we may go on adding constraints, as in Figure 18.3, until the frontier is composed of many straight-line segments meeting at corners. It looks more and more like an ordinary production possibility frontier, only one made up of linear segments instead of a smooth curve. We shall reconsider this point in Section 18.7, but we see at once that, however many linear constraints we add, the frontier will not be continuously differentiable.

Next, let us alter the third equation in the technology matrix so

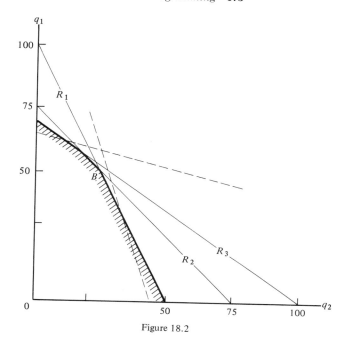

Figure 18.2

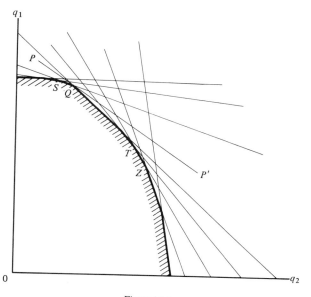

Figure 18.3

that the third constraint does alter the solution. We choose

$$q_1 + \tfrac{1}{2}q_2 \leq 50 \quad .$$

This gives a q_1-intercept of 50, which is the value of q_1 at B, whence B is now unattainable. The new constraint is illustrated by the line labeled R_3' in Figure 18.1. Evidently the profit-maximizing point is now C, and R_2 *does not bind*. To solve the program, all we have to do is drop the second equation, replace the inequalities with equalities in the first and third equations, and solve. Thus

$$q_1 + 2q_2 = 100$$

and

$$q_1 + \tfrac{1}{2}q_2 = 50 \quad ,$$

which are solved by $q_1 = q_2 = 33\tfrac{1}{3}$. The value of the program is $(2)(33\tfrac{1}{3}) + (3)(33\tfrac{1}{3}) = 166\tfrac{2}{3}$. This is naturally less than the value of the program we first solved, since the profit-maximizing point is closer to the origin.

Surveying these rather naïve examples, one common feature emerges. In each case, two, and only two, constraints bind at the optimal point. This is one of the most interesting results of linear programming: *in general, the number of constraints that bind will not exceed the number of goods it pays to produce.* We shall not offer any general proof of this proposition, but we may consider it further. Two phrases need attention, the qualification "in general" and the words "will not exceed" (not "will be equal to").

The qualification "in general" is needed because of the possibility of a "degenerate case." Consider the solution at C in Figure 18.1. Now suppose that R_2 were moved toward the origin until it just passed through C. C would remain the optimal point, and three constraints would "just" bind. This case is clearly a pure fluke.

Now suppose that the price of q_1 were to fall. To make any given profit, it would be necessary to produce *more* q_1. The iso-profit lines would accordingly all become steeper. Thus imagine P_2 in Figure 18.1 pivoting clockwise around B. As it changes slope, it corresponds to different levels of profit, since absolute prices are changing, but B continues to give optimal quantities (although with different values of the program) until it pivots "far enough." If it pivots far enough, it will exactly coincide with R_1. Points on R_1 above B are still unattainable, but *all points* on R_1 between B and the horizontal axis yield the same profit (including B and the point $q_1 = 0$, $q_2 = 50$). It therefore simply does not matter which point is chosen. If it is B, then two constraints bind; if it is anywhere between B and the axis, then only one constraint binds, although two goods are produced; and if it is the point on the axis, then the number of binding constraints and the number of goods produced are again equal.

Finally, let P_2 pivot a little more, so that it lies *inside* R_1 below B. Then there are points on R_1 below and to the right of B that yield *more* profit than does B. Indeed, the farther down R_1 one goes, the greater the profit. Now profit is uniquely maximized at the point $q_1 = 0$, $q_2 = 50$, where again the number of binding constraints does not exceed the number of goods it pays to produce. In this case, the price ratio is such that the iso-profit lines are steeper than every segment of the frontier of the feasible set. This leads to a solution on the horizontal axis where $q_1 = 0$. It is easy to see that, if the iso-profit lines were *flatter* than every segment of the frontier, the solution would occur on the vertical axis, where $q_2 = 0$. For an interior point such as B, where both goods are produced, to be a unique optimum it is necessary that the price ratio be such that the slope of the iso-profit lines lies *between* that of two binding constraints. This is what we assumed in the example of Section 18.2.

18.4 THE DUAL

A problem we have not yet solved is how to impute values to our fixed resources. We are clearly dealing with a short-run problem in which the firm has fixed quantities of plant and equipment, say lathes, presses, and drills, or locomotives, freight cars, and passenger cars. In general, these items will have market prices, but we want to know what they are actually worth to the operating unit in the short run. These imputed values may, after all, not be the same as market prices.

We shall go about this problem in a seemingly arbitrary fashion; that is, we shall present a solution first and see why it works afterward.[1] We shall use as an example the program of Section 18.2. We denote the imputed prices of the three resources by V_1, V_2, and V_3 (dollars per unit). The problem is to find the actual values of the V's. We now proceed to turn around everything in the program that we can. For a start, we *minimize* instead of maximizing. We choose as our objective function

$$\text{minimize } 100V_1 + 75V_2 + 50V_3$$

(or, in general, minimize $R_1V_1 + R_2V_2 + R_3V_3$). Our technology matrix was

[1] The procedure we shall adopt is wittily discussed by W. J. Baumol and R. E. Quandt, "Dual Prices and Competition," in *Models of Markets*, A. R. Oxenfeldt, ed., Columbia University Press, New York, 1963. The paper is reprinted in the Penguin readings volume *The Theory of the Firm*, G. C. Archibald, ed., Baltimore, Md., 1971.

$$\begin{bmatrix} 1 & 2 \\ 1 & 1 \\ 0 & \frac{1}{2} \end{bmatrix},$$

and we turn this around by transposition (swapping rows for columns) to get

$$\begin{bmatrix} 1 & 1 & 0 \\ 2 & 1 & \frac{1}{2} \end{bmatrix}$$

(in general, we replace $\mathbf{A}$ by $\mathbf{A}'$). We cannot postmultiply this by the column vector $\{q_1, q_2\}$ because it does not conform with $\mathbf{A}'$ for multiplication. But the column vector $\{V_1, V_2, V_3\}$ does conform, so let us postmultiply by that to get

$$V_1 + V_2$$
$$2V_1 + V_2 + \tfrac{1}{2}V_3$$

(in general, $\mathbf{A}'\mathbf{V}$). Continuing our campaign of turning everything around, we replace "less than or equal to" with "greater than or equal to" — but greater than or equal to what? Well, we have the V's and the values of R_1, R_2, and R_3, and we have put them into the objective function, displacing the (net) product prices. So let us now use the product prices on the right-hand side instead of the R's. We get

$$V_1 + V_2 \geq 2$$
$$2V_1 + V_2 + \tfrac{1}{2}V_3 \geq 3$$

(in general, $\mathbf{A}'\mathbf{V} \geq \mathbf{p}$). Finally, since we do not define negative values here, we have

$$V_1 \geq 0, \quad V_2 \geq 0, \quad V_3 \geq 0$$

(a resource may be worthless but does not impose costs).

If we now assemble our scrambled program, we find we have a new linear program:

$$\text{minimize } 100V_1 + 75V_2 + 50V_3$$

subject to

$$V_1 + V_2 \geq 2$$
$$2V_1 + V_2 + \tfrac{1}{2}V_3 \geq 3$$

and

$$V_1 \geq 0, \quad V_2 \geq 0, \quad V_3 \geq 0 \quad .$$

We write this in general form as follows:

$$\text{minimize } \mathbf{R'V}$$

subject to

$$\mathbf{A'V} \geq \mathbf{p}$$
$$\mathbf{V} \geq 0$$

(where again a prime indicates transposition). This program is called the *dual* of our original program, which in turn is called the *primal* program. You should now check for yourself that, if we attack the dual in exactly the same way that we attacked the primal, we shall recover the primal: *the primal program is the dual of the dual program!* The steps are: maximize instead of minimize; transpose the technology matrix; swap the q's and the V's; swap the p's and the R's; reverse the weak inequalities in the constraints.

At this point one may reasonably wonder what on earth is going on, but it will be easier to understand after we have solved the dual program and considered a geometrical illustration.

Solution in this case is easy, since we already know from Section 18.2 that the third constraint does not bind. This means that V_3 *must be zero.* If a unit of R_3 were taken away, the value of the program would be unaltered, whence it is making no contribution to profit (if half our lathe capacity were lying idle because of the bottlenecks in pressing and drilling, profits would be unaltered if a lathe were taken away or sold for scrap). We can now proceed just as we did in the primal program. We simply drop the constraint that is slack and replace the inequalities with strict equalities. Thus we solve for V_1 and V_2

$$V_1 + V_2 = 2$$
$$2V_1 + V_2 = 3 \quad .$$

Our imputed values are, accordingly,

$$V_1 = 1, \quad V_2 = 1, \quad V_3 = 0 \quad .$$

We now have a very handy check. When we solved the primal problem, we calculated the value of the program from $p_1 q_1{}^* + p_2 q_2{}^*$, where the stars indicate the optimal values of the outputs. If we have correctly valued the resources that contributed to that profit, we should have just exhausted that profit. Substituting our V's $(1, 1, 0)$ into our objective function $(100V_1 + 75V_2 + 50V_3)$, we get 175, just as we should. Suppose that the value of the dual program had turned out to exceed that of the primal. Then we should be attributing to our fixed resources a value greater than the dollar return from operating them in the most profitable possible fashion, which would not make sense. Suppose, on the other hand, that the value of the dual was less than that of the primal. Then there would be some profit not allocated to any particular resource, whence its origin would be a bit of a mystery: this result, if it occurred, would certainly suggest that we had made a mistake somewhere.

Our *procedure,* in the dual, is to look for the *lowest* values of the fixed resources that will *just* account for the prices of the products, given the contribution from each resource required per unit of each product. This is the force of the constraint $A'V \geq p$ on the minimization.

Since only two constraints bind in this simple example, we can illustrate the solution of the dual geometrically. In Figure 18.4 we measure V_1 on the vertical axis and V_2 on the horizontal axis. The first constraint, $V_1 + V_2 = 2$, is simply illustrated by a line of slope minus one between the intercepts 2, 2. The second, $2V_1 + V_2 = 3$, is illustrated by a line of slope minus one half between the intercepts $\frac{3}{2}$ and 3. Now consider the objective function $100V_1 + 75V_2$ (with $V_3 = 0$). Isovalues of this function (which is to be minimized) satisfy $100dV_1 + 75dV_2 = 0$, and are illustrated by lines of slope $-\frac{3}{4}$. One is illustrated by the line with intercepts 3 and 4 [corresponding to a value of the program of $(100)(3) + (75)(4) = 600$]. This line is to be moved, parallel to itself, *toward* the origin until the constraints just bind. The solution is at D, the exact analogue of B in Figure 18.1.

We hope that the dual program has now ceased to be a mystery. You may note that we could have reversed the order of argument, presented the dual first, and then gone on our "turn it around" campaign to discover the primal. There are two further points to notice. The first is that, since the constraints in the dual are "greater than or equal to," they bind "from above": this is illustrated by the hatchings in Figure 18.4. The second is that this frontier is convex *from above.* But this is the way it should be. Think of minimizing costs on an isoquant map, as compared with maximizing GNP on a production possibility map (Sections 11.1 and 11.7). You will also, of course, notice that the slope of the iso-valuation lines lies *between* that of the two binding constraints. We leave it to you to work out what is implied if this condition is not met.

Our imputed prices have one more property that we must discuss. Suppose that we were operating a firm with a technology such that we thought that linear programming was applicable. We collect up the required numbers and give them to a programmer. He elects to solve the dual rather than the primal problem (it may be computationally easier) and tells us the prices to be attributed to our fixed resources.

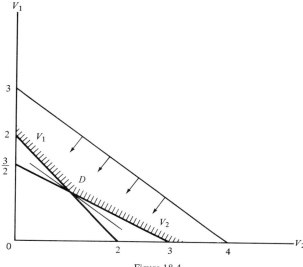

Figure 18.4

Is this useful knowledge? The answer may be surprising, but it is definitely yes. The reason is that the information is sufficient to tell us which goods to produce and which not to produce. Thus suppose that the rth and sth equations of the dual are

$$0.1V_1 + V_2 + 0.25V_3 + 0.5V_4 \geq 2$$

$$0.3V_1 + 2V_2 + 0.1V_3 \qquad\qquad \geq 1.5 \quad,$$

where 2 is the price of the rth good, 1.5 is the price of the sth good, and the numerical coefficients come from the rth and sth *columns* of the **A** matrix, respectively. Now our programmer tells us that he has computed

$$V_1 = 1, \quad V_2 = 0.5, \quad V_3 = 2, \quad \text{and} \quad V_4 = 3 \quad.$$

Substituting in, we find

$$(0.1)1 + (1)0.5 + (0.25)2 + (0.5)3 = 2.6 > 2$$

$$(0.3)1 + (2)0.5 + (0.1)2 \qquad\qquad = 1.5 \quad.$$

This tells us to produce the sth good but *not* the rth. The reason is not that the rth good is unprofitable, but that the *opportunity cost* of making it exceeds its profit. Its gross profit is 2 per unit over and above direct variable cost, but the value of the fixed resources used in making it (2.6) is greater than 2. What this means is that it pays better to use these resources to produce something else, such as the sth good, where opportunity cost and return are equal.

18.5 SHADOW PRICES

The V's we have just discussed are often called *shadow prices,* shadow because they may not appear on any observable price tag. It is clear that the shadow price of a piece of equipment might differ from firm to firm even in the same industry, depending on the capital structure of the firms. It is certain that, if shadow prices differ, they cannot all be equal to market prices. We now ask if there is any mechanism that will tend to equate shadow and market prices.

Suppose that the shadow price of a firm's drills exceeds the market price, whereas that of lathes is less than the market price (even zero). We obviously expect the firm, as soon as it can, to buy more drills and perhaps to sell or scrap lathes. The shadow price of lathes would tend to go up as the stock of drills increased, output rose, and lathes became more useful. The shadow price of drills would certainly fall. The market price of drills would rise, or stay constant (if drills were produced under constant costs). The market price of lathes would fall or stay constant. Whether market prices change or not, it is clear that the long-run adjustment of the firm will tend to push shadow and market prices toward equality. It is intuitively obvious that, if we assume competitive markets, the long-run equilibrium condition *is* equality of shadow and market prices.

This is a very nice result. It reconfirms what we know about competitive markets: in long-run equilibrium they ensure the equality of market price and opportunity cost. We may say that a property of imperfect markets is that they drive a wedge between prices and opportunity costs and thus lead to production of the "wrong" bundle of outputs. As is well known, uncorrected externalities do the same thing.

This result also has an interesting application in the theory of central planning. Suppose, as we did in Question 1 of Chapter 17, that we are called in as consultants by the government of Ruritania. For better or for worse, the country has a central planning bureau. Now, suppose that, in addition to the input–output coefficient matrix we were first given, we are told the resource and capacity constraints (available power supplies, the size of the labor force, and so on). We see that we have the essential information to set up the constraint part of a linear program: all we need is an objective function. The choice of an objective function was suggested in Section 18.1: GNP. But GNP is $\Sigma\ p_i y_i$ (where the y_i's are the final goods), and the obvious problem is the choice of the weights or prices. Who is to determine the relative weight to be attached to shirts and shoes, guns and butter? If the Ruritanian economy is to be centrally planned by linear programming methods, the central planners must do it.

To make the exercise worthwhile, the technology and the constraints must be specified in great detail, and the computational requirements will be huge. Thus central planning will be very costly in its informational and computational requirements (but remember that markets do not work costlessly either). If, however, we solve the primal problem, we can, at least in principle, tell every plant manager how much of each good to produce, and how. We then face the problem of enforcement. We have to set up a system to detect noncompliance with the plan and punish it (Siberia) — or reward compliance. Clearly a market system has one advantage: *if* it is competitive, it is in the interests of all the managers to "behave," and we need incur no enforcement costs over and above the information and transactions costs of the markets themselves.

Suppose now that the central planning bureau solves the dual program instead of, or as well as, the primal problem. It now knows the shadow prices (or opportunity costs) of all Ruritania's scarce inputs, including shadow wages, as well as the prices assigned to all final goods. An intriguing possibility is that it could simply announce the shadow prices and tell all managers to get on with it (maximize), *using the shadow prices in their accounts* whether they were equal to market prices or not. Although the information costs of setting up the program would be unaltered, enforcement costs might be greatly reduced. Indeed, the system would be closely analogous to competitive capitalism, with managers instructed to base their decisions on prices that reflected social opportunity cost.

The whole question of central planning is too complex and controversial to pursue further here. What is important for present purposes is to see that computed shadow prices can serve the same signaling function as competitive market prices.

18.6 APPLICATIONS OF LINEAR PROGRAMMING

The idea of linear programming, as we have seen, is essentially simple: it is maximization under constraint once again. For it to be useful as a practical tool, rather than merely to reinforce our understanding of economic principles, there must exist manageable methods for solving large programs. Analytic solution is not possible: the methods must be numerical. Methods were developed, as it happens, at about the same time in the United States and the USSR under the stimulus of World War II. George Dantzig developed the first method of solution in 1947 while working for the U.S. Air Force.

Initially, the range of applications appeared to be very much at the micro-level. A well-known early example of civilian application was to the planning of an Indian cotton mill. Linear programming appeared to be part of the tool kit of the new discipline of operations research ("how to," or "scientific management"). The technique was applied to the scheduling of airlines and oil tankers, the operation of an oil refinery, the blending of aviation gas, and the organization of delivery systems. By the late 1950s, however, the relationship between linear programming and economic analysis, and its wider application to central planning, were well understood.[2]

One possibly surprising application of linear programming we owe to a Norwegian, Leif Johansen.[3] This application is to the problem of regional economic policy in an unplanned economy. Suppose, for simplicity, that we can divide a country into two "regions," one that is prosperous and one that is relatively depressed (consider, for example, the Appalachian region of the United States). Governments in unplanned capitalist economies commonly intervene with some program of assistance to the relatively depressed regions. In Canada, the United Kingdom, and Norway, for example, the assistance has usually taken the form of subsidization (or some sort of tax relief) to companies investing in designated areas, on the grounds that new investment would both directly create jobs and have favorable local multiplier effects. Johansen was able to show, using linear programming methods *but without numbers*, that this policy is generally mistaken. The reason is very simple.

The two regions have their existing stocks of capital equipment and labor, both immobile, in the short run at least. The stocks of each sort of capital, and of labor of each sort of skill, in each region, provide the constraints in the primal problem. There is obviously no reason why physically identical labor, of the same skills, should have the same shadow prices in the two regions: the shadow prices must depend, among other things, on the capital stocks the labor has to work with in each of the two regions. Consider, on the other hand, new investment that will be made somewhere in the country in the next, say, 12 months. Until it is actually made, it is completely mobile. Thanks to the agency of financial intermediaries, savings made in New York can be invested as easily in Florida or California as in New York and vice versa. It is the forthcoming supply of saving that limits the total of new investment that can be undertaken, irrespective of where it is located. Looking at our linear programming "plan" for the next 12 months, then, we see that there is a *single* constraint for new investment. A single fixed resource can, however, have only one

[2] The classic work on economics and programming is known as "Dossow:" *Linear Programming and Economic Analysis*, by R. Dorfman, P. A. Samuelson, and R. K. Solow, McGraw-Hill, New York, 1958.

[3] L. Johansen, "Regional Economic Problems Elucidated by Linear Programming," *International Economic Papers*, vol. 12, 1967.

shadow price, not two. It follows that the shadow price of new capital cannot differ between the two regions. It follows, in turn, that although the market price of new capital may not equal the shadow price (because of taxation or market imperfections), there is no reason why the government should try to make its price differ between the two regions. This must be the case whatever we choose for our objective function—GNP, or employment, or some linear combination of the two: a single scarce resource enters as a single constraint with a single shadow price.

We notice that relatively depressed regions commonly experience a rate of unemployment chronically higher than that of the rest of the country. The linear programming approach to regional problems offers a particular explanation of this phenomenon. In general, we should not expect the shadow price of a worker with specified skills to be the same in Illinois and West Virginia. It is, however, quite possible that the wage rates are the same in the two places (or that, if they differ, they differ by less than the shadow prices). This suggests, in turn, that wage rates in relatively depressed regions may be above shadow prices, at least for some sorts of workers. In this case, if the government wishes to intervene, it should do so by subsidizing wages, not capital. By doing so, it could bring the effectives wages as seen by employers in line with the shadow prices. It would create, in effect, the competitive solution for firms, who would consider the net (after subsidy) wage in taking their decisions, in spite of the fact of market imperfection.

We see, then, that linear programming, as well as offering practical numerical methods for both micro- and macro-planning, offers useful qualitative results. There is one last practical problem we should consider. It is obvious that the program required for central planning must be enormous, with staggering information requirements. But consider the application of programming to a large corporation such as General Motors. To attempt this on a centralized basis would again be a staggering task. We notice that, in practice, most large firms are subdivided into "divisions" of some sort. This means that they *decentralize* some, at least, of their decisions (often everything except finance and research). An obvious question is whether decentralized decisions "add up" to a global maximum. Usually, no one knows: it has to be taken on faith. The analogous question is obviously, can a linear program be decentralized, or "decomposed," so that the central office need not solve the whole program, but can delegate sections of it to divisions?

The problem of finding what are technically called "decomposition algorithms" for linear programs is obviously of great practical importance. It is perhaps the biggest problem in the theory of central planning today. We are not here concerned with the mathematics but with the economics of the problem. Consider further the decision process of a large corporation that delegates some decisions to its divisions. We might imagine the divisions making their own plans for next year, for inputs, outputs, prices, and expansion. These plans are reported to the head office, which adds them up. It finds, let us suppose, that the output plans together require more of one input than it expects to be able to purchase on favorable terms, whereas the plans for expansion will use up only part of the capital it expects to have available. It communicates this news to the divisions, inviting them to try again. It adds up the new plans, and so on. This is an *iterative* approach to the planning problem (notice that it might not be convergent). The iterative approach is not inconsistent with the possibility that each division sets up its plan as a linear program.

Now suppose that the divisions, instead of being controlled by the large corporation, were independent decision-making firms. Suppose, in fact, that they were small, and that we indeed had competitive markets. This means, of course, that we have decentralized decision making. There is no reason, however, to suppose that any particular set of prices that prevails on a certain day is an equilibrium set. Thus the market system itself must iterate, experimenting with new prices (and quantities) in response to the initial excess demands and supplies. The difference, of course, is that the market system iterates in "real time," making real transactions at disequilibrium prices, whereas the planning system goes through its iterative procedure without transactions. We see that each system is the analogue of the other, and that each imposes its own costs. Which is cheaper is not obvious.

18.7 SUBSTITUTION

It should now be clear that linear programming is more than a numerical technique for the operations researcher: its results complement and reinforce familiar principles of economics. We need not rehearse the relationship between shadow prices and competitive prices, or that between decentralized planning and decentralized markets. We shall conclude by discussing two topics that sometimes cause trouble, substitution in a linear system,[4] in this section, and comparative statics, in the next.

[4] This is particularly well explained in R. Dorfman, " 'Mathematical' or 'Linear' Programming: A Nonmathematical Exposition," *American Economic Review*, vol. 43, 1958. The paper is reprinted in the Penguin readings volume *The Theory of the Firm*, G. C. Archibald, ed., Baltimore, Md., 1971.

In the input–output analysis of Chapter 17, it was assumed that substitution between inputs was impossible. It might well appear that linear programming, with its constant-coefficients technology matrix, rested upon the same assumption. This is not the case, although substitution takes place in a slightly different manner from that in our familiar models in which everything is continuously differentiable. We have to consider substitution in outputs (between goods) and in production (between inputs).

To understand the possibility of substitution between outputs, turn back to Section 18.3 and, in particular, to Figure 18.3. We remarked there that the frontier illustrated in Figure 18.3 looked remarkably like an ordinary production possibility frontier, but composed of straight-line segments and corners instead of being a smooth differentiable curve. To see how substitution works in this case, suppose that relative prices are given by the slope of PP' in Figure 18.3, so that the mix of outputs is given by Q. Now let relative prices alter (pivot PP' around Q). Until the slope of PP' coincides with that of either the segment SQ or the segment QT, nothing happens: the same output mix remains optimal. When PP' coincides with either SQ or QT, then, as we saw in Section 18.3, Q is only one of the set of optimal points in the appropriate segment of the frontier. Let relative prices now change just a little more, so that PP' is even fractionally steeper than QT (but flatter than TZ). Now T is the optimal point, and the production mix has "jumped" from that of Q to that of T. The consequence of linearizing the production possibility frontier has simply been to make substitution proceed in "jumps" instead of smoothly. For sufficiently small changes in prices, nothing happens; in response to larger changes, production takes a discrete jump; and, in between, there is always a set of relative prices such that the optimal production mix is, within a range, indeterminate.

To understand the possibility of substitution between inputs in linear systems we must extend our analysis to what is called "activity analysis." We shall illustrate this approach very briefly. Let us assume that it is possible to make a certain good by combining labor of a certain skill with a machine of certain properties in fixed proportions. Measure labor along the horizontal axis in Figure 18.5 and capital along the vertical axis (in this illustration we shall ignore power and raw materials). With fixed proportions (constant returns to scale) the production possibilities are illustrated by the ray, or vector, $0A$. Distance along $0A$ is proportional to output, and its slope measures the required proportions. This ray illustrates our first *activity*. Now, it is commonly the case that machinery comes in well-specified types. Let us suppose that our first activity involved the use of a high-speed, automatic lathe that required relatively little labor per unit output.

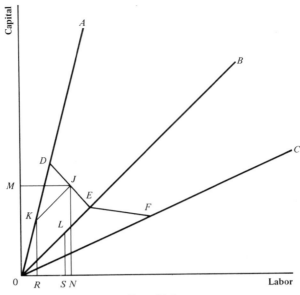

Figure 18.5

We assume that there is available a cheaper and slower model of lathe that requires more labor per unit output. With fixed proportions, the activity that employs this type of lathe is illustrated by the ray $0B$. We may finally assume the existence of a third and more primitive lathe with no automatic devices at all, and illustrate the most labor-intensive activity by the ray $0C$.

Now let us arbitrarily pick a *unit* (which might be 1, 10, or 100 units of actual output). On $0A$ we mark off at D the point that corresponds to the inputs required to make a unit of output. We similarly mark off the "unit" points E and F on $0B$ and $0C$. Can we join up D, E, and F? Assuming divisibility (which is why we might wish to choose a large "unit"), indeed we can. We pick any point, say J, on DE. Construct a line through J parallel to $0B$, and mark off at K its point of intersection with $0A$. Mark off L on $0B$ so that $0L = KJ$. It is easy to show that using the first process to the level $0K$, and the second to the level $0L$, generates the unit output *and* employs inputs given by the coordinates of J ($0M$ capital and $0N$ labor).

To see that we do get unit output at J, that is, that DE is an isoquant, we show that the output corresponding to $0K$, plus that corresponding to $0L$, is equal to that corresponding to $0D$ (or $0E$). Note that output is directly proportional to the distance along a ray from the origin. Note also that KDJ and $0DE$ are similar triangles (by construction). We therefore have (output at $0L$)/(output at $0E$) = $0L/0E$

and (output at $0K$)/(output at $0D$) = $0K/0D$. Also, (output at $0D$) = (output at $0E$). Adding,

$$\frac{(\text{output at } 0L) + (\text{output at } 0K)}{(\text{output at } 0D)} = \frac{0L}{0E} + \frac{0K}{0D}$$

$$= \frac{KJ}{0E} + \frac{0K}{0D} = \frac{KD}{0D} + \frac{0K}{0D} = 1 \quad .$$

It remains to show that the input coordinates $0M$ and $0N$ do "add up." We will consider only labor: the construction for capital is parallel. The labor inputs are $0R$ for the first process and $0S$ for the second. We need to show that $0R + 0S = 0N$. Since JK and $0L$ are equal and parallel by construction, $RN = 0S$. It follows that $0R + 0S = 0R + RN = 0N$, as required.

We could repeat the above argument for *any* point J in DE, or for any point in EF. DEF is therefore an iso-quant. Its correspondence to our familiar smooth convex iso-quant is analogous to that of the frontier of the feasible set in programming to the smooth production possibility frontier. It is easy to see that the substitution possibilities are analogous, too. Cost minimization is familiar. Let relative factor prices be given. Consider the set of parallel iso-cost lines, the slope of which gives relative factor prices. The production plan that minimizes the cost of the output corresponding to DEF is then given by the point at which the iso-cost curve nearest to the origin touches DEF. Suppose that this point is E. Then the cost-minimizing choice of activity is the second. Small variations in relative factor prices cause no change in the input mix. Large enough changes will "jump" it to D or F. At all three points, only one activity is used to produce one good. The degenerate case is familiar.

18.8 COMPARATIVE STATICS

Throughout this book, we have stressed the importance of comparative static analysis, and particularly qualitative comparative statics, as a means of deriving testable predictions from our theories. It remains to review linear programming from this point of view.

First, it is obvious that it is not devoid of qualitative content: our discussions of shadow prices and competition, and of the regional problem, demonstrate that. It is not even totally devoid of qualitative comparative static content, as our discussion of substitution shows: everything goes "the right way," albeit in jumpy increments rather than smoothly. There is, however, little more that can be obtained without numbers. Generally speaking, at least in a program of any size, if one wants to know how the decision variables respond to changes in the parameters, one has to solve the program numerically for each set of parameter values and hope that some intelligible pattern begins to emerge. Effectively, one gets the computer to do for one numerically what, in simple differentiable systems, we have learned to do analytically.

It does not take much imagination to see that the researcher may need considerable ingenuity and a great deal of computer time as he tests a particular linear programming problem for its "sensitivity" to various parameters. It has often been supposed that the absence of analytic results, the meagerness of qualitative results, and the dependence on numerical instances, were great defects in the linear programming approach compared with conventional, continuous, analysis. We should hesitate before we accept this verdict. We saw in Sections 16.9 and 16.10 how easy it is to construct a conventional model that has little or no comparative static content. Indeed, it is much easier than we have represented here: conventional models of any degree of complexity and sophistication are all too often qualitatively empty. Thus perhaps we should give thanks for an approach that at least allows us to proceed by the comparison of numerical instances, even if it has limited generality.

We finally remark that in recent years the programming approach has been rapidly extended, in particular to nonlinear objective functions (nonlinear or dynamic programming) and to stochastic problems. These techniques are beyond the scope of this book, but they are proving of increasing service to economists conducting "pure" research.

QUESTIONS

1. Assume that the technology matrix and resource limitations are those of the first numerical example in Section 18.2 but that net product prices are $p_1 = 3$ and $p_2 = 5$.
   a. Find the profit-maximizing levels of output.
   b. Find the value of the program.
   c. Find the shadow prices of the resources.
   d. The outputs are unchanged by the change in prices from the example in Section 18.2. Why?
   e. What is the easiest way of discovering which constraints bind in this example?

2. With technology and resources unchanged, prices now become $p_1 = 5$ and $p_2 = 1$.
   a. Find the outputs, the value of the program, and the shadow prices.
   b. What is the easiest way of discovering which constraints bind in this example?

3. Alter the third row in the technology matrix, as we did in Section 18.3, to

$$q_1 + \tfrac{1}{2}q_2 \leq 50 \quad,$$

giving, with $p_1 = 2$ and $p_2 = 3$, $q_1 = q_2 = 33\tfrac{1}{3}$. Find the shadow prices.

4. Now suppose that the quantity of the second resource is reduced until R_2 just binds at C in Figure 18.1.
   a. Write the second row of the technology matrix.
   b. What are the shadow prices in this case?

5. Consider the regional problem of Section 18.6. Assume that there are two products, q_1 and q_2, each produced by linear technologies in both regions A and B, and that each region has one type of immobile capital K, and one quality of immobile labor L, each of which can be used in the production of both products. Assume that technological knowledge is the same in both regions.
   a. Assume that the objective is to maximize GNP. Write out in general form the primal problem and the dual.
   b. Suppose that the capital in the two regions is physically identical. Do you expect its shadow price to be the same in both regions?
   c. Suppose that the labor in the two regions is identical in skill, strength, etc. Do you expect its shadow price to be the same in both regions?
   d. On what conditions would you expect the "market solution" to be identical to the solution of linear programming?

6. Consider now a short-run regional planning problem. Assume again two products, each produced in each of two regions. Assume that each region will have otherwise unemployed labor next year in quantities L_A and L_B. The labor is completely mobile between the two industries within each region, and completely immobile between the two regions. In addition, there will be an amount of new capital, I, available for the two regions together next year. The capital can be allocated to either region and used in the production of either good.
   a. Assume that the object is to maximize the contribution to GNP that may be obtained from the newly available resources, L_A, L_B, and I. Write out the primal and dual problems.
   b. Will this objective (maximizing the contribution to GNP) also minimize unemployment among the workers L_A and L_B?
   c. Would it make any difference to the policy result of Section 18.6 (subsidize or tax wages on a regionally discriminatory basis if necessary, but not investment) if the regions produced different commodities?
   d. Why might it be "necessary" to interfere with wages in any case?
   e. Would it make any difference to the policy conclusions if the technology matrices in the two regions were identical?
   f. On what conditions would the "market" solution to this short-run planning problem be identical to the Linear Programming solution?

7. Consider the problem of choosing, from all the foodstuffs available, the cheapest diet that contains certain minimum quantities of protein, vita-

mins, fats, carbohydrates, etc. Can this be set up as a linear programming problem?

8. We have explored some basic macro-models in this book, examining the trade-offs between such things as employment and the balance of payments. Would linear programming help a government to make a sensible policy choice?

9. (for discussion) Can you imagine linear programming being of any help in planning the operations of a university?

10. (for discussion) "Remedial programs undertaken by the federal government are 'problem-oriented' rather than 'location-oriented.' But because poverty problems tend to occur in the same places, the U.S. government has a 'regional' policy whether it knows it or not." Is this true? Can U.S. regional "policy" be elucidated by linear programming methods?

Linear Programming and the Simplex Method

In the last chapter we discussed the mathematical and economic interpretation of a linear program, and while this gives us great insight into many important economic phenomena, historically linear programming had its major impact because it was the first complex optimization problem posed which had a relatively simple and cheap method of solution. The computational technique developed to solve linear programs was known as the simplex method, and it involved nothing more complex than the simple arithmetic operations of addition, division, and multiplication. Its importance to an economist is that it made both central planning and activity analysis computationally feasible.

The basic idea behind the simplex method is quite simple. Consider again the LP problem represented in Figure 18.1 which is reproduced here as 18A.1. As noted previously the feasible set is the shaded area *ODBE*. The corner points of the feasible set are known as *extreme points*. The simplex method consists of examining the extremum points in a systematic fashion. For example, a point such as *B* is picked, and those extreme points adjacent to it such as *D* and *E*. The value of the objective function is examined at each of these points, and if either *D* or *E* yield a higher value than *B*, then the next step consists in moving to that adjacent point giving the higher value and carrying out the same procedure over again. Of course when there are more than two dimensions to the problem, there are many more adjacent points to any extreme point, and the method becomes

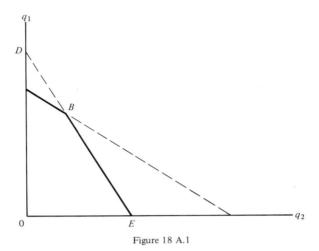

Figure 18 A.1

more complex. It is, however, systematic and computationally efficient.

In order to present a more general version of the simplex algorithm it will be necessary to introduce some more explicit material on vectors. In Question 2 of Section 15.4 the concept of linear dependence of vectors was introduced. We shall now define this more precisely. Let $\{y_i\}$, $i = 1, 2, \ldots, n$ be a set of $m \times 1$ column vectors and $\mathbf{O}_m$ denote an $m \times 1$ column vector of zeros. We then have the following two definitions.

   i. A set of vectors $\{y_i\}$ is said to be linearly dependent if there exists a set of numbers $\{a_i\}$, where some of the a_i are not equal to zero, such that $\Sigma a_i y_i = \mathbf{O}_m$.

   ii. A set of vectors $\{y_i\}$ is said to be linearly independent if for all numbers $\{a_i\}$ such that $\Sigma a_i y_i = \mathbf{O}_m$ it is the case that all $a_i = 0$.

Note that the definitions imply that if a set of vectors is not linearly independent then they must be linearly dependent and vice-versa. It is often convenient to form a matrix from a set of vectors when dealing with linear programming problems. Therefore suppose we had three column vectors

$$\mathbf{y}_1 = \begin{bmatrix} 1 \\ 2 \\ 3 \end{bmatrix} \quad \mathbf{y}_2 = \begin{bmatrix} 3 \\ 6 \\ 7 \end{bmatrix} \quad \text{and} \quad \mathbf{y}_3 = \begin{bmatrix} 8 \\ 0 \\ 2 \end{bmatrix}.$$

We could form the matrix $\mathbf{A}$ as follows:

$$A = [\mathbf{y}_1 \quad \mathbf{y}_2 \quad \mathbf{y}_3] = \begin{bmatrix} 1 & 3 & 8 \\ 2 & 6 & 0 \\ 3 & 7 & 2 \end{bmatrix} \ .$$

More generally consider an n-set of vectors $\{\mathbf{y}_i\}$, where each $\mathbf{y}_i$ is an $m \times 1$ column vector. Then we can construct an $m \times n$ **A** matrix as follows.

$$A = [\mathbf{y}_1 \quad \mathbf{y}_2 \quad \cdots \quad \mathbf{y}_n] \ .$$

With this idea of a matrix consisting of a row of column vectors consider a set of linear equations

$$\mathbf{Ax} = \mathbf{b} \tag{1}$$

where **A** is an $m \times n$ matrix, **x** is an $n \times 1$ column vector and **b** is an $m \times 1$ column vector. Note that in order for this system of equations to have a solution m must be less than or equal to n, that is, the number of equations must not be greater than the number of unknowns. Let us denote by $\mathbf{A}^j$ the jth column of **A**, where $\mathbf{A}^j$ is an $m \times 1$ column vector. We can then write the system of equations as

$$[\mathbf{A}^1 \quad \mathbf{A}^2 \quad \ldots \quad \mathbf{A}^n] \begin{bmatrix} x_1 \\ x_2 \\ \vdots \\ x_n \end{bmatrix} = \begin{bmatrix} b_1 \\ b_2 \\ \vdots \\ b_m \end{bmatrix},$$

or upon rearranging as

$$x_1 \mathbf{A}^1 + x_2 \mathbf{A}^2 + \cdots + x_n \mathbf{A}^n = \mathbf{b} \ .$$

Therefore we can express a system of linear equations as a linear sum of vectors, where the coefficient corresponding to each vector is a variable of the equation system.

We shall now prove a very useful theorem about matrices and vectors, which we shall subsequently use. In Question 3 of Section 15.6 it was demonstrated for a particular case that if $n = m$, that is if the number of vectors forming the **A** matrix was equal to column size, that is, **A**, a square matrix, and the set of vectors forming **A** were linearly independent, then **A** was invertible as its determinant was nonzero. One might suspect then that if $n > m$, then the set of column vectors forming **A** were in fact linearly dependent. Suppose, for example, we have a matrix **A**, 2×3, where

$$A = \begin{bmatrix} 1 & 0 & 1 \\ 0 & 1 & 1 \end{bmatrix} \ .$$

Since the third column vector $\begin{bmatrix} 1 \\ 1 \end{bmatrix}$ is equal to $\begin{bmatrix} 1 \\ 0 \end{bmatrix} + \begin{bmatrix} 0 \\ 1 \end{bmatrix}$, the first plus the second column vector, these three vectors are linearly dependent. In fact this is the case. Let A be an $m \times n$ matrix, $n > m$ and let A^j, $j = 1, \ldots, n$ be the set of column vectors of A, $A = [A^1 \ \ A^2 \ldots A^n]$.

Theorem: Let A be an $m \times n$ matrix, with $n > m$. Then the set of vectors $\{A^j\}, j = 1, \ldots, n$ is linearly dependent.

We shall prove this theorem for the case $n = m + 1$. Clearly if it is true for this case it will be true for any arbitrary $n > m$. The method of proof is by contradiction. That is, we assume that the conclusion of the theorem is false, and then demonstrate that it contradicts the premise of the theorem, and therefore the conclusion must have been true. Suppose $A^1, \ldots, A^{m+1}$ are linearly independent. Then for any set of numbers $(\lambda_1, \ldots, \lambda_{m+1})$ such that $\sum_{j=1}^{m+1} \lambda_j A^j = 0$, we have from the definition of linear independence that $\lambda_1 = 0, \ldots, \lambda_{m+1} = 0$. Now since $A^1, \ldots, A^{m+1}$ are linearly independent, it follows from the definition that any subset of these vectors are linearly independent. Let us choose the first m $A^j, j = 1, \ldots, m$ and denote by $\hat{A}$ the matrix $[A^1 \ \ A^2 \ldots A^m]$. Now choose an arbitrary $\lambda_{m+1} \neq 0$ and consider the linear equation system in the variables $(\lambda_1, \ldots, \lambda_m)$ given by the equation

$$\sum_{j=1}^{m} \lambda_j A^j = -\lambda_{m+1} A^{m+1} \quad . \tag{2}$$

But since the $\{A^j\} \ j = 1, \ldots, m + 1$ are linearly independent, this equation system can have *no* solution, other than $(\lambda_1, \ldots, \lambda_m, \lambda_{m+1}) = 0'_{m+1}$. However (2) is a well-defined linear system of equations given $\lambda_{m+1} \neq 0$ and therefore has a solution, which admits $\hat{\lambda}_{m+1} \neq 0$. This gives us a contradiction. Therefore our supposition is incorrect whence the $\{A^i\}, j = 1, \ldots, m + 1$ are linearly dependent.

With this result we may now turn to consideration of the solution of linear programming problems. Recall the general form of the L.P. problem.

$$\text{MAX } c'x \qquad \text{subject to} \qquad Ax \leq b \tag{3.1}$$

$$x \geq O_n \tag{3.2}$$

where c is $n \times 1$, x is $n \times 1$, b is $m \times 1$, and A is $m \times n$. In order to use the simplex method it is necessary to convert the inequality constraint (3.1) into an equality constraint. We do this by adding to the problem what are known as *slack variables*. The term slack arises because they "take up the slack" in the inequality.

The number of slack variables is equal to the number of constraints in (3). In this case the dimension of the vector of slack variables is m. Therefore let s be an $m \times 1$ vector, $s \geq \mathbf{O}_m$ such that we replace (3.1), (3.2) by

$$\mathbf{Ax} + s = \mathbf{b} \tag{3.1'}$$

$$x \geq \mathbf{O}_n \qquad s \geq \mathbf{O}_m \quad . \tag{3.2'}$$

We can now rewrite the L.P. problem (3) in equivalent form as

$$\text{MAX } \hat{\mathbf{c}}'\hat{\mathbf{x}} \qquad \text{subject to} \qquad (1) \ \hat{\mathbf{A}}\hat{\mathbf{x}} = \mathbf{b}$$

$$(2) \ \hat{\mathbf{x}} \geq \mathbf{O}_{n+m} \tag{4}$$

where $\hat{\mathbf{c}}' = [\mathbf{c}'\mathbf{O}'_m]$, $\hat{\mathbf{x}}' = [\mathbf{x}'\mathbf{s}']$ and $\hat{\mathbf{A}} = [\mathbf{AI}_{m \times m}]$ with $\mathbf{I}_{m \times m}$ denoting the $m \times m$ identity matrix. Hence by the convenient use of slack variables we can convert an inequality constrained L.P. into an equality constrained L.P., and this is the form to which the simplex method applies. For the time being we shall drop our "hats" in (4) and consider the general equality constrained L.P. problem

$$\text{MAX } \mathbf{c}'\mathbf{x} \qquad \text{subject to} \qquad \mathbf{Ax} = \mathbf{b} \tag{5.1}$$

$$x \geq \mathbf{O}_n \quad . \tag{5.2}$$

Now we define a *feasible solution* to the L.P. (5) as an $n \times 1$ vector x which satisfies (5.1) and (5.2). Of fundamental importance to the simplex method is the idea of a basic solution.

> A *basic solution* to L.P. (5) is one which has at most m nonzero elements. A *basic feasible solution* is one which is basic and feasible.

In examining possible solutions to the L.P. problem (5) it would greatly simplify matters if we could restrict our search to solutions which are basic feasible. The following theorem ensures that, if the solution set is nonempty, there do exist basic solutions. In proving the theorem we make use of the result proved earlier on linear dependence.

Theorem: If the L.P. problem (5) has a feasible solution, then it has a basic feasible solution.

Suppose we have a feasible solution x with $k > m$ nonzero elements. Since it is feasible it must satisfy

$$\sum_{j=1}^{n} x_j \mathbf{A}^j = \mathbf{b} \tag{6}$$

where $\mathbf{A}^j$ is the jth column of $\mathbf{A}$. Let us take the last $n - k$ x_j to be zero.

Then (6) can be rewritten as

$$\sum_{j=1}^{k} x_j \mathbf{A}^j = \mathbf{b} \quad . \tag{7}$$

Now since $k > m$, and the $\mathbf{A}^j$ are $m \times 1$ vectors we may apply the theorem we proved on linear dependence. That is there exists a set of weights $\{\lambda_j\}$ not all zero such that

$$\sum_{j=1}^{k} \lambda_j \mathbf{A}^j = \mathbf{O}_m \quad , \tag{8}$$

and we can take at least one of the λ_j to be positive. Now consider the ratios of λ_j/x_j. We use the notation $\Theta = \max_j \lambda_j/x_j > 0$ to denote the maximum of ratios λ_j/x_j over all $j = 1, \ldots, n$.

Then combining (7) and (8) we get

$$\sum_{j=1}^{k} x_j \mathbf{A}^j - 1/\Theta \sum_{j=1}^{k} \lambda_j \mathbf{A}^j = \mathbf{b}$$

and rearranging

$$1/\Theta \sum_{j=1}^{k} [\Theta x_j - \lambda_j] \mathbf{A}^j = \mathbf{b} \quad .$$

Since $\Theta > 0$, and from the definition of Θ we have $\Theta x_j - \lambda_j = 0$ for at least one j, we also have $\Theta x_j - \lambda_j \geq 0$ for all j. Thus the vector with elements $1/\Theta[\Theta x_j - \lambda_j]$ is a nonnegative solution to equation (7), and has $n - k + 1$ zero components.

The reason the vector $\bar{\mathbf{x}}$ whose elements are $1/\Theta[\Theta x_j - \lambda_j]$ has a zero component, which $\mathbf{x}$ did not have, follows from the construction of Θ. Since $\mathbf{x}$ had by assumption $n - k$ zero components, then $\bar{\mathbf{x}}$ will have one more zero element, or $n - k + 1$. Now if $k - 1 > m$ we can carry out this process again, getting $m - k + 2$ zero components and so forth. Once $k = m$ we will have a basic feasible solution and the theorem is proved.

In the examination of feasible solutions to (5) we are of course interested in those which attain the maximum value of the objective function $\mathbf{c}'\mathbf{x}$. Those feasible solutions at which the maximum is attained are called *optimal* solutions. When one has "flat" segments in the feasible set as in the L.P. problem we know there may be more than one optimal solution. The next theorem gives us the very useful result that, in our search for optimal solutions, we may restrict ourselves to those which are basic feasible solutions.

Theorem: If the L.P. problem (5) has an optimal solution then it has a basic optimal solution.

(The proof here is rather difficult and may be omitted on first reading.) Let x^* and y^* be the solutions to problem (5) whose dual is

$$\text{MIN } y'b \qquad \text{subject to} \qquad A'y \geq c \qquad (8.1)$$

$$y \geq O_m \quad . \qquad (8.2)$$

In the context of the activity analysis model, for example, $y'b$ represents factor costs, and the vector c is product prices. We know from Section 18.4 that if $A^{j'}y^* > c_j$, that is if the unit cost of producing the jth good at an optimum is greater than the product price c_j, then $x_j{}^* = 0$, or none of the jth good will be produced. The converse is also true. If $\hat{x}_j = 0$ whenever $A^{j'}y^* > c_j$ then $\hat{x}$, where $\hat{x}$ is a nonnegative solution to $Ax = b$, is an optimal solution. To show this statement is true, recall that at an optimum of the program the optimal activity vector x^* and shadow prices y^* are such that profit is identically zero, $c'x^* = y^{*'}b$. Consider $c'\hat{x}$, and using the hypothesis that $\hat{x}_j = 0$ when $A^{j'}y^* > c_j$, then

$$c'\hat{x} = \sum_{j=1}^{n} c_j\hat{x}_j = \sum_{j=1}^{n}(A^{j'}y^*)\hat{x}_j = (\sum_{j=1}^{n} \hat{x}_j A^j)\, y^{*'} = by^{*'} \quad .$$

Hence $\hat{x}$ is an optimal solution.

Suppose x^* is an optimal solution, and that x^* has $k > m$ nonzero components. Since x^* is feasible it must satisfy

$$\sum_{j=1}^{k} x_j{}^* A^j = b \quad . \qquad (9)$$

Applying the last theorem we proved, we know there exists a basic feasible solution $\bar{x}$, which also satisfies (9).

$$\sum_{j=1}^{m} \bar{x}_j A^j = b \qquad m < k \qquad (10)$$

Now dual to the optimum x^* is the dual vector y^*. If $x_j{}^* = 0$, then $A^{j'}y^* > c_j$. Since (10) was derived from (9), if $x_j{}^* = 0$, then $\bar{x}_j = 0$. Therefore if $\bar{x}_j = 0$, then $A^{j'}y^* > c_j$. Therefore we know that x is an optimal vector.

This theorem and the one preceding it are what make the simplex method "simple." They ensure that if a feasible solution exists at all, then a basic solution exists, and furthermore that by examining only basic feasible solutions we may reach an optimum. For example, suppose the number of variables is ten and the number of constraints is five, then by examining basic solutions only, we have to consider only those solutions with five nonzero elements, a considerable saving of effort. The simplex method consists of systematically checking solutions to the L.P. problem, and applying a number of rather tedious but simple rules at each step. Consider again problem (4)

$$\text{MAX } c'x \qquad \text{subject to} \qquad Ax + s = b$$

$$x \geq O_n \qquad s \geq O_m \; . \qquad (4)$$

This problem has $n + m$ variables and m constraints. In order to solve this problem there are six steps to follow, which must be followed in a sequential fashion. The simplex algorithm involves following steps one through five, with the sixth step being a return to step three. You continue to cycle in this manner until the problem has been solved. This is an example of an iterative process referred to earlier in Section 18.6 when discussing the solution of planning problems.

Step 1: Pick an initial basic feasible solution. For problem (4) this is relatively simple. Set $x = O_n$ and $s = b$. Since s is of dimension m this solution is basic, and by assumption $b > O_m$, and therefore the solution is feasible.

Step 2: Construct the initial simplex tableau. The simplex tableau is a highly convenient way of representing your linear program. Along the lefthand side are the basic variables, which in our initial case are $(s_1, \ldots , s_m)$. Along the top are the nonbasic variables, i.e., those which take the value zero; in our case these are $(x_1, \ldots , x_n)$ in the initial step. Now adjacent to the vector of basic variables is a column of constants, which are the values the basic variables take.

Tableau I

Nonbasic Variables

		x_1	x_2	$\cdots$	$\cdots$	x_n
	0	c_1	c_2	$\cdots$	$\cdots$	c_n
s_1	b_1	$-a_{11}$	$-a_{12}$	$\cdots$	$\cdots$	$-a_{1n}$
s_2	b_2	$-a_{21}$	$-a_{22}$	$\cdots$	$\cdots$	
$\vdots$	$\vdots$	$\vdots$	$\vdots$			$\vdots$
s_m	b_m	$-a_{m1}$				$-a_{mn}$

Basic Variables

For the initial step $s_i = b_i$ is the value of the basic variables. Just below the nonbasic variables is a row of constants, which are given the following interpretation. If the ith nonbasic variable were changed from zero to one, then the constant term immediately below it measures the change in the value of the program due to that change. For the initial tableau this row of constants is just the vector of coefficients in the objective function of the L.P., c'. The lower righthand block of coefficients is a matrix B which generally differs from A, except in the first iteration of the algorithm, and which satisfies the identity

$$x_B = k - Bx_{NB}, \qquad x_B \geq O_m \quad x_{NB} \geq O_n \qquad (11)$$

for x_B, the basic variables, x_{NB} the nonbasic variables, and k a vector of constants, and the set of equations (11) has the same solution set as

$$s = b - Ax, \qquad s \geq O_m, x \geq O_n \quad . \qquad (12)$$

Note that for the initial tableau, $x_B = s$, $k = b$, $x_{NB} = x$, and $B = A$. The upper lefthand corner of the tableau gives the value of the program, $c'x$, given the values taken by the basic variables. In the initial tableau $x = O_n$ and hence the value of the program is zero.

Step 3: Checks to be made for each tableau. We now state three checks to be made on the tableau. Each time the tableau is altered, these checks should be made.

1. *Check for a basic solution* This is done simply by ensuring that none of the nonbasic variables assumes a positive value.
2. *Check for feasibility of basic solutions* The basic solution on the left is feasible if all the constant terms of the lefthand column of the tableau are nonnegative.
3. *Check for optimality* The basic solution is optimal if none of the coefficients in the top row of the tableau corresponding to nonbasic variables are nonnegative.

An intuitive explanation of the last result is that if one of the coefficients were nonnegative, then the value of the program could be increased by increasing the corresponding nonbasic variable. Let us put the L.P. problem of Section 18.2 into the first stage of the tableau form. First we shall rewrite it in the form of (4):

$$\text{MAX } 2q_1 + 3q_2 \qquad \text{subject to} \qquad q_1 + 2q_2 + s_1 = 100$$

$$q_1 + q_2 + s_2 = 75$$

$$\tfrac{1}{2}q_2 + s_3 = 50$$

$$q_1, q_2, s_1, s_2, s_3 \geq 0 \quad .$$

We choose as our initial basic feasible solution $q_1 = 0$, $q_2 = 0$, $s_1 = 100$, $s_2 = 75$, and $s_3 = 50$. Tableau 1 below is the initial tableau for this L.P. problem.

Tableau 1

		q_1	q_2
	0	2	3
s_1	100	-1	$\left(-2\right)$
s_2	75	-1	-1
s_3	50	0	$-\frac{1}{2}$

For this tableau we carry out step 3.

1. Check for basic solution? This holds by construction.
2. Check for feasibility? Yes. The lefthand column is nonnegative.
3. Check for optimality? *No.* There are positive entries in the top row corresponding to nonbasic variables. In this case they are 2 and 3.

Since we do not have an optimal basic solution, the tableau is not in its final form. The next step is to find another set of basic variables such that the value of the program is increased. This involves what is known as the pivoting operation, a seemingly arbitrary step, but is in fact just a simple way of doing the necessary arithmetic, in choosing a new basic solution.

Step 4: Choosing a pivot. We must choose a particular element of the lower righthand matrix of the tableau, which shall be called the *pivot* element. The column from which the pivot is chosen corresponds to the nonbasic variable of the old tableau which is to become a basic variable in the new tableau. The row from which the pivot is chosen corresponds to the basic variable in the new tableau. The following rules apply to choosing a pivot.

Rule 1. Choosing a pivot column: the pivot element is chosen from that column which has the largest positive element. In Tableau 1 of the example, since 3 is greater than 2, the second column is the pivot column.

Rule 2. Choosing a pivot row: take each negative element in the chosen column and divide it into the corresponding element in the first column. The element for which the resulting quotient is smallest in absolute value must be chosen as the pivot.

Considering our example again, from the first element in the second column we compute $100/-2 = -50$, from the second element $75/-1 =$

-75, and from the third $50/-\frac{1}{2}=-100$. Since the first element gives us the smallest absolute value, the first row is the pivot row, and -2 is the pivot element. It is convenient to identify the pivot element by circling it, and -2 is accordingly circled in Tableau 1.

Step 5: Computing a new tableau. The next set of rules tells us how to compute a new tableau. It is quite simple to do, but happens to be rather tedious. For large programs of course, computers do all this for us.

Rule 3. The element which replaces the pivot element is simply the number 1 divided by the old pivot element.

In our example we replace -2 by $-\frac{1}{2}$. This is entered in Tableau 2, given below.

Tableau 2

		q_1	s_1
	150	$\frac{1}{2}$	$-\frac{3}{2}$
q_2	50	$-\frac{1}{2}$	$-\frac{1}{2}$
s_2	25	$\frac{1}{2}$	$\frac{1}{2}$
s_3	25	$\frac{1}{4}$	$\frac{1}{4}$

Rule 4. Other pivot row elements are obtained by changing the sign of the corresponding old elements and dividing by the old pivot element.

In our example we replace the second row of Tableau 1, $(100, -1, -2)$ with $(50, -\frac{1}{2}, -\frac{1}{2})$ for the second row of Tableau 2.

Rule 5. Other pivot column elements. These are obtained by dividing the old column element by the old pivot.

Thus $(3, -2, -1, -\frac{1}{2})'$ in Tableau 1 is replaced with $(-\frac{3}{2}, -\frac{1}{2}, \frac{1}{2}, \frac{1}{4})'$ in Tableau 2.

Rule 6. All other elements. Take any other element in the tableau. First consider its position relative to the pivot element, and the elements, one in the pivot row and one in the pivot column which form a rectangle with the chosen element and the pivot. Now form the cross product c, which is equal to the old element times the pivot element minus the product of the other two elements. Suppose (b_{ij}), $(m+1) \times (n+1)$ is the tableau matrix. Let b_{qp} be the pivot element.

Then define $c_{ij} \equiv (i, j)$th cross product $\equiv b_{ij}b_{qp} - b_{qj}b_{ip}$. The elements of the new tableau matrix are then

$$b_{ij} = c_{ij}/b_{qp} \quad,$$

that is the cross product divided by the pivot element. Tableau 1 is reproduced below for the sake of convenience.

		q_1	q_2
	0	2	3
s_1	(100)	-1	-2
s_2	75	-1	-1
s_3	50	0	$-\frac{1}{2}$

Suppose we wish to find the element with which to replace 50 in the new tableau. Corresponding to 50 are the two corner elements 100 and $-\frac{1}{2}$. Therefore the cross product is $c = 50(-2) - (100)(-\frac{1}{2}) = -50$, and the new element is $-50/-2 = 25$ which takes the place of 50 in Tableau 2. We do this for all elements in the tableau and Tableau 2 is the end result of all these computations.

Step 6: Return to step 3. Once we have computed a new tableau we must make the same checks we made on the original tableau. For Tableau 2 the basic solution is given by $q_2 = 50$, $s_2 = 25$, $s_3 = 25$, $q_1 = 0$ and $s_1 = 0$. The value of the program is given in upper lefthand corner: $150 = 3q_2 + 2q_1 = 3(50) + 2(0)$.

Carrying out the three checks on Tableau 2 we have

> Check 1: basic solution. Yes.
> Check 2: feasibility. $(40, 25, 25)' > O_3$. Yes.
> Check 3: optimality. Since $\frac{1}{2} > 0$ in the top row we do not
> have an optimal solution.

Applying step 4 to Table 2 we see that the pivot element is $-\frac{1}{2}$ in the third row, and this is indicated by the circled $-\frac{1}{2}$. Carrying out the operations in step 5 we get a new tableau, Tableau 3.

Tableau 3

		s_2	s_1
	175	-1	-1
q_2	25	1	1
q_1	50	-2	1
s_3	37.5	$-\frac{1}{2}$	$\frac{1}{2}$

Now go through the checklist of step 3, on Tableau 3.

Check 1: basic solution. $q_1 = 50$, $q_2 = 25$, $s_3 = 37.5$, and $s_2 = 0$, $s_1 = 0$. Therefore the solution is basic.

Check 2: feasibility. The column $(25, 50, 37.5)'$ is positive and therefore the basic solution is feasible.

Check 3: optimality. The row at the top of the tableau $(-1, -1)$ is negative and therefore the solution is optimal.

Since we have found a basic optimal solution, our search has ended and the simplex algorithm is terminated. The final tableau gives us some additional information, in addition to an optimal solution. First the upper lefthand corner tells us that the maximum value of the program is 175. Second since the third slack variable assumes a strictly positive value of 37.5 we know that the third constraint does not bind. Hence the final tableau tells which resources will have positive shadow prices and will be fully utilized.

The algorithm as presented has been considerably simplified in two directions. The first relates to step 1 where an initial basic feasible solution is chosen. In many cases, this is not an easy thing to do, and algorithms have been designed to accomplish this. Secondly, we have completely ignored the problem of degeneracy, which requires a modification of the simplex algorithm. Readers interested in these and other computational problems of linear programming are referred to S. I. Gass, *Linear Programming*, New York: McGraw-Hill, 1958.

Finally, the reader who is not interested in computational methods should realize that, having once struggled through the simplex method, he need never do so again. If he should have a quantitative problem, he may legitimately rely on the experts and their computer. Qualitative problems in economics which are illuminated by linear programming were discussed in Chapter 18, and the reader who is interested in these problems should refer to the literature cited there.

QUESTIONS

1. Consider a country selling two goods q_1, q_2 at prices 1, 2, respectively, subject to the endowment of two resources $R_1 = 5\frac{1}{2}$, $R_2 = 7$, and the technology matrix

$$A = \begin{bmatrix} 1 & \frac{1}{2} \\ \frac{1}{4} & 2 \end{bmatrix} .$$

a. Set this up as a linear programming problem, and solve for the optimal $(q_1{}^\circ, q_2{}^\circ)$.

b. Set up the dual problem and solve for $(V_1{}^\circ, V_2{}^\circ)$.

2. Suppose that another country, with the same technology matrix and the same world prices, has endowments of the resources given by $R_1 = 3$, $R_2 = 2$. Show that the shadow prices of the resources are the same in both countries. This is what is known as the "factor price equalization theorem."

3. Show that any country that specializes in the production of both goods will have the same factor prices. Demonstrate that the condition for the production of both q_1 and q_2 is that the ratio of resource endowments R_1/R_2 lies between $\frac{1}{2}$ and 4. This interval is what is known as the "diversification cone."

4. Solve Questions 1a and 1b again, only let the prices of goods 1 and 2 be 1 and 3, respectively.

5. Using the results of Questions 1 and 4, show that with the increase in the price of good 2, the share of factor 1, $V_1{}^\circ R_1/(V_1{}^\circ R_1 + V_2{}^\circ R_2)$, in the national income goes down. This is an example of the "Stolper-Samuelson theorem." How does this result depend on $\mathbf{A}$?

6. Solve Questions 1a and 1b, only change the endowments of the two resources to $R_1 = 8$, $R_2 = 7$.

7. Using the results of Questions 1 and 6, show that the output $q_1{}^\circ$ is greater for the endowments of Question 6 than for the endowments of Question 1. This is an example of the "Samuelson-Rybczinski theorem."

8. Suppose that a country has only one primary resource but produces two goods. Thus we have the linear programming problem

$$\text{Maximize } p_1 q_1 + p_2 q_2$$

$$\text{subject to } a_1 q_1 + a_2 q_2 \leq R_1 \quad \text{and} \quad q_1, q_2 \geq 0 \quad .$$

Under what conditions will the country diversify, that is, produce both goods? Suppose that R_1 is labor. How might one explain a labor theory of value?

9. Suppose that a country has two activities for producing two goods q_1 and q_2 and one primary resource R_1. We then have the linear programming problem

$$\text{Maximize } p_1 q_1 + p_2 q_2$$

$$\text{subject to } [a_{11} + a_{12}]x_1 + [a_{21} + a_{22}]x_2 \leq R_1 \quad ,$$

where x_1 and x_2 are the levels of the two activities. Recall from the chapter on input–output that

$$q_1 = a_{11}x_1 + a_{21}x_2$$
$$q_2 = a_{12}x_1 + a_{22}x_2 \quad .$$

Show that if the economy produces both goods, then the country will use at most one activity.

Answers to Questions

Chapter 2

1. *a.* Rational   *b.* Irrational   *c.* Irrational   *d.* Rational   *e.* Complex
   f. Rational (-3)   *g.* Irrational

2. *a.* Not pure — depends on price–quantity units
   b. Pure — one percentage divided by another
   c. Not pure — depends on money measure *and* time unit
   d. Pure — same units appear in both numerator and denominator

3. *a.* Yes   *b.* No

4. One inch

5. All are appropriate, but the first might be most helpful in a complicated system because the Y would help to remind us which of the possible functions of w we were dealing with.

6. *a.* 15 falls within both range and domain.
   b. 1000 falls only within the range.
   c. No; 50 is outside the domain.

7. *a.* $f(x) = 0$, where $x = 0$; $f(x) = 0$ is solved by $x = 0$ or $x = -3$; hence the curve goes through the origin and has a minimum point at $x = -\frac{3}{2}$.
   b. $f(x) = -2$, where $x = 0$; $f(x) = 0$ is solved by $x = -2$ or $x = 1$, and the minimum is at $x = -\frac{1}{2}$.

8. We are told that the function is linear, so $q = a + bp$ and $\Delta q / \Delta p = b$. When p goes from 12 to 15, $\Delta p = 3$ and $\Delta q = -15$, whence $b = -5$. q will fall to zero when $p = 22$ since each unit change in p reduces q by 5, and $q = 50$ at $p = 12$. Thus $0 = (-5)(22) + a$, whence $a = 110$.

9. *a.* Yes. The actual rule is simply "for any x, $y = c$." This may sound like a fiddle, but it is consistent with our geometry; we can draw a horizontal straight line at height c above the x-axis. Consider the case of the demand curve to the individual firm in perfect competition.

b. Yes; given x we can read off y. We cannot express the functional rule in convenient symbolic form but have to write it out extensively, but it still exists.

10. *a.* Function; the arguments are x and z.

b. Ambiguous; it may be a function with argument the ratio w/v or a coefficient, depending on context.

c. Coefficient; the function has been written out in full.

d. Ambiguous; it may be a function, with argument $x + z$, or a coefficient, depending on context.

11. *a.* No; yes. *b.* Yes *c.* Yes

12. *a.* The function has neither a kink nor a discontinuity.

b. Yes.

c. $a = 1$, $b = -6$, $c = 9$.

d. $a = 1$, $b = 0$, $c = -3$.

13. *a.* Yes *b.* Yes

14. *a.* The range is 0 to 5000 inclusive.

b. The domain is 0 to 5000 inclusive.

15. *a.* Yes *b.* Yes *c.* No *d.* $S - 7T = 0$ *e.* Yes; yes

16. *a.* S, C *b.* No *c.* One

17. *a.* (i) 1 and $\frac{1}{5}$ (ii) $1 -$ a multiple root

b. (i) is correct.

18. $x = -\frac{5}{4}$

19. *a.* Yes *b.* Yes

20. *a.* 15 *b.* -1

21. *a.* The choice of lettering is arbitrary, but the argument goes like this:

$D = D_1(R)$ (1) where D is the divorce rate and R measures religious belief; decreasing function

$A = A(t)$ (2) where A is attendance at church, and t time; decreasing function

$R = R_1(A)$ (3) religious belief can be measured by church attendance, an essential step in the argument; increasing function

$R = R_2(t)$ (4) an inference from (2) and (3); decreasing function

$D = D_2(t)$ (5) observed; increasing function

b. Only (2) and (5) refer to observation.

c. Both are attributable to common cause, itself an increasing function

of time; compare the increase in purchases of motor cars and phonograph records.

 d. The argument is certainly not inconsistent with observation, which is
the best that can ever be said. But (1) would be more firmly supported
if (3) were based on observation. It would not be a bad plan to inquire
into the divorce rates of church-going and non-church-going married
couples.

22. *a.* Yes; no

 b. Monotonically increasing everywhere

 c. Linear: $x < 0$; quadratic: $x > 0$

 d. $y + x - 1 = 0$ for $x < 0$; $y - x^2 - x - 1 = 0$ for $x > 0$

23. *a.* Yes *b.* Yes *c.* Yes

24. Yes

25. The index is x.

26. *a.* True

 b. False: $9^{2/3} \neq 3^2 = 81^{1/2} = \sqrt[2]{81} \neq 6$

 c. True

 d. False

 e. True

27. The base is a.

28. Yes

29. *a.* $9 = 3^2$ whence $\log 9 = 2 \log 3 = 0.9542$

   $27 = 3^3$ whence $\log 27 = 3 \log 3 = 1.4313$

 b. $4 = 16^{1/2}$ whence $\log 4 = \frac{1}{2} \log 16 = 0.6020$

   $2 = 4^{1/2}$ whence $\log 2 = \frac{1}{2} \log 4 = 0.3010$

 c. $6 = 3 \cdot 2$ whence $\log 6 = \log 3 + \log 2 = 0.7781$

30.

$$2x + 3 > 4$$
$$\underline{-3 - 3}$$
$$2x \quad\ > 1 \quad .$$

Multiplying both sides by $\frac{1}{2}$,

$$x > \tfrac{1}{2} > 0 \quad .$$

31. *a.* $\text{Log } y = \log 7 + \frac{1}{3} \log x$.

 b. No. There is no operation in logarithms to correspond to adding natural
numbers.

 c. No, not in the range $x > 0$, since there are no logarithms of negative
numbers.

32. The form is $\log y = \log a + b \log x$. From the incremental ratio, $b = 3$. The
intercept, $\log y = 1$, gives $\log a$. Hence

$$y = (\text{antilog } 1)(x^3)$$
$$= 10x^3 \quad .$$

33. 0; 2; 3; $\log_{10} 10^n = n \log_{10} 10$. Note that this result agrees with our earlier method for taking powers with logarithms, as in Question 29.

34. No; no—the conditions ($y > 3.5$ and $y < 4.5$) prove the nonsufficiency of $y > 3$ and $y < 5$ for $y = 4$.

35. a is necessary and sufficient for b.

36. (1) Necessary but not sufficient [either (2) or (3) must also be present]
(2) Neither [not necessary because (3) will do instead; not sufficient because (1) must be present]
(3) Neither [for reasons analogous to (2)]
(1) and (2): Sufficient [not necessary because (1) and (3) will do just as well]
(1) and (3): Sufficient [not necessary for the same reasons as (1) and (2)]
(2) and (3): Neither necessary nor sufficient [not sufficient because (1) is needed; not necessary because *either* (2) *or* (3) will do]
(1), (2), and (3): Sufficient but not necessary [it is not necessary to have (1), (2), and (3) because (1) and (3) or (1) and (2) will do; moral: if any subset of conditions is sufficient, the full set cannot be necessary]

37. (1) Neither: there are female civil servants
(2) Neither
(3) Necessary
(1) and (2): Neither
(1) and (3): Sufficient
(2) and (3): Sufficient
(1), (2), and (3): Sufficient

38. $b^2 - 4ac = 4 - 4C$; want $C \leq 1$

39. *a.* $y = 0$ if $x < 4$ *b.* $y = 0$ if $x < t$
        $y = 1$ if $x > t$ $y = 1$ if $x \geq t$

40. $27\sqrt{2}$

Chapter 3

1. Substitute $p = (a - c)/(d - b)$ into $q^s = c + dp$. Only rearrangement is required to find $q = (ad - bc)/(d - b)$. If we find p by assuming that $q^d = q^s$, we must find the price such that we are simultaneously on both the demand and the supply curves. Hence we may read off the corresponding equilibrium quantity from either curve and must get the same answer.

2. $p = 250$ instead of 200, and $q = 700$ instead of 800. The easiest way of obtaining this answer is to substitute into (22) to find p; then subtract 75 and substitute into (5) to find q.

3. $q = (ad - bc)/(d - b) + (\Delta ad - \Delta cb)/(d - b)$. For $\Delta q = 0$ we require $\Delta ad - \Delta cb = 0$ or $\Delta a/\Delta c = b/d$. $\Delta q > 0$ if $\Delta ad - \Delta cb > 0$, and $\Delta q < 0$ if $\Delta ad - \Delta cb < 0$. The shift parameters in the solution for price gives $p = (a - c)/(d - b) + (\Delta a - \Delta c)/(d - b)$. Thus $\Delta p = 0$ requires $\Delta a = \Delta c$. Substitution into the quantity solution shows that $\Delta q > 0$ if $\Delta a = \Delta c > 0$ and $\Delta q < 0$ if $\Delta a = \Delta c < 0$. For $\Delta q = 0$, Δa and Δc must be of opposite sign, and in this case $\Delta p > 0$ if $\Delta a > 0$, and $\Delta p < 0$ if $\Delta a < 0$.

4. Substituting (22) into (1),

$$q = a + b\left[\frac{a - c}{d - b} + \frac{d}{d - b}t\right]$$

$$= \frac{ad - bc}{d - b} + \frac{db}{d - b}t \quad .$$

The intercept parameters do not appear in the coefficient of t. Compare this result with Eq. (12).

5. (a) Yes; (b) no (notice that, if the demand curve is above the supply curve, consumers are willing to purchase at a higher price than suppliers require — the trouble is that they cannot discover an equilibrium — whereas if the supply curve is everywhere above the demand curve, the answer must be that nothing is produced); (c) the two curves coincide.

7. By perfectly inelastic demand, we mean that a given quantity, $\bar{q}$, is demanded, irrespective of price. Hence in place of (1) we have $q^d = \bar{q}$. Together with (20), $q^s = c + dp - dt$, we have $p = [(\bar{q} - c)/d] + t$. This says that price goes up by the full amount of the tax, which is the standard result. By a perfectly elastic demand curve, we mean a vertical one; consumers will take anything they are offered at some given price $\bar{p}$. Proof that the tax falls entirely upon suppliers should now be routine. Consider $q^s = c + d(\bar{p} - t)$, where $\bar{p}$ is a constant.

8. *a.* $k = 1/(1 - b - f)$ and $k = 1/0.1 = 10$
   b. Yes
   c. No, because it is a function of another variable in the model, namely Y

9. From Eq. (39), $\Delta D = \left[1 - \dfrac{t}{1 - c(1 - t)}\right]\Delta G = [1 - (0.2/0.44)\,]5 = \$2.73$ billion.

10. *a.* $MPC = 0.9$, $APC = 5/Y + 0.9$
    b. No
    c. $MPC = 0.9$, $APC = 0.9$, always
    d. Yes
    e. $k = 10$ for both
    f. Yes, but a specific or quantitative comparative static result

11. *a.* No; the multiplier is the entire term.
    b. If $t = 0$, then $k = 20$; if $t = 1$, then $k = 1$.
    c. If $t = 0$, then $\Delta y = \$100$ billion; if $t = 1$, then $\Delta y = \$5$ billion.
    d. In the case of no taxes, $t = 0$, there are no "leakages" from subsequent

rounds of expenditure, whereas at the other extreme the "leakage" back to the government is complete in the first round.

12. *a.* Using Eq. (39), $\Delta D = (1 - tk)\Delta G$; $0.13 \times 5 = \$0.65$ billion.
    b. The deficit would not have changed as the original level of G does not enter into calculation. No; a qualitative comparative static result tells us that the deficit cannot be greater than the expenditure.

13. *a.* The increase in government spending leads to increased income; this increases tax yield; hence the deficit cannot rise by the full amount of the increase in government spending.
    b. $1/[1 - c(1 - 1)] = 1$; income increases by exactly the increase in government expenditure, but so does tax yield, so $\Delta D = 0$.
    c. Obvious error; it is assumed that taxable income is independent of the tax rate.

14. It is necessary to show that $k/(1 - tk) > k$ or that $1/(1 - tk) > 1$. From (39) and (40) we know that $1 - tk < 1$.

15. The slope is k.

16. Starting at S, on the full-employment frontier, an increase in the provision of collective goods requires a transfer of resources from households to the government. This means increased taxation, which is unpopular. If society is inside its production frontier, private consumption and government expenditure are complementary instead of competitive.

17. *a.* Evaluating the multiplier of Eq. (45), we find $k = \frac{25}{13}$. The sum of autonomous expenditures is 299, whence $Y = 575$.
    b. Balance requires $G = T$. $T = tY = tk(I + G + X)$. Hence the answer is provided by solving the following equation for G:

$$G = tk(I + G + X)$$
$$= tkG + tk(I + X) \quad ,$$

whence

$$G - tkG = G(1 - tk) = tk(I + X)$$

and

$$G = \frac{tk}{1 - tk}(I + X) \quad .$$

$tk = \frac{1}{5} \cdot \frac{25}{13} = \frac{5}{13}$, $1 - tk = \frac{8}{13}$; hence

$$G = \frac{5}{13} \cdot \frac{13}{8} \cdot 200 = 125 \quad .$$

c. Balance requires $M = X$.

$$M = mY(1 - t) = m(1 - t)k(I + G + X) \quad .$$

Hence the answer is provided by solving the following equation for G:

$$X = m(1 - t)k(I + G + X) \quad .$$

Rearrangement gives

$$m(1-t)kG = X - m(1-t)kX - m(1-t)kI \quad,$$

whence

$$G = \frac{1 - m(1-t)k}{m(1-t)k}X - I \quad.$$

Substituting in numerical values of m, t, k, X, and I, required $G = 60$. Notice that by transferring I to the left-hand side of the last equation, we have the solution for the level of total home injections that lead to balance of payments equilibrium for a given X.

d. Merely solve for G

$$700 = kG + kI + kX \quad,$$

to find $G = 164$.

e. $M = mY(1-t) = 112$ in this case, so the deficit is 32.

f. (i) $\dfrac{\Delta D}{\Delta Y} = \dfrac{1 - tk}{k} = \dfrac{8}{25}$

(ii) $\dfrac{\Delta D}{\Delta M} = \dfrac{1 - tk}{m(1-t)k} = 2$

(iii) $\dfrac{\Delta Y}{\Delta M} = \dfrac{1}{m(1-t)} = \dfrac{25}{4}$ directly

g. $S + T + M = (1-c)Y(1-t) + tY + mY(1-t) = 299$ if $G = 99$ as in part a. $I + G = 219$ and $S + T = 207$, so home investment is mainly home-financed, and little capital is being imported; there is a balance of payments deficit of 12, as may be verified. It is sometimes said that the export of capital takes place "at the expense" of home investment. Here, at least, this is impossible because I is fixed. A reduction in G will lead to balance of payments surplus, that is, capital exports.

h. Deficit-financed expendituse is required to reach full employment, at which there is a large balance of payments deficit. Consider devaluation, any other measures for reducing the balance of payments deficit, and measures to increase domestic investment.

18. a. Equilibrium values are $Y = 240.012$, $r = 0.06$.

b. New equilibrium values are $Y = 240.014$, $r = 0.07$.

$$\frac{\Delta r}{\Delta b} = -\frac{e}{(1-c)f + eg}$$

$$\frac{\Delta Y}{\Delta b} = \frac{f}{(1-c)f + eg}$$

19. Examples of flow variables: Y, G, C, purchases, quantity demanded Examples of stock variables: supply of money, any inventory variables, stock of capital

Chapter 4

1. *a.*

$$\frac{dq}{dp} = \frac{-1200}{p^2}$$

$$\eta = \frac{dq}{dp} \cdot \frac{p}{q} = \frac{-1200}{p^2} \cdot \frac{p}{q}$$

$$= -\frac{1200}{pq}$$

$$= -\frac{1200}{1200}$$

$$= -1$$

b.

$$\frac{dq}{dp} = -Cp^{-2}$$

$$\frac{dq}{dp} \cdot \frac{p}{q} = -\frac{C}{p^2} \cdot \frac{p}{q}$$

$$= -\frac{C}{pq}$$

$$= -\frac{C}{C}$$

$$= -1$$

2.

$$q = Cp^{-\alpha}$$

$$\frac{dq}{dp} = -\alpha Cp^{-\alpha-1}$$

$$= -\frac{\alpha C}{p^{\alpha+1}}$$

$$\frac{dq}{dp} \cdot \frac{p}{q} = -\frac{\alpha C}{p^{\alpha+1}} \cdot \frac{p}{q}$$

$$= -\frac{\alpha C}{p^{\alpha}q}$$

$$= -\frac{\alpha C}{C}$$

$$= -\alpha$$

3. *a.* (i) $\eta = 1$; (ii) no
   b. (i) $-55p/(100 - 55p)$; (ii) $0 \leq p < 100/55$; (iii) $-55/45$
   c. (i) $50p/(50 + 50p)$; (ii) $\eta = 1$; (iii) $\eta = -2$

4. *a.* $y + \Delta y = (\tfrac{1}{3})(x + \Delta x)^3 = \tfrac{1}{3}(x^3 + 3x^2\Delta x + 3x(\Delta x)^2 + (\Delta x)^3)$

$$\Delta y = \tfrac{1}{3}(3x^2\,\Delta x + 3x(\Delta x)^2 + (\Delta x)^3)$$

$$\frac{\Delta y}{\Delta x} = x^2 + x\,\Delta x + \tfrac{1}{3}(\Delta x)^2$$

$$\lim_{\Delta x \to 0}\frac{\Delta y}{\Delta x} = x^2 = \frac{dy}{dx}$$

Similarly for parts b and c.

5. *a.* $dy/dx = 2(x - 1)$

b. Three; expand and differentiate the power function, chain rule ($z = x - 1$ and $y = z^2$), product rule ($y = (x - 1)(x - 1)$)

6. $\dfrac{dy}{dx} = \lim\limits_{h \to 0}\left[\dfrac{f(x + h) - f(x)}{h}\right] = \lim\limits_{h \to 0}\left[\dfrac{(x + h)(1 + x + h) - x(1 + x)}{h}\right]$

$$= 1 + 2x$$

7. *a.* No; consider $x = 0$.

b. $dy/dx = 1$ if $x > 0$, $dy/dx = -1$ if $x < 0$, kink at $x = 0$.

c. No; the function is not continuous.

8. *a.* (i) 3   (ii) 1   (iii) $2500x^{49}$ (iv) 2500   (v) $2500x^{49}$
(vi) $4(x + 3)^3 + 12(x + 3)$ (vii) $-1/3x^{-4/3}$ (viii) $-1/3x^{-4/3}$
(ix) $(x^2 + 8x - 1)/(4 + x)^2$ (x) 5

b. (i) 0   (iii) $122{,}500x^{48}$ (iv) 0   (vi) $12(x + 3)^2 + 12$

9. *a.* $\dfrac{dy}{dx} = 16x$; $\dfrac{d^2y}{dx^2} = 16$

b. $\dfrac{dy}{dx} = 4x^{-1/2}$; $\dfrac{d^2y}{dx^2} = -2x^{-3/2}$

c. Using the function of a function rule, $dy/dz = 8z + 2$ and $dz/dx = 6x + 1$; hence $dy/dx = 144x^3 + 72x^2 + 20x + 2$; $d^2y/dx^2 = 332x^2 + 144x + 20$.

d. $8x(3 + 2x^2)$; $24 + 48x^2$.

e. $3x^2 - 8x + 10$; $6x - 8$.

10.

$$\frac{dy}{dx} = 3 + 15x^2 + 35x^4$$

$$\frac{d^2y}{dx^2} = 30x + 140x^3$$

$$\frac{d^3y}{dx^3} = 30 + 420x^2$$

$$\frac{d^4y}{dx^4} = 840x$$

$$\frac{d^5y}{dx^5} = 840$$

11. *a.*
$$TR = 1000p - 3p^2$$

$$MR = \frac{1000}{3} - \frac{2}{3}q$$

b.
$$p = AR = a + bq$$

$$TR = pq = aq + bq^2$$

$$MR = a + 2bq$$

c.
$$p = f(q)$$

$$TR = qp = qf(q)$$

$$MR = \frac{dTR}{dq} = f(q) + qf'(q)$$

12. $dA/dr = 2\pi r$, which is the circumference of the circle.

13. *a.* $MPC = b$, $APC = a/Y + b$
   b. Yes; $1/b$
   c. Yes

14. *a.* (i) $\frac{1}{4}$ (ii) 7 (iii) $-5/y^2$
   b. $dy/dx = -2x$ $dx/dy = \pm 1/(2\sqrt{5-y})$, which by substitution yields $\pm\frac{1}{2}x$;
   that is, it is possible, but dx/dy has two values.

15. *a.* (i) $dy/dx = 2$
      (ii) $dy/dx = 2x$
      (iii) $dy/dx = 3x^2$
   b. (i) $dx/dy = \frac{1}{2}$
      (ii) $dx/dy = 1/2x$
      (iii) $dx/dy = 1/3x^2$
   c. (i) $x = (y/2) - 5$
      (ii) $x = y^{1/2}$
      (iii) $x = y^{1/3}$
   d. (i) $dx/dy = \frac{1}{2}$
      (ii) $dx/dy = 1/2y^{1/2}$, but $y = x^2$, so $dx/dy = 1/2(x^2)^{1/2} = 1/2x$
      (iii) $dx/dy = 1/3y^{2/3}$, but $y = x^3$, so $dx/dy = 1/3x^2$

16.
$$\frac{dq^d}{dp} = -5 - 0.3p^2$$

$$\frac{dp}{dt} = 3t^{1/2}$$

$$\frac{dq^d}{dt} = (-5 - 0.3p^2)3t^{1/2}$$

$$= -15t^{1/2} - 0.9p^2t^{1/2} \quad ,$$

but
$$p = 2t^{3/2} \quad ,$$

so

$$p^2 = 4t^3 \quad .$$

Substituting to remove p^2 gives

$$\frac{\mathrm{d}q^d}{\mathrm{d}t} = -15t^{1/2} - 3.6t^{7/2} \quad .$$

Substituting directly into the expression for q^d gives

$$q^d = 1000 - 10t^{3/2} - 0.8t^{9/2}$$

$$\frac{\mathrm{d}q^d}{\mathrm{d}t} = -15t^{1/2} - 3.6t^{7/2} \quad .$$

17. *a.* $6t - 3t^2$; 2 seconds
   b. 4 feet
   c. $6 - 6t$; at $t = 1$

18. *a.* 100 and 0; 8 and 0.
   b. $f(p) = 0.08(p)$. Any function for which $f(0) = 0$, $f(100) = 8$ and which is strictly monotonic increasing between zero and 100 will do.

19. *a.* (i) Kink at a, no discontinuities
      (ii) No kink, no discontinuity
      (iii) Discontinuity at 10, derivative $= 0$ at all values other than 10
      (iv) Discontinuity at every integer multiple of $3 -$ unique derivative of zero at all other points
      (v) Unique zero derivative everywhere the function is defined
   b. (ii) $\mathrm{d}y/\mathrm{d}x = 2(x - 5)$; $\mathrm{d}^2y/\mathrm{d}x^2 = 2$

Chapter 5

1. *a.* $\eta = -0.75$
   b. $\eta = -0.75p^{-0.75}/(20 + 10p^{-0.75})$
   c. $\eta = \alpha p^\alpha/(a + p^\alpha)$
   d. $\eta = 1$
   e. $\eta = 1.25$
   f. $\eta = \alpha b p^\alpha/(a + b p^\alpha)$

2. *a.* Raising the power term causes the tax yield to rise from $5tp^{-1.5}$ to $5tp^{-1.1}$, that is, by a factor of $p^{0.4}$.
   b. Raising the power term causes the tax yield to rise from $5tp^{-0.5}$ to $5tp^{-0.1}$, that is, by the same factor as in part a.
   c. The first tax yield equation is a per unit tax, whereas the second is a tax on total revenue. The change in the power term has a greater impact in the second $-$ total revenue tax $-$ case.

3. $-ck^2 = (-75)/16$; see Eq. (15).

4. *a.* $-(c - m)k^2 = -\frac{375}{169}$.

b. From (20),

$$\frac{d}{dt}\left(\frac{\Delta Y}{\Delta D}\right) = \frac{d}{dt}\left(\frac{k}{1 - tk}\right) = \frac{k^2(1 - c + m)}{(1 - tk)^2} = \frac{125}{32} \quad .$$

c. From (24),

$$\frac{1}{m(1 - t)^2} = \frac{1}{\frac{1}{5}(\frac{4}{5})^2} = \frac{125}{16} \quad .$$

5. *a.* $\dfrac{dk}{dc} = \dfrac{-1}{(1 - c(1 - t))^2}(-1 + t) = (1 - t)k^2 > 0$

b. $\dfrac{\Delta D}{\Delta G} = 1 - tk;\quad \dfrac{d(\Delta D/\Delta G)}{dc} = \dfrac{-tdk}{dc} = -t(1 - t)k^2 < 0$

6. *a.* $\dfrac{\Delta Y}{\Delta B} = \dfrac{\Delta Y}{\Delta M} = \dfrac{\Delta Y}{\Delta G} \cdot \dfrac{\Delta G}{\Delta M}$

and

$$\frac{\Delta Y}{\Delta G} = k(1 - g) \quad ;$$

hence

$$\frac{\Delta Y}{\Delta B} = \frac{k(1 - g)}{g + m(1 - t)k(1 - g)} \quad .$$

b. We may apply the quotient rule to part a or the product rule to take

$$\frac{d}{dt}\left(\frac{\Delta Y}{\Delta G} \cdot \frac{\Delta G}{\Delta M}\right) = \frac{\Delta Y}{\Delta G}\frac{d}{dt}\left(\frac{\Delta G}{\Delta M}\right) + \frac{\Delta G}{\Delta M}\frac{d}{dt}\left(\frac{\Delta Y}{\Delta G}\right)$$

$$= k(1 - g)\frac{d}{dt}\{g + m(1 - t)k(1 - g)\}$$

$$+ \{g + m(1 - t)k(1 - g)\}\frac{d}{dt}\{k(1 - g)\} \quad .$$

Persistent application of the product rule, the use of $dk/dt = -ck^2$, and brute force would be required to take this much further; we should look for an easier way to proceed. We know from Eq. (24) that (d/dt) $(\Delta Y/\Delta B) > 0$ in the case in which there is no import content in the *multiplicand*. If all the import coefficients in the multiplicand are, however, positive fractions, it is impossible that the *direction* of any effect be altered; only magnitudes are affected.

7. *a.* Substituting,

$$Y = a + b(Y - t(Y - I)) + I + G + X - mY \quad ,$$

whence

$$k = (1 - b(1 - t) + m)^{-1}$$

and

$$Y = k(a + btI + I + G + X) \quad .$$

b. $\dfrac{dY}{dt} = \dfrac{dk}{dt}(a + btI + I + G + X) + kbI\dfrac{dt}{dt} \quad .$

Now

$$\frac{dk}{dt} = \frac{-1}{(1 - b(1 - t) + m)^2}\, b = -bk^2 \quad ,$$

whence

$$\frac{dY}{dt} = kbI - bk^2(a + btI + I + G + X) \quad .$$

8. *a.* $MC = 1000 - 1000q + 2q^2$
 b. $dMC/dq = -1000 + 4q$
 c. $C/q = 5000q^{-1} + 1000 - 500q + \frac{2}{3}q^2$
 d. $q = 0$ or $q = 375$ by solving the following equation for q:

$$1000 - 1000q + 2q^2 = 1000 - 500q + \tfrac{2}{3}q^2$$

9. *a.* $MC = 1000 - 1000q + 2q^2 + \frac{4}{5}tq^{-1/5}$
 b. $dMC/dq = -1000 + 4q - \frac{4}{25}tq^{-6/5}$
 c. $AC = (5000/q) + 1000 - 500q + \frac{2}{3}q^2 + tq^{-1/5}$
 d. No; t is the rate to be applied to $q^{4/5}$ instead of q to obtain the tax yield, whence it is not a *unit* tax.

10. *a.* No, because $MC = 1.32 - 0.0004q$ is a decreasing function of q; faced with a constant price, the firm would expand output indefinitely.
 b. No, by part a and the result of Section 5.9,* that diminishing marginal product is *necessary* as well as sufficient for increasing marginal cost given a constant factor price.

11. *a.* $MR = (d/dq)(100q - 2q^2) = 100 - 4q$.
 b. MR falls twice as fast as AR ($4q$ to $2q$).
 c. 50, by putting $100 - 4q = 0$, whence $q = 25$ and $p = 100 - 50$. Note that this occurs at the halfway point between zero and the intercept of 100.

12. *a.* $\dfrac{d(pq)}{dq} = \dfrac{d(aq^{\beta+1})}{dq} = a(\beta + 1)q^{\beta} \quad .$

 b. $\eta = \dfrac{dq}{dp}\cdot\dfrac{p}{q} = \dfrac{1}{\beta a q^{\beta-1}}\cdot\dfrac{a q^{\beta}}{q} = \dfrac{1}{\beta} \quad .$

 Notice that we have written the function in the Marshallian way. The function $q = ap^b$ has an elasticity of b.
 c. If price is to be positive, a must be positive. But a downward-sloping demand curve requires $\beta a q^{\beta-1}$ negative; hence β must be negative.

13. *a.* $\dfrac{dq}{dl} = 3al^2 + 2bl + c$

  b. $AP = al^2 + bl + c + dl^{-1}$

14. To use (41), notice that

$$g(l) = cl + dl^2$$

$$g'(l) = c + 2dl$$

$$f'(q) = b \quad,$$

and, to eliminate q, we have

$$f[g(l)] = a + b(cl + dl^2) \quad.$$

Thus substitution into (41) gives

$$\frac{dR}{dl} = (cl + dl^2)b(c + 2dl) + (c + 2dl)\{a + b(cl + dl^2)\} \quad,$$

and only routine simplification is now required.

15. *a.* From (45)

$$\frac{dV}{dq} = \frac{w}{g'(l)} = \frac{10}{(0.2)(100) - (0.0015)(100^2)} = 2 \quad.$$

  b. $d^2q/dl^2 = 0.2 - 0.003l$. This becomes negative (diminishing returns set in) when l exceeds $66\frac{2}{3}$; hence with constant wages marginal cost starts to increase (see Section 5.9).

16. *a.*
$$MRP = (MPP)(MR)$$

$$MPP = 3al^2 + 2bl + c$$

$$MR = 100 - 4q \quad.$$

  Therefore

$$MRP = (100 - 4q)(3al^2 + 2bl + c) \quad.$$

  b.
$$\frac{d(MRP)}{dl} = \frac{d(MPP)}{dl}MR + \frac{d(MR)}{dl}MPP$$

$$= \frac{d(MPP)}{dl}MR + \frac{d(MR)}{dq}\frac{dq}{dl}MPP$$

$$= \frac{d(MPP)}{dl}MR - 4(MPP)^2 \quad.$$

Chapter 6

1. The sign of x depends on the sign of $-b/2a$; to find the sign of y, substitute:

$$y = a\left(\frac{-b}{2a}\right)^2 + b\left(\frac{-b}{2a}\right) + c \quad .$$

2. a. $x = 25$; maximum
   b. $x = 100$; minimum
   c. $x = 5$; maximum
   d. $x = -5$; minimum
   e. $x = -1$; minimum

3. Maximum at $x = -2$, minimum at $x = 5$, nonstationary inflexional point at $x = \frac{3}{2}$.

4. a. Stationary inflexional point at $x = -1$ (the roots of $dy/dx = 0$ are both equal to -1, and $d^2y/dx^2 = 0$ at $x = -1$); no extreme values.
   b. Maximum at $x = -1$, minimum at $x = 1$, nonstationary inflexional point at $x = 0$ (the roots of dy/dx are $x = \pm 1$, and $d^2y/dx^2 = 0$ at $x = 0$).
   c. Minimum at $x = -\frac{3}{2}$; no other extreme or inflexional values [$(x + 1)$ is a factor of the numerator, so that the function proves to be a quadratic; if the quotient rule is applied directly, the resulting numerator is divisible by $(x + 1)^2$].
   d. Minima at $x = \pm 1$, maximum at $x = 0$, points of inflexion at $x = \pm\sqrt{\frac{1}{3}}$ (to find the first derivative, use the substitution $z = x^2 - 1$; solution of $dy/dx = 0$ gives $x = 0$ *or* $x = \pm 1$; solution of $d^2y/dx^2 = 0$ gives $x^2 = \frac{1}{3}$; by inspection, $y = 0$ when $x = \pm 1$, and increases monotonically for values of $x > 1$ or $x < -1$).
   e. Minimum at $x = 1$, maximum at $x = -2\frac{1}{3}$, point of inflexion at $x = -\frac{2}{3}$ [the required factors are $(3x + 7)$, $(x + 1)$].
   f. This cubic has a maximum at $x = -2$, a minimum at $x = 1$ and a non-stationary point of inflexion at $x = -\frac{1}{2}$.

5. No. This follows from the circumstance we discussed in Section 2.2, that there are no "holes" in the real line. Thus, however close to b we choose x, we can always find an x even closer and a correspondingly larger value of $f(x)$.

6. Let us start with a definition: $y = f(x)$ has a local minimum in a closed interval at $x = \bar{x}$ if $f(x) > f(\bar{x})$ for $x \neq \bar{x}$ in the neighborhood of $\bar{x}$. By definition,

$$\frac{dy}{dx} = \lim_{h \to 0} \frac{f(x + h) - f(x)}{h} \quad .$$

Put $x = \bar{x}$, and choose h negative. Then if $\bar{x}$ is a minimum, $f(\bar{x} + h) - f(\bar{x})$ must be positive and dy/dx negative. Similarly, if h is positive, dy/dx is positive. Continuity assures that the limit as h goes to zero must be zero.

7. If $f''(x) = 0$, where $f'(x) = 0$, we have a nonstationary point of inflexion. If the function is everywhere decreasing, $f'(x)$ is everywhere negative, and we merely look for a point, if there is one, where $f''(x) = 0$.

8. No part of the definition in Section 6.1 needs to be altered; positivity of y and x was neither stated nor implied. A maximum may occur where, for example, both x and y are negative.

9. No, by inspection. It is, however, instructive to search. We have

$$xy = c \quad \text{or} \quad y = cx^{-1} \quad ,$$

whence

$$\frac{dy}{dx} = -cx^{-2} \quad .$$

But if $c \neq 0$, there is no solution to $-cx^{-2} = 0$. The function is discontinuous at $x = 0$ (and $y = 0$). Note that it has two "branches," x and y both positive or both negative if $c > 0$ and of opposite signs if $c < 0$.

10. a. $f' = 0$ is necessary; $f'' > 0$ and $f' = 0$ together are sufficient.
   b. $f' = 0$; $f'' < 0$ and $f' = 0$.
   c. $f' \neq 0$; $f'' = 0$ and $f' \neq 0$.
   d. No. $f'' < 0$ is sufficient *only* if the necessary condition $f' > 0$ is satisfied. We know from Section 6.4 that $f'' < 0$ is not a necessary condition. Notice that a necessary condition and a separate sufficient condition when taken together do not give a single necessary and sufficient condition.

11. The function has no stationary points:

$$y = (x^2 + 5)^{1/2}$$

$$\frac{dy}{dx} = \frac{x}{(x^2 + 5)^{1/2}} = \frac{x}{y}$$

The function has a minimum value at $x = 0$. To express the second function $y^2 = x^2 + 5$ in terms of y, we take the square root of both sides, but we see then that the right-hand side could have a minus in front and still satisfy $y^2 = x^2 + 5$. Thus the two functions are

$$y = (x^2 + 5)^{1/2}$$

$$y = \pm(x^2 + 5)^{1/2} \quad .$$

12. No stationary point exists in the open interval; that is, there is no x in that interval that satisfies $dy/dx = 0$. A stationary point exists in the closed interval at $x = -b/2a$. An interesting point to consider is that given $y = x$ over a certain closed interval, a maximum and a minimum will exist, yet the function has no stationary points.

13. *a.* $y = 0$.

 b. The function is not defined in the given domain.

 c. $y = 5$.

 d. There is no stationary point but a maximum at $x = 10$, $y = 50$.

 e. $x = 10$, $y = 55$.

 f. No maximum.

 g. There is no stationary point within the domain and no maximum.

 h. $x = 10$ and $y = 9$ is a maximum, although not a stationary point. Note that the answers to parts f and g depend on the fact that the interval is open on the lower end; that is, $0 < x$, not $0 \leq x$.

14. Necessary: $\dfrac{dy}{dx} = 0 = x\dfrac{dz}{dx} + z - \dfrac{dw}{dx} = 0$

Sufficient: $\dfrac{d^2y}{dx^2} < 0$ and $dy/dx = 0$

where

$$\frac{d^2y}{dx^2} = x\frac{d^2z}{dx^2} + \frac{dz}{dx} + \frac{dz}{dx} - \frac{d^2w}{dx^2} \quad .$$

15.

$$\frac{dy}{dx} = (x + 1)\frac{d(x - 1)}{dx} + (x - 1)\frac{d(x + 1)}{dx}$$

$$= (x + 1) + (x - 1)$$

$$= 2x$$

$$\frac{d^2y}{dx^2} = 2 \quad .$$

$$\frac{dy}{dx} = 0 \qquad \text{at } x = 0$$

and

$$\frac{d^2y}{dx^2} > 0 \qquad \text{at } x = 0 \quad ,$$

whence we have a minimum at $x = 0$.

16. Let $z = \dfrac{3x + 2}{10}$ whence $\dfrac{dz}{dx} = \dfrac{3}{10}$.

$y = z^{1/3}$ whence $\dfrac{dy}{dz} = \dfrac{1}{3}z^{-2/3} = \dfrac{1}{3}\left(\dfrac{3x + 2}{10}\right)^{-2/3}$

Combining the two, $\dfrac{dy}{dx} = \dfrac{1}{10}\left(\dfrac{3x + 2}{10}\right)^{-2/3}$.

Chapter 7

1. *a.* Adding $3q$ to profit (instead of subtracting tq),

$$\Pi = -7.5q^2 + 150q - 100 \quad,$$

which is maximized by $q = 10$, whence $p = 145$.

b. $AVC = 3 + 7q$; in the short run, it pays to produce at any price above 3. From the demand curve, it is obvious that this can be done without a subsidy. At what price it pays to stay in business, that is, at what price the fixed cost of 100 is covered, is another question.

c. $\Pi = -7.5q^2 + 147q - 100 + sq$. First-order conditions give

$$q = \frac{147}{15} + \frac{s}{15} \quad,$$

whence, writing s for the subsidy per unit,

$$\frac{d\bar{q}}{ds} = \frac{1}{15} \quad \text{and} \quad \frac{dp}{dq}\frac{d\bar{q}}{ds} = (-0.5)\frac{1}{15} = -\frac{1}{30} \quad.$$

2. Substituting directly into (2), Section 7.1,

$$t = \frac{(-2)(0) - (1200)(4)}{(2)(-2)(4)} = \frac{-4800}{-16} = 300 \quad,$$

which is a maximum.

3. Let $C = c(q)$, $AC = c(q)/q$, and $MC = c'(q)$. If there is a value of q that satisfies $dAC/dq = [qc'(q) - c(q)]/q^2 = 0$, that is, if the average cost curve is U-shaped (it could, after all, be monotonically increasing), then $AC = MC$ at that value: $c'(q) = c(q)/q$.

4. With zero MC, Π is maximized by maximizing $TR = pq$. Using the product rule, set

$$p + q\frac{dp}{dq} = 0 \quad,$$

whence

$$\frac{dp}{dq} \cdot \frac{q}{p} = -1 \quad.$$

But this is the elasticity of demand by definition.

5. *a.* Choose w to maximize wl subject to being on the demand curve, that is, to $l = 100 - 2w$. Thus set

$$\frac{d(wl)}{dw} = \frac{d}{dw}(100w - 2w^2) = 100 - 4w = 0 \quad;$$

hence put $w = 25$. Since $w = 25$ maximizes wl, it follows that no larger sum can be extracted from employers consistent with their being in equilibrium. To generalize, follow the Cournot case: Maximize $w \cdot f(w)$, where $f(w)$ is the employers' demand, by setting $d[w \cdot f(w)]/$

$dw = w \cdot f'(w) + f(w) = 0$. It follows that the wages bill is maximized at the wage at which the elasticity of employers' demand is unity. This follows from maximizing a function of the form $x \cdot f(x)$, not from linearity.

b. To maximize $(0.9\bar{w})l$, where $l = 100 - 2\bar{w}$, set $d/d\bar{w}[(0.9\bar{w}(100 - 2\bar{w})] = d/d\bar{w}[90\bar{w} - 1.8\bar{w}^2] = 90 - 3.6\bar{w} = 0$, whence $\bar{w} = 25$, but take-home pay is $(0.9)(25)l$, that is, has been reduced by 10 percent; the workers bear the whole tax. There is nothing freakish about this; it is better to pay tax on the maximum than on anything less. To check, set (d/dw) $[\alpha w \cdot f(w)] = 0$, where α is the proportion of after-tax wage to gross wage ($\alpha = 0.9$ here). If $\alpha \neq 0$, then $w \cdot f'(w) + f(w) = 0$ as before.

6. a. Quite straightforward:

$$q = \frac{a - c}{2(b + d)} \quad \text{and} \quad p = a - \frac{b(a - c)}{2(b + d)} \quad.$$

If cost is to be a monotonic increasing function of output, d must be positive.

b. Now $\Pi = -(b + d)q^2 - (c - a + t)q - k$. Setting the first derivative equal to zero, we find

$$\bar{q} = \frac{a - c}{2(b + d)} - \frac{t}{2(b + d)} \quad,$$

whence obviously

$$\frac{d\bar{q}}{dt} = -\frac{1}{2(b + d)} \quad \text{and} \quad \frac{d\bar{p}}{dt} = \frac{b}{2(b + d)} \quad.$$

7. a. Total cost: $C = C(q)$.
Average cost: $C/q = C(q)/q$.
Marginal cost: $dC/dq = C'(q)$.
b. No. The marginal cost function is the first derivative of the total cost function.
c. Total revenue: $P(q)q$.
Average revenue: $P(q)$.
Marginal revenue: $d(Pq)/dq = q(dP/dq) + P$.
d. (i) Monopolist: Using $\pi = qP(q) - C(q)$.
Necessary: $d\pi/dq = 0 = q(dP/dq) + P - (dC/dq) = 0$, that is, $MR = MC$.
Sufficient: $d^2\pi/dq^2 < 0$ and $d\pi/dq = 0$.
(ii) Perfect competitor: Using $\pi = qP - C(q)$. Necessary: $d\pi/dq = 0 = P - C'(q) = 0$, that is, $MR = AR = MC$. Sufficient: $d^2\pi/dq^2 < 0$ and $d\pi/dq = 0$, where $d^2\pi/dq^2 = -C''(q) < 0$ or $C''(q) > 0$.
Point to note: Although the demand curve of a market generally has price as the independent variable, the monopolist adjusts quantity, that is, quantity is the independent variable in the profit function; he is also setting price by setting quantity. The perfect competitor simply accepts price, so quantity is all he can adjust, whence quantity is the independent variable in his profit function.

8. *a.* $AVC = (1/q)(\frac{1}{3}q^3 - 5q^2 + 30q)$, which is minimized by $q = 7\frac{1}{2}$; with $p = 6$, it pays better to shut down.

9. *a.* Use

$$\pi = 6q - C(q) + 3q$$

$$= 6q - \frac{q^3}{3} + 5q^2 - 30q - 10 + 3q \quad .$$

Now

$$\frac{d\pi}{dq} = 6 - q^2 + 10q - 30 + 3 = 0$$

or

$$q^2 - 10q + 21 = 0 \quad .$$

Thus $(q-7)(q-3) = 0$, and so $q = 7$ is the equilibrium quantity for a profit maximum given the subsidy, which compares with a presubsidy equilibrium quantity of 6. Profits are still negative.

b. If the subsidy were granted to all firms, then all firms would adjust their output levels, whence the price level in the market as a whole would change.

10. The result is the same; the maximization of a function is equivalent to the minimization of the negative of that function. The firm in question is minimizing the negative of its profits.

11. *a.* One need only substitute the equilibrium quantity value of 6 back into the profit function to see that not only is the resultant profit negative but that revenue is insufficient to cover variable cost.

b. This question and subsequent parts is a good test of your knowledge of cost concepts. A necessary condition is that the first derivative of the average cost function be zero—this does *not* say that marginal cost must be zero. An equivalent condition is that $AC = MC$. Specifically, $\frac{1}{3}q^2 - 5q + 30 + 10q^{-1} = q^2 - 10q + 30$. A sufficient condition for this minimum is that $d(AC)/dq = 0$ and $d^2(AC)/dq^2 > 0$. Consider the second part:

$$\frac{d^2(AC)}{dq^2} = \frac{2}{3} + 20q^{-3} > 0 \quad .$$

As this inequality is always satisfied for positive quantities, the sufficient condition is simply that $d(AC)/dq = 0$. Hence, for this particular function $d(AC)/dq = 0$ is both a necessary and a sufficient condition for a minimum given that $q \geq 0$.

c. Yes, to one decimal place. This can be proved by substituting the value into the first-order condition.

d. Now $\pi = 12.56q - \frac{1}{3}q^3 + 5q^2 - 30q - 10$. Then $d\pi/dq = 0 = 12.56 - q^2 + 10q - 30$, which solves to $q = 7.75$ or $q = 2.25$ and where the former is found to be the appropriate value. The firm's profit is then zero.

12. No. Consider the analysis of the impact of parametric shifts in supply and demand curves on equilibrium price and quantity.

Chapter 8

1. *a.*
$$f_x = 6x + 4y$$
$$f_y = 4x + 2y$$
$$f_{xx} = 6$$
$$f_{yy} = 2$$
$$f_{xy} = f_{yx} = 4$$

b.
$$f_x = 3x^2 + 2xy + 2y^2$$
$$f_y = x^2 + 4xy + 6y^2$$
$$f_{xx} = 6x + 2y$$
$$f_{yy} = 4x + 12y$$
$$f_{xy} = f_{yx} = 2x + 4y$$

c.
$$f_x = ay^{-2}$$
$$f_y = -2axy^{-3}$$
$$f_{xx} = 0$$
$$f_{yy} = +6axy^{-4}$$
$$f_{xy} = f_{yx} = -2ay^{-3}$$

d.
$$f_x = -x^{-2}y^{-1}$$
$$f_y = -x^{-1}y^{-2}$$
$$f_{xx} = +2x^{-3}y^{-1}$$
$$f_{yy} = +2x^{-1}y^{-3}$$
$$f_{xy} = f_{yx} = x^{-2}y^{-2}$$

2.
$$f_c = (1 - t)k^2$$
$$f_m = (t - 1)k^2$$
$$f_t = (m - c)k^2$$
$$f_{cc} = 2(1 - t)^2k^3$$
$$f_{mm} = 2(t - 1)^2k^3$$
$$f_{tt} = 2(m - c)^2k^3$$

3.

$$f_x = \lim_{h \to 0} \left[\frac{f(x+h, y) - f(x, y)}{h} \right]$$

$$f_{xy} = \lim_{g \to 0} \left[\lim_{h \to 0} \left[\frac{(f(x+h, y+g) - f(x, y+g))}{h} \right] - \lim_{h \to 0} \left[\frac{(f(x+h, y) - f(x, y))}{h} \right] \right] \Big/ g$$

$$= \lim_{h \to 0} \left[\lim_{g \to 0} \left[\frac{(f(x+h, y+g) - f(x+h, y))}{g} \right] - \lim_{g \to 0} \left[\frac{(f(x, y+g) - f(x, y))}{g} \right] \right] \Big/ h$$

$$= f_{yx}$$

4. *a.* Marginal utility of $x = \partial U / \partial x = \alpha x^{\alpha-1} y^{\beta}$.

Marginal utility of $y = \partial U / \partial y = \beta x^{\alpha} y^{\beta-1}$.

Since $\alpha, \beta < 1$, it follows that $\partial U / \partial x$ diminishes as x increases and that $\partial U / \partial y$ diminishes as y increases. This is obvious from inspection, but you can also take f_{xx} and f_{yy} and show that these necessarily have a negative sign.

b. Holding U constant, we have $x^{\alpha} = \bar{U} / y^{\beta}$ or $x = \bar{U}^{1/\alpha} / y^{\beta/\alpha}$. These are convex indifference curves asymptotic to the x- and y-axes.

$$\frac{dx}{dy} = -\frac{f_y}{f_x} = -\frac{\beta x^{\alpha} y^{\beta-1}}{\alpha x^{\alpha-1} y^{\beta}} = -\frac{\beta}{\alpha} \cdot \frac{x}{y} \quad .$$

This is the general case of which the function in Question 1d was an example in which $\alpha = \beta = -1$. Inspection shows the slope to have the correct sign.

c. $f_{xy} = \alpha \beta x^{\alpha-1} y^{\beta-1}$. As y increases the marginal utility of x decreases.

d. No, as you will see by calculating f_{yx} just as a check.

e. Set $f_x = 0$ to get

$$\alpha x^{\alpha-1} y^{\beta} = 0 \quad .$$

This is true only for $x = 0$ or $y = 0$. The household attaches no utility to consuming one product on its own; if $y = 0$, $f_x = 0$ for all x. If y is held constant at some positive amount, $f_x > 0$ for all positive finite x. As $x \to \infty$, however, $f_x \to 0$, showing that marginal utility gets very small as x gets very large, although it is always positive for any finite value of x.

5. *a.* $\partial q / \partial y = 500p$, $\partial q / \partial p = 500y$, $\partial^2 q / \partial y \, \partial p = 500$, $\partial^2 q / \partial y^2 = 0 = \partial^2 q / \partial p^2$.

b. Substituting, $z = 225x^6 + x^2$, $\partial z / \partial x = dz/dx = 1350x^5 + 2x$ and $\partial^2 z / \partial x^2 = d^2z/dx^2 = 6750x^4 + 2$.

c. $\partial q / \partial y = 500$, $\partial q / \partial p = 500$, $\partial^2 q / \partial y \, \partial p = \partial^2 q / \partial y^2 = \partial^2 q / \partial p^2 = 0$.

6. *a.* (i) Not separable
(ii) Separable
(iii) Separability not relevant because z is a function of either x or y
(iv) Not separable
b. (i) Log-separable

(ii) Not log-separable since $\log z = \log (35x - 35y)$

(iii) Separability not relevant because z is not a function of both x and y

(iv) Not log-separable

7.
$$\frac{dx}{dt} = 3, \quad \frac{dy}{dt} = 6t \quad .$$

Now substitute into $dz/dt = f_x \, dx/dt + f_y \, dy/dt$ to obtain

a. $dz/dt = 18x + 12y + 24xt + 12yt$

b. $9x^2 + 6xy + 6y^2 + 6x^2t + 24xyt + 36y^2t$

c. $3ay^{-2} - 12axy^{-3}t$

d. $-3x^{-2}y^{-1} - 6x^{-1}y^{-2}t$

8. $dC/dS = 1 + L(dW/dS) = 1 + LW'$

9.
$$\frac{dx}{dy} = -\frac{f_y}{f_x} = -\frac{-x^{-1}y^{-2}}{-x^{-2}y^{-1}}$$

$$= -\frac{x}{y} \quad .$$

Of course $dy/dx = -(y/x)$. The slope in either case depends only on the ratio of x to y and not on their absolute values. At $x = 5$, $y = 10$ and at $x = 15$, $y = 30$, $dx/dy = -\frac{1}{2}$.

10. a. $z = x^{1/2}y^{-1/2}$, $z = w^3x^{-4}y$

    b. $z = xy$, $z = w^3x^{-4}y^3$

11. a. Use $dq = q_p \, dp + q_y \, dy$.

    (i) $dp = 2dy$. Therefore, $dq = q_p \, dp + \frac{1}{2}q_y \, dp$, or $dq/dp = q_p + \frac{1}{2}q_y$, or $dq = 2q_p \, dy + q_y \, dy$. Thus, $dq/dy = 2q_p + q_y$.

    (ii) $2dp = dy$. Therefore, $dq/dp = 2q_p + q_y$.

    (iii) $dp = -dy$. Therefore, $dq = q_p \, dp - q_y \, dp$, or $dq/dp = q_p - q_y$, or $dq/dy = q_y - q_p$.

    b. Using Eq. (3), we have

    $$q_y = 20y + 8p^{-2}y^3$$

    $$q_p = -4y^4p^{-3} - 9p^2 \quad .$$

    Then

    (i) $dq/dy = 2q_p + q_y = -8y^4p^{-3} - 18p^2 + 20y + 8p^{-2}y^3$

    (ii) $dq/dy = \frac{1}{2}q_p + q_y = -2y^4p^{-3} - \frac{9}{2}p^2 + 20y + 8p^{-2}y^3$

    (iii) $dq/dy = q_y - q_p = 4y^4p^{-3} + 9p^2 + 20y + 8p^{-2}y^3$

12. Taking total differentials, $2xdx + 2ydy + 2zdz = 0$.

    a. $dy/dx = -x/y$ when $dz = 0$.

    b. Given $dx = 2dy$,

$$2x2dy + 2ydy + 2zdz = 0$$

$$(4x + 2y)dy + 2zdz = 0 \quad ,$$

or

$$\frac{dz}{dy} = \frac{2(2x + y)}{-2z} = \frac{-(y + 2x)}{z} \quad .$$

Similarly,

$$\frac{dz}{dx} = \frac{dz}{2dy} = \frac{-(y + 2x)}{2z} \quad .$$

Chapter 9

1. A simple substitution of $d\alpha = 0$, $d\beta > 0$ and $d\alpha = 0$, $d\beta < 0$ is sufficient to establish $dp = S_\beta d\beta / (D_p - S_p)$. Insertion of $d\beta$ appropriately positive or negative is all that is required.

2. The necessary equilibrium condition is

$$\frac{d\pi}{dq} = 0 = \frac{dp}{dq}q + p - \frac{dC}{dq} \quad .$$

When we treat α and β as variables, care must be taken to consider indirect as well as direct effects; in general dp/dq is a function of α, and dC/dq is a function of β. Thus,

$$d\pi = \left[\frac{\partial p}{\partial q}dq + \frac{\partial p}{\partial \alpha}d\alpha\right]q + p\ dq - \frac{\partial C}{\partial q}dq - \frac{\partial C}{\partial \beta}d\beta$$

$$= \left(q\frac{\partial p}{\partial q} + p - \frac{\partial C}{\partial q}\right)dq + q\frac{\partial p}{\partial \alpha}\ d\alpha - \frac{\partial C}{\partial \beta}\ d\beta$$

is the equation of the tangent plane to the profit function (and this will equal zero when profits are a maximum).

3. Substitute $d\alpha > 0$ and $d\beta = 0$ into (15) and manipulate to obtain

$$\frac{dY}{d\alpha} = \frac{C_\alpha}{1 - C_Y} > 0 \quad .$$

4. *a.* $P = MT^{-1}k^{-1}$.

b.

$$\frac{\partial P}{\partial M} = \frac{1}{Tk} > 0$$

$$\frac{\partial P}{\partial T} = \frac{-M}{T^2k} < 0$$

$$\frac{\partial P}{\partial k} = \frac{-M}{Tk^2} < 0 \quad .$$

Thus an increase in T or k lowers P, but the relation between ΔP and ΔT and ΔP and Δk is not one of simple proportionality (as it is between ΔP and ΔM).

c.
$$dP = f_M \, dM + f_k \, dk + f_T T$$

$$= \frac{dM}{Tk} - \frac{M \, dk}{Tk^2} - \frac{M \, dT}{T^2 k} \quad .$$

5. First take total differentials of

$$Y = C(Y, \alpha) + Z(\beta),$$

$$dY = \frac{\partial C}{\partial Y} \, dY + \frac{\partial C}{\partial \alpha} \, d\alpha + \frac{dZ}{d\beta} \, d\beta$$

or

$$dY = \left(\frac{1}{1 - \partial C/\partial Y} \right) \left(\frac{\partial C}{\partial \alpha} \, d\alpha + \frac{dZ}{d\beta} \, d\beta \right) \quad .$$

Now if α and β shift equally $(d\alpha = d\beta)$, then

$$\frac{dY}{d\alpha} = \frac{dY}{d\beta} = \left(\frac{1}{1 - \partial C/\partial Y} \right) \left(\frac{\partial C}{\partial \alpha} + \frac{dZ}{d\beta} \right) \quad .$$

The second bracketed term in this expression determines, solely, the sign of the slopes, $dY/d\alpha$ and $dY/d\beta$, because $\partial C/\partial Y$ is restricted to lie between 0 and 1.

6. Taking differentials of $Y = (10 + 0.92Y + \alpha) + (600 + \beta)$ we obtain

$$dY = 0.92dY + d\alpha$$

or

$$dY = 12.5 \, d\alpha \quad .$$

Then

$$\frac{dY}{d\alpha} = 12.5 \quad .$$

Similarly,

$$\Delta Y \simeq 12.5\Delta\alpha$$

and specifically

$$\Delta Y \simeq 12.5(30) = 375 \quad .$$

7. *a.* Decreasing returns to labor:

$$\frac{\partial q}{\partial L} = \frac{2K^{2/3}}{3L^{1/3}}, \quad \frac{\partial^2 q}{\partial L^2} = -\frac{2K^{2/3}}{9L^{4/3}} \quad .$$

Similarly for capital.

b. Increasing returns to scale: $(\lambda K)^{2/3}(\lambda L)^{2/3} = \lambda^{4/3}(K^{2/3}L^{2/3})$.

c. $\frac{2}{3}q$ to labor and $\frac{2}{3}q$ to capital, making an (impossible) total of $\frac{4}{3}q$.

8. *a.*
$$\frac{\partial q}{\partial L} = \alpha A C^\alpha L^{\alpha-1} \quad .$$

If marginal product of L is to be constant, $\partial^2 q/\partial L^2$ must be zero for positive L and K and $\partial q/\partial L$ must be a constant. By inspection if $\alpha = 1$, $\partial q/\partial L = AC$, $\partial^2 q/\partial L^2 = 0$. Similarly for capital.

b. Increasing returns to scale are just strong enough so that the scale effects of raising output, even by raising only one input, just counterbalances the effect of changing factor proportions.

9.
$$f_x = 2xz^{-1}$$
$$f_z = -x^2 z^{-2} \quad .$$

According to Euler's theorem,

$$y = f_x x + f_z z \quad .$$

Thus

$$y = (2xz^{-1})x + (-x^2 z^{-2})z \quad ;$$

with $x = 2$, $z = 4$ this gives $y = 1$. Now substitute into $y = x^2 z^{-1}$ to get $y = 1$ also.

10. Euler's theorem: $Z = f_X X + f_Y Y + f_W W$.

Total differential: $dZ = f_X \, dX + f_Y \, dY + f_W \, dW$.

Euler's Theorem is valid only if f is homogeneous of degree 1. The total differential is always valid on f as long as it is continuous and without kinks at the point at which the differential is evaluated.

11. *a.* Homogeneous of degree $\frac{5}{2}$.

b. Not homogeneous by virtue of constant term.

c. Homogeneous of degree 1, i.e., Cobb-Douglas function.

d. Same as (c) — idential function.

12. *a.* $z = x^{1/2}y^{-1/2}$, $z = w^3 x^{-4} y$.

b. $z = xy$, $z = w^3 x^{-4} y^3$.

Chapter 10

1. *a.* $x = 25$, $y = 50$.

b. $dy/dx = -y/x = r$. $dr/dx = y/x^2 > 0$. Thus the larger is x, the smaller is the amount of y that will be sacrificed at the margin for yet more x.

c. $x = 50$, $y = 100$.

d. None. Replacing the multiplicative constant 2 by 10 only means that "utility" is 5 times as large. Equilibrium values are unchanged, and so are they if a constant is added.

2. *a.* $x = 75$, $y = 30$.

   b. Substitute into Eq. (15), or note that $f(x, y) = 20x^{1/2}y^{1/2}$ is an objective function of the Cobb-Douglas form discussed in Section 10.6 with $A = 20$, $\alpha = \beta = \frac{1}{2}$.

3. *a.* $x = 52$, $y = 25$.

   b. Positive first derivatives at the point $(52, 25)$ are

$$f_x = (20)(25) - (2)(52) > 0$$

$$f_y = (20)(52) - (2)(25) > 0 \quad,$$

   and negative second derivatives are

$$f_{xx} = f_{yy} = -2 \quad.$$

4. *a, b.* Both functions are linear. If the slope of $f(x, y)$ is not equal to that of $F(x, y)$, corner solution; if it is, anywhere on $F(x, y)$ is optimal.

   c. Perfect substitutes; slope of iso-f curve $= -a/b$, a constant.

5. The result would be unaffected. To see this, let $-\lambda = \psi$; then let $+\psi$ rather than $-\lambda$ be used in the Lagrangian.

6. *a.* No, we do not have a maximum; the constraint slopes upwards, cutting through all the iso-f lines and hence precludes a tangency solution.

   b. Write $-x$ or $-y$ (but not both).

7. *a.* $x/y = \frac{1}{2}$

   b. $x/y = -\frac{1}{2}$

   c. $x/y = -\frac{10}{18}$

8. *a.* There is some ambiguity in economic literature on this point: generally, a Cobb-Douglas *production* function is homogeneous of degree 1 (constant returns to scale), whereas a Cobb-Douglas *utility* function simply implies homogeneity of any positive degree. (The reason is that, since production is cardinally measurable whereas utility is usually assumed to be only ordinally measurable, the degree of homogeneity is critical for production functions but unimportant for utility functions.)

   b. Yes; it is homogeneous of degree 0.

   c. It is inappropriate as a production function because the marginal product of factor y is negative for *all* positive values of y.

9. *a.* $x = y = 1/\sqrt{2}$; value of maximand $= 2/\sqrt{2}$

   b. $x = y = \sqrt{10}$; value of maximand $= 2\sqrt{10}$

   c. $x = y = 1/\sqrt{2}$; value of maximand $= 2/\sqrt{2}$

   d. $x = y = \sqrt{10}$; value of maximand $= 2\sqrt{10}$

   e. $x = 1$, $y = 2$, $z = 3$; value of maximand $= 108$

Chapter 11

1. One to one. The function is the form of (13), and the answer may be obtained by substitution into (15).

2. The elasticity for both functions is 1; indeed for all "Cobb-Douglas" functions, even those for which constant returns to scale do not hold, the elasticity of substitution is 1.

3. *a.* The second expression for σ involves the equilibrium conditions $MPK = r$ and $MPL = w$ and hence is not a definitional relationship.
   b. (i) Yes.   (ii) Yes, remember that log $(w/r) = \log w - \log r$.

4. *a.* $x = y = 50$.
   b. The rationing is effective; see points S and Q in Figure 10.5. With unchanged prices, only 40 can be spent on x, so consumption of y becomes 60. The Lagrangian method will not work; there is no tangency.

5. The slope of the iso-U curve is $-U_x/U_y$, which is the marginal rate of substitution. Specifically, $MRS = -y/x$. The value of the MRS in equilibrium is -1; this is also the value of the (constant) slope of the budget constraint.

6. Cardinality is lost in transforming V_4 to V_5. Ordinality is lost in transforming V_5 to V_6 by virtue of a negative transformation.

7. Maximizing one objective function subject to a given value of another, we have a convex iso-f curve and a concave constraint. If a linear constraint is sufficient, so, a fortiori, is a concave one.

Chapter 12

1. *a.* False   *b.* True

2. *a.* Excess demand is defined as $E = q^d - q^s$; hence

$$\frac{dE}{dp} = \frac{dq^d}{dp} - \frac{dq^s}{dp} .$$

   b. Yes; the function is a first-order approximation for any finite change in price relative to the equilibrium price, that is, $\Delta E \simeq ((dq^d/dp) - (dq^s/dp)) \, \Delta p$.
   c. The function of part *a* above is the general version of (5) in the text, since in a linear system $dq^d/dp = b$ and $dq^s/dp = d$.

3. *a.* Market 1: $p = 150$
   $q = 300$
   Market 2: $p = 300$
   $q = 1500$.
   b. Market 1 is stable since $A = -\frac{1}{3}$.
   Market 2 is unstable since $A = -\frac{5}{4}$.

		Market 1	Market 2
c.	p_0	350	280
	p_1	83	325
	p_2	172	269
	p_3	143	339
	p_4	152	251
	p_5	149	361

d. Eventually the price falls to zero ($q^d > q^s$ at $p = 0$). In the next period $q^s = 0$, and there can be no price in subsequent periods if nothing is produced. On this interpretation the oscillations cease to increase in magnitude as soon as p reaches zero. If we were not constrained to the positive quadrant, the oscillations would grow without limit.

4. *a.* Using the equilibrium condition $q_t^d = q_t^s$, we obtain $p_t = ((a - c)/d) + (bp_{t-1}/d)$ from which $\hat{p}_t = A\hat{p}_{t-1} = (b/d)\hat{p}_{t-1}$, that is, $A = b/d$.

b. As in the supply lag model, oscillations will occur with normal slopes of the demand and supply curves (in which case b and d are of opposite sign). The convergence, or divergence, of these oscillations can be analyzed as before, as long as the terms "slope of the supply curve" and "slope of the demand curve" are interchanged.

c. When *both* supply *and* demand are lagged the same period of time, only one price will clear the current market, and this price coincides with the equilibrium price.

5. Generally, we wish to ensure (i) that $d(dp/dt)/dE > 0$, and (ii) that $dp/dt = 0$ is implied when $E = 0$, that is, the reaction function should be homogeneous.

a. Fails first condition

b. Fails first condition; consider a fall in E

c. Fails first condition

d. Passes both conditions

e. Equation of part d and hence passes both conditions

f. Fails second condition

6. *a.* Macro theory tells us that $\alpha < 0$; Y falls when $Y > C + I$ and rises when $Y < C + I$.

b. The graph will be a straight line through the origin with a slope of α. (dY/dt is on the Y-axis and $Y - C - I$ on the X-axis.)

c. We require expenditure to exceed income for $Y < Y^*$ and expenditure to be less than income for $Y > Y^*$.

d. At equilibrium income equals expenditure. $dY/dY = 1$, and thus we require for part c that $dE/dY < 1$ (where E is expenditure and is the same thing as $C + I$). This is easily established:

$$E = C + I$$
$$= a + cY + \bar{I}$$
$$\frac{dE}{dY} = c \quad \text{(the marginal propensity to consume)} \quad .$$

Therefore we require $c < 1$, which is the familiar condition that the aggregate expenditure line should have a slope less than the 45° line. We also require $a > 0$ to ensure that the aggregate expenditure line cuts the 45° line in the positive quadrant.

7. The driver corrects, so he displays negative feedback; but he may over correct and oscillate, and increasing oscillations will probably be fatal.

8. The thermostat responds to the difference between a pre-set (equilibrium) temperature and actual room temperature. It gives the furnace a negative-feedback signal; but this is not a sufficient condition for stability.

9. *a.* Perhaps hogs, corn, coffee, broiler chickens (you may well have other examples).
   b. They would buy when the price was low and sell when it was high. Entry of speculators would tend to reduce the oscillations in price, so that, in equilibrium, they would not make super-normal profits.
   c. Yes. When the price was high it would pay to contract now to supply the commodity next period (when the price at which the contractor could obtain it would be low). Note that a futures market could work even if the commodity were perishable.
   d. Very difficult: we should have to model their expectations (discussed in Chapter 14).
   e. No. People are not so dumb.

10. Positive. The increased fee will reduce next year's registration; and so on.

11. *a.* Writing F for the number of foxes and R for the number of rabbits, the behavior of foxes is given by

$$F_t = a_0 + a_1 R_{t-\tau}$$

where τ is the lag. The behavior of rabbits is given by

$$R_t = b_0 + b_1 F_t \quad .$$

This is a pair of simultaneous equations, of which the first is a difference equation. We shall not need the method of solution in this book (although in this case it is quite easy, as you will see, if you substitute from the second equation into the first and set $\tau = 1$).
   b.
$$F_t = a_0 + a_1 R_{t-1}$$
$$R_t = b_0 + b_1 F_{t-1} \quad ,$$

a pair of simultaneous difference equations which we shall not solve.

Chapter 13

1. As these are all indefinite integrals, they require a constant of integration, C.
   a. $\frac{2}{3}x^3 + C$
   b. $\frac{1}{61}x^{61} + C$
   c. $e^x + C$

d. $e^x + \log_e x + C$

e. $\frac{5}{2}x^2 + C$

f. $3x + C$

2. $TC = 100 + 10x - 0.005x^2 + 0.0003x^3$. The constant of integration is fixed cost, here equal to 100.

3. *a.* $TR = 100q - 5q^2 + C$; $AR = 100 - 5q + (C/q)$.

   b. When nothing is sold nothing can be earned; hence the total revenue function must pass through the origin: C is zero.

4. *a.* $dE/dY = m + c = 0.2 + 0.7 = 0.9$.

   b. $E = C + 0.9Y$. The constant C stands for all forms of expenditure that do not vary with income.

5. *a.* $y = x^3 + C$

   b. $y = \frac{1}{12}x^4 + C$

   c. $y = 2x^3 + \frac{3}{4}x^4 + C$

   d. $y = \frac{1}{6}x^{3/2} + C$

   e. $y = \frac{9}{2}x^{2/3} + C$

   f. $y = \frac{1}{3}x^3 - \frac{1}{2}x^2 + C$

6. *a.*   (i) $y = 3x + C$.

      (ii) $y = \frac{3}{2}x^2 + (C_1)(x) + C_2$.

      (iii) $y = e^x + \frac{1}{3}(x^3) + C$.

   b.   (i) $10 = (3)(0) + C$, therefore $C = 10$.

      (iii) $10 = e^0 + (\frac{1}{3})(0^3) + C$; therefore $C = 9$ (not 10).

   c.   (i) $15 = (3)(5) + C$; therefore $C = 0$ [also true for $30 = (3)(10) + C$].

      (ii) $15 = (\frac{3}{2})(5^2) + 5 \cdot C_1 + C_2$, and $30 = (\frac{3}{2})(10^2) + 10 \cdot C_1 + C_2$ solve for $C_1 = -19.5$ and $C_2 = 75$.

7. *a.* $dz = ye^{xy}\, dx + xe^{xy}\, dy$.

   b. We know that a *necessary* condition for a maximum is that all first-order partials be zero, that is, in this case, $\partial z/\partial x = \partial z/\partial y = 0$. But this means that $ye^{xy} = xe^{xy} = 0$, which implies that the *only* possibility for a maximum is at $x = 0$ and $y = 0$. At $x = y = 0$ the value of the function is unity. If there were a maximum at this point, the value of the function could not exceed unity for any other values of x and y. However, when $x = 1$ and $y = 1$ the value of the function *is* greater than unity ($e^{xy} = e > 1$), proving that the function does not have a maximum.

8. *a.* $0.09e^{0.03x}$.

   b. $-\frac{1}{4}e^{-x/4}$. (Notice that $e^{-x/4} = e^{(-1/4)x}$, and the rule $(d/dx)e^{ax} = ae^{ax}$ may be applied at once.)

9. *a.* $e^{0.1x} + C$

   b. $3e^{2x} + C$

10. All but the expression in part d are equivalent; it should be $\sigma = (d \log L - d \log K)/(d \log r - d \log w)$.

11. *a.* $y = y_0 e^{rt}$. This answer is verified as follows: $dy/dt = ry_0 e^{rt}$ and

$$\frac{1}{y}\frac{dy}{dt} = \frac{ry_0e^{rt}}{y_0e^{rt}} = r \quad.$$

b. $y = 4e^{0.1}$.

12. a. $\frac{2}{3}$ of 1 percent.
b. $\frac{1}{3}$. "Percentage response" is elasticity, by definition, and $\eta_{y.x} = d \log y/d \log x$. Thus the exponents in the Cobb-Douglas function are the elasticities of output with respect to the inputs.

13.
$$\frac{d \log q}{d \log p} = -\frac{1}{4}$$

$$d \log q = -\tfrac{1}{4} d \log p$$

$$\int d \log q = \int -\tfrac{1}{4} d \log p$$

$$\log q = -\tfrac{1}{4} \log p + \log C$$

$$q = Cp^{-1/4}$$

14. Provided you remembered that x^{-1} cannot be integrated by the power function rule, you should have had no trouble: $\int x^{-1} dx = \log x + C$.

Chapter 14

1. a. We know by Section 14.1 that stability depends on the sign of $\alpha y = \alpha((dp^d/dp) - (dq^s/dp)) = 5(-15 - 15) = -150$, which implies that this model is stable.
b. Now $\alpha y = 5(15 + 15) = 150$, so this model is explosive. Note that by using a differential equation we preclude oscillations in the model: Compare Section 14.1 with Section 12.3.

2. You should answer the question in the following steps.
a. Calculate the equilibrium level of income Y°.
b. Derive an expression for the deviation of actual income Y from its equilibrium Y°. Call this $\hat{Y}$.
c. Substitute into the adjustment function to obtain an expression for dY/dt.
d. Integrate this expression to get $\hat{Y}_t = Ae^{\alpha(1-c)t}$.
e. Inspect the solution to show that an arbitrary disturbance $\hat{Y}_0$ gets progressively smaller as time passes. (Given that $\alpha < 0, 1 - c > 0, t > 0$.)

3. a.
$$\frac{\partial q}{\partial L} = \alpha A_0 e^{rt}L^{\alpha-1}K^{1-\alpha}$$

$$\frac{\partial^2 q}{\partial L \, \partial t} = \alpha r A_0 e^{rt}L^{\alpha-1}K^{1-\alpha}$$

and, for the proportionate rate of change,

$$\frac{1}{\partial q/\partial L} \frac{\partial^2 q}{\partial L \, \partial t} = r \quad,$$

and similarly for capital.

b. It does not, since α is unaffected, so both marginal products grow at the same rate. Thus the shapes of the iso-quants are unaffected; they simply move toward the origin. Technical progress that does not alter the *MRS* may be called neutral.

c. They are not, since they depend only on α.

d.
$$\frac{1}{q} \frac{dq}{dt} = r \quad.$$

e.
$$dq = \frac{\partial q}{\partial t} dt + \frac{\partial q}{\partial L} dL + \frac{\partial q}{\partial K} dK$$

or

$$\frac{dq}{dt} = \frac{\partial q}{\partial t} + \frac{\partial q}{\partial L} \frac{dL}{dt} + \frac{\partial q}{\partial K} \frac{dK}{dt} \quad.$$

f. From part e,

$$\frac{1}{q} \frac{dq}{dt} = \frac{1}{q} \frac{\partial q}{\partial t} + \frac{1}{q} \frac{\partial q}{\partial L} \frac{dL}{dt} + \frac{1}{q} \frac{\partial q}{\partial K} \frac{dK}{dt} \quad.$$

Evaluating this,

$$\frac{1}{q} \frac{dq}{dt} = r + \frac{1}{q} \alpha A_0 e^{rt} L^{\alpha-1} K^{1-\alpha} \frac{dL}{dt} + \frac{1}{q}(1-\alpha) A_0 e^{rt} L^{\alpha} K^{-\alpha} \frac{dK}{dt} \quad.$$

Substituting for the q's in the denominators of the right-hand side and simplifying,

$$\frac{1}{q} \frac{dq}{dt} = r + \alpha \frac{1}{L} \frac{dL}{dt} + (1-\alpha) \frac{1}{K} \frac{dK}{dt}$$

$$= r + \alpha m + (1-\alpha)n \quad.$$

Hence output grows at rate r *plus* the rates of growths of inputs, each weighed by its elasticity coefficient.

4. *a.*
$$Y_t^1 = Ae^{nt}$$

$$Y_t^2 = Be^{rt} \quad.$$

Set $Y_t^1 = Y_t^2$ and solve for t

$$Ae^{nt} = Be^{rt} \quad.$$

Taking logs to the base e (ln)

$$\ln A + nt \ln e = \ln B + rt \ln e$$

$$\ln A + nt = \ln B + rt$$

$$nt - rt = \ln B - \ln A$$

$$t = \frac{\ln B - \ln A}{n - r} = \ln \left(\frac{B}{A}\right)\left(\frac{1}{n - r}\right) \quad .$$

Thus the time taken depends on the ratio of their incomes and the difference between their growth rates.

b. If $r > n$, $1/(n - r) < 0$, so $t < 0$. Thus the time at which economy 1 overtook economy 2 is already past; 1's lead will now widen progressively.

c. (i) Let $n = r$, $A > B$.

$$Y_t^1 = Ae^{nt}$$

$$\frac{dY_t^1}{dt} = nAe^{nt}; \quad \frac{1}{Y_t^1}\frac{dY_t^1}{dt} = n \quad .$$

Similarly for 2, so the growth rates are the same.

(ii) $\quad \dfrac{d(Y_t^1/Y_t^2)}{dt} = \dfrac{d(Ae^{nt}/Be^{nt})}{dt} = \dfrac{d(A/B)}{dt} = 0 \quad .$

(iii) The absolute discrepancy D is

$$D = Ae^{nt} - Be^{nt}$$

$$\frac{dD}{dt} = nAe^{nt} - nBe^{nt}$$

$$= ne^{nt}(A - B) \quad .$$

$A - B$ is a constant equal to the initial discrepancy, but as t increases this absolute discrepancy increases steadily. [This is consistent with the finding in (ii) that the ratios of the two countries' (growing) incomes were constant.]

5. a. $r - n$. Let's hope that $r - n > 0$!
   b. Megalomania. Who but Stalin would want to maximize GNP instead of GNP per capita?

6. a. Yes.
   b. Yes.
   c. $M = kPX$; $\log M = \log k + \log P + \log X$; $d \log M = d \log k + d \log P + d \log X$. *Ceteris paribus* implies that $d \log k = d \log X = 0$. Then $d \log M = d \log P$, and the proposition is proved.

7. a. (i) This statement does not characterize the "flight from money" model. The statement expresses Walras' law — that excess demand for goods is identical to excess supply of money — and adds a dis-

equilibrium adjustment response in which reducing money balances causes prices to rise.

 (ii) This statement captures the essential features of "flight from money" models, especially the effect of anticipated changes.

 b. The demand for money equation (19) is a behavioral equation by virtue of the constant k, which is determined by the behavior of money holders. Also, the proposed adjustment function (23), $dP(t)/dt = \alpha(M^s - M^d)$, is a behavioral equation. Of course, any equation which has an expectational term, for example, (31) is a behavioral function.

8. *a.* The solution is an equation having x and y as variables but one that does not include any differentials. Further, the solution will include arbitrary constants. There will be a single arbitrary constant when only the first-degree differential appears.

 b. Yes.

9. *a.* $y = \frac{5}{2} + de^{-2x}$. Now let $y = y_0$ when $x = 0$; then $d = y_0 - \frac{5}{2}$. Then $y = \frac{5}{2} + (y_0 - \frac{5}{2})e^{-2x}$.

Similarly,

 b. $y = (c/a) + (y_0 - (c/a))e^{-(b/a)x}$.

 c. $y = y_0 e^{3x}$.

10. *a.* The "time constant" is $1/\frac{1}{4} = 4$.

 b. It would take four time units.

11. Let K° be your desired stock of knowledge and $K(0) - K^\circ$ be the initial discrepancy in your stock of knowledge. Then a possible stock adjustment model would be $dK/dt = \beta(K^\circ - K(t))$ with a solution $K(t) = K^\circ + (K(0) - K^\circ)e^{-\beta t}$. Note that this implies that you slow down your rate of learning as you get closer to your goal. A different formulation would be required for those who accelerate as they near the finish line.

12. *a.* The α-term would probably be a variable because it represents the speed of response to a discrepancy between the desired and the actual capital stock and would depend, among other things, on general business conditions.

 b. A possible economic variable would be the interest rate. The decision on the speed of replacement of capital might be expected to depend on the value of discounted expected profits, which in turn depends on the interest rate.

13. *a.* No; the statement would be true for per capita output since equilibrium in the model is defined as a constant level of per capita output at full employment.

 b. Yes; if population is constant, then output attains a fixed level at equilibrium, since equilibrium for the model implies a constant level of per capita output.

Chapter 15

SECTION 15.1

1. *a.* 2×2 *b.* 2×5 *d.* 1×1 (well, why not?)

SECTION 15.2

1. *a.* $\begin{bmatrix} 3 & 11 \\ 2 & 9 \end{bmatrix}$ *b.* $\begin{bmatrix} 16 & 18 & 22 & -5 \\ 3 & 21 & 4 & 24 \end{bmatrix}$

   c. Addition impossible

   d. $\begin{bmatrix} 2 & 3 \\ 4 & 5 \end{bmatrix}$

2. *a.* $\begin{bmatrix} 1 & -5 \\ 6 & 1 \end{bmatrix}$ *b.* $\begin{bmatrix} 12 & 12 & 14 & 5 \\ 1 & -15 & -34 & -16 \end{bmatrix}$

   c. Subtraction impossible

   d. $\begin{bmatrix} 2 & 3 \\ 4 & 5 \end{bmatrix}$

3. *a.* $\begin{bmatrix} 4 & 6 \\ 8 & 10 \end{bmatrix}$ *b.* $\begin{bmatrix} \lambda & 0 & 0 \\ 0 & \lambda & 0 \\ 0 & 0 & \lambda \end{bmatrix}$

4. Yes. If $\mathbf{C} = \mathbf{A} + \mathbf{B}$, $c_{ij} = a_{ij} + b_{ij} = b_{ij} + a_{ij}$.

5. If $\mathbf{C} = \lambda(\mathbf{A} + \mathbf{B})$, $c_{ij} = \lambda(a_{ij} + b_{ij}) = \lambda a_{ij} + \lambda b_{ij}$.

6. $d_{ij} = (a_{ij} + b_{ij}) + c_{ij}$. Scalars follow the *associative* law; it does not matter in what order we perform additions. The same holds for matrices.

7. *a.* $\begin{bmatrix} 46 & 66 & 86 \\ 82 & 118 & 154 \end{bmatrix}$.

   b. $\mathbf{A}$ is 2×2 and $\mathbf{B}$ 2×3, whence $\mathbf{AB}$ is 2×3, but $\mathbf{BA}$ does not exist.

8. *a.* $\mathbf{AB} = \begin{bmatrix} 16 & 9 \\ 34 & 21 \end{bmatrix}$ and $\mathbf{BA} = \begin{bmatrix} 11 & 16 \\ 16 & 26 \end{bmatrix}$.

   b. $\mathbf{AB} = \begin{bmatrix} 8 & 5 \\ 3 & 2 \end{bmatrix}$ and $\mathbf{BA} = \begin{bmatrix} 8 & 3 \\ 5 & 2 \end{bmatrix}$.

   Note that in part b $\mathbf{BA} = (\mathbf{AB})'$.

9.
$$\mathbf{AB} = \begin{bmatrix} 5 & 3 \\ 11 & 7 \end{bmatrix}, \quad \mathbf{BC} = \begin{bmatrix} 4 & 4 \\ 6 & 7 \end{bmatrix}$$

$$\mathbf{ABC} = \begin{bmatrix} 16 & 18 \\ 36 & 40 \end{bmatrix} = \mathbf{A(BC)} = \mathbf{(AB)C} \quad.$$

The associative law works in multiplication, too. It can be proved (tediously) by writing out the characteristic elements of **ABC**, **A(BC)**, etc., in full and observing that they are all the same.

10. *a.* (i) Conformable — (n, m) — a matrix.
(ii) Conformable — $(1, m)$ — a row vector.
(iii) Conformable — $(1, 1)$ — a single value.
(iv) Not conformable — but $\mathbf{A}(1, 1)$ is simply a single value and could be treated as a scalar, if that is intended.
(v) Conformable — (m, m) — a square matrix.
(vi) Conformable — (m, m) — a square matrix.
b. Addition is possible only in case (v); **A** and **B** can be added together if and only if they are of identical dimensions.

11. *a.* 0   *b.* 4   *c.* $\begin{bmatrix} 1 & -1 & -1 & -1 \\ -1 & 1 & 1 & 1 \\ -1 & 1 & 1 & 1 \\ -1 & 1 & 1 & 1 \end{bmatrix}$

SECTION 15.3

1. $\mathbf{AI} = \mathbf{IA} = \mathbf{A} = \begin{bmatrix} 2 & 8 \\ 10 & -12 \end{bmatrix}$

2. **C** is 3×2. If **I** is 3×3, **IC** exists and is 3×2 (**C**); if **I** is 2×2, **CI** exists and is 3×2. **IC** = **CI**, for any **C**, choosing **I** of appropriate order, *not* the same for pre- and postmultiplication unless **C** is square. **I** may be called the *identity matrix*.

3. *a.* A diagonal element of $\mathbf{I}^2$ is given by $\sum_k i_{ik} i_{ki}$ (using i for the characteristic element of **I**, whether 0 or 1). But $i_{ik} = i_{ki} = 0$ unless $i = k$, in which case we have $1 \times 1 = 1$. For an off-diagonal, we have $\sum_k i_{ik} i_{kj}$. There is a 1 in each vector but not in corresponding positions, so the sum is zero.
b. We have $\mathbf{I}^2 = \mathbf{I}$. Now

$$\mathbf{I}^3 = \mathbf{I}(\mathbf{I}^2) = \mathbf{I} \cdot \mathbf{I}^2 = \mathbf{I}^2 = \mathbf{I}$$

$$\mathbf{I}^4 = \mathbf{I}(\mathbf{I}^3) = \mathbf{I} \cdot \mathbf{I}^3 = \mathbf{I}^2 = \mathbf{I} \quad,$$

and so on.

4. We have already had an example of the summation:

$$b_{ij} + 0 = b_{ij} - 0 = b_{ij} \quad .$$

Multiplying, we have

$$\sum_k b_{ik} 0_{kj} = \sum_k b_{ik} \cdot 0 = \sum_k 0 \cdot b_{kj} = 0 \quad .$$

5. $\lambda \mathbf{I} = \begin{bmatrix} \lambda & 0 & \cdots & 0 \\ 0 & \lambda & & \\ & & \ddots & \\ & & & \\ 0 & & \cdots & \lambda \end{bmatrix}$

6. $\mathbf{xy} = \begin{bmatrix} 1 & 3 & 0 & 2 \end{bmatrix} \begin{bmatrix} 2 \\ 0 \\ 7 \\ 1 \end{bmatrix} = 2 + 0 + 0 + 2 = 4$

7. *a.* $\mathbf{x}$ is a column vector, whence $\mathbf{x}'$ is a row, and $\mathbf{x}'\mathbf{x}$ is a scalar product, row by column:

$$\mathbf{x}'\mathbf{x} = \begin{bmatrix} x_1 & x_2 & x_3 \end{bmatrix} \begin{bmatrix} x_1 \\ x_2 \\ x_3 \end{bmatrix} = x_1^2 + x_2^2 + x_3^2 \quad .$$

b. $\mathbf{xx}'$ is 3×1 times 1×3, whence a 3×3 matrix:

$$\begin{bmatrix} x_1 \\ x_2 \\ x_3 \end{bmatrix} \begin{bmatrix} x_1 & x_2 & x_3 \end{bmatrix} = \begin{bmatrix} x_1^2 & x_1x_2 & x_1x_3 \\ x_1x_2 & x_2^2 & x_2x_3 \\ x_1x_3 & x_2x_3 & x_3^2 \end{bmatrix} \quad .$$

Note that the product is a *symmetric* matrix.

c. $\mathbf{y}'\mathbf{y}$ is a scalar product, $4 + 0 + 49 + 1 = 54$.

8. $n \times m$ conforms with $m \times 1$, which must be the order of $\mathbf{x}$; the product is $n \times 1$, which must be the order of $\mathbf{y}$.

9. $\mathbf{Ax} = \mathbf{c}$, where

$$\mathbf{A} = \begin{bmatrix} 1 & 2 & 3 \\ 2 & 0 & 1 \\ 2 & -1 & 4 \end{bmatrix}$$

$$\mathbf{x} = \{x_1 \quad x_2 \quad x_3\} \quad \text{and} \quad \mathbf{c} = \{1 \quad 0 \quad 7\} \quad .$$

10. $\mathbf{A}' = \begin{bmatrix} 1 & 3 \\ 2 & 0 \\ 1 & 2 \end{bmatrix}$

11. *a.*

$$\mathbf{A}'\mathbf{A} = \begin{bmatrix} 1 & 3 \\ 2 & 0 \\ 1 & 2 \end{bmatrix} \begin{bmatrix} 1 & 2 & 1 \\ 3 & 0 & 2 \end{bmatrix} = \begin{bmatrix} 10 & 2 & 7 \\ 2 & 4 & 2 \\ 7 & 2 & 5 \end{bmatrix}; \quad 3 \times 3 \quad .$$

$$\mathbf{A}\mathbf{A}' = \begin{bmatrix} 1 & 2 & 1 \\ 3 & 0 & 2 \end{bmatrix} \begin{bmatrix} 1 & 3 \\ 2 & 0 \\ 1 & 2 \end{bmatrix} = \begin{bmatrix} 6 & 5 \\ 5 & 13 \end{bmatrix}; \quad 2 \times 2 \quad .$$

b. $\mathbf{A} \cdot \mathbf{A}$ requires 2×3 times 2×3, which does not conform.

12. $\mathbf{A}$ is symmetric, $\mathbf{A} = \mathbf{A}'$, whence

$$\mathbf{A}\mathbf{A}' = \mathbf{A}'\mathbf{A} = \mathbf{A} \cdot \mathbf{A} = \begin{bmatrix} 5 & 8 & 2 \\ 8 & 14 & 4 \\ 2 & 4 & 2 \end{bmatrix} \quad .$$

For $\mathbf{A}^2$ to exist at all, $\mathbf{A}$ must be square.

13. If $\mathbf{C} = \mathbf{A} + \mathbf{B}$, $c_{ij} = a_{ij} + b_{ij}$, whence $c_{ij}' = a_{ij}' + b_{ij}'$: $(\mathbf{A} + \mathbf{B})' = \mathbf{A}' + \mathbf{B}'$.

14. It cannot be $\mathbf{A}'\mathbf{B}'$ since this would involve multiplying the columns of $\mathbf{A}$ by the rows of $\mathbf{B}$. If c_{ij} is the characteristic element of $\mathbf{AB}$,

$$c_{ij} = \sum_k a_{ik} b_{kj}$$

and

$$c_{ij}' = c_{ji} = \sum_k a_{jk} b_{ki} \quad .$$

Now,

$$a_{kj}' = a_{jk} \quad \text{and} \quad b_{ik}' = b_{ki} \quad ,$$

whence

$$c_{ji} = \sum_k b_{ik}' a_{kj}'$$

and

$$(\mathbf{AB})' = \mathbf{B}'\mathbf{A}' \quad .$$

This is sometimes called the *reversal rule* for the transpose of a product.

15.
$$\mathbf{AB} = \begin{bmatrix} 1 & 0 \\ 0 & 1 \end{bmatrix}.$$

Here **B** is in fact the *inverse* of **A**.

16. No. If **A** and **X** are not of identical dimensions, then at least one of the two operations cannot be performed. In the special case in which **A** and **X** are both $m \times n$ matrices both operations can be performed, but you need only consider the calculation of the first element of **Y** to realize that the two operations do not give the same result.

SECTIONS 15.4 AND 15.5

1. *a.* −2. *b.* 2. (These two examples illustrate the change of sign of a determinant following the interchange of two rows.)
  c. −5 (use the second column).
  d. 1 (the determinant of the unit matrix of any order is 1).
  e. λ^3 (the determinant of the nth order scalar matrix is λ^n).
  f. $-\lambda^3$ (interchange of two rows again).
  g. (Compare part c).
  h. 0 (the first and last columns are identical).
  i. 0 [This illustrates another rule for determinants, to be proved shortly, that one can add a multiple of one row (column) to another without altering the value of the determinant. If the first column is subtracted from the second, in this instance, the remainder is equal to the first column. A determinant with two identical columns is zero. We see that if one column (row) of a determinant is a scalar multiple of another, the determinant vanishes.]
  j. 0 (This extends the rule we have just met. The second column is twice the first plus the third. Subtracting the first and the third from the second, we should be left with a column identical to the first.)
  k. 5 (The determinant is simply the transpose of the determinant in part g. Since one can expand a determinant by either row or column, it is not surprising to find that $|\mathbf{A}| = |\mathbf{A}'|$.)

2. $|\mathbf{A}| = \Sigma_i\, a_{ji} A_{ji}$. If we now add, element by element, λ times row r to row j, we find

$$|\mathbf{A}| = \sum_i (a_{ji} + \lambda a_{ri}) A_{ji}$$

$$= \sum_i a_{ji} A_{ji} + \sum_i \lambda a_{ri} A_{ji}\ .$$

The first term is $|\mathbf{A}|$. Since λ is a constant, it can be factored out of the summation, giving $\lambda\, \Sigma_i\, a_{ri} A_{ji}$. But the summation is now expansion by alien cofactors, which vanishes. It is pretty obvious what happens in the cases

$$\sum_i (a_{ji} + \lambda a_{ri} + \mu a_{si}) A_{ji},\quad \text{etc.}$$

If one vector is composed entirely of multiples of other vectors in this way, it is said to be *linearly dependent* on them.

3. Write the determinants $[\mathbf{x}^{(1)}\mathbf{x}^{(2)}\mathbf{x}^{(3)}]$, where the $\mathbf{x}^{(i)}$'s are column vectors. Then for determinant i, $\mathbf{x}^{(2)} = 2\mathbf{x}^{(1)}$. For determinant j, $\mathbf{x}^{(2)} = 2\mathbf{x}^{(1)} + \mathbf{x}^{(3)}$. Using the proof of Question 2, we can reduce $\mathbf{x}^{(2)}$ to a column of zeros without altering the value of the determinant, but any determinant with a column (row) of zeros obviously vanishes.

4. *a.* -3.

   b. There is no determinant because the matrix is not square.

   c. There is no determinant because the product is a scalar.

   d. The product is

   $$\begin{bmatrix} 1 & 1 & 1 \\ 1 & 1 & 1 \\ 1 & 1 & 1 \end{bmatrix}.$$

   All three rows are identical; therefore the determinant vanishes, that is, it has a zero value. Note that two identical rows and columns are sufficient to make the determinant vanish.

   e. The second and fourth rows are identical; hence the determinant vanishes.

SECTION 15.6

1. *a.* **I**, from the fact that $\mathbf{I} \cdot \mathbf{I} = \mathbf{I}$.

   b. $(1/\lambda)\mathbf{I}$.

   c. The matrix of cofactors is

   $$\begin{bmatrix} 3 & -1 \\ -1 & 2 \end{bmatrix}.$$

   Transposing, the adjoint matrix is the same. The determinant is 5, whence the inverse is

   $$\frac{1}{5}\begin{bmatrix} 3 & -1 \\ -1 & 2 \end{bmatrix}.$$

d. cofactors: $\begin{bmatrix} 1 & -1 & 0 \\ 0 & 1 & -1 \\ 0 & 0 & 1 \end{bmatrix}$; adjoint: $\begin{bmatrix} 1 & 0 & 0 \\ -1 & 1 & 0 \\ 0 & -1 & 1 \end{bmatrix}.$

   Det $= 1$, whence the adjoint is the inverse.

2. Not matrix a since the rows are linearly dependent; the first is twice the second, whence the determinant vanishes (the matrix is singular). Not matrix b for the same reason (second column twice the third).

Not matrix d; not square.
Not matrix e; singular since first and last rows are identical.

3.

$$\frac{1}{2}\begin{bmatrix} 0 & 2 & -6 \\ -1 & 1 & -2 \\ 2 & -2 & 6 \end{bmatrix} \ .$$

Note: You should always check that an inverse is correct by multiplying out $\mathbf{AA}^{-1}$.

4. *a.*

$$\mathbf{A}^{-1} = \begin{bmatrix} \dfrac{1}{a_{11}} & 0 & 0 \\[2ex] \dfrac{-a_{21}}{a_{11}a_{22}} & \dfrac{1}{a_{22}} & 0 \\[2ex] \dfrac{a_{21}a_{32} - a_{22}a_{31}}{a_{11}a_{22}a_{33}} & \dfrac{-a_{32}}{a_{22}a_{33}} & \dfrac{1}{a_{33}} \end{bmatrix} \ .$$

b. Inverting the matrix in this case is unnecessarily cumbersome, although it is worth checking that the inverse of a triangular matrix is triangular. The equations are

$$a_{11}x_1 \qquad\qquad\qquad = c_1$$
$$a_{21}x_1 + a_{22}x_2 \qquad\quad = c_2$$
$$a_{31}x_1 + a_{32}x_2 + a_{33}x_3 = c_3 \ .$$

The method of "elimination," taught at school, is the simple method. From the first equation, $x_1 = a_{11}{}^{-1}c_1$. Putting this into the second equation,

$$a_{21}a_{11}{}^{-1}c_1 + a_{22}x_2 = c_2 \quad ;$$

that is,

$$x_2 = a_{22}{}^{-1}(c_2 - a_{21}a_{11}{}^{-1}c_1)$$

$$= \frac{c_2}{a_{22}} - \frac{a_{21}c_1}{a_{11}a_{22}} \quad ,$$

and so on. You should complete the solution for x_3, and compare the results with $\mathbf{A}^{-1}$ above. A system of equations whose coefficient matrix is triangular is said to be *recursive*. The procedure is to start at the thin end, and chew your way along.

5. In this case again, elimination is quickest. The equations are

$$x_1 \qquad\quad + \ x_3 = 1$$
$$x_1 + 6x_2 + 3x_3 = 0$$
$$2x_2 + \ x_3 = 0 \ .$$

The first gives $x_3 = 1 - x_1$, whence the third gives $x_2 = \frac{1}{2}x_1 - \frac{1}{2}$. Substituting for x_2 and x_3 in the second equation,

$$x_1 + 6\frac{x_1}{2} - \frac{6}{2} + 3 - 3x_1 = 0 \quad,$$

whence $x_1 = 0$, $x_3 = 1$, and $x_2 = -\frac{1}{2}$. Notice that we have *not* built up the inverse; if we are required to find x for a new c vector, we have all our labor to do again.

SECTION 15.7

1. See the answers to Questions 4b and 5 in Section 15.6.

2. The general 3×3 determinant was given in Section 15.4. We require Δ_1, Δ_2, and Δ_3:

$$\Delta_1 = \begin{vmatrix} 0 & a_{12} & a_{13} \\ 1 & a_{22} & a_{23} \\ 0 & a_{32} & a_{33} \end{vmatrix} = -(a_{12}a_{33} - a_{13}a_{32})$$

$$\Delta_2 = \begin{vmatrix} a_{11} & 0 & a_{13} \\ a_{21} & 1 & a_{23} \\ a_{31} & 0 & a_{33} \end{vmatrix} = a_{11}a_{33} - a_{13}a_{31}$$

$$\Delta_3 = \begin{vmatrix} a_{11} & a_{12} & 0 \\ a_{21} & a_{22} & 1 \\ a_{31} & a_{32} & 0 \end{vmatrix} = -(a_{11}a_{32} - a_{12}a_{31}) \quad.$$

$x_i = \Delta_i / |A|$. Looking back to Section 15.4, we see that no cancelation is possible, since the general determinant does not factor.

3. $\{1 \quad 0 \quad 0\}$ yields $x_1 = \frac{0}{2}$, $x_2 = -\frac{1}{2}$, $x_3 = \frac{2}{2}$.
$\{0 \quad 1 \quad 0\}$ yields $x_1 = \frac{2}{2}$, $x_2 = \frac{1}{2}$, $x_3 = -\frac{2}{2}$.
$\{0 \quad 0 \quad 1\}$ yields $x_1 = -\frac{6}{2}$, $x_2 = -\frac{2}{2}$, $x_3 = \frac{6}{2}$.

If we compare these results with the inverse obtained in Question 3 of Section 15.6, we see that the solution for $\{1 \quad 0 \quad 0\}$ has yielded the first column of the inverse, that for $\{0 \quad 1 \quad 0\}$ the second column, and so on.

4. a. $\begin{bmatrix} 3 & 7 \\ 2 & 7 \end{bmatrix}\begin{bmatrix} x \\ y \end{bmatrix} = \begin{bmatrix} 20 \\ 20 \end{bmatrix}$; then $x = \dfrac{\begin{vmatrix} 20 & 7 \\ 20 & 7 \end{vmatrix}}{\begin{vmatrix} 3 & 7 \\ 2 & 7 \end{vmatrix}} = \dfrac{0}{7} = 0 \quad.$

b. $\begin{bmatrix} 1 & 1 & 1 \\ 2 & 2 & 1 \\ 2 & 1 & 2 \end{bmatrix} \begin{bmatrix} y \\ z \\ x \end{bmatrix} = \begin{bmatrix} 10 \\ 20 \\ 30 \end{bmatrix}$; then $x = \dfrac{\begin{vmatrix} 1 & 1 & 10 \\ 2 & 2 & 20 \\ 2 & 1 & 30 \end{vmatrix}}{\begin{vmatrix} 1 & 1 & 1 \\ 2 & 2 & 1 \\ 2 & 1 & 2 \end{vmatrix}} = \dfrac{0}{-1} = 0$.

c. $\begin{bmatrix} 1 & 1 \\ 2 & 2 \end{bmatrix} \begin{bmatrix} x \\ y \end{bmatrix} = \begin{bmatrix} 10 \\ 50 \end{bmatrix}$; then $x = \dfrac{\begin{vmatrix} 10 & 1 \\ 50 & 2 \end{vmatrix}}{\begin{vmatrix} 1 & 1 \\ 2 & 2 \end{vmatrix}} = \dfrac{-30}{0}$, that is, no solution.

(Note that $x = 0/n = 0$ is a perfectly good solution, just as is $x =$ any other number, but that $x = n/0$ means that there is *no* solution for x.)

Chapter 16

1. The investment schedule shifts out by db. Totally differentiating,

$$\begin{bmatrix} 1 - c(1-t) & -g \\ e & f \end{bmatrix} \begin{bmatrix} dY \\ dr \end{bmatrix} = \begin{bmatrix} db \\ 0 \end{bmatrix} .$$

We already have $\Delta = f\{1 - c(1-t)\} + eg < 0$, since $f, g < 0$, e, $\{1 - c(1-t)\} > 0$. We compute

$$dY = \frac{\begin{vmatrix} db & -g \\ 0 & f \end{vmatrix}}{\Delta} = \frac{f}{\Delta} \, db > 0$$

and

$$dr = \frac{\begin{vmatrix} 1 - c(1-t) & db \\ e & 0 \end{vmatrix}}{\Delta} = -\frac{e}{\Delta} \, db > 0 .$$

We have not, however, finished; we still have to find the change in I (*not* equal to db) and in C (or S), the variables eliminated by substitution. We obviously need not solve for dI and dS, but let us find dI and dC.

$$dI = db + g \, dr$$

$$= \left(1 - \frac{eg}{\Delta}\right) db .$$

Evidently sign depends on $eg/\Delta \lessgtr 1$, that is, on $eg/[f\{1 - c(1 - t)\} + eg] \lessgtr 1$. Ordinary manipulation shows it to be <1, whence

$$0 < \frac{\mathrm{d}I}{\mathrm{d}b} < 1 \quad ,$$

as we should expect. Now

$$\mathrm{d}C = c(1 - t) \ \mathrm{d}Y = f\frac{c(1 - t)}{\Delta} \ \mathrm{d}b > 0 \quad .$$

2. *a.* We have

$$\Delta = f\{1 - (1 - t)(c - m)\} + eg < 0 \quad .$$

(i)
$$\mathrm{d}z = \{0, \mathrm{d}M_0\} \quad ,$$

whence

$$\mathrm{d}Y = \frac{g}{\Delta} \ \mathrm{d}M_0 > 0$$

$$\mathrm{d}r = \frac{\{1 - (1 - t)(c - m)\}}{\Delta} \ \mathrm{d}M_0 < 0$$

and
$$\mathrm{d}I = 0 + g \ \mathrm{d}r$$

$$= \frac{g\{1 - (1 - t)(c - m)\}}{\Delta} \ \mathrm{d}M_0 > 0$$

$$\mathrm{d}C = c(1 - t) \ \mathrm{d}Y = \frac{c(1 - t)}{\Delta}g \ \mathrm{d}M_0 > 0$$

and

$$\mathrm{d}M = m(1 - t) \ \mathrm{d}Y = \frac{m(1 - t)}{\Delta}g \ \mathrm{d}M_0 > 0 \quad .$$

(ii)
$$\mathrm{d}z = \{\mathrm{d}X, 0\} \quad ,$$

whence

$$\mathrm{d}Y = \frac{f}{\Delta} \ \mathrm{d}X > 0$$

$$\mathrm{d}r = -\frac{e}{\Delta} \ \mathrm{d}X > 0$$

$$\mathrm{d}I = -\frac{ge}{\Delta} \ \mathrm{d}X < 0$$

$$\mathrm{d}C = \frac{c(1 - t)}{\Delta}f \ \mathrm{d}X > 0$$

$$\mathrm{d}M = \frac{m(1 - t)}{\Delta}f \ \mathrm{d}X > 0 \quad .$$

b. As we learned in Chapter 4, we may write

$$\frac{dY}{dB} = \frac{dY/dG}{dB/dG} \quad .$$

Define $B = X - M$; $dB = -dM$ for $dX = 0$. The multipliers are identical for changes in G or X, so from the answers to the last question we write directly

$$\frac{dY}{dB} = -\frac{(f/\Delta)\, dG}{m(1-t)f\, dG/\Delta}$$

$$= -\frac{1}{m(1-t)} \quad ,$$

the expected negative trade-off.

3. *a.* If we put all the endogenous variables on the left-hand side, we have the three equations

$$I - eY = d$$

$$C - bY = a$$

$$-C - I + Y = 0 \quad ,$$

or, in matrix form,

$$\begin{bmatrix} 0 & 1 & -e \\ 1 & 0 & -b \\ -1 & -1 & 1 \end{bmatrix} \begin{bmatrix} C \\ I \\ Y \end{bmatrix} = \begin{bmatrix} d \\ a \\ 0 \end{bmatrix} \quad .$$

b. The determinant of this matrix is $b + e - 1 = \Delta$, say. Thus

$$C = \frac{\begin{vmatrix} d & 1 & -e \\ a & 0 & -b \\ 0 & -1 & 1 \end{vmatrix}}{\Delta}$$

$$I = \frac{\begin{vmatrix} 0 & d & -e \\ 1 & a & -b \\ -1 & 0 & 1 \end{vmatrix}}{\Delta}$$

$$Y = \frac{\begin{vmatrix} 0 & 1 & d \\ 1 & 0 & a \\ -1 & -1 & 0 \end{vmatrix}}{\Delta} \quad .$$

Expanding the determinants, we find

$$C = \frac{-db - a + ae}{b - e - 1} = \frac{a + bd - ae}{1 - (b + e)}$$

$$I = \frac{-d + bd - ae}{b + e - 1} = \frac{d + ae - bd}{1 - (b + e)}$$

$$Y = \frac{-a - d}{b + e - 1} = \frac{a + d}{1 - (b + e)} \quad .$$

Notice that the common denominator is $-\Delta^{-1}$; this is the multiplier. To check, it is only necessary to substitute this answer for Y (which is the usual multiplier result) into $I = d + eY$ and $C = a + bY$, and see that the results agree.

   c. Assuming that $a + d > 0$, it is necessary and sufficient that the multiplier, $\{1 - (b + e)\}^{-1}$, be a positive.

4. *a.* For households we have

$$C = d + cY \quad .$$

Firm's receipts, R, must be equal to total expenditure, consumption plus investment, so

$$R = C + I \quad .$$

Finally,

$$Y = rR \quad .$$

Household income is a fixed proportion of firm's receipts.

  b. We can substitute, or we can use matrix methods. If we substitute we have

$$Y = rR$$

$$= r(C + I)$$

$$= r(d + cY + I) \quad ,$$

so

$$Y - rcY = r(d + I) \quad ,$$

whence

$$Y = \frac{r(d + I)}{1 - rc} \quad ,$$

and

$$C = d + \frac{cr(d + I)}{1 - rc}$$

$$= \frac{d + crI}{1 - rc} \quad .$$

If we use matrix methods, we have

$$
\begin{bmatrix}
1 & 0 & -c \\
-1 & 1 & 0 \\
0 & -r & 1
\end{bmatrix}
\begin{bmatrix}
C \\
R \\
Y
\end{bmatrix}
=
\begin{bmatrix}
d \\
I \\
0
\end{bmatrix} ,
$$

which is pretty familiar.

c. We now have to decide whether government expenditure goes initially to firms or directly to households or to some of each. Thus we have three cases to deal with. It will be sufficient to write the equations in matrix form in each case, since solution is now routine.

(i) Assume that all government expenditure goes to firms (e.g., contracts for road building). We have

$$R = C + I + G ,$$

so we add G to the second element in the vector of exogenous expenditures on the right-hand side of our equations. If household expenditure is a function of disposable income, $Y - tY$, we have

$$C = d + c(1 - t)Y ,$$

whence the equations are

$$
\begin{bmatrix}
1 & 0 & -c(1-t) \\
-1 & 1 & 0 \\
0 & -r & 1
\end{bmatrix}
\begin{bmatrix}
C \\
R \\
Y
\end{bmatrix}
=
\begin{bmatrix}
d \\
I + G \\
0
\end{bmatrix} .
$$

(ii) Assume that all government expenditure goes directly to households (school teachers' salaries). Now

$$Y = rR + G ,$$

and disposable income is $(1 - t)(rR + G)$. We have

$$
\begin{bmatrix}
1 & 0 & -c(1-t) \\
-1 & 1 & 0 \\
0 & -r & 1
\end{bmatrix}
\begin{bmatrix}
C \\
R \\
Y
\end{bmatrix}
=
\begin{bmatrix}
d \\
I \\
G
\end{bmatrix} .
$$

(iii) Assume that hG goes to firms and $(1-h)G$ to households. We have

$$
\begin{bmatrix}
1 & 0 & -c(1-t) \\
-1 & 1 & 0 \\
0 & -r & 1
\end{bmatrix}
\begin{bmatrix}
C \\
R \\
Y
\end{bmatrix}
=
\begin{bmatrix}
d \\
I + hG \\
(1 - h)G
\end{bmatrix} .
$$

As we saw in Chapter 3, the expenditures alter the *multiplicand*, whereas only the tax rate alters the *multiplier*.

d. It is reasonable to assume that export receipts go directly to firms, whereas their share of household expenditure is consumption minus households' imports. This gives

$$R = C + I - M^h + X \quad .$$

If the firms' propensity to import is m, so that the firms' imports are $M^f = mR$, household income is given by

$$Y = (r - m)R \quad .$$

The best plan now is to list the endogenous variables. To the list C, R, and Y, we add M^f and M^h. This makes it clear that we need one more equation, for household imports: $M^h = hY$, say. Now we have

$$\begin{bmatrix} 1 & 0 & -c & 0 & 0 \\ -1 & 1 & 0 & 0 & 1 \\ 0 & -(r-m) & 1 & 0 & 0 \\ 0 & -m & 0 & 1 & 0 \\ 0 & 0 & -h & 0 & 1 \end{bmatrix} \begin{bmatrix} C \\ R \\ Y \\ M^f \\ M^h \end{bmatrix} = \begin{bmatrix} d \\ I + X \\ 0 \\ 0 \\ 0 \end{bmatrix} \quad .$$

This is solved in the usual way. [The multiplier is the reciprocal of the determinant of the coefficient matrix, the common denominator when we solve by Cramer's rule. In this case $\Delta = 1 - (c - h)(r - m)$.] What is the condition for obtaining a finite positive answer? Note that we have assumed no import content in I or X. How would the model be altered if there were import content in I or X?

5.
$$C = C(Y) \tag{1}$$

$$I = I(r) \tag{2}$$

$$Y = C + I + Z \tag{3}$$

$$M^D = L(Y) \tag{4}$$

$$M^S = M \tag{5}$$

$$M^D = M^S \quad . \tag{6}$$

Substituting into (3) and (6), totally differentiating, and expressing in matrix form gives

$$\begin{bmatrix} (1 - C_Y) & -I_r \\ L_Y & 0 \end{bmatrix} \begin{bmatrix} dY \\ dr \end{bmatrix} = \begin{bmatrix} dZ \\ dM \end{bmatrix} \quad .$$

$|\mathbf{A}| = L_Y I_r < 0$. Solving first for dY and then for dr gives $dY/dZ = 0$, $dY/dM > 0$, $dr/dZ > 0$, $dr/dM < 0$. In Section 16.3 we have $M^D = L(Y, r)$. Substituting $M^D = L(Y)$ puts a zero in position a_{22} of the matrix of coefficients. Since the demand for money depends only on Y, there is one and only one Y that will equate M^D with a fixed M; the rate of interest must vary so as to make expenditure $(C + I + Z)$ consistent with that level of Y.

6. Now Eq. (2) of Question 5 becomes $I = I(Y)$ and the usual manipulations produce

$$\begin{bmatrix} 1 - C_Y - I_Y & 0 \\ L_Y & 0 \end{bmatrix} \begin{bmatrix} dY \\ dr \end{bmatrix} = \begin{bmatrix} dZ \\ dM \end{bmatrix} .$$

Since $|\mathbf{A}| = 0$, the model does not have comparative static results. Since no type of expenditure depends on the rate of interest, there is no mechanism to adjust expenditure to give rise to the level of Y that will equate M^D and M^S.

7. Equation (2) remains as $I = I(Y)$, whereas Eq. (4) of Question 5 becomes $M^D = L(Y, r)$. Substituting and differentiating give

$$\begin{bmatrix} 1 - C_Y - I_Y & 0 \\ L_Y & L_r \end{bmatrix} \begin{bmatrix} dY \\ dr \end{bmatrix} = \begin{bmatrix} dZ \\ dM \end{bmatrix} .$$

$|\mathbf{A}| = (1 - C_Y - I_Y)L_r < 0$. Solving first for dY and then for dr gives $dY/dZ > 0$, $dY/dM = 0$, $dr/dZ > 0$, $dr/dM < 0$. Compared with the model of Question 5 it is the monetary sector that must do the adjusting. There is one and only one level of Y for which $C + I + Z = Y$, and the rate of interest must change to make M^D equal the fixed supply of money at that level of Y.

8. *a.* The equations are $C = C(Y, r)$, $I = I(Y, r)$, $Y = C + I + Z$, $M^D = L(Y, r)$, $M^S = M(Y, r) + M$, $M^D = M^S$. [Note the change from $M^S = S(\ )$ in the text to $M^S = M(\ )$ in our answer. Note also that the constant in the M^S function is denoted here by M.] The usual manipulations produce

$$\begin{bmatrix} (1 - C_Y - I_Y) & -(C_r + I_r) \\ (L_Y - M_Y) & +(L_r - M_r) \end{bmatrix} \begin{bmatrix} dY \\ dr \end{bmatrix} = \begin{bmatrix} dZ \\ dM \end{bmatrix} .$$

To sign the individual terms we need some further assumptions: (1) $C_Y + I_Y < 1$ (already discussed); if a higher interest rate induces more saving, we have $C_r < 0$, so $C_r + I_r < 0$. (2) To begin with we assume that the supply of money increases less as Y increases than does the demand for money; thus $L_y - M_y > 0$. (3) Finally, we assume, following Section 16.8, that the supply of money increases as the rate of interest rises; thus $L_r - M_r < 0$. The sign patttern given below yields $|\mathbf{A}| < 0$:

$$\begin{bmatrix} + & + \\ + & - \end{bmatrix} .$$

Routine substitution shows $dY/dZ > 0$, $dY/dM > 0$, $dr/dZ > 0$, $dr/dM < 0$.

b. If there is no exogenous component in the money supply, $M = 0$ whence $dM = 0$. This has no effect on dY/dZ or dr/dZ.

9. The sign patterns are

$$(a) \begin{bmatrix} + & + \\ 0 & - \end{bmatrix} \quad \text{and} \quad (b) \begin{bmatrix} + & + \\ - & - \end{bmatrix} .$$

and routine substitution is all that is required to show that $dr/dz = 0$ in (a) and $dr/dz < 0$ in (b).

10. *a.* Write the two income equations

$$Y_A(1 - 0.8 + 0.1) \quad - 0.2Y_B = 300$$

$$Y_B(1 - 0.6 + 0.2) \quad - 0.1Y_A = 150$$

or

$$\begin{bmatrix} 0.3 & -0.2 \\ -0.1 & 0.6 \end{bmatrix} \begin{bmatrix} Y_A \\ Y_B \end{bmatrix} = \begin{bmatrix} 300 \\ 150 \end{bmatrix} .$$

Using Cramer's rule,

$$Y_A = \frac{\begin{vmatrix} 300 & -0.2 \\ 150 & 0.6 \end{vmatrix}}{\Delta}, \quad Y_B = \frac{\begin{vmatrix} 0.3 & 300 \\ -0.1 & 150 \end{vmatrix}}{\Delta},$$

$\Delta = 0.16$, whence $Y_A = 1312.5$ and $Y_B = 468.75$. We obtain immediately $M_A = 131.25$ and $M_B = 93.75$. Hence A has a deficit of 37.5.

b. A matrix is singular if the value of its determinant is zero (in which case it is said to "vanish"). The condition is

$$\begin{vmatrix} 1 - c_A + m_A & -m_B \\ -m_A & 1 - c_B + m_B \end{vmatrix} = 0 .$$

It is of some interest to expand this determinant and experiment with numbers. It cannot vanish unless we allow some dissaving.

c. If we differentiate the two income equations with respect to Y_A, Y_B, and I_A, we obtain

$$\begin{bmatrix} 0.3 & -0.2 \\ -0.1 & 0.6 \end{bmatrix} \begin{bmatrix} dY_A \\ dY_B \end{bmatrix} = \begin{bmatrix} dI_A \\ 0 \end{bmatrix} .$$

Solving,

$$dY_A = \frac{\begin{vmatrix} dI_A & -0.2 \\ 0 & 0.6 \end{vmatrix}}{\Delta} = \frac{0.6}{0.16} dI_A$$

or

$$\frac{dY_A}{dI_A} = 3.75 .$$

Similarly,

$$\frac{dY_B}{dI_A} = 0.625 .$$

d. If there were no "feedback" from country B, we should merely solve

$$-dM_A = 37.5 = -0.8 \ dY_A = -(0.8)(3.75) \ dI_A$$

for the required value of $-dI_A$. The induced change in B's income must, however, be taken into account. Balance of payments equilibrium requires $M_A = M_B$, or $0.1Y_A = 0.2Y_B$. Suppose that we use this as an additional equation. We can, however, add an equation only if we have an additional endogenous variable. But we have; it is I_A. Thus the system is now

$$\begin{bmatrix} 0.3 & -0.2 & -1 \\ -0.1 & 0.6 & 0 \\ 0.1 & -0.2 & 0 \end{bmatrix} \begin{bmatrix} Y_A \\ Y_B \\ I_A \end{bmatrix} = \begin{bmatrix} 100 \\ 150 \\ 0 \end{bmatrix}.$$

Solving by Cramer's rule, $I_A = -100$! Negative investment is, of course, not impossible. So long as there is a positive multiplicand, which there is, income will be positive. To check, we calculate $Y_A = 750$ and $Y_B = 375$. Balance of payments equilibrium has indeed been achieved — at a cost. A has approximately halved its income. It might be worth thinking of some alternative policies for A.

11. The four equations are

$$Y - C(Y) - I(r) = Z$$

$$L(Y, r, P) = M$$

$$D\left(\frac{W}{P}\right) - S\left(\frac{W}{P}\right) = 0$$

$$Y = f(N) \ .$$

Differentiation of the third equation proceeds as follows:

$$D'\left(\frac{P \ dW - W \ dP}{P^2}\right) - S'\left(\frac{P \ dW - W \ dP}{P^2}\right) = 0 \ ,$$

or $P(D' - S') \ dW + W(S' - D') \ dP = 0$, where D' and S' are the derivatives of the two functions with respect to the single argument W/P. When the fourth equation is differentiated we get $dY = f_N \ dN$. Because N is determined solely by the labor market equation, the value of N cannot change so long as the labor demand and supply curves are given. Thus $dN = 0$, and the last equation reduces to $dY = 0$ (or if we wished we could write $dY = dX$, where dX is an exogenous shift parameter that stands for a shift in either the labor demand or labor supply functions). Complete differentiation now gives

$$\begin{bmatrix} 1 - C_Y & -I_r & 0 & 0 \\ L_Y & L_r & L_P & 0 \\ 0 & 0 & W(S' - D') & P(D' - S') \\ 1 & 0 & 0 & 0 \end{bmatrix} \begin{bmatrix} dY \\ dr \\ dP \\ dW \end{bmatrix} = \begin{bmatrix} dZ \\ dM \\ 0 \\ 0 \end{bmatrix}.$$

Notice that $S' - D' > 0$ $(D' - S' < 0)$ because the demand for labor varies inversely with the real wage rate whereas the supply varies directly with it. Given these signs the rest is routine. The full set of comparative static properties is summarized as follows:

	dY	dr	dP	dW
dZ	0	+	+	+
dM	0	0	+	+

The level of income is determined solely by the labor market; autonomous expenditure influences only the interest rate, and the quantity of money affects only the level of money prices and money wages.

12. The only change in the equations of Question 11 is that the consumption function becomes $C = C(Y, W/P)$. Totally differentiating gives

$$dC = C_Y \, dY + C_{W/P}\left(\frac{P \, dW - W \, dP}{P^2}\right) \quad .$$

The whole system thus becomes

$$
\begin{bmatrix}
1 - C_Y & -I_r & C_{W/P}\dfrac{W}{P^2} & \dfrac{C_{W/P}}{P^2} - \dfrac{C_{W/P}}{P} \\
L_Y & L_r & L_P & 0 \\
0 & 0 & W(S' - D') & P(D' - S') \\
1 & 0 & 0 & 0
\end{bmatrix}
\begin{bmatrix}
dY \\
dr \\
dP \\
dW
\end{bmatrix}
=
\begin{bmatrix}
dZ \\
dM \\
0 \\
0
\end{bmatrix} \quad .
$$

Before working out the full set of results it is clear that dY/dZ, dr/dZ, and dW/dZ are not affected by this "Cambridge addition" to the model; when the solution vector is substituted into each column in turn the principal minor of dZ never includes the first row. The full set of results is as follows:

	dY	dr	dP	dW
dZ	0	+	+	+
dM	0	0	+	+

Compare this with the results obtained in Question 5.

Chapter 17

1. *a.* You notice immediately that the sum of the elements in the first column exceeds unity, whence industry 1 is a national disaster. It *could* be true (in Ruritania), but we cannot use this matrix for planning purposes; we must sort this out. You also notice that the coefficients in the third column are exactly 1.5 times those in the second column. This makes you suspicious; it looks as though there were two identical industries (with suitable choice of units). It should be remembered, by the way, that although this matrix does not possess an inverse (see Question 2 of Section 15.6), the matrix to be inverted here is $\mathbf{I} - \mathbf{A}$, which will have an inverse.

b. You might remember the balance equations,

$$\mathbf{X} - \mathbf{AX} = \mathbf{Y} \quad ,$$

and ask for information on $\mathbf{X}$ and $\mathbf{Y}$ for the period from which the matrix was constructed. You may, of course, just rediscover the route the planners took to construct $\mathbf{A}$ themselves. In this case, if you are still unsatisfied, you are in for some hard work; you will have to start collecting engineering data and so on, at the industry level, to see if the coefficients seem sensible. Alternatively, this may be the way in which the Office of Central Planning built the matrix, in which case the balance equations will provide a check. (You might wish to speculate on what should be done if

(i) the balance equations do not check, or
(ii) figures for X and Y are not available.)

c. A linear operator is a linear operator! For the economy to be properly described by a linear input–output system, we must have constant returns to scale and no interindustry externalities. Thus you can tell the Ruritanians what they should be worrying about.

2. a. By inspection, industry 4.
  b. Industry 3.
  c. If a matrix is triangular, it must contain a number of zeros equal to half the total number of elements minus the number of elements on the principal diagonal, or $\frac{1}{2}(n^2 - n)$. For a four-by-four, this is $\frac{1}{2}(4^2 - 4) = 6$. This matrix has six zeros, although there is no guarantee that they are in the right places. It is, however, clearly possible that the matrix is triangular, whence it is worth trying some rearrangements. Since the third column has no zeros, let us try the effect of putting it in the first place. Swapping the first and third industries, we have

	3	2	1	4
3	a_{33}	0	0	0
2	a_{23}	a_{22}	0	0
1	a_{13}	a_{12}	a_{11}	0
4	a_{43}	a_{42}	a_{41}	a_{44}

This is a triangular matrix, as we hoped. The answer is: recursively.

3. a. It is straightforward, if laborious, to calculate

$$\mathbf{I} + \mathbf{A} = \begin{bmatrix} 1.1 & 0 & 0 & 0.2 \\ 0.05 & 1.01 & 0.05 & 0 \\ 0.1 & 0.2 & 1.1 & 0.05 \\ 0.2 & 0.01 & 0.2 & 1.2 \end{bmatrix}$$

$$\mathbf{I} + \mathbf{A} + \mathbf{A}^2 = \begin{bmatrix} 1.15 & 0.002 & 0.04 & 0.26 \\ 0.0605 & 1.0201 & 0.0555 & 0.0125 \\ 0.14 & 0.2225 & 1.13 & 0.085 \\ 0.2805 & 0.0521 & 0.2605 & 1.29 \end{bmatrix}$$

$$\mathbf{I} + \mathbf{A} + \mathbf{A}^2 + \mathbf{A}^3 = \begin{bmatrix} 1.1711 & 0.01062 & 0.0561 & 0.284 \\ 0.065105 & 1.021426 & 0.059055 & 0.017375 \\ 0.155125 & 0.229075 & 1.141125 & 0.1015 \\ 0.314705 & 0.065521 & 0.286655 & 1.327125 \end{bmatrix} .$$

We shall stop here, and consider accuracy next.

b. To check that a matrix **B** *is* the inverse of a matrix **A** we normally calculate **AB** (or **BA**) and compare it with **I**. Here, however, we have

$$\mathbf{AB} = \mathbf{A}(\mathbf{I} + \mathbf{A} + \mathbf{A}^2 + \mathbf{A}^3)$$

$$= \mathbf{A} + \mathbf{A}^2 + \mathbf{A}^3 + \mathbf{A}^4 \quad .$$

The check calculation simply requires us to compute another term, $\mathbf{A}^5$, in our series. If we desire a closer approximation, we shall do this anyhow. The check we require is to remember our balance equations,

$$\mathbf{X} - \mathbf{Z} = \mathbf{Y} \quad ,$$

where **Z** is intermediate use, so that we may check the equality

$$(\mathbf{I} - \mathbf{A})\mathbf{X} = \mathbf{Y} \quad .$$

To do this, we must solve for some particular **Y**, $\mathbf{Y} = \{1, 1, 1, 1\}$, say. Thus we calculate

$$\mathbf{X} = (\mathbf{I} + \mathbf{A} + \mathbf{A}^2 + \mathbf{A}^3)\mathbf{Y}$$

$$= \{1.52182, 1.162961, 1.626825, 1.994006\}.$$

[This **X** vector is, of course, simply composed of the row sums of our approximation to $[\mathbf{I} - \mathbf{A}]^{-1}$.] The check is now completed by multiplying this vector by

$$I - A = \begin{bmatrix} 0.9 & 0 & 0 & -0.2 \\ -0.05 & 0.99 & -0.05 & 0 \\ -0.1 & -0.2 & 0.9 & -0.05 \\ -0.2 & -0.01 & -0.2 & 0.8 \end{bmatrix}.$$

This gives, without rounding, the vector {0.9708368, 0.99389914, 0.9786674, 0.97384619}. Comparing this with {1, 1, 1, 1}, we can say that nothing catastrophic has gone wrong, but we are certainly not very accurate. Perhaps it would have been worth calculating A^4.

c. No. But we should require more iterations to get a reasonable approximation.

4. a. Postmultiplication of $(I - A)^{-1}$ by Y gives $X = \{14.19, 11.32, 11.12, 30.82\}$.

b. The required output of X_4 is not feasible; this final bill of goods is not attainable. If this *is* final demand (rather than a planning exercise), there will be excess demand for X_4, and its price will rise. This will increase all the coefficients in the last row of the A matrix, *even if it induces no physical substitution*. (Remember that the coefficients have to be expressed in value terms. Why?) Without more information we cannot go much further.

c. To find the value of imports, we need only compute the scalar, or inner product,

$$XM = (11.12)(0.01) + (30.82)(0.1)$$

$$= 3.1932 \quad .$$

We cannot, of course, say what the balance of payments will be without more information: the export component of final demand.

Chapter 18

1. a. $q_1 = 50$, $q_2 = 25$.

b. 275.

c. $v_1 = 2$, $v_2 = 1$, $v_3 = 0$.

d. Because the same constraints bind.

e. Notice that the slope of the iso-profit line, $-5/3$, is still between that of the first and second constraints (-2 and -1), while the third is vertical.

2. a. $q_1 = 75$, $q_2 = 0$; 375; $v_1 = 0$, $v_2 = 5$, $v_3 = 0$.

b. Notice that the iso-profit line is now flatter than any of the constraints. The corner solution at $q_1 = 75$, $q_2 = 0$ is the most profitable.

3. $v_1 = \frac{4}{3}$, $v_2 = 0$, $v_3 = \frac{2}{3}$.

4. a. $q_1 + q_2 \leq 66\frac{2}{3}$.

b. The dual is as follows:

$$\text{Minimize } 100v_1 + 61\tfrac{2}{3}v_2 + 50v_3$$

subject to

$$v_1 + v_2 + v_3 \geq 2 \quad,$$

$$2v_1 + v_2 + \tfrac{1}{2}v_3 \geq 3 \quad,$$

$$v_1 \geq 0,\ v_2 \geq 0,\ v_3 \geq 0 \quad.$$

Since all three constraints just bind, both inequalities are to be replaced with equalities. We now have two linear equations in three unknowns; the shadow prices are indeterminate.

5. *a.* The primal is

$$\text{Maximize } p_1q_{1A} + p_2q_{2A} + p_1q_{1B} + p_2q_{2B}$$

subject to

$$a_{11}q_{1A} + a_{12}q_{2A} \qquad\qquad\quad \leq K_A$$

$$a_{21}q_{1A} + a_{22}q_{2A} \qquad\qquad\quad \leq L_A$$

$$a_{33}q_{1B} + a_{34}q_{2B} \leq K_B$$

$$a_{43}q_{1B} + a_{44}q_{2B} \leq L_B$$

$$q_{1A},\ q_{2A},\ q_{1B},\ q_{2B} \geq 0 \quad.$$

The dual is

$$\text{Minimize } V_AK_A + W_AL_A + V_BK_B + W_BL_B$$

subject to

$$a_{11}V_A + a_{21}W_A \qquad\qquad\quad \geq p_1$$

$$a_{12}V_A + a_{22}W_A \qquad\qquad\quad \geq p_2$$

$$a_{33}V_B + a_{43}W_B \geq p_1$$

$$a_{34}V_B + a_{44}W_B \geq p_2$$

$$V_A,\ W_A,\ V_B,\ W_B \geq 0 \quad.$$

  b. Only if the labor in the two regions is also identical so that each region has the same **A**-matrix.
  c. Only if the capital is also identical.
  d. If *all* the markets were perfectly competitive.

6. *a.* The primal problem is

$$\text{Maximize } p_1q_{1A} + p_2q_{2A} + p_1q_{1B} + p_2q_{2B}$$

subject to

$$a_{11}q_{1A} + a_{12}q_{2A} \qquad\qquad\qquad \leq L_A$$

$$a_{23}q_{1B} + a_{24}q_{2B} \leq L_B$$

$$a_{31}q_{1A} + a_{32}q_{2A} + a_{33}q_{1B} + a_{34}q_{2B} \leq I$$

and

$$q_{1A'}\; q_{2A'}\; q_{1B'}\; q_{2B} \geq 0 \quad .$$

(The "blank areas" could be replaced by zeros in an obvious manner.) On the assumptions given, we should in fact expect $a_{31} = a_{33}$ and $a_{32} = a_{34}$. The dual problem is

$$\text{Minimize } W_A L_A + W_B L_B + V_I I$$

subject to

$$a_{11}W_A \qquad\quad + a_{31}V_I \geq p_1$$

$$a_{12}W_A \qquad\quad + a_{32}V_I \geq p_2$$

$$a_{23}W_B + a_{33}V_I \geq p_1$$

$$a_{24}W_B + a_{34}V_I \geq p_2$$

and

$$W_{A'}\; W_{B'}\; V_I \geq 0 \quad .$$

(a_{11} would equal a_{23}, and so forth, if the workers were of the same skills.)

b. Yes, unless one of the constraints L_A, L_B does not bind at the optimal solution.

c. No. So long as the total amount of new capital, I, is fixed, that is, is independent of its regional allocation, it has only one shadow price.

d. If market prices varied from shadow prices on a regional basis.

e. No. But if new capital I were not sufficient to absorb all the new labor, it would make no difference to GNP which region got the most of it. Consider the results of substituting pairs of equalities for the inequalities in the dual. Speculate on the GNP-maximizing allocation of I if the workers are of unequal skills, and there is not sufficient new capital, I, to employ them all.

f. If *all* the markets were perfectly competitive. Note that the competitive solution requires that all the economic agents be perfectly informed about next year's prices.

7. Let the q_i's be foodstuffs (bread, hamburger, oranges, etc.) and the p_i's their prices. Then the problem can be written

$$\text{Minimize } \sum p_i q_i$$

subject to

$$Aq \geq R \quad ,$$

where **R** is the column vector of the minimum requirements and **A** the "technology matrix" that tells us how much of each requirement we get per unit of each foodstuff.

8. If the trade-offs are everywhere constant (linear models), a linear objective function will always take us to one of the axes (or give an indeterminate solution). We need a nonlinear objective function to get an "interior solution."

Appendix to Chapter 18

1. *a.*
$$\text{Maximize} \quad 1q_1 + 2q_2$$

subject to

$$1q_1 + \tfrac{1}{2}q_2 \leq 5\tfrac{1}{2}$$

$$\tfrac{1}{4}q_1 + 2q_2 \leq 7 \quad .$$

Since $-\tfrac{1}{2}$ (the slope of the objective function) lies between -2 and $-\tfrac{1}{8}$ (the slope of the constraints), both goods are produced. Hence $(q_1{}^\circ, q_2{}^\circ)$ is the solution to the equation system

$$1q_1 + \tfrac{1}{2}q_2 = 5\tfrac{1}{2}$$

$$\tfrac{1}{4}q_1 + 2q_2 = 7 \quad .$$

Solving this gives $q_1{}^\circ = 4$, $q_2{}^\circ = 3$.

b. The dual problem to part a is

$$\text{Minimize} \quad 5\tfrac{1}{2}V_1 + 7V_2$$

subject to

$$1V_1 + \tfrac{1}{4}V_2 \geq 1$$

$$\tfrac{1}{2}V_1 + 2V_2 \geq 2 \quad .$$

As both goods were produced in the primal, we know that both constraints in the dual bind. Hence $(V_1{}^\circ, V_2{}^\circ)$ are obtained by solving the equation system

$$1V_1 + \tfrac{1}{4}V_2 = 1$$

$$\tfrac{1}{2}V_1 + 2V_2 = 2 \quad .$$

Solving, we get $V_1{}^\circ = \tfrac{4}{5}$, $V_2{}^\circ = \tfrac{4}{5}$.

2. To solve for the shadow prices of the resources we must compute the dual problem for $R_1 = 3$, $R_2 = 2$. This is

$$\text{Minimize} \quad 3V_1 + 2V_2$$

subject to

$$1V_1 + \tfrac{1}{4}V_2 \geq 1$$

$$\tfrac{1}{2}V_1 + 2V_2 \geq 2 \quad .$$

Since both $V_1{}^\circ$ and $V_2{}^\circ$ are greater than zero for the solution to this problem (since both constraints continue to bind), they must satisfy the linear equations

$$1V_1 + \tfrac{1}{4}V_2 = 1$$

$$\tfrac{1}{2}V_1 + 2V_2 = 2 \quad .$$

This gives $V_1{}^\circ = \tfrac{4}{5}$ and $V_2{}^\circ = \tfrac{4}{5}$, which is the same as the solution in Question 1.

3. Consider the primal problem of maximizing GNP subject to the resource endowments R_1 and R_2:

$$\text{Maximize} \quad 1q_1 + 2q_2$$

subject to

$$1q_1 + \tfrac{1}{2}q_2 \leq R_1$$

$$\tfrac{1}{4}q_1 + 2q_2 \leq R_2 \quad .$$

Both q_1 and q_2 will be produced as long as there exists a solution $(q_1{}^\circ, q_2{}^\circ) > 0$ to the equation system

$$1q_1 + \tfrac{1}{2}q_2 = R_1$$

$$\tfrac{1}{4}q_1 + 2q_2 = R_2 \quad .$$

This will be the case as long as the two equations intersect in the positive quadrant. For $q_1 = 0$ this requires that $q_2{}^2 = R_2/2$ be less than $q_2{}^1 = R_1/2$, and for $q_2 = 0$ that $q_1{}^2 = 4R_2$ be greater than $q_1{}^1 = R_1$. Hence we must have $R_2/2 \leq R_1$ and $4R_2 \geq R_1$ or $\tfrac{1}{2} \leq R_1/R_2 \leq 4$. Now this condition ensures that the country will produce both q_1 and q_2. Therefore factor prices are given by the solution to the equations

$$1V_1 + \tfrac{1}{4}V_2 = 1$$

$$\tfrac{1}{2}V_1 + 2V_2 = 2 \quad .$$

Since the solution is independent of R_1 and R_2 for countries producing both goods, all those countries will have the same factor prices.

4. The solutions are $q_1{}^\circ = 4$, $q_2{}^\circ = 3$ and $V_1{}^\circ = \tfrac{2}{3}$, $V_2{}^\circ = \tfrac{4}{3}$.

5. For Question 1, $V_1{}^\circ R_1/(V_1{}^\circ R_1 + V_2{}^\circ R_2) = \tfrac{22}{5}/(\tfrac{22}{5} + \tfrac{28}{5}) = \tfrac{22}{50} = \tfrac{11}{25}$. For Question 4, $V_1{}^\circ R_1/(V_1{}^\circ R_1 + V_2{}^\circ R_2) = \tfrac{11}{3}/(\tfrac{11}{3} + \tfrac{28}{3}) = \tfrac{11}{39}$. Since $\tfrac{11}{25} > \tfrac{11}{39}$, the increase in the price of good 2 lowered the share of national income going to the first factor and raised the share of national income going to the second factor. Given the **A** matrix the factor intensity coefficients relative to factor 1 are $I_1{}^1 = a_{11}/a_{12}$ and $I_2{}^1 = a_{21}/a_{22}$. In the above example $I_1{}^1 = 2$, $I_2{}^1 = \tfrac{1}{8}$. Since $I_1{}^1 > I_2{}^1$, we say that industry 1 is relative more factor-1-in-

tensive. Similarly, $I_1^2 = \frac{1}{2}$ and $I_2^2 = 8$, whence industry 2 is relatively more factor-2-intensive. Note that since we raised the price of the second good the relative income of the factor used relatively intensively in that industry increased.

6. Since $R_1/R_2 = \frac{8}{7}$ (which exceeds $\frac{1}{2}$ and is less than 4, i.e., we are still in the diversification cone), the country produces both goods. Solving we have $q_1^\circ = \frac{20}{3}$, $q_2^\circ = \frac{8}{3}$ and $V_1^\circ = \frac{4}{5}$, $V_2^\circ = \frac{4}{5}$.

7. Since $\frac{20}{3} > 4 = \frac{12}{3}$, the output of q_1 increased by increasing the endowment of factor 1. Note that industry 1 is relatively more factor-one-intensive.

8. Clearly, the country will diversify only if $p_2/p_1 = a_2/a_1$, that is, the slope of the objective function is equal to the slope of the constraint. Note that if a country does diversify then relative prices must satisfy the dual equations

$$a_1 V_1 = p_1$$

$$a_2 V_1 = p_2 \quad .$$

Hence relative prices are determined solely by technological conditions and the price of labor, V_1. This is a very crude "labor theory of value."

9. We rewrite the question as

$$\text{Maximize} \quad V_1 x_1 + V_2 x_2$$

subject to

$$b_1 x + b_2 x_2 \leq R \quad ,$$

and

$$b_1 = a_{11} + a_{12}$$

$$b_2 = a_{21} + a_{22} \quad .$$

where

$$V_1 = p_1 a_{11} + p_2 a_{12}$$

$$V_2 = p_1 a_{21} + p_2 a_{22} \quad .$$

In the activity analysis framework, providing the $a_{ij} \neq 0$, the economy must produce both goods. However, from Question 8 we know that unless $V_2/V_1 = b_2/b_1$ the economy will use only one technique, that is, x_1° or $x_2^\circ = 0$.

Index

76 77 78 9 8 7 6 5 4 3 2 1